中国人民大学“一带一路”经济研究院
中国人民大学经济学院　　　　编
中国人民大学国学院

丝绸之路研究

Journal of the International Silk Roads Studies

第一辑

Volume . 1

生活·讀書·新知 三联书店

图书在版编目（CIP）数据

丝绸之路研究. 第一辑 / 李肖主编. —北京：生活 · 读书 · 新知三联书店，2017.10
ISBN 978－7－108－05867－6

Ⅰ. ①丝… Ⅱ. ①李… Ⅲ. ①丝绸之路－文集
Ⅳ. ① K928.6-53

中国版本图书馆 CIP 数据核字（2017）第 262912 号

责任编辑 张 龙
装帧设计 战盈彤
特约校对 叶爱国 王 丁
责任印制 徐 方
出版发行 生活 · 讀書 · 新知 三联书店
（北京市东城区美术馆东街 22 号 100010）
网 址 www.sdxjpc.com
经 销 新华书店
印 刷 北京隆昌伟业印刷有限公司
版 次 2017 年 10 月北京第 1 版
2017 年 10 月北京第 1 次印刷
开 本 880 毫米 × 1230 毫米 1/16 印张 19.25
字 数 300 千字 图 185 幅
印 数 0,001－4,000 册
定 价 98.00 元
（印装查询：01064002715；邮购查询：01084010542）

丝绸之路研究（第一辑）

Journal of the International Silk Roads Studies Volume 1

《丝绸之路研究》发刊词

以国家“一带一路”倡议为研究主题的首部综合性刊物《丝绸之路研究》即将面世，这不仅是相关学术领域里的一个重大标志性事件，也为“一带一路”沿线国家提供了一个展示跨文化及多元文明交流互动的窗口。

在漫长的历史时期，亚欧大陆，甚至包括非洲的部分地区，被以丝绸之路冠名的各种商贸及文化交流的通道所串联，诸如陶瓷之路、茶叶之路、香料之路、玉石之路、朝圣之路等，为古典时期不同文明之间的交流互通建立了桥梁。因此，丝绸之路也等同于文明交流之路、政治交流之路、经济交流之路。

曾几何时，单一文明的价值观、行为规范成为了其他文明强制接受的普遍价值，研究领域也不例外，那些曾经创建高度文明且对其他文明产生重大影响的文化被边缘化、低矮化，某一文化、某一阶段的繁荣与发展被当成永远不变的世界规律，强权与武力扩张被看作文明之间交往的常态，这与今天以全球视野的角度来分析问题的方法相比已经非常落伍。

丝绸之路或“一带一路”既是对历史的回顾，也是对未来的展望；既是对传统“丝绸之路经济带”沿线国家政治经济发展的希望，也是对构架全球化的“丝绸之路经济带”的运行指南。

《丝绸之路研究》是中国人民大学“一带一路”经济研究院、经济学院、国学院与生活·读书·新知三联书店合办的综合性学术刊物。本刊以沟通古代东西方文明交流的丝绸之路为支点，秉承“一带一路”倡议，挖掘丝路沿线历史文化、探索“丝绸之路经济带”的内在动力，致力于打造跨学科、多领域、高水平的国际学术平台，为全球文化交流与共同发展提供学术支撑。

张骞西行，玄奘寻法，梯山悬度成就沟通中西之壮举；粟特驼旅，天方牵星，西域南海始聚异域遗珍。秉承丝绸之路之勇于进取、和平致远的伟大精神，本刊有信心在中外编委和热心于丝绸之路的广大读者们的支持下，办成一本高质量的学术期刊。

李肖

2017 年 5 月

学人寄语

丝绸之路是前近代亚欧大陆的最大通道。大航海之后，世界一体化进程加速，而前近代的世界，亚欧大陆是人类活动的主要舞台。丝绸之路联结着当时各重要文明地区，为世界一体化打下坚实的历史基础。

文明之间的交往，是文明进步的重要方式。各个文明区与文化主体，就文化要素而言，无不你中有我，我中有你。互通有无，彼此促进，共同提高，从来就是文化交流的华美乐章。今天，人类享受世界一体化带来的便利、快捷和多元，是历史长期积累的结果，人类为此不仅付出辛劳，也付出沉重的代价，包括流血牺牲。吸取历史经验，总结失败教训，是今人的义务，也是获取未来幸福的权利。通过历史研究获得启示，是专业工作者责无旁贷的神圣使命。

文化交流一直是丝绸之路上的主旋律。因为环境不同，丝绸之路可以划分为陆上丝绸之路和海上丝绸之路。因为强调的对象不同，也有陶瓷之路、茶叶之路、香料之路、玉石之路、朝圣之路等冠名，两千年间，有多少有形无形的“物品”在丝绸之路上往来，就有多少种认定丝绸之路的方法。把探索世界一体化进程的目光扩展到丝绸之路的世界，就会被人类曾经拥有的和平牧歌所感动，对于未来世界的同样渴望，就可能感动人类世界。

多年以来，丝绸之路沿线的考古学进步，为丝绸之路研究提供了极其重要的第一手资料。丝绸之路历史学的研究，从来没有今天这样的优厚条件。如今的世界，一体化的进程还在经受种种考验，但不能否认的是这一进程正在深化发展。就中国学者而言，中国提出“一带一路”的倡议，不仅给世界带来憧憬，也给学术研究带来动力。“一带一路”的建设可以是经济的、政治的，但对于完整和成功的“一带一路”建设来说，历史与文化学术研究的缺席，是完全不能想象的。

丝绸之路的历史，是文化多样性、观念多元性的大舞台。如果这可以看作丝绸之路固有精神的话，那么《丝绸之路研究》也应当继承这种精神。《丝绸之路研究》是一部以丝路历史与文化研究为主体的连续学术出版物，为了对丝绸之路的整体性有充分体现，我们也会关注丝绸之路经济和政治的研究课题。《丝绸之路研究》的第一原则是学术性，严肃的学术、求实的理念会贯彻始终。

中国人民大学是以文科为主的综合型大学,《丝绸之路研究》是“一带一路”经济研究院、经济学院、国学院与生活·读书·新知三联书店合办的综合性学术刊物，我们希望《丝绸之路研究》在未来成为探索丝绸之路的历史与文化的重要学术平台。丝绸之路涉及文化与历史的多种面向，研究焦点不胜枚举，广邀学界朋友，共襄盛举。

孟宪实

2017 年 5 月

《丝绸之路研究》办刊宗旨与稿约

《丝绸之路研究》是由中国人民大学“一带一路”经济研究院、经济学院、国学院与生活·读书·新知三联书店合办的综合性学术刊物。中国是丝绸之路的起点，在前近代是亚欧大陆文明的中心之一。“一带一路”的倡议不仅给沿线国家的共同发展带来巨大的契机，也给相关的学术研究注入了新的活力。本刊以沟通东西方文明交流的丝绸之路为支点，秉承“一带一路”倡议，挖掘丝路沿线历史文化，探索“一带一路”的内在动力，致力于打造跨学科、多领域、高水平的国际学术平台。

《丝绸之路研究》以“一带一路”的历史、文化、经济和当代政治为主要研究对象，主要栏目包括人文、社科、学术通讯、札记等部分。欢迎海内外学者惠赠佳作（外文稿件请给予本刊首发授权，本刊编辑部负责翻译发表）。

《丝绸之路研究》诚邀中外人士赐稿，同时依托主办单位适时召开相关研究领域的学术研讨会，邀请专家、学者参会讨论，出版专辑。

作者投稿一经采纳发表，即赠样书2册、电子抽印本1份，稿酬酌付。《丝绸之路研究》为半年刊，来稿请参照所附“《丝绸之路研究》用稿声明及引文规范”，以电子版形式发至本刊编辑部。来稿请附作者简历与详细通信地址、邮编、电子信箱等联系方式，赐寄至以下地址（收到稿件后即自动发送回执）：

邮编：100872

地址：北京市海淀区中关村大街59号中国人民大学国学馆234室

李肖　收

邮箱：haidaoqi@ruc.edu.cn

电话：010-62515747　15001371119

《丝绸之路研究》编辑部

2017年5月4日

Journal of the International Silk Roads Studies

Notice to Contributors

Journal of the International Silk Roads Studies, co-hosted by School of Economics and Chinese Classics in Renmin University of China, is a comprehensive academic journal.

The journal is based on the Silk Roads that communicated the ancient eastern and western civilization and supported by the Belt and Road Initiative. The journal aims to build up an interdisciplinary, multi-field, high-level international academic platform for exploring the historical culture along the Silk Roads and internal dynamics of "the Belt and Road". China is the starting point of the Silk Roads and one of the centres of the Eurasian civilizations in pre-modern times. The Belt and Road Initiative not only offers great opportunities for the international politics and economics, but also adds new vitality to relevant academic researches.

The journal devotes to researches on the history, culture, economy and contemporary politics of the Belt and Road. It publishes original research articles on humanities and social science, economics, academic reports and book reviews, etc. Contributions from scholars both at home and abroad are welcome. Manuscripts in non-Chinese languages should not be published or under consideration for publication elsewhere in China. The editorial department will have it translated into Chinese once the paper is accepted.

The journal considers all relevant submissions, and also publishes papers presented to the forums or seminars initiated by the organizers on relevant fields.

Authors will be supplied free of charge with two copies of the relevant issue of the journal and an e-offprints of their contributions. Certain remuneration will be paid to the authors.

The journal will be published biannually. Please prepare your paper according to the format guidelines of the journal. Manuscripts should be submitted in electronic versions, and your brief biographical, full postal and e-mail address should be attached.

For contributions and further information, please contact:

Editor in Chief: Dr. Li Xiao
School of Chinese Classics
Renmin University of China
Beijing 100872
P. R. China

Tel: (+86) 010-62515747
(+86) 15001371119
E-mail: haidaoqi@ruc.edu.cn

目 录

Journal of the International Silk Roads Studies
Volume 1

Contents

Greek Gods and Traces of the Sumerian Mythology

In Carpets from the 6th Century

Duan Qing (Peking University)

Abstract: This paper will describe the characters within the figures of the recently discovered carpets from Ancient Khotan, which may date back to the end of the 6th and the beginning of the 7th century. It will correlate the findings to demonstrate the inherited tradition of Greek mythology and ancient Sumerian civilizations.

Keywords: Greek gods; Sumerian Innana; carpets from Lop museum; Khotan; Gilgamesh epic; pukku and mekku

I. Introduction

I would like to introduce briefly some places, which are connected with the discovery of the carpets. I began with the area of Shampul, the name denotes a barren place where the carpets were found (Fig. 1). Shampul is a desert district of Lop County. In the center of Lop, a new museum has been opened, where the carpets are now preserved. Lop is about one hour and a half drive way from the city of Khotan.

Fig. 1, the place after the archaeological exploration where the carpets have been found. Courtesy to Xinjiang Institute of cultural relics and Archaeology.

The city of modern Khotan is the administrative center of nine counties, but the name Khotan designates a historical kingdom located on the southern edge of the Taklamakan desert. The modern Khotan area, with its counties, covers approximately the area of the former kingdom of Khotan, which, however, a thousand years ago had extended much more to the south, where today the desert extends. About 97 percent of the modern population of Khotan are Islamic Uighurs who speak Uyghur. But in the past history, before the time of the first millennium, —the kingdom of Khotan was a famous center of Buddhism, in particular for the Mahāyāna-Buddhism. Most of the population of ancient Khotan spoke Khotanese—a language, which belongs to the medieval East-Iranian language group. About in the 6th century, Khotanese became the official Language and Brāhmī, the official script. It is easy to deduce from this that the former population of Khotan would have Iranian origin, and their culture may be bearing influence of the ancient Iranian religion, which was supposedly Zoroastrian. Local tradition of Khotan do not seem to have changed from the old days to the present, to which we may mention jade, silk and carpets.

In particular, today the price of jade has been driven so high to an unreal level that the search for Jade has almost become a business. If one travels to Khotan, he will see everywhere on riverbeds excavators busy at work. In the year 2007, some people trying their luck with the search for jade in a former tributary in the area of Shampul, instead of jade, they found carpets, which, according to the description, lay in a pit built with stones.

II. Findings

It was said that originally seven carpets were found, two of which were sold abroad, while the police later confiscated the other five. They are now preserved in the Lop Museum. Among the five carpets, three carpets are of square format measuring 1.18 by 1.18 meters. They have the same pattern and differ from each other only by colors. Of the two large carpets, the larger one (hereafter called the carpet No. 1) is 2.56 meters high and 1.50 meters wide, and the other measures 2.2 meters high and 1.19 meters wide, which will be called carpet No. 2.

In the 3 square ones, one line of Brāhmī script is woven. It contains the same text though a few characters seem a little different:

Spāvatä meri sūmä hodä

"The spāvata-official Meri gave (this) to Sūma".

Both Khotanese and Tibetan sources, we have learned about a Buddhist saint who sacrificed his life to save the small river from drying out. He is still remembered through a toponymical name. The aforementioned place name Shampul, where the carpets were found, is most likely named after him.① *Spāvatä*, however, is an earlier phase of *spāta*, which comes from Old-Iranian *spāda-pati* and means army leader. Before this form appears in the carpets, experts of Khotanese have suspected that *spāta* should have an earlier form like *spāvatä*, but the idea never has been proven until the discovery of the carpets. Now the presumption is confirmed. This older form, however, indicates that the carpets must be products from the 6th century, because Khotanese was written in Brāhmī script most likely not until the 6th century. Before Khotanese came to its official stage, Kharoṣṭhī had been used as official script, and Gandhārī as the official language, followed by Sanskrit/Brāhmī which was introduced in Khotan approximately in later 5th and early 6th century, for a short period of a maximum of fifty years in the scope of the secular world.②

Tablet 1, changing of official languages and scripts in ancient Khotan:

Gandhārī /Kharoṣṭhī to 5th century	Sanskrit/Brāhmī 5th and early 6th century for a short period	Khotanese/ Brāhmī From the 6th century on → disappearance of the ancient Khotan kingdom.

III. The motivation of design of carpets No. 1 and 2

The main topic of today is to give a rather outlined explanation of the illustrations in carpets No. 1 and 2 (Plate I and II). I am more or less trained in Iranian Studies and Indology. That means that I am more able to deal with texts in languages like Khotanese and Sanskrit than with pictures. The carpet No. 1 has 3 Brāhmī signs, and for many years nobody knew what they meant. In order to find out which context the 3 characters stand, in 2013 I began to research more than 20 figures on this carpet.

---

① I have published an article discussing the script and about the saint in detail, see: Duan Qing, "The inscription on the Shampul Carpets", *the Journal of Inner Asian Art and Archaeology*, Vol.5, 2012, Brepols, pp. 95-100.

② Two Sanskrit documents have been read and published, in which a Khotanese king of the early 6th century is mentioned. The two documents offer the evidence that Sanskrit was used as official language in ancient Khotan. About the two documents, see: Duan Qing, "Deed, Coins and King's Title as Revealed in a Sanskrit Cloth Document from the 6 Century", *Eurasian Studies*, English Version IV, edited by Yu Taishan and Li Jinxiu, Asia Publishing Nexus, 2016, pp. 265-283.

While observing the carpets No. 1 and 2, it is ease to have the impression that a whole story about a journey of a hero is displayed on them. The story must start from below and develops in zigzag-direction to the top. Let take the carpet No. 1 (Plate I) as an example: At the beginning, the hero is shown in the middle in the first row (counted from the bottom). In the second row he occurs on the left, in the third row on the right and then on the left in the fourth row, in order to return to the middle in the fifth row, which represents the happy end of the story.

In the first row of Carpet No. 1, conspicuously illustrated is a small male figure in dark blue color, who stands a little behind on the right side of the hero. His hands and feet, however, are in skin color. The small figure is holding something in yellow in his right hand and he is looking towards the hero. Above the head of the dark blue figure is some drawing, which consists of vertical strokes in dark blue color and cross strokes in earth color. Perceiving this as a symbolic drawing of the surface of the earth, it becomes clear that the little dark blue is displayed just underneath the earth while he is still alive because his hands and feet are deliberately shown in skin color. The attitude, how he is looking at the hero, conveys his strong desire to seek help. He wants to get out of the underworld (Fig. 2).

The motif will be clearer when the figure of a boy in the fifth row is taken into a comparison (Fig. 3). Here the boy no longer looks at the hero, but towards another direction. His front leg is slightly bent, and his back foot is not flat on the ground—all these details indicate that the boy is running with outstretched arms towards a cheerful woman. The boy in the fifth row is depicted in a returning scene that is for certain the same one who is displayed in the first row in dark blue color for showing that he is underneath the earth. At this stage, a conclusive point can be marked. It is a story which inevitably involves life and death. The key to disclose the secret of the story is the dark blue figure.

Looking again closer at the details in the fifth row, it is noticed that the hero now is holding a club with both hands (also in Fig. 3). Sequencing the three themes, firstly, the club of the hero, secondly the yellow object of the dark blue figure in his hand while he is illustrated underneath the earth, and thirdly an old man in the third row—all these details hint at an epic, which was circulated in Mesopotamia around 2000 before Christ. The epic has been preserved in cuneiform on the twelfth clay tablet of the Akkadian Gilgamesh epic, but then remained hidden from the world for thousand years. It was not until the end of the 19th century that the whole Gilgamesh epic had been reconstructed from thousands of tiny little pieces of clay. Today we know that the Gilgamesh epic consists of about 3600 lines of text, which is written in 12 clay tablets.① The 12th clay tablet of the Gilgamesh epic is of unique character, which is telling the story of Gilgamesh, Enkidu and the underworld. This implies to me that the 12th tablet is referencing the illustrations of the two carpets from Khotan.

Fig. 2, a figure under earth with a yellow object (*pukku*) in his right hand.

Fig. 3, the returning scene and the hero with a club (*mekku*).

The Gilgamesh epic is well known having the reputation of the first great epic in the world literature.

① I noticed this information through browsing literatures on *Gigamesh* online from a German author, W Röllig by name, whose book is entitled *das Gilgamesch Epos*, published in Reclam, Ditzingen, 2009. It is certainly due to century long efforts that now a bounty of literature on *Gilgamesh* epic is offered. George has noted main scholars and their contributions in the preface of his volumes on the subject, see: R.A. George, *The Babylonian Gilgamesh Epic: introduction, critical edition and Cuneiform texts*, Oxford, Oxford University Press, 2003.

Most scholars who deal with the Babylonian epic are of the opinion that the complete epic end with the 11th tablet, while the 12th tablet has a new story which is the narration of Enkidu going to the underworld for picking *pukku*. In Babylonian, the word *pukku* is signifying a wooden ball, which is a play toy. *Pukku* is to be hit by a tool called *mekku* .① A Sumerian myth narrates that it was Gilgamesh who created the pair of the toys and invented the play. He drew all young men into the day-long game so that their wives complained about it to the gods. As the consequence, the gods let the ball disappear in the underworld. Gilgamesh was sad about it. Enkidu agreed to go to the underworld to fetch the ball. Gilgamesh explained to Enkidu in detail how he should behave in the underworld, for example, that he should go barefoot and not wear new clothes. Despite all the warnings, Enkidu was caught by the earth and could not get out of the underworld. Gilgamesh sought help from the gods. Finally, a god opened a hole in the earth, which released the spirit of Enkidu. Gilgamesh inquired about Enkidu's deceased relatives. Earlier scholars have pointed out that there are many comparable references between the Gilgamesh epic and the Greek Odyssey. Especially on the 12th tablet of the Gilgameš epic, Enkidu comes from the underworld and reports about the situation there. The 24th chapter of the Odyssey tells about the hero going into the underworld and reporting about the deceased being there.②

Hints like two play objects illustrated in carpets lead to the story of Gilgamesh epic. They are the club in the hand of the hero in the 5th row and the yellow object in the hand of the dark blue figure in the first row. The yellow object is supposed to display the ball—the *pukku* in Babylonian Gilgamesh epic, while the club is *mekku*. Because of the depiction of the *pukku* and *mekku* in the carpets a link to the myth of the Sumerian origin is established. The mythic story tells that the toys *pukku* and *mekku* are made of the crown and the root of a willow tree. It was a special willow tree which had been carefully nurtured by Goddess Inanna for many years in her garden in expectation that it would yield wood for a throne and bed. But when the tree had grown up, it was occupied by three evil creatures. Thanks to Gilgamesh, the goddess could finally make use of the tree for her own purpose.③ For the reward, Gilgamesh received the necessary material for creating the toys *pukku* and *mekku*.

Even more evidence to support the possible link between the illustrative narration of the carpets and the remnant of Sumerian myth: The two words *pukku* and *mekku* are surprisingly not only preserved in Khotanese, but also in Pāli, and even in Chinese transliterations. They occur in the parallel versions of *Mūgapakkha-jātaka*—a tale about one of the former lives of Buddha. In Khotanese, *pukku* and *mekku* appear as *mukä-pamka*, in Pāli *mūgapakkha*, and in Chinese *mu po*（慕魄）. Since a paper discussing the specific topic is published ④, it is not necessary here to go to details about the evolution and variation of these two words. Mentioning the two words in Khotanese is aiming to emphasize that it is not an unfounded coincidence to find the illustration of *pukku* and *mekku* in the carpets.

Until now what attempted in the above discussion, is to find out accordance between the illustrations of the carpets with the Gilgamesh epic. However, after analyzing the all images, my conclusion is that the carpets do not offer a parallel visual version of the Gilgamesh epic. It is only the frame of the story of the 12th clay tablet of the Gilgamesh epic that is taken over, and borrowed for the narration of the illustrative carpets. As related in the 12th tablet, the story of the carpets starts with the scene that the ball is fallen into the underworld, but why it is fallen and why a boy is in the underworld for picking it up, —that is not important, what matters is to get the boy out of the underworld.

① R.A. George, *The Babylonian Gilgamesh Epic: introduction, critical edition and Cuneiform texts*, Oxford, Oxford University Press, 2003, p. 899.

② Hans Ulrich Steymans, *Gilgamesch, Ikonogrphie eines Helden*, Orbis Biblicus et Orientalis 245, Academic Press Fribourg, 2010, pp. 331-332.

③ For the whole story translated from Sumerian language, see: Samuel Noah Kramer, *Gilgamesh and the Ḫuluppu-Tree: A reconstructed Sumerian Text*, the Univeristy of Chicago Press, Chicago, Illinois, 1938; for analysis of the story, see: Diane Walkstein and Samuel Noah Kramer, *Inanna, Queen of Heaven and Earth: her stories and hymns from Sumer*, Harper & Row, Publishers, New York, 1983, p. 140.

④ I have published a paper in Chinese discussing the two words and their variation, see: Duang Qing, "Metaphor of the wooden ball", *A Collection of the Sino-Iranica Cultural Exchange on the Silk Rood International Conference*, ShangHai, ZhongXi Book Company, 2016, pp. 31-40.

Equally as to the 12th tablet, the hero in the illustration of the carpets starts on a journey for seeking help. However, the deities he turns to, are total different than those in the Akkadian epic of Gilgamesh. The end of the story is totally different as is the goal of the narrations. In the following, I will refer to the dark little figure as Enkidu and the hero Gilgamesh. Whether the two figures actually did so in Khotanese is not discussed at this time.

It is said that an epic is always the story of a hero. The depictions of the carpets, however, do not transmit the impression of any combat scene. The attitude of the hero in the first row of the two carpets looks more like help-seeking. Now Gilgamesh is seeking help, because as a human being he is not able to get a man out of the underworld. Consequently, he is a hero seeking help. In this sense, his action – to seek for help – will determine the course of the story. To realize the identity of the hero as a human being and his role as help-seeking one is necessary. It gives a starting point for the orientation of the further research for, the figures to which Gilgamesh turns on his journey for seeking help must be deities who, according to myth or legends, do not only possess superhuman abilities but also are endowed with responsibility of ruling over the spiritual world. The logic of seeking help determines the end of the story; as soon as the hero reaches his goal, and in this case, as soon as Enkidu is out of the underworld, the story is over. Nevertheless, a fact is hidden behind the logic. For those who are not able to grant the final rescue to the hero are degraded whereas the one who does give the last rescue wins the most worship amongst the people. Following the course of the representation of the carpets, it is a goddess who rescues Enkidu from the underworld. Hence, the goddess is the highest deity among all the illustrated divine beings on the carpets. This conclusion leads to the real motif of the carpets No. 1 and 2; they are dedicated to the goddess. In other words, the illustration of the carpets is as good as the manifestation of the goddess. They are remnants of the local cult of the ancient Kingdom of Khotan.

IV. Identity of the Greek Gods

Who are the divine beings to whom the hero turns? First, a consideration of Hindu deities can be ruled out[①], for, as revealed through the Brāhmī script, the carpets are most likely products made in the 6th century, and by this time the important Hindu gods are fully developed to their maturity. This means that they are already fixed in terms of their typical attributes, mounts and weapons. No single aspect of the figures points to Hinduism. Since Sumerian and Akkadian traces are disclosed, the search field must be wide enough including ancient Mesopotamian and Iranian pantheons which are as huge as an ocean.[②]

Hermes

In the first row on both carpets on the far right is the first deity the hero visits. The deity has two serpents lying on his side, one is colored symbolizing life of this world, and the other black symbolizing death (Fig. 4). Searching in the area of the Indo-European pantheon, only the Greek deity Hermes appears on the surface. Frothingham, the former professor of art history and archaeology of Princeton University, called it 'the Snake-god'.[③] Hermes is always given two snakes as attribute who also bears the surname psychopompos. The Greek myth tells that Hermes is the one who sends the deceased through the Lethe into the underworld, and who has the ability to go back and forth between the worlds of the living and the dead. Hermes was the one who had brought back Persephone from the underworld from the side of Hades. The role of Hermes fits well into the context of the representations of both carpets. If

① That the figures on the carpets should be the unexpected representations of the Hindu god Krishna, is supposed by Zhang He. See: Zhang He, "Figurative and Inscribed Carpets from Shanpula, Khotan: Unexpected Representations of the Hindu God Krishna", *the Journal of Inner Asian Art and Archaeology*, Vol. 5, 2012, Brepols, pp. 59-79.

② However, Greek deities are well known while fortunately, the book of Shenkar provides the basic references for the Iranian deities. See: Michael Shenkar, *Intangible Spirits and Graven Images: The Iconography of Deities in the Pre-Islamic Iranian World*, Leiden, 2014. For Sumerian and Akkadian literature sources I benefit from broad knowledge of my colleague professor Gong Yushu at Peking University.

③ L. A. Frothingham, "Babylonian Origin of Hermes the Snake-God, and of the Caduceus I", *American Journal of Archaeology*, Vol. 20, No. 2, Apr.-Jun., 1916, published by Archaeological Institute of America, p. 175.

the hero is looking for some divine beings who consorts with both worlds, he should first turn to the one who had access to both worlds.

Evidently Hermes could not help him, otherwise the visual story would come to an end. It seems however that Hermes was helpful and gave hints for further orientation. Persephone was the next goddess whom the hero visited. This brings us to the second row of figures on the two carpets.

Fig. 4, Hermes with two snakes of carpet No. 1 and 2.

Persephone

Having found the first deity to be of Greek origin, the gods in the second row should also be of Greek origin. This is confirmed. There are three reasons to identify the female figure as Persephone. Firstly, Persephone is always shown in a skirt and holds in her hand a bunch of grain. Here I took pictures of a publication by Paul Carus from 1900. The representation of the cereal bundle in Persephone's hand is similar to that in the carpets, in which the stem of grain is particularly depicted as a long staff (Fig. 5).

Fig. 5, Persephone with a long staff of grains. Pictures are copied from Carus 1900, (98-100), which are redrawn and processed by my colleague Ye Shaoyong.

Secondly, Greek mythology tells of Persephone as the daughter of Zeus and Demeter. When, following the scent of Narcissus, she came to the earth to pick this flower, Hades climbed out of the underworld and kidnapped Persephone. She became the wife of Hades and Queen of the Underworld. In this myth of Persephone, the Narcissus flower plays an important role, as it was the favorite flower of Persephone. Depicted in the hand of the hero is a dark blue flower, which must be a Narcissus

Fig. 6, Narcissus in the right hand of the hero. Persephone with a long staff of grains as depicted in carpets No. 1 and 2.

(Fig. 6). The dark blue color, which is identical with that of Enkidu in the underworld, stands for the color of the underworld. Since Narcissus did not grow in ancient Khotan, this type of flower would only exist in the imagination of the narrators when talking about Persephone. Very likely, Narcissus were thought as an important instrument, should a visit to Persephone been made possible. In the representation on the carpets, the flower in the hand of the hero is obviously intended as a springboard. This is a creative development based on Greek mythology. Such creative applying of Greek mythology for the purpose of the narrative can only be possible for those who were very familiar with Greek mythology.

The third point for supporting that the female main figure in the 2nd series is Persephone comes from the text, which consists of 3 Brāhmī characters (Fig. 7), which, dark-colored between the heads of the figures, can be clearly read. These three signs are *ha dī vä*, of which *dīvä*, a loan word from Sanskrit *dvīpa* - the 'island; Continent' . This meaning has been tested several times in Khotan texts, as, for example, in chapter 16 of the Book of Zambasta. There the verse 38 contains *tcūratasä dīvä uttarūvä*, which Emmerick reproduced in his English translation of "the four-cornered Uttara-dvīpa". The first part *hadi*, however, originates from the Greek Hades, meaning underworld, and at the same time god of the underworld. Thus 'hadīvä' is a composite, composed of Greek Hades and Khotanese *dīvä*, under which, in the context of the representation of the carpets, the 'Greek underworld' is to be understood.

Fig. 7, 3 Brāhmī characters which read ha dīvä.

At this point one has to ask why a composite is necessary of a Greek and a Khotan word, since the word for hell exists in the Khotan vocabulary. As well known, in ancient Khotan the main religion was Buddhism. In the Buddhist theory, *naraka* 'hell' is an important concept of religious significance. The fact that a special composite for the underworld in the term of the Greek religion was created clearly shows that various religious concepts and cults were popular in old Khotan. The historical Khotanese were very aware of the diversity of the religious concepts and they knew how to differentiate them in a philosophical sense. For them *naraka* is certainly a Buddhist concept of a *karma* term which is imbedded in the existential causal law of Buddhist philosophy. From this aspect, a hell is not understood as the final destiny of every human being. Falling into a hell is only the result of evil deeds. Many, however, will be reborn in another better or worse existence, depending on how many good deeds they have achieved during their existence. In contrast to the concept of the Greeks, the underworld is a place where everyone goes after death. Since the religious connotations of the Greek underworld on the one hand and a Buddhist hell on the other totally differ, it is compelling to create the new word—the composite *hadīvä* to express Hades. Persephone is the goddess of the Greek underworld.

Hephaestus, Aphrodite und Ares

The third row of carpets No.1 and 2 does not look identical. While carpet No. 1 shows two groups of figures in

Fig. 8, rights above the hero with two instruments and under him Ares. Links above Hephaestus and under him Aphrodite.

the illustrations, the illustrations in carpet No. 2 shows only one group of figures. The man in the 3rd row on the far right is the hero. His walking appearance suggests that he is the visitor. The older man in the group on the right, I identified him as Ūta-napišti from the Babylonian Gilgamesh epic. Accordingly, as man he had survived the great flood and acquired immortality. His name has been preserved as Xisuthros in Greek. His immortality is expressed through combination with the figure of a young man. The two figures represent the same man. ①

The group of figures on the far left of the third row the carpet No. 1 is of particular interest (Fig. 8). The scene is unfolded in the whole third row of carpet No. 2. Every deity of a cult or a religion has its fixed special symbol and attributes, so that their followers can recognize them and align themselves with them. The established symbolic and attributes are important for different cults and religions, in order to be able to distinguish themselves from each other. Where the characteristics of a deity are not self-evident enough, they must be recognizable by other ways, such as by a scene. The left group shows four figures. Of these, the figure in the upper right is the hero. Here he is now equipped with two tools, one of which looks like an axe, and the other looks like a stick. This indicates that he stands before a master craftsman from whom he has received tools. We know from the Babylonian Gilgamesh epic that Gilgamesh is equipped with two tools, one of which is an axe, the second tool has no specific identification. Some believe it is a 'sky-bolt' and Professor George of London University identified it as a meteor.②

In Greek mythology, Hephaestus is the God of forge and a master craftsman. He is an ugly cripple. His wife is the most beautiful goddess Aphrodite, who had an affair with the war god Ares. Homer tells that Hephaestus created an elaborate "net" when he discovered the affair of the two gods. Aphrodite and Ares were caught together in bed in Hephaestus' home. At first Hephaestus summoned the gods as spectators in order to embarrass the two. Ugliness, beauty and crippling are not enough specific to be perceived as symbols of a deity. The elaborate "net" is something special and it can be considered as a special feature because only Hephaestus is capable of making this. It is amazing to observe that the "net" is unmistakably woven into both carpets (Fig. 9).

Fig. 9, Ares in net as designed in carpets No. 1 and 2.

From the development of the story the visit of the hero to Hephaestus is apparently necessary because

① This is of course only my assumption. I am not sure about this identification.

② About the second thing there is no agreed exploration. Some said that it is a "sky-bolt", see: Stephanie Dalley, *Myth from Mesopotamia*, Oxford, Oxford University Press, 1989, p. 57. George explained it as a meteore, see: R.A. George, *The Babylonian Gilgamesh Epic: introduction, critical edition and Cuneiform texts*, Oxford, Oxford University Press, 2003, p. 793.

the hero has to prepare himself for fulfilling his wish. According to a Sumerian story, it was Gilgamesh who, with his hatchet, cut the willow tree to make a bed for the goddess Inanna.① The carpets are apparently telling a new version, according to which it is Hephaestus who equips the hero with the necessary tools. With this I come to the fourth row.

V. The traces of Sumerian mythology

Analyzing the figures in the 4th row, the hero is depicted on the far left. Carpet No. 2 has only 3 figures in this row. The goddess stands in the middle between two trees, one yellow and the other more or less skin-colored. The two trees remind of Iranian mythology. According to Bundahisn, one of the most important literature about Iranian mythology, there are two divine trees—the haoma tree and the tree of many seeds. But there is no goddess standing underneath the trees in the Old Iranian religion. As mentioned above, the identification of the goddess between the trees is indicated by the club of the hero in the 5th row of carpet No 1. As known from a Sumerian story, it is the goddess Inanna, who gives the crown of a willow tree to Gilgamesh after he has helped her to chase away the evil beings. The club is made from the crown of the willow tree. The Sumerian mythology worships Inanna as the goddess of heaven and earth.②

In the fourth row of the the both carpets, the dark blue figure reappears. Over his head is again the depiction of designs indicating the earth. The appearance of the dark blue figure at this stage has the function to remind the core of the whole representation, to get him out of the underworld. Though hidden in the background, a Sumerian story can be perceived, namely the descent of Inanna into the underworld. When talking about the hidden story, a question is inevitable, which version of the descent of goddess is indicated in the background? Handed down from Mesopotamian ancient time are two versions, the Sumerian version relates to the descent of Inanna, while the Akkadian version relates to the descent of Ishtar where the goddess Inanna is transformed into Ishtar in the Akkadian world. It is to differentiate between the two versions. Which one is hidden in the background of the carpets? The two figures on the far right of the fourth row render the key to disclose the secret (Fig. 10).

Through comparing the two versions of the goddess' descent, it turns out that the Sumerian one is hidden in the background. The relating Akkadian story of the Ishtar's descent is shorter. In order to bring Ishtar out of the underworld, Ea, the god of wisdom, created only one god-like playboy,③ while in the Sumerian story two sexless creatures are created which played the pivotal role in the process of invigorating Inanna. Without them it would be impossible that the goddess Inanna came out of the underworld.

Fig. 10, the figures in the 4th row of carpet No. 1.

Before continuing with the Sumerian story, it is necessary to recapitulate some aspects from the

① Samuel Noah Kramer, *Gilgamesh and the Ḫuluppu-Tree: A reconstructed Sumerian Text*, the Univeristy of Chicago Press, Chicago, Illinois, 1938, pp. 9-10.

② Inanna, Queen of Heaven and Earth, so called is the book of Wolkstein & Kramer 1983. It is expressed in a hymn attributed to Inanna (Diane Walkstein and Samuel Noah Kramer, *Inanna, Queen of Heaven and Earth: her stories and hymns from Sumer*, Harper & Row, Publishers, New York, 1983, p. 95).

③ Stephanie Dalley, *Myth from Mesopotamia*, Oxford, Oxford University Press, 1989, pp. 158-161.

Fig. 11, two children's figures above the screen of Viśa Sambhava. The painting is sketched by professor Zhang Huiming, Paris.

Fig. 12, the two sexless figures with ribbons in their hands are illustrated on a square carpet found in Shampul.

real world of ancient Khotan. The ancient kingdom of Khotan was known as the center of Mahāyāna Buddhism. Nevertheless, traces in Khotanese manuscripts and wall paintings of Dunhuang are noticed that ancient people of Khotan had always cultivated a local religion until the disappearance of their country. For instance, in the collection of Aurel Stein preserved in the British Library there is a long Khotanese paper scroll that Stein took from the hidden cave of Dunhuang.① Several texts are written on it, among which one text contains a typical invocation to all deities according to Khotanese pantheon. In the group subscribed to deities indigenous in Khotan, Ttaśa and Ttara are named in the list.② The Tibetan tradition has preserved legends coming down from the ancient kingdom of Khotan. The two names reappear in *Liyul Lung Bstan-pa*, spelt as Daci and Dara in Tibetan. The legend accounts Daci and Dara as two kings of dragons who were protectors of a Buddhist monastery. In one of the best-known wall paintings from Dunhuang, where the image of the Khotan king Viśa Sambhava is painted from the first half of the 10th century③, two children's figures are illustrated above his screen (Fig. 11), which apparently are playing the role of granting blessings. It is supposed that the two divine figures are portrayed as children, in order to avoid emphasizing any clear gender. The same purpose can be observed in all the three square carpets which, unearthed together with the two carpets on discussion, show separately the same two figures whose gender cannot be identified as either female or male. They each carry a long band in their hands (Fig. 12). In the ancient Iranian culture this long band is called farn or xvarra in Phalavi, which means royal glory.④

Every deity of a cult, whatever it may be, must have a mythological legend, otherwise his cult cannot be explained. It is until the discovery of the carpets that nothing was known about the origin and story of Ttaśa and Ttara. However, it is surprisingly and at the same time unimaginable that the tales about the origin and divinity of these two Khotanese deities are to be found in the remote Sumerian story of the descent of Inanna. Now let's turn to the story as translated by Samuel Noah Kramer, the famous Sumerian cuneiform expert:

"From under his fingernail Father Enki brought forth dirt.

① The complete inventory number of this long paper scroll is Or8210 / S2471 (O. P. Skjærvø, *Khotanese Manuscripts from Chinese Turkestan in the British Library, a Complete Catalogue with Texts and Translations*, The British Library, 2002, pp. 32-34).

② Ttaśa and Ttara are to be read as two separate names as confirmed with Daci and Dara in Tibetan source. About more detailed discussion, see: Duan Qing, *Das Khotanische Aparimitāyuhsūtra. Studien zur Indologie und Iranistik*, Dissertation Band 3. Dr. Inge Wezler Verlag für Orientalische Fachpublikationen,1992, pp. 22-25.

③ The painting of Khotanese king Viśa Sambhava（李圣天）is in cave 98 of Mogao.

④ This topic has been discussed by my in a Chinese paper, see: Duan Qing, "Haloes and Ribbons as Symbolic for Good Fortune according to Zoroastrians", *The Stady of Art History*, Vol. xvii, 2015, pp. 153-166.

"He fashioned the dirt into a *kurgarra*, a creature neither male nor female.

"From under the fingernail of his other hand he brought forth dirt.

"He fashioned the dirt into a galatur, a creature neither male nor female.

"He gave the food of life to the *kurgarra*.

"He gave the water of life to the *galatur*."

Enki, the great god of intelligence and creation, said to the new created creatures:

"Go to the underworld,

"Enter the door like flies."

In the underworld, Ereshkigal, the queen of the underworld according to Sumerian myth, was moaning:

"Oh! Oh! My inside!"

And the two creatures created by Enki moaned after her:

"Oh! Oh! Your inside!"

She moaned:

"Ohhhh! Oh! My outside!"

They moaned:

"Ohhhh! Oh! Your outside!"

……

Then follows a long imitation of the two creatures to the moaning of Ereshkigal, the queen of the Sumerian underworld. Finally, Ereshkigal stopped and looked at them. She said:

"Who are you, moaning—groaning—sighing with me? …… Speak then! What do you wish?"

They answered:

"We wish only the corpse that hangs from the hook on the wall."

……

The corpse of Inanna was given to them.

"The *kurgarra* sprinkled the food of life on the corpse. The *galatur* sprinkled the water of life on the corpse. Inanna arose…."①

Beside of the mythology of the two genderless divine beings, the Sumerian version of the descent of Inanna describes also in detail Inanna's disguise, jewelry and things that she holds in her hand. When comparing the description of the story with the representation of the highest goddess as depicted on the carpets, several consistencies can be made ascertained. According to the Sumerian story, Inanna had to go through seven gates, before she could meet her sister Ereshkigal, who dominated the underworld. At each gate she had to put down one important thing. Now let follow Inanna's walk into the underworld and see what she was wearing, and what she held in her hand:

"When she entered the first gate,

"From her head, the *shugurra*, the crown of the steppe, was removed.

……

"When she entered the second gate,

"From her neck the small lapis beads were removed.

……

"When she entered the third gate,

"From her breast the double strand of beads was was removed.

---

① The whole story of *kurgarra* and *galatur* I have quoted or retold according to Diane Walkstein and Samuel Noah Kramer, *Inanna, Queen of Heaven and Earth: her stories and hymns from Sumer*, Harper & Row, Publishers, New York, 1983, pp. 64-67.

......

"When she entered the fourth gate,

"From her chest the breastplate called 'come, man, come!' was removed.

......

"When she entered the fifth gate,

"From her wrist the gold ring was removed.

......

"When she entered the sixth gate,

"From her hand the lapis measuring rod and line was removed.

......

"When she entered the seventh gate,

"From her body the royal robe was removed.①

......

It is lucky enough that an entire description of Inanna's adornments and attributes is provided by the Sumerian literary source. Bearing the seven attributes of Inanna in mind, an examination and comparison of the details of the figure, which supposed to be Inanna in the carpets, can be carried out. In the depiction several similar motifs are clearly visible: Firstly, let's observe the blue painted necklace and the golden ring around the wrist which is emphasized through yellow color of woolen thread. Nevertheless, most strikingly noticeable are the two rod-shaped things with white and blue dots, which apparently represent the distance marker of a measuring instrument (Fig. 13). If they were not the lapis measuring rod and lapis measuring line, what else could be portrayed? Each deity has its peculiar attributes. The lapis measuring rod and line belong to Inanna as her attributes, as it is described in the Sumerian text of the descent of Inanna. Apropos, the measuring rod and line, they must have been symbols of royal authority in ancient Sumerian time, since according to Sumerian literature, Dumuzi, the king of Sumer and husband of Inanna, possessed scepter, crown, measuring rod and line, fields, meadows, and forests—all these were needed for him to rule his kingdom.② The identification of the white and blue doted lines portrayed in the carpets with the measuring rod and line of the Sumerian Goddess is of significant interest because it is much supposed that they were the forerunner of rod and ring, which formed together a symbol signifying the divine power, and are often observed as attributes of gods in the wide area of Mesopotamia.③ However, the lapis measuring rod and line never have been noticed in any former iconographies. Although their identification is going to be confirmed through another evidence, the carpets have already provided one exemplar for future reference.

Fig. 13, lapis measuring rod and line in hands of goddess illustrated on carpets No. 1 and 2.

① For the complete text, see: Diane Walkstein and Samuel Noah Kramer, *Inanna, Queen of Heaven and Earth: her stories and hymns from Sumer*, Harper & Row, Publishers, New York, 1983, pp. 57-60.

② Diane Walkstein and Samuel Noah Kramer, *Inanna, Queen of Heaven and Earth: her stories and hymns from Sumer*, Harper & Row, Publishers, New York, 1983, p. 164.

③ This supposition has been much disputed, as for instance in "the rod and ring", in Michael Shenkar, *Intangible Spirits and Graven Images: The Iconography of Deities in the Pre-Islamic Iranian World*, Leiden, 2014, p. 54, who gave further reference on the topic. George (R. A. George, "Sennacherib and the Tablet of Destinies", *Iraq*, Vol. 48, published by British Institute for the Study of Iraq, 1986, p. 143) is of the opinion that "rod and ring" is plainly an emblem of divine beings.

VI. the Probable name of Inanna in Khotanese

The former discussion of the identification of the main goddess in the fourth row of the carpets with Inanna proves the existence through the two divine beings Ttaśa and Ttara in Khotanese originated from the Sumerian source, and by comparison of the attributes of Inanna as described in the texts. Even though that all the above identifications rely upon interpretations of texts and figures displayed on the carpets, and given that all similarities are reasonable, it cannot be concluded that the goddess portrayed in the fourth row of the both carpets has come down from the tradition of Sumerian culture if her name is not attested in existing Khotanese texts.

Indeed, there is no goddess by name Inanna or Nanna in the entire known Khotanese literature. Nevertheless, a local goddess regularly occurs in the name list of local deities in Khotanese manuscripts which are composed for the purpose of invocations. For example, the long paper scroll of the British Library as stated before, consists of several texts and includes a long invocation text within that all deities are enlisted; firstly, all Buddhas of the 10 heavenly directions are invocated, then all Bodhisattvas, and finally all the protectors of the Khotan kingdom. An entire paragraph is dedicated to kings of dragons whose names are "Nada Upanada Sāgara Grrahadatta Elapatta Myacalena". Though corrupt in spelling, they are certainly familiar names elsewhere known from Sanskrit Buddhist texts. Then follow names such as *sūmapauña, ttaśa, ttara, būjsyaja, sanīraka*—these are found only in the Khotanese local cult. Among them, *būjsyaja* designates the name a goddess which is also found spelt as *būjsaju* or *būjsaṃja*. In Ch ii 001—another Khotanese text from Dunhuang, a sentence reads as following:

mistye jaśta rrīña si' būjsaṃja hastara sti āmūnā jsīna u ......

My translation:

......the great devī, the queen, who is better than *būjsaṃja* (with regard to) our life and...

Although the sentence is broken, the survival words are still transmitting the impression that *būjsaṃja* is goddess in charge with matters of life. This fits in the role of epic carpets endowed to the goddess. As stated before, in the traditional Khotan texts, no goddess named Nana or Inanna is attested. Būjsaṃja designates the only goddess whose name cannot be etymologically searched in Indic sources, it is a Khotanese word. For its etymology Bailey suggests that the *būjsaṃja* is from **baujana-* with female suffix *-čī-* from base *baug-* 'to enjoy, possess, rule'[1]. Bailey's etymology is questionable because Old Iranian *-č-* is attested as -tc- in Khotanese, for instance, Khotanese adverb *nitca* 'outside'< *niš-čā, and noun *ūtcā-* 'water' < **usa- čā* [2]. My thought is that *būjsaṃjā-* is the name given to the goddess portrayed in the fourth row of the two carpets and as supposed, the story around the goddess goes back to Sumerian mythology. I dare to make any further assumtions that the etymology of the name is to be found in Sumerian words. I would see *-ja-* of *būjsaṃja* or *būjsyaja* as a suffixe meaning the source from which something originates [3] while *būjsaṃ-* or *būjsya-* is derived from the Sumerian word *bilga*, which means 'ancestor'.[4] Accordingly the name *būjsaṃjā-* means 'the one originated from the ancestors'. At present I am not able to provide more Khotanese words that may show influence of Sumerian tradition. Needless to say, my assumption is waiting for further supporting evidence.

VII . Conclusion

In conclusion, the current findings show that Greek and Roman influences were wide spread in ancient central

① W. H. Bailey, *Dictionary of Khotan Saka,* Cambridge, Cambridge University Press, 1979, p. 295.

② Almuth Degener, *Khotanische Suffixe*, *Khotanese Suffixe*, Alt- und Neu-Indische Studien, herausgegeben vom Institut für Kultur und Geschichte Indiens und Tibets an der Universität Hamburg, Stuttgart: Franz Steiner Verlag, 1989, xxx.

③ Ibid., p. 209.

④ It is written *bil2/3-ga* in *Sumerian Lexicon.*

Asia and along the ancient Silk Road. The exhibits of Hellenist style can be viewed in every museum of Taxila or Peshawar, the regions of ancient Gandhara, now known as parts of Pakistan. It was surprising or astonishing to find that Greek mythology existed in ancient Khotan, as it is represented in the figures illustrated on the carpets unearthed from the area of ancient Khotan. The stories behind the illustrations demonstrate an evident familiarity of ancient Khotanese people with the Greek myths so that they could fabricate their own stories based on factors of the Greek myths as seen in the case of Narcissus of Persephone.

However, the deities from Greek mythology are definitely foreign factors that cannot be attributed to the local and indigenous beliefs of ancient Khotan. As stated before, the whole narration of carpets No. 1 and 2 serves a religious cult that is devoted to the main goddess as portrayed in the fourth row of the both carpets whose Khotanese name should be *būjsaṃjā-*. It is thought that the illustration of both carpets is as good as a manifestation of the goddess who portrays similar attributes with those of Sumerian Inanna. Did the ancient Khotanese really inherit the tradition stemming from the Sumerian civilization?

Not yet identified is the other goddess next to *būjsaṃjā-* (supposed to be Inanna) in the fourth row of the carpet No. 1, who is portrayed as playing a long lute in her hands.A She might be Ereshkigal, the sister of Inanna and the queen of the underworld as related in Sumerian source. However, Ereshkigal has no flute as her attribute. Also uncertain is the identification of the figure of the old man in the group on the right side of the third row, whom I recognized as Ūta-napišti or Xisuthros in Greek.

There are indeed several uncertainties about my theory of the identifications and interpretations of the figures, and the etymology of the goddess' name cannot be confirmed. However, what one can unmistakably recognize is the whole story ends with a happy ending as displayed in the fifth row of the carpet No. 1. It is for certain that anyone who sees the carpets will agree that nothing prevents us from admiring the literary creativity of the ancient Khotan. Never before we have seen a combination that on one side preserves and continues the ancient civilization of humanity, even probably going back to Sumerians; while on the other hand, the evidence of combining foreign cultures of several civilizations and beliefs are united into one piece of art. The carpets with their representations can be seen as a real miracle, which the old Khotan culture has left for us.

******

This paper was firstly composed for a speech given at Consucius Institute of Lorand University, Budapest, on October 10, 2016. I acknowledge the first English revision to Dr. Patrick Wertmann of Renmin University of China. I acknowledge the final English revision for this publication to Julia Poole, Foreign Expert of PKU, Educational Consultant of Vancouver BC Canada.

******

---

① It reminds compellingly "the queen of the night" of Mozart. In Sumerian tradition Dumuzi is the spouse of Inanna who was used to play a flute, see: Samuel Noah Kramer, "The Weeping Goddess: Sumerian Prototypes of the Mater Dolorosa", *The Biblical Archaeologist*, Vol. 46, No. 2, Published by the American Schools of Oriental Research, 1983, p. 76.

Plate I, carpet No. 1

Plate II, carpet No. 2

希腊化埃及的“末日审判”观念

颜海英（北京大学）

摘　要：古埃及人最早设想出死者在来世要接受众神审判才能获得永生，这种“末日审判”的观念在中王国时期（前 2106—前 1786）出现，在新王国时期（前 1550—前 1069）广泛流传，在希腊化时期的世变和危机中其道德成分得到极大的提升，成为对基督教世界影响最大的古代思想。对“末日审判”观念发展和流传的考察，有助于我们更全面地理解希腊化时期的文化交融。

关键词：埃及；末日审判；希腊化

“末日审判”是古埃及人来世观念中的核心主题，主要内容是死者要在冥世的“真理大厅”接受众神的审判，符合 42 条道德准则的才可通过，加入众神得到永生。“末日审判”的观念最早见于中王国时期的墓葬文献，到新王国时期成为《亡灵书》的重要内容，一直盛行到希腊罗马时期。在上千年的过程中，“末日审判”观念在变化之中，最大的转折点是希腊化时期，本文通过分析这个流变过程来讨论古埃及宗教在古代晚期的影响。

一　“末日审判”思想的形成与演变

荷鲁斯与塞特的神话从古王国时期就零星出现在《金字塔铭文》中，奥赛里斯是埃及一位仁慈的国王，他教人们如何耕种，为他们立法，教他们如何敬神；他还到国外去，教化其他地区的人。他的弟弟塞特及其同伙阴谋反对他，塞特偷偷地量了奥赛里斯身体的尺寸，然后为他量身制作了一个精美的柜子。塞特在一次宴会上展示这个柜子，所有的神都对它赞美不已，想据为己有，塞特说谁躺在里面最合适这柜子就是谁的。当然奥赛里斯最合适，但他刚一躺进去，塞特及其同伙就关上了盖子，锁上它，然后把它扔进尼罗河，让它顺着河漂向大海。①

奥赛里斯的妻子伊西斯听说这个消息后，哀恸不已，她四处寻找，最终在腓尼基的拜布罗斯（Byblos，今 Jubay）找到了它。但是当她带着柜子回到埃及时，塞特设法再次得到了奥赛里斯的身体，并把尸体分割成 14 块，分别扔到埃及的各地。然后伊西斯第二次出去寻找奥赛里斯，把找到的每一块都就地掩埋（因此埃及有许多奥赛里斯的墓）。她还在奥赛里斯死后感而受孕，有了奥赛里斯的遗腹子，即童年的荷鲁斯。奥赛里斯成为来世之王，荷鲁斯与塞特为争夺王位继承权而斗争，除了正面

① M. Lichtheim, *Ancient Egyptian Literature, Vol.II, The New Kingdom*, Berkeley, University of Californian Press, 1976, pp. 81-83.

冲突外，也在众神的法庭上争执，最终荷鲁斯获得了胜利。[①]

现存的4个版本中，《孟菲斯神论》对众神的审判描述得最为详细。该版本刻于沙巴卡石碑（Shabaka stone），是大英博物馆第498号展品，该石碑以黑色花岗岩制成，约92厘米×137厘米，是25王朝国王沙巴卡（约前710）命人抄录的古王国时期的作品，原来的文本写在纸草上，因虫蚀损毁。该铭文的主要内容是普塔创世，但开篇先讲述了天神盖伯对荷鲁斯、塞特之争的裁决过程。[②]

在这个神话中，塞特是死亡的化身，通过众神的判决，奥赛里斯战胜死亡获得永生。法庭和审判因两神的争执而起，审判是针对死亡本身而非死者。

中王国时期开始，随着来世信仰的系统化，"末日审判"的观念从荷鲁斯神话中脱颖而出，并且产生了质变：所有的死者都要经过奥赛里斯的审判大厅，在那里接受众神的审判，通过之后才可以踏上通往西方乐土的旅程。下面是《石棺铭文》和《亡灵书》中对末日审判的描绘：

在审判大厅中，奥赛里斯是主审，另有42个神陪审。大厅中间有个天平，天平的一端是象征正义和真理的羽毛，另一端是死者的心。天平旁边是负责记录的文字之神图特，还蹲着一个集合了四种动物特征的怪兽。死者首先要陈述自己一生的功过，有两个罪过单，分别列有40项和42项罪名（两个单子的部分内容是重叠的），死者要一一否定这些罪名。他对着奥赛里斯否认40项罪名的单子，对着陪审团否认42项罪名的单子。这期间他的心放置在天平上。如果死者有罪，天平就朝心的一边倾斜，怪兽就会扑上去把心吞噬，这就意味着"二次死亡"，也就是真正的死亡，死者将永远不得超生。[③]

在荷鲁斯神话中，死者奥赛里斯向众神起诉死亡——塞特，而在"末日审判"中，所有的死者都要面对自己的罪恶，永生的希望要通过正义的审判来实现。古埃及人第一次在来世观念中把永生与正义联系在一起。这是来世观念走向道德化的重要一步。

那么，何为"正义"？或者说，死者所否定的那些罪过都是什么？上述的82项罪过，可以归纳为

（图片来源：R.O. Faulkner, *The Ancient Egyptian Book of the Dead*, British Museum, 1985, pp. 34-35）

---

① M. Lichtheim, *Ancient Egyptian Literature, Vol.II, The New Kingdom*, Berkeley, University of Californian Press, 1976, pp. 84-86.

② M. Lichtheim, *Ancient Egyptian Literature, Vol.I, The Old and Middle Kingdoms*, Berkeley, University of Californian Press, 1976, pp. 51-58.

③ R.O. Faulkner, *The Ancient Egyptian Book of the Dead*, British Museum, 1985, pp. 34-35.

三类：一类是最基本的，如“我没有杀人”“我没有欺诈”等；一类是更为具体的，如“我没有弄脏流水”“我没有与他人的妻子有染”等；还有一类是关乎职业道德的，如“我没有缺斤短两”“我没有让耕地荒芜”等。

我没有行不义之事。
我没有暴力抢劫。
我没有对任何人施暴。
我没有偷窃。
我没有杀过男人或女人。
我没有缺斤少两。
我没有欺诈。
我没有窃取上帝的财物。
我没有说过谎话。
我没有掠夺别人的财物。
我没有说恶毒的话。
我没有掠夺别人的食物。
我没有欺诈行为。

我没有发脾气和生气。
我没有侵犯他人。
我没有屠杀属于上帝的动物。
我没有让耕地荒芜。
我没有打探他人消息并捉弄他人。
我没有说他人的坏话。
我没有无端发怒。
我没有犯通奸罪。
我没有玷污自己。
我没有与他人的妻子有染。
我没有吓唬他人。
我没有怒气冲冲地发言。
我没有对正义和真理之词置若罔闻。
我没有让他人哭泣。
我没有说亵渎神明的话。
我没有实施过暴力。
我没有心急。

我没有向神报复。

我没有夸夸其谈。

我没有犯欺诈罪，没有看邪恶的东西。

我从未诅咒过国王。

我没有弄脏流水。

我没有言过其实。

我没有诅咒上帝。

我没有傲慢无礼。

我对人一视同仁。

我没有夺他人的财富以增加自己的财富。

我没有诅咒上帝的东西和我身边的东西。

我从未想过藐视尘世的神。①

这些琐碎而具体的内容，令人想起当时社会生活中的基本道德准则。对比同时期的教谕文献（当时社会的行为准则与指南），甚至神庙祭司的“守则”或者“禁忌”，都会发现很多内容是高度一致的。公元前1400年的一个贵族墓志铭上的自传部分，直接提到“末日审判”中的律法就是他在生活中的处世准则：

我按照“玛阿特”行事，因此得到好运，

我努力遵守“真理大厅”的律法，

因为我想清白地抵达冥界，

不对任何人犯罪，

不做任何让神谴责的事情，

不令自己的名声受到玷污。②

由此可见，“末日审判”既是当时社会道德标准的反映，也反过来对人们的行为规范有制约作用。

在审判大厅中出现的42个陪审的神，象征着埃及的42个诺姆——自古王国后最基本的行政区划，意味着审判是向全世界公开的。死者一生功过的判断，不在世俗的权威，而是交由众神，这是道德神圣化的关键性标志。

二　希腊化时期：超越人世的审判

自新王国结束以后，埃及不断遭受外族入侵和统治，文化上也出现倒退，在外族统治的间歇期间，埃及一度恢复独立，建立了本民族的统治——26王朝（前656—前525），也叫赛易斯王朝，并

---

① R.O. Faulkner, *The Ancient Egyptian Book of the Dead*, British Museum, 1985, pp. 31-32.

② Jan Assmann, *Death and Salvation in Ancient Egypt*, Cornell University Press, 2005, pp. 80-81.

且倡导古典文化的复兴，较突出的成就是“世俗体文字”的问世，用这种文字创作的文学，叫“世俗体文学”。散文故事《善腾·哈姆瓦斯的故事》，便是这种文学的代表作。

《善腾·哈姆瓦斯的故事》讲述拉美西斯二世的第四个儿子——王子哈姆瓦斯的传奇故事。他是孟菲斯城普塔神的大祭司，学识渊博，而且崇尚古代文化，修复过多处神庙。这个故事由两部分组成。第一部分保存在开罗博物馆第30646号纸草上，成文于托勒密王朝。故事主要讲述哈姆瓦斯寻找魔法书过程中经历的种种奇遇。①

故事的第二部分见于大英博物馆第604号纸草的反面，主要是讲哈姆瓦斯之子西奥塞尔的故事。西奥塞尔自幼天赋过人，聪敏异常，12岁时就成为优秀的书吏，学问胜过了孟菲斯城所有的人。故事很大篇幅讲述幼年的西奥塞尔带父亲去观看阴间的奇迹。②

这段故事以两个葬礼的描述开始，一天，哈姆瓦斯看到一个显赫富有的贵族的葬礼，规模浩大，全城的人都来哀悼，随葬品和棺椁都极尽奢华。不久之后，他又看到一个死去的穷人被一张破席裹着，孤零零被拖去沙漠埋葬。哈姆瓦斯不禁感叹：“做个有钱人多好，葬礼如此风光！看那穷人，身后何其凄凉！”西奥塞尔说：“父亲，让我带你去冥府看看他们都有什么样的际遇。”于是父子俩到了冥界，看到了审判大厅，奥赛里斯，42个陪审神。他们看到一个人穿着上好的亚麻衣服，站在奥赛里斯身旁，对他的宣判是：因为他生前的善行，他得以通过“末日审判”，加入众神的行列，从此得到永生。此人竟然是哈姆瓦斯之前看到的那个死去的穷人。而那个举办了风光葬礼的贵族，则被判有罪，被拉去地狱受罚。③

这个故事值得注意的有两点：一是活人入冥府的情节，这在以往的古埃及文学中从来没有出现过，却是两河流域和希腊文学传统中常见的主题，如苏美尔语的《吉尔伽美什、恩启都与阴间》，阿卡德语的《吉尔伽美什史诗》第12块泥版，都描述了恩启都进入冥府而不得生还的故事④，希腊神话中，冥神哈迪斯把农神德墨忒尔的女儿珀耳塞福涅抢到冥府，使得德墨忒尔悲伤过度，从此大地一片荒芜。在宙斯的调停下，哈迪斯答应让珀耳塞福涅回到母亲的身边，但每年必须有3个月居住在冥府；只有俄耳甫斯、赫拉克勒斯、奥德修斯、埃涅阿斯等极少数英雄曾进入冥府又活着回到人世。最悲哀的是奥菲斯入冥府寻找亡妻的故事，冥王与冥后为奥菲斯哀伤的歌所打动，同意他将妻子欧律狄克带回人间，但在两人走出冥府之前，奥菲斯不能回头看跟在身后的妻子。就在即将走出冥府的那一刻，奥菲斯忍不住回头看了妻子一眼，结果欧律狄克被拉回了冥府。

《善腾·哈姆瓦斯的故事》中描述的一些冥府的细节，也与希腊神话惊人的相似。如哈姆瓦斯在冥府见到编织绳子的人，绳子刚刚编好，就被旁边的驴子吃掉了；还有些人眼睁睁看着悬在空中的食物，但眼前横着的水坑使得他们永远够不到那些食物。这些场景令人联想到希腊神话中在地狱备受折磨的坦塔罗斯，他因得罪了神祇而被打入地狱受罚，他站在一池深水中间，却喝不到水；岸边排排果树，累累果实，但他就是无法摘取；他的头顶还悬着一块巨石，随时可能掉下来砸向他。

《善腾·哈姆瓦斯的故事》另一个值得注意的地方，是死者在来世的境遇与现世完全逆转。贵族

---

① M.Lichtheim, *Ancient Egyptian Literature, Vol.III, The Late Period*, Berkeley, University of Californian Press, 1976, pp. 125-138.

② Ibid..

③ Ibid..

④ 段晴：《新疆山普鲁古毛毯上的传说故事》，《西域研究》2015年第1期，第41—43页。

下地狱，穷人得永生。这个故事是埃及传统故事与希腊和犹太传统的奇妙混杂。传统的“末日审判”最典型的是公元前1300年安尼纸草的描绘，写在纸草上的《亡灵书》其功能就是保佑死者通过“末日审判”，没有戏剧性的逆转结局。审判的标准与世俗的道德标准是一致的。

这种大逆转的情节在此前关于“末日审判”的描述中从未出现过。普塔荷太普教谕中有“贪婪者没有坟墓”的句子，但是基本上“末日审判”的依据与社会道德标准是一致的，而没有超越其上。人们只要遵循“玛阿特”的原则，在人间可以功成名就，在冥世也能顺利通过“末日审判”。《善腾·哈姆瓦斯的故事》中颠覆性的逆转是审判标准的变化，活着时被尊敬受赞扬的人在冥世被判有罪，而活着时穷困潦倒的失意者却获得荣耀。这让我们想起《圣经》中拉撒路的故事，他生前贫病交加，死后却得到耶稣的祈祷复活，而为富不仁者却在地狱中受煎熬——“人类所赞誉的恰是神所憎恶的”。哈姆瓦斯的故事超越了传统埃及主题。

在传统的来世信仰中，死后救赎概念的核心是奥赛里斯——作为神在人间化身的国王。王权与战胜死亡始终结合在一起。“末日审判”内容的大逆转，也是新王国之后伴随着王权的衰落，古埃及宗教转型的体现。18王朝埃赫纳吞宗教改革不仅重创了传统文化，也严重地动摇了国王在人们信仰体系中的地位。之后埃及先后经历波斯人、希腊人的统治，本土法老的时代成为永远的过去。埃及人也在漫长的外族统治时期完成了从跟随国王拜众神到直接追随众神的转变。

在公元前206年到前186年之间，底比斯的埃及祭司领导了反抗托勒密王朝的起义，在将近20年的时间里，底比斯及其附近的公证文献不是用托勒密国王的名字纪年，而是用本土的法老年号。他们的疆域南至艾德福，北至阿苏耶特（他们可能没有攻克象岛上的要塞）。祭司们在罗塞达石碑上表彰托勒密五世击败三角洲叛乱的时候，几乎整个埃及南部都在这些人控制中。当然，罗塞达石碑并没有提及这一点。两位叛乱国王的名字分别读作Haronnophris和Anch-onnophris。后面还有一个头衔：“为伊西斯所爱，为众神之王阿蒙－拉所爱”，表明他们为底比斯的阿蒙神庙所承认。①

埃及人对托勒密王朝的反抗最终失败了。在费莱第二教令中，托勒密庆祝了对他们的胜利。在文献中，Anch-onnophris的名字被丑化成hr-wnf，后面还加上失败的敌人的限定符号。正如我们从托勒密国王那里所见的那样，王室名字一般都包含着某种政治信息，叛乱法老Haronnophris和Chaonnophris的名字在内涵上有着一种连续性。在现实中，两位国王的纪年也是延续的：Haronnophris统治了七年，Anch-onnophris就从第八年开始算起，而且持续了另一个十年。不过，他们名字的含义更加意味深长。Hr即荷鲁斯，onnophris则是奥赛里斯神的一个名字，意思是“好的事情，完美的事情”。Haronnophris就是“荷鲁斯－奥赛里斯”。根据古埃及的命名习俗，国王的名字中一定会有神名出现，但是作为冥世之王，奥赛里斯从未出现在法老时代的王名中。然而，到了后期埃及，即埃及在外族统治期间，这种写法变得普遍起来。这个名字令人联想起奥赛里斯死而复生的神话：奥赛里斯是埃及的第一个法老，他被弟弟塞特所杀害，后者想取代他的位置。不过，塞特却被奥赛里斯的儿子荷鲁斯所击败。荷鲁斯为他的父亲复了仇，并成为人间的王。而奥赛里斯成了冥界之王。每个活着的法老都是荷鲁斯的化身，每个去世的法老都成为奥赛里斯。“荷鲁斯－奥赛里斯”这个名字在传递这样一个信息：这个国王既是荷鲁斯又是奥赛里斯，死去的奥赛里斯又回归了。以死神的复活寄托恢复国

① G. Hölbl, *A History of the Ptolemaic Empire*, New York, 2001, pp. 79-86.

家独立的心愿。这就是公元前200年的弥赛亚信息，那时包括犹太人在内的许多古老民族都在盼望着一位弥赛亚的到来。Anch-onnophris 的意思是“活着的奥赛里斯”，这个名字所包含的信息更加显而易见：希望并没有随着 Har-onnophris 的去世而失去，它依然还在，因为“神－国王 onnophris 依然活着”。现在，我们可以明白为什么 Anch-onnophris 在费莱教令中的名字会被毁坏：这样一个名字不能给予叛乱者，即合法统治者托勒密的敌人。这就是最后一个本土法老的名字的秘密。①

古埃及宗教的核心是对死亡的解读和超越。从古王国到希腊化时代，古埃及人的来世观念经历了一个逐渐道德化的过程。古王国时期，众神的法庭只出现在纷争产生之时；中王国和新王国时期，每个死者都要面对“末日审判”，通过遵守社会道德和仪式的操作，审判结果是可预期的；而到了希腊化时期，“末日审判”有了更高不可测的标准。在这个过程中，审判的标准逐渐在提升，逐渐超越人的掌控。这个转变的根本原因是作为古埃及宗教核心的王权的衰落或者说是消亡。奥赛里斯的神话告诉我们王权可以穿越死亡的门槛，但伴随着最后一位以奥赛里斯为名的本土法老被镇压，人们把永生的希望更多地寄托于众神。

从中王国到希腊化时期，两千多年的历史演变中，“末日审判”观念不仅完成了“世俗化”的过程，成为大众信仰的重要组成部分，而且在来世信仰中达到了道德化的关键性超越。无论贫富贵贱，所有死者要在众神面前通过道德审判，这已经是对等级社会道德观的超越。而在希腊化时期的文学作品中，为富不仁也会在“末日审判”中被判有罪，贫贱但道德高尚一样可以得到永生，“末日审判”观念的发展史，是神逐渐超越世俗社会及王权的历史，是后世基督教创建“上帝之国”的开端。

三　希腊化时期的文化交融

19世纪末期的牛津英语词典，如此定义希腊化这个词：a. 希腊语的变体，有许多外国成分，应用于亚历山大大帝之后的埃及、叙利亚等国家；b. 或者指与这个时期的希腊人有关的，即真正的希腊特性被外国成分所改变的时期。这反映了当时欧洲的一种传统观点：亚历山大之后的“堕落的”希腊世界不配被称作希腊的，应使用希腊化的（Hellenistic-Greekish），而不是以希腊的这个名称来称呼亚历山大之后和罗马人完全征服这个地区之间三个世纪的地中海东部地区的文化。②

长期以来人们认为从亚历山大远征（前331）到屋大维将埃及变为罗马一个行省（前30）这300年间的时期，定居在近东的希腊人后代不再是希腊人，而变成了希腊－叙利亚人、希腊－埃及人，以及其他的混杂人。这个观点的代表人物是古斯塔夫·德莱臣（Johann Gustav Droysen），他也是第一个使用“希腊主义”这个词的人。他认为希腊化时期是为基督教时代做准备的时期，这个时期的主要特点是东方文化和西方文化融合成了一种新的文明，一种混合式的文化。这种观点的理论基础是黑格尔的历史哲学，即历史是正、反两面的综合。③

现在学者们已经不再接受民族和文化大融合这样的观点了，以克莱尔·普鲁克斯（Claire Préaux）为代表，认为文化是不同的、分离的观点占据上风。她认为西方文化和东方文化是并存的关系，彼此之间没有真正的相互影响或渗透。克拉瑞斯（Willy Clarysse）则进一步提出托勒密埃及是一个

① G. Hölbl, *A History of the Ptolemaic Empire*, New York, 2001, pp. 79-86.

② N. Lewis, *Greeks in Ptolemaic Egypt: Case Studies in the Social History of the Hellenistic World*, Clarendon Press, 1986, p. 1.

③ 威利·克拉瑞斯：《希腊化时期的埃及——一个双面的社会》，《古代文明研究》2002年第2期。

“双面社会”，希腊文化和埃及文化以“一体连面”的形式共存且并行发展，一个人可能同时有两种文化身份，两种文化在长期共存中，互相影响难以完全避免，到罗马时期，终于融合成为社会文化发展的主流。[①]

自19世纪楔形文字解读以来，随着两河流域大量泥版文献的出土和发表，学者们不断地发现《圣经》故事的“原型”，如“大洪水的故事”、创世故事等，继而发现《圣经》的很多文学体裁如预言、教谕、法典等，都扎根于古代近东的土壤之中，与之有着千丝万缕的联系。随着我们发现越来越多这种文化和文学上的相似性，我们更惊异于希伯来《圣经》的最后创作者如何巧妙地以诸多古老的文学形式表达出全新的世界观。

虽然目前学术界还不能证明究竟《出埃及记》有多少真实的历史背景，但埃及作为古代以色列人创立自己宗教时的对立面，这是毫无疑问的。犹太教萌芽于古代近东文明大家族之中，又革命性地与古代近东的传统宗教决裂，是从古代文明母体中突变出来的。

古代晚期出现的基督教，关乎来世的内容及仪式与古埃及宗教有着诸多相似之处。相反，犹太教及希腊宗教中，却很少有灵魂永生及来世的承诺的内涵。埃及宗教中正义与永生之间是因果关系，而对古代以色列人来说，上帝的承诺体现在历史中，惩恶扬善都在尘世而非彼岸。即使今生不能兑现，也会在若干世代之后展现，上帝承诺的不是个人在来世的永生而是全体选民在现实世界的永存。在关于来世的问题上，基督教是对传统宇宙神宗教的回归。

前170年至前160年，塞琉古的马加比起义被镇压的过程中，殉道者将进天堂的观念开始传播，犹太教信徒们需要为付出的生命代价做出解释。再后来，钉到十字架上的耶稣以自己的死战胜对死亡的恐惧，开启了通往天堂的大门，他的信徒通过受洗而分享永生。从此之后，来世信仰和末日审判成为基督教的重要内容。

青铜时代晚期，地中海地区各古代文明共同经历着帝国的衰落、社会的危机，现实矛盾的不可调和，促使人们突破原有宗教的阈限来寻求解脱。古埃及人在来世中完善“永生”的梦想，末日审判观念中的道德因素逐渐增强，他们通过末日审判观念及其仪式在“正义”和“永生”之间搭建起桥梁，实现了宗教与政治的分离，而基督教则在此基础上最终完成了对“上帝之国”的构想，为其信徒指出“因信称义”的救赎之路。在古代晚期的危机中，源自对抗宗教的与源自宇宙神宗教的，重新汇流，把第一代文明留下的遗产注入到即将到来的基督教文明时代。正如末日审判所描绘的，通过审判，得到了永生。

正如罗斯托夫采夫所说：

> 对于古代世界历史多年的仔细研究使得我相信，希腊化时期，即亚历山大之后的300年，是世界发展的最重要的时代之一。我确信，如果我们希望理解希腊天才的特性和后来的文明史，这个时代是与希腊政治辉煌时期和罗马世界帝国时期同等重要的……雅典蕴育了美与思想的永久的种子。希腊化时期的希腊人，继续着雅典人的努力，使得这些种子繁衍至百万。他们将之传递给我们，并使得我们能够以此来确立先是欧洲现在是整个世界文化的基础。[②]

---

① C. Preaux, *Le monde hellénistique. La Grèce et l'Orient de la mort d'Alexandre à la conquête romaine de la Grèce*, Vol II, Presses Universitaires de France, Paris, 1978, pp. 545-679.

② N. Lewis, *Greeks in Ptolemaic Egypt: Case Studies in the Social History of the Hellenistic World*, Clarendon Press, 1986, p. 3.

The Hellennized Egyptian Concept of “Judgement of the Dead”

Yan Haiying (Peking University)

Abstract: The Egyptians were the first to have the concept of salvation from death through vindication, this is so called “Judgement of the Dead”. This was the central idea of ancient Egyptian afterlife and their most important contribution to western world. This concept appeared in Middle Kingdom (2106BCE-1786BCE) and became popular during New Kingdom (1550BCE-1069BCE). Its development was a history of moralizing of afterlife. During Hellenistic time, in the Demotic story of Setne Khaemwese, with the reversal of earthly circumstances, the verdict of the Judgement became completely independent of the men and highly moralized, it was due to this important change that ancient Egyptian religion can remain present in cultural memory of Europe till today.

Keywords: Egypt; afterlife; Judgement of the Dead

“逾界”与“求诉”

——从《伊施塔入冥府》神话的两大主题看古代两河流域伊施塔崇拜的一些特质

贾妍（北京大学）

摘　要：本文从古代两河广为流传的《伊施塔入冥府》故事入手，围绕“逾界”与“求诉”两个神话中不断重复的主题，通过对苏美尔语及阿卡德语两个神话文本的梳理和分析，以及对相关考古、图像材料的探寻和解读，试图说明：因“欲”而“逾”，由“阈”及“求”，不仅是本篇神话主题的表达，同时也道出了古代两河流域伊施塔崇拜至关重要的“阈”与“求”的特质。

关键词：伊施塔 / 伊南娜；冥府；古代两河；死亡；神话；阈限性

在古代两河的神话世界里，伊南娜－伊施塔（苏美尔语 Inanna，对应阿卡德语 Ištar）女神是一个十分特殊的存在。在自然宇宙体系中，作为金星化身的伊施塔占据重要的地位，她是天神安（An）的女儿，太阳神乌图－沙玛什（Utu-Šamaš）的妹妹，集无上美貌、智慧和法力于一身①；在社会政治体系中，作为主司性爱与战争的女神，伊施塔可通过“圣婚”仪式与国君结合，进而护佑王权的昌盛与万物的繁衍②。她的吸引力和破坏力鲜有人可抵挡，毋论对敌对友。在保存下来的两河流域文献与图像材料中，伊施塔展示出一种二元对立、多面一体的复杂形象。她狡黠、多变、喜怒无常；同时又勇

① 两河神话系统中的伊南娜－伊施塔有多位父神，除天神安（An）外，还包括“大力神”恩利尔－埃利尔（Enlil-Ellil，前者为苏美尔语神名，后者为阿卡德语神名，以下同），智慧神恩基－埃阿（Enki-Ea），及月亮神南纳－辛（Nanna-Sîn）。伊施塔最常见的神话家族是以月亮神南纳－辛为父，宁格儿（Ningal）为母，太阳神乌图－沙玛什（Utu-Šamaš）和雷雨神伊什库尔－阿达德（Iškur-Adad）为兄弟。中亚述时期开始出现的以数字标识神名的系统中，月亮神辛的数字符号为 30，即阴历一个月的天数；而金星伊施塔作为辛神之女，其数字标识为 15，即月中出现满月的日子。参见：Pirjo Lapinkivi, *The Neo-Assyrian Myth of Ištar's Descent and Resurrection*, Vol. 6, State Archives of Assyria Cuneiform Texts, Helsinki, Neo-Assyrian Text Corpus Project, 2010, pp. 35-36。

② 苏美尔传统中的“圣婚”仪式一直是近东研究里关注度比较高的课题，近年来对这个问题的研究比较全面的一部专著是 Pirjo Lapinkivi, *The Sumerian Sacred Marriage: In the Light of Comparative Evidence*, Helsinki, Finland, Neo-Assyrian Text Corpus Project, Helsinki University, 2004；此外，较早些的重要研究成果包括：Piotr Steinkeller, “On Rulers, Priests, and Sacred Marriage: Tracing the Evolution of Early Sumerian Kingship”, in *Priests and Officials in the Ancient near East. Papers of the Second Colloquium on the Ancient near East — the City and Its Life Held at the Middle Eastern Culture Center in Japan (Mitaka, Tokyo)*, ed. Kazuko Watanabe, Heidelberg, Universitätsverlag C. Winter, 1999；Jerrold S. Cooper, “Sacred Marriage and Popular Cult in Early Mesopotamia”, in *Official Cult and Popular Religion in the Ancient near East*, ed. E. Matsushima, Heidelberg, Universtatsverlag C. Winter, 1993；Samuel Noah Kramer, “The Dumuzi-Inanna Sacred Marriage Rite: Origin, Development, Character”, in *Actes de la XVIIe Rencontre assyriologique internationale. Université libre de Bruxelles, 30 Juin-4 Juillet 1969*, ed. André Finet, Ham-sur-Heure, Belgium, Comité belge de recherches en Mésopotamie, 1970, 等等。

敢、坚定、一往无前。① 她亦善亦恶，亦男亦女，亦长亦幼；她的身上兼具贞洁与淫荡、高贵与低贱、人性与神性的特征。② 分析伊施塔的这些矛盾个性，借用亚述学家韦斯滕霍尔茨（J. G. Westenholz）的话来说，就像欣赏一个万花筒，文献类型与历史时期的变换带动着万花筒的旋转，而女神在其中的形象随之呈现出纷繁复杂的模式，引人入胜，却也难以捉摸。③

这样一位复杂难测，集挑逗与危险性于一身的女神，在两河诸多神祇中偏偏身居高位，并受到上至国君贵族、下至普通民众的广泛尊崇与欢迎。④ 从两河文明初期发源之地乌鲁克（Uruk），到后期亚述帝国首府重镇尼尼微（Nineveh），伊施塔崇拜在两河流域兴盛了三千余年；⑤ 甚至在亚述、巴比伦帝国渐次消亡几个世纪以后，仍可以在侵入文化的信仰体系中找到她的依托和身影⑥。正如《伊施塔大颂祷辞》（*Great Prayer to Ištar*）中所写："何处不闻你圣名，何处不筑你祭台，何处不现你神力？"⑦

伊施塔女神深入人心的魅力关键在何处？是什么因素使得伊施塔崇拜在语言变换、族群迁移、王朝更迭等不稳定因素主导文明常态的两河流域得以长盛不衰？这样看似简单的问题实则耐人寻味。带着这些问题，本文从《伊施塔入冥府》神话文本出发，借由故事叙述中的几个关键因素，结合其他相关材料，解析伊施塔女神区别于两河其他诸神的个性和职能特征，以及伊施塔崇拜在两河信仰体系中所代表的深层含义。

一 《伊施塔入冥府》文本比较及情节解析

两河神话中的《伊施塔入冥府》是一个颇具"奇幻"色彩的故事，讲述了伊施塔女神穿越七重门来到冥府，经历"死亡"、求助、得救，最终逃出生天返回阳间的经历。和古代两河流域的很多文学作品一样，《伊施塔入冥府》也有苏美尔语和阿卡德语两种传本。苏美尔语原诗大约成文于公元前两

---

① 关于伊施塔复杂而又矛盾的性格解析，可参见：Rivkah Harris, "Inanna-Ishtar as Paradox and a Coincidence of Opposites", *History of Religions* 30, No. 3, 1991, pp. 261-289。

② 同上，第 272 页；另见：Caitlín E. Barrett, "Was Dust Their Food and Clay Their Bread? Grave Goods, the Mesopotamian Afterlife, and the Liminal Role of Inana/Ishtar", *Journal of Ancient Near Eastern Religions* 7, No. 1, 2007, p. 21。

③ Joan Goodnick Westenholz, "Inanna and Ishtar in the Babylonian World", in *The Babylonian World*, ed. Gwendolyn Leick, New York & London, Routledge, 2007, p. 332.

④ 古代两河流域的诸神通常是按照地位和职能的重要性划分层级的。在苏美尔神话系统中，处在第一层级的大神包括天神安，"大力神"恩利尔，山神宁胡尔萨哥（Ninhursag），以及智慧神恩基；作为金星化身的伊南娜（阿卡德时期以后称伊施塔）处在第二层级，与之地位相当的包括月亮神南纳，太阳神乌图。伊南娜是七位主神中唯一的一位女神，可见其地位的特别。事实上，阿卡德王朝掌握政权后，伊施塔女神被奉为国家主神受到无限推崇。新亚述时期，特别是公元前 8 世纪后半叶的萨尔贡二世（Sargon II）执政时代，伊施塔的崇拜再度掀起高潮。关于以上诸神在两河宗教系统中的地位和作用，可参见：Thorkild Jacobsen, *The Treasures of Darkness: A History of Mesopotamian Religion,* New Haven, Yale University Press, 1976, pp. 93-143；其中伊施塔相关部分见第 135—143 页。

⑤ 乌鲁克的伊阿那（E-ana）神庙和尼尼微的伊施塔神庙分别代表了两河文明早期和后期伊南娜-伊施塔崇拜的祭祀中心。关于尼尼微的伊施塔神庙，可参见：Julian E. Reade, "The Ishtar Temple at Nineveh", *Iraq,* Vol. 67, No. 1, Nineveh, Papers of the 49th Rencontre Assyriologique Internationale London, 7-11 July 2003, Part Two, 2005, pp. 347-390. 关于伊南娜-伊施塔神庙在两河的分布以及文献记录，可参见：Andrew R. George, *House Most High: The Temples of Ancient Mesopotamia*, Mesopotamian Civilizations 5, Winona Lake, Ind, Eisenbrauns, 1993。

⑥ Miroslav Marcovich, "From Ishtar to Aphrodite", *Journal of Aesthetic Education* 30, No. 2, 1996, pp. 43-59.

⑦ Westenholz, "Inanna and Ishtar in the Babylonian World", p. 332.

千年初，现保存下来的版本有四百余行；[1] 阿卡德语版本约成文于公元前一千年初，在保留基本故事情节和叙述框架的基础上，对苏美尔语原诗进行了大幅缩减，同时有一些细节的增补，现存版本共计138行。[2]

将两版《入冥府》故事对照阅读，苏美尔语传本由于文字较长，故事情节相对丰富，人物刻画也更显细腻。文本开始用超过全文1/6的篇幅（第1—72行）来介绍伊南娜下冥府之前的诸项准备工作：女神遗弃了苏美尔诸城，离开了“天庭”，离开了“尘世”，集齐了七件护身法器，孤注一掷地向“冥府”而去。预见自己此行必然有去无回[3]，伊南娜向尾随前行的忠实侍女宁叔布（Ninšubur）交待了自己抵达冥府之后的一系列仪式需求[4]，并叮嘱宁叔布分别向她的三位父神，即居于尼普尔（Nippur）的恩利尔，居于乌尔（Ur）的南纳，以及居于埃利都（Eridu）的恩基求助。伊南娜同时预言，即便前两位大神拒绝出手相救，拥有“生命草”与“生命水”的恩基定能让她复活再生。

较之苏美尔语版本，阿卡德语的《入冥府》故事则完全略去了行前准备的过程；取而代之，在神话开篇增补了对“冥府”的一段白描。短短9行文字，一派幽冷阴暗的惨淡景象跃然纸上。在全文不足140行的故事叙述中，这段不吝笔墨的场景描绘显得弥足珍贵；特别是这段文字并未出现在苏美尔语原诗中，更加凸显了它的重要性。鉴于冥府描述在本文接下来的论述中还要不断回顾，这里摘录如下：

4　去到那幽暗的府邸，埃尔卡拉神的住地，
5　去到那有进无出的屋，
6　踏上那有去无回的路，
7　去到那寄居者们渴求光明的府邸。
8　那里尘埃为食，泥土为饼。

---

① 苏美尔语版本《伊南娜入冥府》的最新转写和英译，参见牛津大学东方学院创建的“苏美尔文学电子文库”(The Electronic Text Corpus of Sumerian Literature，以下简称ETCSL): ETCSL 1.4.1 “Inana's descent to the nether world”（网址：http://etcsl.orinst.ox.ac.uk/cgi-bin/etcsl.cgi?text=t.1.4.1#）；较早的译注参见S. N. Kramer的系列文章：Samuel Noah Kramer, “Inanna's Descent to the Nether World”. The Sumerian Version of ‘Ištar's Descent’”, *Revue d'Assyriologie et d'archéologie orientale* 34, No. 3, 1937, pp. 93-134; “Additional Material to ‘Inanna's Descent to the Nether World’”, *Revue d'Assyriologie et d'archéologie orientale* 36, No. 2, 1939, pp. 68-80; “Ishtar in the Nether World According to a New Sumerian Text”, *Bulletin of the American Schools of Oriental Research*, No. 79, 1940, pp. 18-27; “ ‘Inanna's Descent to the Nether World' Continued”, *Proceedings of the American Philosophical Society* 94, No. 4, 1950, pp. 361-363; “ ‘Inanna's Descent to the Nether World' Continued and Revised”, *Journal of Cuneiform Studies* 4, No. 4, 1950, pp. 199-214; “ ‘Inanna's Descent to the Nether World' Continued and Revised. Second Part: Revised Edition of ‘Inanna's Descent to the Nether World' ”, *Journal of Cuneiform Studies* 5, No. 1, 1951, pp. 1-17.

② 阿卡德语版本《伊施塔入冥府》最新校注英译本为：Lapinkivi, *The Neo-Assyrian Myth of Ištar's Descent and Resurrection*；Lapinkivi在原有文本的基础上，依据一些新的泥版材料又增补了10行左右。汉译版本参见：拱玉书：《伊施塔入冥府》，《北京大学学报·外语语言文学专刊》，1995年，第58—62页。

③ 事实上“冥府”在苏美尔语中的一种常用说法KUR.NU.GI$_4$.A（抑或简写作KUR.NU.GI$_4$），字面意思即是“有去无回之地”。参见：Wayne Horowitz, *Mesopotamian Cosmic Geography*, Winona Lake, Ind.: Eisenbrauns, 1998, p. 268。

④ 这些需求有可能与苏美尔文化的丧葬仪式相关；关于《入冥府》文本与古代两河丧葬仪式的联系，可参见：Nicola Laneri, “The Discovery of a Funerary Ritual: Inanna/Ishtar and Her Descent to the Nether World in Titriš Höyük, Turkey”, *East and West.* 52, No. 1/4 , 2002, pp. 9-51; Dina Katz, “Inanna's Descent and Undressing the Dead as a Divine Law”, *Zeitschrift für Assyriologie und vorderasiatische Archäologie.* 85, No. 2, 1995, pp. 221-233。

9 居者不见光明，常在暗处，
10 像鸟一样，身着羽衣。
11 门扉与门闩上积满了尘土。
11a 门梁上沉浸着死亡的静寂。[1]

经过开篇行前准备（苏美尔语）或冥府描绘（阿卡德语）的铺陈，两版入冥府神话分别进入女神下冥府的过程叙述。从伊南娜–伊施塔站在冥府门前挑衅叫门，到她一道一道地穿越七重门，并在每一扇门前"依照冥府女主的老规矩"卸下一件代表神力的护身法器；[2] 待到伊南娜–伊施塔置身于冥府中央，被带到她的姐姐，幽冥女神埃丽施吉嘉（Ereškigal）面前时，她已经一丝不挂，法力全无了。这段故事情节两版神话大体一致，只是苏美尔语文本中保留了更多的细节刻画，比如埃丽施吉嘉听到冥府守门人带来的伊南娜闯冥府的消息后，"捶着大腿""咬着嘴唇"思考对付伊南娜的计策，非常生动有趣。

阿卡德语版本中，埃丽施吉嘉得到伊施塔到来的消息后，她的反应先是又惊又怒——"脸变青，青得像割断的柽柳，唇变紫，紫得像窟泥努的瓶口"[3]；惊怒之余，埃丽施吉嘉开始理性地思考伊施塔抛弃人间来到冥府的原因和后果：

31 是什么促使她来到我这里？我为何会引起她的欢喜？
32 看啊，在这里我与阿努那基共饮[4]，
33 以泥土为饼，泥水为酒。
34 我是否该为那些被迫离开妻子的年轻男儿们哭泣？
35 我是否该为那些从情人膝头被掠走的少女们哭泣？
36 我是否该为那些婴孩，那些未竟天年而早夭的幼儿哭泣？[5]

这段描绘中，透过埃丽施吉嘉之口，我们可以对司掌性爱、护佑生殖的伊施塔在人间的作用窥见一斑。事实上，为了强调伊施塔对人间的重要性，阿卡德语传本接下来的段落中，对伊施塔入冥府后

---

① 此处译文在参考拱玉书教授汉译版的基础上，依据 Lapinkivi 2010 年最新整理出版的阿卡德语《伊斯塔入冥府》文本有增补（第 11a 行）和修改（第 7、11 行）。Lapinkivi 的英译参见：Lapinkivi, *The Neo-Assyrian Myth of Ištar's Descent and Resurrection*, pp. 6, 29.

② 在苏美尔语版本中，伊南娜卸下七件护身法器的顺序依次为：头巾（第一道门），青金石项珠（第二道门），蛋形乳珠（第三道门），胸饰（第四道门），金环（第五道门），青金石量杆与测线（第六道门），帕拉裙（第七道门）；在阿卡德语版本中，伊施塔卸下法器的顺序依次为：神冠（第一道门），耳环（第二道门），蛋形项珠（第三道门），胸针（第四道门），生日石腰带（第五道门），手足镯（第六道门），神裙（第七道门）；尽管两版传本中女神在门前卸下的七件法器略有不同，它们都是伊南娜–伊施塔神力的象征。

③ 拱玉书：《伊施塔入冥府》，第 59 页。

④ 阿努那基（Anunnaki）早期为无名之神的一个总称；后期与"天神组"（Igigû）相对应，主要用以指代"地神组"和"冥神组"，这里或可理解为"幽冥判官组"。参见：Jeremy A. Black and Anthony Green, *Gods, Demons, and Symbols of Ancient Mesopotamia: An Illustrated Dictionary*, London, The British Museum Press, 1992, p. 34。

⑤ 此段译文为作者在 Lapinkivi 的阿卡德语转写和英译基础上译出，参见：Lapinkivi, *The Neo-Assyrian Myth of Ištar's Descent and Resurrection*, pp. 6, 10, 30。

人间的惨淡景象还有一段直接的描写：

76 在伊施塔女主深入冥府以后，
77 牡牛不同牝牛交配，公驴不给母驴授精，
78 年轻男女不在街上做爱，
79 男儿一人寝，
80 姑娘独自眠。[①]

此段描写的伊施塔离开人间后造成的动物及人类停止交配、孕育的恶果，在天界神侍帕婆苏卡尔（Papsukkal）代伊施塔向父神辛（苏美尔语南纳）和埃阿（苏美尔语恩基）求助之时，又重复咏叹了一遍（第 85—90 行）；见到世间生灵凋敝的景象，对人类向来富有同情心的智慧神埃阿[②]，创造了一个雌雄同体的精灵“英俊哥”[③]，派它潜入冥府解救已经“死去”的女神伊施塔。

伊南娜－伊施塔在冥府经历“死亡”、获救，后又“还阳”的过程在两个版本的神话叙述中出入比较大。在苏美尔语传本中，伊南娜在通过冥府最后一道门并卸下最后一件护身法器之后，被剥光衣服，屈蹲在埃丽施吉嘉面前。不服输的伊南娜仍执意篡取埃丽施吉嘉冥府女主的尊位。最后，“幽冥判官组”用“死亡的目光”“愤怒的话语”以及“重罪的呼叫”处置了伊南娜。失去所有神力，经历死亡审判，仅剩一副皮囊的伊南娜被挂在地府的钩子上，与死尸无异。

在阿卡德语传本中，冥府女主埃丽施吉嘉处置闯入者伊施塔的方式则是传唤自己的侍臣纳木塔（Namtar），放出 60 种疾病施与伊施塔全身：“眼病给她的眼睛，臂病给她的胳膊，脚病给她的脚，心病给她的心，头病给她的头。”[④] 这样，伊施塔整个身心为疾病所累，成为空壳。[⑤]

伊南娜在苏美尔传本中获救的过程与她临行前预言的分毫不差：伊南娜的侍女宁叔布按照女神的嘱托，分别向恩利尔和南纳求救并遭拒后，终于在智慧神恩基那里得到援手。这段细节很有意思：恩基从自己的指甲尖里抠出两坨泥，做成两个小精灵，分别授以“生命草”和“生命水”，并嘱以施救方法。这两个小精灵按照恩基的授意，像苍蝇和幽灵一样从冥府的门缝与门轴间潜入埃丽施吉嘉的府邸，巧言逢迎，讨得幽冥女神的欢心，并最终求得伊南娜的“皮囊”作为奖赏。两精灵合力在伊南娜的“皮囊”上施撒“生命草”和“生命水”，后者得以复苏。

在阿卡德语《入冥府》中，开篇省略了伊施塔行前准备的铺陈，求救和获救环节的叙述也相应

---

① 此处译文在参考 Lapinkivi 版本的基础上，基本遵照拱玉书教授原译。

② 在古代两河大洪水的故事中，诸神欲降洪水诛灭人类，也是智慧神恩基－埃阿出于同情吐露了洪水将至的消息，才有乌塔纳佩什提（《圣经》中“诺亚”的原型）造方舟得以逃脱的结局。关于洪水故事，可参阅《吉尔伽美什史诗》第 11 块泥板的描述：Andrew R. George, *The Epic of Gilgamesh: The Babylonian Epic Poem and Other Texts in Akkadian and Sumerian,* London, Penguin Books, 1999, pp. 88-99。

③ 此精灵名曰 Aṣûšu-namir，字面意思是“他的外表很明亮”，因此拱玉书教授将其译为“英俊哥”。参见拱玉书：《伊施塔入冥府》，第 62 页，注 27。

④ 拱玉书：《伊施塔入冥府》，第 60 页。

⑤ 阿卡德语原文直译过来是：“让它们（作者按：疾病）掏空她（作者按：伊施塔）的身体，掏空她的所有”（第 75 行）；这也与后文中将伊施塔尸身的“皮囊”喻为“水袋”相呼应（第 98、99 行）。参见：Lapinkivi, *The Neo-Assyrian Myth of Ištar's Descent and Resurrection*, pp. 6, 31。

地进行了调整和简化。如前所述，这里代伊施塔向诸神求救的是天界神侍帕婆苏卡尔①；智慧神埃阿（苏美尔语恩基）虽创造出精灵"英俊哥"潜入冥府解救伊施塔，"英俊哥"也试图讨取埃丽施吉嘉的欢心，可是他甫一提出索要伊施塔"皮囊"的赏赐，解救计划即被冥府女主识破，自己也受到重责。出于各种考虑，埃丽施吉嘉最终授意侍臣纳木塔（也就是之前放出60种疾病"掏空"伊施塔的那位）在"幽冥判官组"的面前施撒"生命草"和"生命水"于伊施塔的尸身，令其复生。②

复苏后的伊南娜-伊施塔在两版神话中都经历了离开冥府、重返人间的"还阳"之旅。在苏美尔语版本中，女神"还阳"的情节用了超过全文1/4的笔墨（第282—412行），过程和细节都描述得十分细致。复苏后的伊南娜刚想要从冥府出去，就被"幽冥判官组"捉住，后者表示入冥府得以全身而退者从未有先例，伊南娜要出冥府，须得先为自己找一个"替身"方可。于是伊南娜开始在大小鬼怪组成的"幽冥方阵"簇拥下踏上了"还阳"的路，在找到"替身"之前，无论伊南娜走到哪里，这些鬼怪都亦步亦趋、寸步不离。伊南娜返回世间，首先遇到了在冥府的大门外守候她的女仆宁叔布，后者蓬头垢面、衣衫不整，显然还沉浸在痛失主人的哀伤之中。随从鬼怪们提议带走宁叔布作为女神在地府的"替身"，被伊南娜拒绝了，因为宁叔布在女神"死后"严格遵照她的嘱托行事，女神的获救她功不可没。伊南娜与"幽冥方阵"继续巡行苏美尔诸城，中途鬼怪们提议的另外两位可作"替身"之人也被女神以对其忠诚为由拒绝了；直到伊南娜行至库拉巴平原的大苹果树处，见到亦兄亦夫的谷牧神杜牧兹（Dumuzid）身着华服、高居王座，无半点哀伤之色，一怒之下令鬼怪将杜牧兹作为"替身"带回冥府。惊恐的杜牧兹向妻兄太阳神乌图哭诉求救，乌图助其逃脱鬼怪的捉拿；伊南娜女神在失去丈夫后，也似有懊悔之意；在一只苍蝇的帮助下，伊南娜寻到了杜牧兹的踪迹。故事的最后，伊南娜与埃丽施吉嘉达成协议，杜牧兹一年中有半年居于人间，另外半年则作为伊南娜的死亡"替身"居于冥府。③

较之苏美尔语原诗，阿卡德语传本中对女神"还阳"的描写着墨不多（第118a—138行），叙述精简到只保留了塔牧兹（Tammuz，即苏美尔语版本中的杜牧兹）作为死亡"替身"这一主线；不过与开篇女神入冥府的过程相呼应，新诗增补了伊施塔出冥府时再次穿越七重门的情节——在每一道门前，女神都复穿戴上一件当初褪去的代表神力的护身法器。文本的最后叙述比较模糊，似乎是为塔牧兹举行的祭仪或葬礼。④

二 "逾"与"阈":《入冥府》故事中"门"的神话与文化寓意

在前一部分中，通过对《入冥府》故事苏美尔语和阿卡德语两个传本的对照阅读，在捋清神话基本叙事脉络和情节的基础上，比较了两个文本的同与异。⑤ 作为古代两河流域流传最广、最为人所熟

① 与苏美尔语传本相比照，恩利尔在求救的诸神中被省略，可能是由于阿卡德语传本成文时期，恩利尔的崇拜已经衰落。参见：Lapinkivi, *The Neo-Assyrian Myth of Ištar's Descent and Resurrection*, p. 70。

② 阿卡德语传本中并没有提到"生命草"和"生命水"的具体来源，有可能也是埃阿授予"英俊哥"带到地府中的，只是文本在叙述中省略了。

③ 杜牧兹（阿卡德语名为塔牧兹）半年居于人间、半年居于冥府的安排传统上常理解为季节更替的象征。作为司掌谷牧之神，杜牧兹的"葬礼"在夏季谷物收割后举行；而他返还人间与伊南娜的"圣婚"庆典则安排在春季"新年"伊始，那时万物复苏，象征着谷神的回归。参见：Jacobsen, *The Treasures of Darkness: A History of Mesopotamian Religion*, p. 62; Mark E. Cohen, *The Cultic Calendars of the Ancient near East,* Bethesda, Md., CDL Press, 1993, pp. 476-481。

④ Lapinkivi, *The Neo-Assyrian Myth of Ištar's Descent and Resurrection*, pp. 6, 90.

⑤ 关于两个版本异同点的比较，亦可参见：Katz, "Inanna's Descent and Undressing the Dead as a Divine Law", pp. 228-233。

知的文学作品之一，《入冥府》从苏美尔语原文发展到阿卡德语新诗，在跨越千年的时空里，从最初的400余行浓缩到后来的138行，情节的增删与细节的修改不仅仅透露出字面的讯息，更多传达的是历史的选择和文化的记忆。① 从“神话”背后的“文化”所彰显的“记忆”选择与保存这个层面来讲，对一个文化现象中的“动点”与“定点”的观察显得至关重要：哪些元素是相对稳定，“以不变应万变”的？哪些元素是较为活跃，却“万变不离其宗”的？事实上，在古代近东文化历史研究领域，“变化”与“延续”的主题是近二三十年来学术思考的一个热点方向。② 沿着这个思路，在接下来的两个部分中，我将继续以《入冥府》文本为基础，探讨在神话流传的过程中被刻意保留并不断强化的两个主题——“逾界”与“求诉”——进而追问这两大主题与伊施塔崇拜在两河的长盛不衰是否有必然联系。

由于阿卡德语版本的《入冥府》成文较晚又短小精悍，从这个文本出发进行主题追踪似乎更加合适。为篇幅所限，阿卡德语传本中剪掉了许多细节的枝蔓，使得故事进展更快，但是某些环节不但尽量完整地保留了下来，还在后期刻意地加以增补，这便是伊施塔穿越七重门，入、出冥府的过程。经过这样的增补，整个故事首尾呼应，结构上更加完整紧凑；七重门的铺排增强了冥府描绘的“空间感”；与此同时，女神七进七出冥府之门，并在每道门前卸下或重拾护身法器的一系列动作，也凸显了女神阴阳穿梭过程的仪式感。③ “门”的元素，在《入冥府》的神话里，显然不仅是一种故事情节的助力，更是一个文化符号的表征。那么我们不禁追问，这个故事里面，“门”的象征所指究竟何在呢？

作为建筑中空间建构的关节点，门以自身的“开”与“阖”联结并分隔“内”与“外”，控制行人的“进”与“出”，进以表达空间本身的“通”与“阻”，以及空间对人的“容”与“拒”。④ 在许多古代文化中，“门”都是充满象征意义的仪式性场所。以中国为例，《礼记》中有“祈于庙门”的记载；而《周易 · 系辞上》中“阖户谓之坤，辟户谓之乾，一阖一辟谓之变，往来不穷谓之通”，则以乾坤、阴阳变通对门的象征意义给予了贴合中国文化神韵的阐释。⑤

---

① 关于“文化记忆”的理论，可参考德国学者扬 · 阿斯曼（Jan Assmann）及阿莱达 · 阿斯曼（Aleida Assmann）夫妇的一系列著作，现已译成中文的包括扬 · 阿斯曼：《文化记忆：早期高级文化中的文字、回忆和政治身份》，金寿福、黄晓晨译，北京大学出版社，2015年；阿莱达 · 阿斯曼：《回忆空间：文化记忆的形式和变迁》，潘璐译，北京大学出版社，2016年。

② 近年来近东学界关于“变化”与“延续”主题的探讨，比较重要的包括：Liverani, Mario, “Assyria in the Ninth Century: Continuity or Change? ” in *From the Upper Sea to the Lower Sea: Studies on the History of Assyria and Babylonia in Honour of A. K. Grayson*, ed. Grant Frame, Leiden: Nederlands Instituut voor het Nabije Oosten, 2004, pp. 213-226; Stephanie Dalley, “The Transition from Neo-Assyrians to Neo-Babylonians: Break or Continuity? ” *Eretz-Israel,* 2003, pp. 25-28; Michael Roaf, “Continuity and Change from the Middle to the Late Assyrian Period”, *Migration und Kulturtransfer: Der Wandel vorder- und zentralasiatischer Kulturen im Umbruch vom 2. zum 1. vorchristlichen Jahrtausend*, ed. R. Eichmann and H. Parzinger, Bonn, Habelt, 2001, S. 357-359, 等。

③ 事实上，阿卡德语传本中增补的伊施塔女神再次跨越七重门“还阳”的过程，在神话学的表征系统中是一个不可或缺的环节，具有深刻的象征意义。对此环节含义的发掘或可参考美国神话学家坎贝尔（Joseph Campbell）在其名著《千面英雄》中“跨越归来的阈限”一节进行的阐释，参见约瑟夫 · 坎贝尔：《千面英雄》，黄珏苹译，杭州：浙江人民出版社，2016年，第192—201页。

④ 关于“门”在建筑空间中的功能与寓意，本文作者在2014年完成的博士毕业论文中有更为详细的探讨，参见：Yan Jia, *Imperial Doors of Assyria: Monumentality, Spatiality, and Rituality of the Neo-Assyrian Architectural Doors from Balawat*, PhD dissertation, Department of History of Art and Architecture, Harvard University, 2014, Ch. III 3.1 “Space and Spatiality”。

⑤ 杨昌鸣、徐磊、李湘桔：《门里乾坤——门的文化、心理含义解析》，《天津大学学报》（社会科学版）2004年第3期，第203—206页。

在现代学术界，首次对"门"在仪式中的象征意义和关键作用进行了深度讨论的，是法国学者范甘热内普（Arnold van Gennep）。20世纪初，范氏出版了理论名著《通过仪式》（*Rite de Passage*），他认为门的重要性在于其表征了一种"界限"（boundary），在普通民居中可能是"坊"与"宅"的界限，在宗教庙堂中则可以是"俗"与"圣"的界限。从这种意义上讲，"通过仪式"可以比作跨越门槛的行为：参与者在仪式中仿佛步入一个"新世界"，并与之融为一体。①

在范甘热内普理论的基础上，著名人类学家维克多·特纳（Victor Turner）进一步发展深化了"通过仪式"的理论体系，特别是挖掘并解析了"阈限性"（liminality）的概念。② 从词源学上来讲，这个概念的拉丁语词根"*limin*"意为"threshold"，也即"门槛"，与中文里"阈"的语义相吻合，所以"阈限性"是比较准确的译法。从"门槛"的本意出发，特纳将"阈限性"定义为一种由"门前"到"门后"，由"此境"到"彼境"，具有过渡性质和超越意义的"模棱两可"（Betwixt and Between）的状态。③ 仪式中跨越"阈限"的过程就像迈过门槛的一步，是极具象征性的事件和关键环节所在，仪式主体通过这一步的跨越可以体验到一种"移势换境"的效果。④ 此境到彼境，沧海桑田，仅在跬步之间。

从笼统意义上回归到古代两河流域特定的历史、文化情境下，"门"在建筑中的空间枢纽作用，以及在仪式中的"超越通道"作用，其实很早就引起两河先人的重视了。在两河流域的神话宇宙系统中，上至天堂下至冥府都有"门"（苏美尔语KÁ，对应阿卡德语*bābu*）⑤，这些门连接并分隔不同的宇宙领域和神话世界，往往既是守卫森严的禁区，又是往来必经的通道。比如传说中太阳神乌图－沙玛什每日必经的东西地平线上各有一座天门，日升日落之时，天门守卫会将门扉敞开，供乌图－沙玛什通行（图1）；未经授权者是不能随意穿越天门的，即便地位尊崇的国君、本领超凡的英雄吉尔伽美

---

① 引自范甘热内普《通过仪式》的英译版：Arnold van Gennep, *The Rites of Passage*, trans. Monika B. Vizedom and Gabrielle L. Caffee, Chicago, University of Chicago Press, 1960, p. 20; 法文原版出版于1909年：Arnold van Gennep, *Les rites de passage: étude systématique des rites*, Paris, é. Nourry, 1909。

② 这个概念最初也是由范甘热内普提出，在《通过仪式》中，范氏建立了三段论仪式体系的框架，即 preliminality--liminality--postliminality，其中 liminality，即"阈限"的概念是这个理论体系的核心。自20世纪60年代起，维克多·特纳在范氏的理论架构上，通过一系列重要著作，将"通过仪式"的理论进行了关键性的发展和深化，其中最著名的包括：Victor Turner, *The Forest of Symbols: Aspects of Ndembu Ritual,* Ithaca, N.Y., Cornell University Press, 1967; *The Drums of Affliction: A Study of Religious Processes among the Ndembu of Zambia,* Oxford & London, International African Institute, 1968; *The Ritual Process: Structure and Anti-Structure,* New York, Aldine de Gruyter, 1969; *Process, Performance, and Pilgrimage: A Study in Comparative Symbology,* New Delhi, Concept, 1979, pp. 141-168; "Social Dramas and Stories About Them", *Critical Inquiry* 7, No. 1, On Narrative, 1980, pp. 141-168; *From Ritual to Theatre: The Human Seriousness of Play,* New York, PAJ Publications, 1982; *The Anthropology of Performance,* New York, PAJ Publications, 1988 等。

③ 特纳最重要的论著之一：*The Forest of Symbols: Aspects of Ndembu Ritual*, 现已有中译本：维克多·特纳：《象征之林——恩登布人仪式散论》，赵玉燕、欧阳敏、徐洪峰译，北京：商务印书馆，2006年；其中关于"阈限性"概念的重要阐释出自论文："Betwixt and Between: The Liminal Period in *Rites de Passage*", 中文译作《模棱两可：通过仪式中的阈限阶段》。

④ 所谓"移势换境"为本文作者所译，特纳的原文为"transitions between states"，见 Victor Turner, "Betwixt and Between: The Liminal Period in *Rites de Passage*", *The Forest of Symbols*, pp. 93-94。

⑤ 在阿卡德语中，天堂之门与冥府之门分别写作 *bāb šamê* 和 *bāb erṣetu*，鉴于名词 *bābu* 本身指代的是墙体上开出的用于穿行的通路，这两种表达显然指示的不是建筑上可以开阖的"装置"之门，而是连接、沟通空间的"通道"之门；不过在这些通往天堂和地府的通道上，确也装有"门扉"（苏美尔语 ^{GIŠ}IG，对应阿卡德语 *daltu*），通过开阖来控制进出，并设有护门神专职看守。关于古代两河与门相关的词汇讨论，详见本文作者博士论文 *Imperial Doors of Assyria*, Ch. 1.1.3.1. "'Doors' vs. 'Gates': Reflections on Assyrian and Modern Terminology"。

图 1　阿卡德时期滚印及现代印迹，描绘太阳神乌图 - 沙玛什经过天门的场景，约公元前 2350—前 2150 年，藏于大英博物馆

什，也曾受过天门守卫的阻拦。① 从这个意义上讲，两河神话中的“门”都可以看作“阈限”的象征，标志着自然的天与地、日与夜的边界，也标志着超自然的人与神、生与死的边界。

《入冥府》神话中反复出现的冥府之门其实便是生与死间“阈限”的形象表达。能突破人所不能的“阈限”，是神性的根本，不过在两河，生死之间界限森严（七重门禁的象征），即便是神亦难逾越。伊施塔是两河神祇里的“女汉子”，是充盈着蓬勃生命力的爱神兼战神，面对“生死之阈”也并非无往而不胜。文本写到女神赤裸的身体如抽干的皮囊般挂在地府深处的那段很隐晦，仅着只字片语，却透出无力抗拒的苍凉。即便伊施塔最终在恩基的帮助下得以复苏，连幽冥女神都网开一面时，“生死之阈”仍然坚不可摧地存在着——如苏美尔语传本中幽冥判官组所言：冥府有进无出，有来无回的规矩不能破！于是才有了后来女神“还阳”路上献出自己的丈夫杜牧兹为死亡“替身”的情节。伊施塔最终逃出生天的结果看似是女神挑战“阈限”的一次胜利，在某种程度上其实也是一种无可奈何的妥协。

不过归根结底，《伊施塔入冥府》的故事树立了两河世界里突破重重“门禁”下入冥府又能全身而退的唯一先例，也使得伊施塔成为挑战生死“阈限”的一个成功典范。事实上，在几乎所有伊南娜 - 伊施塔的相关神话中，这位女神都是一个规矩的破坏者，她似乎乐于找到一切现有的“门槛”，或者设法跨越，或者加以破坏，就像她在《入冥府》中威胁门卫所叫嚣的那样：“嘿，快把门打开让我进来！如果你不打开门，不让我进来，我将击碎门，折断闩，砸烂门框，掀翻门扉……”这样的个性特点和行事风格赋予伊施塔有限的神权职责之外不可小觑的潜力和无限的可能。② 以“门”为象征符号，《入冥府》神话中传达出伊施塔女神特有的“阈限性”特质，与神话中另一重复强化的主题——“求诉”密切相连，在下一节里，我将对此加以具体分析。

三 “欲”与“求”:《入冥府》的叙述线索及伊施塔神话的“求诉”主题

苏美尔和阿卡德语两个传本的《入冥府》故事中，另一个不断重复并强化的主题是伊南娜 - 伊施

① 这段情节记录在《吉尔伽美什史诗》第九块泥板中，参见：George, *The Epic of Gilgamesh*, pp. 70-75。

② 亚述学泰斗雅克布森（Thorkild Jacobsen）在他研究两河宗教史的奠基之作《黑暗的宝藏》中认为伊施塔在两河宗教系统中所代表的即是“无限变化”（Infinite Variety），参见：Jacobsen, *The Treasures of Darkness*, pp. 135-143。

塔女神的求诉——一方面是觊觎冥府，想要破门而入的求叫，另一方面是濒临死亡，想要出离冥府的求援；前者是为了求权，后者是为了求生，本质上都是欲望的诉求。以下将对女神在两部分不同的求诉态度和策略进行简要的回顾，并结合其他相关材料分析"求诉"主题在伊施塔神话及信仰中的关键作用。

《入冥府》中前一个部分的"求诉"是女神的直接求叫。两版传本中，对于伊南娜－伊施塔站在冥府重重门禁之前大声叫嚣，威胁门卫开门放其通行的情节有着类似的生动描述。以阿卡德语版本为例：

12　伊施塔一到冥府门前，
13　就对门卫开了言：
14　"嘿，门卫，把门给我打开！
15　把门打开让我进来！
16　如果你不打开门，不让我进来，
17　我将击碎门，折断闩，
18　我将砸烂门框，掀翻门扉。
18a　我会打破衡杆，扯掉把手！
19　我会挑逗死者来吞噬生灵，
20　死人必将会比活人还要多！"[1]

这一段的叫门与其说是求诉，不如说是威胁。短短几行文字，鲜明勾勒出伊施塔女神莽撞、暴力的性格以及与之相连的巨大破坏力。

《入冥府》神话后一个部分的"求诉"是女神授意或委托的间接求援。[2] 在苏美尔原诗中，伊南娜入冥府三昼夜而不归，侍女宁叔布遵照女神之托前往诸父神面前寻求救援，原话如下：

父神恩利尔／南纳／恩基啊，
不要让任何人在冥府中杀死你的女儿。
不要让你那贵重的金属与冥府的尘埃熔为一体。
不要让你珍爱的天青石在那里被劈开，并与匠人的糙石混为一谈。
不要让你的黄杨木在那里被砍成碎屑，并与工匠的木材搅在一块。
不要让年轻的伊南娜小姐在冥府中丧生。[3]

这段以"求诉"为主题的悲叹，宁叔布在三位父神面前分别咏诵了一次，加上伊南娜临行前自己

① 此处译文在参考拱玉书教授汉译版的基础上，主要依据 Lapinkivi 2010 年出版的《入冥府》英译版所译，参见：Lapinkivi, *The Neo-Assyrian Myth of Ištar's Descent and Resurrection*, pp. 6, 29。此段18a行中"衡杆"一词，阿卡德语原文为*gišrinnu*，可能是"门上的一个部件"（参见 *The Assyrian Dictionary of the Oriental Institute in Chicago*, Vol. 5, p. 106），此处暂译为"衡杆"。

② 阿卡德语传本中天界神侍帕婆苏卡尔向诸神的求助虽然没有直接说明，但应该也是出自伊施塔的授意，因为帕婆苏卡尔本身也是伊施塔的侍者。参见上书，p. 70。

③ 此段为作者依据 ETCSL 提供的英译文所译，参见：ETCSL 1.4.1 "Inana's descent to the nether world"，第 41—64 行（网址：http://etcsl.orinst.ox.ac.uk/cgi-bin/etcsl.cgi?text=t.1.4.1#）。

交待的三次，总共重复了六遍。从这些不厌其烦的反复咏叹中可见女神求援的关键在于强调自己的特别之处，这与阿卡德语传本中天界神侍帕婆苏卡尔代伊施塔向诸神提出的求诉有异曲同工之妙。

这样类似的“求诉”在伊南娜－伊施塔相关神话中时有出现，甚至可以说构成了一个不断重复的母题；引起此类“求诉”的动因永远是女神不可抑制的欲望驱动，为权利、情爱抑或生命；故事情节往往会围绕“求诉”的过程与结果展开，形成这样的叙事线索：欲动—求诉—冲突／援助—结果。

《入冥府》神话的苏美尔语原诗即以伊南娜的“欲动”开篇：“从天庭她将心思放到了冥府。从天庭女神将心思放到了冥府。从天庭伊南娜将心思放到了冥府”。（第 1—3 行）经过再三咏叹，女神的欲念终于转化成了不可抑止的行动，出发向冥府而去！在接下来的行文中，伊南娜的权力欲望又借由父神恩利尔和南纳之口被加以强调。在拒绝女神侍者宁叔布的求助时，两位父神说出了同样的理由（第 190—194、204—208 行）：

我的女儿渴望天庭，又觊觎冥府。
伊南娜她渴望天庭，又觊觎冥府。
冥府的神权是不应被觊觎的神权，
因为任何得此权者必须永归冥府。
有哪一位去过那里的，
能够企望再复归来呢？①

类似的欲望促动下的“逾界”与“求诉”，还体现在伊南娜－伊施塔相关的其他文本中。如苏美尔语神话《伊南娜与天神》描写了伊南娜从自己的父亲天神安的手里抢走伊阿那神庙作为自己居所的大逆不道之举②；《伊南娜与恩基》的故事里③，女神灌醉了智慧神恩基，从后者那里巧取了诸多文化礼仪之“道”（苏美尔语 ME）④。由此可见，伊南娜－伊施塔权力欲望的诉求不仅仅限于冥府，天神的居所、智慧神的“道”，都成为了她觊觎的目标和争夺的对象；而在后两个例子中，女神的确获得了成功。

伊南娜－伊施塔有如此多的欲望诉求，与这位女神在两河神话中的性格与职能设定密切相关。在苏美尔语神话《恩基与世界秩序》中⑤，智慧神恩基为诸神都安排了职能，唯独落下了女神伊南娜；后

① 此段为作者依据 ETCSL 提供的英译文所译，参见：ETCSL 1.4.1 “Inana's descent to the nether world”（网址：http://etcsl.orinst.ox.ac.uk/cgi-bin/etcsl.cgi?text=t.1.4.1#）。

② ETCSL 1.3.5 “Inana and An”（网址：http://etcsl.orinst.ox.ac.uk/cgi-bin/etcsl.cgi?text=t.1.3.5#）.

③ ETCSL 1.3.1 “Inana and Enki”（网址：http://etcsl.orinst.ox.ac.uk/cgi-bin/etcsl.cgi?text=t.1.3.1#）.

④ 对于苏美尔语“ME”学界解释不一，一般认为是一个抽象的“文化范畴”的概念。北京大学的拱玉书教授最近的研究中，将 ME 在苏美尔文化中的内涵进行了全面而深刻的剖析，并将其与中国哲学中“道”的概念进行了比较，释“ME”为“道”，以“道”论“ME”，是近年来中外学术界对这一文化概念做出的最有力度的阐释之一。参见：拱玉书：《论苏美尔文明中的“道”》，《北京大学学报》（哲学社会科学版）2017 年第 3 期，第 100—114 页。除此之外，关于 ME 的论述可参考：Samuel Noah Kramer and John R. Maier, *Myths of Enki, the Crafty God*, New York：Oxford University Press, 1989, p. 57；Bendt Alster, “On the Interpretation of the Sumerian Myth ‘Inanna and Enki’ ”, *Zeitschrift für Assyriologie und vorderasiatische Archäologie* Vol. 64, No. 1, 1974, pp. 33-34；Barrett, “Was Dust Their Food and Clay Their Bread? Grave Goods, the Mesopotamian Afterlife, and the Liminal Role of Inana/Ishtar”, pp. 21-22, note 50.

⑤ ETCSL 1.1.3 “Enki and the world order”（网址：http://etcsl.orinst.ox.ac.uk/cgi-bin/etcsl.cgi?text=t.1.1.3#）. 对于《恩基与世界秩序》的一个较新的解读，参见：Richard E. Averbeck, “Myth, Ritual, and Order in ‘Enki and the World Order’”, *Journal of the American Oriental Society* 123, No. 4, 2003, pp. 757-771。

者向恩基哭诉抱怨分配不公，恩基向伊南娜解释，自己已经赋予了她所有女性的魅力：悦耳的声音、华美的服饰、纺锤与发夹……然而在这些美好的特质之余，恩基表示也将赋予"少女伊南娜"一些纠结矛盾的个性，比如"将直线搅乱，将乱线捋直"。同时，恩基还指出伊南娜好战暴虐又爱慕虚荣的品行："堆叠人头如丘垒，播撒人头如种子""破坏不应被破坏的，创造不应被创造的""对爱慕者的目光永不厌倦""完全不知如何在深井上系上绳索"。[①] 从父神恩基的叙述中，我们可以大致勾勒出女神伊南娜的形象和性格特点：一位美丽、自恋、无畏、好奇、莽撞、叛逆、尚斗的少女形象——这一形象与她在文学作品中一以贯之的性格特点和行事风格相吻合：觊觎权力，迷恋情爱，为此不惜挑战权威、逾越界限。

图 2　古巴比伦时期的"夜女王"浮雕版，约公元前 1830—前 1531 年，藏于大英博物馆

事实上，近年来学界有关于伊施塔作为人类灵魂的象征的讨论。[②] 此种观点在图像上的支撑是伊施塔常常被刻画成一位带翼的女神，与两河文献中将灵魂描绘为"鸟状"形态相吻合[③]；大英博物馆收藏的古巴比伦时期（约前 1830—前 1531）"夜女王"浮雕版（图 2）为此提供了最好的范例。[④] 在这块浮雕版上，伊施塔赤身裸体，头戴象征神力的多层角冠，双臂弯举于身侧，手持量杆与测线[⑤]，身着羽翼，大腿以下呈鸟状，立于尾部相抵的两只幼狮背上，狮身两侧各有一只体型较大的猫头鹰。[⑥]

以"夜女王"浮雕版为典型，伊施塔女神在图像上也展示出不同于两河其他诸神的特征，即常以正面形象示人。从图像学的角度来说，侧面形象能较好地突出图像间的关系和作用力，正面形象则更加强调图像本身对于观者的作用力：浮雕版的观者被女神的

① 此段为作者依据 ETCSL 提供的英译文所译（网址：http://etcsl.orinst.ox.ac.uk/cgi-bin/etcsl.cgi?text=t.1.1.3#）.

② 关于这一说法，参见：Lapinkivi, *The Neo-Assyrian Myth of Ištar's Descent and Resurrection*, pp. 6, 38-39。

③ 例如在阿卡德语《伊施塔入冥府》故事开篇对冥府的描绘中，人死后的状态是"像鸟一样，身着羽衣"，在两河观念里人类"灵魂"可能具有类似状态。参见上书，pp. 37-38。

④ 对于这块浮雕版的研究，参见：Dominique Collon, *The Queen of the Night*, London, The British Museum Press, 2005。

⑤ 量杆与测线是伊南娜 - 伊施塔女神的法器，在苏美尔语《入冥府》故事里，伊南娜在第六道门前被迫取下青金石量杆和测线。参见第 29 页注②。

⑥ 在古代两河图像传统中，狮子是伊施塔女神最常见的伴随，可视作女神的象征；猫头鹰的形象也与伊施塔密切相关，甚至有时被认为是后者的化身。参见：Lapinkivi, *The Neo-Assyrian Myth of Ištar's Descent and Resurrection*, pp. 6, 38。

注视牢牢抓住，目光交错之间，神性的力量得到即时传达，并被观者领悟和吸收。[①] 从这种意义上讲，伊施塔的正面形象本身即具有一种连接、沟通图像世界（神）与现实世界（人）的功能，也即一种“阈限性”，这与神话文本中通过女神“逾界”的故事所传达的精神是一致的。

四 “两个世界的主宰”：关于伊施塔崇拜特质的一些思考

通过以上对《伊施塔入冥府》苏美尔语和阿卡德语传本的对照阅读，并借助符号分析和情节解析的方法对神话中“逾界”与“求诉”两大主题加以考察，现在我们可以尝试回到最初的问题：伊施塔女神有什么特殊的魅力，使得伊施塔信仰在两河三千年历史变革中长盛不衰？

美国神话学家约瑟夫·坎贝尔在其名著《千面英雄》中归纳了“人类同一个伟大故事”中的“英雄”的形象及其成长历程，其中非常重要的一个环节即在于能够“跨越归来的阈限”“从时间幻象的世界跨越到因果关系的深层世界”，进而成为“两个世界的主宰”。[②] 这个过程揭示了纷繁复杂的神话故事背后贯穿始终的精神内核，也暗示了宗教与信仰产生的原动力：一方面人类意识到“界限”的存在，于是有了“两个世界”的划分；另一方面人类意识到“界限”面前自身能力的不足，于是有了神话中能够轻盈穿梭于“两个世界”的舞者——神的存在！从这个角度来讲，宗教崇拜的重要目的即在于尽可能地突破现有的“界限”，从此岸到彼岸，从一个世界到另一个世界，获得自由与解脱；而在这种追求突破的过程中，人往往无法独立渡过，需要求诉于一个能够起到沟通作用的媒介，成为他与另一个世界之间的桥梁和通道。

在古代两河的信仰体系中，伊施塔便是这样一位能够起到沟通作用的神祇。入冥府神话中伊施塔不顾一切冲破以“门”为象征符号的“逾界”的行为，带给她一种独有的“阈限性”，使之成为两河神话世界里上天入地无所不能的存在。尽管女神跨越生死的事迹在两河传统里前无古人、后无来者，未必会给现世的人们带来任何“人死可以复生”的企望或暗示；[③] 但是她的成功穿越，以及在地府中经历的生死之间的“临界”状态，赋予了伊施塔其他诸神所不具有的连接生死、沟通三界的特性。或许正是因为这一特性，伊施塔对于崇拜者来说具有了超越其本身司掌领域以外的吸引力——通过对女神的求乞，信仰者希冀自己的愿望能够上通天庭、下达地府。事实上，像伊施塔这样具有“阈限性”的神祇存在于很多宗教体系之中，往往因其逾界贯通的本领而得到尊崇的地位和广泛的欢迎，典型的例子如古代埃及女神哈苏尔（Hathor），因具有沟通现世与来世的能力而备受尊崇。[④]

当神话照进现实，便在历史里留下影踪。在以《入冥府》为代表的诸多神话故事里，伊施塔自身“逾界”与“求诉”行为的引导下，两河的伊施塔崇拜也蒙上了“阈”与“求”的特质——人们怀着各自不同的世俗欲望向女神求助，促使伊施塔由神话体系中的求诉主体转化为崇拜体系中的求诉对象。例如在两河著名的神话史诗《伊塔那》中，人间的君主伊塔那苦于没有子嗣继承王位，于是乘神

---

① 关于伊施塔正面示人在图像学上作用的讨论，参见：Donald P. Hansen, “Through the Love of Ishtar”, in *Of Pots and Plans: Papers on the Archaeology and History of Mesopotamia and Syria Presented to David Oates in Honour of His 75th Birthday*, ed. Lamie Al-Gailani Werr et al., London, Nabu Publications, 2002, p. 99。

② 约瑟夫·坎贝尔:《千面英雄》，第 192—210 页。

③ 关于《入冥府》的故事与古代两河来世观念的讨论，可参见：Barrett, “Was Dust Their Food and Clay Their Bread? Grave Goods, the Mesopotamian Afterlife, and the Liminal Role of Inana/Ishtar”。

④ 关于哈苏尔女神的专项研究，可参见：Lesley Jackson, *Hathor: A Reintroduction to an Ancient Egyptian Goddess*, London, Avalonia, 2014。

鹰上到天堂向伊施塔女神求助，想要获取生育草进而得到子嗣。① 由于史诗的结尾部分残缺，所以故事的结局不甚明了，不过推测伊塔那应该是如愿以偿地从女神那里得到了生育草，因为依据《苏美尔王表》，伊塔那王的确有一个名为巴利荷（Balih）的儿子继承了他在基什（Kish）的王权。②

另一个比较著名的伊施塔作为求诉对象的历史案例是阿卡德王朝的创建者萨尔贡王（Sargon of Akkad，前2334—前2279年在位）获取王位的故事。《萨尔贡的传说》中记载萨尔贡是一个"江流儿"，被基什国王的园丁救起收养，长大后凭借自己的能力在基什宫廷中获得了"持杯者"（Cup-holder）的高位。③ 得权后的萨尔贡为基什国王嫉恨，几次三番加以陷害，但都得到了女神伊施塔的庇护。正是由于女神的爱，萨尔贡后来成功夺取基什王权，并创建了盛极一时的阿卡德王朝。在这种"神话色彩"渲染下建立的阿卡德政权将伊施塔崇拜提升到了国家层面。萨尔贡的女儿，古代两河著名的女诗人恩黑杜阿娜（Enheduanna）写了多篇献给伊施塔的赞美诗，传扬女神之伟力并乞求她的护佑。④ 阿卡德王朝另一位著名君主那拉姆辛（Naram-Sin）则将对伊施塔的崇拜与诉求，以及女神对自己王权的恩宠以图像的方式更为直观地传达出来（图3）。⑤

图3　从那拉姆辛石制盾牌模具上脱模出来的伊施塔女神与那拉姆辛形象，约前2220—前2184年，现由美国纽约乔纳森及珍妮特·罗森（Jonathan and Jeannette Rosen）家族收藏⑥

对于伊施塔女神的求诉不仅仅局限在国君与贵族的阶层，还广泛渗透到古代两河普通民众的生活之中。一方面，人们通过在家中供奉伊施塔来乞求夫妻生活的和美及子孙的繁盛，类似于"夜女神"浮雕版的伊施塔小像常常发现于两河民居之中，作为护身符日常佩戴的印章上也多有伊施塔女神的形

---

① 关于《伊塔那》史诗，参见：James V. Kinnier Wilson, *The Legend of Etana,* Warminster: Aris & Phillips, 1985; Jamie R. Novotny and Simo Parpola, *The Standard Babylonian Etana Epic,* State Archives of Assyria Cuneiform Texts, Helsinki, Neo-Assyrian Text Corpus Project, 2001; Stephanie Dalley, ed. *Myths from Mesopotamia: Creation, the Flood, Gilgamesh, and Others,* Oxford, Oxford University Press, 2000, pp. 189-202等。

② ETCSL 2.1.1 "The Sumerian king list"（网址：http://etcsl.orinst.ox.ac.uk/cgi-bin/etcsl.cgi?text=t.2.1.1#）.

③ ETCSL: "The Sargon Legend"（网址：http://etcsl.orinst.ox.ac.uk/section2/tr214.htm）. 关于"持杯者"的具体职位和权力，文献中没有详细的记载，不过在古代两河的图像传统中，君主常常以"持杯者"的形象出现，也许此处是对萨尔贡未来获得王权的暗示。关于古代两河的国王持杯图像的研究，可参见：Irene J. Winter, "The King and the Cup: Iconography of the Royal Presentation Scene on Ur III Seals", *Insight through Images: Studies in Honor of Edith Porada*, edited by Marilyn Kelly-Buccellati, Paolo Matthiae and Maurits Van Loon, Malibu, Undena Publications, 1986, pp. 253-268。

④ 这些诗篇中最著名的是《伊南娜赞美辞》（*The Exaltation of Inanna*），参见：William W. Hallo and J. J. A. Van Dijk, *The Exaltation of Inanna* , New Haven, Yale University Press, 1968。

⑤ 对于那拉姆辛石制盾牌模具上图像（图3）的分析，请参见：Hansen, "Through the Love of Ishtar"。

⑥ 图片引自 Aruz, Joan, and Ronald Wallenfels, eds, *Art of the First Cities: The Third Millennium B.C. From the Mediterranean to the Indus,* New York, The Metropolitan Museum of Art Press, p. 206, pl. 133。

象；[①] 另一方面，也许是受到《入冥府》中女神逾界而还的感召，在古代两河不同时期的墓葬中也多有伊施塔的图像或神符出现，或意在护佑死者冥府之行的平顺。[②]

“历史成为传说，而传说成为神话。”《魔戒》中这句著名的开场白，其实道出了一个人类学上的基本事实，也即扬·阿斯曼所言：“过去向具有奠基意义的历史或曰神话的转型。”[③] 神话本是历史的婴儿，顺时光之河漂流而下；如何溯源而上，借神话探究历史的原貌，这个问题当下正越来越为文化研究者们所重视。带着这样的领悟，本文从古代两河广为流传的《伊施塔入冥府》故事入手，围绕“逾界”与“求诉”两个神话中不断重复的主题，通过对神话文本的梳理和分析，以及对相关考古、图像材料的探寻和解读，试图说明：因“欲”而“逾”，由“阈”及“求”，不仅是本篇神话主题的表达，同时也道出了古代两河流域伊施塔崇拜至关重要的“阈”与“求”的特质。

“Trespassing” and “Pursuing”:

Some Characteristics of Ishtar Worship in Ancient Mesopotamia through the Two Major Themes of the Myth *Ishtar's Descent to the Nether World*

Jia Yan (Peking University)

Abstract: This article aims to examine the characteristics of Ishtar worship in ancient Mesopotamia through the widespread myth *Ishtar's Descent to the Nether World*. By comparing and analyzing the Sumerian and Akkadian versions of the myth, and by investigating related archaeological and visual evidence, the author intends to argue that “trespassing” and “pursuing”, as the two mayor themes repeatedly expressed throughout the texts of the myth, are to be understood on the basis of the “liminality” of Goddess Ishtar, whom as a mythological exemplar of a trespasser and pursuer, was always to be linked with godly and worldly desires in religions and political life.

Keywords: Ishtar/Inanna; nether world; ancient Mesopotamia; death; myth; liminality

① 参见：Jean Bottéro, “Love and Sex in Babylon” in *Everyday Life in Ancient Mesopotamia*, ed. Jean Bottéro, Edinburgh, Edinburgh, University Press, 2001, pp. 90-111; 关于两河滚印中伊施塔女神形象的考察，可参见：Collon, Dominique, *First Impressions: Cylinder Seals in the Ancient near East*, London, British Museum Press, 1987, pp. 167-170。

② 参见：Barrett, “Was Dust Their Food and Clay Their Bread? Grave Goods, the Mesopotamian Afterlife, and the Liminal Role of Inana/Ishtar”。

③ 扬·阿斯曼：《文化记忆：早期高级文化中的文字、回忆和政治身份》，第 74 页。

“生命树”与古埃及来世信仰

张悠然（北京大学）

摘　要:“生命树”是古埃及信仰体系中重要的象征符号，也是埃及宗教典籍和墓葬壁画频繁出现的元素，表达埃及人对来世的种种想象。然而，埃及学界对“生命树”的研究仅止于材料的搜集整理，缺乏对这一形象的发展脉络和其在来世信仰中的象征意义的探讨。本文试图整合考古、文本和图像材料，分析“生命树”这一象征符号自古王国到新王国时期的扩散过程，对“生命树”在来世信仰体系中的作用做出阐释。

关键词:“生命树”；来世信仰；古埃及宗教

对树的崇拜在古代文明中极为普遍，常见于美索不达米亚、以色列、印度、伊朗与埃及等地。① 古埃及的信仰体系中树的内涵尤为丰富，自古王国到托勒密时期，“生命树”一直是墓葬文献和图像中最基本的元素，埃及每个诺姆（nome）都有各自的圣树崇拜列表。在古王国时期的《金字塔铭文》中，就有对“生命树”的详细描述，自新王国开始，“生命树”常以女神形象出现，为死者提供来世所需食物、水源和保护。“生命树”是古埃及来世信仰中复活观念的核心象征。

虽然“生命树”这一象征符号的重要地位毋庸置疑，但限于考古遗存中树种分析的难度、图像材料中树木辨认的复杂情况以及相关材料的纷繁琐碎等原因，埃及学界目前的研究多数局限于考古资料的整理和图像资料的汇总，对其在来世信仰中具体的象征意义、在宗教仪式中的重要性，没有深入系统的讨论。如对花园这一空间的研究经常把对“生命树”的研究囊括在内，艾利克斯·威尔金森（Alix Wilkinson）于 1994 年发表的论文和 1998 年出版的同主题著作《古埃及的花园》(*The Garden in Ancient Egypt*)，以及莫林·卡罗尔（Maureen Carroll）2003 年的著作《尘世天堂：历史和考古中的古代花园》(*Earthly Paradises: Ancient Gardens in History and Archaeology*）都对埃及树木相关的考古材料做了一定程度的整理和解读，从中可以得到一些“生命树”崇拜在物质遗存和图像材料方面的信息。但是限于这类著作介绍花园的主要目的，对“生命树”的挖掘并不十分深入。这方面更加有代表性的研究是 1947 年玛利亚－露易丝·布罗（Maria-Louise Buhl）发表于《近东研究》(*Journal of Near East Studies*）上的论文《埃及树木崇拜中的女神们》(The Goddesses of the Egyptian Tree Cult）。这篇文章纵横古今，从史前埃及的树木崇拜谈到现代埃及人对树木的祭祀，重点关注三位“树女神”即哈托尔（Hathor）、努特（Nut）和伊西斯（Isis）相关的祭祀活动，对拟人化的神树进行了精彩的分析。但她的研究仅仅针

① 关于古代伊朗的“天树”崇拜，参见段晴:《天树下娜娜女神的宣言——新疆洛浦县山普鲁出土毛毯系列研究之一》,《西域研究》2015 年第 4 期，第 159 页。

对图像资料中的“生命树”，没有结合墓葬文献中“生命树”的相关文献进行综合分析。

当我们整合“生命树”相关的典籍、图像和考古材料时，发现了一个有趣的现象：虽然“生命树”崇拜自古王国时期就有了考古和文献资料的证据，但是“生命树”的图像表达是在新王国时期突然且大量地集中出现，将“生命树”拟人化的形象成为典型的样式。本文将从古埃及人来世信仰发展的角度，分析这类象征符号广泛应用与宗教典籍自上而下扩散的关系，对这一现象进行探讨。

一　复活神话与“生命树”

“树”这个词在象形文字中转写为 nht，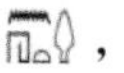，限定符号为一棵小树，如果将这一限定符号换成“房屋”（pr）的符号，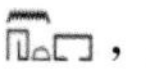，则可表达“庇护、掩蔽”之意。这正是拥有高大树冠的树木在气候炎热的埃及可以提供的重要功能；多种树木的果实更是埃及人生活中常用的食物和药品。埃及人的花园一向树木繁茂，不仅日常居住的房屋周围设有花园，墓葬和神庙前面也有宽阔整齐的花园或林荫大道。可见树木在埃及人生活中是不可或缺的植物。

对古埃及“生命树”进行研究，主要可以依靠以下几类材料：（1）考古遗存；（2）宗教典籍；（3）墓葬壁画；（4）仪式活动。实际上后三种材料是一脉相承的，是古埃及人来世观、宗教观的三种表达方式。[①] 其中宗教典籍指古王国时期（前 2686—前 2160）的《金字塔铭文》（*Pyramid Texts*）为核心的墓葬文学并以奥赛里斯（Osiris）神话为基础的复活故事，这类典籍在中王国时期（前 2055—前 1650）发展为《石棺铭文》（*Coffin Texts*），在新王国时期（前 1550—前 1069）变得更为实际，这就是图文并茂的《亡灵书》（*Book of the Dead*）。墓葬壁画是这类典籍内容的图像表达，而仪式活动更是围绕这些主题进行种种庆典与祭祀。基于对上述材料的整理，可以发现全国性的“生命树”崇拜主要集中在无花果树、金合欢树、柽柳以及椰枣等树上。

在宗教典籍之中，奥赛里斯的复活神话作为一切复活神话的基础，蕴含了“生命树”原初的功能和意义。在古埃及庞大的神祇系统中，奥赛里斯是其中最为长寿、影响最为深远的一位。“他是所有复活之神的原型，这些复活之神死去，只是为了再一次复活。”[②]

简要地说，这是一个贤王被害最终复活的故事。奥赛里斯继承了父亲盖伯（Geb）的王位统治埃及，他登基后实行的统治措施将埃及人从缺吃少穿和远离文明的野蛮生活状态中解脱出来。他教会埃及人认识土地上出产的各种果实，为埃及人制定法律，教他们尊敬神灵。奥赛里斯发现了小麦和葡萄酒，促进了农业的发展，也让人民更加敬畏他。然而，这样一位贤王却被嫉妒他的弟弟塞特（Seth）谋杀。塞特计划周详，先按照奥赛里斯身体的长度做了一个精美的匣子，命人在一次宴会上抬上来，并说哪个人躺在里面最合适便把匣子送给这个人。宾客们逐一躺进箱子里却发现没有一个人的身材适合，奥赛里斯躺进去后，整个身子都能够在棺材里舒展开来。突然间情势骤变，全体宾客冲过去把匣子盖上，一些人在外面钉上钉子，另一些人用熔化的铅来封口，此后他们把装有奥赛里斯的匣子扔入河里漂进大海。

这匣子在叙利亚海岸的毕布洛斯城（Byblos）漂上岸来，竟是有一棵大树从那里茁壮生长，将匣

① 关于古埃及宗教典籍的研究，参见：Eric Hornung, *The Ancient Egyptian Books of the Afterlife,* Ithaca, NY, Cornell University Press, 1999, pp. 1-24。

② 简·艾伦·哈里森：《古代艺术与仪式》，刘宗迪译，北京：生活·读书·新知三联书店，2008 年，第 5 页。

子完全包住。那里的国王见这树挺拔茂密，便将它砍下来做了房梁。奥赛里斯的妻子伊西斯自从听到奥赛里斯被害的消息后，一直拼命寻找丈夫的尸首，当她赶到毕布洛斯时，那棵树已经被砍下来做了房梁。她现出原形，向国王乞要那根房梁，并剖开木头拿出了匣子。随后，在伊西斯出发到布托（Buto）去看她的儿子荷鲁斯（Horus）之前，她把奥赛里斯的棺木藏在隐蔽之处，但是塞特于一个月明之夜发现了这个匣子，他把奥赛里斯的尸体分成42块，抛散在埃及全境的各个诺姆中。随后伊西斯和奈芙缇丝（Nephthys）一起踏遍埃及寻找奥赛里斯的尸体，"她们的悲痛哀悼也成为埃及人关于悲伤最神圣的表达"[①]。当她们把奥赛里斯的尸块找齐拼回人形后，又将他制成木乃伊下葬。此后奥赛里斯的坟墓中长出一棵无花果树，树冠庞大，枝叶婆娑，恰恰可以笼罩奥赛里斯的尸身，"这棵圣树即是奥赛里斯不灭生命的可见象征"[②]。神话的结局中，奥赛里斯和伊西斯的儿子荷鲁斯长大成人后，为奥赛里斯复仇，成功地从塞特手中夺回王位，成为上下埃及之王，而奥赛里斯也得以复活，成为冥世之主。父子二人分别为冥界之王和人间之王，这就是后来一代一代的死去的国王与继任的国王的神化形象。

这个神话对"生命树"的形象进行了高度浓缩和升华，其治愈、保护与庇佑之力在神话中都得到了充分展现。这种治愈力量在医学纸草中也有所体现[③]，比如无花果树可以被用来治愈多种疾病，是古埃及人实施医学魔法的重要工具。此处笼罩奥赛里斯的大树正是上一节中圣树为神和人提供保护的源头。随着奥赛里斯崇拜的不断发展，奥赛里斯墓中长出的圣树逐渐成为独特的象征符号。

出于对奥赛里斯的崇拜，埃及各地都有所谓"奥赛里斯墓"，每个祭祀场所都有圣树用于让神的巴鸟栖息。阿拜多斯（Abydos）、孟菲斯（Memphis）和赫里奥波利斯（Heliopolis）都是奥赛里斯崇拜盛行的地方。菲莱（Philae）则有一棵雪松被作为奥赛里斯的"生命树"，根据普鲁塔克的版本这是奥赛里斯灵魂的栖息之地。而迪奥斯波里斯·帕尔瓦（Diospolis parva）的一处墓葬中，奥赛里斯墓被置于柽柳的荫蔽之下。[④] 神话中那棵包裹着奥赛里斯棺木的树，据说立在丹德拉（Dendera）的奥赛里斯南神殿中；而其中盛着奥赛里斯鹰隼头木乃伊的棺木被描绘成"嵌在树中"的样子。[⑤] 所谓"奥赛里斯墓"，是一种以土堆覆盖墓室，又在土堆上种植树木的设计，这也是一种对创世神话中原初之水中出现的土丘的模仿。塞提一世（Seti I）在阿拜多斯为纪念奥赛里斯而建造的墓葬是其中非常典型的一个。整体建筑全部被土堆覆盖，周边有6棵树，都植于至少15米深的树坑中。树坑边上的近半圆形的围墙用砖和石灰岩块垒成，里面有柽柳和针叶树的遗存。[⑥] 虽然各地圣树种类各不相同，然而考虑到各个诺姆的圣树崇拜自有差别，"生命树"的广泛门类也当属自然。

与复活神话紧密相连的重要习俗之一是每年制作奥赛里斯小圣像的仪式。这是一个将奥赛里斯看作"树神"的仪式，弗米卡特·马特纳斯（Firmicus Maternus）[⑦]、普鲁塔克都描述过这种仪式[⑧]。简要地说，人

① J. H. Breasted, *Development of Religion and Thought in Ancient Egypt*, University of Pennsylvania Press, 1972, p. 26.

② Ibid., p. 28.

③ 关于无花果树在古埃及医学中的使用，参见：Cyril P. Bryan, *The Papyrus Ebers*, London, Geoffrey Bles, 1930, pp. 48, 52, 54, 63, 108, 115, 130, 132。

④ J. G. Wilkinson and S. Birch, *The Manners and Customs of the Ancient Egyptians*, London, J. Murray, 1878, III, p. 349.

⑤ James G. Frazer, *The Golden Bough: A Study in Magic and Religion*, London, Macmillan, 1907, IV, p. 341.

⑥ Alix Wilkinson, *The Garden in Ancient Egypt*, London, The Rubicon Press, 1998, p. 65.

⑦ James G. Frazer, *The Golden Bough: A Study in Magic and Religion*, IV, p. 340.

⑧ 参见普鲁塔克:《论埃及神学与哲学》，段映虹译，北京：华夏出版社，2009年，第50页。

们将松树砍下挖空，用挖出的木料雕成奥赛里斯小像，然后将这小雕像如埋尸体一般埋葬在树的空洞中，这正是一种埋葬奥赛里斯的假想。回归树木长眠的圣像正如死者回归母亲的子宫，而子宫里正孕育着下一场复活。生命流转不息，最终还是要回到最初之地。这样的圣像会在树洞内保存一年，新的一年就要把它取出来烧掉，制作新的圣像。这正是奥赛里斯神话衍生出的对复活的无数演绎中的一种。

"生命树"崇拜的内涵在奥赛里斯神话的基础上不断发展，并在宗教典籍、民间习俗和考古材料中得到反映。古王国和中王国时期对"生命树"的描述基本集中在宗教典籍之中。鉴于宗教典籍一脉相承的特性，古王国时期的《金字塔铭文》和中王国时期的《石棺铭文》中的"生命树"可以联系起来考察，以便与新王国时期图像上的变化做一对比分析。

二《金字塔铭文》与《石棺铭文》中的"生命树"

古王国时期的《金字塔铭文》是埃及最古老的宗教咒语集成，铭文刻在金字塔墓室内部，密密麻麻的象形文字布满墓室的天花板和四壁，其中并没有图像。这是一种"来世指南"，旨在帮助死去的国王升入天堂、成为众神的一员。这个过程需要种种物质或精神上的辅助，比如进入天空的天梯、帮助国王的神祇、进入来世所需的神秘知识等，这都是《金字塔铭文》的重要内容。《金字塔铭文》是国王专用的墓葬文献。中王国时期，这种"来世指南"演变为贵族官员也可以使用的《石棺铭文》，《石棺铭文》内容上继承了《金字塔铭文》的大部分咒语，主要刻在棺椁上，偶尔配有一些插图。对这两份文献进行整理，辅之以当时的考古材料，可以勾勒出古王国至中王国时期"生命树"崇拜的多重内涵。

树木的高大形态可以展现保护的姿态，正如《金字塔铭文》中对树与神的位置关系的描写："无花果树保护着神，那些冥界之神都立于树下。"① 站在树的荫蔽之下便获得了神树的保护之力。下面两条铭文可以更生动地展现"生命树"如何保护死去的国王：

> 蛇盘踞天上，荷鲁斯的蜈蚣伏于地上，荷鲁斯穿着拖鞋踏入其洞。哦，SnT－蛇，我将不会被敌对！我的无花果树就是它的无花果树，我的庇护就是它的庇护，我会找到我的路，把它一块块地吞食。②
>
> 你的无花果树是你的粮食，你的粮食就是你的无花果树！你的尾巴在你的嘴中，哦，SnT－蛇！转身，转过身去；哦，雄壮的公牛！……被诅咒的人已经逃离。哦，sA－tA－蛇，当心大地！哦，sA－tA－蛇，当心……！③

以上两条铭文都是国王在进入来世路上遇到的危险生物之一——蛇（Apophis）的情况下用到的咒语，无花果树提供的保护可以让国王安全通过这条漫漫长路，进入来世，与神并行而达成永生。在古代近东神话中，神树与蛇经常同时出现，带来危险的大蛇与提供保护的神树是一对经典意象。另外，上条铭文中"你的无花果树是你的粮食，你的粮食就是你的无花果树！"是在告诫死者，通往来世路上多艰险，不能随意吃喝，只有无花果树才是安全的、有益的。"生命树"为死者提供另一个世界中的保护与食物，满足了死者延续生命的基本需求。

---

① R. O. Faulkner, *The Ancient Egyptian Pyramid Texts*, Warminster: Aris& Phillips, 1969, p. 299.

② Ibid., p. 89.

③ Ibid., p. 129.

"生命树"还可以满足死者更高层次的精神需求。在《石棺铭文》中多次提到生者为死后所作的准备之一便是"在西方建一方领地，挖出池塘，种植无花果树"[①]。埃及人相信神是居住在神庙或花园的树中的。人间的统治者法老也乐于在宫殿周围的花园里嬉游。花园、池塘和树木构成了一个令人着迷的小世界。在来世重生的死者渴望与在生时的日常生活保持一致，比如依然可以在种有无花果树的花园中沿着池塘散步，享有充沛的水、空气和树荫的遮蔽，这是埃及人日常生活中重要的乐趣之一。这种与在世时的"一致"意味着埃及人追求的永恒。墓葬壁画中经常展现死者在树荫下前行的情景，图像旁边的铭文也经常提到那些树正是墓主生前亲手所植，可以为他提供与在生时一样的荫蔽。一场葬礼过后，树的主人去而复返，其身份已经由花园的主人变更为"来世的一员"，树木却依旧葱翠如故。常青的植物为变动不居的世界提供了一个相对稳定的锚点，这正是永恒的一种象征。

"生命树"不仅是死者在来世享受生活之乐的缩影，更是灵魂的栖居之地。大部分学者认为古埃及人的"巴"指的是"灵魂"，或是个体的精神与物质范畴的一部分。[②] 巴的外形是人头鸟，展翅飞翔的巴鸟能够让死者回到阳间与生者自由交流。这种"栖居"正如鸟儿在树上休息，"生命树"为死者的灵魂提供了一个休憩的空间，让他享受天堂的甜美安详。

天堂的门口正是由两棵树并立构成。这类图像在宗教典籍和新王国之后墓室壁画中频繁出现，比如一轮红日从两棵树之间冉冉升起的场景。在古埃及宇宙观中，太阳活力的恢复需要经过一个被天空女神吞入口中再重新出生的过程。天空女神弯曲的身体犹如穹顶，身下的地平线两端则各有一棵树，太阳就这样从女神腹部出现，照耀大地。这说明两棵树并立的形象构成了一道"门"，这是一种关键地点的指示和对空间的区隔。

《金字塔铭文》第470条中有这样一段死去的国王与其母神的对话：

> "你要去往何处？"
>
> "我要去往天上见我父亲，去见拉神。"我这样回答。
>
> "去那高丘还是那赛特之丘？"
>
> "高丘将会把我送到赛特之丘上，那里高大的无花果树矗立天穹之东，枝叶繁茂风过有声，神祇就坐于树上，因为我是探索苍穹的鹰隼；因为我是掌舵之人……"[③]

第568条则描写了国王升入天空的情景：

> ……梯子为他搭好，他可以借此升入天空；不灭星辰助他上船渡河。公牛弯下角来让他过去，来到那冥界之湖，公牛说道："哦，王！不要摔倒在地！"
>
> 国王抓住天边的两棵无花果树，叫道："渡我过河！"他们便把国王送到天穹之东。[④]

进入那两棵树之间，便是进入天堂。入口是一个充满魔力、能够赋予人"转变"能力的地方。天堂入

---

① R. O. Faulkner, *Ancient Egyptian Coffin Texts*, Warminster: Aris& Phillips, 1973, I, pp. 108, 111; III, pp. 171, 173.

② J. Assmann, *Death and Salvation in Ancient Egypt*, Ithaca, NY, Cornell University Press, 2015, pp. 89-90; "Egyptian Mortuary Liturgies", *Studies in Egyptology Presented to Miriam Lichtheim*, ed. Sarah Israelit-Groll, Jerusalem: Hebrew University, 1990, pp. 1-45.

③ Faulkner, *The Ancient Egyptian Pyramid Texts*, p. 159.

④ Ibid., pp. 221-222.

图 1　梅克特拉墓中房屋及花园模型，彩绘木制，底比斯墓葬 280 号，11 王朝（约前 1990）

口处作为一个关口性质的存在，其中的空间与周围其他空间并非同质，当人踏入其中，便会感受到神显之地的独特力量。正是这种不同，让死者得以完成存在形式的重大转变——成为阿赫（Akh），加入神的行列，实现永恒的存在。①

考古报告中神庙、墓葬周围的大量树坑和其中的植物遗存都可表明神性建筑对“生命树”力量的依赖。② 中王国时期，阿拜多斯的一座坟茔前面的庭院种植了两棵树来作为入口的标志。③ 另外，这一时段大臣梅克特拉（Meket-re）的墓中置有一个木制房屋模型（图 1），这类小模型一般用来保证墓主在来世的一切生活所需，这个房屋前的庭院内有七棵无花果树围绕池塘。宗教典籍中两棵树并立的形象在生活中得到了实践，这类建筑上饱含深意的设计可能会帮助墓主顺利进入天堂。总的来说，古王国和中王国时期，对“生命树”象征内涵的描述集中在文本中，而新王国时期“生命树”崇拜的表达方式从文本转向了图像。

三　新王国时期“生命树”形象的拟人化

在宗教经典文献这方面，新王国时期出现了写在纸草上的大众版本的《亡灵书》。《亡灵书》在内容上侧重对普通人寻求复活之路上种种行为的引导，纸草上有大量配图，其中有很多展现“生命树”和女神合为一体的图景，旁边的咒语正是对这一场景需要念诵的内容。另外，这一时期底比斯（Thebes）的私人墓葬中出现了大量关于树女神哈托尔、伊西斯或努特哺育死者的壁画，这种哺育实际上是一种供奉。古王国时期的壁画常见一队侍者手捧供奉，面向坐在供桌前的死者走去。然而，新王国时期这类供奉仪式在图像中的执行者变成了树女神。根据埃及人的灵魂观念，卡和巴都需要酒食④，所以提供酒食的供奉仪式是复活必不可少的一环。“生命树”在新王国时期以树的拟人化形式出现在大量的墓葬壁画中。

18 王朝（前 1550—前 1295）时期，官员南荷特（Nakht）墓的南墙壁画是目前发现这类图像中最早的一个（图 2）。⑤ 女神站在摆满供品的供桌一侧，手举食物托盘，她头顶的无花果树强调了其树神身份。这一时段中的经典图像是中级官员尼巴曼（Nebamun）墓中壁画展示花园的一幕（图 3），画面

① 阿赫是古埃及灵魂观念中“人”的一种存在形式，广义上说可以分享一些拉神（Re）的特质，死者经历了一系列葬礼仪式、成功通过末日审判之后便会成为阿赫。阿赫的重要能力则是在不同的空间中穿梭，即跨越阳间、阴间与神域。关于阿赫的研究，参见 Jiří Janák, “Akh”, *UCLA Encyclopedia of Egyptology*, ed. Jacco Dieleman and Willeke Wendrich, Los Angeles, 2013, pp. 1-6, http://digital2.library.ucla.edu/viewItem.do?ark=21198/zz002gc1pn。

② 参见：Alix Wilkinson, *The Garden in Ancient Egypt*, pp. 110-113。

③ Alix Wilkinson, *The Garden in Ancient Egypt*, fig. 57, p. 112.

④ 关于古埃及人灵魂概念的研究，参见：Jan Assmann, *Death and Salvation in Ancient Egypt*, pp. 87-104。

⑤ Marie-Louise Buhl, “The Goddesses of the Egyptian Tree Cult”, *Journal of Near Eastern Studies*, 1947, Vol. 6, No. 2, p. 92.

右上角也有一位女神出现在无花果树中，端出水和果实。还有掌印官赛贝克霍特普（Sebekhotep）墓中壁画表现花园的场景（图4），他和妻子在花园中穿行，花园中有无花果树等树木，枝叶繁茂。图像中间一行的右边出现了一位树女神，她的身体就是树干，伸出手来为死者递上供奉。仅18王朝内就出现了这类图像的三种基本形式，分别为女神头顶无花果树、女神上半身出现在无花果树中以及女神身体与树干融为一体。

图2　南荷特墓壁画，底比斯墓葬52号，卢克索，18王朝（约前1550—前1295）

19王朝（前1295—前1186）的一位在王室祭庙中服务的官员乌瑟海特（Userhet）墓中，死者和妻子及母亲一起坐在巨大的无花果树之下，树荫富有保护意味，同时也给予他们与在生时一样的欢娱（图5）。他们前面是一个小的T型池塘，上面有两只人头巴鸟在喝水。两位女性头上有两只巴鸟在飞翔。努特女神立于他们对面，女神头上有一棵小树。女神站在小池塘岸上，手拿祭酒瓶和盛有各种面包的托盘，作为对死者的供养，这正是一幅灵魂和身体都得到满足的场景。同时代的工匠塞内杰姆（Sennedjem）墓中这幅墓主夫妇敬神图（图6）也十分典型，墓主夫妇身着节日盛装，刚刚进入冥界，他们跪在树中露出上半身的女神面前，伸手去接女神播撒的生命之水。这幅图旁边配的铭文则是这一时期平民使用的“来世通关密语”《亡灵书》第59章，即“让死者在来世拥有足够的空气和水之咒语”：

图3　尼巴曼墓壁画，底比斯（约前1400）

图4　赛贝克霍特普墓壁画（约前1500—前1295）

图 5 乌瑟海特墓壁画，底比斯墓葬 51 号，19 王朝（约前 1295—前 1186）

图 6 塞内杰姆墓壁画，底比斯墓葬 1 号（约前 1294—前 1213）

图 7 《亡灵书》第 59 章插图，引自 Raymond O. Faulkner, *The Ancient Egyptian Book of the Dead* (British Museum Publications, 1989), p. 68

图 8 奈斯帕乌舍皮棺椁，底比斯西部，21 王朝（约前 1069—前 945）

图 9 晚期《亡灵书》纸草，第 7 页，大英博物馆，EA10086/7

“啊，这棵努特的无花果树，你拥有充足的水和空气，请你赐予我其中的一点……”[①] 当我们在《亡灵书》中寻找第 59 章所配插图（图 7）时，可以发现相似的图景再次出现。图中右侧部分，死者阿尼（Ani）和他的妻子站在池塘中，弯腰从池塘中捧水送到唇边；左边则是阿尼跪在树中女神面前的图景，他伸手接过树中露出上半身的女神赐予的饮食。

这类图像不仅出现在墓葬壁画上，也会出现在棺椁外壳上。比如 21 王朝（前 1069—前 945）书吏奈斯帕乌舍皮（Nespawershepi）棺椁上刻画的图像（图 8），树女神自身构成了树干，周身环绕着枝叶，向死者的巴鸟提供生命之水。树、水、巴鸟和女神是经常同时出现的意象，“生命树”是得到这一切的通道和手段，而水则是复生所必要的基本元素。这类图像的终极简化则是略去女神本身，直接将手与树结合，即枝叶茂密的树中伸出手臂来为死者提供饮食。比如埃及后期《亡灵书》的插图（图 9），此图左上角和右下角展现了树中伸出手臂的情景，那一页上的咒语依然是上文提到的《亡灵书》第 59 章。可以发现新王国时期这类图像的使用是与宗教典籍《亡灵书》互相配合的，《亡灵书》虽然内容上承袭《石棺铭文》，但却更关注进入来世过程中的实用技巧和巫术，而非晦涩难懂的神秘知识。

① R. O. Faulkner, *The Ancient Egyptian Book of the Dead*, London, British Museum Publications, 1985, p. 68.

在18王朝的地方官员克那蒙（Kenamun）墓中，树女神图像旁配的铭文可以更好地概括这类图像：

> 我是努特，我来是为你带来礼物。你坐在我下方，在我的枝叶下享受这份凉爽。我允许你吮吸我的乳汁，在我双乳的滋养下生活；为了其中的乐趣和健康……你的母亲给你生命。她将你放在她怀孕的子宫里……我为你带来我的面包、我的啤酒、我的牛奶、我的饭菜、我的无花果……①

可见树女神作为母神形象的代表，将古王国和中王国宗教典籍中“生命树”的种种内涵集于一身，不仅为死者提供荫蔽，还为死者提供饮食，最重要的则是让死者进入女神的子宫之中。这种“回归来处”的意味正如奥赛里斯小圣像每年都要被封入树洞的仪式所代表的意义，以及太阳被努特女神吞下又生出的过程，人的永生正与“生命树”代表的回归原初一样，是通过不断返回创世之初完成的不断发生的复活。

综观“生命树”崇拜表达方式自古王国到新王国发生的变化，可以发现其中经历了一个从文本到图像、从官方到民间的过程。这个过程背后的原因非常值得探究。

四　新王国时期来世信仰的世俗化

纵向来看，通过梳理“生命树”崇拜自古王国到新王国的发展变化，可以窥见埃及宗教发展的轨迹。古王国时代的埃及人服从王作为“神在人间的代言人”的统治，通过崇拜国王来获得神的保护。中王国时代《石棺铭文》较之《金字塔铭文》使用阶层的下移已经对后来的发展趋势做出了暗示。新王国时代的《亡灵书》则是直接简化为方便大众理解使用的版本，关注实用性和可操作性，并且着重展现了巫术的作用。然而，这一时期又出现了一批新的国王专用的“来世指南”——《来世之书》（*Books of the Netherworld*），其中包括《杜阿特之书》《天之书》《地之书》《门之书》等。鉴于复活和来世在埃及人精神世界中的核心地位，可知“来世指南”的阶层分化是整个社会最深刻的分化。国王专用的墓葬经典藏在帝王谷的墓室之中，内容也极为晦涩难懂，似乎是拒绝被人解读和使用。

这样的情况要联系新王国时期整体的宗教状况来分析。著名埃及学家扬·阿斯曼（Jan Assmann）认为，新王国时期的宗教经历了两个剧变，一是埃赫那吞（Akhenaten）改革对多神信仰的冲击，一是个人虔信（personal piety）的出现与发展。② 个人虔信指这一时期人们开始直接对神进行祈祷，国王作为人神之间中介的身份开始失效。人们不再像中王国时期依赖国王的护佑，而是直接向神寻求保护。这一观念上的剧变也反映在埃及人对“生命树”的崇拜中。神的形象直接和树结合在一起，赐予死者饮食。如果人们依然像古王国时代那样对王保持崇敬，那供奉的含义则是国王将供品分享给死者。如今死者得到的供奉却是神直接给予的。这种人与神／王互动关系的转变，结合宗教典籍出现的巨大分化，可以发现国王为了维护自己独一无二的地位、保存埃及精英阶层的智慧结晶，将最复杂深奥的《来世之书》深藏于帝王谷的密室之中，是一种对当时来世信仰世俗化大潮的反抗。

---

① Norman de Garis Davies, *The Tomb of Kenamun of Thebes,* New York, Arno Press, 1930, p. 46.

② 关于个人虔信的研究，参见：J. Assmann, *The Mind of Egypt: History and Meaning in the Time of the Pharaohs*, Cambridge, Mass., Harvard University Press, 2003, pp. 229-247。

横向来说，“生命树”信仰是透视古埃及人来世信仰的一扇窗。植物自身的再生能力仅仅是大千世界中的一环，其蕴含的思想观念也只是古埃及复活观念的一个方面。人们对树女神的崇拜是将母神崇拜和复活渴望结合起来的产物。母神给予生命，“生命树”助人复活。在埃及人的生死观中，生与死本就是一体。“回到女神的子宫之中”这类铭文与树女神的图像共同构成死而复活的循环。这种向一切起点处的不断回归正是被对创世之初的怀念所驱动的行为，埃及人循环的时间观念与这种回归相吻合。永恒循环的时间中，埃及人不断重复这片土地上的生活。

The “Tree of Life”and Belief in Afterlife in Ancient Egypt

Zhang Youran (Peking University)

Abstract: “Tree of Life” is a significant symbol in the ancient Egyptian religion, also a common element in the funerary texts and tomb reliefs, which reflects Egyptians’ popular imagination of afterlife. However, the fragmentary materials limit the scholars to collect the materials and hinder us from researches on the development of the image of “Tree of Life”, as well as the symbolic meaning of “Tree of Life” in afterlife. This paper will combine textual, archaeological, and iconographical evidence to analyze how this religious symbol was disseminated from Old Kingdom to New Kingdom, and elaborate the role of “Tree of Life” in the afterlife belief.

Keywords: “Tree of Life”; afterlife belief; ancient Egyptian religion

《王叔和脉诀》在伊朗 *

时光（北京大学）

摘　要：《伊利汗中国科技珍宝书》（*Tanksūqnāmah*）是由伊朗伊利汗王朝宰相拉施特主持翻译编订的一部介绍中国科学技术的著作，全书共有四部，目前仅有介绍中国医学的第一部存世。作为首部编译成波斯语的古代中医学著作，该书对研究中世纪中国与西亚地区的文化交往，尤其是医学方面的交流提供了相当丰富的一手材料，具有极高的价值。

《伊利汗中国科技珍宝书》收录了中国古代脉学著作《王叔和脉诀》中基本完整的歌诀，对每句歌诀进行了波斯文释义，并附上了一些中国名医对歌诀的点评。由于《王叔和脉诀》的原始版本及历史上部分点评著作已经佚失，因此翻译、整理及研究该书对还原《王叔和脉诀》的文本具有极大的参考价值，在本文中将以现存的中医古籍作为参考，对《伊利汗中国科技珍宝书》中《王叔和脉诀》部分进行对比研究，并对其文本的记录过程进行分析。

关键词：中医；王叔和脉诀；伊朗

一 《伊利汗中国科技珍宝书》中的《王叔和脉诀》

《伊利汗中国科技珍宝书》①（*Tanksūqnāma-yi Īlkhān dar Funūn-i ʿUlūm-i Khatāyī*）② 是由伊朗伊利汗王朝宰相拉施特（1247—1318）③ 主持翻译编订的一部介绍中国科学技术的波斯文著作，全书共分四部，目前仅有介绍中国医学的第一部存世，其手抄本孤本被藏于土耳其伊斯坦布尔阿雅·索菲亚（Aya Sophia）图书馆，抄写者穆罕默德·本·艾哈迈德·本·马赫穆德（Muhammad Bin Ahmad Bin Mahmūd），成书于伊斯兰教历 713 年（1313）。1972 年伊朗德黑兰大学出版了该书的影印本，著名历史学家莫季塔巴·米诺维（Mujtabā Mīnuvī）为该书作序，介绍了有关这部作品的创作背景。

主持编订该书的拉施特出生于伊朗西部城市哈马丹（Hamidān），在担任伊利汗王朝统治者合赞汗（1295—1304 年在位）宰相期间，拉施特在贴必力思（Tabrīz）④ 附近修建了一座拥有学校、图书馆、天文台、作坊、医院、药房、清真寺、公共浴室等设施的科技文化中心，后被称为“拉施特镇”

* 本文为教育部人文社会科学研究青年基金项目“波斯语手抄本《中国医学宝书》校注与研究”（项目编号：11YJC752017）阶段性研究成果。

① 以下简称为《珍宝书》（*Tanksūqnāmah*）。

② 本文涉及的波斯语、阿拉伯语词汇采用 IJMES 转写系统，其中带有阿拉伯语词汇冠词词汇按照太阴、太阳字母读音规则转写。

③ 本书中如无特别说明或注释，年代均为公元纪年法。

④ 今伊朗西北部城市大不里士。

（Rab‘-i Rashīdī）。通过一些历史文献可以得知，在当时的“拉施特镇”里有一些来自中国的医师，他们把针灸、脉诊、制作草药等传统中医疗法以及一些著名的中医学著作介绍给了当地的伊朗人。英国医学家西里勒·洛伊德·埃勒古德（Cyril Lloyd Elgood，1892—1970）在其所著的《伊朗医学史》一书中关于伊利汗时期医学一章中曾提到：“在其中一封书信中说：在该医院中有五十名医师，他们其中有一些人来自世界各地，例如埃及、中国、印度、叙利亚。每位医师均负责教授十名学生，除了这支规模庞大的团队，还有一些外科手术大夫、眼科医师与骨损伤医师在这家医院中工作，他们每人也有至少 5 名学生。”①

作为第一部编译成波斯语的古代中医学著作，《珍宝书》对研究中世纪中国与西亚地区的文化交往，尤其是医学方面提供了相当丰富的一手材料，具有极高的价值。《珍宝书》中提到了一部名为《脉诀》的中医著作。《脉诀》又名《王叔和脉诀》②，是一部以歌诀形式写成的中医脉学著作，相传为西晋名医王叔和（201—280）撰。《脉诀》在中国宋元时期由于其流传甚广，曾传有多种不同的版本。至北宋时期，一些医学家逐渐发现《脉诀》一书的作者其实并非王叔和，而是六朝人士高阳生。高阳生用歌诀形式创作了此书，是为了使平常人士更容易理解记忆，之所以托名王叔和是因为王氏乃古代名医，可使该书更受到世人的关注，因此尽管高氏本人并非名医，《脉诀》一书却迅速广为流传于民间。至两宋时期，一些医学家逐渐发现了这部作品中的一些错误之处，开始对《脉诀》中的诸首歌诀进行了点评与批判。

部分汉文《脉诀》注释点评著作如下：

（北宋）刘元宾：《通真子补注王叔和脉诀》

（北宋）池荣：《脉诀注解》（佚失）

（南宋）李駉：《脉诀集解》（佚失）

（南宋）黎民寿：《决脉精要》

（金）张元素：《洁古老人注王叔和脉诀》

（元）戴起宗：《脉诀刊误》

（明）熊宗立：《王叔和脉诀图要俗解大全》

（朝鲜）许浚：《纂图方论脉诀集成》（1581，图 1）

《珍宝书》中的《脉诀》部分与上述汉文点评著作形式相似，编译者首先用波斯文字母及一些特殊符号转写了《脉诀》中各首歌诀的汉字发音，然后附上多位中国古代名医点评语录及中医学经典名作中对歌诀内容相关的阐述。

《珍宝书》中引用语录的名医包括：

通真子：即刘元宾，号通真子，北宋名医，著有《通真子补注王叔和脉诀》。

纂圖方論脈訣集成卷之二
○五臟六腑
布范曰 素問云五臟者藏精氣而不瀉者也故滿而不能實六腑傳化物而不藏故實而不能滿
潔古曰 五臟六腑有餘有不足故實爲有餘虛爲不足有餘法當先時不足法當後時當曰實塞而不通故曰有餘瀉其子以流之逾洎不息子母之虛也當補以留之行留流住爲之子母言補瀉證也補瀉者爲夫婦虛實

图 1 《纂图方论脉诀集成》卷二《五脏六腑》

① Cyril Elgood (translated by Mohssen Javidan), *Tārīkh-i Pizishkī-yi Īrān*, Tehrān, Iqbāl, 1973, pp. 447-448.

② 以下简称为《脉诀》。

池大明：即池荣，号大明，南宋名医，著有《脉诀注解》，该书今已佚失。

李子野：即李駉，字子野，范子，南宋名医，著有《脉诀集解》，该书今已佚失。

黎民寿：字景仁，南宋名医，著有《决脉精要》。

无求子：即朱肱，字翼中，号无求子，北宋名医，著有《南阳活人书》。

张仲景：名机，字仲景，东汉末年名医，被后人尊称为医圣，著有中医学名作《伤寒杂病论》。

杨玄操：唐朝名医，曾校注过《难经》，著有《黄帝八十一难经注》，今已佚失。

杜光庭：字圣宾，号东瀛子，唐末五代道士，道教学者，被认为是脉学著作《玉函经》的著者。

陈藏器：唐代名医、药学家，著有药学著作《本草拾遗》，今已佚失。

许进之：即许国祯，字进之，元代名医，著有《御药院方》一书。

玄晏先生：三国西晋名医皇甫谧，幼名静，字士安，自号玄晏先生。

还有数位医师其姓名暂不可考，其中四位在书中被称为“太医”，分别为：虞太医①、盛太医、沈太医及魏太医，此外还有两位名叫 Dīn dāi schin、D.n čāi 的医师。

《珍宝书》中《脉诀》部分引用的中医典籍包括：

《难经》：相传为秦越人（扁鹊）所作，成书于东汉之前。

《素问》：中国现存最早的中医学理论著作，相传为黄帝创作，大约成书于春秋战国时期。

《病源》：又称《诸病源候论》，著者为隋朝名医巢元方。

《千金方》：著者为唐代名医孙思邈。

《甲乙经》：又称《黄帝三部针灸甲乙经》，中国最早的一部针灸学著作，著者为三国西晋名医皇甫谧。

《珍宝书》是历史上最早译成波斯文的汉文著作之一，这部作品中涉及的中医学知识之广泛与丰富，令人惊叹。虽然遗憾的是随着 1318 年拉施特遭他人政治陷害后被杀，“拉施特镇”亦毁于之后的劫掠，《珍宝书》这部作品在伊朗未能得到进一步的推广，书中介绍的中医学，特别是脉学的理论与疗法在本书问世之后至近现代，在伊朗及其周边地区也没有关于其传播与应用的记载，然而对此书的透彻研究可以还原宋元时期医学在中国的发展状况，通过对《珍宝书》中《脉诀》的歌诀及中国医学家点评的整理归纳，可以复原《脉诀》文本，并与现存《脉诀》点评著作中记录的《脉诀》文本进行版本的对比与研究。

二　波斯文版与汉文版《王叔和脉诀》比较研究

本节选用北宋名医刘元宾所著的《新刊通真子补注王叔和脉诀》② 及明朝名医熊宗立所著的《王叔和脉诀图要俗解大全》③ 作为《珍宝书》中《脉诀》部分歌诀转写的参考与对比文献。之所以选择这两部著作进行歌诀对比，主要是由于刘元宾生活的时代距《珍宝书》较近，在波斯文抄本中也多处直接引用了他本人对《脉诀》的点评。虽然书中对池大明④、李子野⑤等医师的引述也较多，但这几位

---

① 有可能是指北宋医学家虞庶，著有《虞庶注难经》一书。

② 以下简称为《通真子》。

③ 以下简称为《熊宗立》。

④ 即池荣。

⑤ 即李駉。

医师的《脉诀》点评著作目前已经失传。熊宗立的著作中则引用了“通真子[①]（3处）、朱氏[②]（1处）、池氏[③]（62处）、晞范[④]（16处）、杜氏[⑤]（1处）、黎氏[⑥]（3处）等诸家的文字”[⑦]，这些医师的语录在《珍宝书》中均有记录。

将《珍宝书》中的《脉诀》部分与《通真子》一书进行对比，可以发现两者的各卷章结构、标题及内容基本相似。如均以“诊候入式歌”开篇，接下来为“左右手分诊五脏四时脉歌”[⑧]“七表脉”“八里脉”“九道脉”“诊杂病生死候歌”（含“诊暴病歌”“形脉相反歌”“诊四时病五行相克歌”[⑨]“五脏歌”“产后伤寒歌”“小儿生死候歌”“阳毒歌”[⑩]“阴毒歌”[⑪]“伤寒歌”“诊四时虚实脉歌”等）“诸杂病生死脉歌”[⑫]（含“霍乱歌”“鼻衄歌”“心腹痛歌”“头痛歌”“中风歌”“内实歌”“气喘歌”“唾血歌”等）与“察色观病人生死候歌”[⑬]，最后以“诊妇人有妊歌”（含“诊妇人有妊歌”“妊娠漏急候歌”“妊娠心腹急痛歌”“妊娠倒扑损伤歌”“产难生死候歌”“新产生死歌”“妊妇伤寒歌”“小儿外证十五候歌”等）作为结尾卷章。虽然章节内容基本相同，但在部分卷章的顺序上两者依然存有差异，如《通真子》中“七表脉”“八里脉”“九道脉”“阳毒候歌”“阴毒候歌”“论伤寒歌”“诊四时虚实脉歌”出现在该书第二卷中，而在《珍宝书》中这几首歌诀均出现在第三部分中。

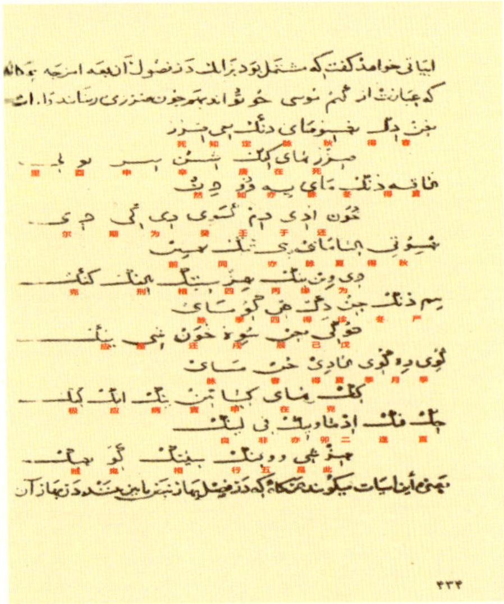

图2 《珍宝书》影印本，第434页

《脉诀》以歌诀形式写成，其中大多为七言歌诀，少许为五言、四言歌诀。经翻译整理，可统计出《珍宝书》波斯文抄本中共抄录《脉诀》歌诀802句[⑭]，其中七言歌诀637句，五言歌诀143句，四言歌诀22句。在抄本中还有不少明显为转写汉文歌诀所留出的空白部分，参考现存的其他《脉诀》点评著作共计可补充七言歌诀86句，五言歌诀22句，填补歌诀中残缺汉字16处及删除错误转写的重复或无意义音节5处，这样计算下来，《珍宝书》编译时计划收录《脉诀》中910句完整歌诀，是一部最为完整的外文《脉诀》点评著作。

图2为抄本中记录的一首《脉诀》歌诀。

① 即刘元宾。

② 即北宋医学家朱肱。

③ 即池荣。

④ 即李晞范。

⑤ 即杜光庭。

⑥ 即黎民寿。

⑦ 熊宗立：《王叔和脉诀图要俗解大全》，《海外回归中医善本古籍丛书》（第一册），北京：人民卫生出版社，2002年，第429页。

⑧ 《通真子》中称为“左右手诊脉歌”。

⑨ 《通真子》中称为“诊四时病五行相克脉歌”。

⑩ 《通真子》中称为“阳毒候歌”。

⑪ 《通真子》中称为“阴毒候歌”。

⑫ 《通真子》中称为“诸杂病生死候歌”。

⑬ 《通真子》中称为“察色观病生死候歌”。

⑭ 指单行歌诀，即每联双行歌诀中的半联，下同。

从《脉诀》歌诀文本来看,《珍宝书》中收录的歌诀与《通真子》及《熊宗立》这两部著作多处存有差异，据统计在《珍宝书》的《脉诀》歌诀字词中至少有108处与其他两部书中的记载皆不同，有39处仅与《通真子》不同，18处仅与《熊宗立》不同。此外，在这些差异中有24个汉字（26次在歌诀中出现）疑似为抄写者误转写的别字（详见下表）。

《珍宝书》中《脉诀》歌诀中的别字

《珍宝书》抄本歌诀中的转写发音及疑似别字（括号内为《珍宝书》中的页数及行数[②]）	《通真子》与《熊宗立》歌诀中的汉字
giu—古（253—05）	舌
kiāy—家（268—03）	客
lun—沦（287—15）	浓
shin—胜（303—07，362—14）	胫
fi—肺（306—13）	脉
yū—有[③]（313—03）	又
bū—不（398—06）	木
she—胁（413—02）	肋
vi—胃（413—08）	肾
khū—和（426—01）	知
tsez—四（434—08）	丁
gi—己（434—10）	巳
id—二（434—13）	乙
gim—今（446—04）	令
liāu—了（liǎo）（446—06）	子
ren—认（448—03）	冷
teu—土（466—01）	上
kān—干（476—01）	千
yuang/yung—用（496—14，500—12）	往
kiei—已（498—04）	已
tū—土（501—13）	右
yen—延（509—11）	诞
fān—反（510—14）	及
gim—检（512—09）	验

此外有一些歌诀仅出现在《珍宝书》之中，例如“小儿外证十五候歌”中的几句歌诀：“泄止不泄”[③]“丹透遍身”[④]“身上黑斑”[⑤]“恶叫时频”[⑥]。而在其他《脉诀》点评著作中出现的部分歌诀在《珍宝书》中也未收录，例如：“积因肥气得，杯覆胁隅傍。翠羽身将吉，颜同枯草殃。四斤余四两，七叶

① 指1972年德黑兰大学出版社影印本。

② 抄本中该汉字波斯文转写旁边被注释为“存在；有”之意，因此转写汉字应为“有”，疑因“又”“有”发音近似，抄本汉字转写者误以“有”字含义解释。

③ Rashīd ud-Dīn Fażl Allāh Hamidānī: *Tanksūqnāmah*, Tehran University Press, 1972, p. 516.

④ Ibid., p. 517.

⑤ Ibid., p. 519.

⑥ Ibid.

两分行”① “溢关涎出口，风中见羁孤”② 等。

在中国历史上，元朝以前从未出现过综合了多位名医点评《脉诀》的著作，因此《珍宝书》中的《脉诀》部分也并不是编译者对一部中医学著作的完全的翻译，而是一部综合吸收了大量的中医学经典名作及多本《脉诀》点评著作的合集。仅在中医脉学方面便有如此完整的“参考书目”，这也在另一方面佐证了当时在“拉施特镇”内确实已拥有相当丰富而完备的汉文书籍。

三　波斯文版《王叔和脉诀》文本记录分析

根据前节中对《珍宝书》相关内容分析研究，可以分析出波斯文版《脉诀》的文本记录过程绝非中国人朗读歌诀、抄本抄写者用波斯文直接记录其发音这样简单，而是有可能一些懂得汉语的伊朗学者也参与了《脉诀》歌诀的波斯文转写工作。原因如下：

第一，在拉施特镇中曾建立过比较正规的外语人才培训机构，包括中国在内的各国学者在这里教授伊朗学生学习各国的语言与文化知识。据信是由拉施特亲笔完成的《珍宝书》序言部分中有这样一段记述：

> 努力在大师中找到一位使语习医学与逻辑学、勤奋努力、品行端正、认真严谨、睿智聪颖，在各类技艺与学艺均好学上进且出类拔萃的年轻人，他是学者之国的毛拉，这一时代独一无二的大学者，国家与宗教的精英，被尊为智者之王的大毛拉。我们安排他师从中国贤哲 Siu Se，还安排一位懂得语言、善于记述的“怯里马赤”③ 跟随他，在这样的条件下学习中国的文字与语言，努力学会他们的术语。在一年之后他学会了这门语言……④

由此可见在当时的拉施特镇中，既有努力学习汉语的伊朗英才，也有已经通晓汉语的翻译人员。关于“怯里马赤”，《珍宝书》正文部分还有一段记载：

> 乞台学者关于此脉说法众多，但对此未作解释。我们所记录的每位医师均有自己的讲述，在此我们无法知晓，所以未写下各医师的名字，留下少许空白，待寻到“怯里马赤”时，我们仔细问询后再做抄写。⑤

根据上述几段讲述，可以确定《珍宝书》中的汉语转写工作是由“怯里马赤”或学习汉语的伊朗英才所完成的。在波斯文抄本中汉字转写部分的笔迹明显与其他不同，并用红色字体标出。抄本中多处未填写歌诀的空白，也是由于他们未能及时转写而留下的遗憾。

第二，在《珍宝书》抄本中，同一汉字存在不同的波斯文转写形式，这种现象并不少见，而且有时会出现在同一页甚至邻近的几行以内，如果是由中国学者朗读，伊朗抄写者根据发音记录，应该不

① 《通真子补注王叔和脉诀》卷一《肝脏歌一》。

② 《通真子补注王叔和脉诀》卷一《脾脏歌三》。

③ 波斯文抄本原词为“kalamachī”，即外语译员之意。元末明初学者叶子奇（约 1327—约 1390）在其著作《草木子》中将该词译为“怯里马赤”。

④ Rashīd ud-Dīn Fażl Allāh Hamidānī: *Tanksūqnāmah*, pp. 23-24.

⑤ Ibid., p. 326.

会出现如此之多一字多形的情况。因此很可能是中国学者首先将歌诀的发音与含义以教学的形式讲述给学习汉语的伊朗英才，让其记录，之后再誊抄至《珍宝书》之上。出现一字多形可能是由于中国学者方言口音存在差异，且伊朗学生记录不准确、记录仓促或记录顺序错误而造成的。

第三，学习汉语的伊朗英才或“怯里马赤”有可能独自转写了少量《脉诀》歌诀。在前节《珍宝书》中《脉诀》文本中别字的表格中，我们可以看到一些中国人通常不会误读的汉字被错误地按照其他汉字发音转写，例如：舌→古，巳→己，令→今，千→干，而在现存汉文《脉诀》点评著作记录的歌诀中并没有此类错误。此外，在某些歌诀转写中还出现了用汉文中其他近义词发音代替了原来汉字的发音，如用“二”的发音转写“乙”字，用“四”的发音来转写“丁”字等。从这两点可以分析出转写者知晓汉语，但对某些字形相似的汉字出现了误读，对另外一些汉字只知其含义但不知其发音，因而错误地按照与其字形相近的词汇或同义词的发音进行了转写。

综合上述分析，波斯文版《脉诀》的歌诀记录过程可以被设想为一名或多名中国学者（如引言部分中提到的 Siu Se）首先将歌诀朗读给学习汉语的伊朗英才或“怯里马赤”，让其用波斯文记录歌诀中汉字的发音，并向他们讲解了歌诀含义、名医点评及中医典籍中相关段落。之后，这些伊朗人首先将汉文歌诀发音转写为波斯文，然后又将歌诀内容进行了释义并把歌诀点评等译成了波斯文。由于中国学者存在不同的方言口音，在记录转写中出现了部分错误，某些转写成波斯文的歌诀之中出现了一字多音、歌诀词句不全、转写发音不准、转写词汇有误等情况。此外，因为《脉诀》篇幅较大，伊朗英才或“怯里马赤”可能直接完成了少量歌诀的波斯文转写工作。总而言之,《珍宝书》的成书体现了当时丝路沿线地区文化间的密切交流，是历史上中国、伊朗两国学者共同努力合作的成果，如其书名，不愧为丝绸之路文明留给后人的璀璨珍宝。

Impulse Formula of Wang Shuhe in Iran

Shi Guang (Peking University)

Abstract: *Tanksūqnāmah*, the translation and editing of which were conducted by prime minister Rashīd al-Dīn of Il-Khan dynasty of Iran, was an masterpiece giving an introduction to Chinese technologies. The book included four volumes, but only the first volume, which introduced the Chinese technologies, still survived. As the first book on ancient Chinese medicine translated to Persian, it is of great value to study of the cultural communication between China and Western Asia in Middle Ages, especially it offers rich first hand materials for the communication of medicines.

Tanksūqnāmah included basically intact formula in verse in ancient Chinese masterpiece of sphygmology *Impulse Formula of Wang Shuhe*, explained every formula in verse in Persian, and attached some comments of the Chinese famous doctors. Since the original version of Impulse Formula of Wang Shuhe and some comments on it in history has lost, translating, collating and studying *Tanksūqnāmah* offers important referential value to restore the texts of it. The paper will use the existing ancient Chinese books as a reference and compare them with the texts of *Impulse Formula of Wang Shuhe* in *Tanksūqnāmah*, and analyze the recording process of the texts.

Keywords: Chinese medicine; *Impulse Formula of Wang Shuhe*; Iran

欧亚大陆视野下的汉唐丝绸之路

荣新江（北京大学）

“丝绸之路”现在是一个热门话题，如何理解丝绸之路，学者、政治家、一般民众各有各的看法，即便是学者，因为所学专业不同，出发点各异，所以观点也有很大的不同。我们没有必要让大家的观点一致，但是，对于有关丝绸之路的一些误解，则是需要加以辨明的。而这些误解的产生，大多数是因为只是从某一时点、某个地域来看丝绸之路。对于这样一个沟通旧大陆的交通道路，而且包含海上和陆上的东西交往通道，我们需要用宏观的视野来观察。本文则只限于讨论公元前 2 世纪到 8 世纪的陆上丝绸之路，希望从欧亚大陆的视野下，来观察历史上的丝绸之路，把不同时期的兴衰、特征加以概括。丝绸之路的内涵广阔，这里更多地是从沟通与贸易来加以叙述，间或涉及政治、文化等方面。

一　汉、罗马、帕提亚、贵霜之间丝绸之路大国贸易的建立

虽然在汉代以前丝绸之路就已经存在，北方游牧民族一直推动着东西方物品的交换。但现存的零星记载和考古发现，还不能让我们构建出当时丝绸之路的总体图像，因此，具有一定规模的丝路贸易，应当从汉代说起。早在 1877 年，德国地理学家李希霍芬（F. von Richthofen）就把汉代中国和中亚南部、西部以及印度之间的以丝绸贸易为主的交通路线称作“丝绸之路”（德文作 Seidenstrassen，英文作 the Silk Road），显然是很有见地的。到了 1910 年，德国历史学家赫尔曼（A. Hermann）根据新发现的文物考古资料，进一步把丝绸之路定义为中国古代经由中亚通往南亚、西亚以及欧洲、北非的陆上贸易交往的通道。虽然经过一百多年的讨论，丝绸之路从时空两个方面都有很大的外延，但其基本定义应当说是没错的，我们今天讨论的欧亚大陆上的陆上丝绸之路，仍是在这个基本定义的范围内。

为什么“丝绸之路”以汉代为开端，这固然是因为汉武帝时张骞通西域，史称“凿空”，也就是首次打通中国与西部世界的联系，开始了贸易往来。更重要的原因，是从公元前 2 世纪到公元后 2 世纪，沿着欧亚大陆的交通干线，自东向西有四大帝国并列其间，即东亚的汉朝（前 206—220）、中亚的贵霜（约 30—226）、西亚的帕提亚（安息，前 3 世纪中叶—226）、欧洲的罗马（前 30—284）。在公元前后，四大帝国都处在国势昌盛的时期，积极向外扩张，彼此交界，使东西方世界得以直接联系起来。

各个帝国中间，都有完善的交通驿路。我们从居延、敦煌发现的汉代《传置道里簿》木牍上，可以看到从汉帝国的都城长安，到边塞城市敦煌，每一个传置（驿站）和相互之间的道里数[①]，而出敦煌后，沿着长城和障塞，道路一直通向罗布泊的楼兰王国，然后分向南北，进入西域南北道。月氏

---

① 何双全：《汉代西北驿道与传置——甲渠候官、悬泉汉简〈传置道里簿〉考述》，《中国历史博物馆馆刊》总第 30 期，1998 年，第 62—69 页；郝树声、张德芳：《悬泉汉简研究》，兰州：甘肃文化出版社，2009 年，第 106—133 页。

西徙，占领大夏（Bactria，巴克特里亚）之地，逐渐统一各个分裂小邦，最后由贵霜翕侯建立贵霜王国，东西南北拓地，成为1世纪时的中亚帝国。贵霜帝国除有跨越帕米尔高原的道路通向塔里木盆地的绿洲王国外，还从都城犍陀罗（Gāndhāra）开通了到印度西北海岸的重要港口婆楼割车（Barygaza，在古吉拉特）的道路，从而与印度到罗马的海上通道相连。帕提亚王国从都城和椟城（Hekotompylos）到小亚细亚的以弗所（Ephesus）有“御道”沟通，东部则自巴比伦到巴克特里亚有驿道，设置驿站和旅馆，供使者和商人换马或休息。罗马帝国也有发达的交通网络，海道可以直达印度。

汉文史料比较丰富，可以看出当时丝绸之路的一些情况。公元前138—前126年张骞第一次出使，只是把道路开通，因为中间被匈奴俘虏，所以谈不上贸易。当公元前119年张骞第二次出使乌孙时，情形就完全不一样了，《史记》卷一二三《大宛列传》说：

> 天子以为然，拜骞为中郎将，将三百人，马各二匹，牛羊以万数，赍金币帛直数千巨万，多持节副使，道可使，使遣之他旁国。……骞因分遣副使使大宛、康居、大月氏、大夏、安息、身毒、于窴、扜罙及诸旁国。……其后岁余，骞所遣使通大夏之属者皆颇与其人俱来，于是西北国始通于汉矣。[①]

这个三百人的使团带着大批价值昂贵的金币、丝绸，显然目的不只是外交，而是要与西方各国做买卖。所遣之国最远到西亚的安息，即帕提亚王国，还有南亚的身毒（印度），而主要是中亚的大宛（今费尔干纳）、康居（今乌兹别克斯坦塔什干一带）、大月氏（巴克特里亚地区）。史称与张骞副使返回长安的，有中亚的大夏之属。

《史记·大宛列传》继续说：

> 汉始筑令居以西，初置酒泉郡以通西北国。因益发使抵安息、奄蔡、黎轩、条枝、身毒国。而天子好宛马，使者相望于道。诸使外国一辈大者数百，少者百余人。……汉率一岁中使多者十余，少者五六辈，远者八九岁，近者数岁而反。[②]

可见从张骞第二次出使之后，汉武帝派出的使者最远到达奄蔡（Ossetes，今高加索）、犁靬（罗马帝国）、条支（叙利亚）地区。而且使团的规模大者数百人，小者也有百余人。派遣的频率很高，一年中多者有十余辈，少者五六般，数年往返。

《汉书》卷九六上《西域传》也有类似的记载：

> 初，武帝感张骞之言，甘心欲通大宛诸国，使者相望于道，一岁中多至十余辈。
>
> 自乌孙以西至安息，近匈奴。匈奴尝困月氏，故匈奴使持单于一信到国，国传送食，不敢留苦。及至汉使，非出币物不得食，不市畜不得骑，所以然者，以远汉，而汉多财物，故必市乃得所欲。及呼韩邪单于朝汉，后咸尊汉矣。[③]

这里所说可与《史记·大宛列传》互补，西域诸国因为直接受到北方匈奴的威胁，所以对待汉使和匈

① 《史记》（点校本二十四史修订本）卷一二三，北京：中华书局，2013年，第3818—3819页。

② 《史记》卷一二三，第3820页。

③ 《汉书》卷九六上《西域传》，北京：中华书局，1962年，第3876、3896页。

奴使者不完全相同，这段来自《史记》的话，也有司马迁批评武帝遣使西域的意思，但却透露出不仅汉朝此时与中亚诸国直到安息之间从事大规模的贸易交往，而且北方的匈奴也继续做着同样的买卖。《汉书》所增加的，主要是说呼韩邪单于入朝汉后（前 49），匈奴衰弱，中亚诸国才对汉朝使者不那么苛刻。也说明到汉宣帝时，汉朝与中亚、西亚的贸易持续不断。

西汉末，王莽乱政，中原动乱，与西域联系一度中断，匈奴重新控制西域。到东汉初，班超经营塔里木盆地西域诸国，汉与西域的联系时断时续。和帝永元六年（94），班超平定西域南北道，于是永元九年（97）派甘英出使大秦（罗马帝国）。《后汉书》卷八八《西域传》记载：

> 和帝永元九年，都护班超遣甘英使大秦，抵条支。临大海欲度，而安息西界船人谓英曰：海水广大，往来者逢善风三月乃得度，若遇迟风，亦有二岁者，故入海人皆赍三岁粮。海中善使人思土恋慕，数有死亡者。英闻之乃止。[①]

这里的条支指叙利亚的安条克（Antiochia），大海一说指红海。安息（帕提亚）人极力夸张大海难渡，阻止甘英与罗马沟通，这显然有着经济的考虑，就是要由自己来承担丝绸等货物的中转贸易，赚取货物转贩过程中的高额利润。从现存的汉朝和罗马的史料来看，也的确没有中国与罗马直接贸易的任何记载，虽然双方的物品都抵达了对方的领地。

敦煌悬泉置出土的汉简，也印证了两汉与中亚、西亚各个国家交往的史事。这批汉简的年代，最早者为汉武帝元鼎六年（前 111），最晚者为东汉安帝永初元年（107），所记录的往来使者，有来自葱岭以西的大月氏、康居、大宛者，有天山南北的乌孙、疏勒、姑墨、龟兹、焉耆、车师、于阗、莎车、精绝、楼兰（鄯善）者，最远的大概是西亚的乌弋山离的使者。有的使团人数逾千，携带有骆驼、马匹，甚至狮子，既是外交使团，又做朝贡贸易，与《史记》《汉书》《后汉书》的记载相吻合。[②]

罗马为了绕开帕提亚，同时海上的交通运输费和过境费的成本都要比陆路少得多，所以在公元前 1 世纪后半叶季风规律被发现和利用以后，罗马帝国开通了从红海直航印度西海岸的海上贸易通道。[③]罗马与印度之间的贸易，使得大量罗马钱币流入印度，老普林尼（Pliny the Elder，23—79）在《自然史》中指出：

> 最低估算，印度、赛里斯（Seres）和阿拉伯半岛每年要从我国带走一亿枚塞斯特斯（sesterce）银币，这是我们的奢侈品和妇女花费的总额。[④]

1 世纪中期的佚名著作《厄立特里亚海航行记》记载，印度西北海岸的港口婆楼割车（Barygaza）

---

① 《后汉书》卷八八《西域传》，北京：中华书局，1965 年，第 2918 页。

② 胡平生、张德芳：《敦煌悬泉汉简释粹》，上海古籍出版社，2001 年。张德芳：《悬泉汉简中若干西域资料考论》，收入荣新江、李孝聪主编：《中外关系史：新史料与新问题》，北京：科学出版社，2004 年，第 129—147 页；郝树声、张德芳：《悬泉汉简研究》，第 177—258 页。

③ 有关罗马与印度海上贸易的情况，参见 E. H. Warmington, *The Commerce between the Roman Empire and India*, Cambridge, Cambridge University Press, 1928 (rev. ed. in 1974); R. E. M. Wheeler, *Rome beyond the Imperial Frontiers*, London, the Camelot Press, 1955。

④ Pliny the Elder, *Natural History*, Vol. 3, 12.41.84, tr. with copious notes and illustrations by J. Bostock & H. T. Riley, London, Henry G. Bohn, 1855, p. 137.

和马拉巴尔（Malabar）海岸诸港口曾进口大量罗马钱币。[①]考古发现也证实了这些文献记载，据统计，印度半岛迄今出土的罗马钱币总数大约有8000枚，其中包括1200余枚金币和接近7000枚银币，以及少量铜币。[②]贵霜王国崛起后，到了2世纪中叶的迦腻色伽一世（Kanishka I）统治时期，势力最盛，领土包括阿姆河流域、印度河流域和恒河流域的大部分土地，从塔里木盆地绿洲王国转运而来的中国货物，可以经犍陀罗地区南下，越兴都库什山（Hindu Kush），经呾叉始罗（Taxila）到达印度西海岸的港口，再乘船前往罗马。[③]贵霜的参与，使得罗马与印度的贸易中心向印度西北海岸移动，而贵霜的商人很可能也参与到印度洋的海外贸易当中，这可以从位于亚丁湾与印度洋的交接处索科特拉岛（Socotra）发现的贵霜使用的大夏文和佉卢文题铭得到印证。[④]

总起来看，由于汉、贵霜、帕提亚、罗马各个大国在势力达到一定范围之后，都积极推动对外贸易，汉与贵霜、帕提亚之间，贵霜与汉、罗马之间，帕提亚与罗马、汉之间，罗马与印度、贵霜、帕提亚之间，都存在着一定规模的贸易往来。而由于大国作为这种贸易的坚强后盾与有力支撑，所以这个时期的贸易更多地是以官方贸易、长途贸易的方式进行，其贸易团队往往动辄数百人，甚至上千人，交换物以高档的奢侈品、丝绸、金银货币为主。不能排除当时有个体或家族商队从事丝路贸易，但他们往往也被视作是某个国家的贸易使团。

到了2世纪末3世纪初，随着丝绸之路上的四大帝国走向衰落，战乱频仍，阻断丝路的畅通；丝路上兴起一些新的国家、民族，除了收取过往的商税之外，也逐渐参与到丝路贸易当中；大国贸易被分割，旧有的贸易格局也不复存在。

二　中古时期丝绸之路贸易的重建——粟特商人的贡献

3世纪以降，大国衰亡，给丝绸之路上的小国提供了生存发展的机会，中亚地区，不论是西北印度、吐火罗斯坦、粟特地区，还是塔里木盆地，形成大大小小的王国，虽然北方匈奴帝国衰亡以后，又有鲜卑、柔然、突厥汗国相继称雄漠北，但曾经控制中亚的柔然和突厥，对于绿洲王国采用匈奴式的征收赋税，而不是直接占领。萨珊波斯王朝（224—651）、印度笈多王朝（319—500）虽然都曾把势力深入到粟特地区和吐火罗斯坦，但也都没有断绝这些王国的王统。从北方南下的嚈哒（Hephthalites）在4世纪后期曾征服粟特地区，最后定居在巴克特里亚，成为中亚的强国，但其他小国仍然存在。552年，新兴的突厥灭柔然汗国；558年又和萨珊波斯联合灭嚈哒，以阿姆河为界，瓜分其领土。中国从220年开始三国时代，以后虽有西晋的短暂统一，但很快分裂为十六国和南北朝，直到589年隋灭陈，重新统一中国。618年唐朝建立后，很快向西域扩张势力，到658年灭西突厥汗国，

---

① *The Periplus Maris Erythraei*, Chs. 49, 56, Text with Introduction, Translation, and Commentary by L. Casson, Princeton, Princeton University Press, 1989, pp. 81, 85.

② R. E. M. Wheeler, "Roman Contact with India, Pakistan and Afghanistan", in W. F. Grimes (ed.), *Aspects of Archaeology in Britain and Beyond: Essays Presented to O. G. S. Crawford*, London, H.W. Edwards, 1951, pp. 374-381; P. J. Turner, *Roman Coins from India*, London, Royal Numismatic Society, 1989, pp. 23, 45-91; F. de Romanis, "Julio-Claudian *Denarii* and *Aurei* in Campania and India", *Annali dell'Istituto Italiano di Numismatica* 58, 2012, pp. 180-185. 上面的数字是罗帅根据以上三家的统计所做的总计，见所撰《印度半岛出土罗马钱币所见印度洋贸易之变迁》，收入吐鲁番学研究院、吐鲁番博物馆编：《古代钱币与丝绸高峰论坛暨第四届吐鲁番学国际学术研讨会论文集》，上海古籍出版社，2015年，第108—109页。

③ 赫德逊：《欧洲与中国》，李申等译，北京：中华书局，2004年第2版，第39、56页。

④ I. Strauch (ed.), *Foreign Sailors on Socotra. The Inscriptions and Drawings from the Cave Hoq*, Bremen, Hempen Verlag, 2012, pp. 202-203, 205-206.

葱岭东西、天山南北各国及各部，都归于唐朝羁縻统治之下，但各个绿洲国家并未灭绝。与此同时，阿拉伯人兴起于阿拉伯半岛，向东征服，651 年灭萨珊波斯，进入粟特地区，但并没有直接占领。661 年立都大马士革的倭马亚王朝积极扩张领土，到 8 世纪初，阿拉伯占领粟特核心地区。751 年阿拉伯军队与唐军在怛罗斯会战，唐朝败北。随之而来的是 755 年唐朝发生安史之乱，唐军只在塔里木盆地坚守，而阿拉伯势力也没有越过葱岭。

在大国纷争、战乱频仍的岁月里，官方的贸易商队往往会被敌对方劫掠，正是在这样的环境下，中亚粟特商队开始出现在丝绸之路的地平线上。因为粟特商队不是官方贸易使团，所以历史文献中没有正式的记录，但我们把零散的文献记载和考古发现结合起来，仍然可以清理出 3 世纪中叶到 8 世纪中叶粟特商人在丝绸之路上活跃的情形。以下大体按照年代先后，阐述粟特商人在魏晋南北朝时期的活跃情形。

三国曹魏明帝太和年间（227—232），仓慈出任敦煌太守，抑制欺辱“西域杂胡”的当地豪族，商胡“欲诣洛者，为封过所；欲从郡还者，官为平取，辄以府见物与共交市，使吏民护送道路”①。其中的“西域杂胡”应当包括来自粟特地区的商胡②，这种说法应当是有道理的。由此我们知道，他们以敦煌为根据地，有的前往洛阳兴贩贸易，有的由此返回家乡，表明从粟特到敦煌，再到洛阳，存在着一条粟特人的经商道路，而这种递进式的经营方式可以得到粟特文古信札的印证。

所谓粟特文古信札是斯坦因（A. Stein）在敦煌西北长城烽隧下面发现的一组粟特文书信，目前已经完整解读出第 1、2、3、5 号信札的内容，所记是 4 世纪初从撒马尔罕（康国）来的一个粟特商团，以凉州武威为大本营，派出商人前往洛阳、邺城、金城（兰州）、敦煌等地从事贸易活动③，还没有完整翻译的第6号信札提到粟特人要去楼兰进行贸易的事情④。虽然西晋末年中原的动乱，使得在洛阳经商的粟特人蒙受了沉重的打击，但通过这组信札，我们可以知道他们从撒马尔罕来到中国的河西走廊东部，以一个大本营（武威）为基地，四处派出商团倒卖货物的经营方式，以及经营的货物品种——香料、药材、布匹、丝绸、谷物等。

粟特文古信札对粟特商团的记录，也得到其他相关地点的考古资料的印证。斯坦因在罗布泊西北楼兰古城遗址中，曾发掘到一些粟特文木简，年代与粟特文古信札一样古老，属于4世纪初的遗物。⑤

① 《三国志》卷一六《魏书·仓慈传》，北京：中华书局，1959 年，第 512 页。

② 马雍：《东汉后期中亚人来华考》，原载《经济理论与经济史论文集》，北京大学出版社，1983 年；此据马雍：《西域史地文物丛考》，北京：文物出版社，1990 年，第 53 页；吴玉贵：《凉州粟特胡人安氏家族研究》，《唐研究》第 3 卷，北京大学出版社，1997 年，第 302 页。

③ N. Sims-Williams, “The Sogdian Ancient Letter II”, *Philologica et Linguistica: Historia, Pluralitas, Universitas. Festschrift für Helmut Humbach zum 80. Geburtstag am 4. Dezember 2001*, eds. M. G. Schmidt and W. Bisang, Trier 2001, pp. 267-280; F. Grenet, N. Sims-Williams, and É. de la Vaissière, “The Sogdian Ancient Letter V”, *Bulletin of the Asia Institute*, XII, 1998, pp. 91-104; N. Sims-Williams, “Towards a new edition of the Sogdian Ancient Letters: Ancient Letter 1”, *Les Sogdiens en Chine*, eds. É. de la Vaissière and É. Trombert, Paris 2005, pp. 57-72; 毕波：《粟特文古信札汉译与注释》，《文史》2004 年第 2 辑，第 88—93 页。

④ N. Sims-Williams, “The Sogdian Merchants in China and India”, *Cina e Iran da Alessandro Magno alla Dinastia Tang*, ed. A. Cadonna e L. Lanciotti, Firenze 1996, p. 49；尼古拉斯·辛维廉撰：《中国和印度的粟特商人》，毕波译，收入周伟洲主编：《西北民族研究》第 10 辑，北京：中国社会科学出版社，2014 年，第 36 页。

⑤ H. Reichelt, *Die soghdischen Handschriftenreste des Britischen Museums*,II, Heidelberg, 1931, p. 42; N. Sims-Williams, “The Sogdian Fragments of the British Library”, *The Indo-Iranian Journal*, XVIII, 1976, p. 43, n. 10; F. Grenet and N. Sims-Williams, “The Historical Context of the Sogdian Ancient Letters”, *Transition Periods in Iranian History*, Leuven, 1987, p. 111, n. 42.

大谷文书 6117 号粟特文残片很可能是与李柏文书（写于 328 年）同出于楼兰遗址的材料。① 值得注意的是，与其中四件粟特语木简同出于一个遗址的 L.A.I.iii.1 号汉文木简上，记有“建兴十八年（330）三月十七日粟特胡楼兰（中残）一万石钱二百”的出入帐目②，时间恰好与上述粟特文木简的年代吻合。从帐目所记一万石的交易数量来看，这里的粟特人当不在少数，他们应当就是和武威粟特商人有联系的群体。

再往西就是尼雅遗址，1994 年中日共同尼雅遗迹学术考察队在尼雅 93A27 遗址发掘出一个用毛绳捆扎起来的小纸包（编号 93A27F1:3），内容是一封粟特语书信，年代应该是在 3 世纪后半到 4 世纪初，纸包中是一些粉末状的物品，或许是书信作废以后，用来包裹某种香料。93A27 遗址曾发现带有汉文“鄯善都尉”印的佉卢文木简，推测可能是驿站的一个附属机构或客馆之类的地方。③ 此外，斯坦因从尼雅发掘的另一件佉卢文书（Kh.35）说道：“目前没有商贾从中国来，因此现在不必去清查丝债。……当有商贾从中国过来时，再行清查丝债……”④ 这些从中国来的商人应当会带来丝绸，可以帮忙清理丝债，而这些商人或许就是带来丝绸、香料的粟特商人。

丝路南道再向西，就是于阗。斯坦因在安迪尔（Endere）发现的一件佉卢文契约文书（No.661），其中买卖的一方是粟特人 Nani Vandhaga（意为娜娜女神之仆）。⑤ 这件用于阗王纪年的佉卢文书的年代众说纷纭，大体应当与尼雅出土的佉卢文书年代相距不远，因为 4 世纪以后，包括安迪尔的于阗王国就使用于阗文作为日常生活用语了。前人还指出，这里的粟特人 Nani Vandhaga 的名字，与敦煌发现粟特文第 2 号古信札的发现人 Nanai-vandak 同名。⑥ 虽然不能说两者就是同一人，但娜娜女神是当时早期来华粟特人的共同信仰，两者的年代应当相距不远。这件契约文书，证明了粟特商人也在于阗经商贩易。

从于阗向西，经渴槃陀（又作汉盘陀、喝盘陀，今新疆塔什库尔干），经瓦罕山谷，越帕米尔（葱岭）高原，到巴基斯坦北部印度河上游。德国和巴基斯坦两国的考古学者 20 世纪七八十年代曾沿着印度河上游的古代丝绸之路进行考古调查，在奇拉斯城（Chilas）、夏提欧村（Shatial）、洪札（Hunza）等地，发现超过六百条粟特文题记，表明有来自粟特地区塔石干（Tashkent）的石国人、弭秣贺（Maymurgh）的米国人、片吉肯特（Panjikent）附近的 Farn-mēthan 人、瑟底痕（Ishtikhan）的西曹国人、撒马尔干（Samarkand）的康国人、屈霜你迦（Kushanika）的何国人等，年代在 4 至 6 世纪。⑦ 这些题记表明粟特商人经巴克特里亚，南下与印度人贸易。同时其中有一条题记记载，也有人从这里

---

① Yutaka Yoshida, “Additional Notes on Sims-Williams’ Article on the Sogdian Merchants in China and India”, *Cina e Iran da Alessandro Magno alla Dinastia Tang*, pp. 69-70. 该文书的转写翻译，见百济康义、ヴェルナー・ズンダーマン、吉田豊:《イラン语断片集成・大谷探检队收集・龙谷大学所藏中央アジア出土イラン语资料》，京都：法藏馆，1997 年，解说编第 105—106 页，图版编 32 页。

② 胡平生:《楼兰出土文书释丛》,《文物》1991 年第 8 期，第 41—42 页。

③ 辛维廉、毕波:《尼雅新出粟特文残片研究》,《新疆文物》2009 年第 3—4 期，第 53—58 页。

④ T. Burrow, *A Translation of the Kharosthī Documents from Chinese Turkestan*, London 1940, p. 9.

⑤ A. Stein, *Serindia*, IV, Oxford 1921, pl.XXXVIII; A. M. Boyer, E. J. Rapson & E. Senart, *Kharosthi Inscriptions*, I. Oxford 1920, p. 249; Burrow, *A Translation of the Kharosthi Documents from Chinese Turkestan*, p. 137.

⑥ J. Brough, “Comments on the Third-century Shan-shan and the History of Buddhism”, *Bulletin of the School of Oriental and African Studies 28*, 1965, p. 594；林梅村:《敦煌出土粟特文古书信的断代问题》,《中国史研究》1986 年第 1 期，第 98—99 页。

⑦ N. Sims-Williams, “The Sogdian Inscriptions of the Upper Indus: a preliminary report”, *Antiquities of Northern Pakistan. Reports and Studies*, 1: Rock inscriptions in the Indus Valley, ed. K. Jettmar, Mainz 1989, pp. 131-137. 这些题记已由同一作者刊布：*The Sogdian and Other Iranian Inscriptions of the Upper Indus*, I, London 1989, II, 1992。

出发，去向葱岭以东的渴槃陀，使得粟特商人的贸易路线，与于阗相接。由于北方有柔然的威胁，所以早期来华的粟特商人，显然选择的是塔克拉玛干沙漠南缘的丝路南道向东前进，从于阗、尼雅、楼兰到敦煌。

相对来讲，塔克拉玛干沙漠北缘丝绸之路上的粟特商人要稍迟一步。大概从4世纪中期以后，或许更晚的时间里，龟兹壁画上出现粟特商人的形象。① 焉耆地区也曾发现可能是4—5世纪的粟特银器。② 这也可能是现存材料的缺乏之故，而出土文献较多的吐鲁番，提供给我们更多的信息。

吐鲁番安乐城出土的《金光明经》题记证明，430年时高昌城东就有一所地标性的胡天祠，根据粟特商人在丝路沿线建立的殖民地中往往设立袄祠的惯例，此时的高昌城东应当有粟特人的聚落。③ 麹氏高昌国时期（502—640）的《高昌内藏奏得称价钱帐》，是一件高昌市场上征收商税的记录，在整个三十多笔交易中，买卖双方主要是康、何、曹、安、石五姓的粟特人，卖者当来自西方，买者在高昌本地，但双方都是粟特人。买卖的商品有金、银、丝、香料、郁金根、硇沙、铜、鍮石、药材、石蜜，除了丝之外，大多数是西方的舶来品，而且都是大宗交易。④ 这件文书反映了粟特人在高昌地区进行贵金属、香料、丝绸等贸易的情形，从西方来的粟特商人把大宗货物运载到高昌，由高昌的粟特商人买下来，再分散或整批运至河西或中原地区兴贩，生动地反映了粟特人的商业运作模式，与粟特文古信札等材料所记相吻合。

正如古信札所记录的那样，敦煌以东也是粟特商人的贸易天地。第2号信札所记粟特商团的大本营武威，就是一个重要的据点。第5号信札也说明，4世纪初武威是粟特人贸易集散中心，他们把转运贸易的货物贮存在那里，并派商人四处转贩。⑤ 更能说明问题的是《北史》卷九七《西域传》"粟特国"条的记载："其国商人先多诣凉土贩货，及魏克姑臧，悉见虏。文成初，粟特王遣使请赎之，诏听焉。"⑥ 可见，北魏灭北凉、攻占其首都姑臧时（439），掠走了大批居住在武威的粟特商人，把他们安置在北魏都城平城（今大同）及其附近地区，以粟特人的财富充实都城地区。到452年后不久，粟特王特意遣使来赎这些粟特商人，表明这些粟特商人对于粟特本国的重要性，也透露出他们的丝路贸易不能断绝。

凉州武威因为是河西首府，所以聚集的粟特商胡最多。史籍记载："后魏安难陀至孙盘婆罗，代

---

① 荣新江：《萨保与萨薄：佛教石窟壁画中的粟特商队首领》，收入荣新江、华澜、张志清编：《粟特人在中国——历史、考古、语言的新探索》，北京：中华书局，2005年，第49—71页；影山悦子：《粟特人在库车：从考古和图像学角度来研究》，同上书，第191—204页。

② J. Watt et al. (eds.), *China. Dawn of a Golden Age, 200-750 AD*, New York, The Metropolitan Museum of Art, 2004, pp. 185-188；毕波：《粟特人在焉耆——从焉耆七个星发现的纳骨器说起》，"粟特人在中国——考古发现与出土文献的新印证"国际学术研讨会论文，银川，2014年8月。

③ 荣新江：《吐鲁番出土〈金光明经〉写本题记与袄教初传高昌问题》，收入朱玉麒主编：《西域文史》第2辑，北京：科学出版社，2007年，第1—13页。

④《吐鲁番出土文书》壹，北京：文物出版社，1992年，第450—453页。参见朱雷：《麹氏高昌王国的"称价钱"》，《魏晋南北朝隋唐史资料》第4期，1982年，第17—24页；姜伯勤：《敦煌吐鲁番文书与丝绸之路》，北京：文物出版社，1994年，第138—139、175页。

⑤ F. Grenet, N. Sims-Williams and É. de la Vaissière, "The Sogdian Ancient Letter V", pp. 91-104；毕波：《粟特文古信札汉译与注释》，第88—93页。

⑥《北史》卷九七《西域传》，北京：中华书局，1974年，第3221页。

居凉州，为萨宝。”① 大概与此同时，凉州还有被北周皇帝封为凉州萨保的史君，而同样是北周末年的同州萨保安伽，也出身凉州。② 一个萨保代表一个胡人聚落的存在，而一个聚落源自一个数百人的粟特商团，可见北朝末年，武威粟特人势力之盛，这也就是安兴贵、安修仁兄弟能够易如反掌地消灭凉州李轨政权，把河西土地献给新兴的唐朝的原因。

近年来在北周长安城东郊陆续发现粟特首领康业、史君、安伽等人的大型墓葬，表明粟特人在长安拥有的势力。《通典》卷一四六《乐六》“龟兹乐”条记：“周武帝聘突厥女为后，西域诸国来媵，于是有龟兹、疏勒、安国、康国之乐。帝大聚长安胡儿，羯人白智通教习，颇杂以新声。”③ 表明当时北周的宫廷中，也有大量从事音乐、舞蹈的胡人。④《周书》卷二二《柳庆传》记载，雍州有一胡人家被劫 ⑤，其原因应当是他们身为商贾而较为富裕的缘故。作为当时北周的都城，长安一定是粟特贸易之路上的一个重要的支点。

洛阳是粟特商人在中原贩易的另一个重要支点，上举《三国志・魏书・仓慈传》就提到“欲诣洛者，为封过所”，表明粟特商人很早就到达这里，并把这里作为一个贸易目的地。粟特文古信札证明，西晋末年武威的粟特商人也前往洛阳经商。494 年，北魏孝文帝迁都洛阳，这里再次成为北方中国的中心，外来商人更加不断。《洛阳伽蓝记》卷三记：“自葱岭已西，至于大秦，百国千城，莫不款附。商胡贩客，日奔塞下，所谓尽天地之区已。乐中国土风因而宅者，不可胜数。是以附化之民，万有余家。”⑥ 这里面当然有粟特商人。

东汉末，曹操封魏公，居邺城，邺城的地位在三国时十分重要。粟特文古信札提到的最东面的经商地点是邺 ⑦，说明粟特人很早就曾到过此地。到了东西魏分裂，邺城成为东魏、北齐的都城，北齐粟特胡人带来的胡化之风为史家津津乐道。北齐职官中有京邑萨甫、诸州萨甫，萨甫即萨保，是胡人聚落首领，可见胡人在北齐的势力之强。安阳曾出土粟特石棺床，围屏上描绘着粟特首领出行、宴饮等图像，有人推测这可能来自一个萨甫的墓葬。⑧

粟特商人还帮助北齐做跨国贸易，如《周书》卷五〇《吐谷浑传》记，西魏废帝二年（553），以青海为中心的吐谷浑国“又通使于齐氏，凉州刺史史宁觇知其还，率轻骑袭之于州西赤泉，获其仆射乞伏触扳、将军翟潘密、商胡二百四十人、驼骡六百头、杂彩丝绢以万计”⑨。这个吐谷浑国派往北齐而返回的使团，显然同时也是一个商队，首领是吐谷浑仆射乞伏触扳和将军翟潘密，而队伍的主体是商胡。这支从北齐来的商队在凉州附近被西魏军队偷袭成功，俘获商胡 240 人，驼骡 600 头、杂彩丝

① 《元和姓纂（附四校记）》“安姓”下“姑臧凉州”条，岑仲勉校记，郁贤皓、陶敏整理，孙望审订，北京：中华书局，1994 年，第 500 页。

② 西安市文物保护考古所（杨军凯、孙武执笔）:《西安北周凉州萨保史君墓发掘简报》,《文物》2005 年第 3 期，第 4—33 页；陕西省考古研究所:《西安发现的北周安伽墓》,《文物》2001 年第 1 期，第 8 页，图 7；第 25—26 页；又《西安北周安伽墓》，北京：文物出版社，2003 年，第 59—63 页。

③ 杜佑:《通典》，王文锦等标点本，北京：中华书局，1988 年，第 3726 页。

④ 有关北周长安的胡人，参见毕波:《北周的胡人与胡化》,《文史》2005 年第 4 期，第 149—171 页。

⑤ 《周书》卷二二《柳庆传》，北京：中华书局，1971 年，第 371 页。

⑥ 周祖谟:《洛阳伽蓝记校释》，北京：中华书局，1987 年，第 132 页。

⑦ W. B. Henning, “The Date of the Sogdian Ancient Letters”, pp. 608-609.

⑧ G. Scaglia, “Central Asians on a Northern Ch'i Gate Shrine”, *Artibus Asiae*, XXI, 1958, pp. 9-28.

⑨ 《周书》卷五〇《吐谷浑传》，第 913 页。

绢以万计，可见是一个颇有规模的商队，因为除了被俘商胡外，应当还有逃散的商人和驼马，包括一些丝绸织品。

魏晋南北朝时期，粟特商人的足迹也进入中国南方地区，一条路是经襄阳南下。僧祐《出三藏记集》所收《渐备经十住胡名并书序》记载：东晋宁康元年（373），凉土沙门慧常将《渐备经》寄托凉州“互市人康儿”，由其“展转送至长安”。这位康国出身的粟特胡商在太元元年（376）五月把经本送到长安。太元二年十月初，长安僧人安法华把此经送至长安的“互市”机构，再由“互市人”送往襄阳。由此可以复原出从姑臧到长安、再到襄阳，粟特互市商人转输物品，往来贸易的情形。[①] 长安僧人安法华，显然是安国出身的粟特人，他在长安担负着转输佛典的任务，当然在长安，也一定有转输货物的粟特商胡。

另一条进入南方的路是从河西走廊经松潘地区南下，到成都，然后顺长江而下，可以直到东晋、南朝的首都建康（南京）。因为南朝与北方的鲜卑政权往往处于敌对状态，所以这条道路的西北枢纽，是青海的吐谷浑国，可以不经北方政权占领的河西走廊，而经青海湖西行，翻过阿尔金山到西域鄯善地区，再西行于阗，或北上高昌。[②]

《续高僧传》卷二六《释道仙传》记：“释道仙，一名僧仙，本康居国人，以游贾为业。梁周之际，往来吴蜀，江海上下，集积珠宝，故其所获赀货，乃满两船，时或计者云：直钱数十万贯。”后来皈依佛门，将所获珍宝沉入江中。[③] 又《隋书》卷七五《何妥传》记：“西城（域）人也。父细胡，通商入蜀，遂家郫县。事梁武陵王〔萧〕纪，主知金帛，因致巨富，号为西州大贾。”[④] 何细胡显然是粟特何国出身的一个商胡，应当也是通过吐谷浑道而进入蜀地的。

粟特人“利之所在，无所不到”，除了进入西域绿洲王国和中国内地之外，也同时进入北方游牧王国。史君墓图像中有粟特商队首领萨保拜访嚈哒首领的场景，安伽墓图像中有粟特萨保与披发突厥首领会盟、宴饮等活动，都说明了这一点。希腊史家弥南德记载，西突厥可汗室点密曾派以粟特人 Maniach 为首的使团到波斯，要求在波斯境内自由出售丝织品，未获允诺。567 年，突厥与波斯断交。568 年初，室点密可汗派（Maniach）率突厥与粟特的联合使团出使罗马，抵达拜占廷，受到查士丁二世（Justin II，565—574 年在位）的热情接待，双方结盟。同年八月，拜占廷使臣（Zemarchus）与 Maniach 一起回访突厥，以后双方使者往来不断，建立了绕过波斯，经高加索到罗马的贸易通道。[⑤] 从史君、安伽墓图像可以看出，粟特商人的东方贸易，受到了北方游牧汗国的保护。

辛维廉（N. Sims-Williams）教授指出粟特人不仅仅是粟特与中国之间贸易的担当者，也是中国与

---

① 朱雷：《东晋十六国时期姑臧、长安、襄阳的“互市”》，原载《古代长江中游的经济开发》，武汉出版社，1988 年；收入作者：《敦煌吐鲁番文书论丛》，兰州：甘肃人民出版社，2000 年，第 327—336 页。

② 夏鼐：《青海西宁出土的波斯萨珊朝银币》，《考古学报》1958 年第 1 期，第 40—50 页，收入《夏鼐文集》（下），北京：社会科学文献出版社，2000 年；周伟洲：《古青海路考》，《西北大学学报》1982 年第 1 期，第 65—72 页；王育民：《丝路“青海道”考》，《历史地理》第 4 辑，1986 年，第 145—152 页。详细的考证，见陈良伟：《丝绸之路河南道》，北京：中国社会科学出版社，2002 年；荣新江：《阚氏高昌王国与柔然、西域的关系》，《历史研究》2007 年第 2 期，第 4—14 页。

③ 《大正藏》第 50 册，第 651 页。

④ 《北史》卷八二《何妥传》同。此处的“西城”，《通志》卷一七四《何妥传》作“西域”，当正之。参见陈寅恪：《隋唐制度渊源略论稿》，北京：中华书局，1963 年，第 78—79 页。

⑤ 沙畹：《西突厥史料》，冯承钧汉译本，上海：商务印书馆，1932 年，第 167—173 页。

印度之间的贸易担当者。[①] 姜伯勤教授也强调粟特人实际上是中古时期丝绸之路上的贸易担当者。[②] 从上面列举的部分例证可以看出，经过长时间的经营，粟特人在粟特本土到中国之间，以及中国与印度之间、北方游牧部落与南方农耕居民之间，从南到北，从西到东，逐渐形成了自己的贸易网络，在这个贸易网络的交会点上，建立起殖民聚落，作为他们东西贸易的中转站。粟特商队由首领萨保率领，一队队从粟特本土出发，来到丝路沿线不同的据点，把货物卸下，一些人返回，一些人继续前行，这样人员不断充实，聚落也得以充实。

因此可以说，在汉、贵霜、帕提亚、罗马四大帝国衰亡后，小国没有力量经营大型贸易，中亚的粟特商人逐渐重建起丝绸之路的贸易网络，他们以商队和聚落相结合的方式，控制了整个中古时期的丝路贸易，即使在突厥、回鹘汗国强盛之际，以及隋唐王朝统治中国的情形下，丝路贸易仍然掌控在粟特人之手，我们从敦煌、吐鲁番和西域出土各种胡汉诸语文书中看到，7 世纪初到 8 世纪中叶，中原与西域的贸易往来，主要是粟特人承担。甚至安禄山在发动叛乱之前，也是利用粟特商人的贸易网络，“潜于诸道商胡兴贩，每岁输异方珍货计百万数”[③]，聚集了大量发动战争的资本。安史之乱后回鹘汗国与唐朝的绢马贸易，也是控制在粟特人之手。虽然有关粟特商人的史料零碎，但把这些分散的不同史料放在一起，就可以看出粟特商人在中古丝绸之路上的伟大形象了。

结 论

丝绸之路是一条交通贸易之路，与中国关系密切，但也与欧亚大陆上的其他国家相关，丝路贸易的兴盛是各国共同经营的结果。

欧亚大陆上的丝绸之路，地理和政治环境并不甚佳，但从来也没有完全断绝。

不同时期的丝路交往与贸易有不同的特点，公元前 2 世纪到公元后 3 世纪是大国长途贸易的时代，而随后的魏晋南北朝混乱时期，则以粟特商队为代表的私人团体，在小国中间做中转贸易，由小到大，由少聚多，重建了丝绸之路的贸易网络。

欧亚大陆上的丝路贸易多数时间里不是一条线通到底，而是层层推进，阶段性发展的。

---

① N. Sims-Williams, “The Sogdian Merchants in China and India” , pp. 45-67.

② 姜伯勤:《敦煌吐鲁番文书与丝绸之路》，文物出版社，1994 年，第 150—226 页。

③ 姚汝能:《安禄山事迹》卷上，上海古籍出版社，1983 年，第 12 页。

“西夷”“西夷西”疑问与汉武帝“指求身毒国”探索*

王子今（中国人民大学）

摘　要:《史记》卷一二三《大宛列传》和卷一一六《西南夷列传》均记载，张骞以西域见闻，判断“邛西”有往“身毒国”的通路，与“大夏”联系“道便近”。于是汉武帝派遣使者“间出西夷西指求身毒国”。“间出西夷西”，《汉书》卷九五《西南夷传》作“间出西南夷”。《史记》研究者对于“间出西夷西指求身毒国”，或理解为“间出西夷，西指求身毒国”，或理解为“间出西夷西，指求身毒国”。就此有必要认真辨析。这是汉代交通史上的重要事件，也是中外文化交流史上的重要事件。所谓“邛西”“西夷西”，是民族构成复杂的地区。“间出西夷西”的交通行为，不仅对于丝绸之路史研究意义重要，也是边疆史与民族史研究者应予特别关注的。

关键词: 张骞；汉武帝；西夷；西夷西；指求身毒国

《史记》卷一二三《大宛列传》和卷一一六《西南夷列传》均记载，张骞根据西域见闻，提出“邛西”有往“身毒国”通路的判断，以为这一路径与“大夏”联系“道便近”，有利于汉王朝向西扩张的战略规划。于是汉武帝派遣使者“间出西夷西指求身毒国”。这是汉代交通史上的大事，也是中外文化交流史上的大事。所谓“邛西”“西夷”“西夷西”，是民族构成复杂的地区。“间出”这一地区的交通行为，也是边疆史与民族史研究者应予特别关注的学术主题。

汉武帝经营西南夷交通，实现了汉帝国西南方向打通国际联系的南越和滇越两条通路。作为实现这一历史性进步的最初步骤，即“西夷”“西夷西”方向的探索，其交通史意义也不宜忽视。

一 《西南夷列传》《大宛列传》“身毒国”信息

张骞西域之行，使得中原人获得了前所未有的关于西域地方比较全面的地理人文知识。其中有涉及“身毒国”的重要信息。《史记》卷一一六《西南夷列传》记载：

> 及元狩元年，博望侯张骞使大夏来，言居大夏时见蜀布、邛竹杖[①]，使问所从来，曰：“从东南身毒国，可数千里，得蜀贾人市。”或闻邛西可二千里有身毒国。骞因盛言大夏在汉西南，慕中国，患匈奴隔其道，诚通蜀，身毒国道便近，有利无害。

*　中国人民大学科学研究基金（中央高校基本科研业务费专项基金资助）项目“中国古代交通史研究”（10XNL001）。

①　裴骃:《集解》:“韦昭曰:‘邛县之竹，属蜀。’瓒曰:‘邛，山名。此竹节高实中，可作杖。’”《史记》中华书局1959年9月标点本作“蜀布、邛竹、杖”，第2995页；1982年11月版作“邛竹仗”；2013年9月“点校本二十四史修订本”作“蜀布、邛竹杖”，第3606页。作“邛竹杖”是。

关于“身毒国”，裴骃《集解》引徐广曰：“字或作‘竺’。《汉书》直云‘身毒’,《史记》一本作‘乾毒’。”骃案:《汉书音义》曰：“一名‘天竺’，则浮屠胡是也。”司马贞《索隐》也说：“身音捐，毒音笃。一本作‘乾毒’。《汉书音义》一名‘天竺’也。”①

《史记》卷一二三《大宛列传》记载：“骞身所至者大宛、大月氏、大夏、康居，而传闻其旁大国五六，具为天子言之。”其中对于“大夏”的介绍涉及“身毒国”：

> 大夏在大宛西南二千余里妫水南。其俗土著，有城屋，与大宛同俗。无大君长，往往城邑置小长。其兵弱，畏战。善贾市。及大月氏西徙，攻败之，皆臣畜大夏。大夏民多，可百余万。其都曰蓝市城，有市贩贾诸物。其东南有身毒国。

关于“身毒国”，裴骃《集解》引徐广曰：“身，或作‘乾’，又作‘讫’。”司马贞《索隐》：“身音乾，毒音笃。孟康云：‘即天竺也，所谓浮图胡也。’”②

《史记》注家所谓身毒国“一名‘天竺’”,“即天竺也，所谓浮图胡也”。指出了其宗教文化的品质。对于“身毒”的初步了解，是中原人西域知识别开生面的内容。来自“身毒”的宗教影响，后来对于中土文化面貌的历史变化发挥了重要的作用。张守节《正义》对于《大宛列传》“身毒”的解说谈到早期佛教：“一名身毒，在月氏东南数千里。俗与月氏同，而卑湿暑热。其国临大水，乘象以战。其民弱于月氏。修浮图道，不杀伐，遂以成俗。土有象、犀、玳瑁、金、银、铁、锡、铅。西与大秦通，有大秦珍物。”张守节《正义》说到“明帝梦金人长大，顶有光明，以问群臣”事。有人回答道：“西方有神，名曰‘佛’，其形长丈六尺而黄金色。”因此导致佛教传入中国，“帝于是遣使天竺问佛道法，遂至中国，画形像焉。万震《南州志》云：‘地方三万里，佛道所出。其国王居城郭，殿皆雕文刻镂。街曲市里，各有行列。左右诸大国凡十六，皆共奉之，以天地之中也’”③。

有关“身毒国”文化信息的传播路径、传播力度和传播效应，以佛教的流布为重要标志，影响了中国社会中古时代的文化走向。文化史进程的这一步骤，无疑与交通开发有重要的关系。

中原社会对“身毒国”文化信息之认识的最初记录，始自张骞“言居大夏时”见闻。这是考察丝绸之路史应当予以特别注意的。而开拓丝路西南重要通道的实践，由自“骞因盛言大夏在汉西南，慕

---

① 《史记》卷一一六《西南夷列传》，第 2995 页。

② 《史记》卷一二三《大宛列传》，第 3166 页。

③ 张守节《正义》又有关于佛教早期传说及文化遗存的介绍：“《浮屠经》云：‘临儿国王生隐屠太子。父曰屠头邪，母曰莫邪屠。身色黄，发如青丝，乳有青色，爪赤如铜。始莫邪梦白象而孕，及生，从母右胁出。生有发，堕地能行七步。’又云‘太子生时，有二龙王夹左右吐水，一龙水暖，一龙水冷，遂成二池，今犹一冷一暖。初行七步处，琉璃上有太子脚迹见在。生处名祇洹精舍，在舍卫国南四里，是长者须达所起。又有阿输迦树，是夫人所攀生太子树也。’《括地志》云：‘沙祇大国即舍卫国也，在月氏南万里，即波斯匿王治处。此国共九十种。知身后事。城有祇树给孤园。’又云：‘天竺国有东、西、南、北、中央天竺国，国方三万里，去月氏七千里。大国隶属凡二十一。天竺在昆仑山南，大国也。治城临恒水。’又云：‘阿耨达山亦名建末达山，亦名昆仑山。水出，一名拔扈利水，一名恒伽河，即经称恒河者也。自昆仑山以南，多是平地而下湿。土肥良，多种稻，岁四熟，留役驼马，米粒亦极大。’又云：‘佛上忉利天，为母说法九十日。波斯匿王思欲见佛，即刻牛头旃檀象，置精舍内佛坐。此像是众像之始，后人所法也。佛上天青梯，今变为石，没入地，唯余十二蹬，蹬间二尺余。彼耆老言，梯入地尽，佛法灭。’又云：‘王舍国，胡语曰罪悦祇国。其国灵鹫山，胡语曰耆阇崛山。山是青石，石头似鹫。鸟名耆阇，鹫也。崛，山石也。山周四十里，外周围水，佛于此坐禅，及诸阿难等俱在此坐。’又云：‘小孤石，石上有石室者，佛坐其中，天帝释以四十二事问佛，佛一一以指画石，其迹尚存。又于山上起塔，佛昔将阿难在此上山四望，见福田疆畔，因制七条衣割截之法于此，今袈裟衣是也。’”《史记》卷一二三《大宛列传》，第 3166 页。

中国，患匈奴隔其道，诚通蜀，身毒国道便近，有利无害”的建议，也是丝绸之路研究者应当予以足够重视的历史现象。而“西夷”“西夷西”方向的探索，尤其值得我们关注。

二 “指求身毒国”方向：西夷·西夷西·西南夷

关于“博望侯张骞使大夏来”言及其东南“身毒国”之后，汉王朝有利用“道便近”的交通条件实现新的战略优势的设想。《史记》卷一一六《西南夷列传》记载汉武帝因张骞建议，试图开通国际道路由身毒国联系大夏的努力。上文已引录：“及元狩元年，博望侯张骞使大夏来，言居大夏时见蜀布、邛竹杖，使问所从来，曰：‘从东南身毒国，可数千里，得蜀贾人市。’或闻邛西可二千里有身毒国。骞因盛言大夏在汉西南，慕中国，患匈奴隔其道，诚通蜀，身毒国道便近，有利无害。”《西南夷列传》接着写道：

> ……于是天子乃令王然于、柏始昌、吕越人等，使间出西夷西，指求身毒国。①

此据中华书局标点本断句。②而泷川资言《史记会注考证》则作“使间出西夷，西指求身毒国”③。究竟是应当读作“使间出西夷西，指求身毒国”，还是应当读作“使间出西夷，西指求身毒国”呢？思考这一问题，也许应当参考《西南夷列传》所记录大概理解并无歧义的“或闻邛西可二千里有身毒国”之“邛西”方位。

现在看来，“使间出西夷西，指求身毒国”与“使间出西夷，西指求身毒国”对这一重要交通探索的空间位置与寻求方向的介绍，似乎并没有根本的不同。所谓“骞因盛言大夏在汉西南，慕中国，患匈奴隔其道，诚通蜀，身毒国道便近，有利无害”，已说这条通路指向“汉西南”，应在“蜀”地之“西”。

关于“西夷”，《史记》还有其他说法。④而《史记》卷一一六《西南夷列传》：“蜀人司马相如亦言西夷邛、笮可置郡。”⑤《史记》卷一一七《司马相如列传》：“是时邛筰之君长闻南夷与汉通，得赏赐多，多欲愿为内臣妾，请吏，比南夷。天子问相如，相如曰：‘邛、筰、冉、駹者近蜀，道亦易通，秦时尝通为郡县，至汉兴而罢。今诚复通，为置郡县，愈于南夷。’天子以为然，乃拜相如为中郎将，建节往使。副使王然于、壶充国、吕越人驰四乘之传，因巴蜀吏币物以略西夷。”“司马长卿便略定西夷，邛、笮、冉、駹、斯榆之君皆请为内臣。除边关，关益斥，西至沫、若水，南至牂柯为徼，通零关道，桥孙水，以通邛都。”⑥这些记述，可以大致说明“西夷”的空间方位，包括蜀郡以西又越巂郡，以及犍为郡部分地方。

《西南夷列传》所见“于是天子乃令王然于、柏始昌、吕越人等，使间出西夷西，指求身毒国”或“使间出西夷，西指求身毒国”，《汉书》卷九五《西南夷传》写作：“于是天子乃令王然于、柏始昌、吕越人等十余辈间出西南夷，指求身毒国。”对于所谓“间出西南夷”，颜师古注：“求间隙而出

---

① 《史记》卷一一六《西南夷列传》，第 2995 页。

② 同上。

③ 司马迁撰，泷川资言考证，水泽利忠校补：《史记会注考证校补》，上海古籍出版社，1986 年，第 1863 页。

④ 如《史记》卷四《周本纪》：“西夷犬戎攻幽王”，第 145 页。这应是西周以当时政治中枢为基点判定的“西夷”。

⑤ 《史记》卷一一六《西南夷列传》，第 2995 页。

⑥ 《史记》卷一一七《司马相如列传》，第 3046—3047 页。

也。”①

将《史记》“西夷”“西夷西”改写作“西南夷”，体现出班固的判断。由“间出西南夷，指求身毒国”句式，可知对《史记》卷一一六《西南夷列传》“西夷”“西夷西”的歧见取“西夷西”的理解可能接近司马迁原意。《通典》卷一八七《边防三·南蛮上·夜郎》“于是乃令王然于间出西南夷，往身毒国”②、《通志》卷一九七《四夷传·南蛮上·西南夷序略》“于是天子乃令王然于、柏始昌、吕越人等十余辈间出西南夷，指求身毒国”③、《太平寰宇记》卷一七八《四夷七·南蛮三·徼内南蛮》“于是乃令王然于、柏始羌等间出西南夷，往身毒国”④、《西汉会要》卷六九《蕃夷中·西南夷》“于是乃令王然于、柏始昌、吕越人等十余辈间出西南夷，指求身毒国”⑤、《文献通考》卷三二九《四裔考六·夜郎国》“于是乃令王然于间出西南夷，往身毒国”⑥等文献载录，均取用《汉书》“间出西南夷”说。

看来，后世史家似乎多不认可《史记》“西夷西”说而信从《汉书》“西南夷”说。

理解《汉书》“间出西南夷”的“西南夷”指向及其与《史记》“西夷西”的逻辑关系，或许应当关注《史记》《汉书》“西南夷”之语义。

三 “西南夷”:“西夷”与“南夷”

方国瑜曾指出，“西南夷”即“巴、蜀以外之南夷与西夷区域”⑦。又如童恩正所说，在《史记》的《西南夷列传》中，“司马迁是以巴蜀为中心，叙述了其南方的贵州北部、西南方的云南滇池区域、洱海区域、四川西昌地区、凉山彝族自治州、西部的雅安地区、西北的阿坝藏族自治州以及北部的赣南武都地区的少数民族，而概括地称之为‘西南夷’。以后一般的研究者即沿袭了这一名词，未加分析。实际上细读《史记》有关部分，我们发现司马迁虽然将篇名成为《西南夷列传》，但实际上又将这些民族分成‘南夷’和‘西夷’两部分”⑧。段渝也指出：“西南夷族类有异，成分复杂。按《史记》有关篇章以及《汉书》的记载，实际上包括西夷和南夷两部分。”“‘西’和‘南’均为方位词。西夷是指位于巴蜀以西的非华夏的民族或族群，南夷是指位于巴蜀以南的非华夏的民族或族群。”⑨《史记》卷一一六《西南夷列传》篇末“太史公曰”总结“西南夷”与中原关系之历史沿革，曾经明确分述“西夷”和“南夷”：

> 太史公曰：楚之先岂有天禄哉？在周为文王师，封楚。及周之衰，地称五千里。秦灭诸侯，唯楚苗裔尚有滇王。汉诛西南夷，国多灭矣，唯滇复为宠王。然南夷之端，见枸酱番禺，大夏杖

---

① 《汉书》，北京：中华书局，1962 年，第 3841 页。
② 杜佑：《通典》，北京：中华书局，1984 年，第 1000 页。
③ 郑樵：《通志》，北京：中华书局，1987 年，第 3163 页。
④ 文渊阁《四库全书》本。
⑤ 徐天麟：《西汉会要》，上海人民出版社，1977 年，第 808—809 页。文渊阁《四库全书》本作“于是乃令王然于间出西南夷，往身毒国”。
⑥ 马端临：《文献通考》，北京：中华书局，1986 年，第 2581 页。
⑦ 方国瑜：《〈史记·西南夷列传〉概说》，《中国史研究》1979 年第 4 期。
⑧ 童恩正：《古代的巴蜀》，重庆出版社，1998 年，第 93 页。
⑨ 段渝：《西南夷考释》，《天府新论》2012 年第 5 期；《先秦汉晋西南夷内涵及其时空演变》，《南方丝绸之路上的民族与文化》，成都：四川民族出版社，2016 年。

邛竹。西夷后揃，剽分二方，卒为七郡。

关于“西夷后揃”，裴骃《集解》：“《汉书音义》曰：‘音翦。’”司马贞《索隐》：“音剪。揃谓被分割也。”关于“剽分二方”，司马贞《索隐》：“剽音匹妙反。言西夷后被揃迫逐，遂剽居西南二方，各属郡县。剽亦分义。”关于“卒为七郡”，裴骃《集解》：“徐广曰：‘犍为、牂柯、越嶲、益州、武都、沈犁、汶山地也。’”①

“西南夷”在司马迁笔下叙写中的“揃”“剽”“分割”，在《西南夷列传》开篇是这样记述的：“西南夷君长以什数，夜郎最大；其西靡莫之属以什数，滇最大；自滇以北君长以什数，邛都最大：此皆魋结，耕田，有邑聚。其外西自同师以东，北至楪榆，名为嶲、昆明，皆编发，随畜迁徙，毋常处，毋君长，地方可数千里。自嶲以东北，君长以什数，徙、筰都最大；自筰以东北，君长以什数，冄駹最大。其俗或土著，或移徙，在蜀之西。自冄駹以东北，君长以什数，白马最大，皆氐类也。此皆巴蜀西南外蛮夷也。”② 开篇前三字“西南夷”，或以为应为“南夷”。童恩正也曾指出：“今本《史记·西南夷列传》一开始就说：‘西南夷君长以什数，夜郎最大’，好像夜郎就是西南夷，而《汉书·西南夷两粤朝鲜列传》则作‘西夷君长以什数’③，这个‘西’字，应为‘南’字之误，王先谦《汉书补注》已有说。④ 所以今本《史记》，一开始也衍了一‘西’字，原文应与《汉书》相同，是‘南夷君长以什数，夜郎最大’，夜郎应属南夷。正因为如此，《正义》才说：‘在蜀之南’。”⑤

《史记》中华书局2013年9月“点校本二十四史修订本”《校勘记》这样写道：

> 西南夷　景祐本《汉书》卷九五《西南夷传》作“南夷”。李笠《广史记订补》卷一〇：“‘南’上本无‘西’字，此以南、西、北方分写，故云南夷长以夜郎为最大，其西靡莫之属滇最大，自滇以北邛都最大。若总言‘西南’，安得以夜郎属之？下文云‘独置南夷夜郎’，亦可证夜郎属南夷？”⑥

这样的处理是正确的。

司马迁的记述，“分写”“南夷”“其西靡莫之属”“自滇以北”“其外西”“自嶲以东北”“自筰以东北”“自冄駹以东北”地方各族，所谓“此皆巴蜀西南外蛮夷也”，指出《西南夷列传》之“西南夷”即“巴蜀西南外蛮夷”其区域及族属是各有别异的。

如果《西南夷列传》开篇“西南夷君长以什数，夜郎最大”应读作“南夷君长以什数，夜郎最

---

① 《史记》卷一一六《西南夷列传》，第2997—2998页。

② 同上书，第2991页。

③ 《汉书》卷九五《西南夷列传》作“以十数”，第3837页。

④ 原注：“在此我们应作一说明。在一般情况下，当然只能用时代在前的书来校正时代较晚的书，而不宜用时代较晚的书校前书。但由于《汉书》西南夷部分基本上是照抄《史记》，而抄的时代又较早，因此当《史记》本身在传抄中发生错误时，《汉书》有关部分反而保存了原意，这是可以理解的。”童恩正：《古代的巴蜀》，第109页。今按：王先谦《汉书补注》：“钱大昭曰：‘西’当作‘南’。南监本、闽本不误。先谦曰：官本作‘南’。”王先谦撰：《汉书补注》，中华书局据光绪二十六年虚受堂刊本1983年9月影印版，第1593页。《汉书》中华书局标点本作“(西)〔南〕夷君长以十数”。校勘记：“钱大昭说‘西’当作‘南’。按景祐、殿、局本都作‘南’。”《汉书》卷九五《西南夷列传》，第3837、3868页。

⑤ 童恩正：《古代的巴蜀》，第93页。

⑥ 《史记》，中华书局2013年9月“点校本二十四史修订本”，第3608—3609页。

大”的意见合理，则是“南夷”称谓明朗的例证。此外，《西南夷列传》还有其他明确分写“西夷”和“南夷”的情形。如言唐蒙建议“通夜郎道，为置吏”，“乃以为犍为郡。发巴蜀卒治道，自僰道指牂柯江”。随后有关司马相如事迹的记述中出现“西夷”和“南夷”：

> 蜀人司马相如亦言西夷邛、筰可置郡。使相如以郎中将往喻，皆如南夷，为置一都尉，十余县，属蜀。①

又汉武帝回应公孙弘对“西南夷”政策的质疑，对西南方向的开发与征服有所收缩，有“西夷”与“南夷”行政的区别：

> 当是时，巴蜀四郡②通西南夷道，戍转相饷。数岁，道不通，士罢饿离湿，死者甚众；西南夷又数反，发兵兴击，秏费无功。上患之，使公孙弘往视问焉。还对，言其不便。及弘为御史大夫，是时方筑朔方以据河逐胡，弘因数言西南夷害，可且罢，专力事匈奴。上罢西夷，独置南夷夜郎两县一都尉，稍令犍为自葆就。

由此可以明确得知，“西南夷”确实是可以“分写”为“西夷”和“南夷”的。“独置南夷夜郎两县一都尉”句下，裴骃《集解》：“徐广曰：‘元光六年，南夷始置邮亭。’”③随后的记述，即前引“元狩元年，博望侯张骞使大夏来，言居大夏时见蜀布、邛竹杖”，“骞因盛言大夏在汉西南，慕中国，患匈奴隔其道，诚通蜀，身毒国道便近，有利无害”，于是汉武帝“乃令王然于、柏始昌、吕越人等，使间出西夷西，指求身毒国”。显然，此“西夷”“西夷西”，是承接上文“西夷”语的连续性记述。

《西南夷列传》还有两处文字说到“南夷”：“及至南越反，上使驰义侯因犍为发南夷兵。”④“上使王然于以越破及诛南夷兵威风喻滇王入朝。”⑤

前引《史记》卷一一七《司马相如列传》：“是时邛筰之君长闻南夷与汉通，得赏赐多，多欲愿为内臣妾，请吏，比南夷。天子问相如，相如曰：‘邛、筰、冉、駹者近蜀，道亦易通，秦时尝通为郡县，至汉兴而罢。今诚复通，为置郡县，愈于南夷。’天子以为然，……”所谓“比南夷”“愈于南夷”者，即“西夷”。司马贞《索隐》：“晋灼曰：‘南夷谓犍为、牂柯也。西夷谓越巂、益州。’”⑥《史记》注家对“西夷”“南夷”的空间区分有所说明者，又见于司马贞《索隐》对于司马相如“四面风德，二方之君鳞集仰流，愿得受号者以亿计”语所谓“二方”的解释：“谓西夷邛、僰，南夷牂柯、夜郎也。”⑦

分析《史记》“西南夷”及“西夷”“南夷”文字，可以知道《西南夷列传》“使间出西夷西，指求身毒国”或者读作“使间出西夷，西指求身毒国”的说法是合理的。《汉书》改说“间出西南夷，指求身毒国”，取用更笼统的表述方式，当然也并没有什么错误，只是没有《史记》准确具体而已。但是“间出西南夷，指求身毒国”之说也容易导致强调“南夷”方向而忽略“西夷”方向的

---

① 《史记》卷一一六《西南夷列传》，第 2994 页。

② 裴骃《集解》：“徐广曰：汉中，巴郡，广汉，蜀郡。”

③ 《史记》卷一一六《西南夷列传》，第 2995 页。

④ 同上书，第 2996 页。

⑤ 同上书，第 2997 页。

⑥ 《史记》卷一一七《司马相如列传》，第 3047 页。

⑦ 同上书，第 3051—3052 页。

成见。

四　以“蜀犍为”为出发点“四道并出”及“邛西”交通探索

听到张骞有关身毒国“去蜀不远”，“从蜀宜径，又无寇”[①]，“道便近”，“有利无害”[②]的报告，“天子乃令王然于、柏始昌、吕越人等，使间出西夷西，指求身毒国”，进而谋求联系“大夏”事，《史记》卷一二三《大宛列传》有情节更为具体的记述。对于他们交通道路探索的方向与路线，司马迁保留的信息十分珍贵：

> 骞曰：“臣在大夏时，见邛竹杖、蜀布。[③]问曰：‘安得此？’大夏国人曰：‘吾贾人往市之身毒。身毒在大夏东南可数千里。其俗土著，大与大夏同，而卑湿暑热云。其人民乘象以战。其国临大水焉。’以骞度之，大夏去汉万二千里，居汉西南。今身毒国又居大夏东南数千里，有蜀物，此其去蜀不远矣。今使大夏，从羌中，险，羌人恶之；少北，则为匈奴所得；从蜀宜径[④]，又无寇。”天子既闻大宛及大夏、安息之属皆大国，多奇物，土著，颇与中国同业，而兵弱，贵汉财物；其北有大月氏、康居之属，兵强，可以赂遗设利朝也。且诚得而以义属之，则广地万里，重九译[⑤]，致殊俗，威德遍于四海。天子欣然，以骞言为然，乃令骞因蜀犍为[⑥]发间使，四道并出：出駹，出冄，出徙，出邛、僰，皆各行一二千里。其北方闭氐、筰，南方闭嶲、昆明。昆明之属无君长，善寇盗，辄杀略汉使，终莫得通。然闻其西可千余里有乘象国，名曰滇越，而蜀贾奸出物者或至焉，于是汉以求大夏道始通滇国。初，汉欲通西南夷，费多，道不通，罢之。及张骞言可以通大夏，乃复事西南夷。[⑦]

所谓“复事西南夷”，显示这是汉武帝时代又一次“西南夷”经营。司马迁曾经有奉使前往巴蜀以南甚至抵达“邛、筰、昆明”等地方的交通实践[⑧]，《史记》有关“事西南夷”的记述，可信度是比较强的。正如方国瑜所说，“疑司马迁仕为郎中，奉使西征，即为参与经略西南夷”，“当于元鼎五年（前112）秋出发，至六年（前111）十月以后始归，在西南有一年多时间”。“司马迁既为负有经略西南夷之任务而至巴、蜀以外之南夷与西夷区域，当必从事调查，了解此地区之情况，及以前汉朝对西南夷之交涉事件，此司马迁对西南夷有较深刻认识之由来。后为太史令作《史记》，其《西南夷列传》一篇，信而有征，非寻常著作可比也。”[⑨]

西汉犍为郡治在今四川宜宾。以“蜀犍为”为出发点之所谓“四道并出：出駹，出冄，出徙，出

---

① 《史记》卷一二三《大宛列传》，第3166页。
② 《史记》卷一一六《西南夷列传》，第2995页。
③ 张守节《正义》：“邛都邛山出此竹，因名‘邛竹’。节高实中，或寄生，可为杖。布，土芦布。”
④ 裴骃《集解》：“如淳曰：‘径，疾也。或曰径，直。’”
⑤ 张守节《正义》：“言重重九遍译语而致。”参看王子今：《“重译”：汉代民族史与外交史中的一种文化现象》，《河北学刊》2010年第4期。
⑥ 张守节《正义》：“犍，其连反。犍为郡今戎州也，在益州南一千余里。”
⑦ 《史记》卷一二三《大宛列传》，第3166页。
⑧ 《史记》卷一三〇《太史公自序》：“奉使西征巴、蜀以南，南略邛、筰、昆明，还报命。”裴骃《集解》：“徐广曰：‘元鼎六年，平西南夷，以为五郡。其明年，元封元年是也。’”第3295页。
⑨ 方国瑜：《〈史记·西南夷列传〉概说》，《中国史研究》1979年第4期。

邛、僰”，体现出具有历史民族地理意义的比较明确的历史交通地理信息。所谓“出駹，出冄”，张守节《正义》：“冄、駹之地，在戎州西北也。”[1]唐代戎州治所在今四川宜宾。[2]则“冄、駹”地方，在今四川雅安、荥经、汉源方向。所谓“出徙”，裴骃《集解》：“徐广曰：‘属汉嘉。’”司马贞《索隐》：“李奇云：‘徙音斯。蜀郡有徙县也。’”张守节《正义》：“徙在嘉州。”[3]所谓“蜀郡有徙县”，据《汉书》卷二八上《地理志上》。谭其骧主编《中国历史地图集》标示，“徙”在今四川天全东南。[4]谓“出邛、僰”，张守节《正义》：“邛，今邛州；僰，今雅州：皆在戎州西南也。”唐代邛州治所在今四川邛崃，雅州治所在今四川雅安。[5]有学者指出，唐代邛州“辖境相当今四川邛崃、大邑、蒲江等市县地”，雅州“辖境相当今四川雅安、名山、荥经、天全、卢山、宝兴等市县地”。[6]司马迁所谓“出駹，出冄，出徙，出邛、僰”的交通方向，现在考定大致均在犍为西北。所谓“皆各行一二千里”，考察其形势，使人联想到现今交通道路可延伸至德格—江达，以及巴塘—芒康的路线。

《大宛列传》接着记述：“其北方闭氐、筰，南方闭嶲、昆明。”而“出駹，出冄，出徙，出邛、僰”，似乎并没有涉及“南方”。也许司马迁的叙说次序，本来就是以“四道并出：出駹，出冄，出徙，出邛、僰”，先说“北方”的探索。按照我们今天的历史民族地理和历史行政地理知识，“南方闭嶲、昆明”可能在前说“四道并出”之外。

汉武帝“因蜀犍为发间使，四道并出”之西路和北路面对复杂的民族错居形势。有的治西南民族史者称这一方向的少数民族为“氐羌族群”。[7]考察“駹”“冄”“邛”“僰”的民族构成与区域分布是非常复杂的问题。马长寿曾论“徙为叟，为蜀，莋都或羌，或彝，或纳西，均于氐族无关”。“汉之冄駹即隋唐之嘉良，亦即近代的嘉戎。此族非氐，非羌，乃远古时从西藏琼部东迁出来的一族。”[8]《汉书》卷二八上《地理志上》“蜀郡”条在“绵虒”之后说到“旄牛”“徙”“湔氐道”和“汶江”：

> 旄牛，鲜水出徼外，南入若水。若水亦出徼外，南至大莋入绳，过郡二，行千六百里。徙，湔氐道，《禹贡》㟭山在西徼外，江水所出，东南至江都入海，过郡七，行二千六百六十里。汶江，渽水出徼外，南至南安，东入江，过郡三，行三千四十里。[9]

“北方闭氐、筰”的“氐”，或许即指“湔氐道”等地方。蜀郡“汶江”，谭其骧主编《中国历史地图集》的处理，即写作“汶江道”，位置标示于今四川茂汶羌族自治县。[10]有关“蜀郡”的文字说到“鲜

---

① 《史记》卷一二三《大宛列传》，第3166页。
② 谭其骧主编：《中国历史地图集》第5册，北京：地图出版社，1982年，第65—66页。
③ 《史记》卷一二三《大宛列传》，第3166页。
④ 谭其骧主编：《中国历史地图集》第2册，第29—30页。
⑤ 谭其骧主编：《中国历史地图集》第5册，第65—66页。
⑥ 史为乐主编：《中国历史地名大辞典》上册，第539页；下册，第2532页。
⑦ 马曜：《我国西南民族研究的回顾与展望》，中国西南民族研究学会编：《西南民族研究》，成都：四川民族出版社，1983年，第1页。
⑧ 马长寿：《氐与羌》，桂林：广西师范大学出版社，2006年，第22—23页。
⑨ 《汉书》卷二八上《地理志上》，第1598页。
⑩ 谭其骧主编：《中国历史地图集》第2册，第29—30页。

水出徼外”“峫山在西徼”“溅水出徼外”，所谓“徼外”“西徼”，均值得注意。[①] 而水道里程的记录“行千六百里”，“行二千六百六十里”，“行三千四十里”等，可以读作接近交通史实际的可能经过大致测定获得的数据。而“鲜水”地名对于可能显示此前民族迁徙现象的意义，我们曾经有所讨论。[②]

尽管汉武帝“因蜀犍为发间使，四道并出”尚有许多未知细节，但是这一外交开创与交通探索的意义却是显著的。有的《史记》研究者认为这是西汉体现出进取精神的外交政策中最典型的实例。如凌稚隆《史记评林》卷一二三写道：“自骞既失侯至骞之他旁国一段，与上天子既闻大宛一段暗相应，盖前推武帝好大喜功之心，故欣然以骞言为然，遣使四出；后原张骞失位怏怏，遂致逢君之欲，而拜将中郎。君臣病根，总来只一贪字为累，便贻国家无穷之戚。”[③] 所谓“好大喜功”，所谓“贪”，论者以为“君臣病根”，其实是当时汉民族时代精神之英雄主义与进取追求的表现。

任乃强曾论“蜀布之路”的开拓，认为张骞、王然于、壶充国、吕越人等并未亲自作为使节出行。[④] 其实据《史记》卷一一六《西南夷列传》“天子乃令王然于、柏始昌、吕越人等，使间出西夷西，指求身毒国”，可知“王然于、壶充国、吕越人等”应当就是“四道并出”的使团首领。关于《大宛列传》所谓“乃令骞因蜀犍为发间使，四道并出：出駹，出冄，出徙，出邛、僰，皆各行一二千里”，有学者以为张骞“亲率汉使出四道”[⑤]，而由“令骞因蜀犍为发间使，四道并出”句式，并没有张骞“亲率汉使出四道”文意。从常理说，张骞也不可能分身为“四”。

五 “事西南夷”“通西南夷”“开西南夷”与“通西南夷道”

前引《史记》卷一二三《大宛列传》言“事西南夷”。《史记》又有多处称“通西南夷”。如《史记》卷一一二《平津侯主父列传》：“是时通西南夷，东置沧海，北筑朔方之郡。”[⑥]《史记》卷一一七《司马相如列传》：“相如使时，蜀长老多言通西南夷不为用，唯大臣亦以为然。”[⑦] 又前引《史记》卷一二三《大宛列传》：“初，汉欲通西南夷，费多，道不通，罢之。”

《汉书》卷二四下《食货志下》则记载：“唐蒙、司马相如始开西南夷，凿山通道千余里，以广巴蜀，巴蜀之民罢焉。”[⑧] 所谓“开西南夷”，未见于《史记》，而《后汉书》卷八六《南蛮传》李贤注引孙盛《蜀谱》亦言“汉武帝开西南夷”[⑨]。又《三国志》卷四三《蜀书·吕凯传》裴松之注引孙盛《蜀

---

① 越嶲郡、益州郡也有来自“徼外”的江流。如越嶲郡“遂久”县条下：“绳水出徼外，东至僰道入江，过郡二，行千四百里。”“青蛉”县条下：“临池灊在北。仆水出徼外，东南至来惟入劳，过郡二，行千八百八十里。”益州郡“嶲唐”县条下：“周水首受徼外。又有类水，西南至不韦，行六百五十里。”“来唯”县条下：“从陒山出铜。劳水出徼外，东至麋泠入南海，过郡三，行三千五百六十里。”

② 参看王子今、高大伦：《说“鲜水”：康巴草原民族交通考古札记》，《中华文化论坛》2006年第4期；《康巴地区民族考古综合考察》，成都：天地出版社，2008年；《巴蜀文化研究集刊》第4卷，成都：巴蜀书社，2008年。

③ 凌稚隆：《史记评林》，明万历李瓛堂刊本。转引自杨燕起、陈可青、赖长扬编：《历代名家评〈史记〉》，北京师范大学出版社，1986年，第711页。

④ 任乃强：《中西陆路古商道——蜀布之路》（上），《文史杂志》1987年第1期。

⑤ 龚伟：《汉武帝经略“西南夷”年际考述》，《中华文化论坛》2016年第11期。

⑥《史记》卷一一二《平津侯主父列传》，第2950页。

⑦《史记》卷一一七《司马相如列传》，第3048页。

⑧《汉书》卷二四下《食货志下》，第1157页。

⑨《后汉书》卷八六《南蛮传》，第2847页。

世谱》曰：“汉武帝时，开西南夷，置郡县。”[①] 有学者说，“开西南夷”之“‘开’字延伸为开道（此道指的是开通道路）、开通、开化，都是有文化交流的意思”，汉代文献中“可以看到‘开……道’、‘通’和司马迁称张骞的‘凿空’之举都是同义”。[②]《说文·门部》：“开，张也。”段玉裁注：“张者，施弓弦也。门之开如弓之张，门之闭如弓之弛。”又《说文·门部》：“闢，开也。”段玉裁注：“引申为凡开祏之偁。古多假借辟字。”[③] 看来，“开”有迫使对方开通的含义，与“通”并非简单同义。而“凿空”语义或可依段玉裁“开祏之偁”说予以理解。

《史记》又可见“通西南夷道”。如《史记》卷三〇《平准书》：“汉通西南夷道，作者数万人，千里负担馈粮，率十余锺致一石。”[④] 又《史记》卷一一二《平津侯主父列传》：“是时通西南夷道，置郡，巴蜀民苦之。”[⑤]《史记》卷一一六《西南夷列传》：“通西南夷道，戍转相饷。”[⑥]《史记》卷一一七《司马相如列传》：“唐蒙已略通夜郎，因通西南夷道，发巴、蜀、广汉卒，作者数万人。”[⑦]

实际上，“事西南夷”就是“通西南夷”。前引《史记》卷一二三《大宛列传》：“初，汉欲通西南夷，费多，道不通，罢之。及张骞言可以通大夏，乃复事西南夷。”语句前后照应，已经可以说明这一情形。而“通西南夷”即“通西南夷道”也是明白无疑的。如前引《史记》卷一一七《司马相如列传》：“唐蒙已略通夜郎，因通西南夷道，发巴、蜀、广汉卒，作者数万人。”“相如使时，蜀长老多言通西南夷不为用，唯大臣亦以为然。”

六 “通西南夷道”的世界史意义

所谓“其北方闭氐、筰，南方闭巂、昆明”说到的交通形势，可以通过《汉书》卷二八下《地理志下》“……及犍为、牂柯、越巂，皆西南外夷，武帝初开置，民俗略与巴、蜀同”[⑧] 予以理解。据《史记》卷一二三《大宛列传》，直接的地方民族势力对交通的显著阻隔来自“昆明”，“昆明之属无君长，善寇盗，辄杀略汉使，终莫得通”。不过，“西南夷”道路的“闭”，其实只是西南交通事业发展史上短暂的停顿。汉武帝时代的交通建设者并没有中止西南方向交通开拓的探求。正如《大宛列传》所记载的：“然闻其西可千余里有乘象国，名曰滇越，而蜀贾奸出物者或至焉，于是汉以求大夏道始通滇国。”

“通西南夷道”的事业，使得相对闭塞的巴蜀地方打通了对外联系的经济与文化通道。

一条通道即南越通道，使巴蜀得以通行南越，进而与南洋航路的大港番禺实现联系。[⑨]《后汉书》卷八八《西域传》：“至桓帝延熹九年，大秦王安敦遣使自日南徼外献象牙、犀角、瑇瑁，始乃一通

---

① 《三国志》，北京：中华书局，1959 年，第 1047 页。

② 龚伟：《汉武帝经略“西南夷”年际考述》，《中华文化论坛》2016 年第 11 期。

③ 许慎撰，段玉裁注：《说文解字注》，上海古籍出版社据经韵楼臧本 1981 年 10 月影印版，第 588 页。

④ 《史记》卷三〇《平准书》，第 1421 页。

⑤ 《史记》卷一一二《平津侯主父列传》，第 2949 页。

⑥ 《史记》卷一一六《西南夷列传》，第 2995 页。

⑦ 《史记》卷一一七《司马相如列传》，第 3046 页。

⑧ 《汉书》卷二八下《地理志下》，第 1646 页。

⑨ 参见王子今：《秦汉时期的东洋与南洋航运》，《海交史研究》1992 年第 1 期；章深：《广州：汉代中国海上丝绸之路第一大港》，《学术研究》2015 年第 10 期。

焉。”[①] 这是“日南徼外”与“大秦”国实现交通的记录。抵达“日南徼外”的外国贡献，也可以通过牂柯江水道抵达巴蜀。[②]

另一通道，即滇越通道，即经过今云南进入缅甸通往印度的道路。《史记》卷一二三《大宛列传》所谓“加其眩者之工”[③]，泷川资言《史记会注考证》引张守节《正义》：“言汉人幻人工妙，更加于黎靬”[④]，以为有“黎靬”与“汉人幻人”两种“幻人”。但是“幻人”之术的发明和导入，仍由于“黎靬”。伯希和认为：“此犂靬亦即亚历山大之译音也。当时《史记》《汉书》所记此国之事，惟言纪元前一四〇至八六年间，安息王以犂靬眩人献于汉，当时亚历山大之魔术者，颇著名。《后汉书》亦曾志及其人由印度赴东方也。则当时之犂靬，即指埃及之 Alexandrie。至纪元一世纪末年，中国人与叙利亚（Orient syrien）相接之后，始以大秦名其地。”[⑤]《后汉书》卷五一《陈禅传》中，记载了“幻人”经西南夷地区转入中原的史实：“永宁元年，西南夷掸国王献乐及幻人，能吐火，自支解，易牛马头。明年元会，作之于庭，安帝与群臣共观，大奇之。”[⑥] 对于这一历史事件，《后汉书》卷八六《西南夷列传·哀牢》也有记述：“永宁元年，掸国王雍由调复遣使者诣阙朝贺，献乐及幻人，能变化吐火，自支解，易牛马头。又善跳丸，数乃至千。自言我海西人。海西即大秦也，掸国西南通大秦。明年元会，安帝作乐于庭，封雍由调为汉大都尉，赐印绶、金银、彩缯各有差也。”[⑦] 此次“献乐及幻人”，并不是第一次正式交往。此前通过这一地区的外交活动的记录，还有：“永元六年，郡徼外敦忍乙王莫延慕义，遣使译献犀牛、大象。九年，徼外蛮及掸国王雍由调遣重译奉国珍宝，和帝赐金印紫绶，小君长皆加印绶、钱帛。”汉和帝永元六年即 94 年。莫延“遣使译献犀牛、大象”，在“幻人”因雍由调的友好行为进入内地 26 年之前。此外，“永初元年，徼外僬侥种夷陆类等三千余口举种内附，献象牙、水牛、封牛”史事也值得注意。汉安帝永初元年即 107 年，也在雍由调永宁元年（120）“献乐及幻人”13 年前。有学者指出，汉和帝和汉安帝时代通过这条线路来到洛阳的“掸国”使团，“带来了具有印度或中亚风格的器物”。[⑧] 有学者指出：“掸国就是今缅甸境内的掸邦。”而对于“敦忍乙”“僬

---

① 《后汉书》卷八八《西域传》，第 2920 页。

② 这条路线的文化联系可以发现较早的线索。有学者指出：“中国西南滇桂黔以及越南的青铜文化是在中原商周文化的影响下发展起来的。”“这些地区的商周中原青铜文化的传播都是间接的，云贵青铜文化的中原因素大部分是通过四川传入的，广西的则是通过湖南、四川、安徽等地传入的，越南受到了两个方向的双重影响。”因文化交流的实现，“在中国中原商周青铜文化的影响下，在中国西南地区产生了‘次生型’的青铜礼乐器，如云南、贵州、广东、广西和越南青铜文明中的器物——‘羊角钮铜钟’就是典型事例”。“第二类是中国南方文明的重要礼乐器——铜鼓。”由于西南夷道路的交通作用，“在中国南方贵州、四川、广西、广东、海南、湖南、重庆、湖北等省区和越南、泰国、老挝、缅甸、柬埔寨、马来西亚、印度尼西亚 7 个东南亚国家产生铜鼓和铜鼓文化”。李昆声、陈果：《中国云南与越南的青铜文明》，北京：社会科学文献出版社，2013 年，第 568—569 页。

③ 《史记》卷一二三《大宛列传》，第 3173 页。

④ 司马迁撰，泷川资言考证，水泽利忠校补：《史记会注考证校补》，第 1982 页。

⑤ 伯希和：《犂靬为埃及亚历山大说》，冯承钧译：《西域南海史地考证译丛》七编，北京：商务印书馆，1995 年，第 34 页。

⑥ 《后汉书》卷五一《陈禅传》，第 1685 页。

⑦ 《后汉书》卷八六《西南夷列传·哀牢》，第 2851 页。

⑧ 程爱勤：《古代中印交往与东南亚文化》，郑州：大象出版社，2009 年，第 62 页。

僥种夷”所在，学界虽意见不一，但是都认为在今缅甸境内。[①]

“西南夷道”之滇越道和南越道，与左思《蜀都赋》所谓“邛杖传节于大夏之邑，蒟酱流味于番禺之乡”[②]可以对应。

汉武帝“通西南夷道”以及直接“因蜀犍为发间使，四道并出”的决策，对于交通建设、边疆管理、民族融合均有重要意义，也值得世界文化交流史研究者关注。对于汉武帝开发西南夷的意义，多有学者研究考察，屡有新见发表。[③]有的研究者认为，“不是纯粹为了西南夷的经济发展”“通西南夷”的目的“是为征讨南越寻找便捷通道，以及寻找通往大夏的交通线，而不是为了开发西南夷地区的经济资源”。[④]以为汉武帝时代经营西南夷的努力，主要目的是打通往大夏的国际通道。这样的意见值得重视。

《史记》卷一一六《西南夷列传》说：“至滇，滇王尝羌[⑤]乃留，为求道西十余辈。岁余，皆闭昆明[⑥]，莫能通身毒国。”[⑦]所谓“为求道西十余辈”，决心不可谓不坚定，努力不可谓不持久，然而最终“莫能通”。我们曾经讨论过汉武帝对“西夷西”道路的探索。[⑧]“天子”“指求身毒国”却未能成功的重要原因之一，在于这一地区纷杂的多民族势力的存在，致使“留”“闭”现象发生。有学者分析，对“通身毒国”汉使的“留”“闭”，或许有垄断贸易通道的动机。余英时曾经指出：“西南夷有意识地封锁汉朝使者，可能是因为他们担心汉朝政府对贸易通道的干预和控制会不可避免地剥夺他们在有利可图的对外贸易中所享有的特权地位。”“出于同样的心理原因，安息商人采用欺骗的手段阻止汉朝使者与罗马帝国建立直接的联系……”[⑨]这样的分析，是有道理的。

七 “蜀贾”与“徼外”经济文化联系的民间通道

司马迁是根据西域地方有关蜀地商品如“蜀布、邛竹杖”的发现注意到另一交通方向“蜀贾人

---

① 陈炎：《中缅文化交流两千年》，收入周一良主编：《中外文化交流史》，郑州：河南人民出版社，1987年，第6页；贺圣达：《缅甸史》，北京：人民出版社，1992年，第14页。参见王子今：《海西幻人来路考》，《秦汉史论丛》第8辑，昆明：云南大学出版社，2001年，收入《中西初识二编》，郑州：大象出版社，2002年。有学者分析巴蜀与滇、滇西北系统的青铜文化，童恩正分析“西南夷”地区的铜柄铁剑，以为“发源于云南境内的可能性似乎更大一些”。参见童恩正：《我国西南地区青铜剑的研究》，《考古学报》1977年第2期。宋治民对石棺葬中几种主要的随葬器物如双大耳罐、单耳罐、山字格青铜剑与铜柄铁剑等进行比较分析，提出川西高原石棺墓出土的这类器物只能是由滇西向北传入川西高原地区。参见宋治民：《川西和滇西北的石棺葬》，《考古与文物》1987年第3期。霍巍指出：“牟托石棺墓中所反映出来的总体文化面貌，更加强了这一认识。”他还指出，通过“秦灭蜀后亡国的蜀人南迁”的方向，可以认识“蜀与滇之间的交通路线”。霍巍：《蜀滇之间的考古学》，《西南考古与中华文明》，成都：巴蜀书社，2011年。

② 萧统编，李善注：《文选》，北京：中华书局，1977年，第79页。

③ 高荣：《汉代对西南边疆的经营》，《中国边疆史地研究》2000年第1期；黎小龙：《战国秦汉西南边疆思想的区域性特征初探》，《中国边疆史地研究》2004年第4期；武保宁、吴硕：《西汉经营西南地区的政策及其分析》，《延安大学学报》（社会科学版）2007年2期；李正周：《两汉时期的“西南夷”民族政策》，《烟台大学学报》（哲学社会科学版）2008年第2期；李珍焱：《秦汉时期巴蜀地区通“西南”的道路及其意义》，《金卡工程·经济与法》2009年第12期；罗亭：《论汉武帝时期对西南夷道路的开发》，《河南科技学院学报》2012年第5期。

④ 郭筱磊：《浅探汉武帝开拓西南夷地区的根本原因》，《淮海工学院学报》（人文社会科学版）2014年第1期。

⑤ 裴骃《集解》引徐广曰：“尝，一作‘赏’。”

⑥ 裴骃《集解》：“如淳曰：‘为昆明所闭道。’”张守节《正义》：“昆明在今巂州南，昆县是也。”

⑦ 《史记》卷一一六《西南夷列传》，第2996页。

⑧ 参见王子今：《汉武帝“西夷西”道路与向家坝汉文化遗存》，《四川文物》2014年第5期。

⑨ 余英时：《汉代贸易与扩张》，邬文玲等译，上海古籍出版社，2005年，第99页。

市”的作用，于是推想大夏“诚通蜀，身毒国道便近，有利无害”的。《史记》中三次说到“蜀贾”：

> 及元狩元年，博望侯张骞使大夏来，言居大夏时见蜀布、邛竹杖，使问所从来，曰：“从东南身毒国，可数千里，得蜀贾人市。”①
>
> 昆明之属无君长，善寇盗，辄杀略汉使，终莫得通。然闻其西可千余里有乘象国，名曰滇越，而蜀贾奸出物者或至焉，于是汉以求大夏道始通滇国。②
>
> 建元六年，大行王恢击东越，东越杀王郢以报。恢因兵威使番阳令唐蒙风指晓南越。南越食蒙蜀枸酱，蒙问所从来，曰“道西北牂柯，牂柯江广数里，出番禺城下”。蒙归至长安，问蜀贾人，贾人曰：“独蜀出枸酱，多持窃出市夜郎。夜郎者，临牂柯江，江广百余步，足以行船。南越以财物役属夜郎，西至同师，然亦不能臣使也。”③

枸酱，《华阳国志》卷二《汉中志》及卷四《南中志》作“蒟酱”。④《资治通鉴》卷四三引“班固论曰”亦作“蒟酱”。班固所言“孝武之世”对外扩张，“睹犀布、瑇瑁，则建珠厓七郡；感蒟酱、竹杖，则开牂柯、越嶲；闻天马、蒲萄，则通大宛、安息。自是殊方异物，四面而至”⑤。将西南夷因“蒟酱”故事通南越道路，引“竹杖”故事通滇越道路两事并说。我们在这里更为关注的，是滇越—身毒—大夏交通线路的探索。

《史记》有关“蜀贾”的记载体现了这一社会群体的活跃。他们将“蜀枸酱”“多持窃出市夜郎”，又经历“牂柯”转贩至于“南越”，进入当地民间饮食生活。“蒙归至长安，问蜀贾人”及“贾人”的回答，说明参与长安经济活动的“蜀贾”对他们在各地的经营内容多是熟悉的。如果长安“蜀贾”曾经有经“夜郎”沿“牂柯江”贩运蜀地“枸酱”往“南越”的实践，则说明他们行贾空间的惊人宽广。如果并非如此，则或可反映这一行业群体内业务交流的密切及其凝聚力度。

蜀地出产见于“大夏”，说明“大夏”通过身毒国“得蜀贾人市”的民间商贸通路的确实存在。这种自由贸易形成的商路，虽然当时未被汉帝国执政者利用，却应当是实际畅通的。《西南夷列传》载张骞所谓“身毒国道便近，有利无害”的判断，应当是有可以说服汉武帝的确实依据的。《大宛列传》载张骞所谓“去蜀不远”，“从蜀宜径，又无寇”。这些交通地理知识，应当来自于“蜀贾”的交通实践。言“蜀贾”经济行为之所谓“持窃出市”，所谓“奸出物”“至”，以传统史家立场指出了“蜀贾”谋求商业利润手段违法或说违反制度的性质。然而其开创意识与冒险精神也因此得到反映。⑥

余英时在论说汉地商人在东北边境贸易活动中的积极表现之后，又写道：“在汉帝国向西南扩张的过程中，中国商人起了相似的作用。四川的商人经常非法越过边境去和夜郎进行贸易，他们的贸易行动最终使汉朝政府注意到夜郎地区的军事、政治重要性。结果是，整个西南（今四川之一部以及

① 《史记》卷一一六《西南夷列传》，第2995页。

② 《史记》卷一二三《大宛列传》，第3166页。

③ 《史记》卷一一六《西南夷列传》，第2994页。

④ 常璩撰，任乃强校注：《华阳国志校补图注》，上海古籍出版社，1987年，第69、230页。卷四《南中志》作“〔蒟〕枸酱”，注：“当依《史记》作枸酱。”

⑤ 《资治通鉴》，北京：中华书局，1956年，第1403页。语出《汉书》卷九六下《西域传下》，第3928页，作“枸酱”。

⑥ 参见王子今：《汉武帝“西夷西”道路与向家坝汉文化遗存》，《四川文物》2014年第5期。

云南和贵州）重新向中国开放，好几个蛮夷国家转化成了中国的郡。”“中国与西南夷之间的经济关系在武帝试图开通西南通道之前很久就通过四川的商人而建立起来了。”“由于没有相关记载，我们不知道西南夷是否为了商业目的而去过印度。不过，似乎可以肯定的是，他们中的一些人至少对印度—缅甸—云南贸易通道有所了解。”[①] 也有学者指出，早在“秦汉时官方参与寻求”“西南丝路”之前，“蜀地的商人”以及“缅甸、印度的商人”共同经营着这条道路的“商业活动”。而“蜀地的商人”“早在公元前4世纪”就开辟了这一通路，他们有的在滇越地方驻留，等待外商交易，“有的甚至继续踏上缅印道，或者翻山越岭、渡涉江河，抵达印度平原，或者由伊洛瓦底江航行出海，经海路到印度，与印度和到印度的西方商人交易”。[②]

八 “西夷西”在西南丝绸之路认识中的指向意义

《大宛列传》只言“因蜀犍为发间使，四道并出”，而《西南夷列传》的记载较为具体，说到使节姓名：“王然于、柏始昌、吕越人等”。《史记》卷一一七《司马相如列传》也说到这位“王然于”的事迹：“相如为郎数岁，会唐蒙使略通夜郎西僰中，发巴蜀吏卒千人，郡又多为发转漕万余人，用兴法诛其渠帅，巴蜀民大惊恐。上闻之，乃使相如责唐蒙，因喻告巴蜀民以非上意。”“相如还报。唐蒙已略通夜郎，因通西南夷道，发巴、蜀、广汉卒，作者数万人。治道二岁，道不成，士卒多物故，费以巨万计。蜀民及汉用事者多言其不便。是时邛筰之君长闻南夷与汉通，得赏赐多，多欲愿为内臣妾，请吏，比南夷。天子问相如，相如曰：‘邛、筰、冉、駹者近蜀，道亦易通，秦时尝通为郡县，至汉兴而罢。今诚复通，为置郡县，愈于南夷。’天子以为然，乃拜相如为中郎将，建节往使。副使王然于、壶充国、吕越人驰四乘之传，因巴蜀吏币物以赂西夷。……司马长卿便略定西夷，邛、筰、冉、駹、斯榆之君皆请为内臣。除边关，关益斥，西至沫、若水，南至牂柯为徼，通零关道，桥孙水以通邛都。还报天子，天子大说。”[③] 作为司马相如“副使”者，为“王然于、壶充国、吕越人”，而探求“西夷西”道路的使节，据《西南夷列传》的记载，为“王然于、柏始昌、吕越人等”。而《资治通鉴》卷一八“汉武帝元光五年”写作：“天子以为然，乃拜相如为中郎将，建节往使，及副使王然于等乘传，因巴、蜀吏币物以赂西夷。”卷一九“汉武帝元狩元年”写作：“乃令骞因蜀、犍为发间使王然于等四道并出，出駹，出冉，出徙，出邛、僰，指求身毒国。”突出了“王然于”，略去了“壶充国、吕越人”“柏始昌、吕越人”。此“王然于”显然是一位处理“西南夷”方向边疆与民族问题的专家。据《史记》卷一一六《西南夷列传》，后来“上使王然于以越破及诛南夷兵威风喻滇王入朝”，在汉王朝“以兵临滇”的形势下，“滇王始首善，以故弗诛。滇王离难西南夷，举国降，请置吏入朝。于是以为益州郡，赐滇王王印，复长其民”。[④] 王然于稳定滇国取得了成功。事实上，他“四道并出，出駹，出冉，出徙，出邛、僰，指求身毒国”的交通探索事业，在滇国方向间接取得了进展。“滇王离难西南夷”句，《史记会注考证》：“中井积德曰：‘离难西南夷’五字不通。《汉书》作‘离西夷’三字。颜师古云：谓东乡事汉。愚按‘西南夷’三字，涉下文而衍。‘离难’，滇王

---

① 余英时：《汉代贸易与扩张》，第83、96、98页。

② 胡绍华：《中国南方民族史研究》，北京：民族出版社，2004年，第70—71页。

③ 《史记》卷一一七《司马相如列传》，第3046—3047页。

④ 《史记》卷一一六《西南夷列传》，第2997页。

名。”[1]也许《汉书》“离西夷”之说[2]，是值得思考的。

司马迁写道：“西南夷君长以百数，独夜郎、滇受王印。滇小邑，最宠焉。”又说：“汉诛西南夷，国多灭矣，唯滇复为宠王。”[3]得以“最宠”的原因，或许不仅仅是“始首善”。可能滇国所处于控制往缅甸—印度通道的重要地位，有重要的作用。

就王然于事迹依时序的记录而言，有这样几个时间坐标值得注意。据《资治通鉴》记载：

1. 元光五年（前130），“拜相如为中郎将，建节往使，及副使王然于等乘传，因巴、蜀吏币物以赂西夷”。

2. 元狩元年（前122），“乃令骞因蜀、犍为发间使王然于等四道并出，出駹，出冉，出徙，出邛、僰，指求身毒国”。

3. 元封二年（前109），“初，上使王然于以越破及诛南夷兵威喻滇王入朝。滇王者，其众数万人，其旁东北有劳深、靡莫，皆同姓相仗，未肯听。劳深、靡莫数侵犯使者吏卒。于是上遣将军郭昌、中郎将卫广发巴、蜀兵击灭劳深、靡莫，以兵临滇。滇王举国降，请置吏入朝，于是以为益州郡，赐滇王王印，复长其民”。[4]

汉武帝“使王然于以越破及诛南夷兵威喻滇王入朝”，“未肯听”。“其旁”“同姓相仗”之部“劳深、靡莫”被诛灭后，汉军“临滇”，于是“滇王举国降，请置吏入朝”。“劳深、靡莫”据《汉书》卷九五《西南夷传》。[5]《史记》卷一一六《西南夷列传》作“劳浸、靡莫”：“劳浸、靡莫数侵犯使者吏卒。”[6]所谓“数侵犯使者吏卒”，应当就是前引《西南夷列传》“为求道西十余辈”，而“岁余，皆闭昆明”，即如淳所谓“为昆明所闭道”，于是“莫能通身毒国”的具体原因。

王然于等人自元光五年（前130）至元封二年（前109）之间20年“指求身毒国”的艰苦努力，最终因“滇王举国降”，取得了由滇国往缅甸—印度地方交通联系的局部成功。然而起初“赂西夷”，以及继而包括“西夷西”方向的“四道并出”的探求，并不是没有意义的。

汉武帝最初于“西夷西”方向往身毒国的交通探索，应当有建立在当时交通地理知识基础上的考虑。《西南夷列传》所谓“或闻邛西可二千里有身毒国”，应是起初的直接判断。“邛西”，应当正是“诚通蜀，身毒国道便近”，或说“去蜀不远”，“从蜀宜径”的交通方向。较“南夷”方面经历滇国的路线，这一方向确实也没有地方依恃较强武装力量的民族势力的阻隔，即面对所谓“无寇”，“有利无害”的形势。对于《大宛列传》所谓“从蜀宜径”，余太山有所讨论：“‘从蜀宜径’，《汉书·张骞李广利传》颜注：‘径，直也。宜犹当也。从蜀向大夏，其道当直。’案：张骞在大夏地见到‘蜀物’固系事实，但赴大夏‘从蜀宜径’却只是他的猜度之辞。”[7]其实，考虑“西夷西”“邛西”方向，所谓“从蜀宜径”与“其道当直”，较昆明—缅甸—印度道路而言，显然是有一定的合理性的。

《汉书》卷九五《西南夷两粤朝鲜传》将“西南夷”“两粤”及“朝鲜”三个方向的边疆与民族问

---

① 司马迁撰，泷川资言考证，水泽利忠校补：《史记会注考证校补》，第1864页。

② 《汉书》卷九五《西南夷传》，第3842页。

③ 《史记》卷一一六《西南夷列传》，第2997页。

④ 《资治通鉴》，第685—686页。

⑤ 《汉书》卷九五《西南夷传》，第3842页。

⑥ 《史记》卷一一六《西南夷列传》，第2997页。

⑦ 余太山：《两汉魏晋南北朝正史西域传要注》，北京：中华书局，2005年，第21页。

题的记述合为一传，班固赞曰："三方之开，皆自好事之臣。故西南夷发于唐蒙、司马相如，两粤起严助、朱买臣，朝鲜由涉何。遭世富盛，动能成功，然已勤矣。"[①]是"西南夷""两粤"及"朝鲜"被称作"三方"。有学者指出，《盐铁论·击之》亦称之为"三方"，而《盐铁论·地广》《备胡》及《击之》又三次称此为"三垂"。于是以为"'三垂'或'三方'，西，即西南夷；南，即南越、东越；东，即朝鲜"[②]。"三垂""三方"似是汉代论边疆民族问题习用语。[③]《汉书》卷六〇《杜钦传》："关东诸侯无强大之国，三垂蛮夷无逆理之节。"颜师古注："三垂谓东、南、西也。"[④]《文选》卷八扬雄《羽猎赋》："割其三垂，以赡齐民"，李善注："三垂，谓西方、南方、东方。武帝侵三垂以置郡，故谓之'割'。"[⑤]《汉书》卷二八下《地理志下》："东夷天性柔顺，异于三方之外。"颜师古注："三方，谓南、西、北也。"[⑥]所谓"三垂""三方"其中"西垂""西方"，恐怕"西，即西南夷"的说法是略有不妥的。"西南夷"即"西夷"与"南夷"，称"西垂""西方"，或侧重于"西夷"，如同"南垂""南方"应包括"南越、东越"，但显然是侧重于"南越"的。

还应当注意到，尽管我们看到了比较充备的"南夷"方向滇越路线实现对外文化交流的诸多实证，但是仍然不能排除当时"西夷西"方向往身毒国的交通线路已得初步开拓并有所应用的可能。蓝勇考察"零关道"即"牦牛道"时指出："元狩元年（前122）汉武帝命令张骞从犍为郡发间使四路出使，欲打通巴蜀通身毒道路，其一路便出邛僰（西昌），只是未能如愿。"论者是以"灵关道系古代川滇交通的一条重要交通路线"的思路研究这条"南方丝绸之路的主线"[⑦]之一的，然而"出邛僰（西昌）"是否可能有其他路径"通身毒"，依然值得我们思考。

许多学者根据现有学术信息，重视云南—缅甸—印度通道的意义。但是有些判断，如伯希和认为，"蜀布邛竹杖此种中国西南之出产，似只有缅甸一道可以输出"[⑧]，或许还可以斟酌。有些学者又发表绝对化的论定。如有人说："我认为蜀布邛竹除了取道云南、缅甸、印度而至大夏外，不可能有别的走法。"[⑨]或断言："这条路线只能是从四川盆地中部的成都出发经云南，过缅甸或孟加拉，经陆路入印度或阿富汗等南亚和中亚各国。"[⑩]这样的意见，不大可能完满解释三星堆青铜人像造型以及蜀地发现的早期玻璃器等多种与当地文化渊源不同的文物遗存的真实由来。

也许考虑"西夷西"方向的文化沟通的可能是必要的。今后考古工作的进一步深入，应当可以为这一文化交流路径的历史学探索提供新的信息。

---

① 《汉书》卷九五《西南夷两粤朝鲜传》，第3868页。

② 黎小龙：《〈汉书·西南夷两粤朝鲜传〉三传合一体例与两汉边疆民族思想》，《中国边疆史地研究》2015年第2期。

③ 如《汉书》卷八五《谷永传》："三垂晏然，靡有兵革之警。"（第3451页）《汉书》卷八七上《扬雄传上》："颇割其三垂以赡齐民，……"（第3541页）《汉书》卷九四下《匈奴传下》："唯北狄为不然，真中国之坚敌也，三垂比之悬矣，……"（第3815页）《汉书》卷八七下《扬雄传下》："《玄》三方、九州、二十七部、……"（第3575页）

④ 《汉书》卷六〇《杜钦传》，第2671页。

⑤ 萧统编，李善注：《文选》，第130页。

⑥ 《汉书》卷二八下《地理志下》，第1658页。

⑦ 蓝勇：《南方丝绸之路》，重庆：西南大学出版社，1992年，第16、12页。

⑧ 伯希和：《交广印度两道考》上卷，冯承钧译，北京：中华书局，1955年，第10—11页。

⑨ 桑秀云：《蜀布邛竹传至大夏路径的蠡测》，收入段渝主编：《南方丝绸之路研究论集》，成都：巴蜀书社，2008年，第110页。

⑩ 颜信：《古蜀与中亚经贸交流考》，《中华文化论坛》2013年第12期。

The Problem of “Xi Yi” or the “West of Xi Yi” and the Exploration of Han Wudi’s Search for a Way to India

Wang Zijin (Renmin University of China)

Abstract: Both of the *Records of the Grand Historian* Volume 113 – *Dawan Commentary Section* and Volume 113-- *the Southwestern Nation*（西南夷）*Commentary Section* record that Zhang Qian considered there was a road from the west of Qiong（邛西）to Hindu（身毒国）according to the information of Western Region. They could get in touch with Tochari easily by this way. So the Emperor Wudi of the Han Dynasty sent messengers to find Hindu(身毒国）by passing the path in the west of Xi Yi(西夷西). The records of *Han Shu* Volume 95-- the *Southwestern Nation*（西南夷）*Commentary Section* is different—the messengers would be passing the path in the Southwestern Nation（西南夷）.Some researchers of the *Records of the Grand Historian* take the view of that the messengers would be passing the path in the west of Xi Yi（西夷西）.But the others take the view of that the messengers would be passing the path in the Xi Yi（西夷）,finding Hindu（身毒国）by heading the western way. We should analyze and differentiate this question. This is not only a vital event in the traffic history of the Han Dynasty, but also a vital event in the history of cultural intercourse between China and other countries. Because the west of Qiong（邛西）and the west of Xi Yi（西夷西）were the regions of ethnic diversities, the messengers'traffic behavior is important both to the research of Silk Roads' history and border area history , national history.

Keywords: Zhang Qian; Emperor Wudi of the Han Dynasty; Xi Yi（西夷）; the west of Xi Yi（西夷西）; go and find Hindu（身毒国）

粟特语的再发现

[英]辛维廉(伦敦大学亚非学院)撰
付马(北京大学)译,毕波(中国人民大学)校

以今日乌兹别克斯坦撒马尔干(Samarkand)为中心的粟特地区和当地古代的居民粟特人,自古就闻名于世。在西方,粟特人因公元前4世纪亚历山大大帝的远征而渐为希腊人所熟知。在东方,中国与粟特地区的交往至迟始于前2世纪,一直持续到晚唐以降;其间,粟特人以商胡闻名于汉地。不论中土、西洋,皆有古典文献传世而不绝,是故粟特人之名未尝湮灭。然而,曾在沟通中西的商路上广泛流行的粟特语则几乎无迹可寻。

本讲分为两节。在前一节,我将介绍粟特研究的开端,包括:首批发现的粟特语文书和铭文、粟特文的破译、粟特语的比定,以及为理解这种新发现的语言奠定了基础的最初的文献整理。在后一节,我将较为细致地讲解最古老的一批粟特铭文和文书及其对于研究粟特人的历史、粟特人与中国的关系史的重要价值。

粟特语的重新发现在一定程度上始于德裔俄国学者里尔希(P. Lerch)。他在19世纪60—70年代间对于一些前伊斯兰时代布哈拉钱币上的粟特铭文进行了部分解读。1876年,他在圣彼得堡举办的第三届国际东方学家大会上发表其研究成果。里尔希应当是将这些铭文称为"粟特语"的第一人。他对于铭文的解读仍有可取之处:尤其是他读出了第一个词是"布哈拉"(Bukhara),第二个词是粟特语的"主人"或者"统治者";当然,我们现在已经知道他对一些字母的解读是错误的。

遗憾的是,这些布哈拉钱币铭文过于简短而不足以展现粟特语的全貌。而接下来发现的材料则是内容远为翔实(但保存不佳)的粟特语碑文——1889年于蒙古高原发现的九姓回鹘可汗碑三语铭文。现在我们已知此三语分别是汉语、鲁尼文突厥语和粟特语,而碑文内容则记8至9世纪间回鹘诸可汗的武功军威和其他功业,尤其是第三任可汗尊摩尼教为国教之事。晚近以来,此碑已为学者深入研究,尤以哈密顿(J. Hamilton)、森安孝夫和吉田豊三位贡献最多,使碑文内容大体昭于世人。然而,直到1909年,人们才发现此碑上的第三种语言是粟特语①;而在那以前,这种语言一直被误以为回鹘文突厥语,因此此碑的发现对于粟特语的再发现和解读没有任何贡献。

粟特研究的真正开始实则源于吐鲁番探险活动。俄国探险队自1879年开始的一系列探险活动使世人得知吐鲁番地区存有古代遗址和写本残片。在19世纪90年代中期,一支俄国探险队将一些写本残片样本带回圣彼得堡,其中恰有一件出自吐峪沟的粟特文残片;但其在当时尚不能被世人解读,竟也没有引起任何关注(直到1980年该残片才被刊布)。② 但是,一些国家的学者却已然留意到俄国人

---

① F. W. K. Müller, "Ein iranisches Sprachdenkmal aus der nördlichen Mongolei", *SPAW (Sitzungsberichte der Preussischen Akademie der Wissenschaften)*, 1909, S. 726-730.

② A. N. Ragoza, *Sogdiyskie fragmenty central'noaziatskogo sobraniya Instituta Vostokovedeniya*, Moscow, 1980, pp. 76-77, 89, Pl. LXIX.

对于吐鲁番盆地前伊斯兰时代的古物的报告，大规模的探险活动也随之开始筹划。其中最为重要的是德国的四次吐鲁番探险，第一次发生在1902—1903年间。众所周知，在这次探险的收集品中包括大量以一种当时尚不为人所知的文字书写的写本残片，而这种文字又明显是源出阿拉美文，且在许多方面与福音体叙利亚文相似。这种新文字很快便被缪勒（F. W. K. Müller）所破解，他在1904年将最早的研究成果以两文刊出。[①]他的这些研究成果震惊世人。缪勒不但成功地破解且几乎无误地释读了这种文字，而且还判断出这些残片的内容是摩尼教文献，而摩尼教文献在当时被认为佚失已久。此外，缪勒发现出自吐鲁番的摩尼教写本是由数种不同语言写成的，包括突厥语、中古波斯语、新波斯语和另外一种被他权且称为“中古波斯语方言”的伊朗语。在缪勒1904年刊布的写本中有一件双语文书（M 172）就是以标准的中古波斯语和这种所谓的“中古波斯语方言”写就的，而文书的内容则是先知摩尼本人的著作《彻尽万法根源智经》（*Living Gospel*）中的一段。现在我们已知，所谓的“中古波斯语方言”正是粟特语，而这件文书就是第一件被刊布的粟特文书。除提供了写本的转写之外，缪勒还尝试初步的翻译并做出了语法注解。这主要得益于中古波斯语平行文本的存在。中古波斯语在当时已多见于婆罗钵文（Pahlavi）琐罗亚斯德教文献，且与现代波斯语差别不大，并不难解读。据这件文书的刊布来判断，我认为1904年应当算作粟特研究创立之年，而缪勒应当是粟特研究的奠基人。当然，另有一位学者也有足够的理由被称为粟特语的发现者，他就是安德列斯（F. C. Andreas），他是将缪勒所谓的“中古波斯语方言”认定为粟特语的第一人。

缪勒和安德列斯均是极具天赋的语言学家，皆通晓多种东方语言，但是他们的工作方式则多有不同。其中一点便是：缪勒写作和发表文章的速度很快，而安德列斯几乎不发表。安德列斯为人所知的许多研究成果都是在其身后由他的学生发表的，他的许多最伟大的学术发现却仅能从其他学者文章中所援引自他的通信或是口头交流的记录中得见。很典型的例子就是他将缪勒所谓“中古波斯语方言”比定为粟特语一事仅仅体现在缪勒1904年第二篇文章的一条注释当中[②]；之后不久，在1907年，缪勒又在一条脚注中提到安德列斯曾在其担任东方语文学教授的哥廷根科学院做过有关此事的演讲，但这次演讲的内容似乎从未公开发表。[③]1908年，缪勒又在一条脚注中首次公开了安德列斯比定出粟特语的过程。[④]他援引了一段安德列斯的谈话，安德列斯称其比定的基础在于比较这种摩尼教写本的语言与比鲁尼（al-Beruni）的著作中所征引的粟特语语料。比鲁尼是伟大的穆斯林博学者，生于973年，卒于1048年。他曾用阿拉伯语著有诸多关于科学和古物的著作。他常在书中引用其他语言的科技术语，这些语言包括埃及语、叙利亚语和梵语，也包括各种伊朗语，譬如波斯语、粟特语以及他的母语花剌子模语。这里特别要指出的是，比鲁尼在其名著《东方民族编年史》里列举了许多语言中一年中的12个月和一月中的30日的名称，其中就包括粟特语。这部著作在19世纪末叶已由德国学者扎豪（E. Sachau）整理并译出。安德列斯注意到比鲁尼所引的粟特语词形有两个特征：古代伊朗语的 **θr* 在粟特语中变作 *š*（或者 *xš*），**b* 则变作 *x*。由于同样的音变规律也见于缪勒所谓的“中古波斯语方言”

① F. W. K. Müller, “Handschriften-Reste in Estrangelo-Schrift aus Turfan, Chinesisch-Turkistan”, [I], *SPAW*, 1904, S. 348-352; II, Anhang zu den *APAW* (*Abhandlungen der Preussischen Akademie der Wissenschaften*), 1904.

② 上引第111页；M 172号文书刊布在上引第100—103页。

③ F. W. K. Müller, *SPAW*, 1907（见第88页脚注⑤）, 260 n. 2.

④ F. W. K. Müller, “Uigurica [I]”, *APAW*, 1908, No. 2, 3 n. 3.

中，安德列斯判定这种语言就是粟特语。正如缪勒所指出的，比鲁尼所列的粟特语月份名称与摩尼教文书残片中所见的月份名称完全吻合，这充分印证了安德列斯的判断。整体而言，粟特语的月份与其他语言的皆不相同[①]，只有少数月份名称与其他伊朗语同源，所以这几乎已是铁证。

安德列斯另一伟大贡献也是由他的同行，而非他本人公布于世的。他发现至今仍有人在使用的雅格诺比语（Yaghnobi）实源出一种粟特语方言。只有很少一些人在说这种语言，他们生活在位于撒马尔干以东、杜尚别以北的遥远的雅格诺布河谷地区。1870 年，雅格诺比语由俄国旅行家库恩（A. L. Kuhn）首次记录下来；其后陆续有其他旅行家追随库恩的足迹，并公布了一些简短的词汇和词形变化表。安德列斯发现了粟特语与雅格诺比语之间的密切联系，这个发现由缪勒在 1907 年首次公布于世。在一条脚注中，缪勒提及了两种语言的词汇之间的若干对应关系，正是这些内容使得安德列斯认定这两种语言有密切关系；缪勒还补充了自己找到的一些新例。单从两种语言有类似的月份名称这点也足见两者之间的密切联系，世上尚没有第三种语言有如此特别的一套月份名称。[②]

安德列斯对粟特研究的贡献散见在他日常的通信和谈话中，而缪勒则通过不断地推出力作来记录他的研究成果。1904 年，正当缪勒忙于解读德国第一次吐鲁番探险带回柏林的摩尼教写本时，德国的第二次吐鲁番探险已在勒柯克（A.von Le Coq）的率领下开拔。1905 年，勒柯克的助手巴图斯（T. Bartus）运气很好，在吐鲁番以北 10 公里处的葡萄沟（Bulayïq）遗址掘得一大批叙利亚文基督教写本。今日我们已知该遗址曾是一座基督教修道院。精选的一些照片被寄回柏林，照片上的文字立即由扎豪（即前面提及的比鲁尼《东方民族编年史》的编译者）刊布。[③] 扎豪刊布的写本多为叙利亚文景教礼拜文献，但有一件却是以叙利亚文书写的粟特语文献。扎豪虽只识得这件写本当中的若干词汇（这件写本在粟特文写本中实属极难释读的一件，直到 1985 年才有完整的整理和翻译问世[④]），但却能判断出写本的语言就是缪勒所谓的“中古波斯语方言”。

扎豪在 1905 年发表文章，首次刊布了这种新型的粟特语文献。这种文献在内容上属基督教题材，而非摩尼教；在书写上则以叙利亚文为载体，而非摩尼文。但由于写本内容未能被解读，他的刊布在当时并没有起到推动粟特语研究的直接作用。缪勒则又一次走在了引领学术进步的前列。不久，他就在葡萄沟所获的写本中比定出若干叶译自叙利亚语伯西托本（Peshitta）《圣经》的粟特语《新约》写本。其中数叶写本是双语本，先写一节叙利亚语原文，再写一节粟特语译文，双语交替出现。当 1907 年缪勒刊布这批基督教粟特语圣经文献之时，他恰如其分地称其为理解粟特语的“钥匙”。[⑤] 由于当时叙利亚语已被很好地解读，而粟特语译本又是严格按照原文的措辞来翻译的，所以写本中粟特语部分的几乎每个词和每个语法结构都在理论上可以被解读。

缪勒于 1907 年 3 月在柏林科学院的演讲中首次讲述了他对粟特语《圣经》文献的比定。同年同

---

① 参见 W. B. Henning, “Zum soghdischen Kalender”, *Orientalia,* 8, 1939, pp. 87-95, 文中将粟特文书中出现的历法术语与比鲁尼书中所记一一比对。

② F. W. K. Müller, *SPAW*, 1907（见本页脚注⑤），261 n. 3. 另参见 C. Salemann, “Manichaica II”, *Izvestiya Imperatorskoy Akademii Nauk*, 1907, pp. 531-558, 文章第 532 页提到安德烈斯就此事而写的一封信。

③ E. Sachau, “Litteratur-Bruchstücke aus Chinesisch-Turkistan”, *SPAW,* 1905, pp. 964-978.

④ N. Sims-Williams, *The Christian Sogdian manuscript C2* (Berliner Turfantexte, 12), Berlin, 1985, pp. 69-77.

⑤ F. W. K. Müller, “Neutestamentliche Bruchstücke in soghdischer Sprache”, *SPAW*, 1907, pp. 260-270. 缪勒后来将新约文献结集为《粟特文书》一（“Soghdische Texte I”, *APAW*, 1912, No. 2.）刊布。

月，斯坦因（Aurel Stein）成为第一位亲赴敦煌莫高窟第 17 窟藏经洞的欧洲人。据叶昌炽日记所记，藏经洞在 1900 年即被发现，而在斯坦因到来之前，已有一大批汉文卷子、梵文贝叶写本和绢画被取走。① 但是斯坦因和次年到来的伯希和（Paul Pelliot）却应当是首批攫取粟特文写本之人。

敦煌藏经洞的发现为粟特语研究再开一源。当时已经被解读的或者将要被刊布的吐鲁番出土的粟特语写本均为摩尼教或者基督教文献，要么以摩尼文书写，要么以叙利亚文书写。敦煌发现的粟特语写本则大多为佛教文献，以另一种文字书写——一种粟特人在其本土所使用的文字。今天我们就直接称这种文字为“粟特文”。这种文字相对易读，因为它与书写回鹘语的文字基本相同。吐鲁番文书与敦煌文书的另一重要的不同是后者在整体上保存得更好。吐鲁番文书多为残片，少有整叶，更不见全书。而一部分敦煌出的粟特写本保存有很大篇幅的文字，多达数百行，甚至千行。一些写本几乎保存完整，譬如其中最早被刊布的写本之一《佛说善恶因果经》。

斯坦因携带其从敦煌所获的写本于 1909 年回到伦敦，但是他在寻求高明人士解读这些粟特语写本时却并不顺利。起先，这些粟特语卷子被当作回鹘语，卷子照片被寄往罗斯（E. D. Ross）处求解。罗斯判定文献语言是粟特语，并自告奋勇要求释读这些卷子，但为斯坦因回绝，盖因罗斯并无相关专业知识。② 相反，这项工作被交付给了柏林的缪勒。缪勒也确实有所推进，他利用自己的汉文知识比定出汉文《维摩诘所说经》（*Vimalakīrtinirdeśa-sūtra*）和《观世音菩萨秘密藏如意轮陀罗尼神咒经》（*Padmacintāmaṇidhāraṇī-sūtra*）两经的粟特语译本；但是直到多年以后，方才有正式的出版物刊出，这在一定程度上是因为缪勒忙于整理刊布吐鲁番出土的粟特语和回鹘语写本。伯希和则顺利得多，他获得了一位年轻的伊朗语专家高迪奥（R. Gauthiot）的大力帮助。自 1911 年起，高迪奥开始稳定高产地发表与伯希和带回巴黎的敦煌粟特语写本有关的文章。在他最早的文章里，高迪奥探讨了粟特字母的发展历史，上起其阿拉美文的源头，下至其后来在草体回鹘文中所呈现的面貌。③ 次年，即 1912 年，他又成为首位刊布佛教粟特语文献的学者，刊布了两种文献。一种是《长爪梵志请问经》（*Dīrghanakha-sūtra*）。这是一部简短但完整的作品，高迪奥在佛学家列维（S. Lévi）的帮助下得以比定出粟特语译本的母本是 8 世纪早期义净所译的汉文本。④ 另一种是《太子须大拏经》（*Vessantara Jātaka*）。这是一部长篇叙事文学作品，不似从汉文本或者其他语言已知的本子直接翻译而来，而应当是作者以粟特语复述这则佛教徒耳熟能详的佛陀前世的故事。⑤ 作为故事而非经文，即使在没有已知语言平行文本参照的情况下，《太子须大拏经》也相对比较容易理解；又由于写本尚存有 1800 多行文字，它为世人提供了第一份道地的粟特语句法的翔实样例，而没有基督教文献中那些因为曲意迎合叙利亚语母本的语序而造成的失真。

如果我们把 1904 年，即第一件粟特语文献被刊布的年份，当作粟特语重新被发现的标志，粟特语研究的第一个十年应当说是在 1913—1914 年高迪奥的《粟特语语法》的第一部分付梓之际结束

① Rong Xinjiang, “Ye Changchi: Pioneer of Dunhuang Studies”, *IDP News*, 7, 1997, pp. 1-5.

② U. Sims-Williams, “Behind the scenes: Some notes on the decipherment of the Sogdian manuscripts in the Stein Collection”, *Exegisti monumenta. Festschrift in honour of Nicholas Sims-Williams*, Wiesbaden, 2009, pp. 469-478, esp. pp. 473-476.

③ R. Gauthiot, “De l’ alphabet sogdien”, *Journal Asiatique*, 10th series, 17, 1911, pp. 81-95.

④ R. Gauthiot, “Le sutra du religieux ongles-longs”, *Mémoires de la Société de Linguistique de Paris*, 17, 1912, pp. 357-367.

⑤ R. Gauthiot, “Une version sogdienne du Vessantara Jātaka”, *Journal Asiatique,* 10th series, 19, 1912, 163-193, pp. 429-510.

的。① 在1914年第一次世界大战爆发之际，这本书仅有少量印本得以发行；直到1923年，这一册书才全面发行。因此，此书正式的出版年份写成了“1914—1923年”。然而，此书其实写就于1913年。如此皇皇之作能够在当年完成，距离第一件简短的粟特语文献刊布尚不足十年，充分反映出这一领域在当时发展进步之迅猛。

到此为止，我已经谈了摩尼文粟特语、叙利亚文粟特语和粟特文粟特语文献的发现和解读的经过。但是所有这些文献的年代都属于粟特语历史上非常晚的时期，主要是8世纪和9世纪。而我们知道到那时粟特语已经被文字记录了数百年之久。因此，现在我要开始本次演讲的第二部分——最早的粟特语铭文和文书。

最早也是最重要的粟特语文书，即所谓的“古信札”，是斯坦因在靠近玉门关的一处烽燧遗址中发现的。② 这些书信不仅是最早的，也是最重要的了解粟特商人在中国活动的粟特语文献。信是出自中国西部的粟特商业聚落内部成员之手，其中至少有一封是发自姑臧（粟特语 *k'cn*），两封发自敦煌当地（*δrw'n*）。唯一一封收信地址尚存的是发往撒马尔干的，其他几封可能是发往楼兰或从敦煌到撒马尔干交通路线上某地。没有直接证据表明为何装有这些信的邮包被弃置于此。最有可能的推测是，出于安全考虑这些信被人没收了。

2号信中保留了一些有关当时中国形势的内容：如在洛阳（粟特语 *sry*）发生的一次导致皇帝逃离国都的饥馑，还有匈奴人（*xwn*）和汉人（*cyn*）之间的战争，以及洛阳及邺（粟特语 *'nkp'*，来自早期中古音 *ŋiap*）的被劫掠。根据这些细节，恒宁（W. B. Henning）推断这组信肯定是写于307年邺城和311年洛阳被洗劫事件发生后的一两年之内，葛乐耐（F. Grenet）和我完全支持其看法，并补充了一些资料。③

这批信札对于考察这一时期粟特商人在中国的活动情况提供了很多信息。不过遗憾的是，由于语言学方面的解读困难及信件原件保存状况不佳，信中的很多细节仍不是非常清楚。最为典型的表现就是仅有以下几种商品能够被明确比定出来：金（*zyrn*）、麝香（*yxs-*）、荜拨（*pδ'pδ[y]h*）、龙脑（kprwh）、大麻或亚麻制成的布（*kynpwyn'k*）以及小麦（*''δwkh*）。过去大家以为古信札中没有提到丝绸，如果确是如此的话，那也一定是由于保存下来的内容有限所致，因为丝绸无疑在这一时期的东西方贸易中扮演了重要角色（即使“丝绸之路”这一概念当时尚未被提出）。但最近我已经能够证明在6号信中出

---

① R. Gauthiot, *Essai de grammaire sogdienne,* I, Paris, 1914-1923.

② 对“古信札”迄今唯一全面的整理刊布，参见：H. Reichelt, *Die soghdischen Handschriftenreste des Britischen Museums, II,* Heidelberg, 1931, 但今已过时。其中4封信已被重新整理：1号信札，参见：N. Sims-Williams, “Towards a new edition of the Sogdian Ancient Letters: Ancient Letter 1”, *Les sogdiens en chine,* Paris, 2005, pp. 181-193；2号信札，参见：N. Sims-Williams, “The Sogdian Ancient Letter II”, *Philologica et Linguistica. Historia, Pluralitas, Universitas. Festschrift für Helmut Humbach*, Trier, 2001, pp. 267-280；4号信札，参见：N. Sims-Williams, “The Sogdian Ancient Letter No. 4 and the Personal Name Manavaghichk”, *Estudios Iranios y Turanios,* No. 3. Homenaje a Helmut Humbach en su 95o aniversario, 2017, pp. 171-179；5号信札，参见：F. Grenet, N. Sims-Williams and É. de la Vaissière, “The Sogdian Ancient Letter V”, *Bulletin of the Asia Institute*, 12, 1998 [2001], pp. 91-104. 1、2、5号信札的汉文翻译，参见：尼古拉斯 • 辛维廉撰，Emma Wu 译：《粟特文古信札新刊本的进展》，收入荣新江、华澜、张志清主编：《粟特人在中国——历史、考古、语言的新探索》(《法国汉学》第10辑)，北京：中华书局，2005年，第72—87页；毕波：《粟特文古信札汉译与注释》,《文史》2004年第2辑，第73—97页。

③ W. B. Henning, “The date of the Sogdian Ancient Letters”, *Bulletin of the School of Oriental and African Studies*, 12/3, 1948, pp. 601-615; F. Grenet and N. Sims-Williams, “The historical context of the Sogdian Ancient Letters”, *Transition periods in Iranian history,* Leuven, 1987, pp. 101-122.

现过两次的 pyrcyk 很可能就是粟特语用来表示丝绸的一个词汇。①

有关古信札其他方面的内容，我曾另撰一文详述，读者可参看笔者英文初稿和汉文修订稿②，我不再赘述。下面我想介绍另一组早期粟特文献，它们远不如古信札那般为人熟知。

古信札早在 1907 年就被发现，而我现在要探讨的这组文献的出土时间则比古信札要晚了将近一个世纪。那是在 2006 年 2 月，我从葛乐耐处首次听说哈萨克斯坦南部发现了一些烧制泥砖或泥板，其上以源自阿拉美字母的文字刻有铭文。这批文物皆出自波杜什金（A. Podushkin）教授主持的位于阿雷斯（Arys）河谷的库尔托贝（Kultobe）遗址的发掘活动。遗址之所在恰是汉文文献中所谓的康居古国境内。第一件带有铭文的碎片发现于 1996 年。此后几乎每年都有新的发掘，迄今已获得 14 件碎片，最近的一件出土于 2011 年。最早的一批文物已经在 2000 年发表于波杜什金教授有关（古代）哈萨克斯坦南部古代"阿雷斯文化"的专著中③，但在当时却并未引起广泛关注。

库尔托贝遗址位于河南岸，由一座戍堡（在 20 世纪 40 年代因河流改道而大部被冲毁）和一座带有城防的地势较低的城市构成；似乎该遗址是沿阿雷斯河向西直到讹答剌（Otrar）的防御体系的一环。库尔托贝以及同一地区的其他遗址显示出相同的文化特征，这种文化被遗址的发掘者波杜什金命名为"阿雷斯文化"。该文化或曾兴盛千年，自前 4 世纪存续至 6 世纪。部分刻有铭文的泥板与该文化中被称为"黑丘"（Karatobe）时期的陶器有关联，根据与其密切相关的当地许多游牧民族墓地的外来商品，这一时期可以被断代在 1—4 世纪之间。根据这些遗址的年代和地理位置，似可确定它们应与汉文史料中的"康居"国（或联盟）有关。康居曾长期称雄于阿姆河以北，并在前 2 世纪至 4 世纪之间与中国通使往来，而这段时间恰好在波杜什金给"阿雷斯文化"的断代内。

迄今已知几乎所有带有铭文的残片均出自遗址的西部、靠近阿雷斯河故道的岸边，河水曾冲毁戍堡的大部。根据葛乐耐最先提出的假说，这些有铭文的泥板可能是被用来装饰城墙或者城门大道。铭文皆在泥板烧制之前写上。一些铭文是很小的断片，仅存数词或者数字，但至少还有两方砖存有足够翻译成句的文字。

与这些铭文一同出现的是两个问题：铭文是何种文字？铭文所记为何种语言？铭文的文字显而易见是源自阿拉美文（Aramaic），阿拉美文不但用来书写阿拉美语，也曾用来书写阿黑门尼帝国（Achaemenian empire）境内流行的几乎所有的中古伊朗语。我们很容易认出其中的一些阿拉美文字母；同样可以很容易认出一些阿拉美语词汇。但是，这些阿拉美词汇并不能说明这种语言就是阿拉美语，因为书写中古伊朗语言的特点是，大量词汇使用阿拉美语的词汇作为表意符来替代伊朗语言的同一词汇。④

关于字体，可以看到一些字符的形状具有粟特文字的显著特征，而与其他各种中古伊朗语的字体

---

① N. Sims-Williams, "Towards a new edition of the Sogdian Ancient Letters"（参见第 90 页脚注②）, p. 182.

② N. Sims-Williams, "The Sogdian merchants in China and India", *Cina e Iran da Alessandro Magno alla dinastia Tang* (Orientalia Venetiana, V), Florence, 1996, pp. 45-67（重印于 V. Hansen, ed., *The Silk Road: Key papers*. Part I: *The Pre-Islamic Period*, Vol. 1, Leiden, 2012, pp. 241-255)；（汉文本）尼古拉斯·辛维廉著，毕波译：《中国和印度的粟特商人》，收入周伟洲主编：《西北民族论丛》第 10 辑，北京：中国社会科学出版社，2014 年，第 32—56 页。另可参见：É. de la Vaissière, *Sogdian Traders: A history*, Leiden, 2005, esp. Chapter 2.

③ A. N. Podushkin, *Arysskaya kul'tura Yuzhnogo Kazakhstana (IV v. do n.è. - VI v.n.è.) [The Arys culture of Southern Kazakhstan (4th century B.C.E. - 6th century C.E.)]*, Turkestan, 2000.

④ 可参考书面日语中使用汉字作为意符的情况。

迥然有异。同时应注意到，一些字形显得尤为古朴，例如 samekh，尤其是 he，更甚于其在古信札中的字形。一些正字的使用也是古朴的，例如，[θ] 音和阿拉美文一样以字母 tau 来表示，而不是像在其他粟特文文献那般用字母 lamedh 来表示。尤其是，库尔托贝铭文中出现的阿拉美语文意符和音写的比例与其他粟特文文献中的情况截然不同；后来的粟特文文献主要是以阿拉美字母音写粟特语，仅有少量意符出现，用来表示最常用的词汇；而在库尔托贝铭文中则含有大量阿拉美文意符，以致铭文乍看好似阿拉美文。这些语言和字体上的特征皆显示库尔托贝铭文所写确是粟特语，但是年代明显要早于 4 世纪初的古信札。遗憾的是，目前很难给出一个更为精确的定年。

如前所述，库尔托贝遗址迄今所出的铭文大都仅存片段。其中只有两件记有足够的连续字句，可以整体解读。第一件是 2 号铭文，文字简短，但内容几乎完整①：

1 （ZNH）(k)nth w（β…）	此城……属于
2 （c）'c' nn' pc	石国人民的
3 （s）p'δ ny CWRH	军队领袖
4 （H）WH	本人

这篇铭文中的 7 个词，至少有 2 个是新出现的词。一个是表示系动词的意符 HWH。另一个是表示“将军”的 sp'δny。这是一个合成词，字面意思为“军队首领”。它与形容词 c'c'nn'pc（曾见于一些石国钱币上）一起出现，意为“石国（Chāch）人民的军队领袖”。库尔托贝遗址几乎就在塔什干（Tashkent）的正北，塔什干之名正是取自古代石国。但是在上古时代，石国的都城所在可能是更南方的甘卡（Kanka）遗址。假定我将第一行的 knth 读作 kanθ（粟特语“城市”，在晚期粟特文中写作 knδh）是正确的，则铭文的目的在于声明库尔托贝城是属于石国人民的军队领袖的私产。

最为重要的铭文是 4 号铭文，共有 7 长行（但各行左侧均残）：

1 ZNH knth 'BDt sp'δny (c)[………ZKn………]
2 BRY ZY šwtt TMH KZY ZY [………………]
3 'P ZK n'p ḤLYK 'P ZK wδ'nn'p[ḤLYK ....]
4 ZK symrkntc MR'Y 'P ZK k[š'yk MR'Y 'P ZK]
5 nxšpyk MR'Y 'P ZK nw(k!)my[tn MR'Y 'PZYš]
6 ZK GNZ KL' LK Ḥt 'P ZK・[....... 'P ZK ....]
7 （空白）ḤLYK NP(Š)[H/Y（空白？）]

此城是由石 [……] 的军队领袖，[……] 之子所建立。他前往（？）那里，因此〔我们的〕人民所分得的〔土地〕和游牧民所 [分得的土地] 都 [可能是……；而] 萨末建（Samarkand）之主、

① 所有的库尔托贝铭文（除了最新发现的铭文）的编辑整理见于两篇论文中：N. Sims-Williams and F. Grenet, “The Sogdian inscriptions of Kultobe”, *Shygys*, 2006/1 [2007], pp. 95-111; N. Sims-Williams, F. Grenet and A. Podushkin, “Les plus anciens monuments de la langue sogdienne: Les inscriptions de Kultobe au Kazakhstan”, *Comptes rendus de l'Académie des Inscriptions et Belles-Lettres,* 2007 [2009], pp. 1005-1034.

佉[沙(Kish)之主]、那黑沙不(Nakhshab)之主和忸[密(Nawakmethan)之主同意(?);而他(?)]将所有的财富、[……,以及……]分得的(土地据为)己有。

与2号铭文相同,4号铭文也以“此城”开头。在同行往下不远处又见“军队领袖”字样。如果此句的动词被读作意为“造”“建”的意符(*‘BD*),则“军队领袖”显然是用以指称此城的创立者。尽管文中没有挑明,但我们可以联想到此处提到的这个将军应与2号铭文中所提到的“石国人民的军队领袖”是同一个人。第二行开头有*BRY*“儿子”一词暗示了第一行末所缺失的部分或许有他的名字和他父亲的名字。

在第三行又有一个有趣的新词:合成词*wδ’nn’p*,意为“帐中百姓”,即“游牧民族”。此处的“帐中百姓”与另一仅被称为*n’p*“百姓”的群体相对。“百姓”当指“我们自己人”或者“定居民族”。释读这一段的关键是意符*ḤLYK*。此词可能表示闪米特语词根*ḤLQ*“分配”的被动分词,在此处作名词意指“分配的结果、部分”,则此数行似乎意指游牧民和粟特居民间的领地划分。我们从这里可以获得的信息恰好与考古发现相印证。考古发掘显示库尔托贝等带有城防的聚落与附近的游牧民族墓葬遗址年代相同,且均出土有同样形制的陶器和其他的手工制品。

铭文的第二部分列举了数个粟特小国君主的名字,他们都在一定程度上参与了石国将军的活动。文中以表示族群名称的形容词的形式出现4个粟特城市名称,其中2个保存完好。一是symrknt,即萨末建(康国);一是*nxšpy*或*nxšp*,即那黑沙不,这是今日之卡尔希(Qarshi)城在上古和中古时代的名称。还可复原一个名称*k[š’y]*为Kishāy,即粟特语之佉沙(*Kish*),亦即今日的沙赫里萨布兹(Shahrisabz)。此名的释读推测成分颇多,但是1号铭文和10号铭文的内容可以在一定程度上印证这种读法,它们都是4号铭文的副本。在这两则铭文断片中,形容词*kishâyîk*(“属于佉沙的”)和4号铭文一样出现在专有名词*Nawak-mēthan*(直译为“新的居住地”)之上。此地是布哈拉绿洲古代的都城,其名见于汉文文献,作“忸密”。据此,我们几乎可以肯定4号铭文列举了粟特地区中、南部的四大城市(撒马尔干、布哈拉、佉沙和那黑沙不)的统治者的名号。

我们不禁要问:这些统治者在远离他们自己王国的地方做什么呢?很遗憾,相关的动词已缺失,它可能原本就在第三行末尾的空缺之处。但是,我们也可以推测他们派遣了士兵或者移民去帮助石国民众向北方扩张粟特人的势力。最后一句话的主语是谁,同样不清楚。究竟是四国的统治者,还是石国人民的将军将财宝和土地占为己有?从语法的角度看,两者都有可能。

自我发表对这些铭文的首次释读以来,又有3则铭文断片在最近几季的发掘中出土。现存的字句足以证明新出的12号、14号铭文是之前发现的2号铭文的副本。其内容是对城市所有权的陈述,与2号铭文的内容吻合:这样的语句或许复刻了多次,并被置于城市的不同位置。最后,我必须要提一下13号铭文断片。13号铭文并非像其他铭文一样出土于戍堡下游的沉积层,而是出土于城址的低处。被发现时它平置地面上,显然这不是它的原先所在的地点。城址低处发掘出土的陶器属于1—4世纪,则我们应知一些铭文在很早的时候便被从原先所在的位置移走。这则铭文的内容也是一个副本(或内容较接近正本的副本),其正本则是很长的4号铭文。唯一的不同在于四座粟特城市的名字以不同的方式被列出,萨末建名列其次,而非第一。

既然我们已经发现这些铭文中有为数甚多的内容重复的情况,就有必要去考虑是否其他的铭文也是这样的。5 号铭文就有可能与 4 号以及 13 号铭文内容相同：

1	]w（n）w（n）[	……获胜的（？）……
2	Z]K n' p [	……人民……
3	]' P Z(K)[	……和……
4	]MR(')[Y	……君主……

5 号铭文中残存的词的出现顺序完全与 4 号铭文中出现的一致，除了第一行的 wnwn。此词意为“胜利的”，它也是一个常见名字和命名因素，恰如英语名字 Victor，而且在一些晚期的石国钱币的铭文上，它以石国统治者的名字出现。如果 5 号铭文确实与 4 号铭文内容一致，则 Victor 肯定是石国将军之名，抑或是其父之名的一部分，这两个名均在 4 号铭文的残缺之处缺失。

直到不久以前，我们所知的康居国几乎都源于汉文史籍如《史记》和《汉书》的记载。现在，这些记载可以与库尔托贝铭文以及波杜什金在哈萨克斯坦南部不断发掘的考古资料相互比对。此外，我通过毕波博士的一篇论文[①]获悉，有关康居的最新重要信息还见于一些敦煌附近悬泉置所出汉简上。这些汉简从多个角度证实了汉文史籍所记之准确，比如康居遣使入贡汉朝之事。一则简文提到康居使者与苏薤（即粟特）使者一起入贡，在《汉书》所记康居所辖“五小国”中，苏薤为第一。

尽管对“五小国”的比定尚困难重重，但是毕波提出的将其与库尔托贝铭文上所列的粟特城邦进行比对的建议却颇有见地。无论如何，我们现下至少已经拥有了最新的、粟特本土所出的材料印证了汉文史料对于康居的记载。

① 毕波：《考古新发现所见康居与粟特》，收入张德芳主编：《甘肃省第二届简牍学国际学术研讨会论文集》，上海古籍出版社，2012 年，第 99—109 页。

从出土汉简看敦煌太守在两汉丝绸之路上的特殊作用

张德芳

（出土文献与古代文明研究协同创新中心中国人民大学中心）

摘要： 张骞开通西域后，汉武帝“列四郡，据两关”，河西走廊成为丝绸之路的必经之地。作为最西端的敦煌郡以及地方最高行政长官的敦煌太守，除了日常行政管理外，还在军事防御、物质保障以及对西域东部地区的管理方面，为两汉丝绸之路的畅通做出了特殊贡献。在军事上，南北两线的军事设防长达600多公里，相较其他郡县更见其军事任务的繁重；在物质上，仅提供沿途驿站传置的食宿供应就是一笔数量巨大的开支；在对西域的管理上，西域东部的伊循屯田和车师屯田，敦煌太守也时有公文下达及直接管理的事例。所有这些都说明，当时地处丝绸之路沿线的国家或地区，其地位、作用、影响力是不一样的。敦煌郡之所以能承担如此重要的使命，背后则是朝廷的支持和国家的强盛。

关键词： 丝绸之路；敦煌郡；敦煌太守；汉简；西域

张骞开通西域后，汉武帝“列四郡，据两关”，敦煌郡处在东西交通关键点上。而作为地方最高行政军事长官的敦煌太守，自然承担和发挥了特殊的使命和作用。随着近百年来地下汉简材料的大量发现和实地考察，大大丰富了我们对上述事实的认识。本文结合传统史料和出土汉简，从军事、政治、财政等多个方面对敦煌太守在两汉丝绸之路上的特殊作用做一些初步论述，以求就教于学界同仁。

一

两汉的太守职责，除了正常的行政公务，即“信理庶绩，劝农振贫，决讼断辟，兴利除害，检察郡奸，举善黜恶，诛讨暴残”①外，还要掌管驻郡部队的训练，“会都试，课殿最”，“行障塞烽火追虏”。②边郡告急，太守还要带兵打仗。按照汉制，内地各郡在太守之下设郡都尉，一郡一个，专管军队之事，属于地方部队的性质。河西各郡地处边防，郡太守之下设部都尉，数量不限一个，而是两个、三个、四个不等，属于边防野战部队的性质。敦煌郡特殊，有四个都尉，即玉门都尉、中部都尉、宜禾都尉和阳关都尉。

由于敦煌地区地处广漠戈壁，特殊的自然地理环境和千百年来地广人稀的特点，使得两汉时期遗留下来的汉塞烽燧、城障遗址等格外丰富，直到今天，人们还可在千里河西走廊上看到连绵不绝的汉塞烽燧，这在全国全世界都是仅有的现象。还由于从1907年斯坦因在敦煌边塞掘得第一批出土汉简

① 孙星衍等辑，周天游点校:《汉官六种》，北京：中华书局，1990年，第20页。

② 同上，第48页。

以来，敦煌所发现的大量汉简大都与当年的军事驻防有关。甘肃是汉简大省，全国 80% 以上的汉简都出自甘肃。而甘肃汉简又几乎全部出自河西（甘谷汉简 23 枚除外），河西所出汉简又以敦煌为最。从广义上来讲，所有 6 万多枚河西汉简，都与当年的丝绸之路密切相关，其中很大一部分汉简就是军事屯戍的内容。第三个原因是，近代科学考古学兴起以来，尤其是 1949 年以后，对敦煌地区的考古调查受到了格外重视，除了那些日常的零星调查和有名的发掘外，还有如《疏勒河流域汉代长城考察报告》《河西汉塞调查与研究》[①]，都是对河西汉塞遗迹的全面调查，对了解汉代敦煌地区的军事设防，极具参考价值。还有第四方面的原因，就是第三次文物普查对每一处不可移动的遗址遗迹利用 GPS 技术进行了定点描述。所有这些，都使我们对汉代敦煌郡的军事防御和敦煌太守的军事职责有了更清楚的认识。当时敦煌地区的军事驻防，每个都尉管辖的防区和防线，下属几个候官、候部和烽燧，都有充分确凿的材料来加以说明。甚至我们今天看到的静默了几千年的大部分汉代烽燧，当年叫什么名字，先后有哪几位戍卒驻防，他们分别来自何方，曾经发生过什么事情，等等，都可以得到相当程度的描述。

当年的敦煌郡包括今天的敦煌市、瓜州县和玉门市，加上南北两山和西部沙漠，大致有十多万平方公里的土地。[②] 河西四郡是向西延伸出的一支臂膀，北部要防止匈奴的入侵，南部要防止羌人的袭扰，南北两面都要防守。而四郡中，敦煌郡的防线最长。敦煌郡北部自西向东，玉门都尉下辖大煎都、玉门两个候官；中部都尉下辖平望、破胡（后改为步广）、吞胡、万岁四个候官；宜禾都尉下辖宜禾、鱼泽、昆仑、美稷、广汉五个候官。从敦煌西部榆树泉盆地的广昌燧（40° 07′ 38.80″ N，93° 08′ 22.30″ E）到瓜州桥湾东 2 号烽燧（40° 33′ 39.70N″，96° 52′ 40.50″ E），直线距离 320 公里。敦煌郡的南部还有阳关都尉，负责敦煌西部和南部的防御。阳关都尉的详细情况我们还不太清楚，只知道可能有雕秩候官和博望候官等。南部的防御任务虽然没有北部那样严峻，但防线仍然很长。如果按北部 320 公里计算，敦煌的南北防线就有 600 多公里（还未将西部计算在内）。这样漫长的边境防线，决定了两汉时期敦煌郡特殊的军事位置。劳榦、陈梦家、永田英正、李均明等中外学者在研究居延汉简时对甲渠候官的部、隧数量和人员规模进行过考证。李均明的结论最为近似，他认为甲渠候官通常情况下有吏卒约 400 人左右。[③] 参照这一规模，敦煌郡十多个候官应有常驻吏卒 5000 多人。当然比起万骑大郡来，不算驻军最多的。所谓“边郡太守各将万骑，行障塞烽火追虏”也只是个说法，实际各郡都未必真有万骑。史书记载说：“元朔三年，以上郡、西河为万骑太守，月奉二万。绥和元年，省大郡万骑员秩，以二千石居。”[④] 敦煌郡属边地，从人口数量看，只是个小郡。按始元二年的人口统计，当时的上郡有户 103683 户，人口是 606658 人。西河郡有户 136390 户，人口 698836 人。而敦煌只有 11200 户，38335 人。人口是上郡的 1/16 左右，是西河的 1/18 左右。[⑤] 而这样一个小郡，驻 5000

① 岳邦湖、钟圣祖：《疏勒河流域汉代长城考察报告》，北京：文物出版社，2001 年；吴礽骧：《河西汉塞调查与研究》，北京：文物出版社，2005 年。

② 今天的行政划界大有变动，敦煌、瓜州、玉门有国土面积 7 万平方公里左右，两汉时上述地区的界线向南、北、西延伸很长，实际面积要比现在大得多。

③ 劳榦：《居延汉简考证之部》，见《中研院历史语言研究所集刊》第 30 本上册，1959 年，第 404—407 页；陈梦家：《汉简所见居延边塞与防御组织》，《汉简缀述》，北京：中华书局，1980 年，第 63 页；永田英正：《居延汉简研究》，张学锋译，桂林：广西师范大学出版社，2007 年，第 372 页；李均明：《汉代甲渠候官规模考》，《文史》第 34、35 辑，北京：中华书局，1992 年。

④ 孙星衍等辑，周天游点校：《汉官六种》，北京：中华书局，1990 年，第 49、82 页。

⑤ 梁方仲：《中国历代户口、田地、田赋统计》，北京：中华书局，2008 年，第 22—23 页。

人的军队，足见其军事任务的繁重。

敦煌太守所属之军队不仅要负责平时的边塞防守，战时还要集中调派，出征打仗。西汉时典型的事件就是西羌反叛时，朝廷不仅派后将军赵充国前往金城弹压，还命令破羌将军辛武贤率兵六千一百人，敦煌太守快率兵二千人，酒泉侯冯奉世等率兵四千人配合作战。悬泉汉简中就有这次参战的记录：

简一：

御史中丞臣强、守侍御史少史臣忠昧死言：尚书奉御史大夫吉奏丞相相上酒泉大守武贤、敦煌大守快书，言二事：其一事，武贤前书穬麦皮芒厚，以廪当食者小石三石，少不足。丞相请郡当食廪穬麦者石加

（Ⅰ91DXT0309③：221）

简长23厘米、宽1.5厘米，中间起脊两面坡形，一般称之为两行，胡杨。有字81个。从字面看，是御史大夫丙吉、丞相魏相通过御史中丞强和守御史少史忠上给皇上的一份奏书，或者是已经皇上“奏可”后下发的一份诏书。内容是酒泉太守辛武贤和敦煌太守快一起上书朝廷，涉及两件事情。一是谈到当时发放戍卒的粮食按规定每月小石三石，但所发穬麦因为皮厚有芒，份量不足。请求朝廷批准，每石再加发若干（简文在“石加”后结束）。第二件事写在另一简上，因未找到相应的下文，我们还不得而知。

简文中涉及的人有七位：御史中丞强、守御史少史忠、尚书（缺名）、御史大夫吉（丙吉）、丞相相（魏相）、酒泉太守武贤（辛武贤）、敦煌太守快。敦煌太守快的任职时间在神爵元年至四年（前61—前58）。[①] 酒泉太守辛武贤在神爵元年（前61）下半年至次年上半年大致有一年的时间出任破羌将军，神爵二年（前60）下半年又回到酒泉太守任上（或者在担任破羌将军期间，仍领酒泉太守）。魏相于地节三年（前67）任丞相，死于神爵三年（前59）。御史大夫丙吉亦于地节三年上任，到神爵三年接魏相为丞相。这四个人以其所任官职在简文上相交之时只在神爵元年至二年（前61—前60），所以此简内容所反映史实正当此时。当时羌人反叛，朝廷调六万兵马派赵充国西进之际，酒泉太守辛武贤和敦煌太守快亦在奉调之列。此简的内容，当与此次平羌战争有关。或者在此前，说明正为此而厉兵秣马；或者在此后，说明正在处理善后，医治战乱的创伤。[②]

总之，当时的敦煌太守不仅负责驻防边疆，而且遇到战事还要领兵打仗，这在传世史籍和出土汉简中都可得到论证。至于到东汉，中原与西域“三绝三通”，敦煌太守直接出兵西域、处理西域事务的事例就更多了。[③]

---

① 张德芳：《两汉时期的敦煌太守及其任职时间》，收入《简牍学研究》第5辑，兰州：甘肃人民出版社，2014年，第176页。

② 前揭拙文认为：“此简所言史实或者在神爵元年上半年，或者在神爵二年下半年。但神爵元年上半年羌事正炽，赵充国率兵进驻金城，作为酒泉太守的辛武贤正上书朝廷同赵充国就对羌作战问题一论高下，一个主张速战速决，一个主张屯田积谷，似乎还来不及注意到一石矿麦因皮厚芒长而不足数的问题。所以此事的可能性当在神爵二年下半年。羌事结束后，面对对羌作战中发现的一些弊端诸如粮食发放不足数等问题向朝廷提出了改善的建议。”

③ 王宗维：《汉代河西与西域之间的相互关系》，《新疆社会科学》1985年第3期；刘光华：《论东汉敦煌在中原与西域关系中之重要地位》，收入《1983年全国敦煌学术讨论会文集（文史遗书编）》，兰州：甘肃人民出版社，1987年，第27页。

二

敦煌太守在一些特定的时期，还对西域一些地区进行过直接管理。在东汉的情况已有王宗维、刘光华等先生发文论述过。[①] 至于在西汉尤其是西域都护府建立（前 60 年）前，由敦煌太守直接管理伊循屯田，就是一个典型的例子。

元凤四年（前 77），朝廷派平乐监傅介子刺杀楼兰王，“乃立尉屠耆为王，更名其国为鄯善，为刻印章，赐以宫女为夫人，备车骑辎重，丞相将军率百官送至横门外，祖而遣之。王自请天子曰：‘身在汉久，今归，单弱，而前王有子在，恐为所杀。国中有伊循城，其地肥美，愿汉遣一将屯田积谷，令臣得依其威重。’于是汉遣司马一人、吏士四十人，田伊循以填抚之。其后更置都尉。伊循官置始此矣”[②]。

伊循所处，是丝绸之路南道上的必经之地。所谓“自玉门、阳关出西域有两道。从鄯善傍南山北，波河西行至莎车，为南道”[③]。鄯善的伊循屯田，是汉朝继轮台、渠犁屯田以后的又一处重要战略基地。所以由先期的司马一人、吏士四十人发展到后来的都尉驻屯。鄯善国都扜泥城，一般认为即今婼羌的乞尔其都克古城。那么伊循屯田之处何在？一般认为在今婼羌东北 60 多公里的米兰古城周围。尤其在今新疆生产建设兵团 36 团东南部二三公里处发现了古代的灌溉渠道，由一条总干渠、七条支渠、若干斗渠、毛渠组成的灌溉网络[④]，可能就是汉代屯田留下的遗迹。持此观点的学者较多，林梅村还亲自做过考察并著有专文。[⑤] 但是孟凡人《楼兰新史》认为，“LK 古城似为伊循故城”[⑥]。其地理坐标在北纬 40° 5′ 37.18″，东经 89° 40′ 4.98″。于志勇则认为 LE 古城可能是汉代的伊循城，其位置在北纬 40° 38′ 39.28″，东经 90° 7′ 0.65″。[⑦] 魏坚认为伊循屯田的第一阶段即“司马一人，吏士四十人”时期，所驻伊循城当在 LK，后来发展到伊循都尉屯田时期，所驻地点当在 LE 古城。[⑧] 王炳华《伊循故址新论》则仍然认为西汉的伊循屯田区只能在米兰绿洲上。[⑨] 看来这个问题还要继续讨论下去。

不管伊循城的具体地望在哪里，不影响我们下面的论述，即伊循的屯田在相当一段时间内，行政上属敦煌太守管理。

根据出土汉简，学术界对此问题已有过相当研究并提出过精到的见解。[⑩] 我们在这里继续补充一些相关材料并做一些分析。

---

① 王宗维：《汉代河西与西域之间的相互关系》，《新疆社会科学》1985 年第 3 期；刘光华：《论东汉敦煌在中原与西域关系中之重要地位》，收入《1983 年全国敦煌学术讨论会文集（文史遗书编）》，第 27 页。

② 《汉书》卷九六上《西域传上》，北京：中华书局，1962 年，第 3878 页。

③ 《汉书》卷九六上《西域传上》，第 3872 页。

④ 马雍：《从新疆历史文物看汉代在西域的政治措施和经济建设》，《文物》1975 年第 7 期；陈戈：《新疆米兰灌溉渠道及相关的一些问题》，《考古与文物》1986 年第 3 期；新疆维吾尔自治区编：《新疆维吾尔自治区第三次全国文物普查成果集成·巴音郭楞蒙古自治州卷》，北京：科学出版社，2011 年。

⑤ 林梅村：《1992 年秋米兰荒漠访古记》，《中国边疆史地研究》1993 年第 2 期。

⑥ 孟凡人：《楼兰新史》，北京：光明日报出版社，1990 年，第 110 页。

⑦ 于志勇：《西汉时期楼兰“伊循城”地望考》，《新疆文物》2010 年第 1 期，第 63—74 页，收入《西部考古》第 7 辑，西安：三秦出版社，2013 年。

⑧ 魏坚、任冠：《楼兰 LE 古城建置考》，《文物》2016 年第 4 期。

⑨ 王炳华：《伊循故址新论》，《西域文史》第 7 辑，北京：科学出版社，2012 年，第 221—233 页。

⑩ 李炳泉：《西汉西域伊循屯田考论》，《西域研究》2003 年第 2 期；贾丛江：《西汉伊循职官考疑》，《西域研究》2008 年第 4 期。

简二：

敦煌大守遣守属冯充国上伊循城都尉□印绶御史
以令为驾二封轺传　七月庚午食时□□ □
五凤元年五月戊午朔戊寅受敦煌大守常乐丞□谓□□
□□□驾当舍传舍如律令

（Ⅰ 91DXT0309 ③：193）

木牍，长 23.3 厘米，宽 1.3 厘米，红柳。简文分两栏书写，有三个部分。有些看不清楚的□尚可补释。“敦煌大守常乐丞□”可补释为“敦煌大守常乐丞贤”。因为“敦煌大守常乐丞贤”一起签署的文件还见于另一元凤元年的简文中。“□□□驾当舍传舍如律令”，按照一般过所文字的惯用语词，可补释为“以令为驾当舍传舍如律令”。如此，全简可如此句读：“敦煌大守遣守属冯充国，上伊循城都尉□印绶。御史以令为驾二封轺传。五凤元年五月戊午朔戊寅，敦煌大守常乐丞贤谓□□，以令为驾，当舍传舍如律令。七月庚午食时□□□。”简中“五凤元年五月戊午朔戊寅”，五月二十一日，公元前 57 年 6 月 30 日。“七月庚午”：七月丁巳朔，庚午为十四日，8 月 21 日。此简内容是敦煌太守开具的一份过所文件的录副，意思是派守属冯充国将伊循都尉印绶上交朝廷，要求沿途各地按照规定给予乘车和住宿方面的接待。是年，匈奴中“五单于争立”，是否影响到了西域，不得而知。伊循屯田区发生了什么事情，何以要把“伊循城都尉”的印绶上交朝廷亦无法考实。但是上交印绶的这件事情由敦煌太守来承担，似乎不是偶然的。这跟当时伊循城都尉的隶属关系有关，实际上是敦煌太守领属伊循屯田的一个重要证据。

简三：

七月乙丑敦煌大守千秋长史奉憙守部候脩仁行丞事下当用者小府伊循城都尉守部司こ马こ官候移县置广校候郡库承书从事下当用者如诏书／掾平卒史敞府佐寿宗

（Ⅴ 92DXT1312 ③：44）

此简中间起脊，两面坡形。长 23.5 厘米，宽 1.3 厘米，胡杨。字迹比较清晰，分两行书写，69 字。简文的时间，可从“敦煌大守千秋长史奉憙”的记载来追寻。敦煌太守千秋和长史奉憙根据悬泉汉简的记载，他们俩搭班子的时间从甘露二年（前 52）到初元二年（前 47）差不多六年时间。而在这六年中，七月有“乙丑”的历日一是甘露四年（前 50），一是黄龙元年（前 49），还有初元二年（前 47）。除了初元二年是新旧太守交替的时间外，此简所记“七月乙丑”，只能在上述两个年份。简文内容是敦煌太守逐级下达皇帝诏书的例行公文。全文句读应是：“七月乙丑，敦煌大守千秋、长史奉憙、守部候脩仁行丞事：下当用者小府、伊循城都尉、守部司马、司马官候，移县置、广校候、郡库：承书从事下，当用者如诏书。掾平、卒史敞、府佐寿宗。”从这份下发诏书的行文范围看，伊循城都尉显然在敦煌太守的管辖之内。

简四：

史安世丞博德下郡县官伊循城承书从事下当用者□□
令亡人命者尽知之期尽上赦者人数大守府罪别之□□□

（Ⅰ 90DXT0110 ④ : 4）

两行，上部断残。残长 16.9 厘米，宽 1.4 厘米，上部残缺 6 厘米左右，松木。这是一份朝廷赦令的下达文件。按照已见的文例和格式，它的完整形式应该是：“（某年某月某某朔某某，敦煌太守某、长）史安世、丞博德下郡县官、伊循城，承书从事下当用者，（书到）（白大扁书乡亭市里高显处）令亡人命者尽知之，期尽，上赦者人数。大守府罪别之（如诏书）。”意思是，敦煌郡所属郡县官署以及伊循城都尉，接到朝廷诏书后，要将赦令内容公布在乡亭市里高显处，让那些身负命案而在逃的人都能知道。在一定期限内由太守府上报该赦免的罪犯（或者该赦免的罪犯名单已经下发太守府），按诏书要求办理。

在这一诏书赦令的下达中，我们仍然可以看到，伊循城的隶属在敦煌太守的管辖中。

简五：

伊循城都尉大仓上书□

（Ⅱ 90DXT0114 ④ : 349）

断简，残长 5.8 厘米，宽 0.9 厘米，松木，存字 9 个。

简六：

敦煌伊循都尉臣大仓上书一封□
甘露四年六月庚子上　　　　□

（Ⅱ 90DXT0216 ③ : 111）

断简，残长 6.1 厘米，宽 1 厘米，松木，存字 22 个。

简七：

□敦煌伊循都尉大仓谓过所县□
□传舍从者如律令　　　　□

（Ⅰ 90DXT0111 ② : 73）

木牍，上下均残，残长 7.8 厘米，宽 2 厘米，松木，存字 19 个。

简八：

□伊循城都尉大仓谓过所县□
□舍传舍从者如律令　　　□

（Ⅴ 92DXT1312 ③ : 6）

木简，上下残断，残长 6.7 厘米，宽 1.2 厘米，松木，存字 19 个。

上列简五和简八虽都残断，但都记录了伊循都尉大仓的相关活动。前两简是伊循都尉给朝廷上书途经敦煌悬泉置时留下的记录。后两简是伊循都尉为其派往京师的人员开具的过所经过悬泉置时留下的记录。四枚断简发掘时分别出自不同的探方，不在一处。简六有时间，“甘露四年六月庚子”，即农历六月二十四日，公元前 50 年 8 月 15 日。上列四简中有两简直接作“敦煌伊循都尉”，由此引发了学界的关注。李炳泉认为“敦煌伊循都尉”具有敦煌所领部都尉和属国都尉的双重性质。而贾丛江认为，“敦煌伊循都尉”属敦煌太守领导下的部都尉，类似于其下属的玉门都尉、阳关都尉之类。但不管怎么说，他们意见的共同点就是，此时“敦煌伊循都尉”隶属于敦煌太守。①

我们引列上述简文的目的在于进一步说明，当时的敦煌太守，不仅要管理敦煌六县的日常行政、领导玉门等四个都尉驻防南北六百多公里的漫长边界、把守阳关和玉门关的边关要地，还在相当一段时期里管理伊循的驻军和屯田。就其行政职责看，肩负的责任更为重大，在当时的中西交通和丝绸之路上发挥的作用更特殊。

三

在经济上，敦煌郡及敦煌太守承担了来往于丝绸之路上各类人员的食宿交通等的接待。其中食物的供应，就是一笔重大开支，是经济上对丝绸之路的特别贡献。

睡虎地秦墓出土的《秦律十八种》和张家山汉简的《二年律令》，都有《传食律》一章。根据当时的规定，朝廷的官员使者巡行出使，沿途厩传要根据其身份地位提供食宿接待。而接待消费要由官府承担。② 敦煌郡有九座类似悬泉置的传置机构，它不仅接待朝廷官员，更重要的是接待行进在丝绸之路上东来西往的各国使者。其中的《康居王使者册》中所记载的康居王使者、苏薤王使者来京师路过酒泉时未得到认真接待而上告到朝廷的情况就是典型的例子。③ 根据悬泉置遗址出土的大量这方面的材料，没有发现过路的官员使节吃饭住宿用车后支付费用的记载。显然，这笔巨大的开支要由地方政府来承担。特别之处就在于，敦煌地处边郡，凡西域、中亚、西亚、南亚来汉使者都要当外国使节来对待。尽管西域都护府设立后，西域（今天山南北的新疆地区）的大片土地已毫无疑问地属于汉王朝所有，但汉朝对西域都护府与内地郡县的管理是采取不同的两种制度。西域各小国来汉，同样受到较内地一般官员更隆重的接待。

从汉简材料看，接待外国使者和朝廷出使西域（广义的西域包括中亚、西亚和南亚地区）的官员，除了米、粟、麦等日常饭食外，还必须要有酒肉。而每饭提供酒肉，这在当时的生活条件下，是一种特殊的礼遇。

---

① 李炳泉：《西汉西域伊循屯田考论》，《西域研究》2003 年第 2 期；贾丛江：《西汉伊循职官考疑》，《西域研究》2008 年第 4 期。

② 参见赵岩：《论汉代边地传食的供给——以敦煌悬泉置汉简为考察中心》，《敦煌学辑刊》2009 年第 2 期。

③ 郝树声：《简论敦煌悬泉汉简〈康居王使者册〉及西汉与康居的关系》，《敦煌研究》2009 年第 1 期；《汉简中的大宛和康居》，《中原文化研究》2015 年第 2 期。

简九：

出钱九十，买肉十八斤。以食使者卜君所将外国从者九人，人再食。积十八食，食一斤

（Ⅰ 90DXT0114 ③ : 8）

木简，完整，长 23.4 厘米，宽 0.7 厘米，红柳，存 32 字。此简是敦煌悬泉置接待外国客人时用钱买肉的账目。出钱九十买肉十八斤，肉价是每斤五钱，但简中未说明肉类，是牛肉还是羊肉，不得而知。汉代的度量衡，每斤等于 245 克左右，约今天市斤的半斤。

简十：

出钱百廿，买肉廿斤，斤六钱。以食扜弥、龟慈王使者四人，积八食，食二斤半斤

（Ⅱ 90DXT0113 ② : 39）

完整木简，长 23.8 厘米，宽 0.9 厘米，红柳，存 30 字。出钱买肉招待扜弥王和龟兹王使者的账单。一共四个人，吃了两顿，每顿十斤。每人每顿两斤半，约等于 610 克。肉价是每斤六钱。

简十一：

右出钱四百七十，买肉九十四斤。以食外国王使者、贵人从者卌四人，人再食。

（Ⅱ 90DXT0215 ③ : 26)

完整木简，长 23.5 厘米，宽 0.8 厘米，红柳，存字 30 个。亦为悬泉置出钱买肉招待外国客人的账单。出钱四百七十买肉九十四斤，肉价是每斤五钱。被招待的外国客人四十四人，吃两顿，每人每顿吃 260 克左右，相当于今天的半斤左右。

简十二：

出钱七十二，买肉十二斤。以食使者姚君所送□□□

（Ⅱ 90DXT0216 ③ : 82）

残简一枚，残长 13.4 厘米，宽 0.8 厘米，红柳。这是一枚残简，下部两侧已削去。能释读的字只有 18 个。但仍可看到当时的肉价和买肉的用途。七十二钱买肉十二斤，肉价是每斤六钱。被招待的姚君等人是送客者，也可能同时包括了被护送的外国客人。

简十三：

出　米四升　肉二斤　酒半斗　以食乌孙贵姑代一食西

（Ⅱ 90DXT0314 ② : 355）

完整木简，长 23.4 厘米，宽 0.9 厘米，红柳，存字 20 个，分三栏书写。句读应是：“出米四升、肉二斤、

简一

简二

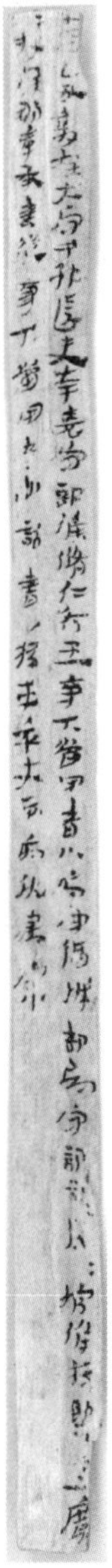
简三

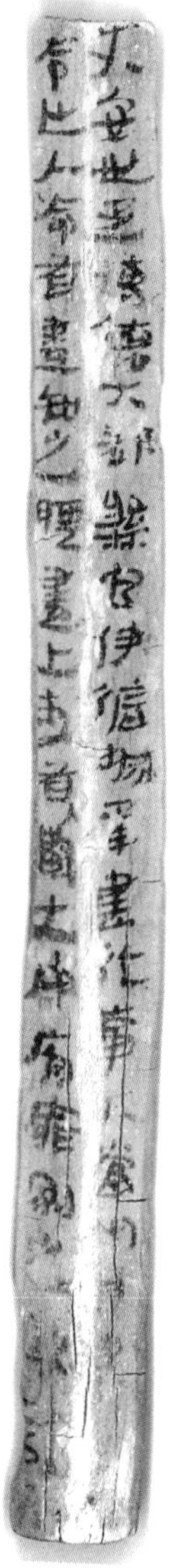
简四

简五

简六

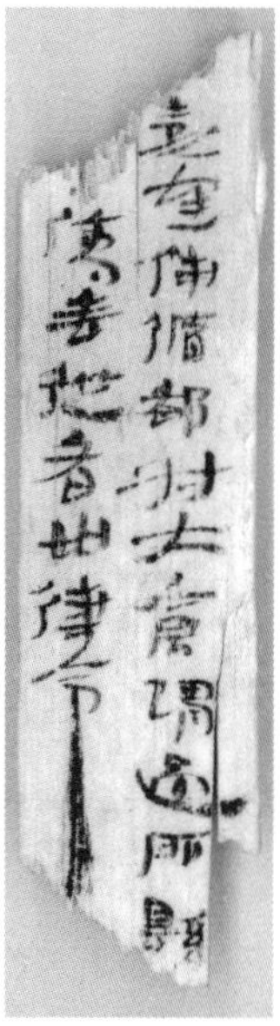
简七

简八

简九

简十

简十一

简十二

简十三

酒半斗。以食乌孙贵姑代，一食，西。”字数虽少，但记录完整。一位乌孙的贵人，名叫姑代，出使中原后从京师回国。路过敦煌悬泉置时，吃了一顿饭，消费米四升、肉二斤、酒半斗。简文“贵”后夺一“人”字。

简十四：

使者贵人百八十九人，用肉千八百七十二斤。A

且末人廿斤，少卌斤·凡少千二百七十三斤。B

（Ⅴ 92DXT1309④：25）

木牍，长22.9厘米，残宽1.1厘米。两面书写，字迹清晰，但内容不完整。正面是“使者贵人百八十九人，用肉千八百七十二斤”，每人用肉十斤左右。背面是“且末人，廿斤，少卌斤·凡少千二百七十三斤”，因为左边残缺，文义不完整。但所招待的“使者贵人”很清楚，在汉简中都指西域诸国客人。而且这次招待的人数规模较大，共189人。不管是累积的人次，还是单独一次的人数，规模都不能算小。用肉1872斤，还少1273斤，用今天的公斤折算，前者是458公斤之多，后者是312公斤左右，这在当时的悬泉置都是一个庞大的数字。

简十五：

疏勒肉少四百廿七斤直千…… 酒少十三石直…… □ A

且末酒少一石直…… □ B

（Ⅴ 92DXT1813③：24）

木牍，残长17厘米，宽1厘米，左边残缺，松木。下部字迹漫漶，两面书写。正面记疏勒肉少若干，酒少若干，需钱多少。背面记且末酒少若干，需钱多少。简文是一种省略的记法，不是说疏勒、且末本身少多少酒、缺多少肉，而是说疏勒、且末等国的客人路过敦煌悬泉置时，还需筹办多少酒肉。同上简所记内容一样。

简十六：

使者廿三人再食 用米石八斗四升
用肉百一十五斤
用酒四石六斗

（Ⅴ 92DXT1309③：20）

木牍，完整，长23.5厘米，宽1.3厘米，红柳。字迹清晰，两栏书写。第一栏一行七字；第二栏三行二十字。二十三人吃两顿饭，用米一石八斗四升，每人每顿四升；肉百一十五斤，每人每顿用肉二斤半，612.5克；用酒四石六斗，每人每顿一斗。

简十七：

六人乘传，当食酒肉。案厨毋见酒、牛羊肉、肉脯□□，唯廷调给。

（Ⅰ 91DXT0309 ③ : 187）

木简，完整。长 23.2 厘米，宽 0.9 厘米，红柳，存字 24 个，其中两字□□未释。按照当时的规定，“乘传”是四马驾的车，不同于一马二马所驾轺传，所以“乘传”者当有一定身份。另从“当食酒肉”看，很可能是接待外国使者。简文说，厨中无现酒，牛羊肉及肉脯也需县廷调给。

简十八：

使者校尉三人食用粺铁干粱饭雉兔牛羊肉鱼以□所食为故

（Ⅴ 92DXT1510 ② : 1）

木简，完整，长 23.6 厘米，宽 0.9 厘米，红柳。存字 25 个，其中一字以□表示。此简为悬泉置招待过往西域官员的记录。使者校尉，是前往屯田渠犁的军官。《汉书·西域传》：“自贰师将军伐大宛之后，西域震惧，多遣使来贡献，汉使西域者益得职。于是自敦煌西至盐泽，往往起亭，而轮台、渠犁皆有田卒数百人，置使者校尉领护，以给使外国者。”[①] 从此简出土的层位看，该层共出纪年简 16 枚，从神爵四年（前 58）到建始四年（前 29），前后 30 年时间，大部分在建昭年间。因此简文时间应该在此段时间及其前后。至于“使者校尉三人”是东来还是西往，看不出来。使者校尉是朝廷派往西域的高级官员，比二千石。所以路过时的招待应有尽有，甚为丰富。主食是“粺铁干粱饭”。“粺”是相对于粝米的一种精米。至于“铁干粱饭”是否与“粺”连读，尚难判断。“铁干”在悬泉汉简中多次出现，有“白铁干粟”“铁干若白糳饭”“铁干粟”“铁干米”“铁干上米”等，似是一种加工更为精细的米。肉类有雉、兔、牛、羊，还有鱼。雉是野鸡，可能是广漠戈壁中一种重要的肉食来源；兔是野兔还是自养，不得而知，很可能也是野物。牛羊是当时主要的肉食种类。鱼是捕捞物。当时的河西及其敦煌比起现在来，散布着更广阔的水域，捕鱼是生机来源之一。简文中没有记载接待这些人的消费数量，但提供的品类则相当丰富。

简十九：

	都护丞以下卅一人	用稗米一石八斗六升直五百五十八
最	吏士妻子私从者二百八人	用粝米十六石二斗一升直二千四百卅
	凡二百卅九人〻再食	用肉八斤直卅二
	积四百七十八食	用果茹百六十一斤直七百九十八
		用酱五斗二升直二百一十
		用盐二石三斗直百七十二

（Ⅱ 90DXT0314 ② : 362）

---

① 《汉书》，第 3873 页。

完整木牍，长23.5厘米，宽2厘米，红柳，存字110个。一份招待西域都护下属人员的总账。顶端一个“最”字，下面分三栏书写。第一栏四行，第二栏五行，第三栏一行。“最”是总计的意思。《史记·卫将军骠骑列传》：“最大将军青凡七出击匈奴，斩捕首虏五万余级。”司马贞《索隐》：“最，谓凡计也。”稗米，当为粺米。稗与粺，古字通。《说文·米部》：“粺，毇也。”段玉裁注：“粺者，粝米一斛舂为九斗也。”也就是说，简中的“稗米”实际是一种比较精细的米。粝米，比粺米较粗的一种米。果茹，当为瓜果蔬菜。简中都护丞以下吏士31人，妻子和私从者208人，总共239人，路过吃两顿饭，用去粺米、粝米、肉类、蔬菜瓜果、酱、盐等若干。这是内宾，没有酒，只用了八斤肉。但这笔消费仍不算小，共4200钱。

上述从简九至简十九，我们集中列举了中外官员和使者路过悬泉置时为其提供接待的特殊账单，一本“酒肉账”。朝廷的官员出使西域除上列简十八、十九以外，最典型的还有《悬泉置元康五年正月过长罗侯费用簿》，简文已有发表，并有多篇论文讨论，原简不再列举。[①]但《长罗侯费用簿》中，列举的食物种类仍然是值得关注的。包括牛肉、羊肉、鸡、鱼、酒以及粟、庚（羹）、豉、酱、鞠（麯）等，主副食和酒肉多达十种以上。

两汉丝绸之路的盛况是：“使者相望于道，一辈大者数百，少者百余人。”“汉率一岁中使者多者十余，少者五六辈，远者八九岁，近者数岁而反。”[②]外国商客来汉的情况是“驰命走驿，不绝于时月。商胡贩客，日款于塞下”[③]。如何接待好丝绸之路上的过往客人？朝廷有规定，地方有义务。作为边关地区的敦煌郡则首当其冲，承担了巨大的物质保障方面的经济责任。上面所列悬泉置的接待账目，只是悬泉置一个置的情况。而当时的敦煌郡有九个类似的接待机构，而每个接待机构的费用开支，都要由敦煌太守统一筹措，这就是我们要说的敦煌太守在物质保障方面为丝绸之路所做的特殊贡献。

总之，我们从军事驻防、行政管理到物质保障等方面，论述了敦煌太守在丝绸之路保障方面所起的特殊作用。旨在说明当时的丝绸之路，东到洛阳、西安，西到中亚、西亚、南亚和地中海沿岸，在无数的经过站点中，每个站点的作用，以及它们对丝绸之路的贡献和丝绸之路对其自身的影响，是不一样的，不平衡的。敦煌地区尤其特殊。尽管目前对“丝绸之路”的概念，言人人殊，对其内涵的宽严有不同的理解。本文所讲的两汉“丝绸之路”，主要指汉王朝与中亚、西亚、南亚和地中海沿岸一带的经济文化交流，以官方外交为主，以朝贡贸易为主。而在这个过程中，丝绸之路沿线的各个国家，其地位和作用是不一样的。谁起主导作用？取决于谁在世界格局中的整体实力。

---

① 张德芳：《〈长罗侯费用簿〉及长罗侯与乌孙关系考略》，《文物》2000年第9期；袁延胜：《也谈〈过长罗侯费用簿〉的史实》，《敦煌研究》2003年第1期；初昉、初师宾：《悬泉汉简拾遗（七）》，收入《出土文献研究》第15辑，上海：中西书局，2016年。

② 《汉书》卷六一《张骞传》，第2694页。

③ 《后汉书》卷八八《西域传》，第2931页。

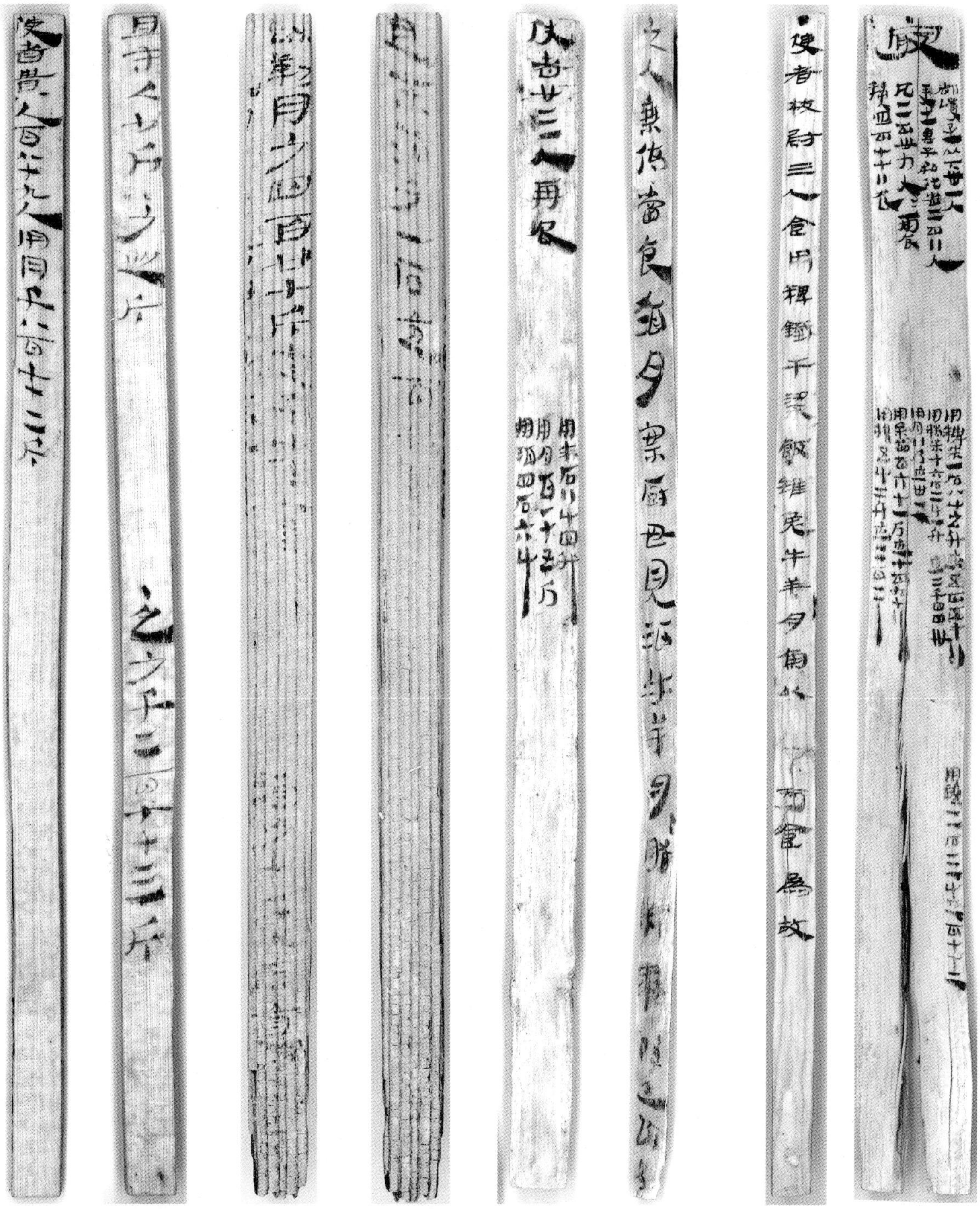

简十四（A） 简十四（B） 简十五（A） 简十五（B） 简十六 简十七 简十八 简十九

The Special Role of Dunhuang Prefecture on the Han Dynasty Silk Roads Based on Unearthed Bamboo Slips

Zhang Defang
(Renmin University of China Unearthed Research and Protection Center)

Abstract: Followed by Zhang Qian opening the Western Regions, Emperor of Wu of Han set up four counties and two gate passes, and Hexi Corridor has become the only access to the Silk Roads. With Dunhuang County being the western end of China, the local highest chief executive Dunhuang Prefecture has made significant contributions to unblock the Han Silk Roads, not only in daily administration, but also in military defense, material support and management of the eastern part of Western Regions. The military defense line from north to south was more than 600 kilometers, so the military tasks were heavier than other prefectures and counties; The supply of the accommodation for the post houses along the road cost huge amount of expenses; In term of the management to Western Regions, Dunhuang Prefecture sometimes sent official documents or straightly administrated the Garrison Reclamation in Yi Xun and Che Shi in eastern Western Regions. All these indicate that, the status, function and influence of the countries and regions along the Silk Roads were different. With the support of the imperial court and the prosperity of Han Dynasty, Dunhuang County was able to take such an important mission.

Keywords: Silk Roads; Dunhuang County; Dunhuang Prefecture; Han Bamboo Slips; Western regions

玄奘《大唐西域记》中所见锡尔河的汉文名称

[日]高田时雄(复旦大学)撰
尤小羽(中山大学)译　王　丁(上海外国语大学)校

今天的锡尔河(Syr Darya),在古代史料中有种种不同的名字。① 古代希腊、罗马作家称之为 Yaksartes,婆罗钵文里的 Yakhšārt 无疑跟这个希腊语词形有关。古突厥碑铭中,它的名字是 Yenčü ügüz。阿拉伯文献中,它叫 Sayhun 或 Sīhun,更晚时代阿拉伯跟波斯语史料中的 Khojend 河,是根据河畔的名城来指称这条河本身。

历代汉文史料中均记载有跟以上词形相对应的词。药杀水(Yaksartes)一名,见于杜佑《通典》对"石国"(今塔什干)的描述②,同时期史籍《北史》③、《隋书》④、《新唐书》⑤ 记载类同。《新唐书》同时引述了锡尔河上游的名字:真珠河和质河(质,中古汉语音 *tśir)。真珠河一名,极有可能是由突厥语 Yenčü ügüz 翻译而来,指今天的纳林河(Narin River)。质河即是今天的锡尔河。《新唐书》此项内容当来自杜环,他于 751 年怛罗斯一役中被俘,其间游历中亚、西亚凡 12 年,终经海路返归中土。杜环所著《经行记》今已散佚,仅在《通典》中保留一小部分。⑥Sayhun/Sīhun 未出现在汉文史料中。⑦ 此外,《明史》⑧ 中的火站一词指称 Khojend 河,显然抄自陈诚的《西域番国志》。Khojend 河的蒙古语形式 Khojend-muren,汉文转写为霍阐没辇,见于《长春真人西游记》,1221 年,丘处机曾前往大雪山(兴都库什)附近的成吉思汗行营,在那里得到成吉思汗的接见。

在此需要提出的是叶河,这是玄奘在《大唐西域记》中为锡尔河记下的一个特殊词形,这是汉文史料中所见 Syr Darya 的最古名称,但在《大慈恩寺三藏法师传》中却作"叶叶河"。⑨ 此种差别值得深究:究竟哪个写法是玄奘原始记录的词呢,叶河还是叶叶河?学者们对此问题久有考辨。为了进一步详考名称,确定本来的写法是很有必要的。在《大唐西域记》中,这条河出现了两次,一次出现在

① 参见标准参考书,如 Pauly-Wissowa, *Real-encyclopädie der classischen Altertumswissenschaft* [Bd. IX, 1181-1189 Iaxartes 条(A. Hermann 撰写)及 *Encyclopedia of Islam*, New Edition, Vol. IX, pp. 659-660, Sir Darya 条(W. Barthold-[C.E. Bosworth] 撰写)]。

② 《通典》卷一九三"石国"条,北京:中华书局,1988 年,第 5275 页。

③ 《北史》卷九七,北京:中华书局,1974 年,第 3235 页。

④ 《隋书》卷八三,北京:中华书局,1973 年,第 1850 页。

⑤ 《新唐书》卷二二一等,北京:中华书局,1975 年,第 6246 页。

⑥ 《经行记》有数种校本,如王国维:《古行记校录》,收入 1928 年《海宁王忠悫公遗书》;张一纯:《经行记笺注》(《中外交通史籍丛刊》),北京:中华书局,1963 年。

⑦ 陈诚于 1412 年受永乐帝派遣出使帖木儿,在其撰写的《西域行程记》中记下"一浑河"的名字。这个名字也许是专名,也许是泛称"水色浑浊的河流"。考以上下文,该河应系 Syr Darya。因此这个汉名或系 Sayhun / Sīhun 的转写形式,亦未可知。参见陈诚:《西域行程记·西域番国志》,收入《中外交通史籍丛刊》,北京:中华书局,1991 年,第 44 页。

⑧ 《明史》卷三三二,北京:中华书局,1974 年,第 8603 页。

⑨ 《大慈恩寺三藏法师传》卷二。该书前五卷由慧立于 664 年完成,其时距离玄奘故去不久。

石国（赭时）一节，另一次出现在窣堵利瑟那国的记述中，这两个出处，在大藏经晚期刻本中都写作叶河。兹将两段文字移录如下（标点略去）[①]：

> 赭时国周千余里西临**叶河**东西狭南北长……（《大唐西域记》卷一）
>
> 窣堵利瑟那国周千四五百里东临**叶河叶河**出葱岭北原西北而流……（《大唐西域记》卷一）

《大慈恩寺三藏法师传》相关文句有所不同[②]：

> 赭时国（唐言石国）西临**叶叶河**
>
> 窣堵利瑟那国，国东临**叶叶河**，河出葱岭北原西北而流

如上所言，两书截然有别，孰者为是，殊不易定。不过，日本古抄本在此有重要异文，为解决问题提供了锁钥。我们且举现存最早的兴圣寺本[③]中对应语句为例：

> 赭时国周千余里西临**叶々河**々东西狭南北长……
>
> 窣堵利瑟那国周千四五百里东临**叶々河**々出葱岭北原西北而流……

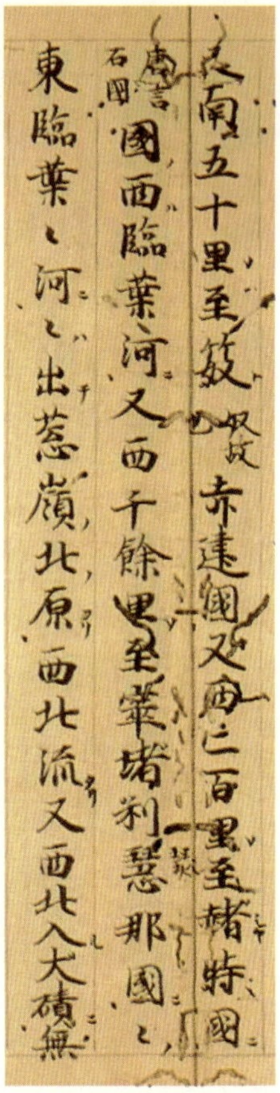
又南五十里至笯赤建國又西南二百里至赭時國
唐言石國 國西臨葉河又西千餘里至窣堵利瑟那國
東臨葉々河々出葱嶺北原西北流又西北入大磧無

这里涉及写本中的重文号问题。在印刷术之前的时代，重文号比现在使用得多得多。按照一般阅读常规，上述兴圣寺本引文应读作“西临叶河，叶河东西狭”及“东临叶河，叶河出葱岭北原”，而非“西临叶叶河，河东西狭”和“东临叶叶河，河出葱岭北原”。我一共查检了七种日本古抄本[④]，其中四种（兴圣寺本、橘寺本、石山寺本、七寺本）使用了重文号，因此我们难以断言这两个句子如何句读。但另三种抄本，即法隆寺本、京都博物馆藏本以及东京国立博物馆藏本都抄对了（见下页表）。即使如此，两段文字中的重文号都导致易被误读。正因如此，叶叶河替代了叶河。《大慈恩寺三藏法师传》中的叶叶河也许就是抄手误解重文号而引起的讹误词形。

有一佳证可以说明这是个讹误。承元四年（1210）《大慈恩寺三藏法师传》抄本[⑤]，其中记述窣堵利瑟那国的文句如下[⑥]：

> 窣堵利瑟那国ヽ东临**叶ヽ河**ヽ出葱岭北原西北流

写本无句读，但我们仍可放心地依据行间夹写的假名附注释读（参看右图）如下：窣堵利瑟那国（ニ至ル），国ノ东叶叶河ニ临ム，河ハ葱岭ノ北ノ原ヨリ

---

① 我们使用的是以高丽大藏经为底本的京都大学本《大唐西域记》卷一，东京：大日本图书，1911年，第20—21页。

② 大正藏，第50册，第227页下栏。

③ 有关兴圣寺本《大唐西域记》，请参见高田时雄：《现存最古大唐西域记写本》，《Itokura》，No.3，2008，第10—11页；《京都兴圣寺现存最早的〈大唐西域记〉抄本》，高启安译，《敦煌研究》2008年第2期，第47—48页。

④ 均为平安时代（794—1192）及镰仓时代（1192—1333）前期抄本。因篇幅限制本文姑不详论。

⑤ 该写本最早为松本文三郎所有，现藏于京都大学人文科学研究所。

⑥ 记述石国（赭时）的一段，该写本作“叶河”而非“叶叶河”，至确。这很有意思，但因本文讨论的是重文号带来的干扰，在此姑不深论。

出デテ西北流タリ（窣堵利瑟那国，东临叶叶河。河出葱岭北原，西北而流）。带重文号的这四个字“叶ヽ河ヽ”，在此读作“叶叶河河”，而不是相应的常规读法“叶河叶河”。

上文对《大唐西域记》的日本写本做了讨论，我们现在对敦煌写本做检核。S.2659Va 几乎保留了《大唐西域记》卷一的全部内容。本文讨论的相应文句如下：

> 赭时国周千余里西临叶叶河东西狭南北长……
>
> 窣堵利瑟那国周千四五百余里东临叶河叶河出葱岭北原西北而流……

第一个句子与《大慈恩寺三藏法师传》对应句全同①，这可以解释为仍是因原文中的重文号引起的误读。

基于以上古本的证据，我们似有充分理由认为，玄奘是把锡尔河叫作“叶河”的，而非“叶叶河”。

版　本	赭时国	窣堵利瑟那国
高丽大藏经本	叶河	叶河叶河
兴圣寺本	叶ヽ河ヽ	叶ヽ河ヽ
橘寺本	叶ヽ河ヽ	叶ヽ河ヽ
石山寺本	叶ヽ河ヽ	叶ヽ河ヽ
七寺本	叶ヽ河ヽ	叶ヽ河ヽ
法隆寺本	叶河叶河	叶河叶河
京都国立博物馆本	叶河叶河	叶河叶河
东京国立博物馆本	叶河叶河	叶河叶河
敦煌写本	叶叶河	叶河叶河

那么，叶河的原型又是什么呢？通过玄奘的音写追溯它的当地名称并不容易。叶，在唐代有两种发音：*iäp 和 *śiäp。据《广韵》，后一种发音仅用于河南汝州的一个县名，《集韵》多了用于姓氏的一项。总之 *śiäp 这一读音似乎仅用于某些专名。那么这一发音是否适用于我们讨论的这个词呢？托马斯 · 瓦特曾试过将 she (*śiäp) 或 ye (*iäp) 解释作 ye-ye 或 ye-she 的简缩形式，据他说，这即是药杀水（Jaxartes）。② 但我们无法接受这一说法，因为如前所述，玄奘的原词不是双音节的“叶叶”，而是单音节的“叶”。

由于没有明确的标准可助确定 she（*śiäp）和 ye（*iäp）这两个发音中的哪一种适用于究明转写而来的叶河这个词，两种可能都应纳入考虑。找到原名以印证音写形式才是最重要的。

我们先假定为 *iäp 河，它的原型很可能是伊朗语（粟特语）中的 āb，义为“水”。这个词素见于地名 Suiyāb 中，在《大慈恩寺三藏法师传》中作“素叶”。锡尔河是该地区最大的一条河，当地人便把它概称为“水”或“河”，似在情理之中。可问题在于玄奘何以使用叶这个字，而不是一个首音节不带有颚化音的更合适的字。玄奘很可能知道，素叶的叶和叶河在词源上其实是一回事。

假若我们采纳 she（*śiäp）这一读音又是怎样的呢？我们知道，撒马尔罕遗迹胜地阿弗拉西阿卜（Afrāsiāb）这个地名，是从塔吉克语 Parsīāb（粟特语 Paršvāb）“黑河之上”亦即 Sīāhāb 或 Siāb 讹变而

① 第二个“河”字显系脱漏，但这与我们在此讨论的主题无关。

② Thomas Watters, *On Yuan Chwang's Travels in India, 629-645 A.D.*, 1904, p. 85.

来的。[①] 倘若我们暂且搁置时期和地点不论，那么音韵上的联系相当之接近。不过，地名 Afrāsiāb 从 17 世纪起才见于使用，因而我们毫无理由把这个词看成玄奘书中 *śiäp 河的原型。

目前尚无明快的办法解决玄奘书中的锡尔河名称，但我更倾向于第一种假设：当地土著将锡尔河称作 āb（义为“河”），玄奘据此记下其音，以汉字叶（*iäp）写之。

在此可以附带论及俄罗斯学者 S.G. Kljaštornij 曾做的考证[②]，他说，古代作家说的 Jaxartes 只能是对该河中上游的指称，这个称呼在当地伊朗语和突厥语两大方言的逐渐同化中消失。Syr 是一古塞语名称，原用于称呼该河下游流域，随后却因 15—16 世纪乌兹别克人对中亚的征服而见用于整条河流。果若如此，参以地理方位，则玄奘在石国和窣堵利瑟那国听到的河流名字应当就是 Jaxartes 或它的某个派生词。

近来 Livshits 教授就 Syr Darya 的古名 Yaxart 发展出一种理论[③]，他主张 Yaxart 为一粟特语词，从词根 xšar 而来，ya 是词首定冠词，tā 是阴性词尾后缀。Livshits 释词根 xšar 为“流、涌”。这种解释颇为诱人，将玄奘的叶（*śiäp）河语源讲通。不过考虑到韵尾不同，该词根与 *śiäp 的关系仍大是问题。毕竟，几无可能确定玄奘的叶（*iäp / *śiäp）河的原来词形。但没准还是如上假设的那样，玄奘仅仅是将当地人对河的称呼记录下来，并未做更多考证。

---

① The article “AFRĀSĪĀB” by G. A. Pugachenkova and E. V. Rtveladze, in *Encyclopaedia Iranica*; Э. Ртвеладзе, *Великий Шелковый Путь*. Ташкенд, 1999, c.188.

② S.G. Kljaštornij, ΙΑΞΑΡΤΗΣ – SĬR-DARJA, *Central Asiatic Journal*, VI, No.1, 1961, pp. 24-26.

③ В.А. Лившиц, “Древнее название Сырдарьи”, *Вестник древней истори*, 2003, No.1, c. 3-10.

Relationship between Sogdiana and Turfan During the 10th - 11th Centuries as Reflected in Manichaean Sogdian Texts

Yutaka Yoshida (Kyoto University)

Abstract: In this article I assemble the three Manichaean Sogdian texts discovered in Turfan which bear out the exchange between Sogdiana and Turfan during the 10th to early 11th centuries. While the first one (Ch/U 6879) proves the importation of cotton cloth from Sogdiana, the other two [LM 20 1552 (23) of the Lushun National Museum and Bäzäklik Letter B] attest the regular correspondence between the Manichaeans of Samarqand and those of Turfan. The Manichaean New Persian texts discovered in Turfan are most likely to represent the literary works of the Manichaeans living in Samanid or Qarakhanid Samarqand. Bäzäklik Letter B was sent by a bishop (aftāδān) of the Manichaean community of the town of Tūdh near Samarqand to celebrate the New Year. The addressee was a Teacher Aryāmān Puhr staying in Turfan. Therefore, in the early 11th century the Manichaeans of Samarqand were under the leadership of a možak or Teacher seated in the church of Turfan, possibly what is now called Ruin K. Finally, I dwell on the problems surrounding the so-called Manichaean Letters i and ii and argue that they are connected to the evacuation of Manichaeans from Mesopotamia reported by al-Nadīm as happening during the reign of al-Muqtadir (908-932 CE).

Keywords: Sogdian; Manichaeism; Turfan; Samarqand; Silk Road

Introduction

The heyday of the Silk Roads is no doubt the first half of the Tang Dynasty (618-906 CE). Many foreigners, in particular Sogdians or *huren* 胡人, came to China and settled in Chinese cities like Changan and Luoyang, where things related to *hu* 胡 such as *hufu* 胡服 "Sogdian dress", *hushi* 胡食 "Sogdian food", etc. were very popular.[①] Many books about the history of the Silk Roads spend the bulk of pages on the relationship between China and the West during and before this period.[②] Consequently, not much is written and known about the Silk Road history after the Anlushan Rebellion (755-763 CE), since when Tang China evacuated Central Asia and lost the interest in what was happening in that area. During this period the Islamization of Sogdiana happened to be underway

① E. Schafer, *The golden peaches of Samarkand. A study of T'ang exotics*, Berkley/Los Angeles/London, University of California Press, 1963, reprint 1985 is still the best book on this subject.

② One may refer to É. de la Vaissière, tr. J. Ward, *Sogdian traders. A history*, Leiden, Brilll, 2005, which has now become a standard work. The third revised edition of its French original, *Histore des marchands sogdiens*, has just appeared in 2016. One of the latest works is V. Hansen, *The Silk Road. A new history*, Oxford, Oxford University Press, 2013. For us Japanese, T. Moriyasu, *The Silk Road and the Tang Empire* (in Japanese), Tokyo, 2007 is the most popular and informative.

and it gives a popular impression that the Silk Road trade came to an end after the Islamization. Nevertheless, the trade did survived and its traces are abundantly found among the Dunhuang documents of the 10th century, where productions of the Islamic West are recorded.① As for another oasis city Turfan, one may refer to a passage in Gardīzī's *Zayn al-Akhbār* (ca 1049-1052 CE); in connection with the residence of a qaghan of the West Uighur kingdom or the Toğuz Oğuz country it records as follows: His (i.e. qaghan's, Y.Y.) floor-coverings are made of felt. But over these are spread carpets made by Muslims ..."② In fact fragments of the textiles produced in the Islamic world have been discovered among the Turfan remains.③

In this article, I assemble the three Turfan Sogdian texts of Manichaean affiliation that point to the relationship or exchange between Sogdiana and Turfan during the 10th to the early 11th centuries.

I Cotton cloth of Sogdiana and Qarašahr

First let us see the text and translation of an unpublished fragment Ch/U 6879④, which attests an interesting expression *swyδ'ny wš'yny* "cotton cloth of Sogdiana". It is a fragment of 21,6 cm x 11,2 cm and is written on the backside of a Chinese Buddhist text corresponding to *Taisho Tripitaka*, vol. 7, 700c12-23, part of the Chinese version of the *Mahāprajñāpāramitāsūtra*. Judging from the width of the fragment (11,2 cm), more than half is missing from the left-hand margin of the original paper, which was more or less 26 cm wide. Consequently, one cannot provide consecutive translation of the text. Manichaean affiliation of the text is made certain by *δyn''βr'y* "elect, Manichaean monk". Since the bulk of Manichaean texts discovered in Turfan are believed to go back to the 10th to the early 11th centuries⑤, there is practically no doubt that this manuscript written in late cursive script is also dated to the same period.

Ch/U 6879⑥: TEXT

1 [ ](..w ...)rt['yw''xr'ny ?]
2 ẓm'š''yky kwrδy o nw'[ ]
3 'δry 'rk-c'ny wš'yny (.)[ ]
4 'rk-c'ny o 'βt' kwm'n[ ]
5 wš'yny oo ctβ'r 'yw''x(r.)[ ]
6 δyn''βr''y wx(w)šw pr(t)[ ]

① Rong Xinjiang's article may be referred to: "Khotanese felt and Sogdian silver: Foreign gifts to Buddhist monasteries in 9th and 10th-century Dunhuang (in Chinese)", in idem, *The Silk Road and cultural interaction between East and West* (in Chinese), Beijing, 2015, pp. 263-277.

② Cf. A. P. Martinez, "Gardīzī's two chapters on the Turks", *Archivum Eurasiae Medii Aevi,* Tomus II, 1982, pp. 109-175., esp. p. 135; Professor T. Moriyasu drew my attention to a passage in the *Songhuiyaojigao*, Vol. 197, p. 7720, where the nine ministers of the Uighur Kingdom are mentioned as wearing garments of brocade and damask produced in *Dashiguo* "Islamic countries".

③ K. Sakamoto, "Two fragments of luxury cloth discovered in Turfan: Evidence of textile circulation from West to East", in D. Durkin-Meisterernst, et al. (eds.), *Turfan revisited - The first century of research into the arts and cultures of the Silk Road*, Berlin, Dietrich Reimer Verlag, 2004, pp. 297-302.

④ On this fragment see Ch. Reck, *Mitteliranische Handschriften. Teil 1. Berliner Turfanfragmente manichäischen Inhalts in soghdischer Schrift* (Verzeichnis der Orientalischen Handschriften in Deutschland Band XVIII, 1), Stuttgart, Franz Steiner, 2006, p. 282, no. 394.

⑤ For the exact dating of the Turfan Manichaean texts one may refer to the so-called Manichaean calendars written in Sogdian and Uighur. So far the following dates have been proposed: Sogdian, (1) M796 = 929-930 CE, (2) Otani 6191 = 932-933 CE, (3) M148=984-985 CE, (4) M5268 = 1000-1001 CE; Uighur, (5) Ch/U 6932 = 988- 989 CE, (6) U495 = 989-990 CE, (7) No. 88 in the *Tulufankaoguji* of Xuang Wenbi = 1002-1003 CE. On the Sogdian texts see Yoshida, "Buddhist influence on the bema festival?" in C. G. Cereti, M. Maggi and E. Provasi (eds.), *Religious themes and texts of pre-Islamic Iran and Central Asia. Studies in honour of Professor G. Gnoli on the occasion of his 65th birthday on 6th December 2002,* Wiesbaden, Reichert, 2003, pp. 453-458. For the Uighur calendars see J. Hamilton, "Calendriers manichéens ouïgours de 988, 989, et 1003", in J.-L. Bacqué-Grammont and R. Dor (eds.), *Mélanges offerts à Louis Bazin par ses disciples, collègues et amis,* Paris, 1992, pp. 7-23.

⑥ For the photograph see the following web-site: http://turfan.bbaw.de/dta/ch_u/images/chu6879versototal.jpg (accessed on 12th August 2016).

7 pncw prt kwm'n[ ]
8 'yw xw'nš'y wcny w(r)[nh?]
9 swγδ'ny wš'yny kwrδy[ ]
10 (w)[š'yn](y) 'yw knpy 20+20+20 oo[ ]
11 [ty]m δβrw 10+iii 'rk-c'ny[ ]
12 (wxw)šwmy m'xy wx[w]šw[sγty']
13 δy[n'']βr(''y[a] p)ncw prt(w)[ ]
14 (ZY 'δry kw)[m'n?]

(a) What I read *βr* looks more like *kr*.

TRANSLATION

"... a tunic for a novice(?). Nine ... three (pieces of) cotton cloth of Ark ... [made out of cotton cloth] of Ark. Seven (pairs of) trousers(?) ... <5> cotton cloth. Four novices(?) ... For an elect six (pieces of) silk cloth ... five (pieces of) silk cloth for(?) trousers. ... One tablecloth(?), old wool(?) ... Cotton cloth of Sogdiana for a tunic. ... <10> cotton cloth 59 (pieces) ... [More]over, I gave(?) 13 (pieces of) [cotton cloth] of Ark ... The sixth month, on the six[th day] ... (for) an elect five pieces of silk cloth ... and three pairs of trousers(?)"

COMMENTARY

2.1 *ẓm'š''yky* "novice(?)".[1] This strange looking word is most likely to be connected with yet another enigmatic word *ẓ-m'š'yktw 'yw'rx'ny* encountered in Bäzäklik Letter A (line 120).[2] Commenting on the word, I also referred to *'ywrx'ny ẓ-m'štyk* found in a Manichaean Uighur text studied by T. Moriyasu.[3] In the both texts the expressions in question appear to denote Manichaean monks of relatively low rank, whence my translation "novice". It is to be noted that *'yw''x(r.)[ ]* of line 5 seems to be the same word as *'yw'rx'ny* or *'ywrx'ny*, although the spellings differ slightly from each other. Minor discrepancy in spellings is again shared by *ẓm'š''yky*, *ẓ-m'š'yktw*, and *ẓ-m'štyk*. The most plausible explanation for this unusual vacillation in the spellings may be looked for in their foreign origin, although the etymologies of the two words are not known. Different order of the two words may perhaps imply that the two words denote two different kinds of novices. Among the Turfan Manichaean wall paintings and miniatures one actually finds two groups of young monks wearing headgears different from those worn by ordinary monks. One is those wearing a flat white hat and the other with a black hat, cf. left side of MIK III 4979 a, b.[4]

In view of *δyn''βr''y* in line 6 and possibly in line 13, an unusual spelling of word medial -''- may belong to our scribe's orthographic peculiarity. Cf. also *ẓm'š''yky* and *'yw''x(r)[ ]*.

2.2 *kwrδy* "tunic, shirt". On this word see also Chr. *qwrθy*.[5] It no doubt denotes a white robe worn by electi or Manichaean monks.

3.1 *'rk-c'ny* "of (the city) of Ark (i.e. what is now Qarašahr in Xinjiang)". The feminine form of this adjective is

① Reck, *op. cit.*, p. 282, no. 394 reads *ẓm'š'n'ky*. The two letters before *k* look very similar and Reck's reading is equally possible. See also my comment on the spelling of *δyn''βr''y* below.

② On the three Manichaean Sogdian letters (A, B, C) unearthed from Bäzäklik and my edition see section III below.

③ Cf. T. Moriyasu, *Die Geschichte des uigurischen Manichäismus an der Seidenstraße,* Wiesbaden, Harrassowit, 2004, (originally published in Japanese in 1990-1991), pp. 85-86.

④ It is reproduced in Zs. Gulácsi, *Manichaean art in Berlin collections*, Turnhout 2001, pp. 71, 245. Youg monks wearing a flat hat are also seen in two different art objects, cf. Gulácsi, *ibid.*, pp. 90, 204. Gulácsi remarks as follows: "... its (flat hat, Y.Y.) connection with a specific rank, geographic or ethnic group within the Manichaean church is uncertain", cf. *ibid.*, p. 204. Yet another word meaning "novice" is suggested in Sims-Williams and Durkin-Meisterernst, *Dictionary of Manichaean Sogdian and Bactrian,* Turnhout, Brepols, 2012, p. 94a s.v. *jw'nwtr*.

⑤ On this word see W. Sundermann, "Nachlese zu F. W. K. Müllers 'Soghdischen Texten I', 2. Teil", *Altorientalische Forschungen* 3, 1975, pp. 55-90, esp. p. 85, n. 146.

attested in L44, line 7: *'rkc'nch (x't'wnh)* "(Uighur) queen of Ark".①

3.2 *wš'yny* "cotton cloth". This word was first recognized by Sims-Williams, cf. Sims-Williams and J. Hamilton, *Documents turco-sogdiens du IXe-Xe siècle de Touen-houang,* London 1990, pp. 56-57.② In the light of the words surviving in the text one may suppose that it is a document recording expenditure of textiles for making the dresses of Manichaean monks and novices. A similar Chinese text of 747 CE is known among the Turfan Chinese documents.③ It is a document issued by a certain Buddhist temple and records the expenditure of cotton cloth for making the spring/summer dress (*chunyi* 春衣) worn by the workers attached to the temple. Three kinds of dresses are mentioned there: (a) *shan* 衫 "shirt", *kun* 裈 "drawers", and *ku* 袴 "trousers".

4 *kwm'n* "trousers(?)". Since *kwrδy* could be the Sogdian equivalent of *shan* 衫 "shirt", one may compare *kwm'n* with Khotanese *kaumadai* "trousers"④, although the phonetic similarity is admittedly slight.⑤

5 *'yw''x(r.)[ ]* "novice(?)". On this word see above.

6 *prt* "silk cloth(?)"⑥. I take the word for a Sogdianized form of Skt. *paṭa* "silk cloth, etc.". On Niya Prakrit *paṭa* and related forms see H. Lüders, "Textilien im alten Turkistan", *APAW*, no. 3, Berlin, 1936, pp. 24-28. On the pleonastic *r* in transcribing the Indian retroflex sound, cf. also *kwrty* "ten million" for *koṭi* and *pwrny'nyh* "religious merit" for *puṇya.*

8.1 *xw'nš'y* "tablecloth(?)". My translation is a simple guess based on the assumption that *xw'n* is an element corresponding Middle Persian *xw'n* "table" widely used in Manichaean Sogdian and Uighur texts in the meaning of "cloth set with food, communal meal". Recently, the Chinese equivalent *shidan* 食单 was discovered by Wang Ding.⑦ On the other hand, if *xw'n* corresponds to *guan* 冠 "cap, head dress" (Middle Chinese **kuân*⑧), *xw'nš'y* may be taken to mean "headgear, crown", but I am not able to find the suitable Chinese character for the second element *š'y.*

8.2 *w(r)[nh]* "wool". This restoration is again nothing more than my conjecture. On Sogdian *wrnh* "wool" found in a medical text Pelliot sogdien 19, see E. Benveniste *Textes sogdiens*, Paris 1940, p. 232.⑨

11.1 *δβrw.* My translation "I gave" is based on the presumption that it is an error for *δ'βrw.* In the light of the impersonal neuter preterite *xwrtw* "it was eaten" attested in Mug documents⑩, it may also be possible to take it for an error for **δβrtw* "it was given". Whatever the case may be, 1 sg. injunctive of *δβr-* "to give" is most unexpected in the context.

11.2 A short line is drawn between lines 11 and 12. Since a date is entered in line 12, this short line may mark the end of the preceding entry or section, which would have been headed by another date earlier than the 6th of the 6th month.⑪

---

① Cf. Sims-Williams and Durkin-Meisterernst, *op. cit.*, p. 18a.

② See now also its English version: *Turco-Sogdian documents from 9th-10th century Dunhuang,* London, SOAS, 2015, pp. 67-68.

③ The text is published in O. Ikeda, *Ancient Chinese household registers and related documents* (in Japanese), Tokyo, 1979, p. 472, no. 214. For the text and translation see Appendix below.

④ Cf. H. Bailey, *Dictionary of Khotan Saka*, Cambridge: Cambridge University Press, 1979, p. 58b.

⑤ It may also be compared with Skt. *kaupina,* of which the Chinese equivalent is *kun* 裈 "drawers", cf. W. Ogihara (ed.), *Sanskrit-Japanese dictionary with reference to the Chinese equivalents*, reprint, Tokyo, 1979, p. 382b. Cf. also *kwmp'n* discussed below.

⑥ In Sims-Williams and Durkin-Meisterernst, *op. cit.*, p. 144a, *prt* is translated "roll of cloth" with a query and Lüders's work is referred to. It is interesting to see that when *prt* is attested three times in this text, it is always accompanied by *δyn''βr'y*. Different textiles, cotton and silk, appear to have been issued respectively to novices and ordinary monks.

⑦ Wang Ding, "Tablecloth and the Chinese Manichaean hymn *Shou shidan ji* 收食单偈", in *East Asian studies. Festschrift in honor of the retirement of Professor Takata Tokio,* Kyoto, 2014, pp. 438-454.

⑧ Middle Chinese forms are cited from B. Karlgren, *Grammata Serica Recensa*, Stockholm, Museum of Far Eastern Antiquities, 1957.

⑨ *wrn'* attested in a medical text, So 14822 (unpublished), seems to be the same word.

⑩ Cf. Yoshida, "Sogdian", in G. Windfuhr (ed.), *The Iranian languages*, London and New York, Rautledge, 2009, pp. 279-335., esp. p. 301.

⑪ This may have been the 6th day of the first month, if the second section beginning in line 12 records the issue of cloth covering the latter half of the year. Is it just a coincidence that the sixth day of the first month is the very last day of the fast lasting 28 days beginning on the 8th day of the preceding month?

The two kinds of cotton cloth mentioned in the text are *'rk-c'ny wš'yny* "cotton cloth of Ark"① and *swγδ'ny wš'yny* "cotton cloth of Sogdiana". Similarly in the contemporary Chinese documents from Dunhuang two kinds of cotton cloth are encountered: *moluxie* 末禄緤 "cotton cloth of Merv" and *anxixie* 安西緤 "cotton cloth of Anxi, i.e. Kucha", cf. E. Trombert, "Une trajectoire d'ouest en est sur la Route de la Soie", in: *La Persia e l'Asia centrale de Alessandro al X secolo*, Rome 1996 (Atti dei convegni Lincei 127), pp. 205-227. I venture to suppose that the two expressions in the Sogdian text correspond to the two in Chinese respectively, especially because Ark is a next oasis city to the east of Kucha usually referred to as Anxi.② The cotton cloth produced in Western Turkestan may have been referred to as either "cotton cloth of Sogdiana" or "cotton cloth of Merv" in China. In the eyes of the scribe of Ch/U 6879, one kind of cotton cloth was produced in Sogdiana and the other in Ark or Qarašahr. In any case the former must have been imported from or via Sogdiana.③ Accordingly, this document suggests the trade conducted between Sogdiana and Turfan.

In concluding this section, I should like to cite yet another similar Manichaean Sogdian document belonging to the Otani collection now preserved in the Lushun National Museum, China. All these manuscripts were discovered in Turfan by the Otani expedition. The text in question bears a signature LM20 1514/528 in the museum and was reproduced in: Lushun Museum and Ryukoku University (eds.), *Selected fragments of Chinese Buddhist texts from Xinjiang region in Lushun Museum,* Kyoto 2006, p. 160. It measures 5.9 cm x 38.3 cm. Approximately three quarters of the sheet are lost from the left hand margin and only one or two words have survived from each line. The Sogdian text is written on the backside of a Buddhist Chinese text, which is again a part of the Chinese version of the *Mahāprajñāpāramitāsūtra* but is too small to be identified with a particular place in this gigantic and repetitive Chinese text.④

LM20 1514/528 verso

1	δyn''βr['y?	elect ...
2	kwrδy XII[	a tunic, 12+x ...
3	XI prt'y[	eleven pieces of silk cloth(?) ...
4	'yw'x'[rny?	novice ...
5	'βt'[	seven ...
6	'δw p'n(.)[	two ?⑤ ...
7	tym '(y)[w	moreover, one ...
8	tym 'ny(w)[	yet another ...
9	'yw prt(')[y	one piece of silk cloth ...
10	kwmp'n[	trousers(?) ...
11	wšyny kw[rδy	cotton cloth, a tunic ...
12	'δry wr[nh(?)	three pieces of woolen cloth(?) ...

prt'y could be the same word as *prt* or a form derived from it. *'yw'x'[ ]* is likely to be compared with *'yw'rx'ny*, etc., while *kwmp'n* may be a spelling variant of *kwm'n* discussed above.

① Professor T. Moriyasu drew my attention to the Uighur equivalent *solmï böz* "cotton cloth of (the country) Solmï or Qarašahr" found in an Uighur letter, cf. S.-Ch. Raschmann, *Baumwolle im türkischen Zentralasien,* Wiesbaden, Harrasowitz, 1995, p. 55.

② Cf. Trombert, ibid., p. 225.

③ Nevertheless, every oasis city of Turkestan could have its own cotton cloth. An oasis of Phema near Khotan was famous for its fine cotton cloth named *ganchengxixie* 紺城細緤 "fine cotton cloth of Gancheng or city of Phema", cf. Rong Xinjiang, art. cit., p. 271. See also idem, "Reality or tale? Marco Polo's description of Khotan", *Journal of Asian history* 49, 2015, pp. 161-174, esp. p. 171.

④ After line 12 a blank space of two lines and several incomplete lines follow. However, only beginnings of words are left and their relationship to the main text is hard to see. Here in this article I omitted this part.

⑤ Since either a name of a textile or dress is expected, *p'n* "table" does not seem to suit the context.

II Mention of Samarqand in a Manichaean Sogdian text

Yet another text belonging to the Otani Turfan collection preserved in the Lushun National Museum, LM 20 1552 (23) P. 22. 9, is an oblong fragment measuring 11.0 cm by 27.0 cm.① It is written only on one side and the verso is left blank. One can see a place where two sheets of paper were glued together, which indicates that the fragment comes from a longer scroll. Its Manichaean affiliation is made certain by such expressions as *'δw wkry 'ncmn* "twofold community" and *δy-np'šyt pryšty-(t)* "angels protecting the (Manichaean) religion".② Being a Manichaean text discovered in Turfan, the manuscript is also likely to be dated to the 10th century; this dating seems to be corroborated again by its late cursive handwriting. Unfortunately, what has been preserved in this fragmentary text is too meagre to identify the contents. Nevertheless, the fact that the text was written on a scroll of which the verso was left blank leads one to presume that it comes from a long letter like the two letters discovered in Bäzäklik. As we shall see below, the surviving words are compatible with this assumption, because the parallel expressions occur in the two Bäzäklik letters.

LM 20 1552 (23) P. 22. 9: TEXT

1 [ ](.m. . ZY s)[ ](. . . .)[ ](m)γwnw
2 [mδy-c]yk 'δw wkry 'ncmn[a] o βγ'nyk 'nt'c ZY sγtm'nw
3 [ ](y-)t šyrxwz-yty 'pryw (o) pr 'nẕ-'wy-n'kw[b] xwβw []
4 ['yšwy](r) o Z(Y)[mγw](n) δy-np'šyt pryšty-(t)[]
5 [prn ZY w'xšykt?]ptnw smr[kn](δ)[h][c]
6 [ ](..) 'x[ ]

(a) A short line is written across the final stroke of *-n*. It is not clear what this short line is meant to be. (b) Two dots below the letter *ẕ*. (c) The typical upper part of a letter *δ* (lamed) has survived and there is no doubt about the restoration of *δ*.

TRANSLATION

"... the whole twofold community staying [here]; together with the holy assembly and the entire [... and] friends; by [...] of the redeeming lord [Jesus]; [... all] the angels protecting the religion, [guardian spirits ...] the town of Samar[qand ...]"

COMMENTARY

2.1 *[mδy-c]yk* "(residing) here". My restoration is a sheer guess. In principle *[tδy-c]yk* is equally possible.

2.2 *'δw wkry 'ncmn* "twofold community". The combination also appears in M 697A and in Bäzäklik Letters A and B edited by me.③ Its Uighur counterpart *iki ančman* is rendered by P. Zieme as "zwei Konvente (consisting of male and female believers)".④ This assumption is supported by the Kephalaion 87: "Now the holy church exists in two forms: in the brothers and the sisters".⑤ Differently A. van Tongerloo⑥, who considers the two communities to be consisting of clerical and secular congregations.

---

① This text was once published by me: "Sogdian materials in the Lushun Museum (in Japanese)", in Lushun Museum and Ryukoku University (eds.), *Buddhist manuscripts excavated in Central Asia,* Kyoto, 2012, pp. 39-53, esp. pp. 41-44, 53.

② The two expressions are encountered in the Bäzäklik letters to be discussed in the next section.

③ For the three Bäzäklik letters and my edition see the next section.

④ Cf. idem, "Ein uigurischer Text über die Wirtschaft manichäischer Klöster im uigurischen Reich", in L. Ligeti (ed.), *Researches in Altaic languages,* Budapest, 1975, pp. 331-338, esp. pp. 332-333.

⑤ Cf. I. Gardner, *The Kephalaia of the teacher*, Leiden / New York / Köln: Brill, 1995, p. 225.

⑥ van Tongerloo, "L'identité de l'église manichéenne oriental (env. 8e s. ap. J.-C.). La communauté des croyants: ir. hnzmn/'njmn, ouig. ančm(a)n", *Orientalia Lovaniensia Periodica* 12, 1981, pp. 265-272, esp. p. 272.

3 *βγ'nyk 'nt'c ZY sytm'n [ ](t) šyrxwz-yty 'pryw* "together with the holy assembly and the entire [... and] friends". This expression may perhaps refer to the divine or holy group of people, i.e. clergymen, and secular supporters of the Manichaean church.①

3-4 *'nz- wy-n'kw xwβw ['yšwy]* "redeeming lord Jesus". For the restoration of *'yšwy* cf. *'nz-'wn'y xwβw 'yšwy* encountered in Bäzäklik Letter A, lines 76 and 106. On the combination of the preposition *pr* and *'yšw* see *pr xwβw*② *'yšwy frm'nw δstwβry* (Bäzäklik Letter A, 19; Bäzäklik Letter B, 77-78) "one who has authority by the command of Lord Jesus".③ Therefore, it is tempting to restore *['yšwy δstwβr](y)*, but the damaged letter does look like *r* rather than *y*.

4-5 *[myw](n) δy-np'šyt pryšty-(t) [prn ZY w'xšykt]*. On this restoration see *mywnw δyn-p'šytw pryšt'kt(y)[prn] ZY w'xšykty* (Bäzäklik Lettetr A, 77-78) "all the guardian angels, [glories] and guardian spirits of the religion".

5.1 *ptnw* "town". This word was borrowed from Indian *pattana* "id.". It has been attested not only in Manichaean but also Buddhist Sogdian texts④ and was well naturalized in Sogdian.

5.2 *smr[kn](δ)[h]*. The original name of Samarqand has been attested once on the envelope of Ancient Letter II: *sm'rknδh*. An adjective derived from it is encountered in Ancient Letter II, Mug documents, and the Ladakh inscription;⑤ in all the texts it is spelled *sm'rknδc* except for one Mug document A14, where *smrknδc* is attested twice.⑥ Since very few words begin with *smr-* followed by *δ*, there is practically no doubt about this restoration.

Mention of Samarqand in this text is presumably understood as indicating that it was dispatched either to or from Samarqand, and hence that during the 10th century exchange was held between the Manichaeans of Turfan and those of Samarqand. In fact existence of the Manichaean community in the Samarqand area in the 10th century was witnessed by such contemporary Islamic scholars as Ibn al-Nadīm (932-990 CE) and Al-Bīrūnī (973- ca. 1050 CE); Manichaeism is also mentioned in the *Hudūd al-'Ālam* (982/983 CE) in connection with Samarqand.⑦ See also the fact that one ruler of the West Uighur Kingdom showed special concern about the ill fate of those Manichaeans who escaped from Babylon and took refuge in Samarqand during the reign of al-Muqtadir (908-932 CE). I cite Reeves's translation of the relevant passage of Ibn al-Nadīm's *Fihrist*:⑧

> The last time when they were visible was during the reign of al-Muqtadir (908-932 CE), when they kept close to Khurāsān. Out of fear for their lives, those of them who were left concealed their affairs and roamed about

① If this interpretation is correct, it lends support to van Tongerloo's understanding of *'δw wkry 'ncmn* nentioned above. However, since the notion of two communities comprising clergymen and clergywomen is so common not only in Manichaeism but also in Buddhism (cf. *erbuseng* 二部僧 "two groups of monks consisting of male and female"), I stick to my understanding of the expression.

② In Letter B one reads *xwt'w* instead of *xwβw*.

③ Cf. also *pr xwβw 'yšwy-y δstwβry* (Bäzäklik Letter B, 13-14) "one who has authority by (the help of) Lord Jesus".

④ Cf. W. B. Henning, "Ein manichäisches Bet- und Beichtbuch", *APAW* 1936, No. 10, p. 83, s.v. 698 and Sims-Williams, "Indian Elements in Parthian and Sogdian." In K. Röhrborn et al. (eds.), *Sprachen des Buddhismus in Zentralasien,* Wiesbaden, Otto Harrassowitz, 1983, pp. 132-141.

⑤ Samarqand is referred to in one of the old inscriptions discovered in Kultobe, Kazakhstan. In the inscription the adjective is spelled *symrkntc*, cf. Sims-Williams with F. Grenet and A. Podushkin, "Les plus anciens monuments de la langue sogdienne: Les inscriptions de Kultobe au Kazakhstan", *Comptes rendus des séances de l'Académie des Inscriptions et Belles-Lettres,* 2007, pp. 1005-1034. On the employment of *t* instead of *δ* in this very early monument see Sims-Williams, "From Aramaic to Manchu: Prehistory, life and after-life of the Sogdian script", in Rong Xinjiang and Luo Feng (eds.), *Sogdians in China: New evidence in archaeological finds and unearthed texts*, Beijing, 2016, pp. 414-421.

⑥ For the editions of these texts see the following publications: (1) Ancient Letter II: Sims-Williams, "The Sogdian Ancient Letter II", in M. G. Schmidt and W. Bisang (eds.), *Philologica et Linguistica, Pluralitas, Universitas. Festschrift für H. Humbach zum 80. Geburtstag,* Trier, 2001, pp. 267-280; (2) Mug documents: V. A. Livshitz, *Sogdian epigraphy of Central Asia and Semirech'e,* London, 2015; (3) Ladakh inscription: Sims-Williams, "The Sogdian inscriptions of Ladakh", in K. Jettmar (ed.), *Antiquities of northern Pakistan*, Vol. 2, Mainz, 1993, pp. 151-163 + plates.

⑦ Relevant passages of the three Islamic sources are collected and translated by J. Reeves, *Prolegomena to a history of Islamicate Manichaeism,* Sheffield / Oakville, 2011, pp. 227-230.

⑧ Reeves, *ibid.*, p. 228.

> in this region. (Eventually) around five hundred of their members gathered together in Samarqand. When their business became public, the governor of Khurāsān sought to put them to death. Then the king of China — I think it was (actually) the lord of the Toghuzghuz — sent a message to him saying: 'In my country there are many more Muslims than there are people of my religion in your country,' and he swore to him that if he should kill a single one of them, he would kill the whole community (of Muslims) who were with him. (He also promised) he would demolish the mosques and leave among the remaining lands lookouts against the Muslims in order to (identify and) kill them. So the governor of Khurāsān refrained from harming them, and accepted the *jizya* from them.

Since al-Nadīm's *Fihrist* was drafted in 987 CE, the ruler of the Toghuzghuz mentioned by him is to be identified with one of the West Uighur qaghans, who were supporters of the Manichaean religion.

III Bäzäklik Letters

In 1981 three Manichaean Sogdian and five Uighur letters were unearthed from one of the caves in Bäzäklik. The three Sogdian texts were edited by the present author in: Turfan Antiquarian Bureau (ed.), *Studies in the new Manichaean texts recovered from Turfan,* Beijing, 2000, pp. 3-199. Three letters are called Letters A, B, and C. Letter A measures 26 cm by 268 cm and comprises 135 lines. Its left-hand margin is badly damaged and the damage is greater towards the end than the beginning. Letter B (79 lines) measures 26 cm by 133 cm and Letter C (29 lines) 30 cm by 45.5 cm; the both are preserved almost intact. While Letter C is written on one sheet of paper, Letters A and B are scrolls consisting of several sheets of paper glued together. Letter A differs from Letter B in that it shows a miniature between lines 25 and 26; it depicts a mitre of a Teacher or možak and two musicians in full colour. The miniature is painted on a narrower sheet of paper than the others and was glued between two sheets of paper constituting the body of the letter.

III-1 Dating of the letters①

Letter C is sent by a monk called Shāh Wispuhr (*š'y wyspwxr*) to his elder Khwar Zādag (*xw'r z-'δ'k*) and is more private than the others; it mentions as many as 19 acquaintances of the addressor bearing Uighur names such as Lord Inčü Bilgä Tiräk (*'yncw pylk' tyr'k xwβw*) and asks the addressee to send his greetings to them. Letters A and B were sent to one and the same addressee named Mār Aryāmān Puhr (*mr 'ry'm'n pwxr*), who was a možak or Teacher of eastern diocese (*xwrsncyk mwz'k*). The two were dispatched to celebrate the New Year and are very similar to each other in that they share almost identical hyperbole expressions praising the Teacher. They also share the feature of bearing crimson seal impressions in various places of the letters, which seems to indicate more official nature of the letters. Nevertheless, while the body of Letter A consists in the wish of auspiciousness for the New Year, Letter B lists the religious services conducted by the addressor and his colleague monks during the month of fast (*cxš'pt m'x*), which is the 12th luni-solar month preceding the New Year.

When I first published the letters I dated them vaguely to the latter half of the 10th century, because it was once shown by Taqizadeh that toward the end of the 10th century in the West Uighur Kingdom, the month of fast was moved ahead by one month from its original position, and because there seemed to me to be no other indication specifying the exact date.② However, it was Professor T. Moriyasu who drew my attention to the fact

① This is a somewhat enlarged version of my discussion published in the following article: Yoshida, "Manichaean Sogdian letters discovered in Bäzäklik", in *Annuaire résumé des conférences et travaux* (École Pratique des Hautes Études. Section des sciences religieuses) Tome 109, 2000-2001[2002], pp. 233-236.

② Originally, the Manichaean month of fast fell on the first luni-solar month of the Chinese calendar, cf. Taqizadeh *apud* Henning, "The Manichaean fasts", *JRAS* 1945, pp. 146-164, esp. p. 160. Letters A and B are in fact dated toward the end of each letter. While almost nothing is left from this part of Letter A, Letter B states that it was written on Monday the sixth day of the month of Pushnu (*pwšnw*) or the first luni-solar month. This dating is far from specific enough to find the exact year.

that a name with a title Isig Ädgü Totoq Ögä (*'ysyk 'δkw twtwγ 'wyk'*) appears both in Letter C and the two Uighur stake inscriptions of 1008 and 1019 CE, (respectively, Stake Inscriptions I and III) and suggested that the two could represent one and the same person.① Following his suggestion I compared the proper names found in the three letters with those of the two stake inscriptions.② Apart from one suggested by Moriyasu, another three names were discovered in the two groups of texts: (1) Alp Totoq Ögä (*'lp twtwx 'wyk'*: Letter A and the two Uighur inscriptions), (2) Sarïγ Baš Tarqan (*sryy p'š trx'n*)③ and (3) Asmïš Tängrim (*''smyš tnkrym*)④ (Letter C and the inscription of 1008 CE).

Especially noteworthy is Alp Totoq Ögä. Letter A (line 123) mentions him as a leader (after the qaghan) heading the lay community of Qočo, where the Teacher was seated: *tδy βyk(k)[yr'nw nywš'kptw] 'lp twtwx 'wyk'* "there (where you are), outside (with respect to secular matters,) [the leader of the auditors] Alp Totoq Ögä". The Uighur minister (Ögä) bearing the same name appears in the following titles: *qočo balïq bägi alp totoq ögä* "the head of the City of Qočo, Alp Totoq Ögä (Stake Inscription I, line 18) and *[el] ögäsi alp totoq ögä qutluγ qočo ulušuγ bašlayur ärkän* "the prime minister Alp Totoq Ögä is the head of the fortunate country of Qočo" (Stake Inscription III, lines 3-4). Accordingly, Alp Totoq Ögä was promoted from the head of the City of Qočo to the prime minister who was in charge of the entire country of Qočo by 1019. Although one does not know what title Alp Totoq Ögä bore in Letter A, the three names shared by Letter C and Stake Inscription I of 1008 CE induce one to date Letters A, B and C nearer to Stake Inscription I of 1008 CE than to III of 1019 CE.⑤ Letter B is dated on Monday the 6th of the first month, and if one looks up the Chinese calendar of the early 11th century, the sixth day of the first month falls on Monday in the years 1007 (27th January), 1010 (23rd January), and 1014 (8th February). In any case, all the three Bäzäklik letters are most likely to go back to the early 11th century.⑥

III-2 Twδ kδ, the place of dispatch mentioned in Letter B

The West Uighur Kingdom had two capitals; one for winter is Qočo and the other for summer, Bešbalïq or Beiting 北庭, today's Jimsar located some 120 km to the north of Qočo. In Letter A (lines 42-44 and 96-97) the Uighur qaghan is mentioned as staying with Aryāmān Puhr; it is most expected that the qaghan stayed in the winter capital during the New Year's season. Since princes and princesses, the members of the royal family, are mentioned with the addressor (lines 125-127), the most likely place of dispatch for Letter A is the winter capital Bešbalïq. In the light of the fact that Letter C mentions the several people bearing Uighur names as having departed from the place where the addressor is staying, it is fitting to suppose that the letter was sent from a locality well within the territory of the West Uighur Kingdom. In this respect Letter B differs from the other two in that no Uighur names are found in it. This situation suggests that Letter B was dispatched from the place outside of the kingdom. In fact the place of dispatch is referred to in Letter B as *twδ-kδ*: *mδy ms twδ-kδcykw prn-w'xšykw* (line 70) "here again, the guardian spirits of the town of Tūdh". In my old study published in 2000, I suggested identifying

---

① His idea is mentioned in Yoshida and Moriyasu, "Manichaean Sogdian and Uighur letters unearthed in Bäzäklik, Turfan (in Japanese)", *Studies on the Inner Asian Languages*, Vol. 15, 2000, pp. 135-178., esp. p. 178.

② The two inscriptions were driven into the ground when stupas were built and the names of donors were written on them. For the text and translation of the two inscriptions see Moriyasu, "Uighur Buddhist stake inscriptions from Turfan", in L. Bazin and P. Zieme (eds.), *De Dunhuang à Istanbul. Hommages à J. R. Hamilton,* Turnhout, 2001, pp. 149-233.

③ I now abandon my old reading Sarïγ Bars Tarqan (*sryy prs trx'n*) in favour of Moriyasu's Sarïγ Baš Tarqan.

④ Moriyasu reads Ašmïš, but for the reading of Asmïš see Sims-Williams and Hamilton, *Documents turco-sogdiens ...*, p. 59.

⑤ On the other hand, as Sundermann argued, not only Buddhism spread but also Manichaean literature flourished in particular under the qaghan mentioned in Stake Inscription III, Kün Ay Tängridä Qut Bulmïš Uluγ Qut Ornanmïš Alpïn Ärdämin Il Tutmïš Alp Arslan Qutluγ Köl Bilgä Tängri Xan, and the Bäzäklik letters may possibly be considered against this historical background, cf. Sundermann, "Iranian Manichaean Turfan texts concerning the Turfan region", in: A. Cadonna (ed.), *Turfan and Tun-huang. The texts,* Florence, 1992, pp. 63-84., esp. p. 70.

⑥ This dating no doubt applies to the other five letters in Uighur, which were discovered with the Sogdian letters.

twδ with a place named Tūdh which is recorded in an Islamic source as located within three farsangs or some 18 km from Samarqand.①

Later when I came to recognize through Dodge's translation of the *Fihrist* that Tūnkath (*twnkθ*) is mentioned by al-Nadīm as a town in Sogdiana where numerous Manichaeans were resident in his time, I proposed to identify *twδ-kδ* with al-Nadīm's *twnkθ*, which could have been a corruption of **twδkθ* due to the similarity of Arabic letters *n* (nūn) and *δ* (dhāl).

> This people [the Manichaeans], who are called Ajārā, are at Rustāq, Samarqand, Ṣughd (Sughd), and especially Tūnkath.②

In his note, Dodge infers that *twnkθ* was located in the Shash or Tashkent region. In the meantime, Moriyasu and I discovered that one Manichaean Uighur text mentions a donator originating from the area around Talas, and that the text can be shown to date back to the early 11th century.③ Thus, my suggestion of identifying *twδ-kδ* with al-Nadīm's *twnkθ* seems to be supported. However, later I came to understand that Dodge's translation is not the only possible rendering of the Arabic original, but several other versions have been proposed.

> (1) Diese Manichäer heissen Adschârî und leben auf den Dörfern von Samarqand, Sogd und vorzugsweise in Nûnkaṭ. (Flügel)④
>
> (2) An-Nadīm sagt aber auch, daß zu seiner Zeit Manichäer in Samarkand, Suǧd und insbesondere *Nawēkaθ lebten. Nawēkaθ ist eher Nawqad Quariš von Samarkqand, zwischen Nasaf und Kiš (...) als Nūkath in Shāsh und Īlāq. (Sundermann)⑤
>
> (3) the remaining Manichaeans in Khurasan are in the district of Samarqand and Sogdiana and especially in Nawēkaθ. (de Blois)⑥
>
> (4) Those people whom they term 'ajārā live in the rural districts of Samarqand, Sogdia, and especially Nawīkath. (Reeves, ibid., p. 229)

What Dodge read *twnkθ* has been read Nawēkath, etc., i.e. *nwykθ*, by the other scholars. Unfortunately, where to locate Nawēkath has not yet been settled⑦, although it is often searched for in the area surrounding Samarqand. It is to be noted that the anonymous author of the *Ḥudūd al-ʿĀlam* clearly indicates that in his time the area designated as Sughd was located between Buchara and Samarqand, much narrower than what we understand under the

① Cf. W. Balthold, *Turkestan down to the Mongol invasion,* 2nd ed., London 1957, p. 132. On a personal name *twδ'yc* possibly derived from this place name see Sims-Williams, *Sogdian and other Iranian inscriptions of the Upper Indus*, vol. II, London 1992, p. 74.

② Cf. B. Dodge, B. 1970: *The Fihrist of an-Nadim*, New York, 1970, p. 803.

③ Cf. Moriyasu, "Four lectures at the College de France in May 2003. History of Manichaeism among the Uighurs from the 8th to the 11th centuries in Central Asia", in: T. Moriyasu (ed.), *World history reconsidered through the Silk Road*, Osaka 2003, pp. 23-111; Yoshida, "Dating of linguistic changes encountered in the texts unearthed from the Silk Road (in Japanese)", *Ex Oriente,* vol. 11, 2004, pp. 3-34.

④ Cf. G. Flügel, *Mani, seine Lehre und seine Schriften. Ein Beitrag zur Geschichte des Manichäismus aus dem Fihrist*, Leipzig, 1862, p. 106.

⑤ Cf. Sundermann, "Ein manichäischer Lehrtext in neupersischer Sprache", in L. Paul (ed.), *Persian origins — Early Judaeo-Persian and the emergence of New Persian,* Wiesbaden, 2003, pp. 243-274, esp. p. 244.

⑥ Cf. F. de Blois, F. *apud* de Blois and Sims-Williams (eds.), *Dictionary of Manichaean texts.* Vol. II. *Texts from Iraq and Iran*, Turnhout, 2006, pp. 26-27, 82-83.

⑦ Since the presence of Manichaeans in the Talas area is suggested by the Uighur text just mentioned, Moriyasu and myself propose to identify Nawēkath with the city referred to as *nwykt* in a Mug document, cf. Yoshida, *Studies of the Chinese Manichaean paintings of South Chinese origin preserved in Japan* (in Japanese), Kyoto, 2015, p. 35. The town called *nwykt* is generally believed to be the old name of today's Krasnaya Rechka on the left bank of the Chu, cf. Livshitz, *op. cit.*, p. 22 with note 3. On this problem see also P. B. Lur'e, "O sledax manixeizma v Srednej Azii", in P. B. Lurje et al. (eds.), *Sogdijcy, ix predšestvenniki, sovremenniki i nasledniki,* St. Petersburg, 2013, pp. 219-251, esp. p. 251.

name of Sogdiana or Sogdian speaking area.① In any case, the town of Tūdh near Samarqand is most likely to be equated rather with what al-Nadīm calls "district of Samarqand" than Nawēkath. Consequently, Letter B was sent from Samarqand to Turfan and betrays the correspondence or exchange between the Manichaean communities of the two cities during the early 11th century.

IV The so-called Manichaean Letters: Letters from Samarqand?

The conclusion reached in the last section induces one to ask whether one can find any other Iranian texts originating from Samarqand among the Turfan materials. One will soon think of those Manichaean New Persian texts discovered from Turfan as likely candidates. Actually, in connection with the dating and the place of origin of the New Persian text studied by him, Sundermann states as follows: "das mit größter Wahrscheinlichkeit im 11. Jahrhundert entstand und dessen Heimat Samarkand oder die Sogdiana im weiteren Sinne war".② In view of the fact that it is written on parchment rather than paper, one may also assume that one Middle Persian text discovered by A. Stein from the Ruin K (Kao. 0111 = Or. 12452D/3) was also copied in Samarqand.③ If this assumption is correct, the miniature of the manuscript was also produced there and requires fresh studies from the viewpoint of the history of Manichaean art.

Here I should like to propose that the two so-called Manichaean Letters once studied by Henning and Sundermann were also dispatched from Samarqand.④ In the letters, in particular Manichaean Letter i, the addressor, who appears to be an indigenous elect, complains about the foreign elects' misbehaviours, which, in his eyes, obviously transgress the precepts. The fact that the names of two schismatics Mihriyya and Miqlāṣiyya are mentioned in the forms of *myhry'nd* "adherents of Mihr" and *mkl'syktyy* "adherents of Miklās" lead both Henning and Sundermann to date the letters to the period before the closing of the schism, which, according to Henning, happened before 880 CE.⑤ Sundermann also paid attention to the fact that no Uighur element is found in the two letters, and assumed that they were written before the Uighurs' evacuation from Mongolia in 840 CE.

However, *myhry'nd* and *mkl'syktyy* appearing in damaged and different places, one cannot see the exact relationship between the two adherents. Moreover, even if the schism was closed the adherents of the fractions and consequently their names could continue to exist. In my opinion *myš'nd rymnyt kmbyt swrykty* (Manichaean Letter ii, line 15) "these dirty mean Syrians" are to be identified with those approximately 500 Manichaeans mentioned by al-Nadīm who left Mesopotamia for Samarqand during the reign of al-Muqtadir (908-932 CE). It would certainly be odd if one cannot find any Turkish word or proper name in the Sogdian letters written in the 10th century Turfan.

---

① Cf. V. Minorsky, V. (tr.) *Ḥudūd al-'Ālam. 'The Religions of the World.' A Persian Geography 372 A.H. -- 982 A.D.,* 2nd ed., London, 1970, p. 113. This understanding of the area covered by Suγd is corroborated by Kāšγarī's statement about Soγd: "They (= Soγdāq) are from Soγd which is between Bukhara and Samarqand", cf. R. Dankoff and J. Kelly (eds.) 1982-85: *Maḥmūd al-Kāšγarī, Compendium of the Turkic Dialects (Dīwān Luγāt at-Turk).* 3 vols., Cambridge, Massachusetts, 1982-1985, p. 352.

② Cf. Sundermann, "Ein manichäischer Lehrtext ...", p. 251. Since the language of Samarqand and Bukhara of the 10th century reported by al-Muqaddasī is nothing but a local variety of New Persian (cf. Yoshida, "Sogdian", 2009, p. 330), Sogdian began to lose its ground by that time.

③ This manuscript was studied by Zs. Gulácsi, U. Sims-Williams, and W. Sundermann, "An illustrated parchment folio from a Middle Persian Manichaean codex in the collection of the British Library", Or. 12452/D (Kao. 0111), *Journal of Inner Asian art and archaeology,* Vol. 1, 2006, pp. 149-155.

④ Henning, "Neue Materialien zur Geschichte des Manichäismus", *ZDMG* 90, 1936, pp. 1-18; Sundermann, "Probleme der Interpretation manichäisch-soghdischer Briefe", in J. Harmatta (ed.), *From Hecataeus to Al-Ḥuwārizmī,* Budapest 1984, pp. 289-316; idem., "Eine Re-Edition zweier manichäisch-soghdischer Briefe", in M. Macuch et al. (eds.), *Iranian languages and texts from Iran and Turan. Ronald E. Emmerick memorial volume,* Wiesbaden, 2007, pp. 403-421. The English translation of the two letters was published in D. Durkin-Meisterernst, "Was Manichaeism a Merchant Religion?", in Academia Turfanica / Turfan Museum (eds.), *Journal of Turfan Studies. Essays on Ancient Coins and Silk: Selected Papers, the Fourth International Conference on Turfan Studies,* Shanghai, 2015, pp. 245-256.

⑤ As far as I can see, neither Henning nor Sundermann gives the basis for this dating.

Nevertheless, it would come as no surprise if letters sent from Samarqand during the 10th century lack Uighur elements. As a matter of fact, no Uighur form is encountered in Letter B. It may be worth noting that Sundermann himself seriously considered the possibility of connecting the situation described in the Manichaean Letters with the evacuation of Manichaeans from Babylon during the reign of al-Muqtadir. He remarks as follows: Es liegt nahe, das Vordringen der manichäischen Syrer nach Zentralasien dann mit diesem Ereignis (i.e. flight of Manichaeans from Babylon to Samarqand, Y.Y.) zu verbinden und in das 10. Jh. zu datieren.①

If my assumption concerning the date and the place of dispatch of Manichaean Letter i proves to be correct, the verbs *sn-* "to go up" and *'wxz* "to go down" found in Manichaean Letter ii may directly refer to the elects' going back and forth between Samarqand and Turfan:② *'rty cw w'nw w'β'nd skwn kt srδ(ng)t pr 'ywp'zky' sn'(nd) [']ty δβtyk 'wxz'nd δymyδ w'xš i p'ryk n's xcyy* (ii, lines 16-17) "And when they are saying that the leaders go up on the visit and come down again, in this word there is altogether destruction". Obviously možak Māhdād went up to Turfan for replacing the late možak Mihrīzad, but there was no gain from that: *pr βγrw'n myh(r'y)[zd] (mwj'k)yy sryy m'hd'd mwj'k sttyy cn(d)n (f)[rtry' 'krtw] (δ)'rt* (ii, lines 18-19) "Možak Māhdād went up (from Samarqand to Turfan) for replacing the late možak Mihrīzad. (But) how much improvement did he do?".

When dating the Manichaean Letters, Henning, and for that matter Sundermann as well, did not pay attention to the Uighur text written on the verso of Manichaean Letter i, which, according to Menges, was written much later and had nothing to do with the Sogdian text on the recto.③ When Moriyasu re-edited the Uighur text published by Geng Shimin and Klimkeit, he was able to establish the exact date of the text; he considered the description of the year in Indian terms, which was identified by M. Yano, a specialist of the Indian astrology, with 983 CE.④ The text was written by an elder (qoštar) named Käd Oγul, who complains about the ill fate of one Manichaean temple in Qočo, from which several ornaments were taken away to decorate and to equip a Buddhist temple. Although no connection can be seen between the Sogdian letter and the Uighur text, my dating of the Sogdian letter places the two texts well within the 10th century, when the bulk of the Turfan Manichaean texts are dated.

Since the first half of the 10th century onward when the Mesopotamian Manichaeans came to join the congregation of Samarqand, the organized Manichaean community existed only in Central Asia.⑤ The sender of Bäzäklik Letter B who lead the church of Samarqand was Mānī Wahman (*m'ny wxmn 'βt'δ'nw*) and bore a title of bishop (aftāδān). Thus, he was inferior to Aryāmān Puhr, who was seated in Turfan and headed the entire community including the Manichaeans of Samarqand. This situation seems to suggest that Aryāmān Puhr was not just a Teacher of the eastern diocese but could also be an archegos of the whole Manichaean church. This assumption may be vindicated by the fact that Aryāmān Puhr is called *pš'γryw* "successor, deputy" in Letters A and B. As Sundermann once proved, the word *pš'γryw* refers to the paraclete and the successor of Mani.⑥ Towards the very end of Central Asian Manichaeism during the early 11th century the centre of the entire Manichaean world is likely to have been situated in Turfan.

---

① Cf. Sundermann, "Probleme ...", 1984, p. 302. Sundermann himslef rejects this possibility on the ground that the language and the contents point to much older period.

② On these expressions see also Sundermann, "Probleme ...", pp. 207-208. One may remember that in Sogdian *'sky kyr'n* "lit. upwards" and *c'δr kyr'n* "lit. downward" also mean respectively "eastward" and "westward", cf. F. Grenet, in *Bulletin of the Asia Institute* 21, 2007[2012], pp. 171-175, esp. p. 175, n. 54.

③ Cf. Henning, art. cit., pp. 17-18, n. 4.

④ Cf. Moriyasu, *Die Geschchte* ..., 2004, pp. 174-181. The text was re-edited by L. Clark and Gulácsi cites Clark's still unpublished translation in her recent work, *Mani's pictures,* Leiden, 2015, pp. 118-123.

⑤ The contemporary Manichaeans of Southern China may well be ignored in this context.

⑥ Cf. Sundermann, "Der Paraklet in der ostmanichäischen Überlierefrung", in P. Bryder (ed.), *Manichaean studies. Proceedings of the First International Conference on Manichaeism,* Lund, 1988, pp. 201-212.

V Conclusion

In this article I assembled the three Manichaean Sogdian texts discovered in Turfan which bear out the exchange between Sogdiana and Turfan during the 10th to early 11th centuries. While the first one (Ch/U 6879) proves the importation of cotton cloth from Sogdiana, the other two (LM 20 1552 (23) of the Lushun National Museum and Bäzäklik Letter B) attest the regular correspondence between the Manichaeans of Samarqand and those of Turfan. The Manichaean New Persian texts discovered in Turfan are most likely to represent the literary works of the Manichaeans living in Samanid or Qarakhanid Samarqand. Bäzäklik Letter B was sent by a bishop (aftāδān) of the Manichaean community of the town of Tūdh near Samarqand to celebrate the New Year. The addressee was a Teacher Aryāmān Puhr staying in Turfan. Therefore, in the early 11th century the Manichaeans of Samarqand were under the leadership of a možak or Teacher seated in the church of Turfan, possibly what is now called Ruin K. Finally, I dwelled on the problems surrounding the so-called Manichaean Letters i and ii and argued that they are connected to the evacuation of Manichaeans from Mesopotamia reported by al-Nadīm as happened during the reign of al-Muqtadir (908-932 CE).

Appendix

1 天宝六载四月十四日给家人春衣历

已上肆人々各给緤

2 常住　大及　■子　■奴　一段充衫八尺充裈

3 祀奴　末如　已上两人々各给一段充衫祀奴八尺充裈

4 可　付緤一段充衫　胡尾子付緤一丈二尺充袴

5 右件緤玖段每段用钱贰伯贰买到用给上件

6 家人春衣谨以为案请僧连署　僧无生

7 僧　　僧玄藏　僧法藏　僧澄练

1 Ledger of spring clothes given to the house workers (attached to a certain Buddhist temple) on the 14th of the 4th month in the 6th year of Tianbao era (= 747 CE).

2 Changzhu, Daji, ???zi, ???nu: (Given) to each of the above mentioned four people one *duan* 段 (equivalent to 20 *chi*s 尺 ① "foot") of cotton cloth for making a shirt; eight feet (of cotton cloth) for making (one pair of) drawers.

3 Sinu, Moru: Given to each of these two people one *duan* 段 of cotton cloth for making a shirt; (Given) to Sinu eight feet (of cotton cloth) for making (one pair of) drawers.

4 Given to Keseng one *duan* 段 of cotton cloth for making a shirt. Given to Huweizi one *zhang* 丈 (= 10 feet) and two feet of cotton cloth for making (one pair of) trousers.

5-7 The above mentioned nine *duan*s 段 of cotton cloth: For each *duan* 段 of cotton cloth 202 copper coins were spent; the cotton cloth was purchased and given to the above mentioned house workers for making their spring clothes. This register document is prepared humbly by us. The monks are requested to sign jointly: (Signatures) Monk Wusheng,② Monk (left blank), Monk Xuanzang, Monk Fazang, Monk Chenglian.

---

① I am grateful to Professor Takao Moriyasu for clarifying the value of *duan* for me.

② Underlined names are the signatures.

玄奘之媲摩与马可波罗之培因再研究 *

罗　帅（中山大学）

摘要： 玄奘所载于阗以东之媲摩城（Phema）即马可波罗提到的培因城（Pein）。唐代文献还经常提到一个跟媲摩密切相关的名字，即坎城（Kamdva）。以往很多学者根据赫定 24 号汉语—于阗语双语文书，将二者勘同。但实际上，它们是相距很近的两座城，二者组成一座城镇共同体。其中，媲摩城也被称作大城，兼具宗教和行政地位；坎城被称作内堡，是于阗东部的军事中心，先后作为唐朝和吐蕃军队的驻地。坎城的历史最早可追溯到汉代，其沿革为扜弥城（Khema）、捍麽城、坎城、建德力城、绀城、肯汗城（Kenhān）。到 12 世纪，肯汗城毁于一次伊斯兰征服战争。明清时期，附近又建起克列牙城儿，又称克勒底雅城、克里雅城。媲摩、坎城均位于克里雅河畔今于田县城附近，而不在老达玛沟的乌宗塔提一带。媲摩地区在古代是多种宗教并存的地方，前伊斯兰时代，佛教尤盛。在唐代早期出现的老子于阗化胡说中，媲摩被描述成老子化胡成佛之所。媲摩之名，意为瑞像，得名于玄奘所描述的媲摩城雕檀瑞像。赫定 7 号于阗语文书记载有媲摩功德使，并称媲摩城高僧众多。媲摩地区的重要物产，据马可波罗记载，一为玉石，二为棉花，其精良者敦煌文书谓之绀城细緤。

关键词： 媲摩；坎城；培因；玄奘；马可波罗

1273 年，著名的旅行家马可波罗（Marco Polo）行经塔里木盆地南道，他在行纪中提到了沿途的六个地名，即可失合儿（今喀什）、鸦儿看（莎车）、忽炭（和田）、培因、阇鄽（且末）和罗卜（若羌）。其中，唯有培因不见于其他蒙元时期的文献。不过，更早时期的文献对这个地方有不少记载，并保留了此地的多个不同名称。例如，玄奘之传、记称其为媲摩，并不惜笔墨详述了当地的瑞像传闻。1906 年，斯坦因（M. A. Stein）撰文《玄奘之媲摩与马可波罗之培因》，立足于实地考古调查，分析和比较了玄奘与马可波罗的文本以及宋云关于捍麽的记载，将培因、媲摩、捍麽勘同，并将它们的位置推定在今策勒县达玛沟乡北部的乌宗塔提（Uzun-Tati）一带。① 他的这些结论影响很大，为大多数学者所接受。然而，百余年来新的出土文献提供的新线索，对其部分观点带来了巨大的挑战。因此，笔者认为，有必要对培因、媲摩的相关问题重新进行审视。

---

* 本文在写作过程中承蒙荣新江先生悉心指导，谨此致谢。

① M. A. Stein, “Hsüan-tsang’s Notice of P’i-mo and Marco Polo’s Pein”, *T’oung Pao*, 2nd series, 7/4, 1906, pp. 469-480; also in: idem, *Ancient Khotan: Detailed Report of Archaeological Explorations in Chinese Turkestan*, Vol. I, Oxford, Clarendon Press, 1907, pp. 452-463（汉译本：巫新华等译：《古代和田》第 1 卷，济南：山东人民出版社，2009 年，第 494—499 页）.

一　地名演变史

（一）培因即媲摩

《马可波罗行纪》结束忽炭州一章后，紧接着就描写了培因的情况，内容包括该州的居民、宗教、城镇、物产、风俗等各个方面。为便于下文讨论，现节录相关片段如下：

> 培因乃一小（TA）州，广五日行程，位于东方与东北方之间。*此州*（LT）居民崇拜摩诃末，且*同样*（P）臣属于大汗。*治下*（VB）有众多城镇和乡村，*全州*（V）最宏大城市名培因，乃该区之首府。有一条*河流经其地*（Z），河中可以找到*数量*（V）非常大的珍*贵*（LT）宝石，人们称之为碧玉和玉髓。*此州*（Z）百姓*拥有极为*（VB）丰富的*一切必需*（Z）品。*该地也*（V）盛产棉花。人们*更多地*（VB）以贸易和手艺为生。[①]

培因在《马可波罗行纪》诸本中的写法各有差异，在F本中写作Pein。伯希和（P. Pelliot）认为，最初的拼法当以-m结尾，因此，正确的形式是Z本的Pem。[②]

贞观十八年（644），玄奘在于阗得诏，获允东归。《大慈恩寺三藏法师传》记其于阗以东行程为："自发都三百余里，东至媲摩城。城有雕檀立佛像……从媲摩城东入沙碛，行二百余里，至泥壤城。"[③]《大唐西域记》所载略同，称于阗国都以东300余里为古战场，又30余里为媲摩城。[④]此外，由于媲摩城雕檀佛像乃于阗著名瑞像之一，因此媲摩之名屡见于敦煌石窟汉文瑞像题记以及敦煌文书P. 3033和S.2113A，但其中"媲"字往往误作"娓"，或写作俗字形式。[⑤]

1871年，玉尔（H. Yule）最先将马可波罗之培因比定为玄奘之媲摩。[⑥]此后，除了沙海昂（A. H. J. Charignon）之外[⑦]，几乎所有的研究者都赞同此说。玉尔的观点在地理位置和语音学方面是讲得通的。在《大慈恩寺三藏法师传》回鹘语译本中，媲摩写作Bim。[⑧]伯希和将媲摩（晚期中古音pɦji-mua[⑨]）的本名准确地复原为*Phema或*Phima。[⑩]现在我们已经知道，在和田地区出土的8世纪于阗语文书

---

① A. C. Moule & P. Pelliot (trans. and annotated), *Marco Polo. The Description of the World*, Vol. I, chap. 55, London, Routledge, 1938, p. 147. 译文在北京大学马可波罗项目读书班译定稿的基础上，略有修订。其中，正体字为《马可波罗行纪》F本的内容；斜体字为其他诸本的内容，其后括注版本信息。版本缩略语参见原书第509—516页表格。

② P. Pelliot, *Notes on Marco Polo*, II, Paris: Imprimerie nationale, 1963, p. 801.

③ 慧立、彦悰撰：《大慈恩寺三藏法师传》，孙毓棠、谢方点校，北京：中华书局，2000年，第124页。

④ 玄奘、辩机原著：《大唐西域记校注》，季羡林等校注，北京：中华书局，2000年，第1026—1029页。

⑤ 张广达、荣新江：《敦煌"瑞像记"、瑞像图及其反映的于阗》，原载《敦煌吐鲁番文献研究论集》第3辑，北京大学出版社，1986年，第69—147页；收入作者《于阗史丛考》（增订本），北京：中国人民大学出版社，2008年，第166—223页。

⑥ H. Yule (ed. & trans.), *The Book of Ser Marco Polo, the Venetian: Concerning the Kingdoms and Marvels of the East*, revised by H. Cordier, London, J. Murray, 1903, p. 192 (original edition in 1871).

⑦ 沙海昂以诸本中培因有作Pein、Peim、Poin、Poim者，与两《唐书》里的"播仙"音近，因而将二者勘同，见沙海昂注《马可波罗行纪》新1版，冯承钧译，北京：中华书局，2003年，第159—167页。

⑧ Л. Ю. Тугушевои, *Фрагменты уйгурской версии биографии Сюань-цзана*, Москва, Наука, 1980, c. 28.

⑨ E. G. Pulleyblank, *Lexicon of reconstructed pronunciation in Early Middle Chinese, Late Middle Chinese, and Early Mandarin*, Vancouver, UBC Press, 1991, pp. 217, 236.

⑩ P. Pelliot, *Notes on Marco Polo*, II, p. 801.

中，媲摩写作 Phema[①]；而在敦煌文书钢和泰藏卷于阗语《使河西记》（写于 925 年[②]）中，媲摩城作 Phịmāṇa kaṃtha[③]。于阗语文书中的这两种形式与伯希和所拟完全一致。在古藏语文献《牛角山授记》中，媲摩被写作 Phye-ma 和 Bye-ma。[④]10 世纪的阿拉伯诗人兼旅行家米撒儿（Abū Dulaf Mis'ar bin al-Muhalhil）声称，他曾奉中亚萨曼王朝（Samanids）异密之命出使过中国，其行纪在于阗（Khatiyān）之后，紧接着描写了一个叫作 Pima 的地方。[⑤]

此外，唐代早期老子化胡说里出现了一种"于阗化胡说"，声称于阗有毗摩城（或言比摩寺、毗摩寺、毗摩伽蓝、毗摩城伽蓝[⑥]），为老子化胡之所。此说在敦煌十卷本《老子化胡经》卷一（S.1857、P. 2007）里有详细表述。[⑦] 目前所知，这种说法最早见于《隋书》（成书于 636 年）："于阗西五百里有比摩寺，云是老子化胡成佛之所。"[⑧] 所谓的比摩寺跟玄奘之媲摩在方位、里程方面均对不上，但综合"于阗化胡说"的各种描述来看，二者应指同一个地方。刘屹对"于阗化胡说"进行了深入研究，认为此说的兴起与李唐皇室直接有关，它首先在 635 年进入起居注一类的皇家实录，并被次年成书的《隋书》所采录，后来更是为多种文献所传袭；而《化胡经》中的毗摩寺，乃是道士们据《宋云行纪》《大唐西域记》等记载虚构出来的。[⑨] 张广达、荣新江亦指出，《老子化胡经》是远离于阗的中原道士虚构之作，有关比摩寺的记载除了见诸老子化胡传说之外，别无他证。[⑩] 这些论断皆切中肯綮。唯《隋书》"比摩"一名源自何处？尚需探讨。玄奘之传、记均提到了媲摩，但他归国较《隋书》成书晚九年。南宋释志磐《佛祖统纪》云："《隋史 · 西域传》、魏宋云《西行记》、唐太子实录，皆言于阗有毗摩寺，是老子化胡处。"[⑪] 然而，今辑佚本《宋云行纪》并未言及"比摩"，原本也许记载有"毗摩寺"，或未可知。南宋谢守灏《混元圣纪》载称："（贞观）九年（635）二月丁卯，于阗王

---

① 根据文欣的统计，提到 Phema 的于阗语文书有近 30 件，见文欣：《中古时期于阗国政治制度研究》，北京大学历史学系硕士学位论文，2008 年，第 91—92 页，表 4—5。

② E. G. Pulleyblank, "The Date of the Staël-Holstein Roll" , *Asia Major* 4, new series, 1954, pp. 90-97.

③ H. W. Bailey, "The Staël-Holstein Miscellany" , *Asia Major* 2/1, new series, 1951, pp. 2, 10; J. Hamilton, "Autour du manuscrit Staël-Holstein" , *T'oung Pao* 46, second series, 1958, p. 117.

④ F. W. Thomas, *Tibetan Literary Texts and Documents Concerning Chinese Turkistan, Part I: Literary Texts,* London, The Royal Asiatic Society, 1935, p. 24; Ibid., Part II: Documents, London 1951, pp. 309-310；朱丽双：《唐代于阗的羁縻州与地理区划研究》，《中国史研究》2012 年第 2 期，第 79 页。

⑤ 费琅：《阿拉伯波斯突厥人东方文献辑注》，耿昇、穆根来译，北京：中华书局，1989 年，第 238 页；冯承钧：《大食人米撒儿行纪中之西域部落》，收入《西域南海史地考证论著汇辑》，北京：中华书局，1957 年，第 186 页。伯希和对米撒儿的相关记载表示严重怀疑（P. Pelliot, *Notes on Marco Polo*, II, p. 801）。马雍对米撒儿出使中国一事进行过探究，指出此事系其杜撰，所载沿途地名、部落皆得自传闻（马雍：《萨曼王朝与中国的交往》，原载《学习与思考》1983 年第 5 期，收入作者《西域史地文物丛考》，北京：文物出版社，1990 年，第 174—182 页）。不过，我认为米撒儿有关于阗、媲摩的描述虽非其亲历所见，但亦非虚构，当抄自前人著作。

⑥ 释念常：《佛祖历代通载》卷二二，收入《大正藏》第 49 册 2036 号，台北：佛陀教育基金会，1990 年，第 719a 页；释祥迈：《大元至元辨伪录》卷二，收入《大正藏》第 52 册 2116 号，第 761c 页。

⑦ P. 2007 号文书录文参见罗振玉编：《敦煌石室遗书百廿种》，收入黄永武主编：《敦煌丛刊初集》（六），台北：新文丰出版公司，1985 年，第 257 页；S.1857 号文书录文参见李小荣：《敦煌道教文学研究》，成都：巴蜀书社，2009 年，第 412 页。

⑧ 《隋书》卷八三《西域传》，北京：中华书局点校本，1973 年，第 1853 页。

⑨ 刘屹：《敦煌十卷本〈老子化胡经〉残卷新探》，收入荣新江主编：《唐研究》第 2 卷，北京大学出版社，1996 年，第 101—120 页。

⑩ 张广达、荣新江：《于阗佛寺志》，原载《世界宗教研究》1986 年第 3 期；收入作者《于阗史丛考》（增订本），第 238—239 页。

⑪ 释志磐：《佛祖统纪》卷四〇，收入《大正藏》第 49 册 2035 号，第 372b 页。

遣子来朝贡，语及其国土所有，云西有毗摩伽蓝，相传是老子化胡之所。”[①] 据此，《隋书》“比摩寺”之名也可能来自这位于阗王子。无论如何，《隋书》的记载表明，在玄奘归国之前，媲摩及其佛教即已蜚声中原。因此，唐初的“于阗化胡”论者才将其视作佛门重地，说成是老子化胡成佛之所。

（二）媲摩与坎城

媲摩与坎城之关系是一个错综复杂的问题。沙畹（E. Chavannes）最早将培因、媲摩与坎城勘同，而赞同者颇多。[②] 也有一些学者，如亨廷顿（E. Huntington）[③]、哈密屯（J. Hamilton）[④]、孙修身[⑤]，认为二者不是同一个地方。近年，文欣、段晴提出新的看法，认为媲摩即坎城；媲摩是一定范围的区域名称，同时也可以指这个区域内的一座城。[⑥] 今按，前说均有未安者，以下试析之。

关于坎城，《新唐书·地理志》云，“于阗东界有兰城、坎城二守捉城”，又据贾耽《皇华四达记》“边州入四夷道”指出，“于阗东三百里有坎城镇，东六百里有兰城镇”，“西经移杜堡、彭怀堡、坎城守捉，三百里至于阗”[⑦]。其中，兰城乃蔺城之误，即玄奘之所谓尼壤城。[⑧] 由此可知，唐朝在于阗国都以东 300 里处设有坎城镇、守捉。但这里的三百里、六百里显系取整的约数。

坎城之名经常出现在和田地区出土的汉文文书里。在古藏语文献里，其名写作 Khaṃ sheng、Kam sheng 或 sKam sheng[⑨]，乃汉文名称之音译。而汉文“坎城”可能来自于阗语文书中的地名 Kaṃdva[⑩]。另外，于阗语文献里还有一个名字也可能跟坎城有关，即赫定（Hedin）42 号文书中的 Khaṃśarāña。这件文书是一份残损的驻军分布名单，在总共 30 个驻军地点中，所列的第一个便是 Khaṃśarāña，其他地点包括 Abīyāgïri、屋悉贵（Ustāki）、Mattiskāña、Salā 等。这个名字在赫定 4 号和 64 号文书中分别写作 Khaśarāṃ 和 Khaśarāña。赫定 4 号文书是一封于阗某王（尉迟曜）二十一年（784）的书信，由 Khaśarāṃ 的居民 Budasaṃga 所写，信的前半部分讲述他收到一批债务还款时，特意提到小麦

① 谢守灏：《混元圣纪》，收入《道藏》第 17 册，北京：文物出版社，1988 年，第 856b 页。

② 沙畹：《宋云行纪笺注》，冯承钧译，收入《西域南海史地考证译丛》第 6 编，北京：中华书局，1956 年，第 13—14 页；H. W. Bailey, *Khotanese Texts*, Vol. IV, Cambridge, Cambridge University Press, 1961, pp. 135-137; 王北辰：《古代西域南道上的若干历史地理问题》，原载《地理研究》1983 年第 3 期，收入《王北辰西北历史地理论文集》，北京：学苑出版社，2000 年，第 320—321 页；又《新疆地名考五条——和田、于田、若羌、鄯善、罗布泊》，原载《干旱区地理》1985 年第 4 期，收入《王北辰西北历史地理论文集》，第 410—413 页；吉田豊：《有关和田出土 8—9 世纪于阗语世俗文书的札记》（一），广中智之译，收入《敦煌吐鲁番研究》第 11 卷，上海古籍出版社，2008 年，第 177 页；又《有关和田出土 8—9 世纪于阗语世俗文书的札记》（二），荣新江、广中智之译，收入朱玉麒主编：《西域文史》第 3 辑，北京：科学出版社，2008 年，第 81 页；又《有关和田出土 8—9 世纪于阗语世俗文书的札记》（三）中，田卫卫译，收入《敦煌学辑刊》2012 年第 2 期，第 172 页；又《有关和田出土 8—9 世纪于阗语世俗文书的札记》（三）下，田卫卫译，收入《敦煌学辑刊》2012 年第 3 期，第 157 页。

③ E. Huntington, *The Pulse of Asia. A Journey in Central Asia Illustrating the Geographic Basis of History*, London, Archibald Constable, 1907, pp. 191, 387-388.

④ J. Hamilton, “Autour du manuscrit Staël-Holstein”, pp. 117-118.

⑤ 孙修身：《莫高窟佛教史迹故事画介绍（二）》，《敦煌研究》1982 年第 1 期，第 108—110 页。

⑥ 文欣：《中古时期于阗国政治制度研究》，第 90—91 页；段晴：《Hedin 24 号文书释补》，收入新疆吐鲁番学研究院编：《语言背后的历史——西域古典语言学高峰论坛论文集》，上海古籍出版社，2012 年，第 74—78 页。

⑦ 《新唐书》卷四〇《地理志四》，第 1048 页；卷四三下《地理志七下》，第 1150—1151 页。

⑧ 朱丽双：《唐代于阗的羁縻州与地理区划研究》，第 80—82 页。

⑨ R. E. Emmerick, *Tibetan Texts Concerning Khotan*, London, Oxford University Press, 1967, pp. 88-91; 朱丽双：《〈于阗国授记〉译注》（上），《中国藏学》2012 年 S1 期，第 244 页；又《唐代于阗的羁縻州与地理区划研究》，第 79 页；荣新江、朱丽双：《于阗与敦煌》，兰州：甘肃教育出版社，2013 年，第 256 页。

⑩ 文欣：《中古时期于阗国政治制度研究》，第 90 页。

和大麦使用的度量单位是“汉人的升”（cemgāṃ ṣṣaṃgna）；赫定64号文书是下达给六城的勿日桑宜（Vaśa'rasaṃgä）的文牒，令其征收布匹并遣送某人至Khaśarāña，其中还提到Khaśarāña有军队指挥官（troop-commanders）。① 通过这三件文书，我们大致了解到Khaṃśarāña是一个有驻军且受汉人文化影响较大的地方。我们知道，赫定文书主要得自和田以东老达玛沟一带，42号文书也提到了六城的屋悉贵，如果这件文书记载的是于阗东部的驻军情况，那么我认为排在首位的Khaṃśarāña很可能是指坎城。这是基于以下三点考虑：首先，从语言学的角度看，这个名字像是汉语“坎城”（晚期中古音kʰam-ʂɦiajŋ②）的完整音译，它跟古藏文的Khamsheng基本一致；其次，出土文书和《新唐书》等文献都表明，坎城是于阗东部的军事镇防中心③，驻守有唐朝的军队；再者，大量和田地区出土文书都揭示了六城向坎城输送人力、物力的情况，而4号和64号文书体现的正是六城与Khaṃśarāña之间的人员和物资往来。概言之，汉语“坎”城最初可能节译自于阗语地名Kaṃdva的首音节，但后来在于阗语文书里又出现了对译汉语“坎城”的名字Khaṃśarāña。

赫定24号文书为厘清媲摩与坎城之关系提供了最关键的线索。其正面是一件贞元十四年（798）的汉语—于阗语双语文书，背面是一份于阗语士兵名籍。正面汉文第4行有“人畜一切尽收入坎城防备”等字句④；根据贝利（H. W. Bailey）和施杰我（P. O. Skjærvø）的译文，于阗文的相应部分为“将此区域内的人畜全部转移到媲摩城（Phẹmāña kiṃtha）”⑤。由于这种对应关系，将坎城与媲摩城勘同貌似无可厚非。然而，实际上这并不合理。因为，既然坎城在于阗语中存在Kaṃdva和Khaṃśarāña这样的对应名字，而且它们在多件文书中被使用，那么这里为何不用这两个名字来对译？

这件文书使用汉语和于阗语双语的用意何在？总的说来，所有的双语文书都是因为牵涉的人群包含有使用这两种语言的人。但具体到不同的文书类别，如宗教文书、经济法律文书、军事行政文书，其意义又不尽相同：若是佛经，可能是为了经文的转译对照；契约和收据，是为了明示一致的法律效力；下达的公文文牒，是就某件事通知不同的人群。前两种无疑需要文本内容高度一致，最后一种却未必。具体到赫定24号文书，其于阗文与汉文夹行相间，于阗文写于每行汉文左侧，但二者并非逐行对译，于阗文内容较汉文简略。⑥ 相关的背景是，于阗既存在唐朝的汉人军队，也存在于阗的土著居民和军队。这份牒文要指示的事情是，敌军来袭，牒文所达，辖区内一切汉胡人等均需做好防备。荣新江正确指出了该文书的功用：“这种双语文本可以供当地的唐人和于阗人官吏共同使用，而在再次转发的时候，可以分别写成汉文和于阗文，转发到唐人和于阗人集中的小吏手中”，“于阗语在汉语的行间或汉语部分的后面书写，不另起草新的文书，这也增加了行政的效率”。⑦ 也就是说，这件由安西节度副使、毗沙都督府都督、于阗王尉迟曜签署的文书之所以使用双语，是为了提高传递效率，

① H. W. Bailey, *Khotanese Texts*, Vol. IV, pp. 74-79, 151-152, 165-166; idem, *Saka Documents, Text Volume*, London: Percy Lund, 1968, pp. 2, 4.

② E. G. Pulleyblank, *Lexicon of reconstructed pronunciation in Early Middle Chinese, Late Middle Chinese, and Early Mandarin*, pp. 54, 170.

③ 沈琛：《吐蕃统治时期的于阗》，北京大学历史学系硕士学位论文，2015年，第52—54页。

④ 张广达、荣新江：《8世纪下半叶至9世纪初的于阗》，原载荣新江主编：《唐研究》第3卷，1997年，第339—361页；此据作者《于阗史丛考》（增订本），第242页。

⑤ H. W. Bailey, *Khotanese Texts*, Vol. IV, pp. 135-138; idem, *Saka Documents. Text Volume*, pp. 12-13; P. O. Skjærvø, “The End of Eighth-Century Khotan in Its Texts”, *Journal of Inner Asian Art and Archaeology* 3, 2008 [2009], p. 120.

⑥ 关于赫定24号文书汉语、于阗语夹行相间的原貌录文及讨论，参见荣新江：《汉语—于阗语双语文书的历史学考察》，收入新疆吐鲁番学研究院编：《语言背后的历史——西域古典语言学高峰论坛论文集》，上海古籍出版社，2012年，第20—22页。

⑦ 荣新江：《汉语—于阗语双语文书的历史学考察》，第30—31页。

当它抵达下层机构之后，汉文和于阗文文本将被分别抄出，转发给相应的人群。其汉文部分的接受者是于阗东部的唐朝镇守军，于阗文部分则是这一带的土著军民。俄藏于阗语文书 SI P 103.49 明确提到 cemgāña Kaṃdvāña（汉人之坎城）①，这是因为在唐朝统治时期，坎城由唐朝军队驻守，是一个军镇。赫定 24 号文书命令唐朝军队进入坎城即 Kaṃdva 防守，于阗语部分不使用 Kaṃdva，恰恰表明媲摩城（Phẹmāña kiṃtha）和坎城不是同一个地方。这件文书并非让当地的土著军民也涌入坎城，而是另有去处，即前往媲摩城。

英藏于阗语文书 Or.11344/8 提到了 Pheme Kaṃdvāṣṭa，即“媲摩之坎城”②，表明媲摩和坎城存在着密切关系。在和田地区出土文书中，类似的两个地名连用的情况还有六城质逻、六城杰谢、杰谢合川、拔伽屋悉贵等，反映的关系均是一种包含关系：前一个是更高级别的行政单位，后一个从属于前者（当然，也有质逻六城的用法，质逻是六城的治所）。据此看来，坎城应在媲摩之辖区内。另一些文书也提示了媲摩与坎城之关系，如 Or.6399/1.5 和 Or.6401/2.2 均提到 Phema śūkṣuha③，吉田豊将 śūkṣuha 比定为汉文中的“守捉”④，这个词组的意思是“媲摩守捉”。而《新唐书》提到了于阗东部有坎城和兰（蔺）城两个守捉，文书里又见到坎城守捉和杰谢守捉，这里的媲摩守捉当是指坎城守捉。坎城即《新唐书》里提到的守捉城。

总体来看，以上材料反映了坎城与媲摩（城）之间难以捉摸的微妙关系。我认为，造成各种困惑的根源可能是中亚普遍存在的大城现象（笔者姑且称之为城镇共同体）。刘迎胜讨论过这种现象。他援引了 14 世纪穆斯林作家乌马里（Ibn Faḍl Allāh al-ʿUmarī，1301—1349）《眼历诸国纪行》中的一条史料：

> 自撒麻耳干至汗八里的路程应〔为〕：自撒麻耳干至养吉 20 日程。养吉由 4 座城组成，互相距离为一个帕剌伤，各有自己的名字：养吉、养吉八里、肯切克和塔剌思。自上述城市养吉至阿力麻里为 20 日程。⑤

根据这则材料，刘先生指出，养吉、养吉八里、肯切克和塔剌思四座城构成一座大城，名曰养吉（意为“新城”）。帕剌伤（Parasang）为波斯长度单位，约当今 13 华里，因此这几座小城彼此相距一二十里。由几个邻近的小城镇合为一座大城的情况在古代中亚很常见。例如，元代别十八里（唐

---

① R. E. Emmerick & M. I. Vorob'ëva-Desjatovskaja, *Saka Documents. Text Volume, III: The St. Petersburg Collections*, London, School of Oriental and African Studies, 1995, p. 156.

② H. W. Bailey, *Khotanese Texts*, Vol. II, Cambridge: Cambridge University Press, 1954, p. 34; idem, *Saka Documents, Text Volume*, p. 36; P. O. Skjærvø, *Khotanese Manuscripts from Chinese Turkestan in the British Library. A Complete Catalogue with Texts and Translations*, with contribution by U. Sims-Williams, London, British Library Publishing, 2002, pp. 111-112.

③ H. W. Bailey, *Khotanese Texts*, Vol. V, Cambridge, Cambridge University Press, 1963, p. 12; P. O. Skjærvø, *Khotanese Manuscripts from Chinese Turkestan in the British Library. A Complete Catalogue with Texts and Translations*, p. 19.

④ 吉田豊：《有关和田出土 8—9 世纪于阗语世俗文书的札记》（三）中，第 172 页。

⑤ Ibn Faḍl Allāh al-ʿUmarī, *Das mongolische Weltreich. Al-ʿUmarīs Darstellung der mongolischen Reiche in seinem Werk Masālik al-abṣār fī mamālik al-amṣār*, Mit Paraphrase und Kommentar hrsg. von Klaus Lech, Wiesbaden, Harrassowitz, 1968, S. 111. 汉译文引自刘迎胜：《海路与陆路——中古时代东西交流研究》，北京大学出版社，2011 年，第 306—307 页；又《西北民族史与察合台汗国史研究》，北京：中国国际广播出版社，2012 年，第 169 页。

代的北庭）本身就是五城的意思。[①] 大城现象在塔里木盆地各个狭小的绿洲上显然也容易出现。北魏《宋云行纪》提到在末城以西22里有捍麽（早期中古音ɣanh-ma，晚期中古音xɦan-mua[②]）城[③]，这个名字无疑来自汉代的扜弥：捍、扜同音同义；又，斯坦因所获214、272、506、709等号佉卢文文书中，扜弥作Khema[④]，可见早期中古汉语以“弥”译-ma，晚期中古汉语则以“麽、摩”译之。捍麽城亦即唐代之坎城——此城在唐代因为由汉军驻守而被称为汉人之城，并有了汉语名称“坎城”（试比较khem- > ɣanh > kham 坎）。宋云所谓的末城即后来的媲摩城，“末”是对Phema第二个音节的省译（更可能的情况是，今辑佚本《宋云行纪》“末”字前有阙文，原作“□末城”）。捍麽城与末城仅相距22里（当今23里），暗示了当地存在城镇共同体的可能。

根据以上分析，我认为存在一座名为媲摩的城镇共同体：它以媲摩城为首，至少还包括坎城，也许还有其他城镇、村落以及军事据点、设施。Pheme Kaṃdvāṣṭa指的是媲摩城镇共同体里的坎城；当然，也可能存在更上一级的行政单位媲摩州。

和田地区出土文书里有两组文书，分别提到了“大城”和“内堡”，它们也暗示了媲摩城镇共同体的存在。第一组文书是中国人民大学博物馆新近入藏的和田汉文文书中的三个残片（出土地可能是丹丹乌里克 / 杰谢）[⑤]，里面均包含有“大城”字样。这三个残片在内容上相关联，可能来自同一件文书，其中一片给出的正式编号是GXW0106，定名为《武周某年事目历》。这件事目历记录的是六城跟坎城镇、大城之间的公文书往来情况。在三个残片中，一共出现领送坎城牒5次，使牒坎城镇1次，领送大城牒2次。显然，其中的坎城与大城存在密切关系。我认为，“大城”指的是媲摩城，其于阗语形式可能为Cheṃjsa-purrāṃ，详见下文讨论。媲摩城的规模比坎城大，是当地城镇共同体的主城，因此被称为“大城”，其名也因此用作整个城镇共同体的名字。

关于媲摩城镇共同体，唐宋扬州城可提供有益的参考。唐代扬州城包括子城和罗城两座相邻的城。子城，又称牙城、衙城，由内城、外城和附郭东城组成，居于蜀岗之上，为官府所在；罗城，又称大城，居于蜀岗之南、运河岸边的平地，为商业区。子城面积约2.828平方公里，罗城约13.1平方公里，后者称作“大城”名副其实。到了宋代，扬州城又演变成宋大城、宝祐城和夹城的三城格局。[⑥] 造成扬州二城或三城的原因是地形的限制。早期的扬州城在蜀岗高地之上，到唐代随着长江北岸向南推移了近30里[⑦]，蜀岗南面形成大片沉积平地，后来就在平地的运河沿岸增筑了罗城作为商业区。媲摩城镇共同体的成因自然不同，但是，唐宋扬州城之布局与中亚大城模式遥相呼应，无疑为媲

① 刘迎胜：《西北民族史与察合台汗国史研究》，第169页。

② E. G. Pulleyblank, *Lexicon of reconstructed pronunciation in Early Middle Chinese, Late Middle Chinese, and Early Mandarin,* pp. 119, 217.

③ 余太山：《“宋云行纪”要注》，收入《早期丝绸之路文献研究》，上海人民出版社，2009年，第272页。

④ T. Burrow, *The Language of the Kharoṣṭhī Documents from Chinese Turkestan,* Cambridge, Cambridge University Press, 1937, p. 86; idem, *A Translation of the Kharoṣṭhī Documens from Chinese Turkestan,* London: the Royal Asiatic society, 1940, pp. 40, 49, 99, 142; J. Brough, “Comments on Third-Century Shan-shan and the History of Buddhism”, *Bulletin of the School of Oriental and African Studies,* 28/3, 1965, p. 593.

⑤ 非正式编号为034A、034B、035-1。

⑥ 中国社会科学院考古研究所等：《扬州城：1987—1998年考古发掘报告》，北京：文物出版社，2010年；又《扬州城遗址考古发掘报告：1999~2013年》，北京：科学出版社，2015年。

⑦ 罗宗真：《扬州唐代古河道等的发现和有关问题的探讨》，《文物》1980年第3期，第22页。又《试述扬州港开始繁荣于唐代的原因》，收入陈玉寅主编：《江苏省考古学会1983年考古论文选》，南京：江苏省考古学会，1983年；收入南京博物院编：《罗宗真文集·历史文化卷》，北京：文物出版社，2013年，第174页。

摩城镇共同体提供了很好的注脚。

南宋朝廷降元后，扬州宋朝守将李庭芝凭借“宋三城”的坚固防御布局，还继续抵抗了相当长的一段时间。① 因此，扬州“宋三城”的布局在我国军事史、城防建筑史上具有极其重要的地位。② 这样的城形成了掎角之势，扩大了攻城的战线。这从侧面暗示了为何坎城在唐、吐蕃统治时期一直是于阗东部的军事防御中心。

第二组文书包括多件于阗语文书，其中均提到了“内堡”（haṃdara prū）。③ 贝利和施杰我将这个词译作 Inner Fort/ Inner Military Fort/ Inner Military Post，表明它是一个军事据点。这些文书均是内堡从六城征调人力和各种物资的内容。在现今已知的和田出土文书中，向六城下达的征调事牒，汉文文书绝大部分来自坎城；于阗语文书主要来自媲摩（Phema），其次就是这些内堡文书。我认为，内堡指的就是坎城，它只出现在于阗语文书中，是坎城军事化之后于阗人对它的另一个称呼。它是媲摩城镇共同体里面的军事据点，所以称作内堡。

这两组文书反映了自唐朝军队驻守坎城以来，汉胡军民对媲摩区域内的地名的几个有趣称呼。综合上文的讨论，可总结如下：唐朝军队驻守在媲摩城镇共同体内的 Kaṃdva 城之后，将其汉译作坎城，此后该城作为唐军的活动基地，于阗土著有时将其称作 ceṃgāña Kaṃdvāña（汉人之坎城）；久而久之，于阗人甚至将汉语“坎城”完整音译回于阗语 Khaṃśarāña；此外，于阗本地居民有时也将其称作内堡。另一方面，汉胡军民将 Phema 城称作大城（Cheṃjsa-purrāṃ）；熟悉玄奘传、记的佛教徒（敦煌相关瑞像的制作者）也根据玄奘的叫法，使用其汉文名字“媲摩”；宋云则可能省译了首音节，将其称作末城。

（三）捍麽城、末城、绀城、肯汗城诸名

相关的文献提供了一组各个历史时期跟坎城有沿革关系的地名——扜弥城、捍麽城、建德力城、绀城、肯汗城。汉代文献所载之扜弥（多误作扞弥）、拘弥城，即《宋云行纪》里的捍麽城，亦即《新唐书》之建德力城。关于扜弥城与建德力城，笔者拟撰专文别论。以下，试对另外几个名称略作阐释。

1. 捍麽城、末城

捍麽城之名见于《洛阳伽蓝记》卷五所载之宋云、惠生行纪中，二人于 519 年西行途经塔里木盆地。其相关片段如下：

> 从左末城西行一千二百七十五里，至末城。城傍花果似洛阳，唯土屋平头为异也。
>
> 从末城西行二十二里，至捍麽城。〔城〕南十五里有一大寺，三百余僧众。有金像一躯，举高丈六，仪容超绝，相好炳然，面恒东立，不肯西顾。父老传云：此像本从南方腾空而来，于阗国王亲见礼拜，载像归，中路夜宿，忽然不见，遣人寻之，还来本处。王即起塔，封四百户以供洒扫。户人有患，以金箔贴像所患处，即得阴愈。后人于此像边造丈六像者及诸像塔，乃至数千，悬彩幡盖，亦有万计。魏国之幡过半矣。幡上隶书，多云太和十九年、景明二年、延昌二

① 《宋史》卷四二一《李庭芝传》，北京：中华书局，1977 年，第 12600—12602 页。

② 中国社会科学院考古研究所等：《扬州宋大城西门发掘报告》，《考古学报》1999 年第 4 期，第 515 页。

③ 关于内堡文书的统计和介绍，参见沈琛：《吐蕃统治时期的于阗》，第 60—62 页。

年。唯有一幡，观其年号是姚兴时幡。

从捍麽城西行八百七十八里，至于阗国。……[①]

按，左末城即且末城。许多学者将引文中描述的捍麽城瑞像视作玄奘记载的媲摩城瑞像，并认为捍麽城即媲摩城。然而，仔细对比，我们可以发现宋云和玄奘所描述的瑞像实际上有诸多不同，捍麽城并非媲摩城。为便于比较，援引玄奘《大唐西域记》的相关内容如下：

战地东行三十余里，至媲摩城，有雕檀立佛像，高二丈余，甚多灵应，时烛光明。凡有疾病，随其痛处，金薄帖像，即时痊复。虚心请愿，多亦遂求。闻之土俗曰：此像，昔佛在世憍赏弥国邬陀衍那王所作也。佛去世后，自彼凌空至此国北曷劳落迦城中。初，此城人安乐富饶，深着邪见，而不珍敬。传其自来，神而不贵。后有罗汉礼拜此像。国人惊骇，异其容服，驰以白王。王乃下令，宜以沙土坌此异人。时阿罗汉身蒙沙土，餬口绝粮。时有一人心甚不忍，昔常恭敬尊礼此像，及见罗汉，密以馔之。罗汉将去，谓其人曰："却后七日，当雨沙土，填满此城，略无遗类。尔宜知之，早图出计。犹其坌我，获斯殃耳。"语已便去，忽然不见。其人入城，具告亲故。或有闻者，莫不嗤笑。至第二日，大风忽发，吹去秽壤，雨杂宝满衢路。人更骂所告者。此人心知必然，窃开孔道，出城外而穴之。第七日夜，宵分之后，雨沙土满城中。其人从孔道出，东趣此国，止媲摩城。其人才至，其像亦来，即此供养，不敢迁移。闻诸先记曰：释迦法尽，像入龙宫。今曷劳落迦城为大堆阜，诸国君王，异方豪右，多欲发掘，取其宝物。适至其侧，猛风暴发，烟云四合，道路迷失。[②]

两相比较，可知宋云和玄奘所描述的瑞像有以下差别：首先，瑞像所在的位置明显不一致，宋云谓瑞像在捍麽城南 15 里大寺内；玄奘所云瑞像在媲摩城中。其次，瑞像的高度相差较大，宋云谓像举高丈六；《大唐西域记》所载像高二丈余，《大慈恩寺三藏法师传》甚至言其高三丈余。再者，瑞像的来历不一样，宋云只道像自南方腾空而来；玄奘则云瑞像先从憍赏弥国凌空飞至曷劳落迦城，此城遭沙埋后又飞到媲摩城。最后，有关瑞像的民间传说不同，宋云听到的是于阗国王试图迁像和起塔的故事；玄奘听到的则是瑞像的飞来过程和沙埋曷劳落迦城的传言。[③] 此外，敦煌莫高窟第 231、237 窟西壁佛龛顶均同时绘有媲摩城瑞像和坎城瑞像，二像差异明显。敦煌文书和石窟瑞像题记亦称，媲摩瑞像自憍赏弥国飞来，坎城瑞像则从汉国来。荣新江和朱丽双认为，后者暗示了坎城与唐朝的密切关系。[④] 孙修身已指出，宋云记载的捍麽城金像即莫高窟第 231、237 窟所绘之坎城瑞像。[⑤] 我赞同此说，坎城和媲摩城各有瑞像，它们分别被宋云和玄奘描述。玄奘所记媲摩城在于阗以东 330 余里，而坎城在于阗以东 307 里，[⑥] 可知坎城在媲摩城以西 20 余唐里；又，宋云谓捍麽

---

① 余太山：《"宋云行纪"要注》，第 272—273 页。

② 《大唐西域记校注》，第 1025—1030 页。

③ 有关沙埋曷劳落迦城故事之研究，见田卫疆：《塔里木盆地"沙埋古城"的两则史料辨析》，收入殷晴、田卫疆主编：《历史时期新疆的自然灾害与环境演变研究》，乌鲁木齐：新疆人民出版社，2011 年，第 336—348 页。

④ 荣新江、朱丽双：《于阗与敦煌》，第 259—260 页。

⑤ 孙修身：《莫高窟佛教史迹故事画介绍（二）》，第 98—110 页。

⑥ 此据两《汉书》和《新唐书》等文献提供的数据换算得出，关于这一点，笔者拟另文专论。

城在末城以西22里，约当22唐里。[①] 两组距离差可比拟。因此，若捍麼城即坎城，则末城当媲摩城在方位和里程上是讲得通的。

贝利推测，媲摩之名可能来自于阗语 pĕma“像”（image，佛教梵语 pratimā）。[②] 我认为其说颇有见地。媲摩城先从西方请回一尊雕檀瑞像，城以像闻名，遂被称作“（瑞）像城”。后来，坎城也得到了瑞像，其像据传来自汉地。这一传言可从宋云的记载中得到印证：在捍麼瑞像周围上万件彩幡中，魏国之幡过半，其上以隶书题写北魏晚期年号；而末城“城傍花果似洛阳，唯土屋平头为异”，均暗示这一地区在北魏时期存在汉人并深受汉文化影响。无独有偶，在讲述左末（且末）城时，宋云亦写道：“城中图佛与菩萨，乃无胡貌，访古老，云是吕光伐胡时所作。”[③] 对此，许多学者指出，彼时且末城为汉人或汉化的土著所居，且中原佛教艺术波及此城。[④] 根据这些线索，我认为在北魏时期曾有一批汉人徙居塔里木盆地南道东段，并带来汉地佛教艺术的回流影响。

最后，尚有一个相关问题仍需解决：如果宋云时期就存在捍麼城（坎城）和末城（媲摩城）两处瑞像，为何宋云和玄奘均只记载了其中的一处？根据宋云的记载，捍麼城仅在末城以西22里，远不足一日之程。宋云描述末城十分简洁，且言末城“城傍花果似洛阳”，“城旁”二字暗示他未入城，只是途经此地，可见，他是赶往捍麼城歇脚的。玄奘在于阗获诏之后，东归心切，行程匆匆，《大唐西域记》于阗以东沿途记载相当疏阔。玄奘应该停住媲摩城，但没有作过多逗留。由于坎城、媲摩城一带佛像众多，他们只记载了各自所停歇的那座城的瑞像，而没有时间去打听另一座城的瑞像情况。

2. 绀州、绀城

后晋天福三年（938），于阗王李圣天遣使入贡。晋廷遣供奉官张匡邺假鸿胪卿，彰武军（驻延州，今延安一带）节度判官高居诲为判官，回使于阗，册封李圣天为大宝于阗国王。当年冬十二月（939），张匡邺等自灵州（今宁夏吴忠）出发，历二载（940）至于阗，至七年冬（942）乃还。高居诲记录了沿途的山川道里，保留在《新五代史》等典籍中，称《于阗国行程记》。其所记塔里木盆地南缘经行路线为：

> 匡邺等西行入仲云界，至大屯城，仲云遣宰相四人、都督三十七人候晋使者，匡邺等以诏书慰谕之，皆东向拜。自仲云界西，始涉碱（原字为“醶”）碛，无水，掘地得湿沙，人置之胸以止渴。又西，渡陷河，伐柽置水中乃渡，不然则陷。又西，至绀州，绀州，于阗所置也，在沙州西南，云去京师九千五百里矣。又行二日至安军州，遂至于阗。[⑤]

---

① 丘光明推定北魏后尺为29.6厘米（丘光明：《计量史》，长沙：湖南教育出版社，2002年，第313页），则1北魏里 = 0.296 × 1800 = 532.8米。

② H. W. Bailey, *Dictionary of Khotan Saka,* Cambridge, Cambridge University Press, 1979, pp. 249, 263. 关于媲摩名称之来源尚有其他一些说法，参见《大唐西域记校注》，第1028—1029页注释所列，但均不足为据。

③ 余太山：《“宋云行纪”要注》，第271页。

④ M. A. Stein, *Serindia: Detailed Report of Archaeological Explorations in Central Asia and Western-most China*, Oxford, Clarendon Press, 1921, pp. 297-298（汉译本见巫新华等译：《西域考古图记》第1卷，桂林：广西师范大学出版社，1998年，第187页）；李肖：《且末古城地望考》，《中国边疆史地研究》2001年第3期，第38页；金维诺：《新疆的佛教艺术》，收入《中国美术史论集》中卷，哈尔滨：黑龙江美术出版社，2004年，第21页；李树辉：《试论汉传佛教的西渐——从突厥语对“道人”（tojin）一词的借用谈起》，《新疆师范大学学报》2006年第4期，第51页。

⑤《新五代史》卷七四《四夷附录》，北京：中华书局点校本修订本，2015年，第1039页。

引文表明，9世纪中叶以后，于阗摆脱了吐蕃的统治，其行政区划效仿唐朝统治时期，列州而治，在国都周边即今和田县境置安军州，其东置绀州。殷晴认为绀州辖有今于田、策勒一带[①]，即唐朝统治时期的坎城和六城地区。另外，俄藏敦煌汉文文书 Dx.2148（2）+ Dx.6069（1）《于阗天寿二年（964）弱婢祐定等牒》第11—12行记载："又绀城细緤寄三五十匹东来，亦乃沿窟使用。"[②]所谓"绀城"，应即高居诲《于阗国行程记》提到的绀州之州治，其地当在原来的坎城。

3. 肯汗城

格瑞纳（F. Grenard）曾摘译过喀布里（Maḥmūd Karam Kābulī）著作中的一个片段，其中讲述了12世纪一支伊斯兰军队在征服阿克苏后，沿克里雅河南下，攻击上游异教徒的肯汗州（the province of Kenhān）。[③]肯汗的镇将是一位称作"突厥达干"的犹太人，他隶属于基督徒努墩汗（Nūdūn Khān），后者是西辽委任的于阗统治者。穆斯林军队击败突厥达干后，占领并洗劫了富庶的吴六杂提城（Ulūgh-Ziārat），接着攻占了质逻（策勒），继而向于阗进发。吴六杂提城邻近都城肯汗城，后者在遭受这次蹂躏之后便奇迹般消失了。

斯坦因指出，肯汗州的范围包括克里雅至策勒一带的诸绿洲。[④]这跟唐朝统治时期坎城镇的军事辖区一致，亦跟高居诲之绀州、马可波罗之培因州的行政疆域一致。而且，肯汗州与坎城、绀州一样，隶属于阗。因此，我认为如同 Kenhān 跟坎、绀在语音上是一脉相承的一样，肯汗州也正是坎城镇、绀州的延续，肯汗城即坎城、绀城。另外，吴六杂提意为"圣地"，而媲摩意为"瑞像"，吴六杂提城与肯汗城毗邻，媲摩城与坎城亦如此，这些都暗示了吴六杂提城即媲摩城、培因城。肯汗城在这支12世纪的穆斯林军队劫掠之后消失了，表明扜弥城—捍麽城—坎城—绀城—肯汗城沿袭至此而废弃。吴六杂提城则劫后重生，得以复苏，并成为该地区唯一的政治中心。因此，当13世纪马可波罗经过此地时，只见到培因城，而未闻有肯汗城。

二　位置与交通

1907年，亨廷顿指出马可波罗之培因在克里雅[⑤]，即今于田县城。同时，斯坦因在《古代和田》中则论证培因在老达玛沟之乌宗塔提。[⑥]此后，伯希和等学者纷纷附和斯坦因的意见。[⑦]20世纪80年代，王北辰根据玄奘所记载的路程，指出坎城在今克里雅河流域于田县城附近。[⑧]近年，文欣和朱丽双亦

---

① 殷晴：《唐宋之际西域南道的复兴——于阗玉石贸易的热潮》，《西域研究》2006年第1期，第38页。

② 关于此文书的录文与相关研究，参见荣新江：《绵绫家家总满——谈十世纪敦煌于阗间的丝织品交流》，原载包铭新主编：《丝绸之路·图像与历史》，东华大学出版社，2011年；后以《于阗与敦煌间的丝织品交流》为题作为荣新江、朱丽双《于阗与敦煌》一书第八章，第234—237页。

③ F. Grenard, J.-L. Dutreuil de Rhins, *Mission Scientifique dans la Haute Asie 1890-1895*, Vol. III, Paris, E. Leroux, 1898, pp. 43-45; M. A. Stein, *Ancient Khotan*, Vol. I, p. 449（汉译本《古代和田》第1卷，第492页）。

④ M. A. Stein, *Ancient Khotan*, Vol. I, p. 463; 汉译本《古代和田》第1卷，第505页。

⑤ E. Huntington, *The Pulse of Asia*, pp. 191, 387-388.

⑥ M. A. Stein, *Ancient Khotan*, Vol. I, pp. 452-457; 汉译本《古代和田》第1卷，第494—499页。

⑦ P. Pelliot, *Notes on Marco Polo*, II p. 801; J. Hamilton, "Autour du manuscrit Staël-Holstein", p. 118; 冯承钧原编：《西域地名》（增订本），陆峻岭增订，北京：中华书局，1982年，第75、101页；吉田豊：《有关和田出土8—9世纪于阗语世俗文书的札记》（一），第177页。

⑧ 王北辰：《古代西域南道上的若干历史地理问题》，第320—321页；又《新疆地名考五条——和田、于田、若羌、鄯善、罗布泊》，第410—413页。

撰文[①]，赞成其说。此外，黄文弼和李吟屏先后指出，坎城应在今策勒县北沙漠中的卡纳沁遗址。[②]

笔者从近年新发现的和田汉文文书中检出一则材料，足证亨廷顿、王北辰之说可信。这件文书属于中国人民大学博物馆藏和田文书，内容为《杰谢百姓牒稿为放免正税事》（GXW0062），刘子凡刊布了其录文，现转录如下：

1 ］杰谢百姓等

2 ］勿萨踵是杰谢乡百姓，其乡去坎城及坎城守捉远四百余里，道路

3 ］往来于□，放免正税，钱输纳不阙，其□杂差

4 ］新造使薄钱恐不□□牒送留须

（后缺）[③]

其中，“坎城及坎城守捉”“远”“道”“免”“正”、“恐”等字均为行右添字。可见，这是一份文书的草稿，加之纸张保存状况较差，甚为残破，这些都给我们理解文意造成一定困难。文书的内容，大致讲的是杰谢乡百姓被要求输送税赋到坎城及坎城守捉，他们以道路险远为由，申请放免正税。刘子凡认为其中提到的“正税”是指百姓需要按例缴纳的常规性税赋，并引用《唐六典》卷三《户部郎中员外郎》的记载“凡诸国蕃胡内附者，亦定为九等，四等以上为上户，七等以上为次户，八等以下为下户；上户丁税银钱十文，次户五文，下户免之”[④]，指出文书所说的“正税”钱，很可能就是这种唐朝对内附民按户丁征收的银钱。[⑤]然而，据文意，所谓的正税恐怕是指按例须缴纳的粮食（青麦、小麦、粟等）、柴草、纺织品等税物，它不是以钱币的形式缴纳。杰谢百姓大概申请用钱的形式来缴纳，盖因路途遥远，实物难以运输。

这件文书中有一句话对判断坎城的位置非常重要，即杰谢乡“其乡去坎城及坎城守捉远四百余里，道路……”杰谢乡即今丹丹乌里克遗址，在策勒县城以北约 90 公里的沙漠中，这一点学界已达成共识。四百唐里约合 212 公里。斯坦因谓培因 / 媲摩在今达玛沟乡以北 19 公里之乌宗塔提遗址，然而，该遗址仅在丹丹乌里克以南 70 公里，远小于文书所说的“四百余里”。如果从丹丹乌里克顺古河、渠道下到策勒绿洲（六城州治质逻），再沿今天的道路到于田县城附近的话，路程刚好在 200 公里左右。[⑥]由此可见，若坎城位于今克里雅河畔于田县城附近，则正符合文书提到的杰谢与坎城之间的里程。

赫定 7 号于阗语文书提到，屋悉贵寺与媲摩城分隔遥远（详下）。屋悉贵即六城拔伽乡的治所，拔伽与杰谢均属六城州。这里反映的情况正与上件文书互相呼应。而乌宗塔提与屋悉贵均位于老达玛沟遗址群，二者自然称不上分隔遥远，这也印证了媲摩城不在乌宗塔提。

---

① 文欣：《中古时期于阗国政治制度研究》，第 90—93 页；朱丽双：《唐代于阗的羁縻州与地理区划研究》，第 78—80 页。

② 黄文弼：《罗布淖尔考古记》，北平研究院史学研究所，1948 年，第 50 页；又《塔里木盆地考古记》，北京：科学出版社，1958 年，第 47—48 页；李吟屏：《古于阗坎城考》，收入马大正、杨镰主编：《西域考察与研究续编》，乌鲁木齐：新疆人民出版社，1998 年，第 236—262 页。

③ 刘子凡：《于阗镇守军与当地社会》，《西域研究》2014 年第 1 期，第 17 页。

④ 《唐六典》卷三，北京：中华书局，1992 年，第 77 页。

⑤ 刘子凡：《于阗镇守军与当地社会》，第 17 页。

⑥ 从丹丹乌里克遗址向东穿越沙漠到克里雅河下游，然后溯河而上，至今于田县城，距离亦在 200 公里左右。

三 宗教

马可波罗只提到培因居民信仰伊斯兰教，但更早时候，此地曾是多种宗教并存的局面。上文论及，10 世纪的穆斯林作家米撒儿记载，从 Khatiyān 旅行 20 日后，来到一个叫作 Pima 的国家：

> 我们到了皮麻（Pima）国，这里棕树密布，蔬菜葡萄遍野。有一座城郭，有很多村镇，乃一叫皮麻国王的治地。城里有伊斯兰教徒、犹太人、基督教徒、祆教徒和偶像崇拜者。〔当地人〕有固定节日。这里有一种绿石，可治眼眵，有一种红石可治脾病。这里有一种红色靛蓝（原文如此），质量极好，放在水上，轻而不沉。我们旅行四十日。〔时而〕平安无事,〔时而〕担惊受怕。[①]

关于 Khatiyān 和 Pima，玉尔和冯承钧皆认为指于阗和媲摩[②]，这是没有问题的。米撒儿关于中国西北部族、地名的描述得自早期传闻[③]，应当抄自八九世纪的波斯阿拉伯语地理著作。关于媲摩城的宗教，米撒儿声称该城居住着伊斯兰教徒、犹太教徒、基督教徒、祆教徒和佛教徒。这表明，在喀喇汗王朝征服之前，于阗境内已经有穆斯林传教布道。其他几种宗教是否也存在过呢？斯坦因曾在丹丹乌里克遗址发现了一件 8 世纪下半叶的犹太波斯语信札残片（Or.8212/166）[④]；近年，中国国家图书馆入藏了一件来自同一地区、同一时代的犹太波斯语信札（X-19）[⑤]。在唐代，于阗有很多粟特人聚落[⑥]，例如六城州就存在名为“粟特村”的村庄[⑦]。可见，这一带在唐代生活着犹太教徒和祆教徒是没有问题的。上文论及，肯汗州的长官是一位犹太人，暗示了到 12 世纪这里仍存在犹太教徒。关于基督徒，马可波罗提到了塔里木盆地西缘与河西走廊众多城镇存在基督教徒和教堂，但在塔里木盆地南道的忽炭、培因、阇鄽、罗卜等地，只谓当地居民信奉摩诃末，未言及有基督徒，而米撒儿在这里罗列了基督教徒。二人的记载与阙载，也许反映了唐元间基督教在塔里木盆地南缘的发展变化。

媲摩的佛教，除了有关坎城瑞像和媲摩瑞像的记载外，我们还可以从出土的于阗语文书中探知一些情况。瑞典探险家斯文·赫定（Sven Hedin）曾在和田东北一带掘得一批纸质文书，其中第 7 号文书是一件双面书写的于阗语文书，年代为吐蕃统治时期。正面 11 行，内容为《某年二月二十六日赞摩（Tcarma）寺法师尉迟跋陀罗（Viśābhadra）致媲摩城诸法师书》。[⑧] 发信人是于阗城南赞摩寺的尉迟跋陀罗，收信人为媲摩城的五位高僧：两藏法师 Yaśi-pramña、三藏法师上座 Pumña-mittra、上座三

---

① 费琅：《阿拉伯波斯突厥人东方文献辑注》，第 238 页。亦参见 H. Yule, *Cathay and the Way Thither. Being A Collection of Medieval Notices of China*, vol. 1, London, The Hakluyt Society, 1866, pp. 189-190；冯承钧：《大食人米撒儿行纪中之西域部落》，第 184—187 页。

② H. Yule, *Cathay and the Way Thither*, Vol. I, pp. 189-190；冯承钧：《大食人米撒儿行纪中之西域部落》，第 187 页。

③ 马雍：《萨曼王朝与中国的交往》，第 179—180 页。

④ M. A. Stein, *Ancient Khotan*, Vol. I, pp. 570-574; 汉译本《古代和田》第 1 卷，第 622—627 页。

⑤ 张湛、时光：《一件新发现犹太波斯语信札的断代与释读》，收入《敦煌吐鲁番研究》第 11 卷，上海古籍出版社，2009 年，第 71—99 页。

⑥ 荣新江：《西域粟特移民聚落考》，原载马大正等主编：《西域考察与研究》，乌鲁木齐：新疆人民出版社，1994 年；收入作者《中古中国与外来文明》（修订版），北京：生活·读书·新知三联书店，2014 年，第 19—24 页。

⑦ 文欣：《中古时期于阗国政治制度研究》，第 83、88 页。

⑧ H. W. Bailey, *Saka Documents*, Vol. I, London: Lund Humphries, 1960, pl.VI; idem, *Khotanese Texts*, Vol. IV, pp. 25, 32, 82-86; idem, *Saka Documents, Text Volume*, pp. 11-12.

藏法师 Mittra-pramña、上座三藏法师 Nāgasthira、三藏法师 Bhadriśvaramittra。尉迟跋陀罗在信中表达了对他们的问候和赞美，以及对他们曾提供帮助的谢意。在这封信里，媲摩城被写作 phimāña kimtha，kimtha 意为“城郭”，吉田豊认为相对于质逻等六“城”，这似乎是一种破格的待遇。①

背面 9 行，为《媲摩僧侣为财产纠纷事上僧正状》。② 其内容有助于我们了解吐蕃统治时期媲摩地区寺院的组织、管理、僧众等情况。兹将贝利的释读文本转译如下：

> 我们向僧正申诉。住在屋悉贵寺的众弟子……被隔绝，远离尊长者。摩陀罗婆诃（Madravaha）叩拜十戒上首……。上座众多，达五六十位。他侵夺了比丘们的财产，对众弟子不利。王室供养物……仆役、例赠，都被他侵夺了。我们曾向教授阿阇黎和上首维摩罗什罗（Vimalaśila）申诉此事。他们为此向住在媲摩的阿阇黎们下达命令，说：“你们应向上座们通告此事，并向我们回馈结果。”随后，他和吐蕃人一起为我们执行。他下令束缚并杖责其他的阿阇黎。媲摩功德使命令就此事备案。他们让我们签名，说：“你们务必声明此事处理得当。”上首立刻同意了。我们不能接受；那只是上首的个人陈词。因此，寺院僧众打算提出友善的抗议。上首与吐蕃人处理此事时于我们不利。他帮他们在各种困难中对付我们。他侵夺了住在大城的众弟子的财产，侵夺了我们在拘尸那寺的僧房。现在，我们只能祈求阿阇黎菩萨的庇护。

这份诉状反映的情况是，一些原居住在媲摩城的僧人被某位上首侵夺了他们在拘尸那寺的僧房，并被驱逐到遥远的屋悉贵寺。他们向教授阿阇黎以及上首维摩罗什罗申诉此事。③ 二者责成媲摩的诸阿阇黎来处理。随后，媲摩功德使要求双方就处理结果陈词备案。上首独自写了状词并要求僧人们签名。但这些僧人觉得事情并没有得到妥善解决，因此又向僧正提起申诉。

可以想见，文书正面提到的五位媲摩城法师收到了赞摩寺法师尉迟跋陀罗的来信，后来，他们中的一位或多位遭遇了上述不幸事件，因此用信件的背面书写了这份诉状。状词中提到的地名除了媲摩外，还有 Chemjsa-purrām、屋悉贵寺和拘尸那寺。关于 Chemjsa-purrām，贝利解释 chem 即古藏语 chen“大”，purrām 即古藏语 phrom“城镇、军镇”。上文论及，中国人民大学博物馆所藏和田汉文文书中有一件《武周某年事目历》（GXW0106），里面多次提到地名“大城”。我认为，“大城”即 Chemjsa-purrām 之意译，指媲摩城。拘尸那寺（Jyūsna-vri）是上状僧人们原来所居住的寺院，也即五位收信法师所居住的寺院，它可能位于媲摩城中或附近。五位收信人中的三位拥有上座身份，四位拥有三藏法师的称号，另一位拥有两藏法师称号。另外，诉状提到“上座众多，达五六十位”，由于这句话前面有阙文，我们不能确定它描述的对象是谁，但很可能说的就是拘尸那寺的情况。通过这些信息我们可以获知，这座寺院的规模十分宏大，僧侣的佛学水平也很高，其影响力必不小。它应该就是

---

① 吉田豊：《有关和田出土 8—9 世纪于阗语世俗文书的札记（一）》，广中智之汉译，收入《敦煌吐鲁番研究》第 11 卷，第 177 页注 2。

② H. W. Bailey, *Saka Documents*, Vol. I, pl.VI; idem, *Khotanese Texts*, Vol. IV, pp. 26, 86-92; idem, *Saka Documents, Text Volume*, pp. 11-12; R. E. Emmerick & P. O. Skjærvø, *Studies in the Vocabulary of Khotanese*, Vol. III, Wien, Verlag der Österreichischen Akademie der Wissenschaften, 1997, p. 180.

③ 在敦煌于阗语文书 Or.8212/162 中亦出现了维摩罗什罗之名，是一位高僧，“ttayą śī 大师 Vimalaśila”，参见 H. W. Bailey, *Saka Documents, Text Volume*, p. 26; P. O. Skjærvø, *Khotanese Manuscripts from Chinese Turkestan in the British Library. A Complete Catalogue with Texts and Translations*, p. 47。当然，我们不敢确定两件文书提到的是否为同一个人。

敦煌瑞像题记以及玄奘提到的那座拥有瑞像的寺院。诉状中也提到了媲摩功德使，说明媲摩城存在官衙。可见，媲摩城是一座兼具政治、宗教功能的综合性城市。

功德使是唐至元代中原王朝设置的管理全国僧尼事务的官职，起初可以由僧人或非僧人充任，在唐德宗贞元四年（788）后一度由宦官专任。[①]唐朝的功德使是一种中央政府官职，于阗将其引进，并在地方上如媲摩也设立此职。[②]过去我们通过出土文书了解到，于阗语借用了汉语的“大使”“刺史”“守捉”“兵马使”等词汇[③]，暗示了唐朝对于阗的政治军事影响。在这份诉状中，功德使的于阗语形式为 kū-thaigä-ṣī，直接借自汉语，进一步表明唐朝对于阗的统治是深入的，唐朝制度的影响不仅表现在行政和军事层面，也表现在宗教管理方面，而且这些影响甚至延续到了唐朝统治结束以后。

关于屋悉贵寺，贝利将其释作 the saṃghārāma in Ustāka，即“位于屋悉贵的伽蓝”[④]。可见，这件诉状实际上并没有提到这座寺院的名字。我们不清楚它是否有正式的名字，这里用村庄的名字来指称它，暗示屋悉贵可能只有一座寺院。20 世纪初，斯坦因在策勒县的麻扎托格拉克（Mazar Toghrak）获得了一些仓库记账用的汉语—于阗语双语木简，其中，在 Or.12637/13 号上面，汉语“屋悉贵”和于阗语 Ustāka 对应出现，吉田豊首先据此将二者勘同。[⑤]近年，在和田地区新发现了更多的这种双语木简，再次出现了二者对应出现的例子，荣新江和文欣的研究表明，屋悉贵是六城州拔伽乡的一个村，且为乡治所在地。[⑥]吉田豊指出，斯坦因发现的巴拉瓦斯特（Balawaste）遗址之名是拔伽（Birgaṃdara）名称遗留下来的音译。[⑦]屋悉贵村的位置应当就在这一带。斯坦因在哈达里克遗址所获的一枚于阗语木简（遗物编号 Kha.ix.40，馆藏编号 IOL Khot Wood 12）中也提到了屋悉贵寺，写作 Ustāvi (= Ustāki) saṃghārāma。[⑧]近年，中国国家图书馆新获的一件于阗语案牍文书《高僧买奴契约》（BH4-66），也跟屋悉贵的僧人有关。段晴对这件契约进行了译注和研究，可知契约的买方是屋悉贵的高僧阿阇黎起贤（Udayabadri）。[⑨]我们不敢断言诉状中提到的 Ustāka 是否就是拔伽乡下属的这个屋悉贵村，但这种可

① 汤一介：《功德使考——读〈资治通鉴〉札记》，《文献》1985 年第 2 期，第 60—65 页。

② 关于媲摩功德使，尚有未明了的地方。唐朝的功德使是中央政府设置的管理僧尼事务的最高官职，在唐朝统治于阗时期，这一官职及其名称应该不能借入于阗和于阗语里。像“刺史”等官职名称被借入于阗语中，是因为唐朝在于阗设立了这些职位。但是，唐朝统治时期于阗应该不能设置功德使一职——如果设了此职，说明功德使在某个时期出现了变化，可以设置在地方。在唐朝统治时期，于阗设置的更可能是僧统、僧正一类的地方僧官。更有可能的是，在吐蕃统治于阗时期，吐蕃设置了新的僧尼管理体系，并借用了唐朝的功德使等官职。

③ 吉田豊：《有关和田出土 8—9 世纪于阗语世俗文书的札记（一）》，第 159—164 页。

④ H. W. Bailey, *Khotanese Texts*, Vol. IV, p. 87.

⑤ 吉田豊：《有关和田出土 8—9 世纪于阗语世俗文书的札记（一）》，第 177 页；吉田豊：《有关和田出土 8—9 世纪于阗语世俗文书的札记（二）》，荣新江、广中智之汉译，第 82 页。

⑥ 荣新江、文欣：《和田新出汉语—于阗语双语木简考释》，收入《敦煌吐鲁番研究》第 11 卷，上海古籍出版社，2009 年，第 45—69 页；Rong Xinjiang & Wen Xin, “Newly Discovered Chinese-Khotanese Bilingual Tallies”, *Journal of Inner Asian Art and Archaeology* 3, 2008, pp. 99-118.

⑦ 吉田豊：《有关和田出土 8—9 世纪于阗语世俗文书的札记（二）》，第 80 页。

⑧ H. W. Bailey, *Khotanese Texts*, Vol. V, Cambridge, Cambridge University Press, 1963, p. 185; idem, *Saka Documents, Text Volume,* pp. 40, 42; P. O. Skjærvø, *Khotanese Manuscripts from Chinese Turkestan in the British Library. A Complete Catalogue with Texts and Translations*, p. 562.

⑨ 段晴：《于阗语高僧买奴契约》，收入《敦煌吐鲁番研究》第 11 卷，2009 年，第 11—27 页；修改后收入作者《于阗·佛教·古卷》，上海：中西书局，2013 年，第 245—266 页；节略本又收入作者《中国国家图书馆藏西域文书：于阗语卷（一）》，上海：中西书局，2015 年，第 67—80 页。

能性极大，因为诉状中提到这里与媲摩分隔遥远。如果它们确实是同一个地方，那么当时媲摩功德使的管辖范围包含了六城地区。

四　物产

（一）玉石

《马可波罗行纪》谈论培因的物产时写道："有一条河（按，克里雅河）流经其地，河中可以找到数量非常大的珍贵宝石，人们称之为碧玉（jasper）和玉髓（chalcedony）。"最近，荣新江撰文，对这条记载进行了深入讨论。① 玉文化是中国传统文化的重要组成部分，于阗玉在古代中国最负盛名。马可波罗在描述阇鄽的碧玉和玉髓时指出："他们（按，商人）将此宝石售往契丹，从中获利巨丰，因为它们量多且非常优质。"② 可见，他也清楚地意识到了昆仑玉石在中国人心目中的价值。然而，在讲述忽炭时他并没有提及于阗玉，甚至也没有提到产玉的于阗河；反而在讲述培因和阇鄽时，均提到当地河流出产碧玉和玉髓两种玉石。这颇令人费解。不过，仔细分析当时的历史背景，笔者发现，马可波罗关于昆仑山北麓玉石出产情况之记载，以及对忽炭极其简短之描述，正是至元间（1264—1294）塔里木盆地南道历史最真实的反映。

马可波罗提到的碧玉和玉髓实际上皆属石英，并非真正的玉类，这跟于阗玉（软玉类）迥然不同。关于这一点，闻广认为马可波罗所谓碧玉和玉髓实指于阗青玉和白玉。西方玉（jade）及软玉（nephrite）之名是哥伦布发现新大陆之后才陆续出现的，马可波罗比哥伦布早二百多年，其时西文玉的名词尚未有之，于阗玉遂被当作颜色相似的 jasper 与 chalcedony。③ 这种说法貌似合理。然而，于阗玉有白玉、青玉、青白玉、墨玉诸色。④ 忽必烈指示于阗贡玉"必得青黄黑白之玉"⑤，高居诲《于阗国行程记》亦称于阗玉河包括白玉河、绿玉河及乌玉河⑥。马可波罗若果真以西方jasper等相似物类指称于阗玉，必以三词当之，何故独遗墨玉而不表？

我认为，马可波罗在培因与阇鄽两章所言碧玉和玉髓并非指于阗玉。它们可能是指昆仑软玉，也可能确实指碧玉和玉髓，更可能是对这一带所产各类玉石之泛称。⑦ 斯坦因指出，软玉在所有发源于昆仑山北麓而流入塔里木盆地的大河河床中，都有出产；而碧玉和玉髓也广泛分布于这一带。他曾在罗布沙漠采集到大量这两种材料的制成品，年代属于新石器时代⑧；贝格曼（F. Bergman）在且末和瓦石峡两地所获亦不少，但年代不明⑨。

至元间，塔里木盆地西南历经阿里不哥、八剌、海都之乱，连年兵祸致使民户逃散，社会经济凋

---

① Rong Xinjiang, "Reality of Tale? Marco Polo's Description of Khotan", *Journal of Asian History* 49, 2015, pp. 161-174; 荣新江：《真实还是传说：马可·波罗笔下的于阗》，《西域研究》2016 年第 2 期，第 39—42 页。

② A. C. Moule & P. Pelliot (trans. and annotated), *Marco Polo. The Description of the World*, Vol. I, chap. 56, p. 147.

③ 闻广：《〈马可波罗行纪〉中地质矿产史料》，《河北地质学院学报》第 15 卷第 2 期，1992 年，第 207 页。

④ 殷晴：《唐宋之际西域南道的复兴——于阗玉石贸易的热潮》，第 40 页。

⑤《永乐大典》卷一九四一七《站赤二》，北京：中华书局，1986 年，第 7199a 页。

⑥《新五代史》卷七四《四夷附录三》，第 918 页。

⑦ 中国古代对玉石并无严格定义，石之美者即为玉。以此观之，碧玉和玉髓当然可以称作玉石，但相较于和田河出产之软玉，无疑属于次等玉料。

⑧ M. A. Stein, *Serindia*, p. 299；汉译本《西域考古图记》第 1 卷，第 188 页。

⑨ 贝格曼：《新疆考古记》，王安洪译，乌鲁木齐：新疆人民出版社，1997 年，第 303—324 页。

敝。马可波罗途经忽炭前不久，其地遭到了八剌的蹂躏，拉施特（Rashīd al-Dīn）在《史集》中言简意赅地写道："八剌的军队洗劫了忽炭。"① 宏达迷儿（Khwandamīr）《旅行者之友》（*Habīb al-Siyār*）亦称："在统治之初，八剌就重新组建了一支军队，并制定了远征斡端的计划。他将忽必烈合罕派驻其地的人赶走，然后便开始劫掠。"② 这种情势，令马可波罗在忽炭停留短暂，因此在行纪中对忽炭着墨不多，他没有记载于阗玉石的主要原因也可能在此。除此之外，还有另外两方面的原因导致他忽略了著名的于阗玉。

首先，马可波罗可能错过了忽炭的捞玉季节，他行经忽炭时根本没有机会见到当地的捞玉场景。高居诲《于阗国行程记》描述了大宝于阗国时期，于阗玉河及采玉的相关情况：

> 玉河在于阗城外。其源出昆山，西流一千三百里，至于阗界牛头山，乃疏为三河：一曰白玉河，在城东三十里；二曰绿玉河，在城西二十里；三曰乌玉河，在绿玉河西七里。其源虽一，而其玉随地而变，故其色不同。每岁五六月，大水暴涨，则玉随流而至。玉之多寡，由水之大小。七八月水退，乃可取，彼人谓之捞玉。其国之法，官未采玉，禁人辄至河滨者。③

从这段记载中可知，玉河即于阗河作为最优质玉石之产地，其采玉活动受到于阗官府的严格控制。④ 玉河之玉由河水从昆仑山上冲刷携带而来。塔里木盆地南缘的河流基本都靠昆仑山的冰川和融雪补给，水量受制于气温，每年五六月份为汛期，此时正当盛夏，气温高，融水足，河流水势浩大，人们无法下河捞玉；只有待到七八月份天气转凉，进入枯水期之后，水位下降，方可下河采玉。于阗河的采玉季节到来时，官府先行采捞，且禁止人们到河滨；官府采毕，百姓才可以下河捡漏。采玉的季节是短暂的，进入严冬之后，河水冰凉刺骨、坚冰覆盖，自然无法采玉。于阗河的这种捞玉政策可能延续到了马可波罗时代。如果马可波罗不是在适合采玉的秋季经过忽炭的话，他就见不到官方及随后民间的大规模捞玉活动。即便他在秋季较早的时候到达这里，也会因为河禁而无法目睹捞玉场面。所以，只有当他在秋季稍晚的时候到达忽炭，才可能见到捞玉场面，并在民间作坊和市场上见到大量的于阗玉。

其次，马可波罗行经之时，正值皇家玉课兴起，而其淘玉地点在远离忽炭城的匪力沙。《元史·食货志》记载："产玉之所，曰于阗，曰匪力沙。"⑤ 又言元代玉课之情况：

> 玉在匪力沙者，至元十一年（1274），迷儿、麻合马、阿里三人言，淘玉之户旧有三百，经乱散亡，存者止七十户，其力不充，而匪力沙之地旁近有民户六十，每同淘焉。于是免其差徭，与淘户等所淘之玉，于忽都、胜忽儿、舍里甫丁三人所立水站，递至京师。此玉课之兴革可考者然也。⑥

---

① 拉施特主编：《史集》第3卷，余大均、周建奇译，北京：商务印书馆，1986年，第108页。

② Khwandamīr, "Histoire des khans mongols du Turkistan et de la Transoxiane, extraite du *Habib essiier* de Khondémir, (2e article)", traduite du persan et accompagnée de notes par M. C. Defrémery, *Journal Asiatique* 19, 1852, pp. 251-252; 刘迎胜：《察合台汗国史研究》，上海古籍出版社，2011年，第173—175页。

③ 唐慎微原著：《大观本草》卷三，艾晟刊订，尚志钧点校，合肥：安徽科学技术出版社，2002年，第74页。高居诲《于阗国行程记》原文已佚，内容保存在《新五代史》等著作中。此段文字为北宋苏颂《图经本草》（此书亦佚）摘引，继而为唐慎微《证类本草》转引，见于今存大观本、政和本中。

④ 荣新江、朱丽双：《于阗与敦煌》，第193页。

⑤ 《元史》卷九四《食货志二》，北京：中华书局，1976年，第2378页。

⑥ 《元史》卷九四《食货志二》，第2380页。

匪力沙，位于喀拉喀什河上游，今皮山县赛图拉镇东南约30公里之苏盖提①，即《新唐书·地理志》所载于阗南600里（约合320公里）之胡弩镇②。《元史·世祖纪》记载，至元十一年春正月丙午"立于阗、鸦儿看两城水驿十三，沙州北陆驿二。免于阗采玉工差役"③。其中，"于阗、鸦儿看两城水驿"即《食货志》中"忽都、胜忽儿、舍里甫丁三人所立水站"；"免于阗采玉工差役"即《食货志》所载免匪力沙旁近民户之差徭。马可波罗行经忽炭大约在1273年下半年，于阗玉课在此之前已然开始。《经世大典》站赤条记载，至元十年（1273）六月十八日：

> 兵刑部侍郎伯术奏："〔可〕失呵儿、斡端之地产玉，今遣玉工李秀才者采之。合用铺马六匹，金牌一面。"上曰："得玉将何以转致至此？"对曰："省臣已拟令本处官忙古·拔都儿，于官物内支脚价运来。"上曰："然则必得青黄黑白之玉。复有大者，可去其瑕璞起运。庶几驿传轻便。"④

刘迎胜指出，"本处官忙古·拔都儿"即忙古带，其名可还原成蒙古语 Monggholtai Ba'atur，而"本处官"应指斡端的镇守官。⑤《元史》和《经世大典》的这些记载反映了两个重要史实：一是历经阿里不哥、八剌等叛乱之后，忽炭民户锐减，以淘玉之户为例，1274年的户数不及乱前的四分之一；二是至元间皇家淘玉地点在忽炭城西南320公里处的匪力沙。上有所好，下必甚焉。既然忽必烈对于阗玉课有所指示，于阗地方自当全力以赴，忽炭城的淘玉之户无疑都被调往匪力沙，即便如此，仍然"其力不充"。忽炭城附近的于阗河畔，即使不存在河禁，也会因为缺乏劳动力而见不到足够引人注目的捞玉场景。

昆仑山北缘其他河流出产的次等玉石大概不受官方的采集限制。南道其他河流要么比于阗河小，要么水流不及其湍急，上游矿床也不如于阗河优质。水量较小较缓使得它们携带的玉石较少较次，水位较低则使当地适合下河捞玉的时间比于阗河早。马可波罗很可能正是在夏末初秋之际经过忽炭，这时于阗河尚未退水，不适合下河捞玉；当他经过培因、阇鄽的时候，正值当地河流的采玉季节，他可以很容易看到当地的采玉场面，了解到当地出产玉石的具体情况。所以，他在培因、阇鄽两章里提到了当地的河流出产玉石，并正确地指出这两个地方出产的是碧玉和玉髓这类次等玉石。

（二）棉花

关于培因之物产，除玉石之外，可称道者尚有桑蚕⑥、棉花等项。马可波罗提到培因的棉花，兹试取唐宋文献相关记载以释之。

---

① 谭其骧主编：《中国历史地图集》第7册，察合台汗国图，北京：中国地图出版社，1982年，第38—39页；蔡美彪等：《中国通史》第7册，北京：人民出版社，1994年，第635页。

② 《新唐书》卷四三下《地理志七》，第1147页。

③ 《元史》卷八《世祖纪》，第153页。

④ 《永乐大典》卷一九四一七《站赤二》，北京：中华书局，1984年，第7199a页。

⑤ 刘迎胜：《蒙元帝国与13—15世纪的世界》，北京：生活·读书·新知三联书店，2013年，第231—232页。

⑥ 段晴：《于阗文的蚕字、茧字、丝字》，收入李铮、蒋忠新主编：《季羡林教授八十华诞纪念论文集》上册，南昌：江西人民出版社，1991年，第45—50页；又《于阗绝绌，于阗锦》，收入《伊朗学在中国论文集》第4—5合集，待刊；段晴、李建强：《钱与帛：中国人民大学博物馆藏三件于阗语—汉语双语文书解析》，《西域研究》2014年第1期，第29—38页。

出土文书表明，于阗所辖之多处绿洲各有颇具声誉之特色农产品。例如，段晴曾指出，六城地区出产的丝织品“絁紬”具备特殊的质地，属于进奉于阗官府的物品，上达王公贵族之家。① 在坎城地区，进奉官府的农业特产则是优质的棉织品。上文论及，俄藏敦煌汉文文书 Dx.2148(2) + Dx.6069(1)《于阗天寿二年弱婢祐定等牒》第 11—12 行记载：“又绀城细緤寄三五十匹东来，亦乃沿窟使用。”② 所谓“绀城”，即唐代的坎城。

“緤”是“氎”的俗字，可指棉布或毛布，这两者于阗都有出产，故难以判断这里具体所指。不过，《大唐西域记》描述于阗国“少服毛褐毡裘，多衣絁紬白氎”③，其中的“白氎”应指白色棉布。荣新江先生认为，“绀城细緤”若指坎城特有的精细棉布，在敦煌显然是很亮丽的衣料；若指坎城特有的细毛布，也是完全讲得通的。④ 如果结合《马可波罗行纪》此处关于培因“盛产棉花”的记载，那么，我认为它指当地出产的优质棉布的可能性更大。信中要求一次寄送敦煌的数量多达三五十匹，可知其产量很大。

结语

唐代于阗东部的历史，六城地区因有丰富的出土文书而被深入探究。另两个地名，媲摩（Phema）和坎城（Kaṃdva），虽然在文献中亦屡有提及，但因材料零散，二者的关系、地望以及文化面貌等问题一直扑朔迷离。本文在前人研究的基础上，系统梳理和分析了各种文献记载，对这些问题一一进行了考订。

自赫定 24 号汉语—于阗语双语文书解读以后，多数学者倾向将媲摩与坎城勘同。然而，于阗的这类军事行政文书使用双语是为了提高传递效率，双语内容无须严格对应，这件文书中的 Phẹmāña kiṃtha 与坎城并不形成对译关系。另两组和田出土文书提供了重要线索，一组提到大城（Cheṃjsa-purrāṃ），即媲摩城；一组提到内堡，即坎城。此外，还有文书提到 Pheme Kaṃdvāṣṭa，“媲摩之坎城”。这些都暗示了媲摩城与坎城是相距很近的两座城，它们组成了一座城镇共同体。媲摩城可追溯到北魏宋云所载之末城，它在 12 世纪的一次伊斯兰征服战争中遭到洗劫，但旋即复苏。13 世纪马可波罗称其为培因城，是当时的区域中心。坎城最早可追溯到汉代的扜弥城（Khema），宋云称其为捍麽城，并详细描述了城南大寺中的瑞像。唐朝统治时期，坎城为唐军驻地，设有坎城镇、守捉，是于阗东部的军事镇防中心。吐蕃统治时期，坎城同样为区域军事重镇。吐蕃统治结束后，于阗王在于阗东部地区设立绀州，治绀城（坎城）。绀州建制在于阗国灭后得以延续，西辽时期称作肯汗（Kenhān）州，州治肯汗城（绀城），在 12 世纪的伊斯兰征服战争中被摧毁。明清时期，其地附近又建起新城，称克列牙城儿、克勒底雅城、克里雅城。

关于媲摩、坎城之地望，斯坦因推测在老达玛沟的乌宗塔提一带，王北辰、文欣等人根据史籍的记载提出异议，认为应在克里雅河畔今于田县城附近。两件相关文书提供的信息支持了后一种看法。

---

① 段晴：《和田博物馆藏于阗语租赁契约研究》，原载《敦煌吐鲁番研究》第 11 卷，上海古籍出版社，2009 年；稍加修改后收入作者《于阗 · 佛教 · 古卷》，上海：中西书局，2013 年，第 277—278 页。

② 关于此文书的录文与相关研究，参见荣新江、朱丽双：《于阗与敦煌》，第 234—237 页。

③ 《大唐西域记校注》，第 1001 页。

④ 荣新江、朱丽双：《于阗与敦煌》，第 237 页。

中国人民大学博物馆藏和田文书《杰谢百姓牒稿为放免正税事》(GXW0062),明确提到杰谢乡(丹丹乌里克遗址)“去坎城及坎城守捉远四百余里”。这个里数远远超过丹丹乌里克与乌宗塔提之间的距离,而与丹丹乌里克至于田县城的路程相符,亦与赫定7号文书所载屋悉贵与媲摩分隔遥远之情况相呼应。

媲摩地区在古代流行过佛教、祆教、犹太教、基督教、伊斯兰教等多种宗教。在前伊斯兰时代,这里佛教昌盛,声名远播。唐代十卷本《老子化胡经》推出于阗化胡说,媲摩城被描述成老子化胡成佛之所。媲摩之名,源自于阗语 pĕma,意为像、瑞像,乃因玄奘提到的媲摩城雕檀瑞像而得名。赫定7号文书透露了媲摩佛教的更多史实,包括媲摩城高僧同于阗赞摩寺僧人之间的交游、吐蕃统治时期媲摩功德使之设立,等等。

媲摩地区盛产棉花,敦煌汉文文书提到了称作绀城细緤的精致棉布,是当地进奉于阗官府的重要产品。《马可波罗行纪》记载培因的主要物产除了棉花之外,还有克里雅河出产的碧玉和玉髓。马可波罗没有提及于阗玉,而载称培因、阇鄽两地产玉石,这正是至元间塔里木盆地南道战乱频仍、皇家玉课兴起之真实反映。

Restudy on Xuanzang's Phema and Marco Polo's Pein

Luo Shuai (Sun Yat-sen University)

Abstract: Marco Polo mentioned a place named Pein to the east of Khotan, which was called as Phema in Xuanzang's *Xiyuji* and in many Khotanese documents. Phema has been commonly deemed to be identical to Kaṃdva which is often referred in the Tang Dynasty literatures, since the Chinese and Khotanese bilingual document Hedin 24 was deciphered. However, they are actually two different but adjacent places. They composed a city community, among which Phema was also called as *Chemjsa-purrāṃ*, i.e., "the greater city", and Kaṃdva as Inner Military Fort. Phema played a religious and administrative role, while Kaṃdva was the military base in the east of Khotan, where the Tang and Tibetan troops stationed successively. Kaṃdva could trace back to Khema in Han Dynasty, and came down to Kenhān in the Kara Khitai khanate. It was destroyed in an Islamic conquer war in the 12th century. Later, a city named Keriya was set up nearby in Ming Dynasty and lasts to nowadays. Phema and Kaṃdva should be situated on the Keriya riverside near the modern Yutian County, but not at Uzun-Tati in the old Domoko district.

The ancient Phema was a place where many kinds of religions ever existed, such as Buddhism, Zoroastrianism, Judaism, Christian and Islam, among which Buddhism was especially prevailed in the early times. The city was so famous for its Buddhism that it was depicted as the shrine where Laozi turned into Buddha in the Taoist book the ten volumes version *Huahujing*, i.e., "Classic on Laozi's Conversion of the Barbarians", in the early Tang Dynasty. The word Phema derived from the Khotanese *pĕma*, i.e., "(auspicious) image", and named after the carved sandalwood auspicious image in the city which was minutely described in the *Xiyuji* and the *Biography of Xuanzang*. The Khotanese document Hedin 7 revealed more details about Phema Buddhism, e.g., the communication between the learned monks lived in Phema and in the Tcarma temple of Khotan, the official title *kū-thaigā-ṣī* (i.e., "the Regulator of the monks") of Phema during the reign of the Tibetan kingdom, etc. According to Marco Polo's *Description of the World*, the main products in the Pein area were precious stone and cotton, the excellent one of the later was called as the Fine Cotton Cloth from Kaṃdva in the Dunhuang documents.

Keywords: Phema; Kaṃdva; Pein; Xuanzang; Marco Polo

Retracing the Roots of the Early Indo-European Population in Xinjiang

Maria Marinova (Sofia University)

Abstract: The present paper examines evidence from historical records as well as from anthropological, archaeological and linguistic studies of the Indo-European settlers of the Tarim Basin, which bears witness to their connection with the population of Southeast Europe. The author of the article establishes the hypothesis that the Western elements, who reached this remote corner of the world around the beginning or the middle of the 2nd millennium BC, were a branch of the ancient autochthonous population of the Balkans, collectively known as *Thracians*. Since the *Thracians* were a multi-tribal nation and each tribe or clan had its own appellation, the people who crossed over the Eurasian Steppes and eventually settled down in the Tarim Basin after a long journey, probably belonged to the clans of the *Scythians* and the *Getes* – two of the most numerous, non-sedentary and militarily-advanced tribes. In ancient Chinese annals their names were recorded with various transcriptions, among which is also the transcription 大夏 (*Daxia*), the original reading of which corresponds to the ethnonym *Thrakai/Thrakes* (*Thracians*) from the western records, as reconstructed by the author.

Keywords: *Tarim mummies*; *nomads*; *proto-Indo-Europeans*; *Yuezhi*; *Saka*; *Tocharians*; *Scythians*; *Getes*; *Thracians*

INTRODUCTION

Over the past two centuries, the borderline of our concepts regarding the time of the first contact between the Eastern and the Western civilizations has been constantly shifting further back in time. The images and the fates of the first "*proto-Indo-Europeans*" who dared to cross thousands of miles through frozen grassland steppes, rugged mountains and treacherous deserts, still haunt the imagination and inspire the scientific intuition of many scholars from both ends of the Eurasian continent. The questions about the process of formation of the prehistoric Silk Road and the possible migration routes for penetration of "*Western elements*" into the Tarim Basin as well as their ethnic origin, are among some of the most vividly discussed and controversial topics nowadays. Modern science is greatly indebted to a constellation of dedicated scholars for contributing the fruits of decades of hard research work to the solution of these problems, and yet, some key questions still remain unanswered, and there are a number of missing links still awaiting discovery.

It should be noted in the first place, that the aim of this study is not to give an overview of the existing hypotheses regarding the origin and the ethnoracial affiliation of the Europoid elements in the Tarim Basin, but rather to follow those threads in the historical, archaeological, anthropological and linguistic research of the *Tocharians*, which connect them with the population of southeast Europe and could present some new perspectives in future research of the problem.

It is generally accepted that Indo-European racial elements started to penetrate into the lands of present-day China as early as 2000 BC, by which time their migration to the East had already reached the territories between the Kunque River Basin and the Hami Basin in today's Xinjiang Autonomous Region.① Naturally, the presence of Europoid population in this remote corner of the world has left its traces in ancient Chinese literature. In one of the earliest geographical descriptions of China –《山海经》("*Classic of Mountains and Rivers*"), composed between the 5th and the 3rd century BC – "*the country of the white people*" ("白民之国") is mentioned twice: the first time it is situated "*to the north of Longyu*"② , whereas the second time it is located "*in the great wasteland*" ③. A similar type of narrative is also found in the《禹贡》("*Tribute of Yu*") section of China's earliest compilation of documentary records –《尚书》("*The Book of History*") – whose authorship is generally attributed to Confucius (551–479 BC). It describes numerous foreign tribes inhabiting certain regions of pre-imperial China, who, since the time of the Xia dynasty (21st–16th century BC) had to pay regular tributes to the Chinese rulers in the form of gold, silver, jade, bronze, iron, pearls, ivory, salt, linen, silk, wood, gems, furs, rare birds, etc.④

The information, derived from the Shang Dynasty oracle bones further complements the dynamic picture of the political state of the Chinese dynasty in the middle of the second millennium BC, confirming the fact that the area under the direct control of the Shang emperor was surrounded on all sides by numerous alien peoples, whose number even back then exceeded twenty.⑤ These foreign ethnic groups, collectively denoted by the term 方 (*fang* – "*barbarians*"), included the tribes *Tufang* (土方), *Jingfang* (井方), *Bafang* (巴方), *Zhaofang* (召方), *Qiangfang* (羌方), *Yinfang* (印方), *Jifang* (吉方), *Mafang* (马方), *Gongfang* (工方), *Guifang* (鬼方), *Renfang* (人方) and many others.⑥

To what extent these foreign tribal entities were ethnically and racially different from the predominant Han population of the Central China Plain is a question to which historical records cannot give a concrete answer. It's worthwhile noting, however, that their clan leaders were called by the title "*Bai*", written with the Chinese characters 白 or 伯⑦ , the first one meaning "white" and the second one consisting of the components "man" and "white". It is very probable that the choice of these specific characters was not dictated by purely phonetical considerations and that they also contain a certain semantic layer (as is the case with the majority of the ancient sinographemes) and recorded the fact that at least some of the numerous foreign peoples surrounding the Xia dynasty were representatives of the "white" race. In his recent study on the ethnic origin of the *Guifang* (鬼方) – one of the powerful "barbarian" states in northwest China during the Shang and the Western Zhou dynasties, the Chinese scholar Song Yixiao (宋亦箫) – a specialized researcher of the early cultural exchange between the Eastern and the Western civilizations – advocates the Indo-European origin of the *Guifang*. Based on written evidence from oracle bones, historical records and bronze inscriptions, he identifies them as the descendants of the *Tocharians* who remained in Jinnan (晋南), while the other groups migrated westward under the pressure of Mongoloid peoples.⑧ Agreeing with the opinion of

---

① 林梅村:《古道西风：考古新发现所见中西文化交流》，北京：生活•读书•新知三联书店，2000 年，第 5 页。

② "白民之国在龙鱼北，白身披发"，见（晋）郭璞:《山海经》卷七《海外西经》，高雄:台湾书房出版有限公司，1997 年，第 281 页。

③ "大荒中有山名曰明星，日月所出。有白民之国。帝俊生帝鸿，帝鸿生白民，白民销姓，黍食，使四鸟：虎、豹、熊、罴"，见《山海经》卷一四《大荒东经》，第 370 页。

④ 钱宗武，江灏译注:《尚书•禹贡》，高雄:台湾书房出版有限公司，2001 年，第 72—95 页。

⑤ 张创新:《中国政治制度史》，北京：清华大学出版社，2005 年，第 69 页。

⑥ 张创新:《中国政治制度史》，第 69 页；Di Cosmo, N., "The Northern Frontier in Pre-Imperial China", in *The Cambridge History of Ancient China: From the Origins of Civilization to 221 BC*, Cambridge University Press, 1999, p. 907.

⑦ 张创新:《中国政治制度史》，第 69 页。

⑧ 宋亦箫:《鬼方种族考》,《晋阳学刊》2008 年第 4 期，第 33 页。

the Chinese historian Yu Taishan (余太山) that the *Tufang* (土方) tribe group can also be regarded as a *Tocharian* ethnic group ①, Song Yixiao further suggests that the *Tufang* and the *Guifang* were probably kindred tribes of Indo-European origin, who were active in the area around Jinnan.②

Although there is some written and archaeological evidence confirming the presence of Indo-Europeans in the northern and central parts of present-day China, the focus of the present research will be laid upon the "*Western elements*" who settled in the Tarim Basin and which are identified by most scholars as the ancestors of the historically attested *Tocharians*.③

ARCHAEOLOGICAL AND ANTHROPOLOGICAL STUDIES OF THE TARIM MUMMIES

The archaeological excavations on the territory of the Xinjiang Autonomous Region now have a century-old history and were marked by a series of outstanding discoveries made by Chinese and foreign scholars. Some of the most ancient and important sites which illustrate the history of early contacts between the East and the West include the Gumugou (古墓沟) Culture (ca. 2000–1500 BC) and the Xiaohe (小河) tomb complex, the Ke'ermuqi (克尔木齐) Culture (2000 BC), the Yanbulake (焉不拉克) cemetery (1750–1300 BC), the Xintala (新塔拉) Culture (1700–1400 BC), the Zahongluke (扎洪鲁克) site (1200–700 BC), the Aidinghu (艾丁湖) Culture (1400–300 BC) and many others.④ On the basis of the available material it was suggested that at least by the early Bronze Age of that region⑤, Western racial elements had entered into the Lopnur area in the southeastern part of Xinjiang, and that their physical character was close to that of the ancient populations of Central Asia, southern Siberia and the Volga River drainage basin.⑥ "*As far as their racial origins are concerned, they have a direct relationship with the ancestors of the analogous Cro Magnon (Homo Sapiens) type of late Paleolithic East Europe.*"⑦

In this context, the appearance of Mongoloid population in Xinjiang is not evidenced until several centuries later – around 1000 BC, and mainly in the eastern parts of the region, which led some scholars to infer that until the first centuries BC, the eastward movement of the Western race to Xinjiang was more rapid and in a greater scale and rate than the western movement of the Mongoloid people, which probably began around the time of the Han dynasty (206 BC–220 AD).⑧

In his article "The Ayala Mazar-Xiaohe Culture: New Archaeological Discoveries in the Taklamakan Desert, China", the renowned Swiss archaeologist and explorer Christoph Baumer concludes that an Early Bronze Age culture, associated with Indo-European population, "*stretched in the first half of the 2nd millennium BCE from the ancient Keriya Delta*⑨ *in the west over a distance of more than 600 km to the northern Lop Nor graveyards in the east*"⑩. He also as-

---

① 余太山:《大方、贵方、工方与猃狁、匈奴同源说》,《古族新考》,北京:中华书局,2000年。

② 宋亦箫:《鬼方种族考》,第35页。

③ 徐文堪:《新疆古尸的新现与吐火罗人起源研究》,《学术集林》卷五,上海远东出版社,1995年,第304—314页;林梅村:《古道西风:考古新发现所见中西文化交流》,第5页。

④ Romgard J. "Questions of Ancient Human Settlements in Xinjiang and the Early Silk Road Trade, with an Overview of the Silk Road Research Institutions and Scholars in Beijing, Gansu and Xinjiang", *Sino-Platonic Papers*, 185, Nov., 2008, pp. 13-16. Available at: http://sino-platonic.org/complete/spp185_silk_road.pdf. [Accessed: 31 March 2017].

⑤ It is generally assumed that the Bronze Age in China covers the period from 2000 to 771 BC.

⑥ Han Kangxin, "The Study of Ancient Human Skeletons from Xinjiang, China", *Sino-Platonic Papers* [Online], 51 (Nov.), 1994, p. 6. Available at: http://sino-platonic.org/complete/spp051_xinjiang_skeletons.pdf. [Accessed: 20.07.2017].

⑦ Ibid.

⑧ Ibid.

⑨ Situated in the Central Tarim Basin.

⑩ Baumer Ch., "The Ayala Mazar-Xiaohe Culture: New Archaeological Discoveries in the Taklamakan Desert, China", *Asian Affairs*, 42: 1, 2011, p. 68.

sumes that other sites belonging to the same culture may have existed some 3500–4000 years ago in the regions of other ancient inland deltas in the Tarim Basin.①

The desiccated bodies of Caucasoid people, discovered in many of the archaeological sites from the Bronze Age to the Han Dynasty, elevated the research of the early culture of Xinjiang to a fundamentally new level. In the beginning of the 21st century, due to the active research and excavation work undertaken in that area, the number of the Taklamakan mummies reached several hundred, their ages ranging from 1800 BC to 400 AD.②

The genetic analysis of one of the older mummies showed that its DNA belonged to the "*typically European*" Haplogroup H, but since it was also found in peoples of diverse ancestry, the conclusion of the archaeologists was that "*it cannot so far relate the mummies yet to any specific European subgroup; it merely emphasizes once again that the Xinjiang mummies find their closest genetic relations among Europeans.*"③

In 2002 Dr. Cui Yinqiu（崔银秋）from the Jilin University also published the results of her mtDNA analysis of eleven Bronze Age mummies from Lopnur, dated 1800 BC, and of twenty Iron Age mummies from Turfan, dated 1500 BC. She compared their samples with modern mtDNA from Central Asian, East Asian and European populations, and the outcome revealed that "*the earliest mummies of the southern Tarim Basin grouped closely with the modern Sardinian and Basque samples without evidence for any mtDNA contribution from the east.*"④

In recent years a team of Chinese scholars has performed a series of DNA analyses of skeletal remains excavated from the Xiaohe tomb complex – an important Bronze Age site in the eastern edge of the Tarim Basin, which contained the oldest and best-preserved mummies so far discovered in the region, dated around 3500–4000 BP. The results from the first analyses revealed that the dominant haplogroup in the Xiaohe people was the East Eurasian lineage C, implying a connection with the Siberian populations.⑤ But besides the East Eurasian lineage, two West Eurasian mtDNA haplogroups H and K were also found, and since both of them are common in Europe and at the same time rare in Central and East Asia, the researchers concluded that the maternal ancestry of the Xiaohe people might have close relationship with western Europe.⑥ Additionally, the Y chromosomal DNA analyses of seven male mummies from the Xiaohe cemetery revealed the presence of the haplogroup R1a1a, which is most frequently found in Eastern Europe, South Asia and Siberia, and rare in the Middle East and East Asia, suggesting that the parental ancestry of the Xiaohe people originated in Europe or Siberia.⑦

In 2015 the same team of international scholars performed another series of DNA analyses of the Xiaohe mummies of the more recent burial layers, with the aim of obtaining genetic evidence in support of one of the

① Baumer Ch., "The Ayala Mazar-Xiaohe Culture: New Archaeological Discoveries in the Taklamakan Desert, China", *Asian Affairs*, 42: 1, 2011, p. 68.

② Haughton B., *Hidden History: Lost Civilizations, Secret Knowledge, and Ancient Mysteries*, Career Press, 2006, p. 211; Chunxiang Li, Chao Ning, Erika Hagelberg, Hongjie Li, Yongbin Zhao, Wenying Li, Idelisi Abuduresule, Hong Zhu and Hui Zhou, "Analysis of Ancient Human Mitochondrial DNA from the Xiaohe Cemetery: Insights into Prehistoric Population Movements in the Tarim Basin, China", *BMC Genetics* [Online], 2015, p. 3. Available at: https://www.ncbi.nlm.nih.gov/pmc/articles/PMC4495690/ [Accessed: 30 March 2017].

③ Mallory, J. P., V. H. Mair, *The Tarim Mummies: Ancient China and the Mystery of the Earliest Peoples from the West*, Thames and Hudson, 2000, pp. 246-247.

④ Cui Y., *Ancient DNA Analysis of Human Population in Xinjiang, China* (Ph.D. Dissertation, Jilin University), 2002, 转引自 Thornton, Ch., T. Schurr, "Genes, Language, and Culture: An Example from the Tarim Basin", *Oxford Journal of Archaeology*, Vol. 23, Issue 1, 2004, p. 93.

⑤ Li Chunxiang et al. "Evidence that a West-East Admixed Population Lived in the Tarim Basin As Early As the Early Bronze Age", *BMC Biology* [Online],5, 2010, p. 7. Available at: http://bmcbiol.biomedcentral.com/articles/10.1186/1741-7007-8-15 [Accessed: 30 March 2017].

⑥ Ibid., p. 7.

⑦ Ibid., p. 9.

two main theories regarding the origin of the populations in the Tarim Basin, namely: the "*steppe hypothesis*", which maintains that the Tarim region experienced at least two population influxes from the Russo-Kazakh steppe – the earliest settlers being nomadic herders of the Afanasievo culture (ca. 3300–2000 BC), followed by a wave of people of the Andronovo cultural complex (ca. 2100–900 BC); and the "*Bactrian oasis hypothesis*", postulating that the first settlers of the Tarim Basin were farmers of the Bactria-Margiana Archaeological Complex (ca. 2200–1500 BC), followed later by Andronovo people from the northwest.① The analysis of the data "*indicated multiple population influences in the Tarim Basin during 4000–3500 yBP, consistent mainly with the 'steppe hypothesis'*" and west Eurasian lineages H, K, U5, U7, U2e, T, east Eurasian lineages B, C4, C5, D, G2a and the Indian lineage M5 were detected in the Xiaohe mummies.② Since haplotypes H, K, U5 and T are found mostly in Europe, the data suggested genetic affinities with Europe, but of particular interest to our study is the presence of the haplogroup U2e in the Xiaohe mummies, which is thought to have originated in Europe, from where it had been spread into central Siberia in the Bronze Age.③ One of the conclusions drawn from the DNA analysis of the Xiaohe population is that "*people carrying European maternal lineages may have spread east into south Siberia, where they mingled with local populations and eventually spread south into Xinjiang via the Ertix River*"④. The study also reveals two additional facts, relevant to our research: firstly, the cattle excavated from the Xiaohe cemetery carried mainly lineage T3, which is typical of European cattle, and secondly, the presence of the medical plant *Ephedra* in the earliest Xiaohe layer, which "*was used by oasis farmers, whereas it doesn't grow in the Russo-Kazakh steppe, nor is associated with the Afanasievo or Andronovo cultures*"⑤, but at the same time is widely spread in southern Europe, Central Asia and China. Unfortunately, the authors of the above study do not attempt to provide explanation of how the presence of European cattle fits into the "*steppe hypothesis*" or the "*Bactrian-oasis hypothesis*", neither do they try to establish any opinion regarding the European lineage of the Tarim mummies, the attention of their research being directed solely towards Eastern Eurasia. However, the overall studies of the Europoid population in Xinjiang have reached the stage where, without the emergence of new and brave hypotheses in regard to the probable European ancestors of the *Tocharians*, it would be impossible to reconstruct the whole picture of their journey to China.

THE *YUEZHI* AND THEIR EASTWARD MIGRATION

On the basis of the evidence, obtained as a result of complex multidisciplinary research, many Western and Chinese scholars identified the Tarim mummies with the predecessors of the *Tocharians*, who inhabited the same regions in the first centuries BC⑥. On the other hand, it is generally assumed in modern science that the *Tocharians* or *Toharoi*, mentioned in the Pompeius Trogus' "*Historiae Philippicae*"⑦ (1st century BC), Ptolemy's "*Geographia*"⑧ (1st century AD) and the writings of other ancient authors, correspond to the *Yuezhi* ethnic group from the Chinese

① Li Chunxiang et al., "Analysis of Ancient Human Mitochondrial DNA from the Xiaohe Cemetery: Insights into Prehistoric Population Movements in the Tarim Basin, China" , *BMC Genetics* [online], 2015, pp. 1-2. Available at: https://www.ncbi.nlm.nih.gov/pmc/articles/PMC4495690/[Accessed: 30 March 2017].

② Ibid., pp. 8-9.

③ Ibid.

④ Ibid.

⑤ Ibid., p. 9.

⑥ 徐文堪:《新疆古尸的心发现与吐火罗人起源研究》，第 304—314 页；林梅村:《古道西风：考古新发现所见中西文化交流》，第 5 页；Mallory, J. P., V. H. Mair, *The Tarim Mummies: Ancient China and the Mystery of the Earliest Peoples from the West*, pp. 246-247.

⑦ Trogus' Prologue, Book XLII. See: Yardley J. C. (tr.), *Justin: Epitome of the Philippic History of Pompeius Trogus*, The American Philological Association, 1994, p. 284.

⑧ Ptolemy VI.11.6. See: Stevenson E.E. (tr.), *Ptolemy Geographia*, Book VI, New York, 1932, p. 142.

annals, although there are some scholars who disagree with this opinion.① The *Yuezhi* appeared in Northwest China in the pre-Qin period (16th–3rd century BC) and in the Chinese written records from that time their name was transcribed as "禺知" (*Yuzhi*) or "禺氏" (*Yushi*), while in the later sources from the Qin (221–206 BC) and Han (206 BC–220 AD) dynasties, it was recorded as "月氏" (*Yueshi*) *or* "月支" (*Yuezhi*).②

According to《史记》– the "*Records of the Grand Historian*" Sima Qian, written in the 2nd century BC – the *Yuezhi* initially inhabited the lands between Dunhuang (敦煌) and the Qilian (祁连) Mountains③, but were defeated by the *Xiongnu* and migrated further to the west. They passed through the *Yuan* (宛) kingdom in the Ferghana valley, and after attacking and conquering the kingdom of *Daxia* (大夏), set up the court of their king on the northern bank of the Amu Darya River (妫水). But a small number of their people stayed with the *Qiang* nomads (羌, "*Shepherds*") in the region of the Southern Mountains④ and came to be known as "*the small Yuezhi*"⑤.

Sima Qian's report has turned out to be too partial, however, in the light of the latest historical research, which represents the *Yuezhi* not as a small and insignificant ethnic group, but as one of the powerful nomadic tribes, ruling over the greater part of the Mongolian steppes, the Junghar and Tarim Basins, as well as the areas along the upper reaches of the Yellow River.⑥ Until their defeat by the Huns around the 2nd century BC, the *Yuezhi* played a dominant role in Central Asia, comparable to that of the Turks centuries later, inhabiting a vast area, stretching from the Tarim valley in the west, all the way to the Ordos Plateau in the northeast.⑦

The Chinese historian He Guangyue (何光岳), after analyzing the information from ancient and medieval Chinese annals, identified the *Yuezhi* with the nomadic tribe *You* (有族, also spelled 禺夷, 嵎夷, 郁夷), which originally inhabited the border regions between today's Shandong and Jiangsu Provinces.⑧ According to him, the western movement of the *Yuezhi* started in the first years of the Shang Dynasty (16th–11th century BC), and by the time of the Qin Dynasty (221–206 BC), they had already reached Xinjiang and settled in the areas around the Ili River basin.⑨

The more contemporary and systematic study of Song Yixiao (宋亦箫) further develops the historical picture from this period, not only by summarizing the achievements of preceding Chinese scholars, but also by adding on some new written and archaeological evidence to the discussion of the origin of the *Yuezhi*. He points out that scholars from the previous generation⑩ have "*almost unanimously*" concluded that the *Daxia* (大夏) tribe, well attested in both Chinese records and toponyms, were identical with the *Tocharians* from Western sources.⑪ That is why the Han imperial envoy Zhang Qian (张骞) gave them the appellation "大夏" (*Daxia*), which was

---

① Yu Taishan, "The Earliest Tocharians in China", *Sino-Platonic Papers* [Online], 204, June 2010. Available at: http://sino-platonic.org/complete/spp204_tocharian_china.pdf. [Accessed: 31 March 2017].

② 林梅村：《汉唐西域与中国文明》，北京：文物出版社，1998年，第56页。

③ The Qilian Mountains are located on the borderline between today's Qinghai and Gansu Provinces.

④ 南山, probably the Qinling Mountains in today's Shaanxi Province.

⑤《史记·大宛列传》："始月氏居敦煌、祁连间，及为匈奴所败，乃远去，过宛，西击大夏而臣之，遂都妫水北，为王庭。其余小众不能去者，保南山羌，号小月氏。"

⑥ 榎一雄等：《月氏人及其迁移》，《中亚文明史》（第2卷），北京：中国对外翻译出版公司，2002年，第130页。

⑦ 林梅村：《汉唐西域与中国文明》，北京：文物出版社，1998年，第56页。

⑧ 何光岳：《郁夷、大月氏的来源和迁徙》，《新疆社会科学》1986年第5期，第90—95页。

⑨ 何光岳：《郁夷、大月氏的来源和迁徙》，第93—97页。

⑩ 林梅村：《开拓丝绸之路的先驱——吐火罗人》，《文物》1989年第1期，第72—74页；王宗维：《"敦煌"释名——兼论中国吐火罗人》，《新疆社会科学》1987年第1期，第61—69页；黄文弼：《重论古代大夏之位置与移徙》，《黄文弼历史考古论集》，北京：文物出版社，1989年，第81—84页；季羡林：《敦煌吐鲁番吐火罗语研究导论》，台北：新文丰出版公司，1993年；王国维：《西胡考下》，《观堂集林》，石家庄：河北教育出版社，2003年，第310—311页。

⑪ 宋亦箫：《大夏（吐火罗）新探》，《武汉文物》2010年第1期，第15页。

pronounced close to "驮互" (*Tuohu*) in the ancient Chinese language from that period.[1] The substantial written evidence, analyzed by Song, also revealed that the *Tocharians* were recorded with various different names in the Chinese annals, such as: 大夏, 西虞, 西吴, 月氏, 禺氏, 牛氏, 禺知, 虞氏, etc.[2]

Agreeing with the opinion of 徐文堪[3], 林梅村[4], 王欣[5], and other Chinese scholars, that the *Tocharians* were a branch of ancient proto-Indo-Europeans, and taking into account the available written and archaeological data, Song Yixiao further suggests that they were migrants from the northern regions of Central or Eastern Europe, who reached the Altai Mountains and the neighbouring areas around 2600–2200 BC. Some of them stayed there, others continued their journey further to the south, settling down around Lake Lopnur, and still others proceeded in an eastern direction following the Yellow River, until they finally established themselves in the Jinbei(晋北) and Jinnan(晋南) areas.[6] Later on, the eastern branch gradually spread to the north and back to the west, splitting again into several groups by the 4th century BC. One group settled in the lands of the Ili River Basin, and became known to later historians as one of the four Tocharian tribes with Scythian origin. Another group settled in the Gansu region, while a third branch mixed with the Tocharian tribes who originally inhabited the areas of Mount Altai and the regions on the northern and southern side of the Eastern Tianshan Mountains (Fig. 1).[7]

In his extensive research work "The Earliest Tocharians in China", the Chinese historian and researcher of Eurasian nomads Yu Taishan also shares the opinion of Song Yi Xiao that the name "*Daxia*" (大夏), which is found

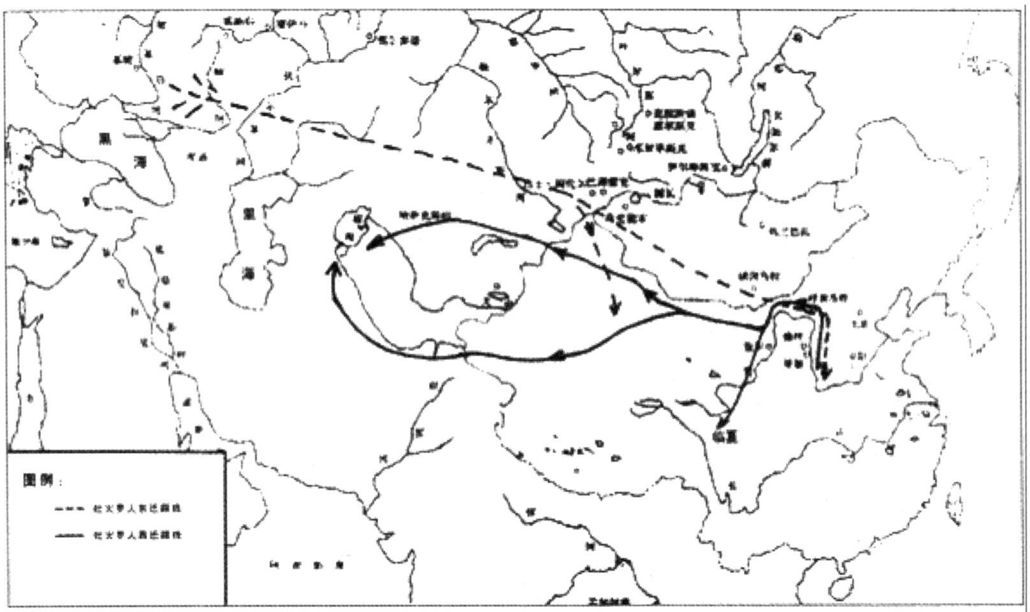

Fig. 1. Paths of Tocharian migration in eastern and western directions, according to Song Yixiao.

---

① 宋亦箫:《大夏（吐火罗）新探》,《武汉文物》2010 年第 1 期，第 15 页。

② 同上，第 15—20 页。

③ 徐文堪:《吐火罗人起源研究》，北京：昆仑出版社，2005 年，第 91—92 页。

④ 林梅村:《吐火罗人的起源与迁徙》,《西域研究》2003 年第 3 期，第 9—32 页。

⑤ 王欣:《吐火罗研究》，北京：中国社会科学出版社，2002 年，第 21—24 页。

⑥ 宋亦箫:《大夏（吐火罗）新探》，第 24 页。

⑦ 同上，第 20—21 页。

frequently in the ancient Chinesc annals, may be taken as an exact transcription of the ethnonym "*Tochari*"①, and should not be regarded as a transcription of the toponym "*Bactria*"②. He further believes that the ancient Chinese historians used the names *Daxia*（大夏）and *Yuezhi*（月氏）for the tribes *Turki* and *Guti* respectively, who left Persia together before the end of the third millennium BC and after a long journey eventually arrived in China.③ It should be noted that the research work of Yu Taishan is based mainly on analysis of existing written records and some linguistic data, used by the author in support of his thesis. The suggested correspondence between *Daxia/Tochari* and *Turki* on one side, and *Yuezhi* and *Guti* on the other, certainly needs to be confirmed by additional archaeological or anthropological evidence, as well as comparison of the material culture and the religious practices between the above groups.

ORIGIN OF THE *YUEZHI/TOCHARIANS*

Concerning their origin, the French orientalist and sinologist Joseph de Guignes (1721–1800) was the first to identify the *Yuezhi* tribe from the Chinese chronicles with the *Getes*.④ In the book *Annals and Antiquities of Rajasthan*, by James Tod, the author equates the *Jats* in Northern India, whom the Chinese called *Yuezhi*, with the *Getes*⑤, and Cunningham⑥ is of the same opinion.

The modern researchers of the Tarim mummies – Prof. James Mallory and Prof. Victor Mair reconstructed the original reading of the Chinese ethnonym *Yuezhi* as *Gwat-ti*, *Go-ti* or *Gut-si*. According to them, this pronunciation phonetically corresponded to several ethnic groups, among which was also that of the *Getes*, who lived northwest of the Black Sea.⑦

Expanding on this line of reasoning, they also assumed that behind the Chinese appellation of the more numerous branch of the tribe 大月支 *Da Yuezhi* (*The big Yuezhi*), lay hidden the name of the *Massagetes* or "*the Great Getes*", since the old-Iranian word "*massa*" meant "*great, big*"⑧.

That the *Massagetes* were most likely ethnical relatives of the *Getes*, can also be inferred from the fact that Herodotus, Strabo, Pliny and Ptolemy all mention several other tribes, whose names contain the root *Getae* – these are the *Thyssagetae*, who lived near the Volga River, the *Tyrigetae*, inhabiting the areas around the Dniester River, also the

---

① Yu Taishan also points out that "*The New Book of the Tang Dynasty*"（《新唐书》), written by a team of scholars during the Northern Song period (960–1126), identified for the first time the term "*Daxia*" with the ethnic group *Tochari*, whose name was recorded in different Chinese records as *Tuhuoluo*（吐火罗；土豁罗）, *Duhuoluo*（睹货逻）or *Tuhuluo*（吐呼罗）. Yu Taishan, "The Earliest Tocharians in China", *Sino-Platonic Papers* [Online], 204(June), 2010, p. 12. Availabe at: http://sino-platonic.org/complete/spp204_tocharian_Ehina pdf. [Accessed: 31 March 2017].

② Ibid., p. 10-11.

③ Ibid., p. 44.

④ "*We learn from De Guignes, that there was formerly a Nomade nation called Yue-chi, or Geté, who inhabited the country west of the Chinese province of Shensy, and who having been invaded by the Huns, about two hundred years B.C., were compelled to emigrate. On this occasion the Geté divided: the greater number proceeded to the north-west, and after having driven before them a tribe named Su, took possession of the country in the vicinity of the river Ili. The lesser division marched towards Tibet, and were distinguished by the title of the Little Geté.*" See *The Asiatic Journal and Monthly Register for British India and Its Dependencies*, Vol. XIV, London, 1822, p. 451.

⑤ Tod J., *Annals and Antiquities of Rajasthan*, Vol. 1, Oxford University Press, 1920, pp. 74-75, 256.

⑥ Cunningham J. D., *Cunningham's History of the Sikhs*, 1853, p. 18. Available at:https://archive.org/details/cunninghamshisto00cunnuoft. [Accessed: 04 April 2017].

⑦ Mallory, J. P., V. H. Mair, *The Tarim Mummies: Ancient China and the Mystery of the Earliest Peoples from the West*, p. 98; See a summary of previous studies and similar conclusions regarding the pronunciation of *Yuezhi* in Jhutti S. S., "The Getes", *Sino-Platonic Papers* [Online], 127, Oct., 2003, pp. 16-19.Available at: http://www.sino-platonic.org/complete/spp127_getes.pdf. [Accessed: 31 March 2017].

⑧ Mallory, J. P., V. H. Mair, The *Tarim Mummies: Ancient China and the Mystery of the Earliest Peoples from the West*, pp. 98-99.

Thyrsagetae, *Euergetae*, etc..① It should be noted that the territories ruled by these various "*Getan*" tribes are located within the boundaries of Great and Little Scythia, but at the same time there is no historical evidence or any record of conflicts between *Scythians* and *Getes* or other Thracian tribes.② Much to the contrary, quite often they are described by Herodotus, Strabo and Thucydides as allies or good neighbours.③ Therefore, the *Getes* and the *Scythians* must have been kindred tribes, which could explain the frequent identification of the former with the latter and vice versa, seen in many historical writings since antiquity.④

Herodotus mentions that the Persians called all *Scythians Sacae*⑤, and regarding the *Massagetes*, he informs us that "*they wear the same costumes as the Scythians, and have the same mode of life*"⑥ and that some people "*assert that this nation is Scythian*"⑦. The ethnic kinship of the *Massagetes* and the *Scythians* is also confirmed by Strabo, who documented the presence of *Scythians* in the areas of the Amu Darya River and the Himalayas around the 1st century BC.⑧ He states explicitly that the eastern *Scythians* were called "*Massagetae*" and "*Sacae*", whereas all the other Scythian tribes, among which the *Asii*, *Pasiani*, *Tochari* and *Sacarauli*, were generally called "*Scythians*", although "*each people was given a name of its own*"⑨. This passage from Strabo reveals a very important fact, namely that the *Massagetes* , the *Sakas* and the *Tocharians* all belonged to the Scythian race. Therefore it would be safe to assume that the *Scythians*, the *Massagetes* and the *Tocharians* were either kindred ethnic groups with common descent, or individual tribes of the same ethnic group, which in Central and Eastern Asia was denoted with the collective term "*Scythes*" *or* "*Sacae*".

Another interesting fact that should be pointed out is that the Roman historian Pompeius Trogus, who lived in the 1st century BC, informs us that the *Scythians* were the founders of the *Parthians* and *Bactrians*⑩, and that later the *Scythians* slew the Persian king Cyrus with his whole army.⑪ These events are described in detail in Jordanes' "*Getica*", which was written several centuries later, but in his account it is the *Getes*, from whose "*name or even race*" the stock of the *Parthians* derived its origin.⑫ According to Jordanes, "*Cyrus, king of the Persians... waged a war, fatal to himself against Tomyris, Queen of the Getae.*"⑬ The depiction of the battle between the two mighty nations also contains some interesting facts of historical value: "*the Getae and their queen defeated, conquered and overwhelmed the Parthians and took rich plunder from them... After achieving this victory... Queen Tomyris crossed over into that part of Moesia*⑭ *which is now*

① Jhutti S. S., "The Getes" , pp. 80-81.

② For instance, in 439 BC the Scythians undertook a campaign against the Persian colonies in Thrace, but only attacked and destroyed the Persians and their allies, never raised a hand against the local population. See: Nedelchev N., "Thraco-Scythica: Historical Contacts (7th–4th century BC)" , *Thrace and the Surrounding World*, Sofia: Mif 9, 2005, pp. 21-22. (Неделчев, Н. Thraco-Scythica – Исторически контакти (VII-VI в. пр. н.е.). – В: Тракия и околния свят. София: Миф9, 2005).

③ Ibid., pp. 26-29.

④ For instance, the Church historian Philostorgius (368–439 AD) in his "*Historia ecclesiastica*" wrote that "*of old the Scythians were called Getae, but now they are called Goths*" (Philostorgius II. 5. See in: Amidon, Ph. R. (tr.), "Philostorgius: Church History" , *Society of Biblical Literature*, Atlanta, 2007, p. 20).

⑤ Herodotus. VII. 64. See in: Gaisford T. (tr.), *The Nine Books of the History of Herodotus*, Vol. II, Oxford, 1827, p. 165.

⑥ Herodotus. I. 215. See in: Gaisford T. (tr.), *The Nine Books of the History of Herodotus*, Vol. I, Oxford, 1827, p. 103.

⑦ Herodotus. I. 201-202. See in: Gaisford T. (tr.), *The Nine Books of the History of Herodotus*, Vol. I, p. 98.

⑧ Strabo. XI. VIII.1-4. See in: Bohn H. G. (tr.), *The Geography of Strabo*, Vol. II, London, 1856, pp. 244-246.

⑨ Strabo. XI. VIII. 2. See in: Bohn H. G. (tr.), *The Geography of Strabo*, p. 245.

⑩ Justin. *Epitome of the Philippic History of Pompeius Trogus*. II. 1. See in: Watson J. S. (tr.), *Marcus Junianus Justinus. Epitome of the Philippic History of Pompeius Trogus,* London, Henry G. Bohn, 1853, p. 16.

⑪ Ibid., p. 19.

⑫ Jordanes. VI. 47; VII. 48. See in: Mierow C. C., *The Gothic History of Jordanes*, Princeton University Press, 1915, p. 63.

⑬ Jordanes. X. 61. See in: Mierow C. C., *The Gothic History of Jordanes*, p. 67.

⑭ I. e. Dobrogea (Dobrudja) – a historical region, situated between the Lower Danube River and the Black Sea, shared today by Bulgaria and Romania.

*called Lesser Scythia... and built on the Moesian shore of the Black Sea the city of Tomi*①*, named after herself.*"②

As we can see, the assumption that *Scythians*, *Getes* and even *Massagetes* were varieties of the same ethnic group is attested in many historical documents, therefore it also appeared in the Western historiography around the beginning of the 19th century. In his research work on Herodotus' geographical system, the English geographer and historian James Rennell supposes that "*Massagetae was a term invented and applied by the Greeks to the Eastern Getae, or Scythians, beyond the Caspian and Jaxartes; in contradiction to the Getae or Scythians of the Euxine (the Black Sea), who were the first and more familiarly known to the Greeks.*"③ He further states that in their geographical descriptions of the regions north of Sogdiana and Bactria, the ancient authors also frequently used the ethnonyms *Scythians*, *Sakas* and *Massagetes* as interchangeable terms.④ According to the Chinese scholar Yu Taishan, on the basis of the information derived from Achaemenid inscriptions, it can be judged that during the reign of Darius I (521–486 BC) at the latest, the *Saka* had not yet become the specific designation for a particular tribe.⑤

SCYTHIAN SITES IN CHINA

Various Chinese historical sources, such as《汉书》(*History of the Han Dynasty*, 1st–2nd century AD)⑥, also contain some information about the Scythian settlements in these distant parts of Eurasia. In the section "*Narrative of the Western Territories*" (《汉书・西域传》), the lands inhabited by the Scythian tribes around the first centuries BC are quite well described.⑦ The summarized available data shows that in the period preceding the founding of the Western Han Dynasty in the 3rd century BC, the territories of the Scythians extended from the banks of the Ili River to the Tianshan Mountain, or even further south to the Alailing Mountain (阿赖岭山) and the Eastern Pamirs.⑧ From the same historical sources we learn that at the end of the 3rd century BC, the *Tocharians* migrated westward and conquered the original Scythian settlements in the areas around the Ili River.⑨

The Scythian culture in Xinjiang is also archaeologically attested by such discoveries as the Alagou (阿拉沟), Xinyuan (新源), Zhaosu (昭苏), Nulasai (奴拉赛), Xiangbaobao (香宝宝) and other settlements scattered along the Ili River and the Pamir Mountains, as well as by remnants of Scythian burials, copper mines, bronze and pottery vessels, weapons and other artifacts, dated between 5th and 3rd century BC.⑩ Prof. Mallory also gives information about 30 kurgan burial mounds dated to 550–250 BC in the Zhongyangchang (种羊场) county in the Tian Shan (天山) and the cemetery from the 7th century BC near the Yuansha (圆沙) fortified settlement on the Keriya River (克里雅河), all associated with the *Saka* on the basis of tomb-building techniques, Europoid physi-

---

① I. e. the city of Constanza in present-day Romania.

② Jordanes X. 62. See in: Mierow C. C., *The Gothic History of Jordanes*, pp. 67-68.

③ Rennell J., *The Geographical System of Herodotus, Examined; And Explained by A Comparison with Those of Other Ancient Authors*, London, 1800, p. 217.

④ Ibid., p. 216. See summary of 19th century scholars on the connection between *Massa-Getae, Thyssa-Getae, Thracians* and *Scythians* in: Jhutti, S. S., Op. cit., pp. 20-23.

⑤ Yu Taishan, "The Name 'Sakā'", *Sino-Platonic Papers* [Online], 251, August 2014, p. 2. Available at: http://sino-platonic.org/complete/spp251_Saka_Sacae.pdf. [Accessed: 31 March 2017].

⑥ It should be noted, that in the later Chinese chronicles the Scythians are almost never mentioned, which could be explained by their migration or assimilation during the first centuries of the new era.

⑦ 《汉书・西域传・乌孙》《汉书・西域传・捐毒国》《汉书・西域传・罽宾国》《汉书・张骞李广利传》，载王先谦:《汉书补注》(二、三)，上海古籍出版社，2008年。

⑧ 王炳华:《古代新疆塞人历史钩沉》,《新疆社会科学》1985年第1期，第48—49页。

⑨ 同上，第49页。

⑩ 王炳华:《古代新疆塞人历史钩沉》，第49—52页；Di Cosmo, N., "The Northern Frontier in Pre-Imperial China", pp. 942-944.

cal type and objects of material culture.①

Although the artifacts from these archaeological sites are traditionally associated with similar representatives of the *Saka*-culture from Central Asia, Russia and Ukraine, the problem regarding the homeland or some "typically Scythian" features such as the *kurgan* burial mounds, the animal-style horse decorations, the prototypes of the gold and silver treasures as well as of the Scythian armor and weapons has not been satisfactorily resolved yet. In modern research works on the movements and interactions between ancient Eurasian populations the scholarly focus is usually laid on the eastern parts of the continent as the natural source for associations and ancestry of the later socio-political formations, their material lifestyles and languages. In the case of the *Tocharians*, the Afanasievo and Andronovo cultures, which lie north of the Tarim Basin, are usually employed as candidates for antecedents, although a number of traits in various fields suggest that the lineage of the *Tocharians* is also closely related with Europe and therefore the scope of investigation of parallels in terms of language, material and immaterial culture should be broadened.② A scientific approach which fails to see or neglects the historical links of the Eurasian steppe populations with the highly developed Neolithic and Bronze Age cultures in Southeast Europe will undoubtedly yield limited and marginal results. For instance, the Scythian *kurgan* burial mounds, which are widely spread throughout the Eurasian steppes, and can also be found in Romania and the northern parts of present-day Bulgaria, are very close in terms of building technique and overall designation to the Thracian burial mounds from the first millennium BC, scattered all over the Balkan peninsula. Gold and silver objects, armors and weapons of the *Scythians* and the *Thracians* also provide a lot of parallels in regard to style, purpose, motifs and craftsmanship. For instance, according to scholars, the akinaka swords (Gr. ἀκινάκης), whose appearance towards the end of the Early Iron Age marked a new stage in the development of swords, were spread in a vast area, stretching from Hungary in the west to Southern Siberia in the East.③ However, they are considered specific and emblemat-

Fig. 2. Bronze statue of a Scythian warrior from Xinjiang

Fig. 3. Thracian helmet

Fig. 4. Phrygian hat

---

① Mallory J. P., "Bronze Age Languages of the Tarim Basin" , *Expeditions* [Online], 52.3, November 2010, pp. 49-50. Available at: https://www.penn.museum/sites/expedition/bronze-age-languages-of-the-tarim-basin/. [Accessed: 02 April 2017].

② In her critical paper "When East Met West: Interpretive Problems in Assessing Eurasian Contact and Exchange in Antiquity" , Prof. Irene Good from the Harvard University addresses some epistemological issues of interpretation of the concept of the Andronovo culture: "*Because many scholars consider Andronovo to represent a cohesive group of people in ethnic and language terms, it has been loosely considered a culture. It has also been variously considered to be an archaeological horizon, a culture complex, a set of related cultures, or a set of material culture traits reflecting interaction between different groups. Thus basic questions of definition have remained open to discussion and debate... What has also been lacking up until now is a clear break from simplistic evolutionist and migration models. There is a need to view the archaeological record of Bronze Age Eurasia as an expression of diverse, interacting local culture histories, with visible synchronic changes in regional material culture in specific regions. Moreover the notion of 'nomad' is grossly over-simplified and at times falsely dichotomized into discreet populations of 'settled' vs. 'nomadic'. This oversimplification is particularly pronounced in the literature concerning Central Asia before the first millennium BC*" . See: Good I., "When East Met West: In terpretive Problem in Assessing Eurasia Contact and Exchange in Antiquity " , *Archaologische Mitteilungen aus Iran und Turan*, 42, 2010, pp. 23-45.

③ Bujukliev H., "Weapons of Offence in Ancient Thrace" , *Weapons from Ancient Thrace*, Historical Museum of Shumen, 1995, pp. 7-8. (Буюклиев Хр, "Нападателното въоръжение в Древна Тракия", *Въоръжение от Древна Тракия*, Исторически музей Шумен, 1995, с.7-8).

ic of both the *Scythians* and one of the Thracian tribes – the *Getes.*① To this the typically Scythian pointed hats can also be added, including the hat (or helmet) of the unique 42-centimetre bronze statue of a warrior "with typical European features"② (Fig. 2), which was found in a Scythian burial mound from the Xinyuan county (新源县) in the Xinjiang Autonomous Region in 1989. Visually it bears close similarity to the pointed helmets of the *Thracians* (Fig. 3) and the pointed hats of the *Phrygians* (Fig. 4) – an ancient Thracian tribe, which moved to the south and settled in Anatolia around 1200 BC.

LINGUISTIC TRAITS

The latest linguistic studies of the Tocharian language further confirm the fact that the origin of the *Yuezhi* or the *Tocharians* must be sought among early Europeans rather than the Iranian-speaking peoples of Central Asia. The Tocharian language, which is documented primarily in fairly late written records from the 6–8th centuries AD, is usually described as a "*centum*" Indo-European language, which, as proposed by the Indo-European comparativist and expert in Tocharian Douglas Adams, is placed in the Northwestern Group of the Indo-European languages together with Celtic, Italic, Germanic, Baltic, Slavic and Albanian, while Greek, Iranian, Armenian and Indic are located in the Southeastern Group.③ Adams further believes that *Tocharians* separated themselves very early from the rest of their group (perhaps in the first half of the third millennium BC) and started moving eastward across the North Pontic steppes and then the Central Asian steppes, ultimately settling down in Chinese Turkestan some two thousand years later④ – an opinion which is shared by the modern Chinese scholar Yu Taishan⑤, who also asserts that the birthplace of Tocharian should be sought in Europe⑥. Furthermore, according to Adams, the ties of Tocharian with both Greek and Indic, which belong to the Southeastern Group of the Indo-European languages, reflect the fact that *pre-Tocharians* first had contacts with *pre-Greeks* and later with *pre-Indics* in the course of their long journey to the East.⑦ This presumption is of significant importance to our study, because it sets a specific criterion in the search of the homeland of the *Tocharians* and limits its scope to a small number of ethnic groups whose location would allow contact with pre-Greek peoples before eventually moving to the east. Undoubtedly, a very probable candidate would be the northern neighbour of the *Hellenes* – the Thracian race, which inhabited the Balkan Peninsula in the second millennium BC and was in constant interaction with speakers of pre-Greek. In later historical periods the territories of some of the Thracian tribes are attested to have stretched as far as Asia Minor to the south and the Carpathian Mountains to the north, comprising Scythia Minor and part of the Pontic steppes. The language of the *Thracians*, as preserved in ancient historical records and inscriptions has been studied by a number of Bulgarian and foreign linguists during the past century. Among them the eminent Bulgar-

---

① Rustoiu A., "Thracian Sica and Dacian Falx. The History of a 'National' Weapon", *Dacia Felix*, Studia Michaeli Barbulescu Oblata. Cluj-Napoca, 2007, p. 67.

② 胡笳、钟习政:《新疆密码》，北京：五洲传播出版社，2007 年，第 61—62 页。

③ Adams D. Q., "The Position of Tocharian among the Other Indo-European Languages", *Journal of the American Oriental Society*, 104(3), 1984, p. 401.

④ Ibid.

⑤ Yu Taishan, "The Earliest Tocharians in China", p. 2.

⑥ Nakhleh L., D. Ringe, T. Warnow, "Perfect Phylogenetic Networks: A New Methodology for Reconstructing the Evolutionary History of Natural Languages", *Language*, Vol. 81, No. 2, June 2005, p. 401.It is also interesting to point out, that the latest computerized technologies for reconstruction of *Proto-Tocharian revealed its direct link with Proto-Slavic*, leading to the conclusion, that "*an ancestor of Tocharian was still in Eastern Europe in the last millennium BC, and it seems clear that by the turn of the millennium the speakers of (pre-)Proto-Tocharian were within striking distance of Xinjiang*"; Thornton Ch., T. Schurr, "Genes, Language, and Culture: An Example from the Tarim Basin", *Journal of Archaeology*, Vol. 23, Issue 1, 2004, p. 98.

⑦ Adams D. Q., Op. cit., p. 395.

ian scholar Prof. Vladimir Georgiev has made a great contribution to the understanding of the connection of the *Thracian* language with other Indo-European languages and in his extensive research work *The Thracians and Their Language*①, he compares a number of Thracian glosses, toponyms and personal names with their correspondences in other (pre-)Indo-European languages, including *Tocharian.* Prof. Georgiev discovers three common glosses of *Thracian* and *Tocharian*② :

Thracian ⋆ard– / ⋆arz– = *Toch. A* arki , *Toch. B* arkwi (white)

Thracian bria / ⋆wriya = *Toch. A* ri, *Toch. B* riye (town)

Phrygian bal(l) ē n, bal(l) ē nos = *Toch. A* wäl, wla–, *Toch. B* w(a)lo (king)

At the same time, certain linguists believe that the Tocharian language has many of the characteristics of centum languages, and is especially close to the Hittite language③, spoken in Anatolia④. Owing to the archaeological studies of the Early Bronze Age cultures from Southeast Europe, more and more scholars worldwide acknowledge the fact that the Balkans appear to be the chronological and cultural ancestor of the Early Bronze Age in Anatolia. Hence some of them suggest that not only the material culture, but also the Indo-European languages were introduced to northwestern Anatolia from the Balkans in the centuries around 3000 BC. ⑤

This assumption again brings us back to Southeast Europe where, with a relatively high degree of confidence, we can search for the homeland and the origin of the Tocharian ethnicity, language and culture. As was demonstrated, a lot of archaeological, anthropological and linguistic research data point at that very region in Eurasia, namely the Balkan Peninsula – one of the earliest centers of advanced civilization since Neolithic times – as the highly probable homeland of the people who were capable of expanding their settlements as far as China.

ORIGIN AND EARLIEST SETTLEMENTS OF THE *GETES* AND THE *SCYTHIANS*

The existence of all the evidence cited here, however partial it may be, should serve to expand the boundaries of interdisciplinary studies of the Europoid population in Northwest China, and to give impetus to more targeted and exhaustive research of its origin. So far we have established the association of the ancient Europoid settlers with the *Yuezhi* or *Tocharoi* on one hand, and the kinship relation or identification of the latter with the *Scythae* and the *Getae* on the other – not a new achievement by itself, but rather a synthesis of a series of discoveries made more than a century ago. We shall proceed, therefore, with narrowing down the scope of our investigation and tracing the original habitats of these ancient tribes.

The earliest mentions of *Scythians* and *Getes* are found in the early historical literature in the context of Eastern Europe. Historians from different periods denoted the tribes as inhabiting the regions of Moesia, Thrace and the Northwest Pontic⑥ coast by different names, which confused and hindered the clarity of the historical picture to a certain extent, but was certainly not coincidental. For example, in the time of Herodotus, the *Scythians* lived on the northern side of the Danube River, whereas the territories on the southern side were inhabited by various

---

① Georgiev Vl., *The Thracians and Their Language*, Bulgarian Academy of Sciences, Sofia, 1977 (Георгиев, Вл, *Траките и техния език*, Българска академия на науките, София, 1977).

② Ibid, p. 65, 13, 216.

③ W. Petersen even supposes that Hittite and Tocharian must have constituted for some time a dialectic unity, because they possess in common certain innovations. See in: Petersen W., "Hittite and Tocharian" , *Language*, Vol. 9, No.1, Mar., 1933, p. 12.

④ 林梅村:《吐火罗人的起源与迁徙》,《西域研究》2003 年第 3 期，第 9 页。

⑤ Mallory, J. P., *In Search of the Indo-Europeans: Language, Archaeology and Myth,* Thames and Hudson, 1991, p. 239.

⑥ Πὸντος Εὺξεινος (Pontos Euxeinos) was the name of the Black Sea in antiquity.

Thracian tribes, among which were also the *Getes* – *"the bravest of all Thracians"*①. Furthermore, the Roman historian of Getan descent – Jordanes – informs us, that *"in their first abode the Getes dwelt in the land of Scythia near Lake Maeotis②; in their second in Moesia, Thrace and Dacia, and in their third they dwelt again in Scythia, above the sea of Pontus."*③ Therefore, it appears that in indefinite antiquity the *Getes* not only inhabited some Scythian territories, but also the very regions, which, according to Herodotus, Thucydides, Xenophon and other ancient historians, have always been the homeland of the Thracian tribes. The above record from Jordanes also confirms the explicit statement of Herodotus (IV.93), that the *Getae* were one of the Thracian tribes – an opinion which nowadays has been substantially supported by the results of decades of archaeologico-historical research of the Thracian civilization. One of the famous Greek chronists – Theophanes the Confessor (758–818 AD) in his *"Theophanis Chronographia"* also lists the *Getes* (called *Goths* at that time) among the Thracian nations.④

On the other hand, it has been shown here that the *Scythians* and the *Getes* were only two of the numerous Thracian kindred tribes. Perhaps the Greek grammarian Stephanus Byzantinus was also well aware of that fact, because in his 6th century geographical dictionary "*Ethnica*" ("*Ἐθνικά*") the *Scythians* were defined in the following manner: *"Σκυθαι, ἔθνος Θρακιον"*, i.e. as a Thracian ethnic group.⑤

According to the opinion of the eminent Bulgarian professor Assen Chilingirov – author of more than 400 scholarly works in the field of history and history of arts – the local population of the northeastern part of the Balkan Peninsula was denominated by the ancient authors either with the collective names *"Thracians"*, *"Getes"*, *"Scythians"* or with the names of individual tribes or tribal groups.⑥ He also points out that in the antique historical records the ethnonym *"Getes"* was usually used as a collective term for the ancient autochthonous population of the Black Sea region, which included all homogeneous tribes and nations, inhabiting that region in the past, such as *Thracians*, *Illyrians*, *Dacians*, *Schythians*, *Sarmatians*, etc..⑦ Additionally, Prof. Chilingirov links the etymology of the name *"Scythians"*, which in Bulgarian is pronounced *"Skiti"*, with the old Bulgarian verb *"skita"* ("*to wander*"), thus presuming that ancient authors purposely labelled the nomadic tribes with this term, in order to distinguish them from the settled farmers of the Balkan peninsula (i.e. the *Thracians*).⑧

In modern science the *Scythians* are often treated as Iranian Eurasian nomads or Iranian people, whose influence stretched from the Carpathian Mountains of Europe to the central steppes and the Tarim Basin in Asia. Their ethnic and linguistic affiliation, however, is still a matter of controversy and has given rise to a number of broad hypotheses. The interpretation of the available archaeological and anthropological evidence generally favours their Eastern Eurasian origin, probably because the analyzed Scythian population comes predominantly from burials in the Asian parts of the territories inhabited by them, and not from the "classical" Scythian lands as described in the ancient historical works.

Herodotus outlines in detail the geographical location of the homeland of the *Scythians* at his time (around the 5th century BC). His *"Old Scythia"* (*ἀρχαίη Σκυθική*) is an area with almost square shape, "*commencing*" from the Ister

① Herodotus. IV. 93. See in: Gaisford T. (tr.), *The Nine Books of the History of Herodotus*, p. 310.

② I. e. the Sea of Azov.

③ Jordanes. V. 38. See in: Mierow C. C., *The Gothic History of Jordanes*, p. 60.

④ Theophanis Chronographia. A. M. 5997 (A.D. 504/5). See in: De Boor C., *Theophanis Chronographia*,Vol. I, Leipzig, 1883, p. 145.

⑤ Meineke A. (tr.), *Stephani Byzantii ethnicorum quae supersunt*, Vol. I, Berlin, 1849, p. 578.

⑥ Chilingirov As., "Goths and Getes" , *Goths and Getes: Research on History of Culture*, Vol. I. Ziezi ex quo Vulgares, 2008, p. 67. (Чилингиров, Ас., "Готи и Гети", В: *Готи и Гети: Изследвания по историята на културата,* том I. Зиези екс куо Вулгарес, 2008, с. 67).

⑦ Chilingirov As., "Preface to the Second Edition" , *Goths and Getes: Research on History of Culture*, Vol. I. Ziezi ex quo Vulgares, 2008, p. 3. (Чилингиров, Ас., "Предговор към второто издание", В: *Готи и Гети: Изследвания по историята на културата, том* I. Зиези екс куо Вулгарес, 2008, с. 3).

⑧ Chilingirov As., "Goths and Getes" , p. 96.

(Danube) River delta and bordering with Thrace to the south, stretching to the Tanais (Don) River delta in the east, and the Borysthenes (Dnieper) River in the north.① Almost ten centuries later, Scythia has already moved a lot more to the east – in the geographical work of Pappus Alexandreus from the 4th century, Scythia extends, arc-like, in a southeastern direction from the Etil (Volga) River all the way to the Imaeus (Himalaya or Pamir) Mountains.② Two centuries later, Jordanes gives us almost the same description of Scythia, except that in his account the territories of *"Old Scythia"*, mentioned by Herodotus are also included: *"Now Scythia borders on the land of Germany as far as the source of the river Ister and ... extends as far as the Huns, Albani and Seres."* ③

These geographical descriptions reflect the gradual expansion of the Scythian presence and culture, starting from the northwestern Pontic steppes, stretching through Middle and Central Asia and reaching down to the Amu Darya River Basin and the Himalayas around the 1st century BC at the latest, as documented by Strabo (XI,VIII.1-4).

In further support of our hypothesis that the *Getae* and the *Scythae,* who reached the territories of the later Chinese empire, originally dwelt in the western and the northwestern parts of the Black Sea region, this author shall provide evidence from a source hitherto unknown to the Western scientific circles and the general public – the Bulgarian translation of an important corpus of manuscripts, published in 2010. It contains the translated texts of Syriac, Coptic, Latin and Greek manuscripts, related to the most ancient dynastic history of the early Balkan population, hence the corpus was named by its compilers *"The Thracian Chronicles"*④. This corpus represents a valuable source of previously unknown historical information, which has been only briefly mentioned by other ancient authors. In the annals of the Thracian kings contained therein, we find reflected from a different angle and in a more systematic and detailed manner many important events, which had been described by Herodotus and Thucydides less than a century earlier.⑤ Needless to say, the texts of the manuscripts also provide an enormous number of parallels, factological contexts and points of contact with modern-day archaeology (especially in the territory of Bulgaria, comprising the ancient geographical districts of *Thrace*, *Moesia* and *Dobrogea*, and extremely rich in archaeological sites and finds from the period of the Thracian kingdoms). They also contribute a lot of explicit information about historical events or persons, thus confirming certain scientific hypotheses, which had already been established on the basis of historical or archaeological data alone.

Since *"The Thracian Chronicles"* also shed some light on the problem of the genealogy of the *Getes* and the *Scythians*, which is important to our study, I shall try to translate some of the relevant passages into English, with the hope that a proper English translation of the entire corpus shall be published one day. In *The Book of Navvi* (*Liber Regum Primus et Secundus id est Navvi*⑥), preserved in two Latin transcripts and one fragmentary Greek manuscript, we find the hitherto unknown genealogy of the *Scythae* and the *Getae*: "(*Yatuef* ⑦)... *gave to his third son Odrys and to*

---

① Herodotus. IV. 99-101. See in: Gaisford T. (tr.), *The Nine Books of the History of Herodotus*, pp. 313-314.

② Hewsen R. H., "The Geography of Pappus of Alexandria: A Translation of the Armenian Fragments" , in *Isis*, Vol. 62, No. 2, 1971, p. 204.

③ Jordanes. V. 30-32. See in: Mierow C. C., *The Gothic History of Jordanes*, pp. 58-59.

④ Guide St., Tz. Guaidarski, *The Thracian Chronicles*, The City Foundation, 2010. (Гайд, Ст., Цв. Гайдарски, *Тракийските хроники,* Фондация Градът, 2010).

⑤ And yet, everything indicates that in *"The Thracian Chronicles"* there is no factual borrowing or attempt of imitation of previous historical works, but rather, a different approach and purpose of the historical narrative is demonstrated. For example, Herodotus focuses on the detail and exhaustiveness of the presented information, although quite often it is collected from secondary sources, while *"The Thracian Chronicles"* represent a systematic genealogy of the Thracian dynasts, with an emphasis on the sacred tradition in the royal clan and its continuity between generations.

⑥ The book is also known as *"The Chronicles of Habrozalmoks"*, Habrozalmoks (Habrizelm) was a Thracian king who ruled as a regent in the period 386-383 BC.

⑦ According to the manuscript, Yatuef was a mighty ruler of Thrace, living around the 31st century BC.

*his brother (Bessoi) a share of land along the River*①*, stretching all the way to the Thracian Sea, and to his fourth son Geth, he gave the lands to the north, right up to the Pison (Istros*②*) River... And so, Geth reigned in the north and the east, and became father of all Getae... And Geth had four sons: Getàn, Scyth, Tanak and Tibar. And his firstborn son Getàn succeeded the royal throne of the Getae after his father, and his second son Scyth expanded the borders of his kingdom to the north and became father of all Scythae."* ③

This short citation further confirms our previous conclusion that the *Scythae* and the *Getae*, like the tribes of the *Odrysae* and the *Bessi*, were descendants of the Thracian dynasts, whose share was to rule over the western and northwestern Pontic regions, subsequently migrating further to the northeast. However, the history and manner of life of these mighty people, although quite well attested in numerous archaeological sites, records, inscriptions, philosophical schools, traditions and beliefs, still remain quite obscure and unknown to most Western researchers. This is partially due to the fact that during the last century, which was marked by intensive and systematic archaeological work and hundreds of new important discoveries, revealing many aspects of the Thracian culture, a very small, even negligible number of books and scientific articles by Bulgarian scholars have been published in English, German or French. That is why it is necessary to examine briefly a few ethno-historical characteristics of the Thracian nation, which are important to our study.

WHO WERE THE *THRACIANS*?

The historical development of the *Thracians* as a geographical and ethno-demographic unity of tribes with the same or at least similar socio-economic, state-political, cultural and ideological characteristics starts from the middle or early 3rd millennium BC with the emergence of the oldest state institutions, and conditionally ends by Late Antiquity (3rd–6th cent.) with the rise of new political formations.④ Early Thracian names are documented in Cretan inscriptions in Linear A from the 18–16th century BC, as well as in Hittite and Egyptian written records from the 14th–13th century BC.⑤ Perhaps the first mention of the ethnonym *Thracians* is in Homer's *Iliad*, which is generally accepted as a historical source of information, relating to the time of the Trojan War – 13th or 12th century BC.

Regarding their origin, we have the testimony of Josephus Flavius⑥ (1st century AD), Isidore of Seville⑦ (7th century AD) and other ancient authors, that the *Thracians* were the offspring of Japhet's son Thiras. Herodotus describes them as the second most-numerous people in the world: "*The Thracian people are, next at least to the Indians, the most numerous in the world: and were they under the control of one prince, or could they agree among themselves, they would, in my opinion, be invincible, and by far the most powerful of all nations; but inasmuch as this is impracticable with them, and impossible ever to take place, they are accordingly, on this account, feeble. They bear various names, according to their respective regions: all of them follow, in every respect, nearly the same institutions.*"⑧

---

① Probably the Maritsa River, running through present-day Bulgaria and Turkey.

② I. e. the Danube River.

③ Navvi. VI. 13-18. See in: Guide St., Tz. Guaidarski (comp.), *The Thracian Chronicles*, pp. 175-176.

④ Popov D., *Thracians*, East-West Publishing, 2011, pp. 11-12. (Попов Д., *Траки*, Издателство Изток-Запад, 2011).

⑤ Porozhanov K., "Society and State Organization of the Thracians Mid- 2nd – Early 1st Millenium B. C." , *Studia Thracica*, 6, Sofia, 1998, p. 199. (Порожанов К. "Общество и държавност у траките: средата на II – началото на I хил. пр. Хр.", *Studia Thracica*, 6, София, 1988, с. 199).

⑥ "*Thiras also called those whom he ruled over Thirasians; but the Greeks changed the name into Thracians.*" (Antiquities of the Jews, Book I, 6.1. See in: Flavius Josephus, *The Antiquities of the Jews*, Digireads.com Publishing, 2010, p. 16.)

⑦ "*Tiras, from whom the Thracians; their name is not much altered, as if it were Tiracians.*" (The Etymologies. IX. ii. 31. See in: Barney St. (tr.), *The Etymologies of Isidore of Seville*, Cambridge University Press, 2006, p. 193.)

⑧ Herodotus. V. 3. See in: Gaisford T. (tr.), *The Nine Books of the History of Herodotus*, p. 2.

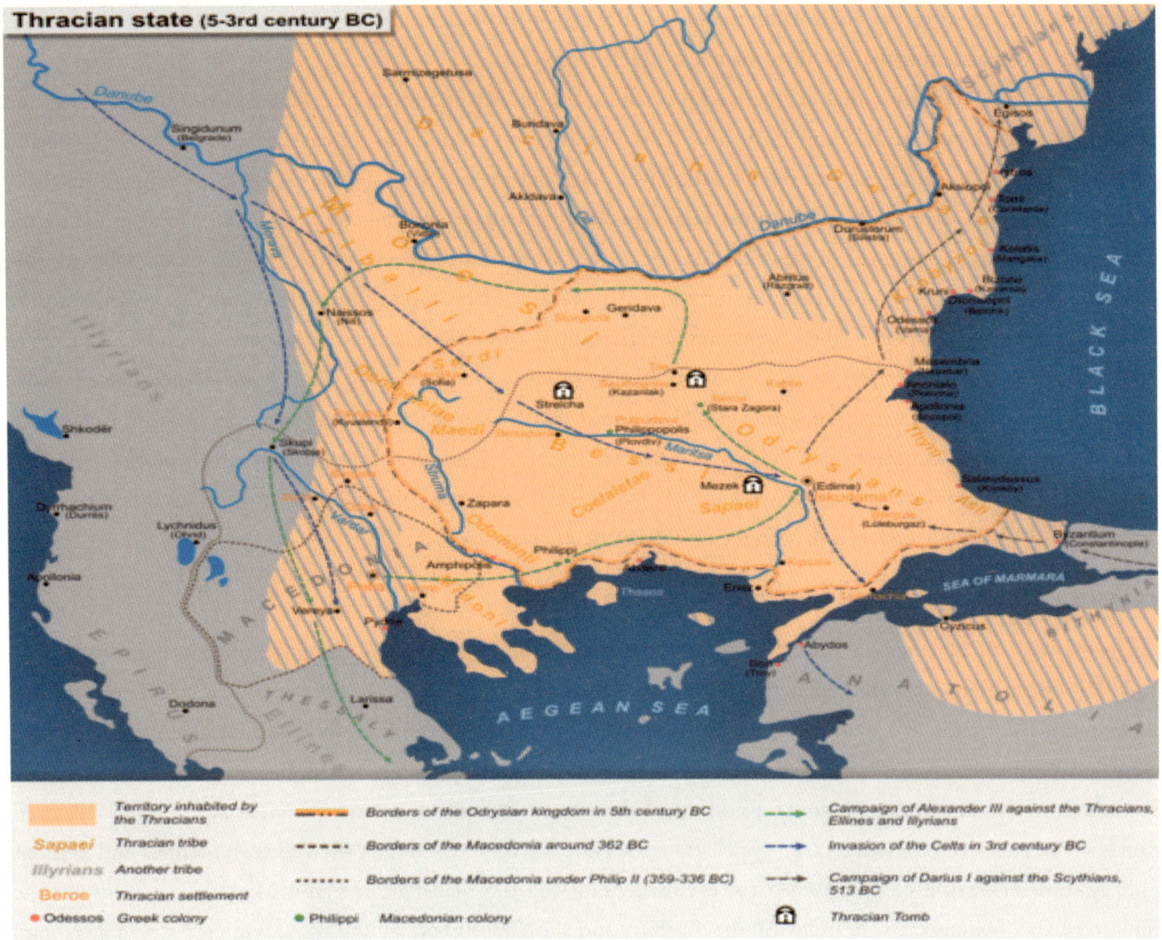

Fig. 5. The lands, dominated by Thracian tribes in the first centuries BC①

The ancient Greek historian Strabo documented more than 20 Thracian tribes, whereas modern Thracology distinguishes over 80 of them, the major ones being the *Getae*, *Bessi*, *Bithyni*, *Phrygi*, *Medi*, *Moesi*, *Odrysae*, *Mygdones*, *Serdi*, *Tribali*, *Edoni*, *Astae*, *Dii*, *Satri*, etc. The center of Thracian culture was the Bulgarian lands, in particular the areas from the Danube river to the Aegean coast and the adjacent islands of Thassos, Samothrace, Lemnos and Imbros.② These territories formed the core of the Thracian diaspora, which in its historical existence extended over a rather wide area – in different historical periods the diaspora of the Thracian tribes also covered the lands between the Carpathian Mountains and the Danube River, certain regions of Asia Minor, parts of the northern Black Sea region and Caucasus, some areas in the Eastern Mediterranean as well as territories in Mesopotamia, Egypt, North Africa and the Roman provinces, which mark the periphery of the Thracian diaspora.③

The military power and skills of the Thracian tribes, as well as the religio-political organization of their society, accounted for the dominant role they played in the key regions between Western Europe, Asia Minor and Central

① Based on the map "*Thracian state (V–III century BC)*", in *Atlas of the History of the Old World*, Integrated Research Institute and Design Mapping, Sofia, 1979. Source: http: //en.wikipedia.org/wiki/File: Tracian_state.png.

② Popov D., *Thracians*, p. 9.

③ Ibid.

Asia (Fig. 5). Even after the Hellenization and the subsequent Roman conquest, the *Thracians* remained a serious threat and a permanent source of disturbance to the newcomers.

It is very likely, therefore, that at least some of the more powerful and mobile Thracian tribes would seek an expansion further into Middle and East Asia. This would be a very natural process, especially to the *Getae* and *Scythae*, inhabiting the lands around the Danube River delta and the northern Pontic steppes, providing a relatively easy access to Asia. Being two of the most numerous, non-sedentary and militarily-advanced Thracian tribes, the *Getes* and the *Scythians* possessed all the characteristics, as well as the actual capacity to undertake a successful expansion or exploration of territories in an eastward direction. A brief look at the world history from the first millennium BC reveals that, during that period, there were only several nations or ethno-culturally homogeneous entities in Eurasia which could be regarded as serious factors in the shaping of the historical picture, the *Thracians* being one of them. Therefore, the Thracian origin of the foreign settlers in the Taklamakan desert not only is a very probable hypothesis, but is also supported by historical records, and the results of anthropological, linguistic and archaeological research, all of which indicate that the Europoid elements that reached the western Chinese territories around the second millennium BC probably originally lived in the northwestern and western Black Sea regions.

CONCLUSIONS AND PERSPECTIVES

On the basis of all evidence provided so far, we can now summarize our working hypothesis, namely that the Indo-European elements, which penetrated into the Tarim Basin around the beginning or the middle of the 2nd millennium BC, gradually expanding their settlements to the northeast, and around the first centuries BC to the west and southwest, were a branch of the ancient autochthonous population of the Balkans, which, in historical records from that and later periods, were collectively known as *Thracians*. Since the *Thracians* were a multi-tribal nation and each tribe or clan had its own appellation, the people who crossed over the Eurasian Steppes and perhaps initially settled down in their eastern parts, eventually crossing the Tianshan or Pamir Mountains after indefinite time, probably belonged to the clans of the *Scythians* and the *Getes* – two of the most numerous, non-sedentary and militarily-advanced tribes. In ancient Chinese annals their names were recorded with various transcriptions, some of which were found to represent the readings of the ethnonyms *Getae* and *Scythae*. The author of this article was especially interested by the transcription 大夏 (*Daxia*), which, according to the Chinese archaeologist Song Yixiao was pronounced close to 驮互 (*Tuohu*) in the ancient Chinese tongue from the first centuries BC.① Following Bernhard Karlgren's reconstruction of Old Chinese, however, the author suggests the following possible pronunciations of the two characters of the name 大夏: [da-ɣa] , [t'ai-ɣa] or [da-g'o]②, where the phoneme [ɣ] should be read as a voiced "h", according to Karlgren. If we also take into account the existence in Old Chinese of the optional medial glide –r–, following the initial consonant, as suggested by Baxter and Sagart③, it is very probable that the character "大" was pronounced as *"tra/dra"*, therefore the old pronunciations of 大夏 could be reconstructed as *"D(r)a – gha"* or *"Th(r)ai-kha"* or *"Dh(r)a-go"*, all of which bear very close similarities with the ethnonyms *Θϱαϰαι* (*Thrakai*), *Θϱαξ* (*Thrax*), *Θϱαϰας* (*Thrakas*) and *Θϱαϰες* (*Thrakes*) as preserved in Greek records. This reconstruction is just an assumption of the author, however, which deserves a more specialized investigation by skilled linguists.

If a direct link between the *Thracians* and the early Europoid population in Xinjiang is established, as hypothetical as it may be, a whole new field of unexplored opportunities for further research should open up. Considering the abundance of the archaeological, linguistic and anthropological material, bequeathed to us by the *Thracians*, comparative studies be-

① 宋亦箫:《大夏（吐火罗）新探》，第 15 页。

② 高本汉:《汉文典》，上海辞书出版社，1997 年，第 19、139、3 页。

③ Baxter W., L. Sagart, *Old Chinese: A new Reconstruction*, Oxford University Press, 2014.

tween their material culture and that of the *Tocharians* could easily confirm or refute the above hypothesis.

In conclusion the author would like to outline a few ideas for further scientific investigation:

1. Comparative DNA analyses between samples from Europoid peoples in the Tarim Basin and genetic material from the early Balkan population①, as well as from their descendants the *Thracians* (1st millennium BC).

2. Comparative study of the set of pre-writing symbols from the Balkans, conditionally termed *"The Danube Script"* ②, and the pictograms, petroglyphs, incised symbols, decorations and pottery marks from *Tocharian* and *Scythian* sites in Xinjiang.

3. Comparative study of *Thracian* and *Tocharian/Scythian* weapons, horse decorations, silver and gold vessels, textiles, dyestuffs, pottery and other emblematic artifacts.

4. Comparative research of burial practices, eschatological beliefs and rituals, with a special focus on burial masks, used by both *Thracians* and *Tocharians*, burial of wooden idols (*Tocharians*) and cenotaphs (*Thracians*), symbolism of phallic symbols, placing of coins in the mouth of the deceased, etc.

5. Linguistic comparison between *Thracian* (and *Pelasgian*) vocabulary and *Tocharian* stem-words.

ACKNOWLEDGEMENTS

The research presented in this paper is partially based on a previous article by the author, published in Bulgarian.③ For all the new information, the author would like to thank the board of the European Association of Chinese Studies and the CCK Foundation for awarding her with the Library Travel Grant in 2013, 2015 and 2016, which allowed her to broaden up the scope of the present research and to gain access to many up-to-date resources. Sincere thanks are also extended to all colleagues and staff from the Leiden University and the Library of the Sinological Institute, and to the staff of the Austrian National Library for their support, advice and encouragement, as well as to colleagues from SOAS, University of London, for their invaluable help.

① Taken, for instance from the Varna necropolis (5th millennium BC) or from the numerous Neolithic burials from the 6th and 7th millennia BC, found in Bulgaria.

② See the works of Marco Merlini and Harald Haarmann.

③ See: Marinova M. "The Ethnic Continuity on the Territory of Little Bukharia in Northwest China" , *The Silk Road*, 2011, pp. 133-144. (Маринова М. "Етническата приемственост на територията на Малка Букхария в Североизточен Китай", –В: *Пътят на коприната*, 2011, с. 133-144).

新疆出土圆锥体耳坠的研究 *

林铃梅（中国人民大学）

摘　要： 新疆共发现了四例圆锥体耳坠：乌鲁木齐柴窝堡古墓葬、乌鲁木齐乌拉泊水库墓葬、哈巴河县东塔勒德墓地、玛纳斯县清水河乡团庄子村墓地。这种圆锥体耳坠在境外有较多发现，且国外学者都对其起源与传播做了较多的研究。研究新疆出土的圆锥体耳坠，结合出土的其他物品，可以管窥新疆作为欧亚草原的一部分，与欧亚草原其他地区的互动与交流。

关键词： 圆锥体耳坠；新疆；欧亚草原；文化交流

耳饰作为一种重要的人体装饰物，在古代社会是身份和财富的象征，也能在一定程度上反映人群的族属。其样式及承载的工艺更是能够反映不同地区不同人群之间的互动与交流。新疆考古调查收集与发掘所得耳饰种类繁多，文化内涵丰富，对了解新疆古代装饰文化具有重要意义，也为研究新疆与周邻地区的文化交流提供了另一套参照系统。其中，新疆发现的圆锥体耳坠是极好的范例。

一　新疆发现的圆锥体耳坠

圆锥体耳坠，指的是圆环下带空心圆锥体耳坠，坠体表面往往装饰细金珠，坠体底部大多焊接带若干孔洞的金片，用于垂挂绿松石等坠饰。目前为止，新疆发现的圆锥体金耳坠有四处，柴窝堡墓地出土一件（M15：3）①、乌拉泊水库墓葬出土一件②、哈巴河县东塔勒德墓地出土一件（IIM3：10）③、玛纳斯县清水河乡团庄子村 M5 号墓出土二件④。

1. 乌鲁木齐柴窝堡古墓葬 M15:3，上部以金丝折一环钩，下穿焊一圆锥体坠饰，上面布满小金珠，底平焊一圆片，下面对称也焊接三个小纽。通长 1.5 厘米（图 1-1）。同一墓地另出了一件金耳坠（M7:15），上环不闭合，下坠一圆锥形金卷，内镶一上小下大的扁圆形蓝色石饰，磨制精细，中穿一孔。通长 2.7 厘米。从形制上来看，这件金耳坠可能属于圆锥体耳坠的变体（图 1-6）。柴窝堡古墓葬

* 国家社科基金重大项目“敦煌与于阗：佛教艺术与物质文明的交互影响”（项目编号：13&ZD087）的阶段性成果。

① 新疆文物考古研究所、西北大学文博学院八九级考古班：《乌鲁木齐柴窝堡古墓葬发掘报告》，《新疆文物》1998 年第 1 期，图 11—12。

② 新疆文物局等主编：《新疆文物大观》，乌鲁木齐：新疆美术摄影出版社，1999 年，第 310 页。

③ 新疆文物考古研究所：《哈巴河县东塔勒德墓地考古发掘简报》，《新疆文物》2013 年第 1 期，第 86 页，图 9。

④ 新疆昌吉回族自治州文物局编：《丝绸之路天山廊道——新疆昌吉古代遗址与馆藏文物精品》，北京：文物出版社，2014 年，图版 207。

还出土了一定数量的金饰件。简报将墓地年代定在约公元前5世纪，相当于中原地区战国前后。

2. 乌鲁木齐乌拉泊水库墓葬出土的金耳坠，环部接口处叠压，圆锥体小坠上饰细金珠，底部有穿孔。长2.5厘米、环径1.5厘米（图1-2）。墓葬年代约在公元前5世纪至前1世纪，相当于中原战国至西汉时期。①

3. 2011年发掘的哈巴河县东塔勒德墓地，虽屡遭盗掘，还是出土了25种大约800件金饰，其数量之多、种类之丰富令人惊叹，包括各种剪刻或錾刻动物纹、几何纹的金饰件、各式金珠饰件、金耳饰、金链饰等。其中在II区的M3，墓中埋葬两人，一位未成年女性及一位成年女性，其中一位墓主盆骨附近出土一件金饰，原报告认为是金指环（IIM3:10），本文认为该墓葬女性墓主盆骨以上部位受到扰乱，这件器物很可能是移位了。新疆发现的指环类器物，往往是环部闭合的，此件器物两端不闭合，且其形制与已经发现的圆锥体金耳坠较一致，由此本文将其认定为金耳坠。耳坠环部以较粗的金丝弯成，环上錾刻了四只变形的鹅喉羚，首尾相连，鹅喉羚前后肢蜷缩在一起，脚紧贴脊背。环部下焊接金坠，金坠表面装饰金珠，并焊有三角形宝石座，内嵌绿松石。坠底部有若干孔洞。环径2.3厘米、丝径0.2厘米，金坠高0.3厘米、径0.6厘米（图1-3）。除此之外，该墓葬还出土了大量金箔饰件，包括蜷曲的雪豹及卧虎图案等，以及绿松石、玛瑙珠等。

东塔勒德I区M32还出土了两件金耳坠，不闭合的圆环下穿圆锥体金箔饰件，内镶嵌绿松石，多数已剥落。环径1.1厘米、口径0.5厘米，圆锥体坠口高0.9厘米、通高2.8厘米（图1-7、8）。形制与IIM3所出应有密切联系。简报中将东塔勒德墓地的年代定在公元前6世纪至前1世纪，相当于中原春秋晚期至西汉。

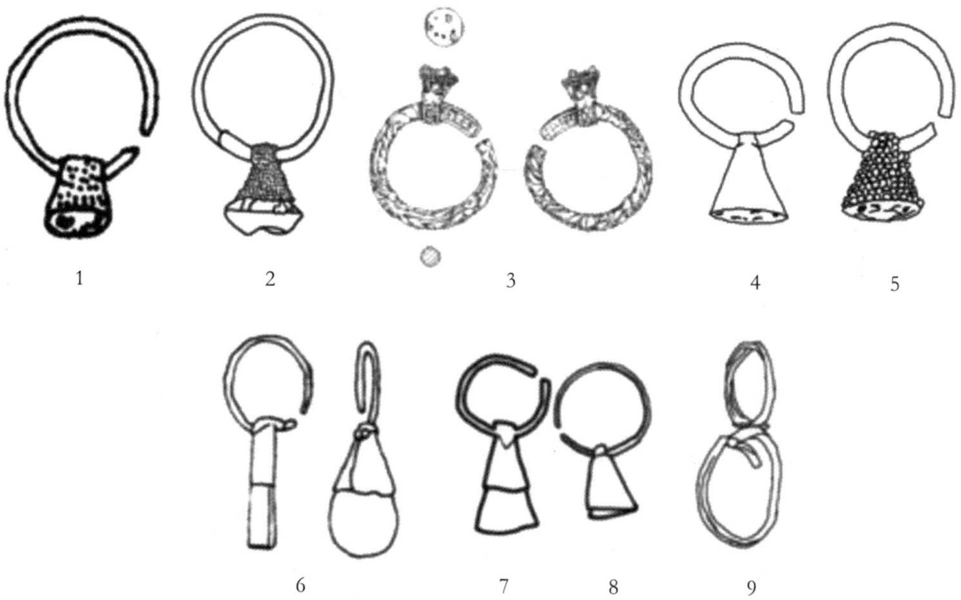

图1　新疆出土的圆锥体耳坠及相关耳饰：1. 柴窝堡古墓葬 M15:3；2. 乌拉泊水库墓葬；3. 东塔勒德墓地 IIM3:10；4-5. 清水河乡团庄子村 M5；6. 柴窝堡古墓葬 M7:15；7-8. 东塔勒德墓地 IM32:4；9. 清水河乡团庄子村 M5

① 王明哲、张玉忠:《乌鲁木齐乌拉泊古墓葬发掘研究》,《新疆社会科学》1986年第1期，第74页。

4. 玛纳斯县清水河乡团庄子村 M5 出土两件圆锥体耳坠，高 2 厘米。其中一件坠部表面光滑无纹，另一件则焊饰了密集的金珠。两件底部都有孔洞。同墓还出土了铁鹤嘴锄、磨刀石、蚀花肉红石髓珠，以及一件双环垂直焊接的金耳环（图 1-4、5、9）。材料的公布者将该墓葬定在公元前 7 世纪，相当于中原地区春秋晚期。

总的来说，新疆发现的这四例圆锥体耳坠集中分布于天山中段北麓地区及阿尔泰山南麓，其所属的墓葬均无较为精确的测年数据，发掘者提供的年代范围过于宽泛。或可以通过与新疆周边地区出土的同类物做比较，对这些圆锥体耳坠甚至所属的墓葬年代有一个相对准确的认识。

二　境外发现的圆锥体耳坠及研究

（一）境外地区圆锥体耳坠的发现

圆锥体耳坠在境外有较多的发现[①]，其分布范围从欧亚草原东端的图瓦地区向西可延伸至伏尔加河下游地区，甚至到南高加索东部地区（图 2）。

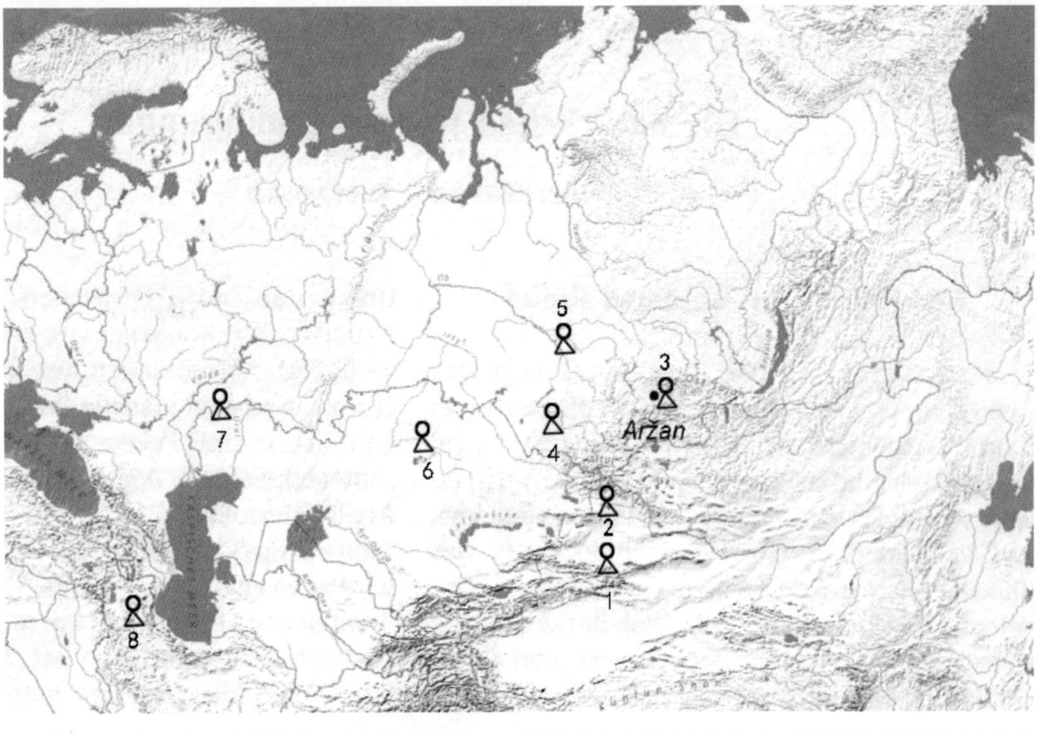

图 2[②]　欧亚草原出土的圆锥体耳坠及出土数量：1. 新疆天山北麓（4 件）；2. 新疆阿尔泰地区（1 件）；3. 图瓦地区（18 件）；4. 阿尔泰山区及边缘（7 件）；5. 库兹涅茨克盆地（1 件）；6. 哈萨克斯坦中部（5 件）；7. 伏尔加河下游（1 件）；8. 南高加索东部地区（2 件）

① 梳理欧亚草原发现的圆锥体耳坠的文章可参考：Вл. А. Семенов, “Синхронизация и хронология памятников алды-бельского типа в Туве”, *Итоги изучения скифской эпохи Алтая и сопредельных территорий*, Барнаул, Изд-во Алтайского университета, 1999, с. 165-169; В. К. Федоров, “Серьги из могильника Сара в Оренбургской области”, *Вестник археологии, антропологии и этнографии,* no. 2(29), 2015, с. 69-79; К. В. Кучунов, “Серьги раннескифского времени Саяно-Алтая (происхождение традиции и типологическое развитие)”, *Исторический опыт хозяйственного освоения Западной Сибири*, Книга 1, Сборник научных трудов под ред. Ю. Ф. Кирюшина и А. А. Тишкина, Барнаул, Изд. АГУ, 2003, с. 386-395。

② 此地图底版出自 Konstantin V. Čugunov, Hermann Parzinger und Anatoli Nagler, *Der skythenzeitliche Fürstenkurgan Aržan 2 in Tuva,* Mainz, Verlag Philipp von Zabern, 2010, S. 2, Abb. 1。

圆锥体耳坠最早发现于图瓦地区，是艾迪拜尔（Aldy-bel）文化（公元前 7 世纪至前 5 世纪）的典型器物。① 我们较为熟悉的阿尔然 2 号墓出土了 10 件圆锥体金耳坠，5、13、20、22、25 号墓葬都有发现（图 3-1 ～ 10）。② 有的环部为光滑的圆环；有的呈扁平状，上面錾刻线纹和绳纹；有的环部制成多面棱角纹样。单环下焊接圆锥体坠，表面布满细金珠，大多有水滴形宝石座，原本或嵌有料珠类饰物。圆锥体坠的底部焊有圆片，上面有一圈的细孔，出土的耳坠经过复原，坠部底面垂挂有绿松石等串珠，这种耳坠并不是直接戴在人耳处，而是环套在另一宽扁的圆环上，再整体悬挂在耳部（图 3-11、12）。③ 阿尔然 2 号墓的年代可以早到公元前 7 世纪。图瓦地区出土圆锥体耳坠的墓葬还有：门噶什—曲力克（Мунгаш- Чирик）40 号墓④、阿塔—赫姆（Ортаа- Хем）III 号墓地 1 号墓 2 号墓室⑤、古伊卢格—赫姆（Куйлуг- Хем）I 号墓地 9 号墓⑥、赫姆曲—邦姆（Хемчик-Бом）III 号墓地 2 号墓 9 号墓

图 3　图瓦地区发现的圆锥体耳坠：1-1a. 阿尔然 2 号墓，M5 墓主 1；2-3. 阿尔然 2 号墓 M5，墓主 2；4-5. 阿尔然 2 号墓 M13A，墓主 2；6. 阿尔然 2 号墓 M13B；7. 阿尔然 2 号墓 M20，墓主 2；8-9. 阿尔然 2 号墓 M22；10. 阿尔然 2 号墓 M25；11. 阿尔然 2 号墓；12. 阿尔然 2 号墓耳饰复原图；13. 门噶什—曲力克 40 号墓；14. 古伊卢格—赫姆 I 号墓地 9 号墓；15. 赫姆曲—邦姆 III 号墓地 2 号墓 9 号墓室；16-17. 萨瑞—布伦 1 号墓 1 号墓室；18. 安郭—哈乌 5 号墓；19. 巴仁郭墓葬

① Konstantin V. Čugunov, Hermann Parzinger und Anatoli Nagler, *Der skythenzeitliche Fürstenkurgan Aržan 2 in Tuva*, S. 165.

② Konstantin V. Čugunov, Hermann Parzinger und Anatoli Nagler, *Der skythenzeitliche Fürstenkurgan Aržan 2 in Tuva*, Tafel. 12, 2-5; 57, 5; 58, 1; 91, 1, 2; 93, 2; 91, 1; 99, 3, 5; 102, 1.

③ Konstantin V. Čugunov, Hermann Parzinger und Anatoli Nagler, *Der skythenzeitliche Fürstenkurgan Aržan 2 in Tuva*, Tafel. 72, 1; S. 214, Abb. 226.

④ Л. Р. Кызласов, *Древняя Тува*, Москва, Изд-во МГУ, 1979, с. 76, рис. 61, 8.

⑤ Вл. А. Семенов, “Синхронизация и хронология памятников алды-бельского типа в Туве”, с. 169.

⑥ А. Д. Грач, *Древние кочевники в центре Азии*, Москва, Издательство «Наука», 1980, рис. 86.

室①、萨瑞—布伦（Сарыг –Булун）1号墓1号墓室②、安郭—哈乌（Ангор-Хову）5号墓③（图3–13–18）。阿塔—赫姆 III 号墓地、古伊卢格—赫姆 I 号墓地及赫姆曲—邦姆 III 号墓地出土的耳坠坠部表面光滑，④后两例在环、坠连接处焊饰有细金珠。此外的几例坠部都有水滴形宝石座并在表面满饰金珠。上述出土圆锥体耳坠的墓葬年代大致都在公元前 7 世纪至前 5 世纪，其中赫姆曲—邦姆 III 号墓地 2 号墓被学者归为萨格利文化（Саглынская культура）时期的墓葬，年代定在公元前 5 世纪至前 4 世纪。⑤图瓦地区的巴仁郭（Баян-Кол）墓葬，位于乌卢格赫姆河（Улуг-Хем）流域。该墓葬出土了一件金耳坠，环部用金丝扭结而成，坠部为双锥形，表面光滑无纹（图 3–19）。⑥其形制与这一地区出土的圆锥体耳坠非常接近，可能是后者的变体。值得注意的是，该墓葬距离出土圆锥体耳坠的安郭—哈乌墓地不远。

阿尔泰山周缘地区也有一些发现。阿尔泰山北麓的贝斯特亚（Быстрянское）墓地 8、14 号墓各出土一件金耳坠，其中 8 号墓所出环部有扭结而成的花纹，坠部表面光滑；14 号墓出土的耳坠坠部残损，表面装饰水滴形宝石座及细金珠（图 4–1、2）。⑦M. П. 格里亚兹诺夫认为这批遗存属于博利谢列切文化（Большереченская культура）的比斯克（Бийск）阶段，公元前 5 世纪至前 3 世纪。⑧巴依德根（Бойтыгем）II 号墓地位于阿尔泰山北麓卡通河支流巴依德根沿岸，其中19号墓出土两件金耳坠，制作精致（图 4–3、4）。⑨墓葬年代定在公元前 7 世纪后半叶至前 6 世纪初。⑩位于阿尔泰山区东部

---

① А. Д. Грач, *Древние кочевники в центре Азии*, рис. 110, 6.

② Iaroslav LEBEDYNSKY, *Les Saces, Les «Scythes» d'Asie. VIIIe siècle av. J.-C. - IVe siècle apr. J.-C.* , Paris, Editions Errance, 2006, p. 117.

③ В. А. Семенов, М. Е. Килуновская, К. В. Чугунов, "Археологические исследования на правобережье Улуг-Хема", *Южная Сибирь в древности*, СПБ, 1995, рис. 2, 3.

④ 阿塔赫姆 III 号墓地出土的耳坠并未见图像，但在学者文章中有对其外形的描述。见 Вл. А. Семенов, "Синхронизация и хронология памятников алды-бельского типа в Туве", с. 165。

⑤ А. Д. Грач, *Древние кочевники в центре Азии*, с. 30-32.

⑥ В. А. Семенов, М. Е. Килуновская, К. В. Чугунов, "Археологические исследования на правобережье Улуг-Хема", рис. 2, 6.

⑦ М. П. Завитухина, "Курганы у села Быстрянского в Алтайском крае: По раскопкам С. М. Сергеева в 1930 г. ", *АСГЭ*, Вып. 8, 1966, с. 62-64, рис. 2, 3; рис. 3, 3; С. И. Руденко, *Сибирская коллекция Петра* I, Свод Археологических источников, Д3-9, 1962, рис. 19, б, а. 贝斯特亚墓地 14 号墓出土的金耳坠最早公布于：М. П. Завитухина, "Курганы у села Быстрянского в Алтайском крае: По раскопкам С. М. Сергеева в 1930 г. ", с. 62-64, рис. 3, 3，后被 М. П. 格亚兹诺夫在其文章 М. П. Грязнов, "Алтай и приалтайская степь," *Степная полоса Азиатской части СССР в скифо-сарматское врем, Серия: Археология СССР,* Москва, Издательство «Наука», 1992, с. 161-178. 中引用，图版中的线图太小，且不清晰。以至于后来学者在再次引用时对其图像产生误解，如 Hermann Parzinger, *Die frühen Völker Eurasiens. Vom Neolithikum bis zum Mittelalter*, Historische Bibliothek der Gerda-Henkel-Stiftung, Band 1, München, Beck, 2006 及 Konstantin V. Čugunov, Hermann Parzinger und Anatoli Nagler, *Der skythenzeitliche Fürstenkurgan Aržan 2 in Tuva* 一书中的线图都将其坠部表面表现为光滑无纹。

⑧ М. П. Грязнов, "Алтай и приалтайская степь", с. 420.

⑨ А. А. Тишкин, "Украшения раннескифского времени из Горного Алтая", *Итоги изучения скифской эпохи Алтая и сопредельных территорий*, Барнаул, Изд-во АлтГУ, 1999, рис. 1.

⑩ А. А. Тишкин, "Украшения раннескифского времени из Горного Алтая", *Итоги изучения скифской эпохи Алтая и сопредельных территорий,* Барнаул, Изд-во АлтГУ, 1999, с. 188.

的库奥（Koo）I 号墓地 2 号墓与巴泽雷克文化的墓葬紧邻，墓中仅出土了一件金耳坠（图 4–5）。① 发掘者根据 2 号墓墓葬形制（地表有石块堆砌的封堆，墓室由石板围砌）、埋葬习俗（屈肢葬）及出土物（圆锥体耳坠）认为它是艾迪拜尔文化类型的墓葬，并指出这一墓葬的发现反映了早期斯基泰时期图瓦地区的文化向阿尔泰地区的渗透，具体表现是图瓦地区文化的特征物品向南传播。② 阿尔泰山西部边缘的塔尔—阿苏（Тар Асу）墓地一座女性墓也出土了两件圆锥体金耳坠（图 4–6、7）。③ 该墓地位于巴泽雷克文化墓葬波内尔（Берел）西南 7000 米处，以及结合墓葬出土的物品，发掘者认为这个墓地属于巴泽雷克文化的范畴，年代定在公元前 5 世纪至前 3 世纪。④

位于阿尔泰山以北、萨彦岭以西库兹涅茨克盆地的卡赞科沃（Казанково）5 号墓地 1 号墓出土了一件金耳坠，圆锥体坠部表面满饰金珠，下部坠有 21 颗绿松石珠组成的葡萄形垂饰（图 4–8）。⑤ 墓葬年代定在公元前 6 世纪至前 5 世纪。⑥

哈萨克斯坦中部塔斯莫拉文化的墓葬中也发现了该类耳坠，卡拉干达地区的热兰迪（Жиланды）墓葬 2 号墓出土一件，2.8 厘米 ×2.2 厘米，耳坠坠部相对较大（图 4–9）。⑦ 塔乐迪（Талды）2 号墓地 5 号墓出土了一件，耳坠底部比较特殊，镶嵌了四个小环（图 4–10）。⑧ 喀拉硕科（Карашокы）墓地 1 号墓出土一件，坠部表面焊饰了密密麻麻的细金珠（图 4–11）。⑨ 别克塔乌亚特（Бектауата）墓

---

① 奥库 I 号墓地出土的这件圆锥体耳坠的材料早在 1992 发掘者的研究论文（А. С. Васютин, “О памятниках Алды-Бельского типа в Саяно-Алтае”, *Античная цивилизация и варварский мир(Материалы III-го археологического семинара)*, часть I, Новочеркасск, Музей истории донского казачества, 1992, с. 34-37.）中发表，但并未提及具体出土墓葬的编号。从 1999 年发掘者再次公布墓葬的材料（А. С. Васютин, А. Ч. Садовой, “К проблеме реконструкции традиционных систем жизнеобеспечения в сопредельных территорий(Восточный Алтай-могильник Коо-I)”, *Итоги изучения скифской эпохи Алтая и сопредельных территорий*, Барнаул, Изд-во АлтГУ, 1999.）来看，两次公布的材料应为同一墓葬，但前后两次公布的耳坠的线描图有细微区别，且早前公布的线描图比例尺有明显错误，所以本文以第二次公布的线描图为准。

② А. С. Васютин, А. Ч. Садовой, “К проблеме реконструкции традиционных систем жизнеобеспечения в сопредельных территорий(Восточный Алтай-могильник Коо-I)”, с. 36；А. С. Васютин, “О памятниках Алды-Бельского типа в Саяно-Алтае”, с. 36.

③ Samašev, Z. S., Bazarbaeva, G. A. und Žumabekova, G. S., “Die „goldhütenden Greife“ des Herodot und die archäologische Kultur der frühen Nomaden im kazachischen Altai. Skythenzeitliche Kurgane von Berel’ und Tar Asu”, *Eurasia Antiqua*, Band 8, 2002, Mainz am Rhein, Verlag Philipp von Zabern, S. 271, Abb. 29, 1, 2; З. С. Самашев, А. П. Франкформ, А. С. Ермолаева и др., “Исследования культуры древних кочевников Казахстанского Алтая”, *Проблемы изучения и сохранения исторического наследия: Материалы Междунар*, археол, конф, Алматы, 1998, рис. 13.

④ Samašev, Z. S., Bazarbaeva, G. A. und Žumabekova, G. S., “Die „goldhütenden Greife“ des Herodot und die archäologische Kultur der frühen Nomaden im kazachischen Altai. Skythenzeitliche Kurgane von Berel’ und Tar Asu”, S. 271.

⑤ Ю. В. Ширин, “Погребения скифского времени в Кузнецкой котловине”, *Итоги изучения скифской эпохи Алтая и сопредельных территорий*, Барнаул, Изд-во АлтГУ, 1999, с. 238, рис. 1, 2.

⑥ Ю. В. Ширин, “Погребения скифского времени в Кузнецкой котловине”, с. 240.

⑦ Grigore Arbore Popescu, Chiara Silvi, Karl Baipakov, *L'UOMO D'ORO, La cultura delle steppe del Kazakhstan dall' età del bronzo alle grandi migrazioni*, Electa, Milano, Elemond Editori Associati, 1998, p. 133, table. 98.

⑧ Arman Bejsenov, “Die Nekropole Taldy 2 in Beziehung zu den Kulturen der frühsakischen Zeit Osteurasiens”, *Unbekanntes Kasachstan Archäologie im Herzen Asiens*, Band II, Bochum, Deutsches Bergbau- Museum Bochum, 2013, S. 598, Abb. 7.

⑨ А. З. Бейсенов, А. О. Исмагулова, Е. П. Китов, А. О. Китова, *Население центрального Казахстана в I тысячелетии до н. э.*, Алматы, Институт археологии им. А. Х. Маргулана, 2015, с. 20, рис. 8, 4.

地 1 号墓出土一件，坠部表面原本有水滴形镶嵌物（图 4–12）。[1] 巴齐布拉克（Бакыбулак）墓地 15 号墓葬出土一件，仅存坠部，表面满饰金珠（图 4–13）。[2] 五处墓葬都属于塔斯莫拉文化早期阶段的遗存，年代定在公元前 7 世纪至前 6 世纪。[3]

西至伏尔加河下游也有个别发现，噶山莫里（Комсомольский）墓地 23 号墓女性墓主左耳佩戴了一件圆锥体耳坠，坠部表面满饰细金珠。上环直径 2.2—2.3 厘米，坠部直径 0.95—1.1 厘米（图 4–14）。[4] 发掘简报中将墓葬的出土物，包括箭头、弓箭袋、长剑、短剑、金饰等与周边地区出土的同类物比较，与南乌拉尔地区早期斯基泰人的遗存有较多共性，推断其年代在公元前 6 世纪后半叶至前 5 世纪初。[5]

南高加索地区也发现了两件近似圆锥体耳坠的材料，均出土于今阿塞拜疆境内。其中一件具体出土地与年代不详，但从公布的线图材料来看，坠部表面不光滑，可能饰有细金珠（图 4–15）。[6] 另一件出土于明格察乌（Мингечаур）墓葬，据学者研究，该墓葬可能反映了到达南高加索地区的斯基泰贵族的遗存，墓葬年代定在公元前 6 世纪至前 5 世纪。[7] 文章并未对耳饰进行描述，但从提供的线描图来看，墓葬出土的耳饰形制非常接近圆锥体耳坠（图 4–16）。[8]

此外，在一些收藏家的藏品中也能看到精致的圆锥体耳坠。17 世纪末 18 世纪初，维钦（Витзен）收藏了一批据说出土于西伯利亚古冢的金饰品，于 1705 年公布于 *Nood-en-Oost Tartarye* 一书中，并于此书 1785 年刊印第二版时增加了他在 1716 年获得的另一批藏品。[9] 藏品中有与图瓦地区所出非常接近的圆锥体耳坠，环部錾刻成波折纹，坠部表面有水滴纹宝石座及焊饰细金珠，坠底部也有一圈小孔（图 5–1）。[10] 另外有两件圆锥体耳坠的变体，坠部表面有用金珠组成的纹样，坠部下方焊接球状饰，并在底部连接一宽扁圆环，圆环中部用金丝编织成麦穗纹（图 5–2、3）。[11] 这种样式的圆环在南乌拉

---

① А. З. Бейсенов, “Поселения и могильники сакской эпохи центрального Казахстана”, *Сакская культура Сарыарки в контексте изучения этносоциокультурных процессов степной Евразии*, Сборник научных статей, посвященный памяти археолога Кималя Акишевича Акишева, Алматы, НИЦИА «Бағазы-Тасмола», 2015, с. 32, рис. 17, 3.

② А. З. Бейсенов, “Поселения и могильники сакской эпохи центрального Казахстана”, с. 32, рис. 17, 5.

③ Grigore Arbore Popescu, Chiara Silvi, Karl Baipakov, *L'UOMO D'ORO, La cultura delle steppe del Kazakhstan dall' età del bronzo alle grandi migrazioni*, p. 133; Arman Bejsenov, “Die Nekropole Taldy 2 in Beziehung zu den Kulturen der frühsakischen Zeit Osteurasiens”, S. 596; А. З. Бейсенов, А. О. Исмагулова, Е. П. Китов, А. О. Китова, *Население центрального Казахстана в I тысячелетии до н. э.*, с. 18.

④ В. В. Дворниченко, В. В. Плахов, М. А. Очир-Горяева, “Погребения ранних кочевников из Нижнего Поволжья”, *Российская археология*, 1997, no. 3, с. 133, рис. 5, 6.

⑤ В. В. Дворниченко, В. В. Плахов, М. А. Очир-Горяева, “Погребения ранних кочевников из Нижнего Поволжья”, с. 138.

⑥ Фазиль Османов, *История и культура Кавказской Албании IV в. до н.э. – III в. н.э.(на основании археологических материалов)*, Баку, «Тахсил», 2006, табл, 12.

⑦ Дж. А. Халилов, “Археологические находки «скифском царстве» на территории Азербайджана”, *Проблемы скифской археологии*, Москва, издательство «Наука», 1971, с. 185.

⑧ Дж. А. Халилов, “Археологические находки «скифском царстве» на территории Азербайджана”, с. 185, рис. 1.

⑨ С. И. Руденко, *Сибирская коллекция Петра I*, с. 4.

⑩ Witsen N. Noord end Oost Tartarye; Tweede Deel: Behelzende de Landschappen Georgia, Mengrelia, Cirkassia, Cirm Astakkia, Altin, Tingoesia, Siberia, en Samojedia. Amsterdam: Francois, 1705. 986 S, table. 3, 3. 转自 В. К. Федоров, “Серьги из могильника Сара в Оренбургской области”, рис. 2, 1.

⑪ С. И. Руденко, *Сибирская коллекция Петра I*, рис. 2; 3.

尔地区的墓葬中多有发现，尤其是在菲力波夫卡墓地有集中表现。[①] 在彼得大帝的西伯利亚藏品中也可以看见圆锥体耳坠的变体，其中一件与维钦藏品中的两件非常接近，另一件可能也是圆锥体耳坠的变体，坠部下端焊接了一个球形装饰，表面焊饰整齐的细金珠（图 5-4、5）。[②]

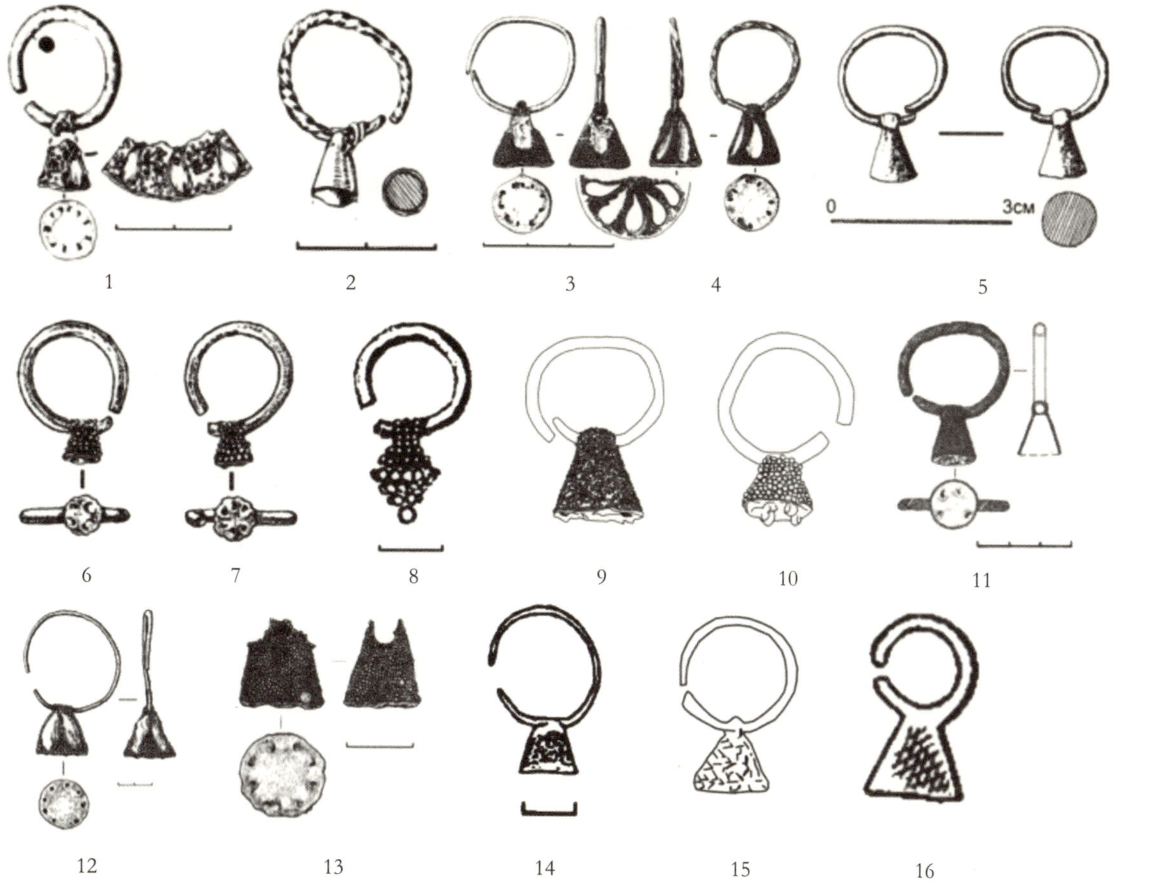

图 4　阿尔泰山麓边缘、库兹涅茨克盆地、哈萨克斯坦中部、伏尔加河下游出土圆锥体耳坠：1. 贝斯特亚 14 号墓；2. 贝斯特亚 8 号墓；3-4. 巴依德根 II 墓地 19 号墓；5. 库奥 I 号墓地 2 号墓；6-7. 塔尔—阿苏墓地；8. 卡赞科沃 5 号墓地 1 号墓；9. 热兰迪墓地 2 号墓；10. 塔乐迪 2 号墓地 5 号墓；11. 喀拉硕科墓地 1 号墓；12. 别克塔乌亚特墓地 1 号墓；13. 巴齐布拉克墓地 15 号墓；14. 噶山莫里墓地 23 号墓；15. 东高加索地区；16. 明格察乌墓葬

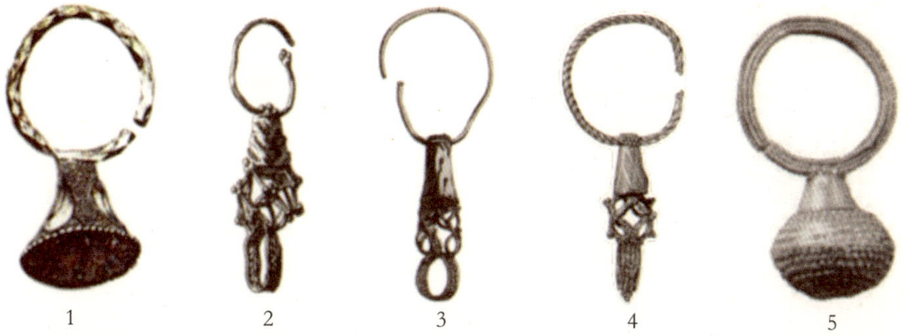

图 5　维钦藏品及彼得大帝西伯利亚藏品中圆锥体耳坠及其变体：1-3. 维钦藏品；4-5. 彼得大帝西伯利亚藏品

① Е. В. Лылова, “Об одном типе серег из погребений ранних кочевников Южного Урала”, *Вестник Челябинского государственного университета*, No. 37(175), 2009, История, Вып. 36, рис. 1.

② С. И. Руденко, *Сибирская коллекция Петра I*, табл. XX, 31; табл. XX, 7.

结合新疆地区及境外发现的圆锥体耳坠，我们可以看到，这种圆锥体金耳坠最早发现于图瓦地区，年代约在公元前7世纪甚至更早。这种耳环样式向四周扩散，向南跨过阿尔泰山区，到了阿尔泰山南麓地区甚至更远的天山北麓一带；向西扩散到阿尔泰山西部边缘、哈萨克草原，甚至远至伏尔加河下游地区。南高加索地区发现的近似例子启示我们，不排除圆锥体耳坠的分布地域跨越了高加索山脉，到达了南高加索地区。若将来我们对这一地区的考古材料有了更全面的掌握，这一情况将被更清晰地了解。目前为止，新疆以东地区未发现有此类耳坠。从出土耳坠的墓葬年代来看，集中在公元前7世纪至前5世纪，被定为公元前5世纪至前3世纪的也有少数。萨彦—阿尔泰地区这类耳坠沿用的时间跨度较长，图瓦地区艾迪拜尔文化和萨格利—巴什（Sargly-Bashi）文化中都有发现。受图瓦地区文化的渗透，阿尔泰山区边缘也出现了相似遗存，至阿尔泰山麓西缘的巴泽雷克文化墓葬也保存了这种耳坠。阿尔然2号墓的报告指出，这种圆锥体耳坠是图瓦北部乌尤克谷地和阿尔泰山前地区往西的草原地带文化的共同特征。同时也提出类似的遗存在阿尔泰山区是否存在的疑问，至少阿尔泰山区公元前7世纪到前6世纪的文化还是存在缺环的。①

从工艺上来看，所有发现的圆锥体金耳坠都延续了焊饰金珠以及坠体底部焊带孔圆片的传统，说明它们的装饰风格也是一脉相承的。但具体来看，随着这种耳坠样式的传播，在边缘地区发现的例子，与最早图瓦地区的同类物相比，也发生了一些变化，表现为耳坠整体的造型灵活性变强，例如哈萨克斯坦卡拉干达地区发现的这件环部与坠部的比例与其他例子很不一样；哈巴河县东塔勒德墓地出土的这件则异常精致、华丽，坠体的表现方式也与众不同；乌拉泊水库出土的这件坠体底部与其他例子不同，不是焊接一圆片，而是呈联体的外凸底部。这些都表现了周边地区的文化接受这种耳坠样式的同时，也进行了大胆的创新，是本地文化与外来文化相结合的生动例子。

这种圆锥体耳坠在欧亚草原早期的鹿石上也有所反映。图瓦苏什村发现的鹿石刻有圆锥体耳坠，年代是春秋到战国时期（图6-1）。阿尔然墓地地表所立鹿石上也可以看到这类耳坠（图6-2）。② 阿

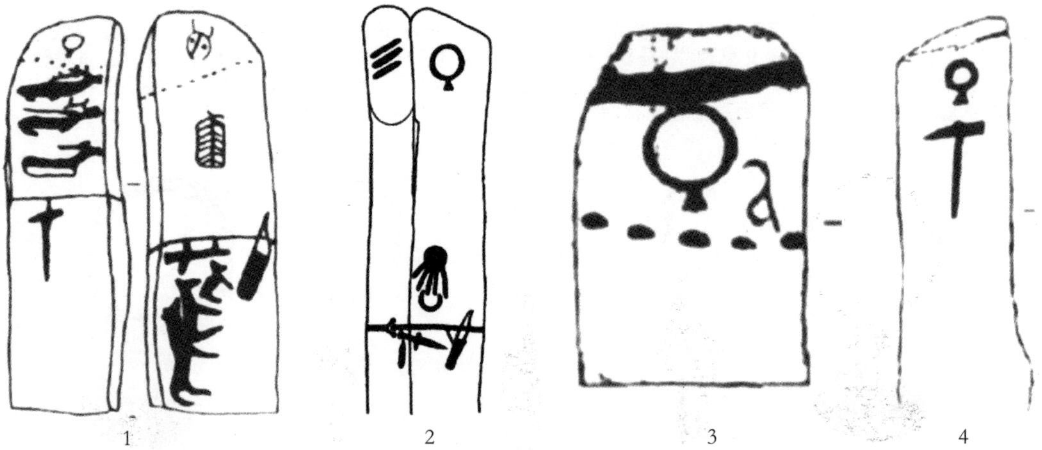

图6　图瓦、阿尔泰山区、蒙古国中西部鹿石反映的圆锥体耳坠形象：1. 图瓦皮伊—赫姆斯基区苏什村；2. 阿尔然墓葬；3. 阿尔泰尤斯季德；4. 蒙古巴彦洪戈尔省博格多县布恩查格敖包2号鹿石

① Konstantin V. Čugunov, Hermann Parzinger und Anatoli Nagler, *Der skythenzeitliche Fürstenkurgan Aržan 2 in Tuva*, S. 313.

② Л. С. Марсадолов, "«Оленные» камни из посёлка Аржан в центре Азии", *Древности Евразии: от ранней Бронзы до раннего средневековья. Памяти В. С. Ольховского*, Сборник статей, Москва, Институт археологии РАН, 2005, с. 309, рис. 6.

尔泰地区发现的鹿石也刻画了较多此类耳坠（图 6-3），鹿石年代早到春秋早期，下限可到战国中晚期。蒙古国巴彦洪戈尔省博格多县布恩查格敖包 2 号鹿石上也有发现这类耳坠，年代在春秋战国时期（图 6-4）。[①] 我们可以知道，刻画圆锥体耳坠的鹿石年代集中在春秋到战国时期，也就是说这种形制的耳坠在这个时间段流行于欧亚草原的东部，包括图瓦、阿尔泰和蒙古国的中西部地区，它的出现可能在春秋早期或更早。这与考古所见耳坠实物的年代也是吻合的。

（二）对圆锥体耳坠来源与传播的探讨

关于圆锥体耳坠更早的来源，国外学者有不少的讨论。Л. С. 马尔沙多洛夫提出最早的这种耳坠可以追溯到亚述的浮雕，如阿舒尔那西尔帕二世（Ашшур нацир апала II，公元前 883 年—前 859 年在位）时期的浮雕（图 7-1、2）。[②] 学者在研究北高加索地区的双锥体耳坠的原型时也倾向于向近东地区前一千纪初的遗存中去寻找，也往往追溯到这处浮雕。[③] 这种推测可能需要更多的中间环节来支撑。

也有学者指出这种带圆锥体坠的耳饰出现于米努辛斯克盆地的卡拉苏克早期遗存（图 7-3）。[④] К. В. 楚古诺夫对萨彦—阿尔泰地区早期斯基泰时期的耳饰进行梳理研究，认为图瓦地区艾迪拜尔文化的圆锥体耳坠应是本地区耳饰序列发展演变的结果，最早可以追溯到安德罗诺沃文化的原型，在此后的卡拉苏克文化及塔加尔文化遗存中都有相似形制的耳坠，他认为从安德罗诺沃文化至艾迪拜尔文化的圆锥体耳坠无论是形制还是制作工艺都是一脉相承的。他也承认，此前的文化遗存中的耳坠没有发现采用金珠工艺的，艾迪拜尔文化圆锥体耳坠上的金珠装饰可能是受到了来自中亚和哈萨克斯坦东部文化因素的影响。[⑤] 值得注意的是，他在文中指出，卡拉苏克文化遗存中有一类耳坠，环部呈弯钩，坠部为喇叭口形，底部四角焊接小钩，不排除小钩是用于垂挂坠饰或用于镶嵌饰物的（图 7-3~5）。这与艾迪拜尔文化圆锥体耳坠底部的功能非常接近。笔者认为，将卡拉苏克文化的这类耳坠视为圆锥体耳坠的原型可能是相对合理的。

关于艾迪拜尔文化的圆锥体耳坠变体也有一些研究。有些学者将南乌拉尔地区别斯—奥巴（Бес Оба）和波克罗夫卡（Покровка）II 墓地 2 号墓出土的耳坠也归为本文所指的圆锥体耳坠（图 7-6、7），[⑥] 这种划归法可能有问题。别斯—奥巴出土的一对耳坠，环部宽扁，不闭合，坠部用金片制成空心圆锥体，底部焊接金片。环坠结合处焊饰金珠，并沿坠部垂直一列及底端一圈金珠。波克罗夫卡 II 墓地 2 号墓出土的一对金耳坠，也和别斯—奥巴所出形制接近，但不见金珠装饰。从尺寸来看，别斯—奥巴出土的耳坠通高 6.7 厘米—7 厘米，波克罗夫卡 II 墓地出土的耳坠通高 4.58 厘米—5.65 厘米。然而目前所见的圆锥体耳坠通高在 2 厘米—4 厘米，尺寸比南乌拉尔地区出土的耳坠小很多。从造型

---

① 潘玲：《论鹿石的年代及相关问题》，《考古学报》2008 年第 3 期，第 326—330 页。

② Л. С. Марсадолов, “Оленные» камни из посёлка Аржан в центре Азии”, с. 309, рис. 6, 1.

③ В. И. Козенкова, *Кобанская культура и окружающий мир(взаимосвязи, проблемы судьбы и следов разнокультурных инфильтраций в местной среде)*, Москва, Таус, 2013, с. 44.

④ Н. Л. Членова, “Памятники переходного карасук-тагарского времени в минусинской котловине”, *Советская археология*, 1963, no. 3, с. 51, рис. 1, 30.

⑤ К. В. Кучунов, “Серьги раннескифского времени Саяно-Алтая (происхождение традиции и типологическое развитие)”, *Исторический опыт хозяйственного освоения Западной Сибири,* Книга 1, Сборник научных трудов под ред. Ю. Ф. Кирюшина и А. А. Тишкина, Барнаул, Изд. АГУ, 2003, с. 386-395.

⑥ Вл. А. Семенов, “Синхронизация и хронология памятников алды-бельского типа в Туве”, с. 165.

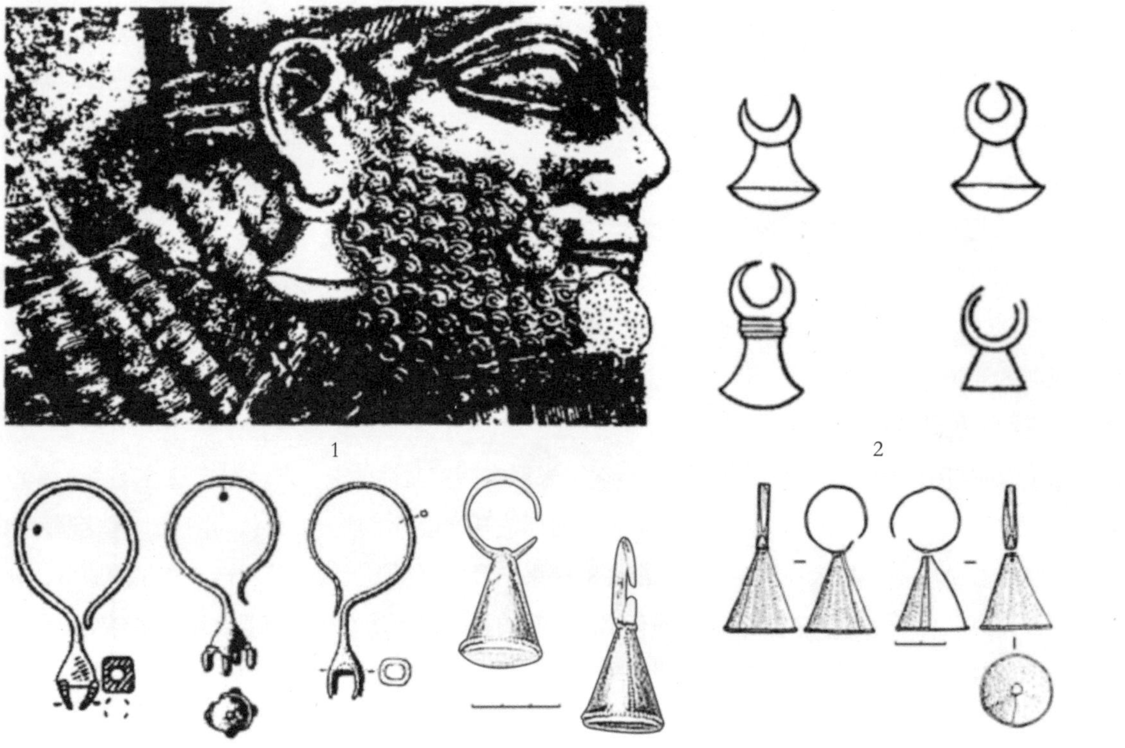

图 7　1. 阿舒尔那西尔帕二世时期的浮雕；2. 亚述雕塑上耳饰的图案；3. 雅尔基（Ярки）出土铜耳坠；4. 图瓦出土铜耳坠；5. 耶罗夫（Еловский）1 号墓出土铜耳坠；6. 别斯一奥巴 3 号墓出土金耳坠；7. 波克罗夫卡 II 墓地 2 号墓出土金耳坠

和装饰风格来看，圆锥体耳坠往往在坠部表面装饰金珠和水滴形镶嵌物，且在底部有孔洞用于垂挂串珠。总的来说，圆锥体耳坠和南乌拉尔地区出土的耳坠差异大于共性，后者的年代在公元前 6 世纪至前 4 世纪，不排除是圆锥体耳坠的变体。①

北高加索地区库班文化晚期（公元前 6 世纪至前 4 世纪）的墓葬中出土了若干带双锥形坠的耳饰（图 8–1–4），经学者研究，这些耳饰在北高加索及南乌拉尔地区游牧人的遗存中可以找到非常接近的例子，他指出这种耳饰样式可能是游牧人南下进入近东地区参与军事行动受到的文化影响，而后将这种耳坠样式带到了北高加索地区，并为当地库班文化居民所采用（图 8–5–9）。这种双锥形耳坠似乎也与圆锥形耳坠有着千丝万缕的联系，尤其是在图瓦地区也发现了双锥形的耳坠样式（图 3–19）。

总的看来，欧亚草原发现的带类似圆锥体坠的耳饰种类繁多，分布范围广，不排除有一个原型的可能（如亚述的耳坠），但中间的连接环节至今未能很好地说明。对具体墓葬年代的分歧，也常常导致对耳饰出现的早晚判断不同，增加了这些中间环节考察的难度。如楚古诺夫认为咸海地区早期塞人墓葬乌因卡拉克（Уйгарак）和萨迦一察卡（Сакар-Чага）4 号墓等可以早到公元前 8 世纪，如此一来，这些墓葬发现的耳坠可能与图瓦地区的圆锥体耳坠同时甚至更早，排除了它们作为圆锥体耳坠变体的

① В. К. Федоров, “Серьги из могильника Сара в Оренбургской области”, с. 76.

图 8 北高加索地区库班文化晚期墓葬出土双锥体耳坠（1–4）及周边地区的同类物（5–9）；1. 普谢达赫（Пседахе）3 号墓；2. 新格罗斯宁（Новогрознен）5 号墓；3. 涅斯捷罗夫（Нестеров）墓；4. 沙卢什卡（Шалушка）大墓（金）；5. 纳尔坦（Нартан）2 号墓；6. 巴达夫什纳（Полтавщина）偶然发现；7. 萨拉（Сара）墓地；8. 帕什科夫（Пашков）墓地 2 号墓 1 号墓室；9. 亚述赛纳克里布（Синнахериба）浮雕上的耳饰形象，公元前 706 年（全部出自 В. И. Козенкова, 2013, рис. 21）

图 9 咸海地区早期塞人墓葬出土耳坠；1–3. 乌因卡拉克 21.22.23 号墓；4. 萨迦一察卡 4 号墓

可能性（图 9–1–4）。① 但事实上，也有不少学者将咸海地区这批早期塞人遗存定在公元前 7 世纪至前 5 世纪。② 对于圆锥体耳坠起源的问题，多个中心各自起源的可能性也应该被考虑到。

三 圆锥体耳坠及相关出土物反映的新疆与周边地区的文化联系

由圆锥体耳坠的研究也延伸到了对欧亚草原早期斯基泰时期各地区文化的考察。关于这方面，国外学者有不少论述，他们指出，图瓦、阿尔泰山区、哈萨克斯坦远至伏尔加河下游的早期斯基泰时期的文化因素趋同。③ 如果将新疆发现的圆锥体耳坠及其相关遗存纳入讨论，对这一现象的考察将

① К. В. Кучунов, “Серьги раннескифского времени Саяно-Алтая (происхождение традиции и типологическое развитие)”, с. 394, 395.

② М. А. Итина, Л. Т. Яблонский, *Саки Нижней Сыркарьи(по материалам могильника Южный Тагискен)*, Москва, Российская политическая энциклопедия(РОССПЭН), 1997, с. 5; О. А. Вишневская, *Культура сакских племен низовьев Сырдарьи в VII-V вв. до н. э., По материалам Уйгарака*, Труды ХАЭЭ, том VIII, Москва, Издательство «Наука», 1973, с. 6.

③ Вл. А. Семенов, “Синхронизация и хронология памятников алды-бельского типа в Туве”, с. 169; А. С. Васютин, “О памятниках Алды-Бельского типа в Саяно-Алтае”, с. 34; Hermann Parzinger, “Der skythenzeitliche Fürstenkurgan Arzan 2 in Tuva-Ergebnisse und weiterführende Betrachtungen”, im Konstantin V.Čugunov, Hermann Parzinger und Anatoli Nagler, *Der skythenzeitliche Fürstenkurgan Aržan 2 in Tuva,* Mainz, Verlag Philipp von Zabern, 2010, S. 311-320.

会更加全面。同时，我们也会对新疆与欧亚草原其他地区之间的文化交流与互动有更深入的认识。

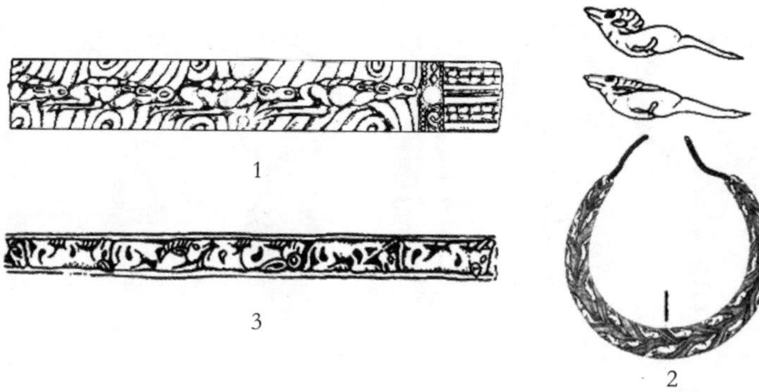

图 10　1. 东塔勒德墓地金耳坠环面图案展开图；2. 阿尔然 2 号墓出土金项饰图案；3. 伊塞克墓出土短剑图案

东塔勒德墓地出土的圆锥体金耳坠，无论是环部錾刻的纹样，还是坠部镶嵌的三角形绿松石，在欧亚草原所有发现的同类耳坠中都是独树一帜的，加之墓葬出土了数量众多的金饰件，反映了很成熟的金器加工水平，由此我们认为，这件耳坠很可能是本地制作的，工匠在外来的耳饰样式的基础上加入了本地的文化元素进行创作。金耳坠的环部錾刻变形的鹅喉羚图案，与草原卷曲的动物纹风格一致（图 10−1）。这种风格的图案不由让人联想到阿尔然 2 号墓 5 号墓葬出土的一件金胸饰，环面錾刻上下两排动物形象，有盘羊、鹅喉羚、鹿、虎等，动物们都向前上方昂首，身体与四肢都自然向后伸展。间隙的线纹和涡旋纹像流水一般裹挟着动物纹，形成流动的美感（图 10−2）。① 动物的形态与饰件整体的纹样构图都与东塔勒德墓地所出极其相似。哈萨克斯坦伊塞克古墓（前 5 世纪—前 4 世纪）出土的一把铁质短剑，表面贴了金箔。柄部顶端为对视的格里芬首，柄部装饰编织纹，剑身中间的装饰带刻画了不同动物，包括鹿、羊、老虎等首尾相接，俯仰相续，作匍匐状的画面。在动物的前后肢位置原来镶嵌有水滴状的绿松石，展现动物肌肉的力量感。尤其是描绘的盘羊和鹅喉羚的形态与东塔勒德墓地戒环上所见如出一辙（图 10−3）。②

于建军、马健已经指出，东塔勒德墓地所出金饰在制作工艺、动物纹种类、造型等方面都与萨彦—阿尔泰地区以及哈萨克斯坦东部地区十分接近。③ 事实上，东塔勒德墓地及其他几处墓地出土的金饰，与哈萨克斯坦中部，西至锡尔河下游及南乌拉尔地区的广大的地域内都有千丝万缕的联系。

东塔勒德墓地出土的错金铁泡（I M32:5），呈圆球状，表面错金成虎逐鹿的形象，金箔表现的线条和图案，与底面的铁形成鲜明的色差（图 11−1）。阿尔然 2 号墓出土了不少错金铁饰物，其中 5 号墓男墓主佩戴的短剑在柄部错金形成两虎相对，身体弯曲，利爪前伸，虎口大张，身上满绘条形纹，形象与东塔勒德墓地铁泡上所见很接近（图 11−2）。④

东塔勒德墓地出土金箔野猪饰件（I M32:8-1）（图 11−3），木垒县也发现了一件野猪纹透雕铜牌饰，为五只野猪围咬虎的图案，中间虎的图案为典型的卷曲成环的动物图案，铜饰直径 13.7 厘米（图

① Konstantin V. Čugunov, Hermann Parzinger und Anatoli Nagler, *Der skythenzeitliche Fürstenkurgan Aržan 2 in Tuva,* Tafel. 79-2a.

② С. Н. Шилов, Р. Исмагил, В. Г. Котов, А. Л. Банников, "Уникальный бронзовый кинжал из Казак-кочердыка (курганская область): типология и семантика", *Уфимский археологический вестник*, 2003 г., Выпуск 4, с. 196, рис. 2, 2.

③ 于建军、马健：《哈巴河县东塔勒德墓地初步研究》，《新疆文物》2013 年第 1 期，第 85—86 页。

④ Konstantin V. Čugunov, Hermann Parzinger und Anatoli Nagler, *Der skythenzeitliche Fürstenkurgan Aržan 2 in Tuva,* Tafel. 40-5.

11–4）。[①] 新疆两处发现野猪的形象与阿尔然 1 号墓出土的短剑柄端上的雕像（图 11–5），以及阿尔然 2 号墓出土的野猪形金饰件十分接近（图 11–7）。[②] 值得一提的是，野猪的形象在阿尔然 2 号墓地表发现的岩刻上也有表现（图 11–6）。[③] 阿尔泰山区巴沙达尔（Башадар）2 号墓棺盖板上也雕刻了野猪的形象，野猪作抵地状，似要向前奔跑，野猪的身上雕刻出涡旋纹（图 11–8、9）。[④] 鄂毕河上游的鄂毕—普列斯（Обские Плесы）2 号墓地 2 号墓出土野猪铜饰件，墓葬年代定在前 5 世纪至前 4 世纪（图 11–10）。[⑤] 额尔齐斯河上游的塔姆拉什（Тамураши）村发现的岩刻上有野猪形象（图 11–11）。[⑥] 东哈萨克斯坦的齐列克塔（Чиликты）墓地（公元前 8 世纪—前 6 世纪）也有出土相似猪图案的金箔饰件（图 11–2）。[⑦] 在哈萨克斯坦中部的卡尔卡拉林斯卡（Каркаралинска）附近也有发现野猪纹样的饰物（图 11–13）。[⑧] 塔斯莫拉 5 号墓地 3 号墓出土的骨饰件上也表现了尖蹄的野猪形象，形象生动（图 11–14）。[⑨] 乌拉尔河下游的菲利波夫卡墓地出土的器物上的金质贴饰也有反映野猪形象的，墓葬年代在公元前 5 世纪至前 4 世纪（图 11–15）。[⑩] 伏尔加河下游也有发现类似的野猪形象，年代在公元前 6 世纪末至前 5 世纪初（图 11–16）。[⑪]

东塔勒德墓地出土的金花饰件（II M3∶2）（图 12–1），在阿尔然 2 号墓也有类似的饰件，是女墓主发饰的一部分，在墓葬出土的带扣上也可以看到相似的纹样（图 12–2~4）。[⑫] 在阿尔泰山区北部边缘的贝斯特亚墓葬也有相似图案的装饰物（图 12–5）。[⑬] 南乌拉尔地区基曲吉诺（Кичигино）I 号墓地 5 号墓出土金箔饰件也有相似的发现（图 12–6）。[⑭] 东塔勒德墓地出土的“S”形金饰片（II M32∶8-2）（图 12–7），在伊塞克墓群（Иссык）也见相似物（图 12–8）。伊塞克墓群年代在公元

① 祁小山、王博：《丝绸之路·新疆古代文化》，乌鲁木齐：新疆人民出版社，2008 年，第 203 页，图 10。

② Konstantin V. Čugunov, Hermann Parzinger und Anatoli Nagler, *Der skythenzeitliche Fürstenkurgan Aržan 2 in Tuva*, Abb. 8、160.

③ Konstantin V. Čugunov, Hermann Parzinger und Anatoli Nagler, *Der skythenzeitliche Fürstenkurgan Aržan 2 in Tuva*, S. 139.

④ С. И. Руденко, *Искусство Алтая и Средней Азии (середина I тысячелетии до н. э.)*, Ленинград, Издательство Академии наук СССР, 1961, рис. 21.

⑤ С. Д. Ведянин, А. Л. Кунгунов, “Грунтовый могильник староалейской культуры Обские Плесы 2”, *Погребальный обряд древних племён Алтая*, Барнаул, Изд-во Алтайского университета, 1996, с. 88-114, рис. 14, 3.

⑥ Е. Ф. Корольков, “Звериный стиль Евразии, Искусство племен Нижнего Поволжья и Южного Приуралья в скифскую эпоху(VII-IV вв. до н. э.)”, *Проблемы стиля и этнокультурной принадлежности*, СПб, Петербургское Востоковедение, 2006, табл. 10, 7.

⑦ Konstantin V. Čugunov, Hermann Parzinger und Anatoli Nagler, *Der skythenzeitliche Fürstenkurgan Aržan 2 in Tuva*, Abb. 286-1.

⑧ А. З. Бейсенов, Г. А. Базарбаева, “Искусство древних кочевников центрального Казахстана: образы, сюжеты, композиции”, *Вестник Южно-Уральского государственного университета*, Серия: Социально-гуманитарные науки, 2013, т. 13, no 2, рис. 1, 5.

⑨ А. З. Бейсенов, Г. А. Базарбаева, “Орнамент в культуре Саков Центрального Казахстана”, *Известия Самарского научного центра Российской академии наук*, т. 16, No 3(2), 2014, рис. 1, 4.

⑩ Е. Ф. Корольков, “Звериный стиль Евразии, Искусство племен Нижнего Поволжья и Южного Приуралья в скифскую эпоху(VII-IV вв. до н. э.)”, табл. 10, 1.

⑪ Е. Ф. Корольков, “Звериный стиль Евразии, Искусство племен Нижнего Поволжья и Южного Приуралья в скифскую эпоху(VII-IV вв. до н. э.)”, табл. 10, 3.

⑫ Konstantin V. Čugunov, Hermann Parzinger und Anatoli Nagler, *Der skythenzeitliche Fürstenkurgan Aržan 2 in Tuva*, Tafel. 54, 4；Tafel. 30, 3, 7.

⑬ Hermann Parzinger, *Die frühen Völker Eurasiens. Vom Neolithikum bis zum Mittelalter*, Abb. 192.

⑭ А. Д. Таиров, С. Г. Боталов, “Погребение сакского времени могильника Кичигино I в Южном Зауралье”, *Археология и палеоантропология евразийских степей и прилегающих территорий,* Сб. статей в честь 60-летия Л. Т. Яблонского, Москва, «Таус», 2010, рис. 4, 17.

图 11　1、3. 东塔勒德墓地；2、6、7. 阿尔然 2 号墓；4. 木垒县；5. 阿尔然 1 号墓；8、9. 巴沙达尔 2 号墓；10. 鄂毕—普列斯 2 号墓地 2 号墓；11. 塔姆拉什村岩刻；12. 齐列克塔墓地；13. 卡尔卡拉林斯卡附近；14. 塔斯莫拉 5 号墓地 3 号墓；15. 菲利波夫卡墓地；16. 伏尔加河下游

前 4 世纪至前 3 世纪。① 东塔勒德墓地出土了金箔弯制的箭叶形饰件（II M3∶1-3），尾部带孔，可以穿绳（图 12-9）。阿尔泰地区巴雷克—库卡（Балык-Соока）1 号墓地出土的金耳坠底部也坠有相似的饰物，呈四片叶状（图 12-10）。墓葬年代在公元前 6 世纪上半叶，属于巴泽雷克文化早期

① K. Akishev, *Ancient Gold of Kazakhstan*, АΛМА•АТА•ӨНЕР, 1983, p. 131.

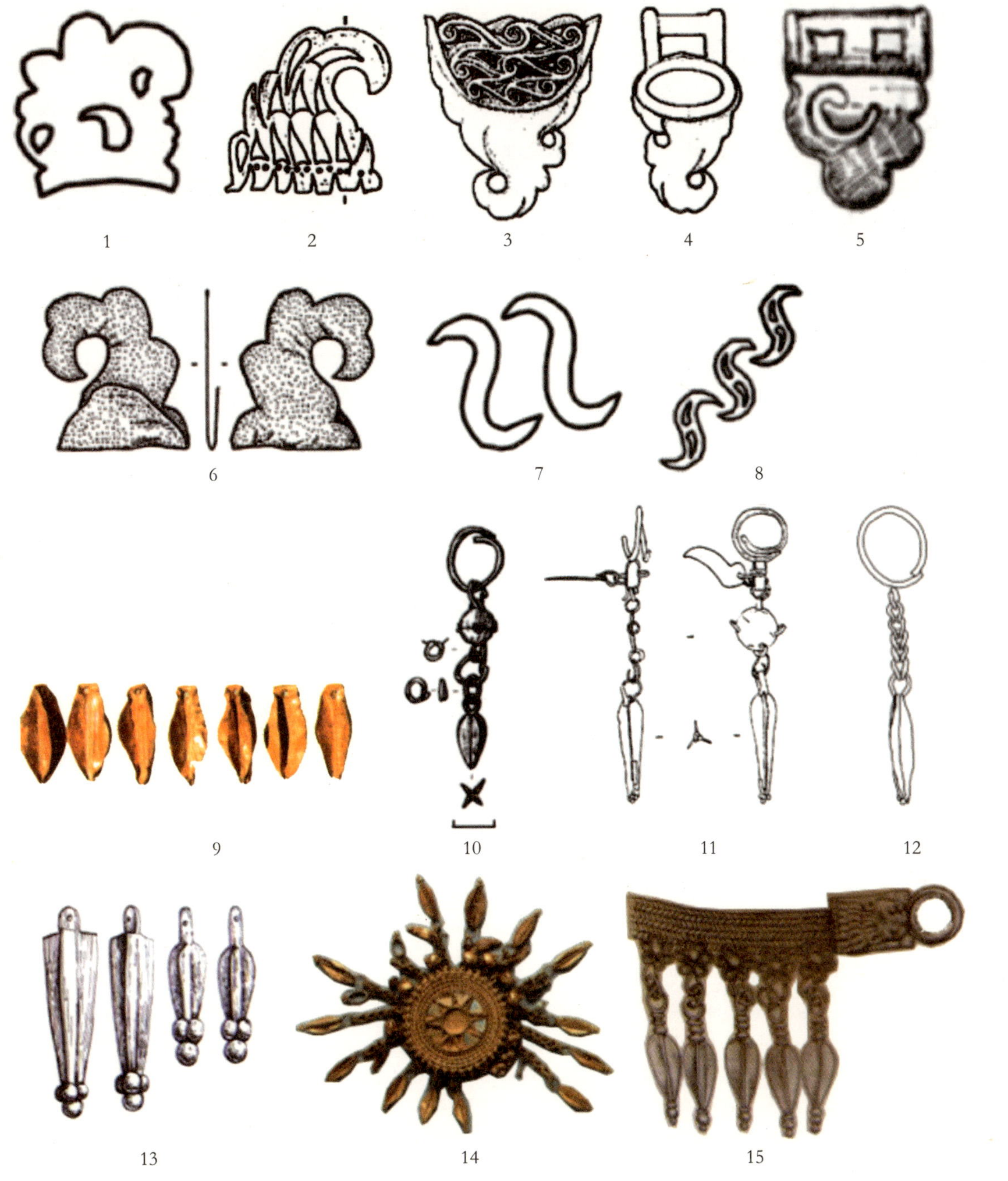

图 12　1、7、9. 东塔勒德墓地；2—4. 阿尔然 2 号墓；5. 贝斯特亚墓葬；6. 基曲吉诺 I 号墓地 5 号墓；8. 伊塞克墓群；10. 巴雷克—库卡 1 号墓地；11. 叶鲁尼纳 II 号墓地 1 号墓；12. 列别杰夫卡墓地；13. 杜鄂根 1 号墓地；14. 菲力波夫卡墓地；15. 黑海北部墓葬

遗存①。位于阿尔泰山西段山麓的叶鲁尼纳（Елунино）II 号墓地 1 号墓出土了一件金耳坠，坠部也

① В. Д. Кубарев, П. И. Шульга, *Пазырыкская культура (курганы Чуи и Урсула)*, Барнаул, Издательство Алтайского государственного университета, 2007, с. 209, рис. 14-3.

有箭叶形饰，墓葬年代约在公元前 6 世纪—前 5 世纪（图 12–11）。① 同样位于阿尔泰地区的杜鄂根（Туэкыин）1 号墓地出土的马饰上也见箭叶形木坠饰（图 12–13）。② 位于哈萨克斯坦西部的列别杰夫卡（Лебедевка）墓葬出土的耳坠，坠部也是金箔制成的箭叶形饰物，末端还焊饰了 3 至 4 颗金珠。墓葬年代大致在公元前 5 世纪至前 3 世纪（图 12–12）。③ 位于乌拉尔河中游的菲力波夫卡（Филипповка）墓地 17 号墓葬，出土了一件坠饰，中间圆盘部分掐丝制成太阳图案，并镶嵌石料，圆盘边缘装饰有一圈金珠、一圈编织纹以及一圈金珠塔。圆盘边缘间隔垂挂箭叶形饰件和石榴饰件，箭叶形饰件在末端和叶片间都装饰有金珠（图 12–14）。菲力波夫卡墓地的年代在公元前 5 世纪至前 4 世纪，一般认为属于早期萨尔马泰文化遗存。④ 黑海北部的墓葬中也有相似的发现，年代在公元前 4 世纪（图 12–15）。⑤

东塔勒德墓地出土了金珠饰件（II M3:1）（图 13–1），在哈萨克斯坦别斯沙图尔（Бесшатыр）2 号墓也发现了相似的饰物，墓葬年代在公元前 5 世纪至前 4 世纪（图 13–2）。⑥ 在菲力波夫卡 I 号墓地 4 号墓 5 号墓室也可以见到同类的饰物（图 13–3、4）。⑦

东塔勒德墓地出土的卧虎形金饰件（II M3:3-1）（图 13–5），在位于哈萨克斯坦中部的塔斯莫拉 5 号墓也有相似的发现，墓地年代约在公元前 6 世纪（图 13–6）。⑧ 位于锡尔河下游的南塔吉斯肯 53 号墓地也出土了相似的猫科动物纹浮雕金饰，墓葬的年代在公元前 7 世纪至前 6 世纪（图 13–7）。⑨ 位于南乌拉尔地区的基曲吉诺 I 号墓地 5 号墓出土装饰在上身衣物的金饰件及金耳坠，均为猫科动物卧姿形象（图 13–8–10）。墓葬年代定在公元前 7 世纪后半叶。⑩ 菲力波夫卡 I 号墓地 4 号墓 2 号墓室出土一件卧虎形金饰，长 8.3 厘米；4 号墓 4 号墓室出土一组 10 件卧猫科动物形金饰件，动物大腿位置还有水滴形宝石座，镶嵌物已遗失，金饰件宽 6.4 厘米至 6.8 厘米（图 13–11、12）。⑪ 这些浮雕金饰，都突出刻画猫科动物的足部，且尾巴末端弯卷成小圆。

木垒县东城乡出土有虎形铜器（图 13-13），甘肃马家塬战国墓地也有发现（图 13-14），⑫ 阿尔然 2 号墓 5 号墓葬男墓主的斗篷上更是装饰了大量这种虎形饰（图 13-16）。⑬ 从萨彦—阿尔泰地区到南乌拉尔地区都可以看到类似虎形饰，如图瓦的古伊卢格—赫姆 I 号墓地 9 号墓，年代在公元前 7 世纪

---

① Ю. Ф. Кирюшин, Я. В. Фролов, “Комплекс памятников эпохи раннего железа в районе с. Елунино”, Сборник научных трудов, *Древние Поселения Алтая,* Барнаул, Издательство Алтайского государственного университета, 1998, с. 136, рис. 11-1.

② С. И. Руденко, *Культура населения Центрального Алтая в скифское время*, М.; Л., Изд-во Академии наук СССР, 1960, табл. LXXYI.

③ *The Centaurs of the Great Steppe*, Tasmagambetov I., 2003.（影像资料附图片）

④ Iaroslav Lebedynsky, *Les Sarmates: Amazones et lanciers cuirassés entre Ourql et Danube VIIe siècle av. J.-C.-VIe siècle apr.J.-C.,* Paris, Editions Errance, 2002, p. 95.

⑤ Н. В. Полосьмак, *Всадники Укока,* Новосибирск, Издательство «ИНФОЛИО-пресс», 2001, с. 267, рис. 160, а.

⑥ K. Akishev, *Ancient Gold of Kazakhstan*, p. 128.

⑦ *Сокровища сарматских вождей(Материал раскопок Филипповских курганов),* рис. 33, 38.

⑧ О. А. Вишневская, “Центральный Казахстан,” *Степная полоса Азиатской части СССР в скифо-сарматское врем, Серия: Археология СССР,* Москва, Издательство «Наука», 1992, табл. 54, 3-6.

⑨ М. А. Итина, Л. Т. Яблонский, *Саки Нижней Сыркарьи(по материалам могильника Южный Тагискен),* рис. 78.

⑩ А. Д. Таиров, С. Г. Боталов, “Погребение сакского времени могильника Кичигино I в Южном Зауралье”, рис. 4, 3-5.

⑪ *Сокровища сарматских вождей(Материал раскопок Филипповских курганов)*, с. 82, рис. 3; с. 93, рис. 21.

⑫ 新疆昌吉回族自治州文物局编:《丝绸之路天山廊道——新疆昌吉古代遗址与馆藏文物精品》，第 252 页，图 263、263a。

⑬ Konstantin V. Čugunov, Hermann Parzinger und Anatoli Nagler, *Der skythenzeitliche Fürstenkurgan Aržan 2 in Tuva*, Tafel. 37.

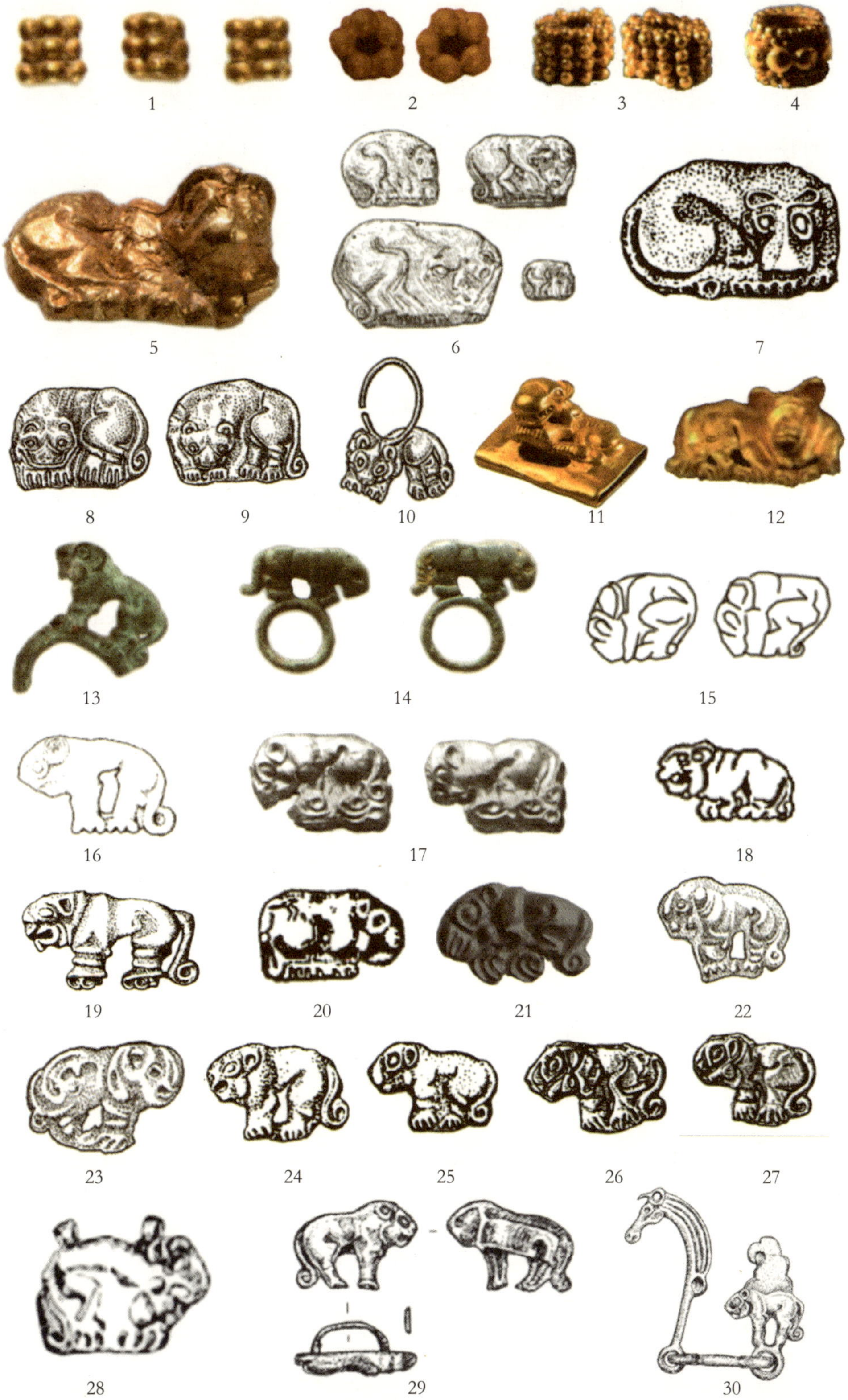

图 13　1、5、15. 东塔勒德墓地；2. 别斯沙图尔 2 号墓；3、4. 菲力波夫卡 Ⅰ 号墓地 4 号墓 5 号墓室；6. 塔斯莫拉 5 号墓；7、24-27. 南塔吉斯肯墓地；8~10.29.30. 基曲吉诺 Ⅰ 号墓地 5 号墓；11. 菲力波夫卡 Ⅰ 号墓地 4 号墓 2 号墓室；12. 菲力波夫卡 Ⅰ 号墓地 4 号墓 4 号墓室；13. 木垒县东城乡；14. 张家川马家塬墓地；16. 阿尔然 2 号墓；17. 古伊卢格—赫姆 Ⅰ 号墓地 9 号墓；18. 科什—贝伊墓地；19. 鄂毕—普列斯 2 号墓地；20. 阿尔泰和鄂毕河上游；21. 塔尔—阿苏墓地；22、23. 塔乐迪 2 号墓地 5 号墓；28. 乌因卡拉克 49 号墓

至前5世纪（图13-17）；[①] 图瓦的科什—贝伊（Кош-Пей）墓地，年代在公元前5世纪至前3世纪（图13-18）；[②] 鄂毕河上游鄂毕—普列斯2号墓地出土铜饰件，年代定在公元前5世纪至前4世纪（图13-19）；[③] 阿尔泰和鄂毕河上游发现的动物纹饰件（图13-20）；[④] 阿尔泰山西缘的塔尔—阿苏墓葬女性墓中既出土了圆锥体耳坠，也出土有类似的动物纹金箔（图13-21）；[⑤] 塔乐迪2号墓地5号墓也出土相似的金饰（图13-22、23）；[⑥] 南塔吉斯肯墓地也出土老虎金饰（图13-24~27）；[⑦] 同样位于锡尔河下游的乌因卡拉克墓地49号墓出土动物形金饰件，墓葬年代在公元前7世纪至前6世纪（图13-28）；[⑧] 南乌拉尔地区的基曲吉诺I号墓地5号墓出土青铜马具饰件（图13-29、30）。[⑨] 东塔勒德墓地出土的雪豹形金饰，其与欧亚草原各处发现的猫科动物纹饰风格一致（图13-15）。

东塔勒德墓地出土了一件动物纹金饰带（I M32:4），残余部分可见模压的山羊首纹样（图14-1）。位于哈萨克斯坦西部的波哈罗夫卡（Прохоровка）大墓也出土有两羊缠绕的金饰件，墓葬年代在公元前5世纪（图14-2）。[⑩] 团庄子村M5号墓出土了一件铁鹤嘴锄（图14-3），阿尔然2号墓也出土了一件铁包金鹤嘴锄（图14-4）。[⑪] 团庄子村墓地出土的砺石（图14-5），在阿尔然2号墓也可以找到相似物（图14-6）。[⑫] 团庄子村墓地出土的蚀花肉红石髓珠，在阿尔然2号墓和塔斯莫拉5号墓也可以见到同类物（图14-7~9）。[⑬] 乌鲁木齐柴窝堡墓地属于战国时期的墓葬，除了出土金耳坠外，还发现了一定数量的各式金饰，用金箔截切、叠合、焊接而成。其中，出土的用于穿系的圆台形中空金部件，在同时期的很多墓葬中都有发现，如阿尔然2号墓和哈萨克斯坦中部的塔乐迪2号墓地5号墓（图14-10~13）。[⑭]

---

① А. Д. Грач, *Древние кочевники в центре Азии,* рис. 86.

② К. В. Чугунов, "Локально-хронологические особенности культуры Тувы в середине 1 тысячелетия до н. э. ", *Евразия сквозь века,* СПб, 2001, табл. 1, 9.

③ С. Д. Ведянин, А. Л. Кунгунов, "Грунтовый могильник староалейской культуры Обские Плесы 2", *Погребальный обряд древних племён Алтая,* Барнаул, Изд-во Алтайского университета, 1996, рис. 14, 2.

④ К. В. Чугунов, "Локально-хронологические особенности культуры Тувы в середине 1 тысячелетия до н. э. ", табл. 1, 25.

⑤ Samašev, Z. S., Bazarbaeva, G. A. und Žumabekova, G.S., "Die „goldhütenden Greife" des Herodot und die archäologische Kultur der frühen Nomaden im kazachischen Altai. Skythenzeitliche Kurgane von Berel' und Tar Asu", *Eurasia Antiqua,* Band 8, 2002, Mainz am Rhein, Verlag Philipp von Zabern, S. 271, Abb. 29-3.

⑥ А. З. Бейсенов, Г. А. Базарбаева, "Искусство древних кочевников центрального Казахстана: образы, сюжеты, композиции", рис. 1, 3, 9.

⑦ М. А. Итина, Л. Т. Яблонский, *Саки Нижней Сыркарьи(по материалам могильника Южный Тагискен),* 1997, рис. 78.

⑧ О. А. Вишневская, *Культура сакских племен низовьев Сырдарьи в VII-V вв. до н. з., По материалам Уйгарака,* табл. 1, 16.

⑨ А. Д. Таиров, С. Г. Боталов, "Погребение сакского времени могильника Кичигино I в Южном Зауралье", рис. 3, 4, 6.

⑩ Grigore Arbore Popescu, Chiara Silvi, Karl Baipakov, *L'UOMO D'ORO, La cultura delle steppe del Kazakhstan dall' età del bronzo alle grandi migrazioni,* p. 173, fig. 263.

⑪ 新疆昌吉回族自治州文物局编:《丝绸之路天山廊道——新疆昌吉古代遗址与馆藏文物精品》，第209页，图204。

⑫ Konstantin V. Čugunov, Hermann Parzinger und Anatoli Nagler, *Der skythenzeitliche Fürstenkurgan Aržan 2 in Tuva,* Tafel. 112-6.

⑬ 新疆昌吉回族自治州文物局编:《丝绸之路天山廊道——新疆昌吉古代遗址与馆藏文物精品》，第211页，图206; Konstantin V. Čugunov, Hermann Parzinger und Anatoli Nagler, *Der skythenzeitliche Fürstenkurgan Aržan 2 in Tuva,* Tafel. 106-7; Grigore Arbore Popescu, Chiara Silvi, Karl Baipakov, *L'UOMO D'ORO, La cultura delle steppe del Kazakhstan dall' età del bronzo alle grandi migrazioni,* p. 143, fig. 151-152.

⑭ Konstantin V. Čugunov, Hermann Parzinger und Anatoli Nagler, *Der skythenzeitliche Fürstenkurgan Aržan 2 in Tuva,* Tafel. 32, 13; А. З. Бейсенов, Г. А. Базарбаева, "Орнамент в культуре Саков Центрального Казахстана", рис. 1, 3, 6.

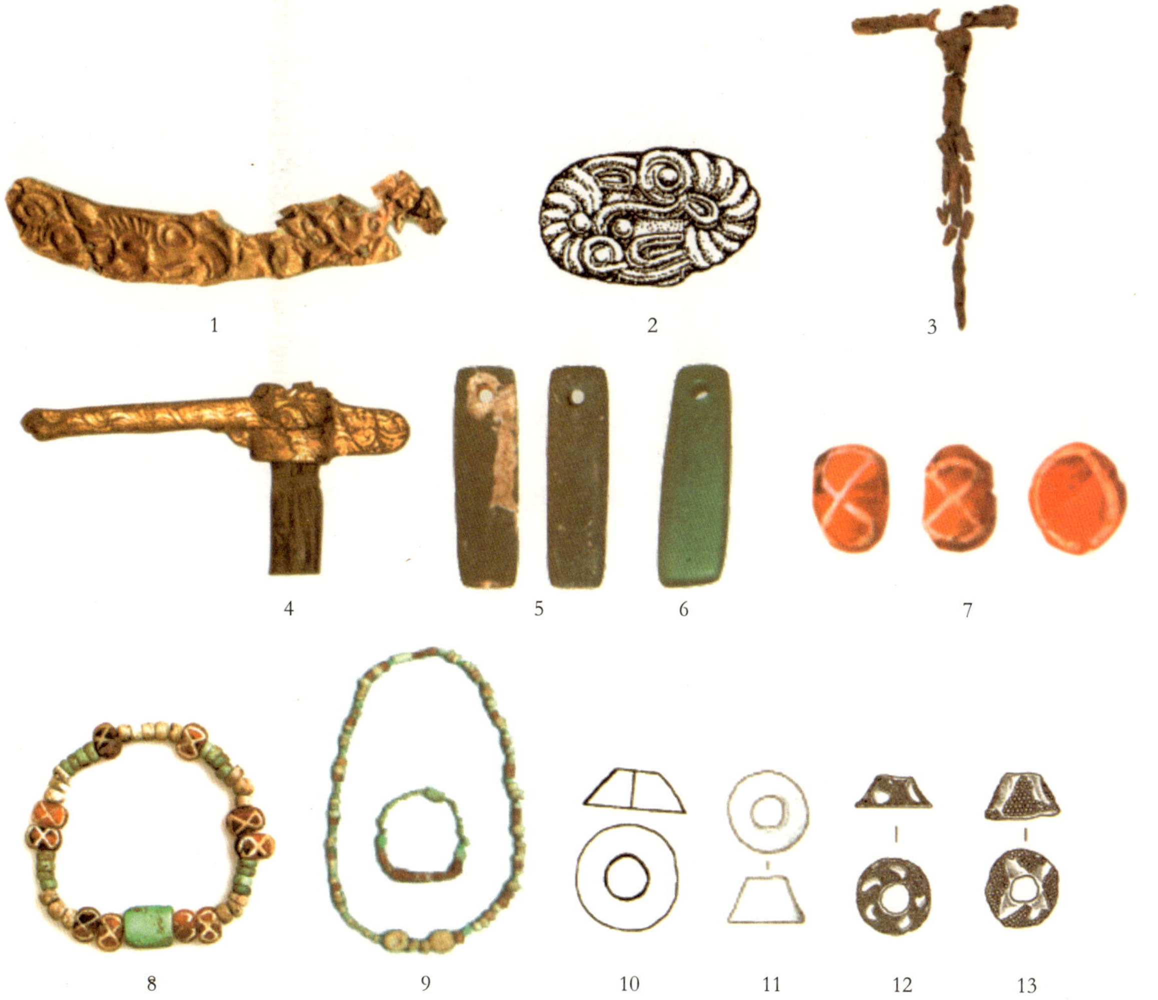

图 14　1. 东塔勒德墓地；2. 波哈罗夫卡大墓；3.5.7. 清水河乡团庄子村墓地；4、6、8、11. 阿尔然 2 号墓；9. 塔斯莫拉 5 号墓；10. 柴窝堡墓地；12.13. 塔乐迪 2 号墓地 5 号墓

可见，圆锥体耳坠及其相关物品的集合，反映了在公元前 8 世纪至前 3 世纪间，新疆境内的天山北麓地区甚至甘青地区，与萨彦—阿尔泰地区、哈萨克草原、锡尔河下游、南乌拉尔地区都存在紧密的联系。这种联系也可以通过圆锥体耳坠的跨文化分布而管窥一斑。事实上，新疆公元前一千纪发现的很多装饰物，在周邻地区都能找到不少的同类物，尤其是萨彦—阿尔泰地区、南西伯利亚、中亚草原地带。国外学者在研究这些装饰物时，由于资料获取上的原因，往往缺乏新疆出土的材料，但事实上，无论是从地理位置还是地域面积来看，新疆都是欧亚草原游牧文明与内亚绿洲农耕文明非常重要的一部分，它对于研究装饰物发展与传播谱系的全面性是不可或缺的。同时，国内学者研究新疆发现的装饰物时，对于境外发现材料的梳理不足，这也使得我们无法很好地掌握其文化内涵。只有将新疆地区放入欧亚草原—绿洲文明交流的大背景中来研究，我们才能对新疆地区的古代装饰文化有更深入的认识。

Study of Earrings with cone-shape pendent found in Xinjiang

Lin Lingmei
(Renmin University of China)

Abstract: Four samples of earrings with cone-shape pendant have been found in Xinjiang: Chaiwopu cemetery in Urumqi, Wulabo Reservoir cemetery in Urumqi, East Talede cemetery in Habahe County, Tuanzhuangzi cemetery in Qingshuihe downship, Manasi county. A number of this type of earrings has been found in foreign areas, and foreign scholars have done some researches on its origin and transmission. Study of the earrings with cone-shape pendant found in Xinjiang, also with some other discoveries, helps us have a better understanding of the interaction and communication between Xinjiang and other zones of Eurasian steppe.

Key words: earrings with cone-shape pendant; Xinjiang; Eurasian steppe; cultural communication

于阗佛教壁画中的非佛教神祇及相关问题 *

[意] 康马泰（中国人民大学）撰
李思飞（中国社会科学院）译

摘　要：在于阗佛教壁画及许愿木板中经常可以见到一些没有印度神祇特征的神灵。它们所呈现的独特风格，引发了一些极具挑战性的身份比定。过去的学者发展出两套理论。根据马尔库斯·莫德（Markus Mode）的观点，这些神祇有可能随粟特人的迁徙而来，所以应被视作琐罗亚斯德教神祇。而马尔沙克（B. Marshak）则认为，他们有可能是当地神祇，不应与粟特神联系在一起。本文将要讨论的是，马尔沙克的假设似乎更为正确，新近在和田地区的考古发现尤其印证了这一点。

关键词：于阗壁画；许愿木板；粟特壁画；佛教；琐罗亚斯德教

最近在塔里木盆地（图 1）古代绿洲王国于阗（今中国新疆维吾尔自治区和田地区）进行的考古发掘，将一批非常有趣的绘画公之于众，其中一些画面上有于阗文题记。这批绘画总是在佛教背景中，作为丹丹乌里克和达玛沟遗址（喀拉墩和托普鲁克墩）当地寺院的装饰组成部分而出现。

自佛陀第一次以人的形象被描绘以来，佛教图像与印度神祇如梵天、帝释天（Indra）等一并出现的画面并不鲜见。他们的共存毫无稀奇之处，这在于阗也不例外。然而，这些绘画经常表现一些特定的神祇，他们的着装、标志物往往不能根据印度图像原则而被完全比定为印度的神。这批新近发现

图 1　和田地区主要考古遗址

* 特此感谢中国外国专家局（State Administration of Foreign Experts Affairs P. R. China）；撰者康马泰先生系中国人民大学艺术学院国际专家。

的绘画可以帮助我们更好地理解于阗宗教艺术，同时也将为探究中亚这一既吸纳了诸多印度文化元素，又保持了自身伊朗背景的独特文明提供一些启迪。

一 于阗王国

于阗王国的历史仅部分地为我们所知，其大部分来源可在中国编年史特别是汉朝对中亚的扩张及西藏历史记述中找到。只有关于8世纪2/3之交的年代有一些直接的资料①，至于2世纪之前的于阗历史仅有钱币为证（汉式钱币、贵霜钱币及当地的“汉佉二体钱”)②，紧随斯文·赫定于19世纪末首次发现组成古于阗王国的主要遗址之后，著名探险家斯坦因来此进行了考古探险并收集了数量可观的艺术品。③

在汉语文献中，于阗以盛产美玉（这是中原王朝大量需求的物品）而著称。于阗也被视为著名艺术家的故乡，《唐书》曾明确提到于阗王的居所装饰着壁画。④根据一份8世纪藏语文献《李国的预言》（*Li Yul lun-bstan-pa*）记载，佛教（这里意指小乘佛教）在公元前1世纪就已由于阗王尉迟散跋婆（Vijaya Sambhava）传入于阗，其后有七位非佛教徒君主。最终确立佛教信仰的是国王尉迟毗利耶（Vijaya Virya）——藏文文献列表上第十一位于阗王。这一讯息应被高度考虑为一个假设，不仅因为它只是保存在于阗域外的文献里，还因为它更像是传说而非史实。⑤

在公元前2世纪到公元2世纪之间，这一地区开始陷入汉帝国与匈奴（或他们在中亚草原的继任者）持续不断的争战状态。在大夏作为贵霜王朝重要王国的崛起过程中（1世纪至3世纪），大部分塔里木盆地南部地区成为汉帝国与贵霜争夺的区域。尽管贵霜人被汉朝将军班超所驱逐，印度—巴克特里亚文化还是得以在新疆这片土地上传播，这可以从古于阗王国，甚至其域外的鄯善王国境内考古发掘的大量钱币、纺织品及其他物品中得到清晰的证实。⑥当中亚这一地区处于匈奴铁骑搅起的混乱之

---

① P.O.Skjaervø, “Iranians, Indians, Chinese and Tibetans: The Rulers and Ruled of Khotan in the First Millennium”, in *The Silk Road. Trade, Travel, War and Faith*, ed. S. Whitfield, London, British Library, 2004, pp. 34-42; 于阗语文书残片（尤其是最早的一批）并不总是由依照科学标准而进行的考古活动发掘的；敦煌藏经洞藏：H. Kumamoto, “The Khotanese in Dunhuang”, in *Cina e Iran. Da Alessandro Magno alla dinastia Tang*, ed. A. Cadonna, L. Lanciotti, Firenze, Olschki, 1996, pp. 79-101.

② J. Cribb, “The Sino-Kharosthī Coins of Khotan. Part I”, *The Numismatic Chronicle*, 144, 1984, pp. 128-152.; J. Cribb, “The Sino-Kharosthī Coins of Khotan. Part II”, *The Numismatic Chronicle*, 145, 1985, pp. 136-149.

③ S. Hedin, *Durch Asiens Wüstens, Leipzig*, 1899; M. A. Stein, *Ancient Khotan: Detailed Report of Archaeological Explorations in Chinese Turkestan*, Oxford, Clarendon Press, 1907.

④ É. Chavannes, *Documents sur les Tou-Kiue (Turcs) Occidentaux*, Paris, 1903, p. 125.

⑤ R. Emmerick, *Tibetan Texts Concerning Khotan*, London: Oxford University Press, 1967, p. 75; G. Gropp, *Archäologische Funde aus Khotan Chinesisch-Ostturkestan*, Bremen, 1974, pp. 30-34. 值得关注的是一些新出的于阗编年史资料佐证了佛教的确早在公元前1世纪就传入了于阗：É. de La Vaissière, “Silk, Buddhism and Early Khotanese Chronology: A Note on the Prophecy of the Li Country”, *Bulletin of the Asia Institute*, 24, 2010, pp. 85-87.

⑥ 几件装饰有典型希腊化主题的毛织物残片出土于中国考古队考察的山普拉（于阗东南部）。另一件带有赫尔墨斯头像及其节杖的残片出土于楼兰墓地：M. M. Rhie, *Early Buddhist Art of China and Central Asia— Volume One: Later Han, Three Kingdoms and Western Chin in China and Bactria to Shan-shan in Central Asia*, Leiden, Boston, Brill, 2007, pp. 272-275. 日本探险队在20世纪初甚至在和田绿洲周边发现了塞拉皮斯—哈尔波克拉特斯（Serapis-Harpocrates）和赫拉克勒斯的陶制小雕像：Ibid., p. 265-266。所有这些物品皆代表了贵霜帝国希腊化主题（甚至神祇）的引入，这些主题往往代表巨大的财富。鄯善王国与贵霜人的文化交往很明显出现在米兰的佛教遗址中：两座饰有彩绘的佛塔（M.III和M.V）无疑显示出根植于早期健陀罗艺术的特征：A. Filigenzi, “From Saidu Sharif to Miran”, *Indologica Taurinensia*, XXXII, 2006, pp. 67-89.; C. Lo Muzio, “Notes on Gandhara Painting”, in *Glimpses of Indian History and Art Reflections on the Past, Perspectives for the Future*, ed. T. Lorenzetti, F. Scialpi, Roma, Sapienza Università Editrice, 2012, pp. 319-335.; H.P. Francfort, “Les peintures de Miran et l' art de l' Asie centrale”, *Monuments Piot*, 93, 2014, pp. 23-64.

际（4世纪至6世纪），于阗成为嚈哒人（西方史学家称为“白匈奴”）的附属国，不久又身陷突厥汗国的第一次领土扩张之中。① 中国宫廷与于阗国保持了良好的关系，那些探求珍贵佛经的僧侣曾多次来于阗寻访。当8世纪下半叶唐帝国遭遇755年至756年安史之乱等一系列内部祸患，再也无力控制塔里木盆地之后，于阗又吸引了吐蕃人的兴趣。840年居于蒙古的回鹘王国崩解后，突厥人开始在塔里木盆地定居下来，他们的活动范围由最初的吐鲁番盆地周边扩散至整个塔里木地区。1006年于阗被喀喇汗国（Karakhanids，840—1212）征服。伊斯兰教逐渐成为这一地区的主要宗教。②

在伊斯兰化和突厥化之前，于阗与其周边主要文明如中国、印度、吐蕃保持了重要的文化联系，经由陆上商旅队踏出的丝绸之路也与萨珊波斯建立了一些交往。来自于阗的异域商品和奴隶一度代表了波斯在伊斯兰时期文学作品如《列王纪》（*Shahnameh*）的主题。毫无疑问，于阗与保护佛教的王国之间存在着一些有益的交流，这也是为什么一些学者在谈论丝绸之路时会以于阗为中心的原因。③

在被维吾尔语取代之前，于阗语属于印欧语系伊朗语族东伊朗语的一支。在塔里木盆地和敦煌考古发掘中出土了用于阗文书写的文书。④ 这些文书均指向于阗地区至少在4世纪就已信奉大乘佛教。⑤ 此外，于阗文是用印度字母拼写而成的，因为印度文化一直在塔里木盆地的这一地区占据主导地位。

尽管考古发掘的题铭数量可观，对于阗文的破解依然问题重重，学界才刚刚开始这方面的研究。本文重点关注的是图像材料，仅涉及少量于阗语和题记。

二　于阗与粟特壁画

近期在丹丹乌里克和达玛沟发现的绘画并不是和田地区唯一的绘画遗存。20世纪初，奥莱尔·斯坦因就在和田地区的几处遗址发现了绘画残片，尤其在丹丹乌里克发现了彩绘许愿木板。这些木板现在部分藏于大英博物馆、艾尔米塔什博物馆及私人藏家如斯克林（Skrine）和特林克勒（Trinkler）手中。⑥ 由于多幅图中所绘神灵既非佛教又非印度教神祇，这些木板画故而成为一些颇有意思的研究对象。这些神祇通常被表现在木板的一面，另一面则有一位佛教偶像。虽然有的木板上刻有题铭，但无一可以解释与之相伴的图像。所有这些画面——壁画和木板画，很可能来自7世纪至8世纪。

① 重建这一阶段的历史是尤为困难的，虽然在汉语文献中反复提到嚈哒附属国的领土向西延伸至波斯，东至于阗。T. Yu, “Records Relevant to the Hephtalites in Ancient Chinese Historical Works”, *International Journal of Eurasian Studies*, 3, 13, 2015, pp. 208, 222, 242, 252, 258.

② V. Hansen, *The Sik Road: A New History*, Oxford, Oxford University Press, 2012, pp. 199-234.

③ E. Forte, “Centralità dell' oasi di Khotan nell' intercultura buddhista del I millennio lungo le vie della seta”, in *Archeologia delle Vie della Seta: Percorsi, Immagini e Cultura Materiale*, ed. B. Genito, L. Caterina, Napoli, 2012, pp. 97-121. 颇为值得注意的是：萨珊钱币并未在和田出土，而吐鲁番、库车和中国中部则出土了大量此类钱币。F. Thierry, “Sur les monnaies sassanides trouvées en Chine”, in *Circulation des monnaies, des marchandises et de biens*, Res Orientales III, ed. R. Gyselen, Bures-sur-Yvette, Leuven, E. Peeters, 1993, pp. 89-139.

④ M. Maggi, “Khotanese Literature”, in *A History of Persian Literature: The Literature of Pre-Islamic Iran*, XVII, ed. R. E. Emmerick, M. Macuch, London, New York: I. B. Tauris, 2009, pp. 330-418; M. Maggi, “Local Literatures: Khotanese”, in *Brill's Encyclopedia of Buddhism*. Vol. 1. Literature and Languages, ed. J. Silk, Leiden, Brill, 2015, pp. 860-870.

⑤ É. de La Vaissière, “Silk, Buddhism and Early Khotanese Chronology: A Note on the Prophecy of the Li Country”, *Bulletin of the Asia Institute*, 24, 2010, p 86.

⑥ N. V. Djakonova, “Materialy po kul' tovoj ikonografii Central' noj Azii domusulmanskogo perioda”, in *Trudy Gosudarstvennogo Ermitazha*, V, ed. T. N. Minasjan, Leningrad: 1961, pp. 257-272; J. Williams, “The Iconography of Khotanese Painting”, *East and West*, 23, 1-2, 1973, pp. 109-154.; G. Gropp, *Archäologische Funde aus Khotan Chinesisch-Ostturkestan*, Bremen, 1974.

在大约出版于25年前的一篇有趣文章中，马尔库斯·莫德表述了这些神祇中的一些形象应被视为来自粟特艺术的观点。① 在5世纪至8世纪间，许多粟特人沿着丝绸之路迁徙。这条由商旅驼队构成的路网，连接起了粟特人的祖国（今乌兹别克斯坦南部及塔吉克斯坦西部地区）与中国。移居中国和塔里木盆地的粟特人主要是商人，虽然他们也从事许多其他领域的事务。② 特别是在诸多6世纪来华入仕粟特人的墓葬被发现之后，一些学者致力于深入研究粟特文明。这些墓葬显示，一些权贵粟特人在许多方面都接受了汉人风俗，但并未完全放弃他们原初的文化特质。③ 粟特人在于阗的活动可以通过考古调查中于阗语和粟特语文书的直接来源为证。④

马尔库斯·莫德提出了一个假说，他认为于阗许愿木板画表现的是粟特神祇，但另一位粟特文化艺术专家马尔沙克则认为这些神祇是于阗本土的产物。⑤ 两位学者都意识到了这些木板画中有一些在以佛教为主要信仰体系的其他伊朗地区如大夏—吐火罗斯坦或巴米扬王国中无法找到的独特之处。除上述两种主要假说以外，我们也不应忽略佛教密宗（金刚乘）的成分。佛教这一神秘莫测的面相通常与西藏文化联系在一起，虽然尚不确知于阗艺术在何种程度上影响了喜马拉雅的佛教图像。一些学者致力于研究于阗—西藏艺术的相互作用，但关于丹丹乌里克木板画上的神祇，尚无人提出实质性的身份比定。⑥

图2　7—8世纪丹丹乌里克许愿木板线描图（大英博物馆）：两位男性神祇和中间的一位女神（娜娜？）

莫德由发现于丹丹乌里克的8世纪装饰有三位神祇的木板画开始他的假说（图2）。三位神祇之一有四只手

① M. Mode, "Sogdian Gods in Exile. Some Iconographic Evidence from Khotan in the Light of Recently Excavated Material from Sogdiana", *Silk Road Art and Archaeology*, II, 1991/92, pp. 179-214.

② 毕波：《中古中国的粟特胡人——以长安为中心》，北京：中国人民大学出版社，2011年。

③ 关于粟特人在中国与中亚的离散寓居，参见 É. de La Vaissière, *Sogdian Traders: A History*, Leiden, Boston: Brill, 2005. 关于入华粟特人墓葬，参见 B. I. Marshak, "La thématique sogdienne dans l' art de la Chine de la seconde moitié du VIe siècle", *Comptes Rendus de l'Académie des Inscriptions et Belles-Lettres*, 1, 2001, pp. 227-264.; J. A. Lerner, "Aspects of Assimilation: the Funerary Practices and Furnishings of Central Asians in China," *Sino Platonic Papers*, 168, 2005；孙武军：《入华粟特人墓葬图像的丧葬与宗教文化》，北京：中国社会科学出版社，2014年；P. Wertmann, *Sogdians in China: Archaeological and Art Historical Analyses of Tombs and Texts from the Third to the Tenth Century AD*, Darmstadt, Verlag Philipp Von Zabern, 2015.

④ H. W. Bailey, *The Culture of the Sakas in Ancient Iranian Khotan*, New York, Caravan Books, 1982, pp. 76-78; B. Bi, N. Sims-Williams, "Sogdian Documents from Khotan, I: Four Economic Documents", *Journal of the American Oriental Society*, 34, 4, 2010, pp. 497-508.

⑤ M. Mode, "Sogdian Gods in Exile. Some Iconographic Evidence from Khotan in the Light of Recently Excavated Material from Sogdiana", *Silk Road Art and Archaeology*, II, 1991/92, pp. 189-190, n. 44.

⑥ 霍巍：《于阗与藏西：新出考古材料所见两地间的古代文化交流》，《藏学学刊》2007年第3辑，第146—156页。感谢北京大学荣新江教授提示了这一注释。入藏于阗人有手工艺人，商人和僧侣。参见 H. H. R. Hoffmann, "The Tibetan Names of the Saka and the Sogdians", *Asiatische Studien*, XXV, 1971, pp. 451-453。在敦煌发现了10世纪用于阗文写成的金刚乘佛教经书，但它们很可能是由藏文原本翻译而来。M. Maggi, "Local Literatures: Khotanese", in *Brill's Encyclopedia of Buddhism*, Vol. 1. Literature and Languages, ed. J. Silk, Leiden, Brill, 2015, p. 867.

臂，戴有王冠。上面的手臂分别托着太阳和月亮，恰如8世纪片治肯特壁画所表现的娜娜（Nana）女神那样。在那些画面中，娜娜通常坐在她的象征动物——一头狮子上，尽管也有些时候她没有坐骑。莫德提出于阗木板画上表现的女神就是没有狮子坐骑的娜娜。大约30年前，N. Djakonova也提出了相同的对该女神的身份比定。① 同一木板画上位于中央女神两侧的男性神祇也表现出强烈的印度特征。如上文所示，虽然这些比定尚存在一些问题，莫德还是确信那些神祇来自粟特艺术。

在粟特本土片治肯特的主要遗址，至少自6世纪起，许多绘有当地神祇的画面已开始展现出清晰的印度图像元素（特别是来自印度教的元素）。② 尽管身着印度服装，粟特神代表的却是琐罗亚斯德教神祇，他们属于汉语文献中称为“祆教”的琐罗亚斯德教的当地形式。③ 最具代表性的例证是绘于片治肯特（XXII/1号房址）的一位神（Weshparkar，古波斯琐罗亚斯德教经典《阿维斯陀》中的风神Vayu），其身份毫无疑问地由其腿上的题字：wšpr(kr)而得以确认。虽然与著名的阿维斯陀神灵有着清晰的联系，在片治肯特壁画中风神Weshparkar仍被表现为湿婆（Shiva），后者的形象特征为三头、多臂、高举的手臂中有一手握有三叉戟（trishula）（图3）。

图3　8世纪早期片治肯特1号房址第XXII区粟特壁画线描图（艾尔米塔什博物馆）：Apam Napat(?)和风神

当贵霜王朝（1世纪—3世纪）早期的印度发展出规范化的佛教图像之时④，在犍陀罗（Gandhara）和马图拉（Mathura），印度教神祇就已开始被表现在佛陀的生平场景中。正如莫德注意到的，在印度境外开凿于5世纪的中国云冈石窟，人们仍可以看到这些继续被表现在佛教背景中的神祇。因此，在于阗佛教绘画中现存的粟特神祇的案例中，印度图像程序的存在表明：早于用“印度教服饰”表现粟特（琐罗亚斯德教）神灵几个世纪或与之同时，印度的佛教系统就已经吸纳了印度教神祇。以此图像学为基础，它们实际上是不可能被区分出来的。总而言之，这是莫德论文的出发点，也将是本文屡屡提及的观点。

在莫德文章之后发表的其他一些论文，对佛教吸纳粟特的印度图像模式的过程的重要性给予了

---

① N. V. Djakonova, “Materialy po kul’tovoj ikonografii Central’noj Azii domusulmanskogo perioda”, pp. 257-272.

② M. Compareti, “The Indian Iconography of the Sogdian Divinities and the Role of Buddhism and Hinduism in Its Transmission”, *Annali dell'Istituto Orientale di Napoli*, 69, 1-4, 2009 ; F. Grenet, “Iranian Gods in Hindu Garb: The Zoroastrian Pantheon of the Bactrians and Sogdians, Second–Eighth Centuries”, *Bulletin of the Asia Institute*, 20, 2010, pp. 87-99.

③ P. Riboud, “Réflexions sur les pratiques religieuses designées sous le nom de xian”, in *Les Sogdiens en Chine*, ed. É. de La Vaissière, É. Trombert, Paris, EFEO, 2005, pp. 73-91.

④ M. Taddei, “Non-Buddhist Deities in Gandharan Art. Some New Evidence”, in *Investigating Indian Art*, Berlin, 1987, pp. 349-362.

批判性的再次考量。① 佛教通常善于接纳并融合当地神祇（不仅有印度教的还有来自中亚的——主要是琐罗亚斯德教神祇），因此我们可以假设在于阗也发生了同样的情形。伟大的于阗语研究专家 H. Bailey 以类似的方式提出，当佛教传入时，当地的琐罗亚斯德信仰形式出现了一些问题。②

对比丹丹乌里克木板画的三人组合神像，莫德考察了片治肯特 III/6 号房间的 8 世纪早期粟特壁画上表现的三座祭坛。在其中一座祭坛上出现了一幅多臂神的图像，因为这一崇信对象必然代表风神 Weshparkar，其图像（正如已观察到的）已被粟特人塑造成湿婆的形象。因此莫德认为在另一祭坛上的神祇有可能是丹丹乌里克木板画中的娜娜和另一位男性神祇。后者应当被比定为 Adbagh，他是粟特人对《阿维斯陀》中主神阿胡拉·马兹达（Ahura Mazda）的特定表现形式。在丹丹乌里克木板画中，Adbagh 的形象以帝释天为基础，所以他的象征动物是大象，以通常画在神祇一只手中的金刚（vajra）为标志。

一些文献资料对部分地佐证上述假说颇有帮助。在涉及 7 世纪至 8 世纪的中国文学作品中，据说组成粟特地区的不同城邦的国王习惯于坐在具有象征性动物造型的王座之上。布哈拉（Bukhara，汉语文献称“安国”）国王坐在一个骆驼形的王座上，骆驼很可能是当地宗教的重要角色。在出土于不同考古遗址的一些陶土小塑像残片中，可以观察到一位持火祭坛的男性神祇坐在一匹骆驼上，更有意思的是，在瓦拉赫沙（Varakhsha）“东厅”的彩绘祭坛上也看到了同样的图像，这一地点被鉴定为 8 世纪布哈拉国王的居所。③ 在粟特地区主要考古遗址片治肯特和撒马尔罕的阿夫拉西阿卜（Afrasyab）发现了大量陶土制成的粟特神祇小塑像。坐在大象宝座上的一位男性神十有八九会被比定为 Adbagh/阿胡拉·马兹达，因为正如上文所指出的，这位神祇是粟特地区对印度教神灵帝释天的叠印表现。④

粟特与印度神祇的这种关联可以在中国西域发现的粟特文书中得到证实，而且这种联系是在一个完全是佛教的环境中产生的。对于这份粟特文书的文本分析似乎指明这一在湿婆和风神之间的图像比定遭遇了一场挑战。⑤ 此类关联至少可在一个例证中被正确考量：我们可以通过在片治肯特壁画中其腿上的题铭而明确认定该神正是风神 Weshparkar（图 4）。

---

① F. Grenet, “The Second of Three Encounters between Zoroastrianism and Hinduism: Plastic Influences in Bactria and Sogdiana (2nd-8th Century A.D.)”, *Journal of the Asiatic Society of Bombay*, James Darmesteter (1849-1894) Commemoration Volume, 69, 1994, pp. 41-57; M. Compareti, “The Indian Iconography of the Sogdian Divinities and the Role of Buddhism and Hinduism in Its Transmission,” *Annali dell'Istituto Orientale di Napoli*, 69, 1-4, 2009, pp. 175-210; F. Grenet, “Iranian Gods in Hindu Garb: The Zoroastrian Pantheon of the Bactrians and Sogdians, Second–Eighth Centuries”, *Bulletin of the Asia Institute*, 20, 2010, pp. 87-99.

② H. W. Bailey, *The Culture of the Sakas in Ancient Iranian Khotan*, p. 1. 根据藏文文献 Prophecy of the Li Country，在于阗的佛教徒与非佛教徒之间产生的这些“问题”与不肯信奉文明宗教的 7 位国王有关，他们在尉迟毗利耶之前统治于阗。又见荣新江：《丝绸之路与东西文化交流》，北京大学出版社，2015 年，第 318—329 页。据《唐书》记载，于阗人崇奉“天国之神”与佛陀。沙畹（Chavannes）确信无疑地将“天国之神”比定为琐罗亚斯德教神祇，É. Chavannes, *Documents sur les Tou-Kiue (Turcs) Occidentaux*, Paris, 1903, p. 125.

③ V. A. Shishkin, Varakhsha, Moskva , 1963: fig. 76; C. Silvi Antonini, “Ob odnom siuzhete v zhivopis’ dvorca Varahshi”, in *Ancient and Mediaeval Culture of the Bukhara Oasis*, ed. C. Silvi Antonini, D. K. Mirzaakhmedov, Rome, Samarkand, 2006, pp. 50-54.

④ M. Compareti, “La Sogdiane et les ‘Autres’. Élements d’ emprunts extérieurs dans l’ art sogdien pré-islamique”, in *Asie centrale. Transferts culturels le long de la Route de la soie*, ed. M. Espagne, S. Gorshenina, F. Grenet, Sh. Mustafayev, C. Rapin, Paris, 2015a, pp. 229-239.

⑤ G. Gnoli, “Some Notes upon the Religious Significance of the Rabatak Inscription”, in *Exegisti Monumenta. Festschrift in Honour of Nicholas Sims-Williams*, ed. W. Sundermann, A. Hintze, F. de Blois, Wiesbaden, 2009, pp. 146-149; A. Wendtland, “Xurmazda and Aδbaγ in Sogdian”, in *From Daena to Din. Religion, Kultur und Sprache in der iranischen Welt. Festschrift Ph. Kreyenbroek*, ed. Ch. Allison et al., Wiesbaden: Harrassowit, 2009, pp. 111-125.

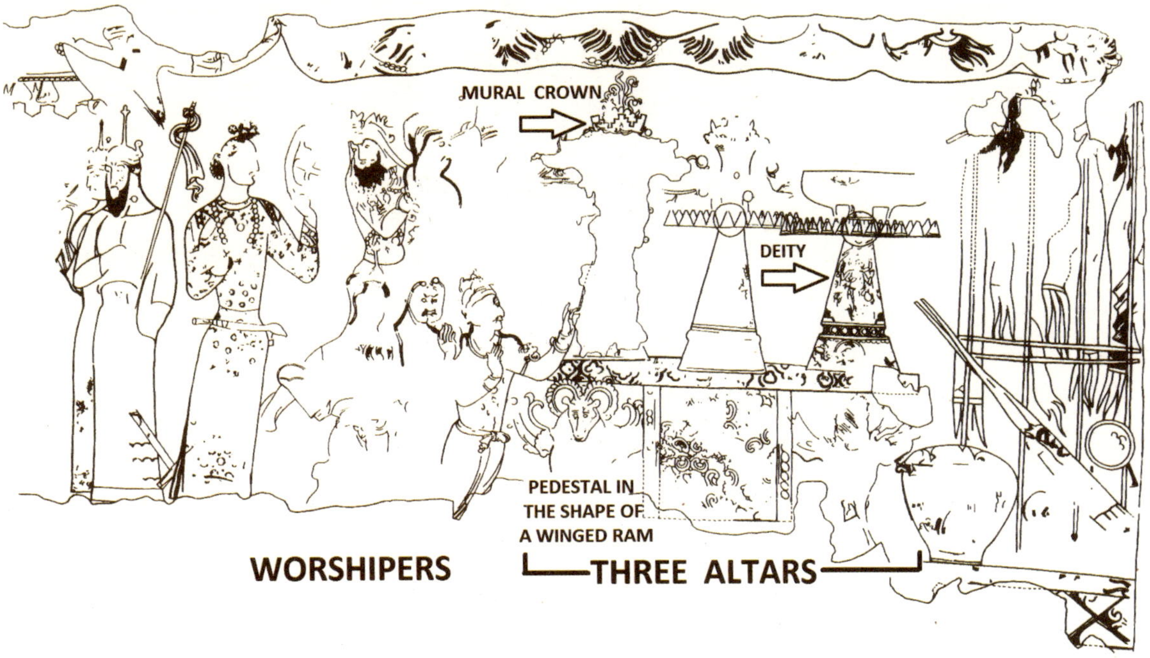

图 4　8 世纪早期片治肯特 6 号房址第 III 区粟特壁画线描图（艾尔米塔什博物馆）：向火祭坛致敬的粟特人

除去风神在粟特的身份识别问题及他与湿婆的联系，为什么粟特的娜娜女神应该与 Adbagh 和风神一并组成这幅三人组合神像画的缘由也不为人所知。实际上，马尔沙克更倾向于将片治肯特 III/6 号房间壁画的三座祭坛看作专门献给三位男性神祇：Adbagh、祖尔万（Zurvan）和风神 Weshparkar 的。①莫德注意到有可能是献给女神娜娜的祭坛上方有雉堞状的王冠，这在中亚艺术中实际上被视作对娜娜的表现，其程式化的造型也出现在丹丹乌里克木板画的女神头上。尽管娜娜女神在中亚人民心中享有很高的地位②，粟特艺术书面文献及其他证据的欠缺均提示我们在做这样的联系之时应采取极度谨慎的态度，因为绘于墙上的王冠也被用于不代表娜娜女神的波斯艺术中，粟特统治者采纳了萨珊王冠的诸多元素（展开的翅膀、新月等），萨珊波斯的神祇也可能由嚈哒人在整个中亚地区迅速传播开来。③

另外需要注意的是，如果奉献给某位特定的粟特神 / 女神的祭坛图像中，某位神祇拥有最好的装饰，那么片治肯特 III/6 号房间壁画中支撑三座祭坛的有翼公羊又扮演了什么样的角色呢？如上文观

---

① A. M. Belenitskii, B. I. Marshak, "The Paintings of Sogdiana", in G. Azarpay, *Sogdian Painting. The Pictorial Epic in Oriental Art,* Berkeley, New York, London: University of California Press, 1981, p. 31.

② 娜娜一定是片治肯特乃至整个粟特地区最受尊崇的神。F. Grenet, B. I. Marshak, "Le mythe de Nana dans l' art de la Sogdiane," *Arts Asiatiques*, 53, 1998, pp. 5-18. 她也在大夏 (D. Potts, "Nana in Bactria", *Silk Road Art and Archaeology*, 7, 2001, pp. 23-35.) 和花剌子模受到崇拜 (M. Minardi, "A Four-Armed Goddess from Ancient Chorasmia: History, Iconography and Style of an Ancient Chorasmian Icon", *Iran*, LI, 2013, pp. 111-143.)。

③ M. Compareti, "The Representation of Foreign Merchants in the Pranidhi Scenes at Bäzäklik", in *Proceedings of the 5th Conference of the Societas Iranologica Europaea. Volume I. Ancient & Middle Iranian Studies*, ed. A. Panaino, A. Piras, Milano: Mimesis, 2006, p. 369; E. Kageyama: Mimesis, "The Winged Crown and the Triple-crescent Crown in the Sogdian Funerary Monuments from China: Their Relation to the Hephthalite Occupation of Central Asia", *Journal of Inner Asian Art and Archaeology*, 2, 2007, pp. 11-22.; S. Hiyama, "Study on the First-style Murals of Kucha: Analysis of Some Motifs Related to the Hephthalite' s Period", in *Buddhism and Art in Gandhara and Kucha Buddhist Culture along the Silk Road: Gandhara, Kucha, and Turfan*, ed. A. Miyaji, Ryukoku, 2013, p. 130,135.

察到的，动物形状的王座或基座（正如此例证中）应该暗示了它们所要承载的神祇或王室人物的象征动物。此外，我们尚不完全明了同一画面里一座祭坛上多臂神的身份，所以不能排除他是另一位“印度教服饰”里的粟特神祇，而并非确指湿婆或风神。

三　于阗佛寺绘画中的神祇

新近于阗佛寺绘画的发现吸引了来自世界各地学者的关注。一些研究致力于探讨出现在佛像及供养人之中的神祇，因为在一些例证[①]中他们的衣着有明确的印度特征，更难以捉摸的是，那些绘在木板上的神祇图像甚至很有可能是献给当地神庙的。[②]

正如前文所述，莫德认为于阗佛寺画中身着印度服饰的神祇是粟特人引入的。然而并不是所有的与于阗佛寺画中佛陀图像一起出现的神祇都可做根植于印度文化艺术的解读，并且同样与娜娜女神相关联的女神的在场愈发清晰地指向了在于阗有相当具体的伊朗元素。莫德注意到了一位骑马或骑驼有头光的神祇，它被称为所谓的“丝绸之神”（此神也曾被他人比定为《列王纪》的主要英雄鲁斯塔姆，Rustam[③]），另一位神则身处两匹相对的马之后。决定这样的神祇是否由于粟特人在塔里木盆地的活动（莫德的假说）而有了一些“与伊朗的接触”，还是他们实际上只是当地神祇，并不是一件容易的差事。而表达关于于阗在前佛教时代的信仰的假设则更为困难，因为文献和考古证据都相当稀少。

（一）手持日月的女神（娜娜女神？）

娜娜是一位美索不达米亚女神，她出现在伊朗神祇中有可能是阿契美尼德王朝时期对中亚扩张的结果[④]，甚或是在更早的年代由西亚传入伊朗文化圈的[⑤]。如果娜娜就是上文所讨论的木板画所表现的女神，那么我们就不能排除她经由贵霜钱币、印章和其他艺术品而到达于阗，因为她正是贵霜货币中所表现的主要女性神祇。在一段很长的时间跨度内，木板画和金属制品由域外（印度、大夏、克什米尔、吐蕃等地）被引入于阗，这一过程实际跨越了于阗佛教王国的整个存续期。[⑥]

---

① C. Lo Muzio, “Culti Brahmanici a Khotan: note sulle pitture del tempio D13 a Dandan Oiliq”, *Rivista degli Studi Orientali*, 79, 1-4, 2006, pp. 185-201；陈粟裕：《从于阗到敦煌——以唐宋时期佛教图像的东传为中心》，北京：方志出版社，2014 年，第 12—13，18—20，27，35，39，55，83，117，141，148 页；E. Forte, “On a Wall Painting from Toplukdong Site no. 1 in Domoko: New Evidence of Vaisravana in Khotan?”, in *Changing Forms and Cultural Identity: Religious and Secular Iconographies. South Asian Archaeology and Art*, ed. D. Klimburg-Salter, L. Lojda, Turnhout: Brepds Publishers, 2014, pp. 215-224；张惠明：《公元 6—8 世纪于阗佛教护法神系中的散脂夜叉图像》,《艺术史研究》第 17 辑，2015 年，第 205—244 页；C. Lo Muzio, “Skanda and the Mothers in Khotanese Buddhist Paintings”, in *Interaction in the Himalaya and Central Asia: Processes of Transfer, Translation and Transformation in Art, Archaeology, Religion and Polity*, ed. E. Allinger, F. Grenet, Chr.Jahoda, M.-K. Lang, A. Vergati, Vienna, 2017, pp. 71-89.

② N. V. Djakonova, “Materialy po kul’tovoj ikonografii Central’noj Azii domusulmanskogo perioda”, pp. 257-272.; J. Williams, “The Iconography of Khotanese Painting”, *East and West*, 23, 1-2, 1973, pp. 109-154.

③ B. Rowland, *The Art of Central Asia*, New York: Crown Publishers, 1974, p. 128.

④ M. A. Shenkar, *Intangible Spirits and Graven Images: The Iconography of Deities in the Pre-Islamic Iranian World*, Leiden, Boston, Brill, 2014, p. 119.

⑤ D. Potts, “Nana in Bactria”, *Silk Road Art and Archaeology*, 7, 2001, pp. 30-31.

⑥ E. Forte, “A Journey ‘to the Land on the Other Side’: Buddhist Pilgrimage and Travelling Objects from the Oasis of Khotan”, in *Cultural Flows across the Western Himalaya*, ed. P. McAllister, C. Scherrer-Schaub, H. Krasser, Vienna, Verlag der Österreichischen Akademie der Wissenschaften, 2015, pp. 151-185.

大夏在贵霜王朝统治中亚这一地区期间和之后与于阗保持了相当重要的关系。① 因此我们可以很显然地想到塔里木盆地南部居民对贵霜的宗教图像是了然于胸的，尽管贵霜钱币的铸造与丹丹乌里克佛寺画的完成中间相隔了约 5 个世纪。然而在于阗，很长一段时间内关于某些贵霜统治者的记忆有可能依旧鲜活，这一点有名为“Kanishkavadana”的文学作品为证。这部书是献给最负盛名的贵霜君主，同时也是佛教最大的保护者迦腻色伽（Kanishka）王的。②

中日联合考古队在丹丹乌里克的最新考古发现之前不久，同一佛教遗迹里其他一些壁画得到了修复。这批新壁画的发现者鲍默（C.Baumer）试图用莫德建立的方法，即从伊朗学观点识别这些佛寺中表现的神祇。鲍默提出对身着印度服装的神祇身份的比定——尽管后来他做出了修正 ③——是应该被摒弃的，因为事实上他们被证明本来就是印度的神。④ 这一点在一个佛教语境中是很明显的。出于这一原因，虽然丹丹乌里克木板画上的神祇图像与中亚的娜娜女神非常相像，木板画的另外两位神祇则可被比定为印度教神祇，很可能左边是帝释天—金刚手菩萨（Indra-Vajrapani），右边是湿婆。另外值得一提的是，在西北印度（一个总能找到伊朗文化元素的地域）贵霜帝国覆灭之后，娜娜女神依然享有很高的知名度，她拥有一头狮子作为特定坐骑 ⑤，不应被混同于其他印度教神祇。

关于于阗佛寺画中女性神祇的表现，尚有最后一点值得考察，即鲍默发现的丹丹乌里克同一佛寺的壁画中，至少可以从两幅壁画里看到身处印度衣着的其他神祇之中，有一位手托一个或多个小孩的女神。目前尚无法完全明了这两幅图中是否为同一个女神诃利帝母（Hariti ?，又名鬼子母）⑥，尽管她手中的小儿可以清晰地将她区别于丹丹乌里克木板画中以手托日月为特征的女神。事实上，如果后者有可能被比定为娜娜女神，就可以排除其图像中小孩的存在，因为在接纳了这位女神的其他族群诸如高度伊朗化的亚美尼亚人中，孩子的出现十有八九是与女神安娜希塔（Anahita）相关联的。⑦

将丹丹乌里克的这位女神比定为娜娜是高度值得商榷的。她在墙上的王冠并未得到很好的保存，而且在于阗佛寺的其他绘画如 CD4 号寺院东墙壁画中也可观察到有高处的手臂托举日月的神，他们均有可能表现的是其他印度神祇。

（二）丝绸之神

关于丝绸之神，在粟特艺术中并未发现对应的神祇（图 5）。因而莫德不得不去辨识这位神在当地的地位。他暗示其他学者将此神比定为鲁斯塔姆仅仅是一种武断的假设，从而拒绝了这一观点。尽管其四只手臂和拉长的耳垂明确指向对印度元素的借用，丝绸之神的特征仍然令人难以界定。他的形象只能在现藏于大英博物馆、艾尔米塔什博物馆和新德里国家博物馆的丹丹乌里克木板画

---

① V. Hansen, *The Sik Road: A New History*, pp. 47-48.

② M. Maggi, “Khotanese Literature”, pp. 364-365.

③ Ch. Baumer, “Dandan Oilik Revisited: New Findings a Century Later”, *Oriental Art*, XLV, 2, 1999, pp. 2-14.

④ C. Lo Muzio, “Culti Brahmanici a Khotan: note sulle pitture del tempio D13 a Dandan Oiliq”, *Rivista degli Studi Orientali*, 79, 1-4, 2006, pp. 185-201.; C. Lo Muzio, “Skanda and the Mothers in Khotanese Buddhist Paintings”, p. 73.

⑤ M. Ghose, “Nana: The ‘Original’ Goddess on the Lion”, *Journal of Inner Asian Art and Archaeology*, 1, 2006, pp. 97-112.

⑥ C. Lo Muzio, “Culti Brahmanici a Khotan: note sulle pitture del tempio D13 a Dandan Oiliq”, p. 192; C. Lo Muzio, “Skanda and the Mothers in Khotanese Buddhist Paintings”, pp. 71-89.

⑦ M. Compareti, “Armenian Pre-Christian Divinities: Some Evidence from the History of Art and Archaeological Investigation”, in *Studies on Iran and the Caucasus: In Honour of Garnik Asatrian*, ed. U. Bläsing, V. Arakelova, M. Weinreich, Leiden, Brill, 2015, pp. 193-204.

图 5　7—8 世纪丹丹乌里克许愿木板画（大英博物馆）："丝绸之神"

上找到。①

来自于阗的其他几块木板画呈现出了有同一位神出现的奇怪场景。对某些学者来说，这些场景暗示了关于丝绸文化传入于阗的传说：一位来自已经知晓制丝工艺的邻国的公主嫁给了当地国王［确切地说是尉迟迟耶（Vijaya Jaya）］。② 据这一传说所描述的，公主将蚕茧藏在头饰中，而木板画中也的确有一个人手指着一位头戴王冠可能是女性的人物。丝绸之神通常坐于王座之上，他的多只手臂持有各种制丝工具，监管丝绸生产的全过程。

在他的重构假说中，莫德将这位神祇高举的右臂中的物体描述为一把勺子而不是缫丝工具。③ 这是一个非常有趣的细节，因为在 A. Naymark 和 T. Mktrychev 对粟特人纳骨瓮的研究中，他们提出在琐罗亚斯德教祭祀中一位腰带内别有勺子的神，可被比定为 Adbagh/ 阿胡拉・马兹达。④ 在 A. Naymark 和 T. Mktrychev 的这一考察之前，至少在一件粟特纳骨瓮上，这位一手托碗和一头风格化小象的神祇并未得到正确的解读。⑤ 如上文已经提到的，大象实为帝释天的象征动物，后者的形象也是粟特神 Adbagh 的图像基础。而于阗木板画表现的丝绸之神并没有大象，还应注意的是，在绘有她和其他两位男性神祇的画面里，娜娜女神的狮子坐骑也没有出现。我们并不清楚莫德为何仅仅根据丝绸之神手中的一把勺子就重建这一比定的假说，这看起来颇像一个武断的决定，而且也不与 Adbagh 相匹配。

木板画中被称为"丝绸之神"的角色毫无疑问是一位神：因为他有四只手臂，这是源自印度传统的一个特征。此外，将其与一位真实的当地神灵或来自粟特的神祇相关联还是颇成问题的。否决"粟特引入说"的一个很好的论据在于至少出现在三处神祇服装上的绿色：一处是现藏大英博物馆由斯坦因发现的木板画，另两处则是保存在艾尔米塔什博物馆的两块木板画。⑥ 从粟特本土片治肯特的多处例证看来，绿色从未出现在粟特壁画里。⑦ 于阗佛寺画的诸多其他神祇大量使用绿色，这种情况哪怕

① N. V. Djakonova, "Materialy po kul'tovoj ikonografii Central'noj Azii domusulmanskogo perioda", pp. 257-272., fig. 1, 5; J. Williams, "The Iconography of Khotanese Painting", pp. 109-154., fig. 57-64.

② 据玄奘和 the Prophecy of the Li Country 记载，这位公主是中国人：É. de La Vaissière, "Silk, Buddhism and Early Khotanese Chronology: A Note on the Prophecy of the Li Country", *Bulletin of the Asia Institute*, 24, 2010, p. 86.《唐书》记述了同样的故事：É. Chavannes, *Documents sur les Tou-Kiue (Turcs) Occidentaux*, p. 126.

③ M. Mode, "Sogdian Gods in Exile. Some Iconographic Evidence from Khotan in the Light of Recently Excavated Material from Sogdiana", *Silk Road Art and Archaeology*, II, 1991/92, pp. 179-214., fig. 17c.

④ T. Mktrychev, A. Naymark, "Ossuary", in *Culture and Art of Ancient Uzbekistan*, ed. K. A. Abdullaev, E. V. Rtveladze, G. V. Shishkina, Moscow, Tashkent, Внешторгиздать, 1991, pp. 64-70.

⑤ F. Grenet, "L'art zoroastrien en Sogdiane. Études d'iconographie funéraire", *Mesopotamia*, 21, 1986, pp. 97-131: fig. 47.

⑥ M. A. Stein, *Ancient Khotan: Detailed Report of Archaeological Explorations in Chinese Turkestan*, pl. LXI; Catalogue Tokyo, 1985, pp. 102-103. 指明绿色是与这位神相结合的颜色是不可能的，因为在某些木板中他衣服上的色彩已经褪尽。例证参见：M. A. Stein, *Ancient Khotan: Detailed Report of Archaeological Explorations in Chinese Turkestan*, pl. LXIII。

⑦ N. Lapierre, "La peinture monumentale de l'Asie centrale soviétique: observations techniques", *Arts Asiatiques*, 45, 1, 1990, p. 34.

是在移居塔里木盆地的粟特艺术家中也是非常罕见的。

（三）骑马的神祇

莫德在一些其他木板画和来自吐鲁番的丝绸画上找到了与骑马神祇相似的表征。在那幅丝绸画上，此神身着一副盔甲。他与丹丹乌里克骑马神祇唯一的共同点在于他举起的手中有一只碗，一只黑鸟正冲碗飞去（图 6）。莫德提出将这些图像与一位粟特神相联系，后者装饰在一个来自 Yakkabag（也被称为“Khirmantepa”，纳骨瓮①）的 7 世纪纳骨瓮上，一同出现的还有女神娜娜。在他看来，这只是毗沙门天王（Vaishravana）经由粟特艺术改造后的另一个面相。在关于于阗国建立的佛教传说中，毗沙门天王发挥了重要作用，于阗艺术中对他的表现相当常见。②

这一身份比定也是颇有问题的，但非常清晰的是粟特艺术中的其他图像以鸠摩罗（Skanda/Kartikkeya，又名“世建陀”）为基础，这位印度教战神的动物坐骑是孔雀，以手中有一只公鸡和一张弓箭为特征。Yakkabag 纳骨瓮上身着盔甲的神祇高举的一只手中有一只鸟。而他众多手中的两只手又举着一张弓箭。弓箭似乎是《阿维斯陀》雨神 Tishtrya 的独有特征，Tishtrya 至少有一次和娜娜一起出现在片治肯特 XXV/12 房间的 8 世纪粟特壁画里。③ 令人好奇的是，在那幅壁画中，他坐在一座由龙支撑的宝座上。从天文学—占星术的角度来看，Tir（Tishtrya 在粟特地区的名字）与水星相联系，在其他文化中他也有明确的对应物，人们常将他与埃及的托特神（Thoth）、希腊的阿波罗和古叙利亚—美索不达米亚的 Nabu 神（在《圣经》中被称为 Nebu）相比对。④ 这些神祇中，Nabu 神绝对是最有意思的一位。他在美索不达米亚地区是非常重要的神，被视为巴比伦众神首领马杜克（Marduk）之子，并且在某些文化传统中也是娜娜的丈夫。⑤ 有时他被表现为与其象征物——龙一起出现，龙也是他父亲马杜克的象征物。⑥ 出于这一原因，Nabu 继续被粟特艺术家表现为与娜娜一齐现身，至少在片治肯特（XXV/12 房间）的一幅壁画中他被描绘成坐在由龙支撑的宝座上。来自极度古老的美索不达米亚文化艺术的范型，仍然在粟特得以传承，观察一下这种现象是非常有趣的。正因为此，在 Yakkabag 纳骨瓮上与娜娜在一起的身着盔甲的神的身

图 6　7—8 世纪丹丹乌里克许愿木板线描图（大英博物馆）：骑马神祇

---

① M. A. Shenkar, *Intangible Spirits and Graven Images: The Iconography of Deities in the Pre-Islamic Iranian World*, fig. 112.

② G. Yamazaki, “The Legend of the Foundation of Khotan”, *Memoirs of the Research Department of the Toyo Bunko*, 48, 1990, pp. 55-80.

③ F. Grenet, G.-J. Pinault, “Contacts de traditions astrologiques de l’ Inde et de l’ Iran d’ après une peinture des collections de Turfan”, *Comptes Rendus de l’Académie des Inscriptions et Belles Lettres*, 4, 1997, p. 1058; M. A. Shenkar, *Intangible Spirits and Graven Images: The Iconography of Deities in the Pre-Islamic Iranian World*, fig. 110.

④ A. Panaino, Tištrya, *Vol. II. The Iranian Myth of the Star Sirius,* Rome: Is. M. E. O., 1997, p. 47-85.

⑤ A. R. Millard, “Nabû”, in *Dictionary of Deities and Demons in the Bible*, ed. K. van der Toorn, B. Beckig, P. W. van der Horst, Leiden, Boston, Köln, Brill, 1999, pp. 607-610.

⑥ J. Black, A. Green, *Gods, Demons and Symbols of Ancient Mesopotamia: An Illustrated Dictionary*, London, British Museum Press, 1992, p. 134.

份只能是 Tishtrya，而不是毗沙门天王。

此外，莫德将于阗神祇视为毗沙门天王的身份比定，至少有两个原因使其看似更不正确。第一，丹丹乌里克木板画上的骑马神祇并没有身穿盔甲，而毗沙门天王从来也不是一名骑马者。第二，有一块被称为“Skrine A”的木板（图 7），展现出有两只黑鸟围绕着的骑马神，与一位身着盔甲的神在一起，后者可以轻易被识别为毗沙门天王。在两位神之间、树的左侧，残缺不全的题字写有绘图者是谁，但是其姓名已经残损。不幸的是没有其他题字留存至今。左边站立的人物具备毗沙门天王的一切特征，如有头光、持矛、左手持一圆顶佛塔。在同一块木板右边，骑马的人物也可以被视为一位神祇，因为他头部后面有头光。他也戴一顶王冠并骑着一匹花斑马，这种花斑马还可在丹丹乌里克的其他木板画中看到。但是这里他手上并没有碗，而且黑色的鸟是两只。无论如何，同样的神似乎不会出现两次，还骑在马上身披盔甲。所以此处意欲表现的很有可能是两位不同的神，只有披甲站立者可被比定为毗沙门天王。

图 7　7—8 世纪丹丹乌里克许愿木板画（来自斯克林收藏）：站在骑马神前面的毗沙门天王

A. 斯坦因曾出版了丹丹乌里克佛寺壁画呈现出的一组骑马男性形象行进的图像（图 8），他们中不止一位骑在花斑马上，这些马与丹丹乌里克木板画中的马极为相似。这些行进的骑者通常处于佛教图像的下方，这大概暗指他们位低一等的身份。另外值得注意的一点是，在神祇队伍行进起始的地方，又产生了一个扑朔迷离的场景：一个男孩正在接近一个似乎沐浴中的裸女，后者正保护着自己的裸体。尚不清楚这是否是佛教传说中关于于阗王国建立的故事的变体，这一传说被载于西藏和其他地方的文献中。[①]

图 8　丹丹乌里克遗失壁画：神话场景？

新近在丹丹乌里克 CD4 寺院（图 9）和达玛沟 2 号寺院（图 10）的考古发掘中，与佛教图像一起出现了更多上面绘有骑马者手端着碗的壁画残片，他们骑马行进，每个人物上方都有一只黑鸟。这些神祇均有头光，马则有不同颜色：白底黑点、全白或淡红棕色。丹丹乌里克 CD4 号寺院北墙上有一个颇为有趣的发现，位于骑者之一身旁的于阗文题记提到了神秘的“八天神”（eight spirits，图

① G. Yamazaki, “The Legend of the Foundation of Khotan”, pp. 55-56.

11）。①

图 9　丹丹乌里克 CD4 号寺院东墙壁画：行进的骑马神祇

将“八天神”作粟特神祇考虑是颇为困难的，因为在粟特本土的撒马尔罕、片治肯特、瓦拉赫沙及其他遗迹里并没有相似的壁画。此外，这样一组神祇在文献中也无处提及。而且数字“八”在伊朗世界里并不意味着大量财富。在波斯伊斯兰文学中，“八天堂”（Hasht Behesht）的故事曾迅速变成一个老生常谈的主题，但并没有明确证据显示类似的故事存在于萨珊波斯。② 八天神的记载或许是一种可以在中国文化中找到的佛教元素，因为与波斯的情形相反，数字“八”在中国文化里（不仅仅是在佛教语境中）有极高的重要性。

因此，这样的图像在塔里木盆地其他人群的宗教（以佛教为主）艺术产品中是全然未知的。如果不是有上文讨论的吐鲁番绿洲出土的那件丝画，看上去冲着骑者的碗飞去的黑鸟并不能构成任何与之对照的语境。③ 在贵霜货币中，身披盔甲有鸟相伴的神，据大夏题记一定被比定为 Yima。莫德

图 10　达玛沟 2 号寺院壁画：行进的骑马神祇

① 我希望感谢罗马大学“La Sapienza”的 Mauro Maggi 教授，他关于这一题铭的解读完全证实了之前的译文。于阗文题铭可以读作：“供养人 Budai 要求在那里画上八天神。祈愿他们保佑他。”

② M. Bernardini, “Hašt Behešt”, in *Encyclopaedia Iranica*, XII, ed. E. Yarshater, Costa Mesa, Mazda Publishers, 2003, pp. 49-51.

③ M. Mode, “Sogdian Gods in Exile. Some Iconographic Evidence from Khotan in the Light of Recently Excavated Material from Sogdiana”, p. 186.

图 11　丹丹乌里克 CD4 号寺院北墙壁画：骑马神和于阗文题记

已经探讨过 Yima 的图像与 Yakkabag 纳骨瓮上有盔甲的神祇之间的联系。在 F. 葛勒内看来，毗沙门天王的形象有可能在粟特与 Yima 的形象有交叠现象，这不仅因为两者皆身穿盔甲，而且他们都代表北方。事实上，在佛教里毗沙门天王是北方的护法天王，而根据琐罗亚斯德教规，人们把 Yima 当作阴间意指北方也就是地狱的神。① 不仅如此，Yima 从未被描画成骑在马上，手中也从未托碗。

粟特神祇手中经常托有一只盘子，上面有象征这位神祇的特定动物。但是在于阗艺术中并未发现此类图像。尽管出现得很神秘，黑色飞鸟还是将这些图像指向了当地的渊源，也不排除来自天文学—占星术的解释可以与之匹配。数字“八”很显然可以使人联想到古代（也包括伊朗的）发光体行星系统，或者组成这一系统的拟人化形象：太阳、月球、水星、金星、火星、木星、土星和地球本身或引起日蚀的龙（Ketu）。② 此外，丹丹乌里克绘画和题记都没有得到很好的保护，所以，我们尚不明了题铭是否明确提及在某些画面中，骑者似乎多于八个。③

骑马神祇有一个非常有意思的对照物，这一对照物可以在离于阗不远的山普拉出土的织物残片中找到，这些织物被断代于公元纪年之初。④ 在一件图案更复杂的毛毯残片中，装饰有反复出现的狩猎场景（图 12），猎者正张弓射向他面前的怪兽图像，在猎者所骑的马的尾巴上方有一只鸟盘旋在猎者身后。虽然猎者身份不明，但这些织物残片很可能是当地前佛教时代民间信仰的反映。它们尤其使人联想到年代晚得多的片治肯特的粟特壁画（VI/41 房间），这组壁画被比定为鲁斯塔姆的事迹。那些

---

① F. Grenet, “Yima en Bactriane et en Sogdiane: nouveaux documents”, in *Yama/Yima. Variations indo-iraniennes sur la geste mythique,* ed. S. Azarnouche, C. Redard, Paris, Collège de France, 2012, pp. 83-94.

② A. Panaino, “Cosmologies and Astrology”, in *The Wiley-Blackwell Companion to Zoroastrianism,* ed. M. Stausberg, Y. Sohrab-Dinshaw Vevaina, A. Tessmann, Chichester, John Wiley & Sons, Ltd, 2015, pp. 235-257.

③ 李翎：《佛教与图像论稿》，北京：文物出版社，2011 年，第 40—41 页。我感谢 Kira Samosjuk，她友善地提示我注意现藏于艾尔米塔什博物馆的一幅出自 Khara Koto 的 13 世纪西夏唐卡，上面有围绕着中心人物 Kubera/ 毗沙门天王的 8 位骑者 (*Sulla via della seta. L'impero perduto. Arte buddhista da Khara Khoto*[X-XIII secolo], curator M. Piotroviskij, Milano-Lugano, 1993, cat. 56)。不仅有几匹马头上的装饰元素看去与于阗壁画上的马风格相近，而且唐卡靠下部位甚至还绘有五只杯子的细节，杯内物品看上去像三叉戟或火焰，甚或飞鸟。令人遗憾的是这一细节并不清晰，在介绍目录中关于这些元素仅被描述为“献祭供品”。虽然两者都确信无疑地处于佛教语境中，但我们尚不明了西夏与于阗壁画之间是否存在一定联系。又见张小刚：《天王与夜叉——试释于阗引雁骑行人物的身份》，《艺术史研究》第 17 辑，2015 年，第 183—204 页。

④ E. Bunker, “The Cemetery of Shanpula, Xinjiang. Simple Burials, Complexe Textiles”, in *Fabulous Creatures from the Desert Sands: Central Asian Woolen Textiles from the Second Century BC to the Second Century AD,* ed. D. Keller, R. Schorta, Riggisberger Berichte, 10: Abegg-Stiftung, 2001, pp. 15-45.

图 12 公元前 3 世纪—公元 3 世纪山普拉早期于阗羊毛织物：与一只猎鹰在一起的神话人物正在射猎怪兽

8 世纪中叶的片治肯特壁画，在不止一个方面体现了与山普拉织物残片的联系。[①] 这也不排除于阗人［说一种被专家称为“于阗塞语”（Saka Khotanese）的语言］与其他伊朗东部居民如粟特人有着共同的史诗神话系统，这一系统在伊斯兰时期被波斯文学（如《列王纪》）所吸纳。

然而，这并不代表于阗的骑马神祇应被比定为来自粟特艺术风格的引入。这位于阗神极有可能是一位与粟特神祇有某种相似之处的当地神祇，因为两者有着相同的伊朗（确切地说是东部伊朗）文化背景。对行进中的神祇（或相似的一些神祇）相同的表现方式看起来源自根植于于阗文化的当地传统，而与粟特艺术无关。

（四）相向而立的马身后的神祇

这一天文学—占星术假说也有可能与另一幅于阗绘画中相向而立的马匹后面的神祇有关。

莫德认为这位神祇与贵霜钱币上的一位神有关联，后者骑在一匹双头马上，手握三叉戟，钱币的题铭为“MOOZDOANO”，在他看来，这一题铭有可能是阿胡拉·马兹达的另一个名字。[②] 但是“MOOZDOANO”已被证实是湿婆的一个别称，因为人物特征凸显了手中的三叉戟。双头马可被解释为湿婆的双重性格，“既善良仁慈，又暴躁易怒”，然而这一解释并不能完全令人满意[③]。不仅如此，MOOZDOANO 神骑的是一匹双头马，而我们所讨论的于阗神则与两匹常规的相向而立的马一同出现。

20 世纪初，德国探险家曾来到和田地区一处尚未识别的遗址（可能是丹丹乌里克）进行调查，在此地出土的木板残片上，这位神祇现身于相向而立的两匹马身后。他的整个面孔几乎褪色殆尽，能够清晰区分的只有两匹马的形状（图 13）。这件艺术品曾是特林克勒的收藏，现在与其他一些

① M. Compareti, “Due tessuti centrasiatici cosiddetti ‘zandaniji’” decorati con pseudo-Simurgh”, in *Le spigolature dell' Onagro. Miscellanea composta per Gianroberto Scarcia in occasione dei suoi ottant'anni*, ed. M. Compareti, R. Favaro, Venezia, Privately Printed, 2013, p. 28; M. Compareti, “Ancient Iranian Decorative Textiles: New Evidence from Archaeological Investigations and Private Collections”, *The Silk Road*, 13, 2015.

② M. Mode, “Sogdian Gods in Exile. Some Iconographic Evidence from Khotan in the Light of Recently Excavated Material from Sogdiana”, p. 187.

③ G. Gnoli, “Some Notes upon the Religious Significance of the Rabatak Inscription”, in *Exegisti Monumenta. Festschrift in Honour of Nicholas Sims-Williams*, ed. W. Sundermann, A. Hintze, F. de Blois, Wiesbaden: Harrassowit Verlag, 2009, pp. 146-149.

图 13　7—8 世纪丹丹乌里克许愿木板线描图（不莱梅特林克勒收藏）：相向而立的马后面的神祇

图 14　丹丹乌里克 CD4 号寺院东墙壁画：相向而立的马后面的神祇

来自和田地区的文物一同保存在不莱梅海外博物馆（Bremen Overseas Museum）①。最近在丹丹乌里克CD4号寺院东墙壁画（图13）发现了保存现状好得多的同一神祇的形象。它被刊登在若干出版物上，但尚无特别清晰的照片。②

CD4 号寺院东墙的场景颇为复杂：在反复出现的坐佛图像周围，有一组身份不明的神祇构成的框架，其中在右下角也有一位神祇处于相对而立的马身后。除了这位神祇之外，所有其他神祇都展现出明确的印度特征，而且有确凿论据证明他们正是鸠摩罗，总是与“母亲神”（mothers）一起出现，如果得到适时的崇奉，这些母亲神可以拯救病儿的性命。C. Lo Muzio 曾对这些神祇提出颇具说服力的身份比定，但至于那位处于两匹相对的马身后的神则没有提出任何印度参照物。③ 这是因为参照印度的文化艺术并不能解释该神祇的图像意涵，而且正如上文所探讨的，他的图像也未显示出充分的证据表明其来自粟特的属性。

因为已经有人提出丹丹乌里克 CD4 号寺院北墙的“八天神”题记与天文学—占星术相关，那么显然我们也可沿着这一思路来研究这位处于两匹相对的马身后的神。此外，值得关注的是 CD4 号寺院东墙的同一壁画上具有印度艺术特征的其他一些神祇，在他们处于高处的手中举着太阳和月亮。尽管尚无法将其比定为印度行星神祇的体现，但上述神祇很有可能与天文学—占星术有某种关联。④

天文学—占星术在古代及中世纪占有重要地位。这在伊朗人中也不例外，尽管目前发现的前伊斯

① G. Gropp, *Archäologische Funde aus Khotan Chinesisch-Ostturkestan*, Bremen, 1974, fig. 81.

② Y. Zhang, T. Qu, G. Liu, “A Newly Discovered Buddhist Temple and Wall Paintings at Dandan-Uiliq in Xinjiang”, *Journal of the Inner Asian Art and Archaeology*, 3, 2008, pp. 157-170, fig. 5.

③ C. Lo Muzio, “Culti Brahmanici a Khotan: note sulle pitture del tempio D13 a Dandan Oiliq”, pp. 193-199; C. Lo Muzio, “Skanda and the Mothers in Khotanese Buddhist Paintings”.

④ 对于 CD4 号寺院东墙壁画与身处相向而立的马身后的神一同出现的神祇，故宫博物院的孟嗣徽老师建议予其天文学—占星术的身份比定。这只是另一种可能性，塔里木盆地（正如古代世界任何其他地方一样）显然高度重视天文学—占星术。一幅在吐鲁番地区发现的现存柏林的装饰有黄道十二宫符号的 8—9 世纪的绘画卷轴展露出非常强烈的印度和伊朗元素，F. Grenet, G.-J. Pinault, “Contacts de traditions astrologiques de l’ Inde et de l’ Iran d’ après une peinture des collections de Turfan”, *Comptes Rendus de l’Académie des Inscriptions et Belles Lettres*, 4, 1997, pp. 1003-1063. 该卷轴上并没有与这位处于相对的马后的神祇相像的形象，但应注意到该图上只有黄道十二宫的符号，没有行星的拟人化表现。

兰时代的记述极为罕见。仅在蒙古统治时期（13—14 世纪）之后，在配有丰富插图的波斯语伊斯兰书籍中，才出现了一份很有意思的资料。一些关于伊斯兰天文学—占星术的研究将行星神祇、黄道十二宫符号、二十八宿、黄道十度分度等演绎为数量繁多的图像解释。在罕见的伊斯兰插图文本如现藏法国国家图书馆（波斯第 174 卷）13 世纪的 Daqa'iq al-Haqa'iq 中，可以清晰地看到印度元素的借用与象征性表现行星之间的关联。在诸多例证中，神奇的生物（动物和人）总呈现出多头、多腿、多臂的特征，甚至其手中的标志器物也恰如典型印度神祇所拥有的那样。[①] 虽然天文学—占星术图像在伊斯兰书籍插图中大量扩散，但令人联想到在相对的马匹身后的于阗神的图像看似并不那么流行。

一幅在 1388 年至 1420 年间完成于巴格达的神秘莫测的 Jayalarid 天文学插图文献表现了黄道十二宫和发光天体的拟人化形象（巴黎法国国家图书馆，波斯第 332 卷增补部分），这些图像仅此一例，别无他处可寻。其中有一幅代表太阳（21v. 对页）的图像与于阗壁画里身处相对的马身后的神像极为相似（图 15）。学界尚不确定这一 Jayalarid 太阳图像符号的来源，尽管它很有可能来自中亚，根植于前伊斯兰时代的传统信仰。[②] 虽然每一个线索都指向这一路径，但要确定于阗艺术家的创作是否归因于“中亚图像特征”仍然并非易事。那幅 Jayalarid 手稿中的太阳图（与其他行星或黄道标志一起）绝非来自波斯或粟特图像传统。事实上，在波斯、粟特及其他伊朗地域如巴米扬王国，主要的太阳神是密特拉（Mithra），其重要特点是头后方射线状的光晕、套着马的双轮马车和用马支撑的宝座。[③]

图 15　约 1388—1420 年波斯 Jayalarid 手稿中代表太阳的图像（法国国家图书馆）：太阳的符号化体现

尽管有一段很长的间隔期（约 7 个世纪）将于阗绘画与 Jayalarid 插图书区隔开来，但它们似乎描绘了相似的主题来表现一位太阳神，这一与众不同的神祇的形象符号来自于中亚的某地而不是粟特地区。值得一提的是，在于阗语（如花剌子模语等一些在今帕米尔地区仍在使用的被孤立的东伊朗语一样）中，太阳叫作“Urmaysde”[④]，所以也不能排除莫德提出的那幅图与阿胡拉·马兹达

① M. Barrucand, “The Miniatures of the Daqā'iq al-haqā'iq (Bibliothèque Nationale Pers. 174): A Testimony to the Cultural Diversity of Medieval Anatolia”, *Islamic Art*, IV, 1990-1991, pp. 113-142.

② A. Caiozzo, “Une conception originale des cieux: planètes et zodiaque d' une cosmographie jalayride”, *Annales Islamologiques,* 37, 2003, pp. 59-78.

③ F. Grenet, “Mithra, dieu iranien: nouvelles données”, *ΤΟΠΟΙ,* 11, 1, 2001, pp. 35-58.

④ H. W. Bailey, *Dictionary of Khotanese Saka*, Cambridge: Cambridge University Press, 1979, p. 40; H. W. Bailey, *The Culture of the Sakas in Ancient Iranian Khotan,* p. 29. 在他对 Bailey 著作（1982 年）的书评中，J. Russell 坚持认为这是一个奇怪的现象。在他看来，于阗语将太阳称为“urmaysde”并不意味着于阗人信仰琐罗亚斯德教，而只是更笼统地说明当地信奉一种不易识别的前伊斯兰时代的伊朗宗教。遗憾的是 Russell 的书评发表距今已逾 30 年，连他本人都记不清是出自哪家出版社。我感谢 J. Russell，他在一场私人谈话中确认了他对于阗人宗教信仰的假设。

有一定关联。无论这一图像符号来自哪里，它都极有可能被用来表现伊朗太阳神，而关于这位神的记忆在伊斯兰时代仍旧存续着。如果这一身处相对的两匹马身后的神可视为与阿胡拉•马兹达的当地形式相关的太阳神的表现，那么就有充分证据使人想到前佛教时代于阗的当地宗教与琐罗亚斯德信仰有着某些共同之处。

（五）骑驼的神祇

丹丹乌里克的木板画上还有最后一位神祇：他骑着骆驼，与骑花斑马的神祇同时出现（图 16）。莫德把此神比定为粟特神 Washagn（《阿维斯陀》中的战神 Verethragna），由此他将琐罗亚斯德教神祇与来自瓦拉赫沙东厅彩绘祭坛上骑驼的神相关联。

图 16　7—8 世纪丹丹乌里克许愿木板画（大英博物馆）：骑马神祇与骑驼神祇

手中端着一只碗的神祇也出现了，但是周围并没有鸟。正如骑马神祇那样，在最近出土于丹丹乌里克 CD10 号佛教寺院的壁画残片上也发现了这位神祇。他现身于至少有两位骑驼神祇的行进队伍中（图 17），这一图像紧随佛教画面出现。图中没有任何涉及神的题记，但这一例证也给人一种此风格是由粟特传入的假说并不成立的印象。

如前文所论，骆驼是构成布哈拉国王王座的动物。布哈拉的主神很有可能被用类似的方式而表现。这位神被假定为 Washagn，尽管尚存很多疑点需要学者更为审慎地研究。[①] 既然此处他有可能是 Washagn 的形象，那么他为何又在一个系列场景中被反复描绘两次甚至更多次呢？这种对神祇的表现方式似乎在于阗很常见，而在粟特地区并不常见。

图 17　丹丹乌里克 CD10 号寺院壁画：行进的骑驼神祇

瓦拉赫沙的红厅壁画装饰由三个层次组成（图 18），画面中在粟特本土前伊斯兰时代为粟特人供奉的神祇的象征动物正列队行进。在第一层中，有反复出现的骑着大象的主要人物与比其小得多的随从与豹子和龙搏斗的场景，一些学者将较大的主要人物比定为阿摩 / 阿胡拉 • 马兹达，这一观点遭遇了 A. Naymark 更具说服力的论据的挑战。实际上，他可能是英武的当地国王，其图像特征以佛教原型普贤菩萨（Samantabhadra）为基础，后者并非直接来自印度，而是源自塔里木盆地。[②] 第二层有一些动物和神兽行进的场景，第三层表现了在中间大树两侧成对相向而

① C. Silvi Antonini, "Ob odnom siuzhete v zhivopis' dvorca Varahshi", in *Ancient and Mediaeval Culture of the Bukhara Oasis,* ed. C. Silvi Antonini, D. K. Mirzaakhmedov, Rome, Samarkand, 2006, pp. 50-54.

② A. Naymark, "Returning to Varakhsha", *The Silk Road Newsletter*, 1, 2, 2003, p. 17.

立的动物，并很有可能重复了第二层画面的内容。让我们聚焦第二层的行进队列。只有动物的下部可被观察到，其中一些动物有马鞍和马镫，它们看似都是四足动物，而其他动物则是由鸟、狮的不同部位组合成的神兽，与格里芬（Griffins）或相仿的神异动物相类似。Naymark 提出，此类动物应被比定为当地神的象征，因为当时阿拉伯人已经开始入侵粟特西部地区，所以这些神并未出现在壁画上，况且对当地统治者来说，公开表露对伊斯兰教之外宗教的依附已变得很不安全。

图 18 根据 Boris I. Marshak 复原方案的 8 世纪早期瓦拉赫沙（布哈拉）“红厅”线描图：第二层仅能看到行进中的当地神祇的坐骑

如此看来，瓦拉赫沙壁画并无意表现一列驼队，而是描绘了包括一头（或多头）骆驼在内的不同动物和神兽列队行进的场景。我们的结论是，粟特人曾（极罕见地）用连续画面表现他们的神及其象征动物在一起，而不是同样的神反复出现。此处更有可能的假设是，在丹丹乌里克壁画反复出现在行进队伍中的骑驼神祇大概根植于于阗前佛教时代的当地宗教。

四 结论

本文同意马尔沙克的意见，无论从图像学观点，还是从其程式化元素来看，于阗佛教壁画的神祇图像都很可能指向当地神灵而非粟特神祇。在这些画面中可辨识出非常强烈的伊朗特征，这也许是源于于阗语言文化的伊朗根基，这一点早已被 H. Bailey 等其他学者注意到了。但是莫德的假设依然展现出颇有意思的面相，这些有趣之处可在一些案例尤其是新近发现的和田绿洲壁画中得到精确的体现。

来自丹丹乌里克和达玛沟的绘画为于阗研究呈现了一个重要的发现。它们正如最近出土于山普拉的织物碎片一样，以相似的方式为于阗前佛教时代的信仰提供了一些解释。这一信仰统称为“前佛教信仰”，大概是琐罗亚斯德教在当地的变体，在 1 世纪时于阗统治者很可能还信奉这种宗教，因为它在《李国的预言》中也得到了保存（虽然并不是公开的）。在改宗新的信仰之后，所有那些当地神祇要么以偶像的形式，要么作为连接佛祖或菩萨与信众的“圣人”身份而留存下来。

目前的研究无法对这些神祇给予更精确的身份比定，任何更充分的证据也只能等待在于阗文化一度繁荣过的地区，期待新的、富有启发性的考古发现来达成了。

The Representation of non-Buddhist Deities in Khotanses Paintings and Some Related Problems

Matteo Compareti (Remin University of China)

Abstract: Some deities that do not present Indian peculiarities can be observed very often in Khotanese paintings in Buddhist temples or on votive wooden tablets. They present unique features which render any identification extremely challenging. In the past, scholars developed two theories. According to Markus Mode, these deities could have been introduced by Sogdian immigrants and they should be then identified as Zoroastrian ones. According to B. Marshak, they are possibly local ones and should not be associated to Sogdian gods. In the present study, it will be discussed as Marshak hypothesis seems to be more correct especially in the light of very recent archaeological discoveries in Khotan. However, in some specific case, Mode's hypotheses could be considered accurate.

Keywords: Khotanese painting; Votive wooden tablets; Sogdian painting; Buddhism; Zoroastrianism

入华粟特人葬具上的狩猎图

[德] 魏骏骁（中国人民大学）

摘　要：过去几十年，在中国北部和西部发现了几座确定为入华粟特人的墓葬。其中在一些墓葬中发现了大件的葬具，主要包括围屏石榻和房形石椁。葬具上雕刻有世俗和宗教题材的图像，通过这些图像我们能够管窥这些中亚人在华夏文化圈的生活。

本文探究其中最常见的一类图像的来源，那就是狩猎图。狩猎图起源于中亚和西亚原型的图像，或能够追溯到公元前 9 世纪的亚述王国时期。葬具上的狩猎图明显地反映了来自萨珊波斯和索格底亚那一带等其他地区艺术的影响。中国各地发现的文物上也能看到同样的狩猎图像，根据这些材料我们能了解到狩猎运动早在战国时代就已经十分流行。

粟特人一定熟悉来自于母国和中国的狩猎图的意义。把这些图像融入到他们自己的葬具上，入华粟特人无疑渴望某一天离开这个世界以后仍然能享受图像所象征的场景。

关键词：入华粟特人；粟特葬具；狩猎图

一　介绍

过去几十年，在中国北部和西部发现了几座确定为入华粟特人的墓葬。其中一些墓葬里主要发现了墓志铭和大件的葬具，尤其是围屏石榻和房形石椁。葬具的屏风或石壁往往雕刻有精彩、生动的图像，使我们能够管窥这些来自中亚的祆教徒在华夏文化圈的生活习俗。①

通过对墓志铭的分析和图像的比较研究，这些大部分为 6 世纪中叶至 7 世纪晚期之间的墓葬被认定为入华粟特人的墓葬。笔者共认定了 37 个与粟特人有关的墓葬或现在被国内外博物馆收藏的单独葬具。② 不过，只有那些墓志铭明确记载墓主人为粟特裔的墓葬才能够确认为和粟特人有关。上述 37 个墓葬或葬具之中有 27 个应该能辨认为粟特的。③ 其中 22 个墓葬发现于新疆（如吐鲁番、吉木萨尔和库车地区）和宁夏（如盐池和固原地区）一带；其他 5 个墓葬出土于中原地区，尤其在西安北郊。其他缺少墓志铭的墓葬只能通过比较研究葬具上雕刻的图像来判断该墓葬是否为粟特人的。不过，在

① 关于粟特历史，考古和艺术请参见荣新江，张志清:《从撒马尔罕到长安：粟特人在中国的文化遗迹》，北京：北京图书馆出版社，2004 年；荣新江:《中古中国与粟特文明》，北京：生活•读书•新知三联书店，2014 年；魏义天:《粟特商人史》，桂林：广西师范大学出版社，2012 年。

② 关于这些墓葬和葬具的详细介绍请参见 P. Wertmann, “Sogdians in China: Archaeological and art historical analyses of tombs and texts from the 3rd to the 10th century AD” , *Archaeology in China and East Asia*, 2015, 5。

③ 同上，第 193—195 页，表 1。

这种情况下判定墓主人的粟特身份是较为困难的。

葬具图像所涉及的题材主要包括宗教和世俗两个方面。① 前者显示出入华粟特人的信仰和宗教习俗，其中大部分是涉及祆教的内容，比如祆教祭司在火坛进行拜火祭祀或者审判之桥的画面；世俗题材表现最多的是狩猎和盛宴场景，后者还经常包括奏乐和舞蹈表演的场面。这些世俗题材让我们了解到当时粟特人，也有可能是墓主人本身在中国的生活环境和生活方式。

本文的焦点是狩猎图，这也是葬具上表现最多的一个题材。狩猎图来源于中亚和西亚的文化传统，或能够追溯到公元前 9 世纪的亚述图像原型。粟特人把这些题材融入他们自己的艺术里，这些图像也由此沿着粟特人的贸易路线到达中国及其他地方。在这个过程中，粟特人的艺术结合了不同地方的传统，反映到图像上则为我们提供粟特人与其在旅途中遇到的不同背景人群的文化交流的证据。

中国各地的考古发现，墓葬和石窟里保存下来的壁画都证明，狩猎题材早在战国和汉代就已经出现了。同一时代的文献记载也反映了当时的狩猎活动。② 根据这些材料我们今天能了解到狩猎活动在古代中国也十分流行，它深受帝王贵族和民众的喜爱。狩猎当时不仅仅是一个习俗和娱乐性活动，而且是一种与练兵和祭祀相关的礼制活动。③ 不过，与中亚、西亚一带狩猎图不同的是，在华夏的图像中一般不是统治者或首领当猎手，而是不知名的人。就入华粟特人而言，因为他们受到西亚的影响，他们葬具上狩猎图所描绘的猎手也许是社会地位高的粟特或其他民族的首领。

二　上流社会狩猎的乐趣

What in this world may compare to the pleasures of chase?
To whom does the goblet of life sparkle so rich?
Lying down in the verdure to the sounds of the horns,
Chasing wild deer through the thicket and pond,

Is princely joy, is manly desire,
It strengthens the limbs and flavours the meal.
If forests and rocks surround us in echoing way,
The freer and joyous the filled goblet resounds!

Yo, ho! Tralalalala!

德国作曲家卡尔・马利亚・冯・韦伯（Carl Maria von Weber，1786—1826）的杰作《自由射手》

① 关于宗教题材，参见 F. Grenet, "Religious Diversity among Sogdian Merchants in Sixth-Century China: Zoroastrianism, Buddhism, Manichaeism, and Hinduism", *Comparative Studies of South Asia, Africa and the Middle East*, 2007, 27.2, pp. 463-478; J. A. Lerner, "Aspects of Assimilation: The Funerary Practices and Furnishings of Central Asians in China", *Sino-Platonic Papers,* 2005, p. 168; J. A. Lerner, "Zoroastrian funerary beliefs and practices known from the Sino-Sogdian tombs in China", *The Silk Road Journal*, 2011, 9, pp. 18-25。

② 参见王丽：《唐代狩猎图案及狩猎俑的初步研究》，西北大学硕士学位论文，2012 年，第 43 页。

③ 参见齐东方：《虞弘墓人兽搏斗图像及其文化属性》，《文物》2006 年第 8 期；顾乐红：《汉画像石狩猎图的祭祀意义研究》，《大众文艺》2012 年第 19 期，第 49 页。

（*Der Freischütz*），是德国最早的一部浪漫派歌剧，它戏剧性地描述了猎手在打猎时所感受到的情绪和激情。在森林里追逐鹿的运动被描述为贵族最纯粹的娱乐和渴望，让猎手感觉到极其自由和兴奋。与打猎活动密切相连的是饮酒的行为和盛宴。这些娱乐活动并不仅仅限于欧洲的贵族，同样也是西亚和中亚甚至远至古代中国的一个社会娱乐活动。

粟特墓葬葬具图像里的猎手一般是国王或首领。有的时候他在步行，但更多的时候他是骑在马背上，或者也骑着骆驼、大象等动物。国王狩猎时使用矛、剑、弓箭和绳索等武器。猎物往往为狮子、野猪、鹿、羚羊等。通常，猎手身旁有一只猎犬伴随他。国王只狩猎动物而绝不和其他人搏斗，这与中亚、西亚等地的一些岩壁或金银器上为人们所熟知的图像程式有所不同。在所有的图案中，国王在神授仪式上被加持而成为与猛兽搏斗的胜利者。

图像中的猎手如果是骑马的弓箭射手，我们经常能看到一个特定的姿势：猎手转身脱缰骑在马背上，一手持弯弓，另一手拉满弦，欲射后方的猎物。猎物往往是一只狮子。这种被称为“安息回马箭”（Parthian Shot）的射击技术成为英雄猎手最流行的技能。这种技术非常有效，因为此时射手把箭头直接瞄准向猎物而无须担心马头会妨碍他。公元前 9 世纪的图案证明该射击技术已经被亚述人运用过。不过，据历史记载是罗马战争时期安息弓箭手擅长这种射击技术。①

三　入华粟特人葬具上的狩猎图和外来的影响

除了西安北郊出土的北周康业墓石棺床②、安阳出土北齐石棺床③和山东青州傅家北齐④等画像石，大部分与入华粟特人有关的葬具包括西安北周的安伽墓石棺床⑤和史君墓房形石椁⑥，在日本美秀美术馆收藏的浮雕⑦和甘肃天水石马坪的石棺床⑧都至少娴熟地展现出一个狩猎图。在这方面，山西

① J. Curtis and N. Tallis, J., *Forgotten Empire - The world of Ancient Persia*, London, British Museum Press, 2005, p. 230.

② 西安市文物保考古所:《西安北周康业墓发掘简报》,《文物》2008 年第 6 期，第 14—35 页；郑岩:《逝者的“面具”——再论北周康业墓石棺床画像》,《艺术史研究》2010 年第 2 期，第 7—14 页。

③ G. Scaglia, “Central Asians on a Northern Qi gate shrine”, *Artibus Asiae*, 1958, Vol. XXI, pp. 9-28； G. Gabbert, *Buddhistische Plastik aus China und Japan. Bestandskatalog des Museums für Ostasiatische Kunst der Stadt Köln*, Wiesbaden, Steiner, 1972； O. Sirén, *Chinese Sculpture from the fifth to the fourteenth century*, Vol. II, Bangkok, SDI Publications, 1998； A. Schlombs, “Miniaturtorbauten eines Totenbettes”, in *100 Jahre Museum für Ostasiatische Kunst Köln, Das Herz der Erleuchtung – Buddhistische Kunst in China 550-600*, 2009, pp. 132-136； S. Priewe, “Das Zhangdefu-Sargbett – Grundlegende Fragen erneut gestellt”, *Ostasiatische Zeitschrift*, 2009, 17, pp. 15-24.

④ 夏名采，山东省益都县博物馆:《益都北齐石室墓线刻画像》,《文物》1985 年第 10 期，第 49—54 页；夏名采:《青州傅家北齐线刻画像补遗》,《文物》2001 年第 5 期，第 92—93 页；郑岩:《魏晋南北朝壁画墓研究》，北京：文物出版社，2002 年，第 236—284 页。

⑤ 陕西省考古研究所:《西安北郊北周安伽墓发觉简报》,《考古与文物》2000 年第 6 期，第 28—35 页；陕西省考古研究所:《西安北周安伽墓》，北京：文物出版社，2003 年。

⑥ 杨军凯:《石刻上的粟特人》,《文明》2004 年第 8 期，第 102—115 页；杨军凯:《北周史君墓》，北京：文物出版社，2014 年；西安市文物保护考古所:《西安市北周史君石椁墓》,《考古》2004 年第 7 期，第 38—49 页；西安市文物保护考古所:《西安北周凉州萨保史君墓发掘简报》,《文物》2005 年第 3 期，第 4—33 页。

⑦ 美秀美术馆，*Miho Museum: South Wing*, Shigaraki, Miho Museum, 1997；美秀美术馆，“Eleven Panels & Two Gate Towers with Relief Carvings from a Funerary Couch”, 2009. http://www.miho.or.jp/booth/html/doccon/00001115e.htm； A. L. Juliano and J. A. Lerner, “The Miho Couch Revisited in Light of Recent Discoveries”, *Orientations*, 2001, 32.8, pp. 54-61.

⑧ 天水市博物馆:《天水市发现隋唐屏风石棺床墓》,《考古》1992 年第 1 期，第 46—54 页；姜伯勤:《天水隋石屏风墓胡人“酒如绳”祆祭画像石图像研究》，收入《中国祆教艺术史研究》，北京：生活・读书・新知三联书店，2004年，第155—170页；宋莉:《甘肃天水石棺床年代考》,《西北美术》2006 年第 1 期，第 44—47 页。

太原市晋源区出土的隋代虞弘墓[①]的石椁，因总共包括13幅狩猎图和两幅野兽搏斗图，对本文研究有特殊价值。与前文所提及的其他葬具不同，虞弘墓石椁上所描绘的图案受到非常强烈的外来文化的影响，这充分显示出墓主人和波斯文化的密切关系。虞弘本人不是粟特人，但他的母国虞国和索格底亚那有共同的文化背景，即可能存在于阿姆河和锡尔河之间的文化区。[②]

安伽墓、史君墓、美秀美术馆及天水石马坪石板上的狩猎图像都有很多相似之处。这些狩猎图像有的雕刻在一整块石板上，有的则雕刻在分割后的单块石板上，如安伽墓正面屏风第二幅图或史君石堂西壁第三幅上部狩猎浮雕。所有狩猎图所描绘的繁茂植被、岩石、山脉和云彩等自然景色都指示着狩猎在山区或森林里进行。浮雕上的猎手一般是自上而下地排列，他们奔跑的方向相同或相反，岩石及其他自然景色不但具有装饰作用，而且有助于把石板上的画面分成几个部分。

安伽墓石屏围榻上总共有四个狩猎图，左侧屏风第二幅有两个（图1）[③]，正面屏风第二幅的下半部（图2）[④]和右侧屏风第一幅各有一个（图3）[⑤]。按照猎手的发型和衣服等装饰风格能推测他们大多数是来自于索格底亚那一带。不过，有些猎手的外貌则显示他们来自于别处，比如右侧屏风第一幅狩猎图有两位猎手应该是突厥人。[⑥]画面下部另外一位猎手头后飘带上扬，左手拿着盘卷的绳索。根据马尔夏克先生的推测，这个人也有可能是粟特的一位王子。[⑦]所有这些猎手骑在奔跑的马上。他们穿上类似中亚草原风格的衣服，包括紧身长袍和靴子。马身上都装备了马鞍、马鞯等马具。

图1 安伽墓石屏围榻左侧屏风第二幅上的狩猎图

图2 安伽墓石屏围榻正面屏风第二幅下半部的狩猎图

图3 安伽墓石屏围榻右侧屏风第一幅上的狩猎图

安伽墓石屏围榻所描绘的猎手都坐在奔跑的马上。他们狩猎的工具包括弓箭、矛、剑、绳索和棍子。猎物有野山羊、公羊、鹿、野猪、虎、狮子等动物。在中亚原型图像所反映的狩猎图中，野猪和狮子的狩猎是最典型的。在这方面，安伽墓石屏正面第二幅下半部的狩猎图突出显示了来自古代伊朗

① 山西省考古研究所、太原市文物考古研究所、太原市晋源区文物旅游局:《太原隋虞弘墓》，北京：文物出版社，2005年。

② 张庆捷:《虞弘墓志中的几个问题》,《文物》2001年第1期；Yu Taishan（余太山），“A Hypothesis on the Origin of the Yu State”，*Sino-Platonic Papers,* 2004, p. 139.

③ 陕西省考古研究所:《西安北周安伽墓》，北京：文物出版社，2003年，第23页。

④ 同上，2003年，第28页。

⑤ 同上，2003年，第35页。

⑥ 同上，2003年，第36页。

⑦ 美秀美术馆，*Miho Museum: South Wing, Shigaraki*, Miho Museum, 1997；美秀美术馆，“Eleven Panels & Two Gate Towers with Relief Carvings from a Funerary Couch”，2009. http://www.miho.or.jp/booth/html/doccon/00001115e.htm；A. L. Juliano and J. A. Lerner, “The Miho Couch Revisited in Light of Recent Discoveries”，*Orientations,* 2001, 32.8, p. 36.

原型的因素。图上有一位粟特弓箭射手，他腰带上挂着一个长的弓箭袋。猎手脱缰骑在奔跑的马上，左手持弯弓，右手拉满弦，欲射前方扑来的狮子。在他的下面还描绘了另外一位猎手。他双手持枪刺向野猪。

右侧屏风第一幅上有一位短发的骑马猎手。他回首注视着身后攻击的狮子，举持短刀准备全力地刺向野兽。猎手的姿势又让我们联想起萨珊银盘上类似的狩猎图。

狩猎是当时伊朗和中亚上流社会非常流行的一项社会活动。国王每次招待贵宾的时候，他经常会带着他们外出打猎。这种娱乐活动无疑是当时对贵宾表示尊重和尊敬的有利方式。同时，国王通过打猎活动也展示了他的至高无上的地位、权力和财富。这种活动显然是在安伽墓石屏围榻右侧屏风第一幅上显示的。图上刻画了一位狩猎狮子的粟特首领和三位异域的猎手。

美秀美术馆浮雕和天水石马坪石棺床围屏上也有类似的狩猎图。偶尔，猎手上方还能看到飞行的鸟，有的是衔绥鸟。这种被称为 hvarnah，基于中亚的原型图像，象征吉祥和神圣荣耀的形象。另外，猎犬也是一个非常流行的图像。在入华粟特人的葬具上和索格底亚那一带的壁画中也都能发现它，比如片治肯特遗址发现的 7 世纪的一幅壁画（图 4）①。

美秀美术馆一块石板上雕刻出一幅典型的驱猎场景（图 5）②。图中有四位弓箭猎手并骑着马。猎手们头上都带上类似于花冠的装饰，最上边的一位身上还束着一条飘带。他们的装饰，尤其穿着的胸襻使人联想到萨珊的图像。四位弓箭射手都脱缰骑马，将弓瞄向鹿和野山羊。第三石板下半部有另外一幅狩猎图。图中有两位骑马的突厥弓箭射手和猎犬在追逐野猪和鹿。

天水石马坪石棺床左侧屏风第一幅描绘在山林的背景前进行的狩猎场景：两位射手和猎犬正在猎杀一只老虎和鹿（图 6）③。图像上部的山林中有一位身穿甲胄的骑马人，他似乎在从山林中察看图像下部所描绘的狩猎场景。

史君墓石堂上所雕刻的狩猎图中有一些令人瞩目的细节：石堂西壁第三幅左侧图中有两位猎手，一位是骑马弯弓射箭的猎手，其后一侍者左手上举着一只隼（图 7）④，他们与猎犬一起在驱赶

图 4　片治肯特遗址公元 7 世纪壁画上的猎犬

图 5　美秀美术馆石板上的驱猎场景

图 6　天水石马坪石棺床左侧屏风上的狩猎场景

① 作者拍摄。

② 日本美秀美术馆藏。

③ 天水市博物馆：《天水市发现隋唐屏风石棺床墓》，《考古》1992 年第 1 期，第 48 页。

④ 作者拍摄。

图7　史君墓石堂西壁第三幅左侧图上的两位猎手

五只动物，包括鹿、羚羊、野猪和兔子等。其中的鹿已中箭倒地，其他的正在逃离。弓箭射手的装饰包括胸襻和头上带双翼、类似萨珊风格的花冠。跟随持弓猎手的骑马猎手长有长辫，推测可能是突厥人。一匹马正在从图像右侧进入现场。这表明有更多的猎手在跟进。

更多精彩的狩猎图刻在石堂的东西底座上（图8）[①]。与介绍的上述图像不同，这些狩猎图一般包括一到两位猎手直接与猎物搏斗。在石堂西外壁能看到三位猎手骑着马。从左到右，一位猎手用矛刺杀野猪，其他两位是弓箭射手。其中一位正在使用安息回马箭瞄准一只袭击的老虎。第二位正在与一只奔跑过来的狮子搏斗。猎手之中两位头上戴着双翼的花冠，肩膀披着长的飘带。他们马身上装饰着流苏。与此相反，中间的猎手戴着一个简单的头饰，腰带上挂着一把短剑。石堂东外壁底座也有三位猎手。其中两位携弓箭，一位持矛，猎手们正在驱两头野山羊。弓箭射手是一位短发的粟特人，长发持矛的猎人应该是突厥人。第三位猎手跪在地上，右手持弯弓，左手拉满弦，欲射前方奔跑的鹿。值得注意的是这位猎手戴双角头饰，也许是用来伪装自己，便于更好地接近猎物。

最后，还需要特别关注的是虞弘墓。虞弘墓石堂浮雕里具有数量最多、风格和构图与波斯和中亚一带原型图像最接近的狩猎或搏斗图。石堂内侧、外侧和底座上都有相关图案，图像中通常能看到一位单独的猎手骑着马、骆驼或大象等动物与一只野兽搏斗。石堂的主要石板画面分成两个部分，上面有一幅大的主画面，下面有一幅小的附属画面，人兽搏斗图一般在主要画面上。石板的构图使人联想到索格底亚那一带的壁画，尤其是在瓦拉赫沙城址红殿和片治肯特遗址蓝殿两处发现的壁画。就红殿而言，主要图像中显示着一位骑马的英雄猎手与一只野兽搏斗。下面的底部通常能看到神兽。虞弘墓

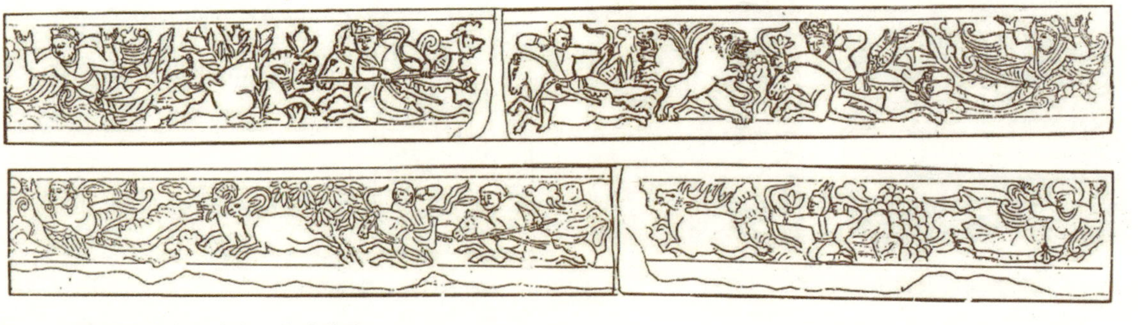

图8　史君墓石堂东西底座上的狩猎图

① 西安市文物保护考古所：《西安北周凉州萨保史君墓发掘简报》，《文物》2005年第3期，第20页。

图 9　虞弘墓石堂墙壁第三幅图骑着单峰骆驼的弓箭射手

图 10　虞弘墓石堂墙壁第四幅图骑着双峰骆驼的长发突厥射手

图 11　虞弘墓石堂墙壁第六幅图的骑象猎手

石堂墙壁第三幅图有一位带光晕的短发弓箭射手，肩膀披着飘带（图 9）①。他骑着一头单峰骆驼，使用安息回马箭射向一只狮子，图中还有一只猎犬，另外一只正在从下方攻击的狮子被单峰骆驼挡住了。狩猎图中的动物几乎围成一个圆圈。这种构图和斯基泰艺术中流行的动物纹饰接近。在石堂墙壁第四幅图的狩猎场景中能看到一位骑着双峰骆驼的长发突厥射手和猎犬（图 10）②。与第一位猎手一样，这位猎手也坐在驼背上射击一只从后面袭击的狮子，另有一只狮子在撕咬这只骆驼的脖子。弓箭手的上方有两只飞鸟，前面的口衔树枝，后面的口衔绶带。这种被认为象征神圣荣耀的图像在中亚一带很流行。第三幅狩猎或搏斗图位于石堂墙壁第六幅中，图像刻画了一位骑着大象的猎手和猎犬（图 11）③。根据猎手的光晕能推测他拥有神圣的身份。他手持两把剑，击刺一只从后面奔跑过来的狮子。猎手的服装和容貌与波斯萨珊摩崖浮雕和银器上所显示的图像十分相似。他有着长胡子和卷发，头戴有飘带的花冠。尤其他穿着以宽松皱褶为特征的裤子使人联想到萨珊类似的图像。大象前面和下面被另外两只狮子袭击，后者被象鼻遮挡了。

石堂里正面屏风下部有两个极其生动而刺激的人狮搏杀图（图 12）④。左侧猎手没有武器，他的头正在被袭击的狮子所吞食，故呈拼命挣扎状。第二位战士的头也已被狮子吞没，不过，他仍右手持剑刺中狮子。这种题材在中国古代传统

图 12　虞弘墓石堂里正面屏风下部的人狮搏杀图

① 山西省考古研究所、太原市文物考古研究所、太原市晋源区文物旅游局：《太原隋虞弘墓》，第 101 页。

② 同上，第 102 页。

③ 同上，第 110 页。

④ 同上，第 106 页。

图 13　虞弘墓石堂左右两侧的狩猎图

图 14　比亚－纳衣曼遗址纳骨器上的拱柱廊结构

图 15　片治肯特木质雕带下骑在狮子上的娜娜女神

图 16　虞弘墓石堂正面外壁左侧的狮牛搏斗图

图 17　虞弘墓石堂里面右侧的狮马搏斗图

文化中难以见到。

第二组狩猎图在石堂的两侧和背面的底部。左右两侧的图是雕刻出来的，原本带有颜色，分上下两部分（图13）①。上半部有连拱柱廊，拱门下有狩猎或搏斗图，底部有壁龛。除了最右边包含一位男人搏斗或驯服一匹双翼飞马的壁龛外，其他壁龛里都是骑马的猎手，其中四位是弓箭射手，他们的猎物包括狮子、鹿、兔子和羚羊或野山羊，大部分的狩猎图里都还有猎犬。除了一位猎手以外，其他的都有光晕，这指示他们拥有神圣的身份，中间有一位长发突厥弓箭射手，其他猎手都是短发的中亚人，拱柱廊的结构和猎手的样子与波斯和中亚一带的原型图像基本一致。比如，连拱柱廊结构曾经在片治肯特出土的木质雕带或在比亚—纳衣曼遗址（Biya-Nayman）也都发现过（图14）②，片治肯特的拱门下有戴花冠的贵族坐在宝座上或娜娜女神骑在狮子上的图像（图15）③，虞弘石堂背面底部图像的风格基本与其相同，不同的是这边的图案不是雕刻出来而是直接画在石堂表面上。除此之外，猎手不是描绘在拱门下而是在壁龛内。

虞弘墓石堂有两个图引起特别的关注。石堂正面外壁左侧浮雕下部和石堂里面右侧浮雕下部各图中能看到野兽之间的搏斗。前者有一幅狮牛搏斗图（图16）④，后者是狮马搏斗图（图17）⑤。值得注意的是，狮马搏斗图中的马前肢生翼，后肢和尾部为鱼状，这就是海马（Hippocampus）。

① 山西省考古研究所、太原市文物考古研究所、太原市晋源区文物旅游局：《太原隋虞弘墓》，第123页。

② 作者拍摄。

③ A. M. Belenitzky and D. V. Belous, *Mittelasien: Kunst der Sogden*, Leipzig, E. A. Seemann, 1980，p. 154. 请参看 A. M. Belenitzky and D. V. Belous, *Mittelasien: Kunst der Sogden*, Leipzig, E.A. Seemann, 1980, p. 192.

④ 山西省考古研究所、太原市文物考古研究所、太原市晋源区文物旅游局：《太原隋虞弘墓》，第114页。

⑤ 同上，第99页。

虽然形成于稍晚的时期，但这些图使人联想起斯基泰艺术中所谓的动物风格。斯基泰艺术中，动物体现特殊的品质，比如敏捷、体力、地位和胜利。① 把这种图像容纳在某一个类似于虞弘石堂的实物上，当时的人们认为这种品质会传递给墓主人。就狮牛搏斗图而言，阿契美尼德时期这种图像就已经出现了，比如公元前 5 世纪波斯波利斯阿波陀那宫殿基墙壁面上雕刻出一幅狮子袭击公牛图。②

伊斯兰时代的细密画表明同样的题材后来还沿用了很长时间。这些插图通常涉及基于更早《卡里来和笛木乃》的《五卷书》里的核心故事。③ 就虞弘墓而言，我们可以从墓志铭来了解他生前因使者的身份与波斯王国有密切的关系。虞弘石堂上发现有这种图像证明他非常熟悉波斯文化和习俗，包括该地区的艺术。由此，虞弘无疑也应该受到波斯文化的影响。

入华粟特人葬具上显示的狩猎图可以一直追溯到美索不达米亚北部的古亚述王国时代（大约前 3000 年—前 608）。在位于现在伊拉克北部一带的尼姆鲁德宫殿和尼尼微宫殿遗址中发现了描绘皇室狩猎的浮雕。其中一些能看到亚述最后一位国王亚述纳齐尔帕一世（公元前 883—前 859 年在位）和皇太子进行猎狮的图像。④ 在古代亚述王国，狩猎狮子被认为是国王的运动，它代表着国王为了保护人民而奋斗的责任。⑤

狩猎题材的另一个起源是公元前 5 世纪至前 4 世纪塞克人或斯基泰人的艺术。例如，西伯利亚南部草原一带发现了一个金质带扣，上面能看到打猎野猪的骑马弓箭射手。⑥ 带扣的年代在公元前 4 世纪至前 3 世纪左右，相当于波斯的阿契美尼德王朝时期。图案的风格和构图与晚期的帕提亚和萨珊王朝甚至与晚期发现的中亚东部乌孙人的遗存有明显的相似之处。另外有两处来自于现在的乌兹别克斯坦南部的发现，第一个是发现在 Takht-e Sangin 遗址（前 4—前 3 世纪）的一批雕刻的象牙牌饰（图 18）⑦，第二个是发现在 Orlat 墓地（1—3 世纪）的一批雕刻的骨头牌饰。两个牌饰上能看到带着明显

① E. Sims and B. I. Marshak and E. J. Grube, *Peerless Images – Persian Painting and its Sources*, New Haven and London, Yale University Press, 2002, p. 7.

② Ibid., p. 285.

③ 这个故事迄今已知有大概二十五个插图，例如 13 世纪晚期或 14 世纪早期 Abu'l-Ma'ali Nasrallah 的一个手稿。在伊斯兰时代晚期的《卡里来和笛木乃》里，围绕狮子，公牛和胡狼的故事是书里的核心故事之一。狮子因为从未见过公牛（Shanzaba），担心它大声地吼叫。为了刻服对它的恐惧，狮子的密友笛木乃（Dimna）建议它应该跟公牛见面。之后，公牛和狮子认识了，很快就成为朋友了。笛木乃变得嫉妒并命令狮子杀它以前的朋友。笛木乃很快就后悔了它的行为而因叛国王受审。请参见：E. Sims and B. I. Marshak and E. J. Grube, *Peerless Images – Persian Painting and its Sources,* New Haven and London, Yale University Press, 2002，pp. 283-284。图案例如参见该书，p. 287。

④ 图片请上大英博物馆官网：http://www.britishmuseum.org/explore/highlights/highlight_ objects/me/s/stone_panel,_nw_palace-4.aspx.

⑤ Historisches Museum der Pfalz Speyer, *Pracht und Prunk der Großkönige – Das persische Weltreich*, Stuttgart, Theiss, 2006，pp. 54-55.

⑥ 狩猎图中有另外一位人隐藏在后面。根据马尔夏克先生带扣上的场面与《沙纳玛》里的一个故事有关的，这就是 Bizhan 打野猪和他朋友 Gurgin 藏在山之中。请参见：E. Sims and B. I. Marshak and E. J. Grube, *Peerless Images – Persian Painting and its Sources,* New Haven and London, Yale University Press, 2002，pp. 103, 105。

⑦ 作者拍摄。请参见：B. A. Litvinsky, “Бактрийцы на охоте” [Bactrians on the hunt], *Memoirs of the Oriental Department of the Russian Archaeological Society (ZVORAO)*, New Series 2002, Vol. I (XXVI), pp. 181-213。

图 18 Takht-e Sangin 遗址发现的象牙牌饰

图 19 Orlat 墓地发现的骨头牌饰

草原特点的骑马人在狩猎鹿、野山羊和老虎（图19）[①]。上述的例子都不显示国王或英雄人物，而似乎只是描绘普通的狩猎者或战士。

波斯人使用过这个题材的原因应该是和他们草原根源有关的。他们在公元前第一个千年早期迁徙到伊朗高原。作为游牧人，他们非常重视马，擅长骑马和在马背上打猎。在他们的艺术中，他们因此就选择了那种品质来表现自己。很有可能他们熟悉亚述和斯基泰的图像而逐渐把它结合在自身的艺术中。[②]

就阿契美尼德人的艺术而言，狩猎图在他们的摩崖浮雕上是找不到的。不过，这个题材出现在别的艺术类型中。比如，年代相当于大流士一世（公元前 522—前 486 年在位）和阿尔塔薛西斯二世（公元前 404—前 359 年在位）时期的阿姆河宝藏中的金质剑鞘。剑鞘上能看到 9 位猎手用长矛或弓箭猎杀狮子。[③] 猎手身穿波斯风格的长袍和头戴高大的头饰，脚上似乎不穿靴子，所骑乘马匹的马鞍下有马鞯，马身上有流苏装饰。[④]

1841 年 C. A. de Bode 男爵在伊朗西南部发现了 Tang-e Sarvak 遗址。它成为埃利迈利王国最重要的圣地遗址之一，在此发现了一批年代为帕提亚帝国时期的石雕（1 世纪—3 世纪）。除了类似于宫廷仪式、战斗与祭仪等题材以外，一块石刻上还发现了两幅狩猎图。第一幅上有一位使用短剑或剑来狩猎野猪的骑马猎手，第二幅上有一位猎手正在勒死一只狮子。[⑤] 按照帕提亚的艺术传统，所有的猎手都是正面地描绘的 [⑥]，他们穿着长袍和宽松的裤子，有的肩膀上还披一件披风。

接下来的萨珊王朝最早的一个狩猎图雕刻在伊朗法尔斯省毕沙普以南 Sar-Mashad 遗址的摩崖浮雕上。该图上能看到萨珊第五位国王巴赫拉姆二世（276—293 年在位）与两只狮子正在进行搏斗的场

---

① 作者拍摄。就 Orlat 墓地牌饰而言，Ilyasov 于 Rusanov 关系到服装和马具。请参见：J.Y. Ilyasov, D. V. and Rusanov, D.V., “A study on the bone plates from Orlat”, *Silk Road Art and Archaeology*, 1997—1998, 5, pp. 107-159。关于 Orlat 墓地牌饰讨论的概述，请参见：M. Mode, “Heroic fights and dying heroes - The Orlat battle plaque and the roots of Sogdian art”, *Ērān und Anērān – Webfestschrift Marshak*, 2003. http://www.transoxiana.org/Eran/Articles/mode.html。

② 请参见：Historisches Museum der Pfalz Speyer, *Pracht und Prunk der Großkönige – Das persische Weltreich*, Stuttgart, Theiss, 2006, pp. 54-55。

③ 图片载于大英博物馆官网：http://www.britishmuseum.org/explore/highlights/highlight_objects/me/c/ceremonial_gold_scabbard.aspx，访问时间：2017 年 2 月 19 日。

④ J. Curtis and N. Tallis, J., *Forgotten Empire - The world of Ancient Persia*, London, British Museum Press, 2005, p. 233.

⑤ 图片请见：E. Haerinck, Tang-e Sarvak, 2005. http://www.iranicaonline.org/ articles/tang-e-sarvak-1。

⑥ Tang-e Sarvak 遗址和雕刻，请参见：E. Haerinck, Tang-e Sarvak, 2005. http://www.iranicaonline.org/ articles/tang-e-sarvak-1。

景。[①] 值得注意的是，国王不只在猎杀狮子，显然也在保护站在他右边并拉着他手的妻子。上述所提到的早期狩猎图能看到善与恶之间的战斗。与此相反，Sar-Mashad 遗址浮雕上的国王还承担着保护妻子的作用。[②] 作为国王的配偶，王后有为国王生育继承人的责任。换言之，她保证王朝的连续性。

到目前为止，没有发现过萨珊王朝的沙普尔二世国王（309—379 年在位）的摩崖浮雕。不过，沙普尔二世的图像能够在银器上找到，比如 1927 年在俄罗斯北部一个窖藏里发现的银盘，该银盘上有骑马的国王使用安息回马箭射向一只狮子的图像。[③] 银盘还有另外一只狮子，第一只攻击国王，第二只被国王的骏马踏死了。与巨大摩崖上的浮雕一样，银盘上的图像象征着授予强大且总是获胜的领袖的神圣荣耀。

萨珊时期最晚的摩崖浮雕之中有受阿尔达希尔二世（379—383 年在位）、沙普尔三世（383—388 年在位）和库思劳二世（591—628 年在位）三位国王委托建造的、保存在伊朗可曼莎塔伊波斯坦遗址中的狩猎图。库思劳二世在位时期的狩猎图有两幅保存至今。其中一幅能看到国王从船上射向一头野猪，第二幅为国王骑马猎鹿。[④] 与沙普尔二世的狩猎图不一样，国王并未穿着象征身份的花冠和胸襻，考虑到打猎时应不使用这些装饰品，图上的描绘是有道理的。虽然如此，国王还是穿着带有精彩图案的、应该是刺绣的丝质长袍，这种衣服在 6 世纪至 7 世纪生活在伊朗以东草原上的突厥人中也很流行。[⑤] 国王有穿着类似衣服的骑马者、侍从和乐师等人随行。

在索格底亚那一带遗址发现的壁画对本文的研究很重要。就 5 世纪至 8 世纪片治肯特遗址的发现而言，尤其是显示骑马者在游行前行或在战斗中的题材，比如蓝殿 VI/41 号庭遗址。[⑥] 该地点发现了包括伊朗英雄鲁斯塔姆故事的图案（图 20）。[⑦] 西壁上能看到两组的全副武装骑马者之间的战斗，踩踏一名战士。

图 20　片治肯特蓝殿 VI/41 号庭遗址的鲁斯塔姆故事图

除了片治肯特蓝殿遗址的战斗图以外，其他房址里还发现了不同的、如狩猎等题材的壁画。比如，在一间原来为两层高、有接待厅的私人别墅里发现了一幅大约 7 世纪的骑马猎手和猎犬图（图 4）。

---

① E. Yarshater, "The Seleucid, Parthian and Sasanian Periods", *The Cambridge History of Iran*, Vol 5 (2), Cambridge University Press 2008，p. 1118；W. Seipel, *7000 Jahre persische Kunst – Meisterwerke aus dem Iranischen Nationalmuseum Teheran*, Wien, Skira, 2001, p. 272. 图片请参见：E. Sims and B. I. Marshak and E. J. Grube, *Peerless Images – Persian Painting and its Sources*, New Haven and London, Yale University Press, 2002, p. 10。

② E. Sims and B. I. Marshak and E. J. Grube, *Peerless Images – Persian Painting and its Sources*, New Haven and London, Yale University Press, 2002, p. 10；E. Yarshater, "The Seleucid, Parthian and Sasanian Periods", *The Cambridge History of Iran*, Vol 5 (2), Cambridge University Press, 2008, p. 1117.

③ 图片请参见：E. Sims and B. I. Marshak and E. J. Grube, *Peerless Images – Persian Painting and its Sources*, New Haven and London, Yale University Press, 2002, p. 105。

④ 图片请参见：http://www.livius.org/ta-td/taqe_bostan/taqe_bostan_large_cave.html, 访问时间：2017 年 2 月 19 日。

⑤ E. Sims and B. I. Marshak and E. J. Grube, *Peerless Images – Persian Painting and its Sources*, New Haven and London, Yale University Press, 2002, p. 10.

⑥ VI 区由三个被走廊关联的部分组成：一间仪式庭 (VI/41)，一间接待庭 (VI/42) 和一间带穹顶的小庭 (VI/55)。

⑦ 作者拍摄。发掘的时候，该庭西北角壁画的高度还是四米。壁画被联珠纹组成的线分成四个横向的部分。

这位猎手穿着一件蓝色的长袍，把弓箭瞄准向他面前的猎物，他头顶上方装饰有菱形的环绕类似于郁金香的图案。猎手的紧身裤子似乎是豹皮质的。一把长剑挂在他腰带上。在 XXIV/7 号庭遗址也发现了一幅相似的图，区别是骑马猎手头上有一只飞行的衔绶鸟。这些发现在私人别墅里的狩猎图其内涵应该跟银器上类似的图案是一致的，这就是财富与吉祥被认为是传递给了房子的主人。

正如我们在片治肯特蓝殿遗址所发现的鲁斯塔姆故事画面能看到的，有的图案基于古代传说、叙事诗或寓言之上，比如菲尔多西的《沙纳玛》或尼扎米的长篇叙事诗《五部曲》等伊朗经典文学作品。有一些考古发现像奥莱尔·斯坦因曾经在敦煌莫高窟第 17 窟发现的描绘鲁斯塔姆的 9 世纪粟特文献证明，伊朗最早的这些著作也包括了主要人物的描述。① 很有可能当时的艺术家使用了这些描述来绘制画中的人物。如银器等其他类型的艺术品证明，这些题材不仅仅是壁画上的题材，上面所提到的北俄罗斯窖藏所出土的沙普尔二世银盘还出土了另外一个银器。② 银盘上能看到萨珊国王巴赫拉姆五世（421—438 年在位）带他妻子阿扎达去打猎的场景。③ 因为国王“Gor”的外号，是波斯语野驴的意思，他也被叫作巴赫拉姆·野驴。

更多的能参考的资料是片治肯特宫殿遗址所发现的木质雕塑和雕带。后者在阿拉伯入侵片治肯特的时候因起火和碳化而幸运地保存下来。④ 这些雕刻上既有装饰又有人物作品。就人物雕塑而言，它们都包括浮雕和圆雕。有的上面能看到由联珠纹围绕的骑马猎手使用安息回马箭射向狮子（图 21）⑤。

除了片治肯特的壁画以外，撒马尔罕阿弗拉西亚卜古城遗址大使厅北壁上的画面提供更多的对比资料（图 22⑥）。壁画左侧能看到唐代公主虚构的一个旅行。她在九位女侍从的陪同下坐在船上，侍

图 21　片治肯特宫殿遗址联珠纹围绕的骑马猎手图

图 22　撒马尔罕阿弗拉西亚卜古城遗址大使厅北壁的狩猎图

① 请参见：S. Whitfield, *The Silk Road: Trade, Travel, War and Faith*, London, Serindia Pubns, 2004, p. 119。

② 图片请参见：E. Sims and B. I. Marshak and E. J. Grube, *Peerless Images – Persian Painting and its Sources*, New Haven and London, Yale University Press, 2002, p. 305.

③ 巴赫拉姆带妻子阿扎达去打猎是巴赫拉姆·野驴传说中的重要场景之一。巴赫拉姆·野驴，这就是萨珊国王巴赫拉姆五世在波斯传统中因他对罗马、突厥和印度人的胜利以及对他的狩猎技巧而闻名。他的名字巴赫拉姆·野驴为他的狩猎技巧给出证据。根据传说，巴赫拉姆为年轻王子的时候和阿拉伯人生活在一起。他们也经常带他去打猎。有一天他骑骆驼准备打猎的时候他妃子阿扎达坐在他后面。阿扎达挑战他作为弓箭射手的技巧，谴责他有恶魔的力量。最终，巴赫拉姆把他妃子从骆驼扔下去并践踏了她。

④ 壁画痕迹尤其是发现在仪式厅里。从 P/2 四柱房出土有灰泥和壁上的画。后者认定的题材其中有围绕衔绶鸟的联珠纹。

⑤ A. M. Belenitzky and D. V. Belous, *Mittelasien: Kunst der Sogden*, Leipzig, E. A. Seemann, 1980, p. 156.

⑥ 作者拍摄。

从或者演奏乐器或者划船。根据《沙纳玛》一书，西突厥射匮可汗请求唐太宗将一个女儿嫁给他，虽然唐太宗答应了射匮可汗的请求，但公主因没有到达西突厥的王廷，婚姻从未发生过。[①] 壁画右侧能看到唐太宗。他骑着马用矛刺杀一只母狮或豹。考虑到他的社会地位，他的形象比其他四位猎手大得多。后者包括两位猎手持着矛，两位猎手拿着弓箭杀狮子或豹等猎物，每一位猎手的艺术风格都相当于早期伊朗或中亚的图案。因为索格底亚那有一段时间在萨珊王朝的统治下，因此能够在他们的艺术作品中找到这个地区的影响是可以理解的。

接下来我还想关注下 5 世纪至 8 世纪瓦拉赫沙城址红殿的壁画。红殿壁画底部能看到一系列反复的、骑在白色大象上的猎手与豹或其他猎物之间的狩猎或搏斗图。这种狩猎图和其构图容易使人联想到古代波斯一带的原型图像。其他方面，尤其是所描绘的英雄的外貌显然起源于印度北部和阿富汗地区古代贵霜帝国和中亚东部。

同样题材更新的例子证明，描绘狩猎图在古伊朗是长久以来的传统，文化意义十分重要。不过，狩猎这个题材不仅仅限制于中世纪时期的艺术，尤其是贵族还继续使用它们很长时间。[②] 比如，在 1427 年来自于阿富汗西部的赫拉特的一本诗和散文集里表现狩猎题材的细密画。图上有骑马的帖木儿的王子拜桑格赫（1399/1400—1433）及随行人员，猎犬和一只鹰一起驱猎。[③] 随行人中有一位正在用箭射向一对山羊，在现场的观众观看他。

另外一个例子证明狩猎图在近代仍被伊朗统治者继续使用。这张图是在伊朗沙太美斯普一世（1524—1576 年在位）尼扎米长篇叙事诗《五部曲》未完成手稿的封面上。该画大约在 1825 年和 1828 年之间受伊朗第二位国王法特赫·阿里沙·卡扎尔（1797—1834 年在位）委托绘制的。[④] 画中的国王是一位骑马的英雄猎手，用矛刺杀一只狮子。国王在为他驱逐鹿和野猪等猎物的侍从的陪同下出猎。

四　中国考古出土文物上的狩猎图

狩猎题材不仅仅限于中亚、西亚一带或者入华异域人的艺术。中国各地的考古发现证明，狩猎题材早在战国和汉代不同文物类型上也已经出现，包括木材、石材、青铜和金银器等材质。[⑤] 中国西北和中原地区包括新疆、青海、甘肃、宁夏、陕西和山西等省在 5 世纪至 8 世纪的考古发现证明，那段时间狩猎图在中国也非常流行。除此之外，墓葬或石窟里的壁画中也都有狩猎图。比如，2013 年在山西忻州市九原岗发现北朝墓葬里中国目前最大面积的一幅狩猎壁画 [⑥] 或者年代在南北朝至隋唐时期之

---

① 据康马泰先生研究，该壁画的内容涉及中国端午节，纪念生活在战国时期楚国而于公元前 278 年自杀的屈原的故事。请参见：M. Compareti, “Further Evidence for the interpretation of the ‘Indian Scene’ in the pre-Islamic paintings at Afrasiab (Samarkand)”, *The Silk Road Journal* 2006-2007, 4 (2), pp. 32-42。

② E. Sims and B. I. Marshak and E. J. Grube, *Peerless Images – Persian Painting and its Sources,* New Haven and London, Yale University Press, 2002, p. 122。

③ 图片请参见：E. Sims and B. I. Marshak and E. J. Grube, *Peerless Images – Persian Painting and its Sources,* New Haven and London, Yale University Press, 2002, p. 108。

④ Ibid., p. 113.

⑤ 齐东方：《虞弘墓人兽搏斗图像及其文化属性》，《文物》2006 年第 8 期。

⑥ 山西省考古研究所、忻州市文物管理处：《山西忻州市九原岗北朝壁画墓》，《考古》2015 年第 7 期，第 51—73 页。

间敦煌佛教石窟里的壁画。[1] 与上述的狩猎图一样，尤其是在墓葬里这些图像用来表现上流社会的日常生活，同时它们也象征墓主人的身份、等级等方面。

图 23　吐鲁番阿斯塔那墓地 101 号墓丝绸残片上的狩猎图

图 24　青海都兰 DRM1PM2 号墓丝绸残片

（一）纺织品上的狩猎图

吐鲁番阿斯塔那墓地 101 号墓发现了一块 5 世纪至 6 世纪之间的丝绸残片（图 23）[2]。上面的装饰是大型的联珠纹各围绕一个图像，其中有大象、狮子、骆驼以及一幅典型的狩猎图。后者是一对对称的骑马弓箭射手使用安息回马箭射向一头鹿。丝绸残片下半部大部分的联珠纹没有保存下来。和在青海都兰 DRM1PM2 号墓发现的一块几乎相同的丝绸残片比较，阿斯塔那丝绸残片下半部的联珠纹里原来应该有古希腊太阳神赫利俄斯的形象（图 24）[3]。不同地方的文化因素在这块丝绸残片上显示出来，包括萨珊波斯的联珠纹、对称的动物形象和使用安息回马箭的骑马射手，以及起源于印度的大象和古希腊神话的赫利俄斯形象。就骆驼而言，这个形象有可能是代表沿着古丝绸之路的贸易网。

图 25　阿斯塔那墓地 191 号墓丝绸上的狩猎图

阿斯塔那墓地 191 号墓还发现了另外一块著名的 7 世纪至 8 世纪早期的染色丝绸。这块丝绸上能看到一幅经典的与前面所述波斯和中亚包括索格底亚那一带风格非常类似的狩猎图。图中有一位骑马的射手正在使用安息回马箭（图 25）[4]。除此之外，图中还有一个驱逐兔子的猎犬，图的上部有一只飞行的鸟。通过马背上写的“飞”字能认识到马应该是皇室饲养的马。[5]

① 参见丛振：《敦煌狩猎图像考》，《石河子大学学报》（哲学社会科学版）2016 年第 2 期，第 21—27 页。

② J. C. Y. Wyatt, *China – Dawn of a Golden Age, 200-750 AD*, New York, Metropolitan Museum of Art, 2004, p. 273.

③ 作者拍摄。

④ J. C. Y. Wyatt, *China – Dawn of a Golden Age, 200-750 AD*, New York, Metropolitan Museum of Art, 2004, p. 342.

⑤ J. C. Y. Wyatt, *China – Dawn of a Golden Age*, 200-750 AD, New York, Metropolitan Museum of Art, 2004, p. 342; Sh. Müller, *Die Gräber der Nördlichen Wei-Zeit (386-534)*, München, Ludwig-Maximilians-Universität München, 2000.

（二）青铜和金银器上的狩猎图

1981 年，山西省大同市发现的 504 年封和突墓出土了一个镀金的银盘，上面有一幅狩猎野猪场景（图 26）[①]。银盘大概生产于现在的阿富汗北部或土库曼斯坦南部的某个地方。这个地区在 6 世纪是在萨珊波斯的统治下。在这个地区发现的几乎相同的其他银盘证实了这个推测。[②] 在大同发现的银盘显示，北魏迁都洛阳后，古都平城仍然继续跟中亚有贸易往来。

1970 年，西安附近的何家村唐代窖藏出土了一批精美的 8 世纪的金银器。[③] 其中发现的杯子和盘子带有明显的外来文化特点，比如多层的表面和联珠纹装饰。尤其是把环杯的风格和表面的图像都使人联想到来自索格底亚那的器皿。比如环把八瓣银杯上有狩猎和奏乐舞蹈图。狩猎图上有一位骑马猎手正在驱逐一只动物，似乎是老虎（图 27）[④]。考虑到它的大小，这杯子很可能不是实用器，而是用于欣赏的。

同样的受波斯或中亚地区影响的图像在别的材质的文物上也出现了，比如龟兹古城皮朗墩遗址曾经采集过的一件铜画押（图 28）[⑤]。画押上雕刻有一位骑象猎手使用安息回马箭射向一只狮子。这幅图和 8 世纪瓦拉赫沙红厅骑象猎豹壁画有相似之处。皮朗墩遗址的那件画押应该沿着古丝绸之路的贸易路线传到了龟兹古国。

另外，陕西省历史博物馆收藏的一个铜镜（图 29）[⑥]。该博物馆另外有一个鎏金铜牌，其上的图像

图 26　山西省大同市封和突墓出土的镀金银盘

图 27　西安何家村环把八瓣银杯上的狩猎和奏乐舞蹈图

图 28　龟兹古城皮朗墩遗址采集的铜画押

① J. C. Y. Wyatt, *China – Dawn of a Golden Age, 200-750 AD*, New York, Metropolitan Museum of Art, 2004, p. 153. 封和突墓出土的银盘上有一位战士用剑打猎一群野猪。与萨珊波斯典型的银盘不同，封和突银盘所描绘的战士不带花冠，所以他很有可能不是国王。不过，尤其是萨珊时期早期（约 3 世纪晚期—4 世纪早期）这种银盘也同时受皇室的王子委托制造的。后者在王国之内担任地方首领。很有可能，封和突银盘上的战士也是这样一位地方首领。就封和突当屯骑驻军首领而言，他也许和来自于西亚的人有某种关系，由此能获得像该银盘之类的奢侈品。请参见考古发掘报告：马雍：《北魏封和突墓及其出土的波斯银盘》，《文物》1983 年第 8 期，第 8—12 页；J. C. Y. Wyatt, *China – Dawn of a Golden Age, 200-750 AD*, New York, Metropolitan Museum of Art, 2004, pp. 152-153.

② 请与 4 世纪晚期至 5 世纪可能在阿富汗生产的萨珊银盘比较。图片请参见：J. C. Y. Wyatt, *China – Dawn of a Golden Age*, 200-750 AD, New York, Metropolitan Museum of Art, 2004, p. 51。

③ 关于何家村唐代窖藏请参见 J. Li and V. Hansen, *The Glory of the Silk Road: Art from Ancient China*, Dayton Art Institute, 2003；齐东方：《唐代金银器研究》，北京：中国社会科学出版社，1999 年；齐东方：《虞弘墓人兽搏斗图像及其文化属性》，《文物》2006 年第 8 期；孙机：《中国圣火——中国古文物与东西文化交流中的若干问题》，沈阳：辽宁教育出版社，1996 年，第 178—197 页。

④ J. C. Y. Wyatt, *China – Dawn of a Golden Age*, 200-750 AD, New York, Metropolitan Museum of Art, 2004, p. 319.

⑤ 祁小山、王博：《丝绸之路 • 新疆古代文化》，乌鲁木齐：新疆人民出版社，2008 年，第 163 页。

⑥ 作者拍摄。

图 29　陕西省历史博物馆收藏的铜镜

图 30　陕西省历史博物馆收藏胡人骑象的鎏金铜牌

图 31　宁夏盐池古峰庄村发现的金质“方奇”

是一位胡人骑象使用安息回马箭技术（图 30）[①]。猎手的姿势显然也使人联想到起源于波斯和中亚图像的例子。大象应该证明了来自印度的影响。

宁夏盐池古峰庄村出土了一件 598 年金质长方并采用镂空装饰制成的隋代“方奇”军用品（图 31）[②]。与上述文物一样，该方奇也显示草原风格的包括一位骑马弓箭射手和两位步行猎手的狩猎图。猎物中有大象和不同的猫科动物以及类似于格里芬的野兽，在中间猎手头上有一只飞鸟。

（三）石质文物上的狩猎图

河北省邯郸市临漳县文管所收藏的一件采集自邺城遗址年代为东魏北齐的石枕上显然也能看到一幅生动的狩猎图（图 32）。[③] 图像背景所雕刻的山丘和树木指狩猎发生在森林或山区里。石枕的左边雕刻有一位弓箭射手骑在飞奔的马上。猎手使用安息回马箭射向两头野猪。野猪的狩猎在中亚原型的图像中是最典型的一种。

图 32　河北省邯郸市临漳县邺城遗址采集的石枕上

（四）壁画和画上的狩猎图

中国境内也有绘制的狩猎图，如在敦煌莫高窟 249 号西魏洞窟里发现的一幅壁画，内有两位猎手在山区骑马射猎。[④] 其中一位使用安息回马箭射向一只狮子类野兽，另外一位正在追逐一群逃离的鹿。

晚唐时期的 156 号洞窟壁画上（约 848—907）有一位射手引弓往前瞄准。[⑤] 他穿着中亚风格的长袍和一条紧身的裤子。在他的腰带上挂着一个长条状弓箭袋。后者的形状和吐鲁番阿斯塔那墓地 188 号墓出土的带木质撑板的弓箭袋实物很相似。阿斯塔那弓箭袋的年代稍微早一点，大约在 7 世纪和 9

---

① 作者拍摄。

② 作者拍摄。

③ 非常感谢中国人民大学毕波副教授向我提示这件石枕和中国人民大学李肖教授为我提供图片。

④ 图片请参见：R. Whitfield et al., *Cave Temples of Mogao – Art and History on the Silk Road,* Los Angeles, Getty Conservation Institute, 2000, p. 58。

⑤ Ibid., pp. 8-9.

世纪之间。[①]弓箭袋的表面描绘有两位骑马的弓箭射手和猎犬在山区打猎。左边的猎手使用安息回马箭技术射向一只老虎，而右边的猎手驱逐一只白色的兔子。猎手们的马背上有圆形的马鞯和马鞍，马具缀有流苏。

五 总结

在山区或森林里进行的上流社会狩猎活动是入华粟特人葬具上最常见的一种题材。骑在马背上或步行的猎手通常无畏地驱逐野兽。猎手使用不同工具来狩猎，包括弓箭、矛、剑、绳索和棍子。猎物中有狮子、野猪、野山羊、兔子和其他野生动物。猎手经常带猎犬随行。

亚述最后一位国王亚述纳齐尔帕一世（公元前883—前859年在位）在古亚述一带的雕刻上已经被描绘成狮子猎手。狩猎狮子被认为是国王的运动，象征他保护人民的责任。正如卡尔·马利亚·冯·韦伯在他创作的《自由射手》歌剧里描述的，看上述的狩猎图就能生动地感觉到猎手进行挚爱的娱乐活动时所扬漾的情绪和激情。这些图引起一种强烈自由和纯原始的感情。在古代波斯，狩猎图中的猎手一般是国王。从猎手在授权仪式所被授予神圣光耀开始，他便成为狩猎或搏斗的胜利者。除了追求个人乐趣之外，狩猎还成为一个很重要的社会活动。狩猎同时也有助于展示炫耀性消费，描绘首领的权力和财富，同时也对贵宾表示尊礼。入华粟特人葬具上狩猎图中能辨认出不同地区和民族的因素。伊拉克北部尼姆鲁德和尼尼微遗址所发现的浮雕上的图像证明其中最早的因素能追溯到美索不达米亚北部的亚述古王国时代（约公元前3000年中叶至公元前608年）。

西伯利亚南部草原一带的考古发现证明，上述的几个狩猎图也似乎受到了公元前5世纪至公元前4世纪塞克人或斯基泰人艺术的影响。很有可能，波斯人熟悉斯基泰人草原风格的图像而逐渐把其中的一些因素结合到他们自身的艺术中。阿契美尼德王朝时期的波斯波利斯阿波陀那类似题材的浮雕支持这个推测，比如狮子和牛之间的搏斗在一定程度上使人联想到斯基泰风格的动物纹饰。

另外一个与入华粟特人狩猎图相关联的似乎是1世纪至3世纪的帕提亚艺术。除了上述伊朗西南部帕提亚时期 Tange Sarvak 遗址所发现的狩猎图以外，同时期狩猎场景中所描绘最多的一个图像是安息回马箭。后者是弓箭射手特定的打猎技术。他骑在马背上转身把箭射向猎物。正如其名称所表明，当归功于来自安息的弓箭射手。不过，公元前9世纪保存下来的图案指示亚述人已经掌握了这项技术。

萨珊王朝时期，所谓的狩猎银盘广泛传播。这些银盘上通常能看到国王成为出色的猎人并狩猎狮子、野猪等强大的野兽。通常，为国王建立了卓越功勋的人被赐予这种狩猎银盘。当时的人们认为银盘所代表的品质会传递给新的物主。作为赠品或奖品，这些狩猎银盘沿着长途的贸易路线到达遥远的地方，且在一定程度上影响当地的艺术。

包括受伊朗第二位国王法特赫·阿里沙·卡扎尔委托，尼扎米未完成的《五部曲》手稿的封面画上的来自于伊朗一带的狩猎图证明，狩猎并不限于古代艺术，而是直到19世纪初在伊朗文化中仍然是十分重要的文化活动。

---

① 图片请参见：V. H. Mair, *Secrets of the Silk Road – An Exhibition of Discoveries from the Xinjiang Uyghur Autonomous Region, China*, California, Bowers Museum, 2010, p. 95。

索格底亚那曾被不同的统治者占领，包括阿契美尼德王朝、帕提亚帝国和波斯萨珊王朝。所有这些统治者明显地影响了粟特文化。索格底亚那所发现的壁画、建筑等遗存证明粟特艺术所受到的异域影响。尤其是片治肯特、阿弗拉西亚卜和瓦拉赫沙城址壁画和木质雕带上狩猎图的结构和风格显示出高度相似之处。

这些题材与粟特艺术相结合，它们沿着贸易路线传播至华夏和其他地方。在这一文化背景下，入华粟特人的葬具上发现这些题材也是很容易理解的。粟特人一定熟悉狩猎图的意义和相关的品质。入华后他们无疑也渴望某一天离开这个世界以后被后代铭记为英勇的首领。达到这个目标的最好办法是把这些题材描绘在他们的葬具上。

最终，上述讨论的狩猎图不仅仅限于索格底亚那和中西亚一带。实际上，中国各地包括丝织品、石器、青铜器、金银器和壁画等诸多 5 世纪至 8 世纪的考古发现证明狩猎图在此也受了同样程度的欢迎。

The Hunting Scenes on Funerary Furniture of Sogdians in China

Patrick Wertmann (Renmin University of China)

Abstract: Over the last decades, tombs attributed to members of the Sogdian community in China were discovered in the north and west of China. Some of them contained large pieces of funerary furniture, in particular screened couches and house-shaped sarcophagi. These were adorned with both secular and religious themes that give insights into the lives of these Central Asians in their Chinese environments.

This paper explores the origin of one of the most frequently depicted themes, i.e. the hunt. The hunting scene can be traced to central and western Asian prototypes that date back as early as the Assyrian kingdom in the 9th century BC. Obvious influences derive, among others, from the arts of Sassanid Persia and the area of former Sogdiana. Identical themes depicted on cultural relics from across China attest to the same popularity of the hunt since the Warring States period.

Sogdians were clearly familiar with the symbolic value and qualities of these motifs both in their homeland and in China. By incorporating them onto their funerary furniture, they must have hoped to enjoy the social values expressed by them even in their afterlife.

Keywords: Sogdians in China; Sogdian funerary furniture; hunting scene

库木吐喇第75窟数码复原及相关壁画题材及题记研究

[日]山部能宜（早稻田大学）　赵　莉（新疆龟兹研究院）
谢倩倩（新疆龟兹研究院）

摘　要： 库木吐喇第75窟是一个方形小窟。该窟正壁上绘有一身坐禅比丘，其周围绘出五趣或六趣的场景。正壁底部有一则题记，严重褪色。我们用数码复原并解读了该题记的部分内容。题记基本的主题是四无量观，阿毗达磨的宇宙论和密教的观想。在右侧壁绘两幅轮回图，已漫漶不清，但用数码复原后的图像则可以显示这两个轮和藏传佛教的生死轮间的密切联系。在左侧壁上，我们复原了前人没有注意到的回鹘文题记。阿不都热西提·亚库甫教授为我们解读了这个题记。我们还复原了在两侧壁底部的供养者壁画和随附的题记。

关键词： 库木吐喇第75窟；数码复原；四无量观；生死轮；回鹘文题记

库木吐喇石窟位于库车县西北约25公里与新和县交界处的渭干河（木扎提河）东岸，北面离克孜尔石窟直线距离约20公里，314国道从其南侧经过。南行大约3公里，有名为库木吐喇的村庄，“库木吐喇”出自维吾尔语，汉译为“沙漠中的烽火台”。库木吐喇石窟是龟兹地区仅次于克孜尔石窟的一处重要石窟群，1961年被列为全国第一批重点文物保护单位。库木吐喇石窟编号洞窟114个，按地理位置分为两区，即谷口区和大沟区，后者也称为窟群区。谷口区位于石窟群南部渭干河流出山口处，靠近314国道。33个洞窟分布在木扎提河东岸崖壁的三条沟谷内。大沟区位于谷口区以北约1.5公里处，由于洞窟所在区域有一条宽约20米的大沟而得名。大沟曲折回转，81个洞窟分布在沟谷内外崖壁上。

大沟区的洞窟大部分集中在木扎提河岸边一带，也有一小部分洞窟散落于背离河流沿山谷的位置。1979年由北京大学考古队发现的第75窟距离石窟主窟群几百米远。①

第75窟平面呈方形，主室面宽156厘米，进深192厘米，高172厘米，纵券顶，前壁左端开拱券顶门道（图1）。

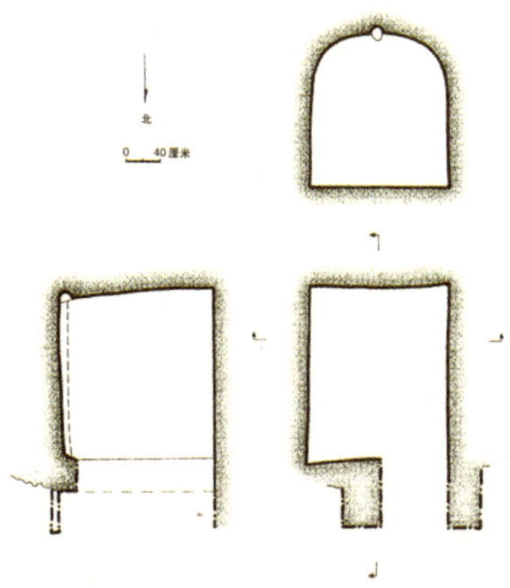

图1　库木吐喇第75窟平、剖、立面图（新疆龟兹研究院绘图）①

正壁绘一幅禅定僧人像，双手捧一钵置胸前。从钵中引出数条墨线连接五道或六道轮回图。两侧壁各绘几列禅定小坐佛、菩萨、僧人像，下部各绘一列供养人像。右

① 晁华山：《库木吐喇石窟初探》，《中国石窟·库木吐喇石窟》，北京：文物出版社，1992年，第183页。

侧壁还绘有两幅轮回图。此外，在正壁和侧壁上有一些题记。早期研究这个洞窟的有晁华山①、马世长②、梁志祥和丁明夷③、贾应逸和买买提·木沙⑤。最近，太史文（Stephen F. Teiser）和森美智代也在探讨这个问题。⑥ 学者们认为该窟是回鹘时期（10—11 世纪）开凿的一个禅窟⑦或是追悼已故僧人的影窟⑧。

由于窟内壁画和题记严重褪色、剥落，导致难以详细观察。新疆维吾尔自治区龟兹研究院与日本东京农业大学合作，将第 75 窟进行了数码复原。这篇文章是此项目的结项报告。⑨

一　正壁

首先让我们来看正壁壁画（图 2）。由于壁画颜料褪色，画面细节在可见光图片下不是十分清晰。但在图像软件加强后的红外线图片中，至少一些线条变得较为清晰（图 3）。⑩ 碳元素吸收红外线，所以壁画中用碳墨绘出的模糊线条常常显现清晰的黑色线。⑪ 同时也会经常消除其他在普通可见光下可见的颜料。⑫ 因此，普通图像和红外图像信息的结合常常是一种

图 2　库木吐喇第 75 窟正壁（可见光）

图 3　库木吐喇第 75 窟正壁（红外线，加强）

① 晁华山：《库木吐喇石窟初探》，第 170—217 页。

② 马世长：《库木吐喇的汉风洞窟》，收入《中国石窟·库木吐喇石窟》，第 211—212 页。

③ 梁志祥、丁明夷：《记新发现的几处洞窟》，收入《中国石窟·库木吐喇石窟》，第 227—229 页。

④ 并参照新疆龟兹石窟研究所编：《库木吐喇石窟内容总录》，文物出版社，2008 年，第 247 页，图 124。

⑤ 贾应逸、买买提·木沙：《历史画廊——库木吐拉壁画研究》，收入《中国新疆壁画全集·库木吐拉》，新疆美术摄影出版社、辽宁美术出版社，1995 年，第 1—26 页。

⑥ Stephen F. Teiser, *Reinventing the Wheel: Paintings of Rebirth in Medieval Buddhist Temples*, Seattle, University of Washington Press, 2006; 森美智代：《クムトラ石窟第七五窟の壁画主題について：ウイグル期亀兹佛教の一側面》，《美术史研究》50(2012), pp. 125-146.

⑦ Teiser, *Reinventing the Wheel: Paintings of Rebirth in Medieval Buddhist Temples*, p. 146；森美智代：《クムトラ石窟第七五窟の壁画主題について：ウイグル期亀兹佛教の一側面》，p. 127.

⑧ 晁华山：《库木吐喇石窟初探》，第 191 页；贾应逸、买买提·木沙：《历史画廊——库木吐拉壁画研究》，第 18 页。

⑨ 这篇论文中的所有图片，除非另有说明，其余都是在 2011—2013 年的实地考察中，由山部能宜和铃木迅一起拍摄的。加强或复原照片的全过程都由山部能宜制作。这项研究受到日本科学研究费（21320014 和 16H05667）的资助。

⑩ 山部能宜对 2011 年拍的照片使用 Adobe Photoshop CS5 进行了处理（那时 Photoshop CC 还未发布）。

⑪ 碳元素吸收红外光，因此含有碳的部分在红外图像下会呈现深色。

⑫ 三浦定俊：《古美术を科学する：テクノロジーによる新发见》，广济堂出版，2001, pp. 16-22; Orna Almogi, Martin Delhey, Claire MacDonald, and Boryana Pouvkova, " Recovering Lost Writing and Beyond: Multispectral Imaging for Text-related and Codicological Studies of Tibetan Paper and Sanskrit Palm-Leaf Manuscripts", *Journal of the International Association of Buddhist Studies*, 36/37(2013/2014［2015］), pp. 165-167.

复原褪色壁画的有效手段（图 4）。[1]

在这张合成图像中，我们可以稍微清楚地观察壁画。僧人手持钵盂，墨线从钵延伸至其周围所绘的各类众生。在正壁的左下方，左边动物（马）的上部[2]，有长条形榜题，但是文字几乎不可辨识（图 5）。[3]

图 4 库木吐喇第 75 窟正壁（加强后的可见光和红外线照片结合）

图5 正壁上的畜生画的题记（可见光）

马世长识别出以下文字[4]：

此□□□□畜生□□□

……乃至〔犛〕□□等。[5]

对于这个榜题，红外线没有起到作用（图 6），可能这些文字不是用碳墨书写的。

然而，加强后的可见光照片，我们能够复原稍微清晰一点的图像（图 7），并且手动加深痕迹，假设复原部分文字（图 8）。[6] 在这些文字中，我们至少可以确定两个字："畜生"（图 6、7）。其余文字几乎都是推测的，但是如果我们的辨识还算可靠的话，那么这则题记列举的是各类动物：

□□〔厉〕畜生〔道〕□□〔兔〕□

〔鸟〕乃至〔蚤尸〕[虫][7]〔虱〕等[8]

〔轮〕　　　〔兀〕[9]

---

① 关于这个方法，参见坂田俊文：《ハイテク考古学》，丸善，1991, pp. 23-27; Gary Hoffmann, *The Application of Spectral Methods of Image Exploitation to Document Restoration*, Final Report, Digital Imaging and Remote Sensing Group and Novel Image Processing and Recording Laboratory, Chester F. Carlson Center for Imaging Science, Rochester Institute of Technology, 2003 (http://www.cis.rit.edu/research/thesis/todo/gdh8512/public_html/thesis/thesis.pdf); L. L. Christensen, R. Fosbury, and R. Hurt, *Hidden Universe*, Weinheim: Willy-VCH, 2009, p. 406, fig. 2-3, 131, fig. 79; 这个方法的更详细的讨论在：Nobuyoshi Yamabe, "Toyok Cave 20: Paintings and Inscriptions", in *Epigraphic Evidence in the Pre-modern Buddhist World*, edited by Kurt Tropper, Vienna: Arbeitskreis für Tibetische und Buddhistische Studien, 2014, pp. 217-261.

② 马世长：《库木吐喇的汉风洞窟》，第 211 页；梁志祥、丁明夷：《记新发现的几处洞窟》，第 227 页。

③ 不确定（推测）识读放于波形括号内；不可见文字基于上下文以存于方括号补充；空白方格表示部分可见但不能识读的文字。下文同此。

④ 马世长：《库木吐喇的汉风洞窟》，第 211 页。

⑤ 梁志祥、丁明夷：《记新发现的几处洞窟》，第 228 页："……畜生…… / ……为……"；庄强华：《库木吐喇石窟总叙》，收入《中国石窟·库木吐喇石窟》，第 272 页："……畜生…… / 为……"。

⑥ 这些方法和技术细节在下文中讨论。

⑦ 这里的"尸"是相当可靠的。"虫"是推测的。"尸虫"即一种以腐烂尸体为食的蠕虫。

⑧ 参见有贺要延：《佛教难字大字典》，国书刊行会，1986，第 234 页。

⑨ 感谢侯冲教授和严耀中教授在辨识题记中给予的帮助。即使在他们的帮助下，这个破译也只是尝试性的。

图 6　库木吐喇第 75 窟正壁左下部的畜生画的题记（红外线，加强）

图 7　库木吐喇第 75 窟正壁左下部的畜生画的题记（可见光，加强）

图 8　库木吐喇第 75 窟正壁左下部的畜生画的题记（可见光，假设复原）

尽管这种识读仍然很不确定，但是由于确定了“畜生”一词，那么这个区域描述的应该是畜生道。

在其上方，我们可以看到一个沸鼎，鼎下有火焰。一个长角的恶魔手持三叉戟立于鼎旁，鼎的架子上似乎有排列的人头。此场景描述的应该是地狱道。《观佛三昧海经》中记载：

狱卒头上有八牛头，一一牛头有十八角。[①]

其上方有七个跪着的身着铠甲的人物，具头光。可能是天人或许是阿修罗（天道或阿修罗道）。

在右下角，绘有两身骨瘦如柴、在火中挣扎的人物。表现的一定是饿鬼（饿鬼道）。在这个画面上方，有四身站立人物，描绘的是人道。在他们上方，绘有须弥山，两侧隐约可见日、月。山顶上看起来像是绘了一座宫殿。这可能是暗指阿修罗攻击帝释天的场景[②]，虽然我们在画面上看不到阿修罗。或者，这可能是对天人的另一描述[③]。因此，依据对此部分的解释，正壁的这幅壁画绘的是五道或六道轮回。在僧人的头部上方，我们看到一棵大树，其上有许多小坐佛。[④]

坐禅比丘周围的轮回画面中众生的布局让我们想起了敦煌的地藏菩萨（图 9—11）。马世长也曾推测：正壁坐着的僧人可能是地藏菩萨。[⑤] 六道或五道轮回的描述很有可能受地藏菩萨像的影响。但

---

① T15:668c15-16 (No. 643).

② 马世长：《库木吐喇的汉风洞窟》，第 211 页。

③ 梁志祥、丁明夷：《记新发现的几处洞窟》，第 228 页。也可以参见森美智代：《クムトラ石窟第七五窟の壁画主題について：ウイグル期龟兹佛教の一侧面》，第 133—134 页。我们也必须考虑在下面讨论的地藏菩萨画（MG. 17793，图 9-10）中右上方的建筑（位置与库木吐喇 75 窟正壁山峦上宫殿的位置一致）有一题记“生天道”（图 10）。

④ 参见新疆龟兹石窟研究所编：《库木吐喇石窟内容总录》，第 246 页；森美智代：《クムトラ石窟第七五窟の壁画主題について：ウイグル期龟兹佛教の一侧面》，第 133—134 页。

⑤ 马世长：《库木吐喇的汉风洞窟》，第 212 页。

图 9　地藏画 (MG. 17793) 局部，法国吉美博物馆，敦煌，10 世纪后半，山部拍摄（可见光，稍加强）

图 10　地藏画 (MG. 17793) 右上部，法国吉美博物馆，敦煌，10 世纪后半，山部拍摄（可见光，稍加强）

图 11　地藏画 (EO. 3580) 局部，法国吉美博物馆，10 世纪，山部拍摄（可见光，稍加强）

是如太史文指出，绘在墙壁上的图像是一个比丘。[①]

树上有坐佛是不寻常的，但是森美智代注意到敦煌壁画中有相似的一棵树（图 12）。

库木吐喇第 75 窟坐禅僧人下方，正壁底端保存有一大幅方形题榜（图 13）。

1979 年洞窟被重新发现时，题记就已褪色、剥落，马世长勉强辨识出[②]：

1. ……………………………无量观门
2. □□界三千大千世界□□□□□
3. ………………作圣四大〔比〕行
4. ……悉□□□使起浊身〔尘〕□
5. ………………………无意识界意识
6. ………………………昏□□□□□
7. ……轮皆次问[③]分为□□放□□
8. ………………广量[④]□□旁□□

图 12　魔鬼来袭画 (EO. 17655) 局部，法国吉美博物馆，10 世纪前半，山部拍摄（可见光，稍加强）

① Teiser, *Reinventing the Wheel: Paintings of Rebirth in Medieval Buddhist Temples*, p. 156, n. 12; 参见森美智代:《クムトラ石窟第七五窟の壁画主題について：ウイグル期龟兹佛教の一側面》，第 130 页以下。

② 马世长:《库木吐喇的汉风洞窟》，第 211—212 页。在贾应逸和买买提・木沙的文章中有非常相似的抄本，见贾应逸、买买提・木沙:《历史画廊——库木吐拉壁画研究》，第 18 页。不同的识读下文也将标出，我们已经添加了行号（以下同此）。

③ 贾和木沙认为是“间”。参见同上。

④ 贾和木沙认为是“度”。参见同上。

9.………………………意想有更为

10. …………白色白光〔势〕及水轮

11. 识下汎[①] 入洛水〔铁〕成水轮□

12.……………金黄色黄光变成金轮

13. ………金轮想自身□□□唵□□

14. ………火轮焚烧不净罪□那[②] 之

15. ……………若见自身身骨即念是

16. ……………无常无我□□□不□

另外一个由梁志祥和丁明夷给出的早期抄本，内容如下[③]：

1. ……………………………………无量观门

2. □□[④] 三千大世界□□□□□□

3. ……………………〔义〕作圣四大〔比行〕

4. ……………〔悉〕[⑤]…使〔起浊〕身[⑥] □□

5. ……………………………□无意识界意识

6. ………………………………〔昏〕[⑦]………

7. ………轮〔皆〕次〔间分〕为放□〔到〕[⑧]

8. ………………………广量□□〔旁〕□□

9.……………………………□〔意〕想有更为

10.…………………白色白光〔变成〕[⑨] 水轮

11. ……〔识〕下汎[⑩] 八洛水〔铁〕成水轮□

12. ………………………金黄色黄光变成金轮

13. ………又金轮想自身〔迦助〕[⑪] □唵□□

---

① 贾和木沙认为是“汎”。参见同上。

② 贾和木沙表明此文字难以辨认。参见同上。

③ 梁志祥、丁明夷：《记新发现的几处洞窟》（中文版），第 228 页；另参见梁志祥、丁明夷：《新発见の石窟について》，《中国石窟 · クムトラ石窟》，平凡社，1985 年（日文版），第 254 页。中文版和日文版的抄本之间有几个重要的不同处。这里我们用日本版的抄本。在庄强华的文章中发现类似抄本，见庄强华：《库木吐喇石窟总叙》，第 272 页。我们已添加行号。

④ 庄认为是“界”。参见同上。

⑤ 庄认为是“〔意〕”。参见同上。

⑥ 庄抄写为“〔使〕起浊身”。参见同上。

⑦ 庄认为是“〔香〕”。参见同上。

⑧ 原抄本中的字体有一点不一样。庄认为是“为□□放□□”。参见同上。

⑨ 庄认为是“〔势及〕”。参见同上。

⑩ 庄认为是“〔讯〕”。参见同上。

⑪ 庄认为是“〔之过〕”。参见同上。

14. ……………火轮焚烧不净罪到①那②之

………………③

15. 若见自身身骨即念是

16. 无常〔我〕……□……不□

然而，由于从那以后题记褪色、剥落更严重，《库木吐喇石窟内容总录》仅记录以下文字④：

1.…………量观门…………

2. …………千世界…………

3. …………作圣四…………

4. …………

5. …………无意识…………

6. ………………………

7. ………………………

8. …………广量…………

9. …………想…………

10. …………白…………

11. …………下水………………轮

12. …………黄…………

13.……………金轮想自身……………

14. ……………焚烧不净那之

15. ………………………

16. ………………………

如果人们看到题记的现存状况（图13），就会明白仅这些的解读实际上已是相当出色的工作。

最近，太史文和森美智代试着辨识此题记内容。他们两个都参观过这个洞窟，并且亲眼看到了题记。由于题记的褪色、剥落情况，他们不得不完全依靠早期记录，没有任何方法确定他们的识读内容。

图13　库木吐喇第75窟正壁下部的题记（可见光）

① 庄认为是“〔罪〕□”。参见同上。

② 梁志祥和丁明夷的抄本有异体字“䣊”，参看龙谷大学佛教文化研究所编：《西域出土佛典の研究》,《附古体字例》，法藏館1980, 71；黄征：《敦煌俗字典》，上海教育出版社，2005年，第283页。庄认为是带有人字旁的“那”。参见同上。

③ 庄没有标明这是空行。参见同上。

④ 新疆龟兹石窟研究所编：《库木吐喇石窟内容总录》，第246页。

根据早期的抄本[①]，关于这个题记太史文提出有两种可能性。第一种假设，他指出题记中提到的轮（盘）接近善无畏（约 637—735）、一行（683—727）汉译的《大毗卢遮那成佛神变加持经》[②] 和一行的注释《大毗卢遮那成佛经疏》[③] 中作为观想对象的宇宙轮。这部经中描述了六种的轮观想，每一类型都要花一个月的时间。[④]

第二种推断，他提出题刻内容可能跟《梵文瑜伽书》（*Yogalerhbuch*）中描述的观想有关。《梵文瑜伽书》是在新疆一些地方（克孜尔、焉耆）发现的一种不知名的梵语禅经。[⑤] 这部经第三章有关六种要素（界）的观想（Dhātuprayoga, 观界），将地轮、金轮、水轮和风轮作为观想对象。[⑥] 这也可能是题刻中所提及的内容。[⑦]

另一方面，森美智代注意到了梁志祥和丁明夷的抄本中所表达的“八洛水”。她认为，“八洛水”就相当于“八洛叉水（八洛叉 =800,000［由旬］)”。在玄奘的汉译本《阿毗达磨俱舍论》（第三章第 45—47 颂）提到水轮的厚度[⑧]：

安立器世间	风轮最居下
其量广无数	厚十六洛叉
次上水轮深	十一亿[⑨] 二万
下八洛叉水	余凝结成金
此水金轮广	径十二洛叉
三千四百半	周围此三倍

在佛教世界观中，世界最底部为风轮。其宽无数由旬，深十六万由旬。风轮之上为水轮，深一百一十二万由旬。其中自底部起的八十万由旬为水，其余部分凝结成金轮。水轮与金轮的直径为一百二十万三千四百五十由旬，周长是其三倍。[⑩]

因此，森美智代得出以下结论：题记内容依据的是《俱舍论》中的宇宙论。相应地，题记中似

① 他基本上用梁志祥和丁明夷的抄本，但几处按照贾应逸和买买提・木沙的抄本修改了。参见 Teiser, *Reinventing the Wheel: Paintings of Rebirth in Medieval Buddhist Temples*, p. 156, n. 13。

② T18: 37a-38a (No. 848).

③ T39: 753b-754a (No. 1796).

④ Teiser, *Reinventing the Wheel: Paintings of Rebirth in Medieval Buddhist Temples*, pp. 156-157.

⑤ Dieter Schlingloff（迪特・施林洛甫）, *Ein buddhistisches Yogalehrbuch: Textband*, Sanskrittexte aus den Turfanfunden, vol. 7, Berlin: Akademie-Verlag, 1964; *Ein buddhistisches Yogalehrbuch: Tafelband*, Sanskrittexte aus den Turfanfunden, vol.7a, Berlin: Akademie-Verlag, 1966; *Ein buddhistisches Yogalehrbuch: Unveränderter Nachdruck der Ausgabe von 1964 unter Beigabe aller seither bekannt gewordenen Fragmente*［再版］, ed. Jens-Uwe Hartmann, and Hermann-Josef Röllicke, Buddhismus-Studien 5, München: IUDICIUM, 2006.

⑥ Schlingloff, *Ein buddhistisches Yogalehrbuch: Textband*, pp. 85-95.

⑦ Teiser, *Reinventing the Wheel: Paintings of Rebirth in Medieval Buddhist Temples*, pp. 157-158.

⑧ T29: 57a8-13.

⑨ 梵文的颂中没有词与汉译中的“亿”直接对应，但是在散文注释中我们发现 lakṣa。在这里 lakṣa 的意思是“十万”。见《阿毗达摩俱舍论》(*Abhidharmakośabhāṣya*), 普拉丹 (Pradhan)，第一版，158.7 以及见《广说佛教语大辞典》该条目：洛叉。

⑩ 定方晟：《须弥山と极乐：佛教の宇宙观》，讲谈社，1973 年，第 13 页。

乎有说一切有部的背景。① 关于这一点，她指出金轮、水轮和风轮出现在都勒都尔—阿乎尔发现的与《梵文瑜伽书》(被认为是说一切有部的)有密切关系的写本中的禅观描述。②

另外，她对《梵文瑜伽书》的以下段落加以注目③：

> [ta]t[o] m ū rdhno [rat]n(amayo vṛkṣo) ’naṃtāṃ lokadhātūn spharitvā tiṣṭhati / tasmiṃ vṛ[k]-(ṣ)e ghanapa[t](r)aśākhāsu Buddhā dṛśyamte dharmaṃ deśayaṃtaḥ taṃmukhaniḥsṛtai [rat]na[p]u[ṣ]-papadmavarṣair [n]ān(ā)varṇair loko (vyava)[k](ī)ry(a)te / vṛkṣamūlāni ca vaiḍūryābhāny antaḥsuṣirāṇi (ca)... y(o)gācārapādatalaiḥ kāṃcanacakre pratiṣṭhitāni dṛśyante /
>
> 然后(宝树)从〔水晶人〕头部竖立，遍及无穷世界。在这棵树繁茂的枝叶上，可见诸佛说法。多彩的宝雨、花雨和莲花从他们〔佛〕口中洒落在世界上。空心树根闪亮如琉璃，连同(?)修行者脚底建立在金轮之上。④

森美智代指出，这一段让人联想起壁画里从禅定僧人头部长出的树，以及树上的坐佛(见图 4 [上部])。因此她断定在所有可以查阅的佛典中，与此幅壁画最为密切相关的就是《梵文瑜伽书》以及有关的禅经。⑤

太史文和森美智代的这些观点非常重要，我们从中受益匪浅。同时，他们的研究也存在一定的局限性。我们首先应该想到，太史文和森美智代仅仅依据早期抄本，并且不能确定他们的识读是否背离原题记。而且，两者都没有彻底研讨过题记第一行所表达的意思：无量观门。因为一份文献常常是开篇点题，我们应该更加注意探讨“无量观门”的意思。另外，我们也应注意到题记(第 14 行)中提到的火轮并未在《俱舍论》宇宙论中出现。⑥

图 14　库木吐喇第 75 窟正壁下部的题记(红外线，稍加强)

没有确定题记识读内容，我们不能给出可靠的论据。因此希望得到更好的图像，我们拍了这个题记的红外线照片。但遗憾的是，我们用红外线拍的照片尚未奏效(图 14)。

我们用艾尼提 (Anyty)3R-ViewTer-500IR(图 15)便携

---

① 太史文也认为《毗卢遮那成佛神变加持经》中轮的观想好像也是以《阿毗达摩俱舍论》宇宙观为依据的。参见 Teiser, *Reinventing the Wheel: Paintings of Rebirth in Medieval Buddhist Temple*, p. 156, n.14.

② 写本的相关的部分 (Pelliot sanskrit no rouge 9.1 recto) 的抄本和英译参见 Nobuyoshi Yamabe(山部能宜), “Fragments of the ‘*Yogalehrbuch*’ in the Pelliot Collection”, in *Ein buddhistisches Yogalehrbuch*(再 版), eds. Jens-Uwe Hartmann and Hermann-Josef Röllicke, München: IUDICIUM, pp. 329-331. 都勒都尔—阿乎尔是靠近库木吐喇石窟的一处重要寺院遗址。

③ Schlingloff, *Ein buddhistisches Yogalehrbuch: Textband*, 127V1-3; Nobuyoshi Yamabe(山部能宜), “The Significance of the ‘*Yogalehrbuch*’ for the Investigation into the Origin of Chinese Meditation Texts”. *Bukkyō bunka* 佛教文化 (Buddhist Culture) 9(1990), p. 30 所引。

④ 在《观佛三昧海经》(T15: 663c16-19，森美智代未提及)中发现了有点相似的段落：“身诸毛孔犹如华树，一一华树上至梵世。诸华叶间，有百千亿声闻比丘。一一比丘着千纳衣，千纳千色。一一色中百千化佛，皆纯金色。”(Yamabe, “The Significance of the ‘*Yogalehrbuch*’ for the Investigation into the Origin of Chinese Meditation Texts”, p. 29 所引)。

⑤ 森美智代:《クムトラ石窟第七五窟の壁画主題について：ウイグル期亀兹佛教の一側面》, 第 138 页。

⑥ 感谢原田和宗提到这一点。

图 15 库木吐喇第 75 窟正壁下部的题记局部（显微图像）

显微镜观察这条题记，文字似乎不是墨书而是用蓝色颜料书写的。如果是这种情况，红外照片自然不会奏效。①

然而，如果仔细观察可见光照片（图 13），我们能看到一些非常模糊的文字痕迹。因此，我们以高分辨率可见光照片为基础，并且用图像修复软件（Capture One 7 以及 Adobe Photoshop CC）来处理。在这个过程中，我们尝试了各种方法，由于整个过程有点复杂而难以在文中全面解释，只能介绍大概：首先用 Capture One 7 做一个初步调整（最重要的是最大程度地提高了清晰度）；然后，用 Adobe Photoshop CC 选择字体颜色并且加深，也选择了背景色并且提亮，调整了色调曲线加强对比，而且最终将整幅图像提亮了一些（因为上文的描述过程已经呈现出一个较清晰但有点暗的图像）。

在这个过程中，我们已经用图像处理软件的“色彩范围”命令选定了相关色彩②，没有基于主观判断特意增加或删除任何内容。从这种意义上来说，图像不是任意操控的结果，应具有一定的客观有效性。在这里最重要的任务是，要把模糊的字迹变得可读，因此我们并未太注重这张图像的色彩。这仅仅是复原褪色、剥落文字的尝试（图 16—17）。

处理之后，我们看到了比原图片上更多的文字。然而，即使加强图像的清晰度也不足以来破译文字，必须采取进一步的措施。

如果仔细观察文字的剥落笔画，我们注意到，虽然笔画多半已剥落，但是笔画的边缘常常会留下一些模糊的痕迹（图 18）。

手动描摹这些边缘模糊痕迹，也许可以圈出曾有笔画的范围。一旦描出明显笔画，我们就可以加深并且假设复原这些笔画。③ 实际上，往往很难辨别剥落的模糊字迹笔画和后代的污迹。所以不能排除这种可能性有时无意描了像字迹的后代污迹。因此，必须强调是高度假设的结果。当然，即使假设识读也比完全放弃破译要好。

尽管如此，还是呈现了我们推测性复原的结果（图 19—20）。

以下是我们尝试性辨识。④

1. ………〔四〕无量观〔门〕………
2. 〔界〕三千大千世〔界界〕□

① 如上面看到过，对碳墨以外的颜料绘出的部分，红外线照片没有效果。

② 感谢城野诚治提到这个方法。

③ 对照：文化财复原中心《画像的文物复原》第 5 页 (http://fukugen.info/wordpress/download/). 美术史学方面，“数码（虚拟）复原”(digital/virtual restoration）的成果不完善的话，常常尝试“虚拟（假设）重建”(virtual/hypothetical reconstruction）。我们的“假设复原”和他们的“虚拟（假设）重建”有相似的意图。参见：Francesco Gabellone, “The Reconstructive Study in Archaeology: Case Histories in the Communication Issues”, *Scientific Research and Information Technology,* 1, no. 1 (2011), pp. 62-65; Gabellone, “Digital Technologies and Communication: Prospects and Expectations”, *Open Archaeology,* 1 (2015), pp. 108-109. 以及参见：Gábor Gercsák, and Mátyás Márton, “New Terminology of Differentiating Digital Facsimiles”, *e-Perimetron,* 5, no. 2 (2010), p. 100。

④ 阿拉伯数字表示行号，数字是我们添加的。

图16　库木吐喇第75窟正壁下部的题记右半（可见光，加强）

图17　库木吐喇第75窟正壁下部的题记左半（可见光，加强）

图18　题记第5行中"意"字的放大图

3. 〔四〕大作圣四大〔由〕

4. ………〔使起〕□身………

5. ………〔亮〕意〔识〕□□〔意识〕

6. 大…………………………

7. 〔轮上之阿字〕□………〔放〕………

8. ………广量〔无〕〔数〕〔变〕………

9. ………〔众〕………想〔有〕………金

10. ………〔白色〕白光〔变成〕水〔轮〕

11. ……〔亦〕下□八洛水〔余成金轮〕金

12. ……□黄〔色黄光〕变①成〔金轮〕

13. 金轮想自身〔求成〕□……

14.〔大〕……火〔轮焚烧〕不〔净罪紉〕那②之

15. 〔行〕〔者若〕見〔自〕身骨〔骨即〕念〔是〕

16. 〔无〕无常〔无我〕………〔否〕

在下文中，我们将关注一些关键性文字，并讨论其意义。

第一个关键性文字是第一行首字（见图16、19）。这一行中，"无量观"相当清晰。最后一个字部分毁坏，但是早期抄本中"门"似乎可以识读。"无"之上，放大后的图片上（图21），我们可以看到一些边缘非常模糊的痕迹。这些痕迹与在第三行的"四"字好像很相似（图22）。显微图像呈现的也好像是"四"（图23）。这些痕迹如此模糊，以至于看起来仅仅像后代的污迹，而且在早期的抄本

① 此题记有一个异体字，见黄征：《敦煌俗字典》，第23页。相似的字，也在第10行。

② 此题记有一个异体字。见龙谷大学佛教文化研究所编：《附 古体字例》，收入《西域出土佛典の研究》，法藏馆，1980年，第1—80页；黄征：《敦煌俗字典》，第283页。

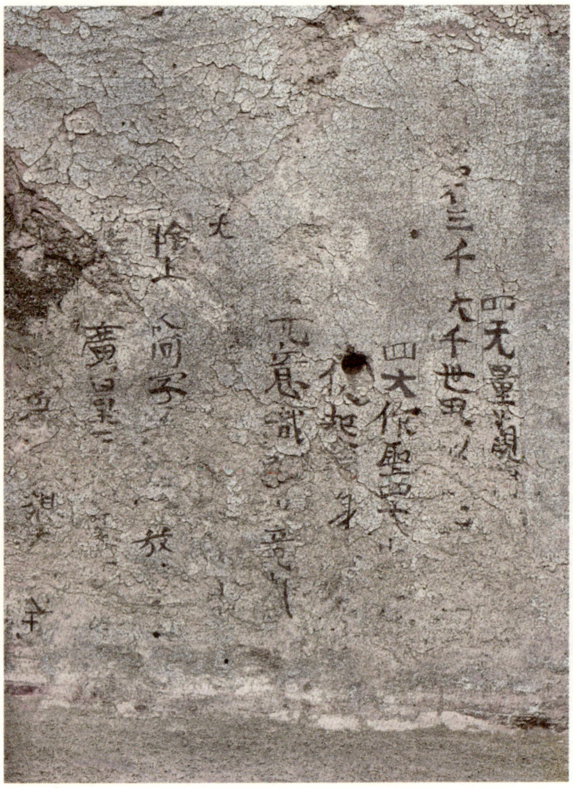

图 19　库木吐喇第 75 窟正壁下部的题记右半（可见光，假设复原）

图 20　库木吐喇第 75 窟正壁下部的题记左半（可见光，假设复原）

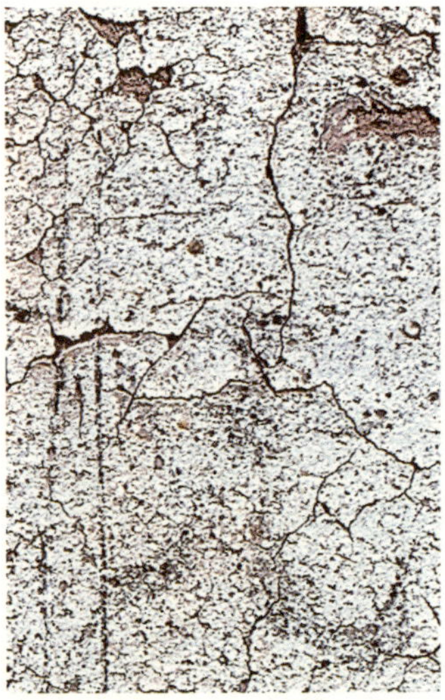

图 21　题记第 1 行模糊字的痕迹放大图（可见光，加强）

图 22　题记第 3 行“四大”字的放大图（可见光，加强）

图 23　题记第 1 行模糊字的痕迹放大图（显微图像，稍加强）

中也未发现“四”字。不过，从上下文来说，其实“四”是很有可能的识读。

尽管从前还没人特别注意此行文字，实际上是一个关键词组，可用来确定这条榜题以及正壁壁画的主题。我们认为，这里的“四无量观门”指友善（慈）、怜悯（悲）、欢喜（喜）、平静（舍）的四种无穷（无量）的观想。这是一种修行项目，而且出现在许多禅经文中，像《梵文瑜伽书》（第七章至第十章）[1] 和《达摩多罗禅经》[2]。

下文中的第二行，我们看到“三千大千世界”，如初期的抄本中曾指出的。这里应该注意到，在四无量修行中，修行者想起众生在三千大千世界中遭受疾苦，见以下摘自《禅法要解》的段落 [3]：

> 行者得此第四禅，欲行四无量心随意易得。……问曰。行者云何得慈心无量。答曰。行者依四禅已，念一城众生愿令得乐。如是一国土，一阎浮提，四天下，小千国土，二千国土，三千大千国土，乃至十方恒河沙等无量无边众生，慈心遍覆皆愿得乐。

因此，根据上下文来看，“四无量”与“三千大千世界”非常匹配。我们应该进一步关注这点：按照其他相关禅经，修行者在四无量观修行中，观想五道中受苦的众生。[4] 见以下出自《达摩多罗禅经》的引文 [5]：

> 修行四无量三昧第十四。……又修行住悲心时，见五趣众生苦痛炽然无量烧迫，深起悲心兴救护想。

在《梵文瑜伽书》第七章中关于“慈”的陈述，如下 [6]：

> tato 'ṣṭau mahānarakān[7] ṣoḍaśotsadamahāparivārāṃ saha śītanarakais[8] tiryakpretamanusyāṃś[9] cāpanīta[10] ...tadupari ṣaṭ kāmāvacarāṃ devān rūpāvacarāṃś ca caturdhyānopapa[nn]āṃ sthānāṃtarapa[ri] ...
>
> 然后〔修行者看到〕伴随着十六个辅助地狱的八大地狱以及寒地狱、畜生、饿鬼、人间以及除……在其上方看到六〔种〕属于欲界的诸天以及那些已得到四禅的属于色界以及中间状态……

同一瑜伽书中关于“悲”的第八章，我们发现以下语句 [11]：

> sa tasya karuṇ(ā) ... [sa]rvāṃś ca satvāṃ nārakāṃ[12] paśyati / puṣparasadhārābhiḥ siṃcyamānān[13] / evaṃ ti[ryā]ṃ [p](r)et[ā](ṃ manusyāṃś ca /) ...
>
> 他，他的怜悯……看到地狱中所有众生都受花香的骤雨。他同样看到畜生、饿鬼以及人间。

---

[1] 此经文内容如下：1. aśubhaprayoga 不净观，2. ānāpānasmṛtibhāvanā 安那波那观，3. dhātuprayoga 观界，4. skandhaparīkṣā 观蕴，5. āyatanaparīkṣā 观入，6. pratītyasamutpādaparīkṣā 观缘起，7. maitrī 慈，8. karuṇā 悲，9. muditā 喜，10. upekṣā 舍，11. anusmṛti: buddha, dharma, saṃgha, śīla, devatā 随念：佛、法、僧、戒、天。

[2] T No. 618. 此经文内容如下：安那波那念（ānāpānasmṛti），不净观（aśubhā），观界（dhātu），四无量三昧（catvāri apramāṇāni），观阴（skandha），观入（āyatana），观十二因缘（pratītyasamutpāda）。

[3] T15: 290a16-26 (No. 616).

[4] 另请参阅《大智度论》，T25: 208c9-11（No. 1509）。

[5] T15: 319c-320b (No. 618).

[6] Schlingloff, *Ein buddhistisches Yogalehrbuch: Textband*, 145R5-6.

[7] 底本：-narakā. 根据 *Ein buddhistisches Yogalehrbuch: Textband*, p. 129, n. 1 订正如上。

[8] 底本：sahaśītanarakais. 根据 *Ein buddhistisches Yogalehrbuch: Textband*（再版）, p. 306 订正如上。

[9] 底本：-manṣyāś. 根据 *Ein buddhistisches Yogalehrbuch: Textband*, p. 129, n. 3 订正如上。

[10] 底本：ca apanītas. 根据 *Ein buddhistisches Yogalehrbuch: Textband*, p. 129, n. 4 订正如上。

[11] Schlingloff, *Ein buddhistisches Yogalehrbuch: Textband*, 149R2-3.

[12] 底本：narakāṃ. 根据 *Ein buddhistisches Yogalehrbuch: Textband*, p. 140, n. 8 订正如上。

[13] 底本：siṃcyamānaṃ. 根据 *Ein buddhistisches Yogalehrbuch: Textband*, p. 140, n. 9 订正如上。

由此看来，“四无量观”很好地阐释了正壁的壁画，好像描述了源于禅定僧心想出来的五道或六道轮回。僧侣应该正在观想轮回中的众生。由此推断，题记中的前两行似乎指出了题记和壁画的总背景。

题记的 8—11 行，我们看到以下内容：

8. .... 广量〔无〕〔数〕〔变〕.........
9. .....〔众〕......... 想〔有〕....... 金
10. ..... 白色白光〔变成〕水〔轮〕
11. .....〔亦〕下□八洛水〔余成金轮〕金

这里，森美智代提出的关键词“八洛水”，在我们的复原（图 20）中似乎也可以读出来。《阿毗达磨俱舍论》宇宙描述中的其他关键词也在题记中发现。比较上引的题记和下引的《阿毗达磨俱舍论颂》(下线的部分)：

安立器世间　　风轮最居下
其量广无数　　厚十六洛叉
次上水轮深　　十一亿二万
下八洛叉水　　余凝结成金①

另一个关键字是在题记第七行发现的（图 24）。马世长识读这一不清楚的文字为“问”以及梁志祥和丁明夷识读为“间”。如果仔细观察处理后图像上的这个字，我们就会发现在此字的左上角上方有一些模糊不清的痕迹（图 25）。

图 26 是假设复原的结果。

推测这可能是“阿”字异体字的一部分（图 27、28）。

如果这种推断识读不是完全空穴来风，因为接下来的文字很可能是“字”（见图 25—26），我们发现了一个词“阿字”。那么极有

图 24　图 16（添加箭形符号）

图 25　题记第 7 行模糊的字的放大图（图 16 局部［可见光，加强］）

图 26　题记第 7 行模糊的字的放大图（假设复原）

① T29: 57a8-11.

可能与密教有关。

让我们再次看看题记抄写本的7—14行：

7.〔轮上之阿字〕□……〔放〕……
8. ………广量〔无〕〔数〕〔变〕……
9. ……〔众〕……想〔有〕………金
10. ……白色白光〔变成〕水〔轮〕
11. ……〔亦〕下□八洛水〔余成金轮〕金
12. ……□黄〔色黄光〕变成〔金轮〕
13. 金轮想自身〔求成〕□……
14.〔大〕……火〔轮焚烧〕不〔净罪纫〕那之

图27 ф096中的“阿”异体字[①]

图28 S.2614中的“阿”异体字[②]

这部分似乎是以密教五轮的观想为依据的。我们在辽代11世纪80年代道殿编著的《显密圆通成佛心要集》[③]中找到以下最为接近的段落：

> 行者顶上想रं嚂字。变成火轮烧尽自己有漏之身。复想大莲华上有अ[④]阿字。生成无漏智身。更想अं暗字灌顶已。又想रं嚂字变成大火。烧此有为世界。如同劫火烧尽无遗。但有空寂。复想建立无为之坛。于最下方遍想खं欠字。杂色而为空轮。于空轮上遍हं含字。黑色变成风轮。风轮上遍想रं嚂字。赤色变成火轮。火轮上遍想वं鍐字。白色变成水轮。水轮上遍想अ阿字。黄色变成金刚地。[⑤]

按年代顺序，道殿（11世纪末）与库木吐喇第75窟壁画（马世长认为，该窟时代为10世纪到11世纪）十分接近。由于在吐鲁番地区发现了辽代高僧诠明（10世纪到11世纪）的作品[⑥]，那么龟兹地区与辽之间的佛教文化与艺术交流也似乎是可能的。综合上述因素，库木吐喇第75窟正壁榜题文字与辽代密教文献之间的相似性似乎不是巧合，因而很明显这条题记后半的内容与密教紧密相关。

通过以上讨论，我们发现库木吐喇第75窟正壁题记和壁画的出处主要有以下：

第一个是梵汉禅经。这些禅经为这条题记提供了基础背景，即“四无量观”。四无量观也可以很好地阐释正壁的五道或六道轮回壁画。

第二个是在《阿毗达摩俱舍论》中发现的宇宙论。毫无疑问，这条题记在一定程度上受了《俱

① 黄征:《敦煌俗字典》，第1页。

② 同上。

③ 见 Robert M Gimello, “Icon and Incantation: The Goddess Zhunti and the Role of Images in the Occult Buddhism of China”, in *Images in Asian Religions: Texts and Contexts*, edited by Phyllis Granoff, and Koichi Shinohara, pp. 225-256, Vancouver, UBCPress, 2004。感谢 Robert Sharf 教授提到这个资料。

④ 这里的原文是悉昙文字，但我们用天城体代替了。以下类同。

⑤ 类似的表现在尧挻:《准提心要》(明代的密教文献)(续藏经[藏经书院版]第104卷，第778—779页)；以及参照安然(841—915?):《胎藏界大法对受记》, T75: 59b19-c9 (No. 2390)。

⑥ 见 Nobuyoshi Yamabe (山部能宜), “Yogācāra Influence on the Northern School of Chan Buddhism”；庄国彬、罗珮心编:《佛教禅修传统：起源与发展》，台北：新文丰出版公司，2014年，第255—256页。

舍论》宇宙论的影响。同时，我们应该注意到，《俱舍论》之宇宙论并没有完全解释这则题记的文字，因为在榜题第 14 行发现的“火轮”，并未包含在《俱舍论》体系中。

因此，我们需要查看另外第三个出处，就是密宗文献。事实上，题记后半的内容好像深受密教五轮和相关梵文字母的观想的影响。

因为此条题记在复原后仍是残破的，我们不能确定其完整内容。不过，前文讨论已经表明，正壁上的题记和壁画是禅经、《阿毗达摩俱舍论》以及密教中要素的融合。

我们应该也注意到，有关的汉梵禅经[①]与密教文献不是完全无关系，因为这些禅经也有一些貌似密教的元素。[②]也许在正壁上的题记与壁画背后所隐含的可能是比这些早期禅经更为密教化的一种修禅传统。

关于技术方面，尽管不是完全成功，但在数码复原方面的尝试已经使褪色、剥落的题记变得可读了。同时，我们应该注意的是，这种方法不是全能的，不同材料需要不同的方法。而且，目标图像越模糊，区分原始图像模糊痕迹和后代的污迹就越困难。因此，总会有一种无意识强调后代污迹的可能性。换句话说，此方法中不可能完全排除主观因素。

然而，我们在一定程度上能够辨识出用其他方式很难看到的内容。我们相信，这种尝试在许多方面都是有帮助的。尽管这项操作很耗时，但值得付出时间和劳动。

二　右侧壁“生死轮”

右侧壁绘有两个轮。我们先来讨论上方的轮（图 29）。这幅壁画褪色很厉害，难以观察其细节。因此，在这里我们再次尝试改善图像（图 30）。

图 29　库木吐喇第 75 窟右壁上方的生死轮（可见光）

图 30　库木吐喇第 75 窟右壁上方的生死轮（可见光，加强）

在此我们也使用了各种方法，但是最有效的方法如下：首先选择蓝色部分并且使用 Photoshop CC 软件做了图层遮罩。通过复制图层只加强目标（蓝色）区域。[③]通过加强后的图像，我们就能更容易地观察到细节。

毫无疑问，此轮描绘的也是生死轮回。正如山部在别处已指出的，生死轮或者缘起轮是修禅中观想的一种形象，如《禅秘要法经》以及《梵文瑜伽书》中所示。[④]

---

① 汉文禅经是五世纪的；《梵文瑜伽书》好像更晚一些。

② Nobuyoshi Yamabe（山部能宜），“The Significance of the ‘*Yogalehrbuch*’ for the Investigation into the Origin of Chinese Meditation Texts”，《佛教文化》，9 (1999), pp. 60-62.

③ 参见：Ctein, *Digital Restoration from Start to Finish: How to Repair Old and Damaged Photographs*, Oxford, Focal Press, 2007, pp. 231-266；藤岛健，谏山研一：《プロの基础基本 Photoshop 编》，株式会社アスキー，2007 年，第 98—100 页。

④ Yamabe, “The Significance of the ‘*Yogalehrbuch*’ for the Investigation into the Origin of Chinese Meditation Texts”, pp. 57-58.

光光七宝色，从胸而出……见光如云绕身七匝。其一一光，化成光轮。于光轮中，自然当见十二因缘根本相貌。①

pratīt[y](asamutpādaṃ② parīkṣya)[m]āṇasya③ dvādaśāṅgaṃ pratītyasamutpādacakraṃ (saṃskā) rasāṃtāṇikaṃ traidhātukaṃ karmakleśāvabaddhaṃ bhramaṇtam abhimukhībhav(a)t(i) dṛṣṭvā cāsya[v] ai[mukhya](m) [u](tpadyate /) ④

对思择缘起的〔修行者〕目前，行相续性、属于三界、被业和烦恼束缚轮回的十二支缘起轮出现。看到〔此生死轮〕，厌恶之情在他〔心中〕升起。

按照《根本说一切有部毘奈耶》，生死轮里描绘五道，所以它与正壁的主题相关联。那么在这儿出现这个轮也是很自然的。

《根本说一切有部毘奈耶》中，有对生死轮设计的解释。依据此律，在中心一圈，应绘代表三种毒的三种动物。

表 1⑤

三种弊病	象征物
食染（rāga）	鸽（pārāvata）
瞋恚（dvesa）	蛇（bhujaṅga）
愚癡（moha）	猪（sūkara）

它们周围，应绘五个区域代表五趣图。

表 2

五　道	象征物
天（devāḥ）	
人（manuṣyāḥ）	四洲（catvāro dvīpāḥ） 东毗提诃（Pūrvavideha） 西瞿陀尼（Aparagodānīya） 北拘卢洲（Uttarakuru） 南赡部洲（Jambudvīpa）
傍生（tiryañcaḥ）	
饿鬼（pretāḥ）	
饿鬼（pretāḥ）	

轮的外缘一周，要绘象征着十二支的十二个象征。

① T15:257a21-25 (No. 613).

② 底本：pratit[y](asamutpādaṃ. 根据 Schlingloff, *Ein buddhistisches Yogalehrbuch: Textband*, p. 163, n.18，订正如上。

③ 底本：-[m]ānasya. 根据 Schlingloff, *Ein buddhistisches Yogalehrbuch: Textband*, p. 163, n. 19，订正如上。

④ Schlingloff, *Ein buddhistisches Yogalehrbuch: Textband*, 159V6-R1，在第 10 章 upekṣā "舍"。

⑤ 表 1 和表 2 依据 Monika Zin, and Dieter Schlingloff, "Samsāracakra: Das Rad der Wiedergeburten in der indischen Überlieferung", *Buddhismus-Studien*, vol. 6, Düsseldorf: EKŌ-Haus, 2007, pp. 21-22 (Divyāvadā〔Cowell and Neil ed., 300.6-15〕所引的梵文《根本说一切有部毗奈耶》) 以及汉译《根本说一切有部毗奈耶》（T23: 811a28-b5〔No. 1442〕)。在这些部分，梵文本和汉文本相当一致。

表3[①]

缘　起	象　征
1. 无明（avidyā）	罗刹（rakṣas）
2. 行（saṃskāra）	瓦轮
3. 识 (vijñāna)	猕猴
4. 名色 (nāmarūpa)	乘船人
5. 六处 (ṣaḍāyatana)	六根
6. 触 (sparśa)	男女相摩触
7. 受 (vedanā)	男女受苦乐
8. 爱 (tṛṣṇā)	女人抱男女
9. 取 (upādāna)	丈夫持瓶取水
10. 有 (bhava)	大梵天
11. 生 (jāti)	女人诞孕
12a. 老 (jarā)	男女衰老
病 (vyādhi)	男女带病
12b. 死 (maraṇa)	舆死人
12.1 忧 (śoka)	男女忧慼
12.2 悲 (parideva)	男女啼哭
12.3 苦 (duḥkha)	男女受苦
12.4 恼 (daurmanasya)	男女挽难调骆驼

描述五道轮回的壁画现存于阿旃陀石窟第 17 窟（图 31），克孜尔石窟第 175 窟（图 32），以及敦煌榆林窟第 19 窟（图 33）。晚一点的是现存于大足宝顶山石刻（图 34）。

在这些图像中，阿旃陀石窟的生死轮仅部分保存下来而且解读并不容易。[⑤] 克孜尔石窟的五道轮回图像似乎与《昆奈耶》中的描述相当不同，并且在此难于讨论。而库木吐喇第 75 窟的生死轮图与榆林窟和宝顶山的图像有共同之处。

意外的是，在这些现存的生死轮中，与库木吐喇第 75 窟壁画最接近的那些图像发现于藏传佛

① 依据义净译《根本说一切有部毗奈耶》(T23: 811b7-18)。参见 Zin and Schlingloff, "Saṃsāracakra: Das Rad der Wiedergeburten in der indischen Überlieferung", pp. 27-28（义净译《根本说一切有部毗奈耶》上揭部分的 Przyluski 的法译），cf. ibid., pp. 37-38（《根本说一切有部昆奈耶》梵文写本［Pelliot sanskrit n° rouge 5.1-3］对应部分的原本和德译）；以及 Teiser, *Reinventing the Wheel: Paintings of Rebirth in Medieval Buddhist Temples*, 10, pp. 55-56（义净译《根本说一切有部毗奈耶》上揭部分的英译）。相比跟中亚的生死轮壁画汉译比梵文更为一致（尤其是，下面提到的保存于鲁宾博物馆的西藏壁画），因此我们主要是依据汉译。

② 参见《中国新疆壁画艺术》编辑委员会编：《中国新疆壁画艺术》，乌鲁木齐：新疆美术摄影出版社，2009 年，图 210。

③ 参见敦煌研究院接待部：《敦煌石窟》，兰州：甘肃文化出版社，2000 年，第 117 页；Teiser, *Reinventing the Wheel: Paintings of Rebirth in Medieval Buddhist Temples*, plate 11。

④ 感谢 Henrick Sørensen 教授提供这张照片。

⑤ 此轮出现了歧义。参见：Schlingloff, *Studies in the Ajanta Paintings: Identification and Interpretations*, Delhi, Ajanta Publications, 1988, pp. 167-174；Zin and Schlingloff, "Saṃsāracakra: Das Rad der Wiedergeburten in der indischen Überlieferung", pp. 43-112；Leela Aditi Wood, *The Buddha and the Shape of Belief: Indic Visual "Jātakamālās"*, Ph.D. Dissertation, University of Michigan, 2005, pp. 538-547; Teiser, *Reinventing the Wheel: Paintings of Rebirth in Medieval Buddhist Temples*, pp. 76-103。

图 31　阿旃陀石窟第 17 窟的生死轮，5 世纪（山部拍照）

图 32　克孜尔石窟第 175 窟的生死轮，8 世纪或以后（新疆龟兹研究院拍摄）①

图 33　敦煌榆林窟第 19 窟的生死轮，10 世纪（敦煌研究院拍摄）②

图 34　大足宝顶山的生死轮石刻，约 1250 年（Henrick Sørensen 教授拍摄）③

图 35　生死轮，西藏，20 世纪早期，布帛上的彩画。鲁宾（Rubin）博物馆（纽约）所藏。从 Navin Kumar 搜集品（纽约）购买的。C2004.21.1 (HAR 65356) ⑤

教地区。比如，注意到一处藏于鲁宾博物馆的 19 世纪的壁画（图 35）。

因此，尽管拿 10—11 世纪的生死轮图与晚至 19 世纪的生死轮图做比较相当不合时宜，但在此我们集中对藏传和库木吐喇第 75 窟的生死轮进行比较讨论。

库木吐喇石窟上方的轮的最内一圈，所能观察到的仅有一条蛇样的图像，如太史文指出的。② 由空间推测，原来很可能绘有其他两种动物，现在几乎完全褪色看不见了（比较图 30 与图 35）。

库木吐喇石窟上方的轮（图 30）的中间一圈，顶部有座宫殿，里面坐有人。如太史文所说，这应该描绘了天界。右手边描绘的是一个坐着的人，正如太史文指出，这描绘了人界。左手边完全褪色，因此我们不能做任何判断。问题在于底部两块区域。我们看到两身相似的红色人物似乎在奔跑，不清楚他们的身份以及为什么两身相似的人物占据了两块单独的区域。也许是由于画师有些困惑导致的结果。我们对此部分需要更多的研究。

现在让我们来看最外圈，描绘十二缘起（dvādaśāṅga-pratītyasamutpāda）的部位。即使复原后，我们仅能在某种程度上观察到三个象征物，也就是猕猴代表识（1:30 的方向），一个人坐在讲台上（？）手持一根木棒代表名色（4:30 的方向）。与鲁宾博物馆的生死轮相比（猕猴在 2:30 的方向 [图 35]），库木吐喇石窟的轮中此物的安排是有点不同的（猕猴在 1:30 的方向），但阿旃陀石窟轮的外圈也是如此，猕猴位于 1:30 的方向（图 31）。因此，这不是个问题。更多的疑问是第四项，代表名色。根据《根本说一切有部毘奈耶》的汉译，这儿应

① 我们感谢鲁宾博物馆的 Michelle Bennett Simorella 女史允许我们用这项作品。参见：Teiser, *Reinventing the Wheel: Paintings of Rebirth in Medieval Buddhist Temple*, p. 10。

② Tesier, *Reinventing the Wheel: Paintings of Rebirth in Medieval Buddhist Temples*, pp. 160-162. 对此范围的议论，以下省略每次引证。

图 36　图 30 局部

图 37　图 35 局部

该有船上坐一人。库木吐喇第 75 窟中的轮也是如此，此人手持一根木棒（图 36），和鲁宾博物馆的轮相似（图 37）。①

然而，这个人看起来更像是坐在一个讲台上而不是船上。也许画师没有完全理解设计的含义，将乘船人的画像与另外一个僧人坐在讲台上的题材混在一起了。僧人坐在讲台上的例子就是在莫高窟第 172 窟的观经变相里发现的（图 38）。

图 38　敦煌莫高窟第 172 窟的观经变相局部③

我们注意到，此轮的右上部（图 29）有一人物手持轮。这种人物在阿旃陀石窟生死轮图的相应部分并未出现。然而，如果我们察看塔波（Tabo）寺庙（图 39）和派东泊（Pedongpo）石窟寺（图 40）的藏式生死轮，就能看到相同的图形。② 这是我们猜测库木吐喇第 75 窟的生死轮可能与藏式生死轮接近的另一证据。

现在，我们来看库木吐喇第 75 窟右侧壁的下方轮。同样，这部分现在褪色非常严重（图 42），因此试图用与处理上方轮同样的方法去复原，以期获得较清晰的图像（图 43），但是即使加强过的图像也不是完全清晰。在内圈，可能有三种动物（现在只有蛇清晰可见）。中间一圈也不是很清晰。右边区域有一人，并且在上方区域可能是一宫殿建筑，但其他部分完全漫漶不清。最成问题的是外圈。太史文认为上方轮和下方轮“几乎完全相同”⑥，但实际上并非如此。即使图像漫漶不清，很多因素都不确定，但并非是关于十二支缘起的描述。许多区域看起来像波浪式的图案，它们是什么呢？

图 39　塔波寺庙正堂前室东壁的生死轮，11 世纪（Christian Luczanits 教授拍摄）④

一种可能性是，这与塔波寺中生死轮外圈内的环状水波纹相一致。⑦ 有情正在穿越一些桶状物，这似乎是描述有情转世。这可能与《根本说一切有部毘奈耶》中描述的相一致：

---

① 感谢 Christian Luczanits 教授提到这点。

② 鲁宾博物馆中的轮由一无常大鬼手持。见图 35。

③ 施萍婷：《敦煌石窟全集》第 5 卷《阿弥陀经画卷》，商务印书馆，2002 年，第 178—179 页，图 164（局部）。

④ 感谢 Luczanits 教授提供这张图片。并参见：Teiser, *Reinventing the Wheel: Paintings of Rebirth in Medieval Buddhist Temples*, plate 12。

⑤ 感谢 Helmut 和 Heidi Neumann 博士提供图 40 和图 41 的照片。并参见：Teiser, *Reinventing the Wheel: Paintings of Rebirth in Medieval Buddhist Temples*, plate 13.

⑥ Ibid., p. 160.

⑦ 我们感谢 Luzcanits 教授指出这个可能性。

图 40　派东泊石窟寺门廊的生死轮，12 世纪。(Helmut Neumann 博士和 Heidi Neumann 博士拍摄)

图 41　派东泊石窟寺门廊的生死轮，右上部 (同上)[①]

图 42　库木吐喇第 75 窟右侧壁的下方生死轮 (可见光)

图 43　库木吐喇第 75 窟右侧壁的下方生死轮 (可见光，加强)

于其辋处应作溉灌轮像。多安水罐画作有情生死之像。生者罐中出头，死者于罐中出足。[①]

在派东泊石窟寺（图 40—41）、榆林窟第 19 窟（图 33）以及宝顶山石刻（图 34）中的轮上有相似的水筒。因为库木吐喇第 75 窟右侧壁下方轮漫漶不清，难以得出一个明确的判断。然而，波纹式模样很可能是生死海的描述，就像我们在塔波寺庙生死轮中看到的。另外，库木吐喇的轮中有一些蓝色物体，可能是水纹间的水筒。特别是 7 点方向的“水筒”的左上方，我们看到似乎某物（或人？）从“水筒”里出来，这可能是一个有情从一世到另一世生死海中的轮回。

库木吐喇第 75 窟是 10—11 世纪的洞窟，而相关的藏式轮的年代是 11—12 世纪。因此，从年代的观点看，库木吐喇第 75 窟生死轮图与藏式生死轮图中的密切关系好像是有可能的。然而，由于吐

---

① T23: 81b5-7.Teiser, p. 55.《根本说一切有部毗奈耶》中的梵文表现有细微区别：aupapādukāḥ sattvā ghaṭīyantraprayogeṇa cyavamānā upapadyamanāś ca kartavyāḥ / (Zin and Schilingloff, “Samsāracakra: Das Rad der Wiedergeburten in der indischen Überlieferung” , p. 23). 应该画（逐字地：作）以水轮的方式死去重生着的化生众生。

蕃基本上是在 9 世纪中期从塔里木盆地退出的，那么 10—11 世纪的回鹘佛教与藏传佛教之间的交流是什么程度呢？这需要今后的更多研究。

三　供养人与题记

在每一侧壁的底端，我们看到有一列供养人，每身人物的左上方（？）都有一个长方形题榜。大部分题榜中的字是褪色严重的，很难识读。在此，红外线图片起到了很好的效果。通过使用红外线，一些题记变得更加清晰。这些题记应该是用碳墨书写。它们似乎都是表明回鹘供养人名字的（图 44—45）。

我们识读到第 7 身供养人的题记："兄骨禄□"。[②] 这里前三个字相当清晰。虽然第 6 身供养人的题记很难识读，但是它看起来像"□□〔禄〕□"。[③]

第 10 身供养人的题记在红外线照片加强下相当清晰："〔妹骨禄〕思力。"[④]

第 8 身供养人的题记可能是："〔骨字母〕思力"，但是前三个字不确定。[⑤] 第 9 身供养人的题记似乎残余了五个字，但是它们难以识读（图 46—47）。

第 15 身供养人的题记识读："弟［子］…〔者〕一［心］供养"（图 48—49）。[⑥]

左侧壁底端左侧末尾，我们看到以下汉文题记（图 50—51）：

在图 50—51 右手边的题榜，我们看到文字"梵"，左手边看到："〔麦〕□〔當〕寺〔蓮〕秀一〔心〕供养"。[⑦]

图 44　右侧壁底部的供养人第 5 到第 7[①]（可见光）

图 45　右侧壁底部的供养人第 5 到第 7（红外线，加强）

① 在右侧壁上我们从右（正壁侧）到左（入口侧）编号供养者。

② 马世长：《库木吐喇的汉风洞窟》，第 212 页；新疆龟兹石窟研究所编：《库木吐喇石窟内容总录》，第 247 页。

③ 同上。

④ 同上。

⑤ 同上。

⑥ 同上。此人物右侧有一空白区域。因为不能确定人物的踪迹，我们认为这一区域为空白。

⑦ 马世长：《库木吐喇的汉风洞窟》，第 212 页；新疆龟兹石窟研究所编：《库木吐喇石窟内容总录》，第 246 页。

图 46　右侧壁底部的供养人第 8 到第 10（可见光）

图 47　右侧壁底部的供养人第 8 到第 10（红外线，加强）

图 48　右侧壁底部的供养人第 15 到第 16（可见光）

图 49　右侧壁底部的供养人第 15 到第 16（红外线，加强）

图 50　左侧壁底端左侧末尾的题记（可见光）

图 51　左侧壁底端左侧末尾的题记（红外线，加强）

因此，在左右两侧壁，红外线照片已捕捉到一些题记内容。这表示在两侧壁，题记是以碳墨书写的。另一方面，正壁题记是用某种蓝色颜料书写的。令人疑惑的是，为什么在如此小的洞窟内没用同样的墨书写所有的榜题文字？关于此问题需要进一步的调查研究。

四　回鹘文题记

在左侧壁中央位置，有一好像空白的区域（图 52），仔细观察仅见一些模糊的绿色颜料痕迹。这样的情况，红外线只会过滤掉这些痕迹。

但是可见光诱导冷光照片①已捕捉到这些字的一些痕迹（图 53）。我们也拍可见光照片，像处理正壁的长篇题记一样，明显化了照片。只是结果不如长篇题记的那么好（图 54）。

在可见光诱导冷光照片中，一些几乎完全褪色的颜料痕迹，通过冷光变得可见。因此，一些字的痕迹在可见光照片下完全不可见，而在可见光冷光中可见。在这张照片中，可以观察到残缺不全的回鹘文题记。我们邀请了中央民族大学的阿卜杜热西提·亚库普教授将这则回鹘文题记进行转写、汉译并注释如下：

转写：

1. ačari čantan y/ [　　]
2. *a*čari(?) ba*h*čı*qa*[　　]
3. suvını tarım // [　　]
4. käsip čang// [　　]

图 52　左侧壁上题记的痕迹（可见光）

图 53　左侧壁上题记的痕迹（可见光诱导冷光，加强）

图 54　左侧壁上题记的痕迹（可见光，加强）

① 见文化庁编:《国宝・高松塚古坟壁画》，中央公论美术出版，2004, pp. 13-14, 18-19；城野诚治:《可视域内励起光を用いた蛍光反応による物质の识别法》,《月刊文化财》，487 (2004), pp. 9-12;《可视域内励起光による蛍光摄影法》,《日本の美术》, pp. 492, 2007, 25-26;《蛍光摄影法を用いた材料の识别》,《凤翔学丛》，8(2012), pp. 4-6.; 井出诚之辅 , 城野诚治 , 山梨绘美子:《Light & Color: 绘画表现の深层をさぐる》，中央公论美术出版 , 2009, pp. 178-223; 并参照 Giovanni Verri, “The Use and Distribution of Egyptian Blue: A Study by Visible-Induced Luminescence Imaging”, in *The Nebamun Wall Paintings: Conservation, Scientific Analysis and Display at the British Museum*, edited by Andrew Middleton and Ken Uprichard, pp. 41-50, London, Archetype Publications, 2008; Almogi, Delhey, MacDonald, and Pouvkova, “Recovering Lost Writing and Beyond: Multispectral Imaging for Text-related and Codicological Studies of Tibetan Paper and Sanskrit Palm-Leaf Manuscripts”, pp. 155-156。

译文：

1. 大师 Čantan y/［　］
2. 对法师（？）大师［　］
3. 把……的水 / 河塔里木 //［　］
4. 砍下［　　］

注释：

1. ačari 源于梵文 ācārya-，意为"大师""法师"，似是通过乙种吐火罗语借入，请与乙种吐火罗语 aśari 比较。作为人名的一部分，该词既可以出现在人名之前又可附在人名之后，如 Ačari K(ä)-ši Qarunadaz Sidu"法师迦鲁纳答思司徒"，Tayto Samtso Ačari"大唐三藏法师"等；详见 Uigurisches Wörterbuch，第 8—10 页。①

Čantana：似是人名，也许源于梵文 Candana"旃檀、白檀"；至于 Candana 的汉译详见荻原云来编：《汉译对照梵和大辞典》，第 458 页。

2. *a*čari（？），也许也念 ačari，但最初一字母不清。回鹘语文献虽有 ačari 和 bahšı 并用的例子，如 bahšı ačariqa"对于大师"，但未见有 ačari 在前，bahšı 在后的例子。需要注意的是，ba*hčıqa* 中 ba 以后的字母都模糊不清。

3. suvını：可译作"把……的水""把……的河"，但开头的字母是否为 s 值得进一步调查，若不是，应念 Uvini 或 Ovini，意义不明。喀什噶里曾提到一条叫作 Usmi Tarim 的河，见 *Dîvânü Lûgati't-Türk*，第 77 页。② 但此处 Tarim 之前的词无法读作 Usmi。若读 Uvini 或 Ovini，应是河名。

4. käsip 为动词 käs-"砍""切"的完成副动词形式。

结　论

正如上面探讨的，我们尝试以数码修复使褪色题记和壁画变得更加清晰。因此，一些以前不可用的以及未知的技术可用于我们现在的研究，并使库木吐喇第 75 窟的壁画与题记更加清楚。

正壁壁画中，动物（马）的上部长条形标题中的"畜生"二字重新证实它描述了坐禅僧人周围的五道或六道轮回。

对于正壁底端的长篇榜题，首先发现了此榜题的基本背景是四无量观以及在各种世界领域受苦的众生的观想。进一步观察到这些元素与同壁上的五道或六道轮回图紧密对应。

我们也注意到，此榜题中的宇宙轮一定程度上与《阿毗达磨俱舍论》中的描述相吻合。然而，宇宙轮以及相关的梵文字母（bīja）的观想与密教更密切相关，而且最为接近的是在辽代道殿的《显密圆通成佛心要集》中发现的。这也表明在塔里木盆地一带与辽之间存在佛教文化与艺术交流的现象。

关于右侧壁的两个生死轮，我们已经注意到其与藏式生死轮极为相似。这表明库木吐喇石窟与吐蕃之间存在佛教文化与艺术的交流。

---

① Klaus Röhrborn, *Uigurisches Wörterbuch: Sprachmaterial des vorislamischen türkischen Texte aus Zentralasien*, II. Nomina — pronomina – partikeln, Band 1, a-asvik, Neubearbeitung, Wiesbaden, F. Steiner, 2015. 感谢笠井幸代博士提供相关的情报。

② Kâşgarlı Mahmud, *Dîvânü Lûgati't-Türk*, Ankara, 1990. 感谢松井太副教授提供相关的情报。

关于两侧壁底部的回鹘供养人，我们已经确定了一些题记内容。尽管他们用汉文书写，但是他们记录了回鹘人的名字。因此，无疑此洞窟是由回鹘佛教徒捐助供养的。

最后，在左侧壁，我们发现了从前没有报告过的回鹘文题记。这个发现再次显示数码复原的有用性。

我们也应该注意到数码修复并不是万能的，不同材料要求不同方法。另外，目标图像越模糊，识别原始图像的痕迹和后代污迹就越困难。因此，总有无意因素强调了后代污迹并且让它们看起来像是原始元素的可能性。换句话说，在此方法中不可能完全排除主观因素。此外，用此方法不能确定无疑地恢复原始色彩。为了达到这个目的，我们需要通过科学分析辨认壁画所使用的颜料，但其研究将超过这次项目的范围。

在此项目中我们运用的是相对简单的方法，不能复原图像的原始色彩，也不能排除复原中的一些不确定因素。然而，我们有时能够辨认出用肉眼难以辨识的内容，值得将来继续研究。

A Digital Restoration of the Paintings in Qumtura Cave 75 and an Examination of Relevant Motifs and Inscriptions

Nobuyoshi Yamabe (Waseda University) Zhao Li (XinJiang Kucha Academy)
Xie Qianqian (XinJiang Kucha Academy)

Abstract: Qumtura Cave 75 is a small but important cave situated some distance away from the main cave complex facing the Muzart River. On its rear wall, there is a painting with a frontal view of a seated meditating monk surrounded by scenes of the five or six realms of samsāra is painted. At the bottom of the same wall, there is a long but badly faded inscription. We have digitally restored and deciphered part of the inscription. The basic context of the inscription is meditation on the fourfold boundlessness, combined with abhidharma cosmology and esoteric visualization. On the left side-wall, we can see two wheels. They too are faded, but the digitally restored images suggest a relation to *samsāracakras* in the Tibetan tradition. On the right side-wall, we have restored and, with the help of Professor Abudrishid Yakup, deciphered a hitherto-unknown inscription in Old Uighur. We have also restored the paintings of donors and the accompanying inscriptions at the bottom of both side-walls.

Keywords: Qumtura Cave 75; digital restoration; fourfold boundlessness; *samsāracakra*; Old Uighur inscription

唐代汉传佛教在龟兹地区的传播及其影响 *

——以佛陀观为中心

苗利辉（中国人民大学／新疆龟兹研究院）

摘　要：有唐一代，龟兹地区生活了大量的汉族军民。随之，汉地佛教的佛陀观也传入龟兹，其内容包括对阿弥陀佛、药师佛、永远的释迦佛、卢舍那佛和三世十方佛的信仰。受其影响，龟兹本地民众也接受了永远的释迦佛和西方阿弥陀佛的信仰。

关键词：汉传佛教；佛陀观；龟兹

一

公元640年，唐军以侯君集为交河道大总管西进，攻灭了勾结突厥势力的麴氏高昌王国。当年八月，以其地置西州。九月，在西州置安西都护府，主要用于对付西突厥，主管伊、西、庭三州军事。贞观十八年（644），由于焉耆王突骑支反复无常，拒不朝贡，还与西突厥结成政治联姻，引龟兹为外援，对建立不久的安西都护府构成了威胁。太宗命安西都护郭孝恪为西州道行军总管，率兵西征焉耆，大获全胜。占领了焉耆后，唐朝打开了通往龟兹的门户。

贞观二十一年（647），太宗以阿史那社尔为昆丘道行军大总管，与契苾何力、郭孝恪、李海岸等将军，发兵讨伐龟兹，打败了西突厥的援军，次年平之。龟兹平定之后，安西都护府移至龟兹都城，“统于阗、碎叶、疏勒，号四镇”①。其军事力量较以前大增。显庆三年（658），唐朝又在今塔里木盆地，西突厥十姓地区，葱岭以西的河中地区和阿姆河以南地区设置都护府州，“西尽于波斯，并隶安西都护府”②。此后，安西都护府先后和西突厥、吐蕃、突骑施展开斗争。特别是长寿元年（692），武则天当政时：

> 武威军总管王孝杰、阿史那忠节大破吐蕃，克复龟兹、于阗等四镇，自此复于龟兹置安西都护府，用汉兵三万人以镇之。既征发内地精兵，远逾沙碛，并资遣衣粮等，甚为百姓所苦。言事

*　本文为国家社科基金重大项目“敦煌与于阗：佛教艺术与物质文化的交互影响”（项目编号：B&ZD087）的阶段性成果之一。

①《新唐书》卷二二一上《龟兹传》，北京：中华书局，2013年，第6232页。

②《旧唐书》卷一九四下《突厥传》，北京：中华书局，2013年，第5187页。

者多请弃之，则天竟不许。[①]

除了三万正规军以外，当还有几倍于此的政府官吏、眷属及移民、流民纷至沓来。估计当时在安西境内，要远远超过三万之数。自贞观十四年（640）直至贞元三年（787），安西都护府前后存续达140多年之久，其驻跸地龟兹境内，聚居了大量的汉人。

随中原人西迁龟兹，在中原发展形成的大乘佛教，应运乘势西渐，中原大乘佛教在龟兹落地发展，很快形成了强大的势力。于是在小乘佛教的龟兹，出现了大小乘和谐并存的历史奇观。这种情况一直延续很久，8世纪初新罗僧人慧超在《往五天竺国记》中载：

又从疏勒东行一月，至龟兹国，即是安西大都护府，汉国兵马大都集处。此龟兹国，足寺足僧，行小乘法，食肉及葱韮等也。汉僧行大乘法……[②]

这种汉传佛教和本地佛教并行发展的情况在现存的石窟中有所反映。

库木吐喇第29窟为一典型的龟兹本地特点的石窟，它位于具有唐代汉地风格的第16窟的西侧，两窟仅相距三十余米。库木吐喇石窟中，龟兹小乘佛教与中原大乘佛教咫尺相存，为世界佛教文化奇观。

关于龟兹地区汉传佛教的情况，以往学者依据文献和保留下来的遗存分别从佛寺系统、石窟艺术和历史发展等方面进行了论述，使我们对它的情况有了深入的了解。[③]然而，从其佛教思想角度的研究尚未展开。有鉴于此，笔者拟在前人研究基础上，对唐代龟兹地区汉传佛教的佛陀观加以探讨，不当之处，还望方家指正为盼。

二

依据目前龟兹地区发现的佛教遗址及有关文书材料，我们可以看到唐代这一地区至少存在以下佛陀信仰：西方阿弥陀佛、东方药师佛、永远的释迦佛、宇宙主卢舍那佛、三世十方佛等。

（一）西方阿弥陀佛

阿弥陀佛又名无量光佛、无量寿佛，意为光明和寿命无限，西方极乐净土的教主。

依据《无量寿经》所载，过去久远劫世自在王佛住世时，有一国王发无上道心，舍王位出家，名为法藏比丘，于世自在王佛处修行，熟知诸佛之净土，历经五劫之思虑而发殊胜之四十八愿。誓愿建立一个庄严的极乐世界，以救度一切念佛名号的众生。其中有三个大愿：

设我得佛，十方众生至心信乐，欲生我国，乃至十念，若不生者，不取正觉。唯除五逆、毁谤正法。设我得佛，十方众生发菩提心、修诸功德，至心发愿欲生我国。临寿终时，假令不与大

① 《旧唐书》卷一九八《龟兹传》，第5304页。

② 慧超、杜环撰，张毅、张一纯笺释：《往五天竺国记笺释》，北京：中华书局，1994年，第159页。

③ 荣新江：《唐代西域的汉化佛寺系统》，收入新疆龟兹学会编：《龟兹文化研究》第1辑，香港：天马出版有限公司，2005年，第130—137页；马世长：《库木吐喇的汉风洞窟》，收入新疆维吾尔自治区文物管理委员会、库车县文物保管所、北京大学考古系编著：《中国石窟库木吐喇石窟》，北京：文物出版社，1992年，第207页；贾应逸、祁小山：《印度到中国新疆的佛教艺术》，兰州：甘肃教育出版社，2002年，第321—331页；霍旭初：《阿艾石窟题记考识》，《西域研究》2004年第2期，第50—59页。

众围绕现其人前者，不取正觉。设我得佛，十方众生闻我名号，系念我国，植众德本，至心回向，欲生我国，不果遂者，不取正觉。①

此后，不断积聚功德，而于距今十劫之前，愿行圆满，成阿弥陀佛，在离此十万亿佛土之西方，报得极乐净土。

基于这些上述的誓愿，因此，在他成佛之后，任何人只要具足信愿行、如法念佛，则一定会得到他的接引，而往生至真至善至美的净土佛国。

阿弥陀佛属于大乘佛身观中的报身佛，是法藏比丘初发心修习，至十地之行满足，酬报此等愿行之果身，为万德圆满之佛身。

《观无量寿经》中说，无量寿佛之身如百千亿夜摩天阎浮檀金之色，他的身高六十万亿那由他恒河沙由旬。眉间之白毫右旋宛转，毫相之大小犹如五倍须弥山之高广；其眼清白分明，眼之大小犹如四倍大海水之纵广。其身有八万四千相，一一相中有八万四千好，一一好中有八万四千光明，遍照十方世界，摄取念佛之众生。②

此佛身，随顺众生种种机类应现，永不消失破坏：

二者依于业识，谓诸菩萨从初发意，乃至菩萨究竟地心所见者，名为报身。身有无量色，色有无量相，相有无量好，所住依果亦有无量种种庄严，随所示现，即无有边，不可穷尽，离分齐相，随其所应，常能住持，不毁不失。③

阿弥陀佛信仰特别强调阿弥陀佛加持的无上效力，加上修行方式简单，对于渴望摆脱世间诸苦和解脱成佛，而又畏难娑婆世界成佛之路的众生来说，无疑具有极大的吸引力。故而，从唐代开始，弥陀信仰成为中国佛教信仰的一个主流。阿弥陀佛信仰的经典主要有《无量寿经》《佛说阿弥陀经》和《佛说观无量寿佛经》，依据这些经典产生了许多与阿弥陀佛有关的经变故事画。

根据绘画内容和形式，龟兹地区此类经变画可以分为两类，一类系依据《阿弥陀经》绘制的阿弥陀经变，保存在库木吐喇石窟第 11 窟、14 窟的主室正壁（图 1）；一类则是依据《观无量寿经》绘制的观无量寿经变，保存在库木吐喇石窟第 16 窟主室左侧壁和阿艾石窟主室正壁（图 2）。

库木吐喇石窟第 11 窟和 14 窟的阿弥陀经变无论是绘制的人物还是构图布局均完全相同。阿弥陀佛位于画面中央，两侧为观世音、大势至胁侍菩萨。佛和菩萨上方的华盖上摩尼珠闪烁。阿弥陀佛和观世音、大势至菩萨上方的空中，天花乱坠，各方诸佛端坐莲中前来赴会，楼阁飘浮在天空中，彩云烘托着的飞天持花盘供养，画面的左右两侧上方绘日、月。阿弥陀佛和观世音、大势至菩萨下方及周围，围绕众菩萨、天人和阿修罗、夜叉、龙王等天龙八部。

库木吐喇石窟第 16 窟主室左侧壁和阿艾石窟的主室正壁绘制的观无量寿经变布局和构图也完全相同，只是均有不同程度的残损。现以阿艾石窟所绘加以介绍。

画面为中堂式布局。画面中央为阿弥陀佛法会图。楼台上，主尊阿弥陀佛位于画面中央，结跏趺

① 《大正藏》，第 12 册，第 267 页。

② 同上，第 343 页。

③ 同上，第 223 页。

图1 库木吐喇14窟主室正壁阿弥陀经变

图2 阿艾石窟主室正壁观无量寿经变

坐于莲台上，手作说法印。佛头光分出数条光芒，光芒上云气，云气上绘一佛二菩萨赴会图，云气下绘有华盖，佛和菩萨上方绘有各种乐器，如筝、阮咸等，不鼓自鸣。佛两侧绘观世音菩萨和大势至菩萨，均结跏趺坐于莲台上，一手置膝上，一手作与愿印。阿弥陀佛和观世音、大势至菩萨周围绘供养天人及花树。楼台前的栏台上，伎乐翩翩起舞，仙鹤驻足。栏台两侧亭中各绘一坐佛，其旁有闻法天人。楼台、栏台间池水中有化生童子嬉戏。栏台以下画面脱落。两侧条幅仅左侧残存部分，为一唐装贵妇合十跪拜一楼阁。

库木吐喇石窟第16窟主室左侧壁中堂部分尚存各种乐器悬浮，不鼓自鸣。水榭楼台中绘菩萨、歌舞伎乐和飞天。残存立轴条幅中，可见汉式宫廷建筑和汉装人物。条幅榜题为："佛从岐阇崛山中没王宫中见韦提夫人自武时"和"韦提夫人观见水变成冰时"。①

此外，库木吐喇第42窟右甬道左侧壁有"南无阿弥□佛"的题记，右侧壁有"□□□势至菩萨"的题记。第45窟右甬道右侧壁有"南无阿弥陀佛"和"南无大势至菩萨"的题记。②

（二）东方药师佛

据《药师琉璃光如来本愿功德经》介绍，药师琉璃光佛为东方药师净土的教主，此佛于过去世行菩萨道时，曾发十二大愿，愿为众生解除疾苦，使具足诸根，导入解脱，故依此愿而成佛，住净琉璃世界，其国庄严如极乐世界：

> 彼佛土纯一清净，无诸欲染，亦无女人及三恶趣苦恼之声。以净琉璃而为其地，城阙宫殿及

① 渡边哲信：《西域旅行日记》，《新西域记》上卷，有光社，1937年，第336页。

② 这些图像主要以笔者亲自田野调查收集为主，对于现已不存的图像，则参照以往学者出版的相关报告和画册中的照片。（参见格伦威德尔：《新疆古佛寺》，赵崇民、巫新华译，北京：中国人民大学出版社，2007年；阿尔伯特·冯·勒柯克、恩斯特·瓦尔德施密特：《新疆佛教艺术》，管平、巫新华译，乌鲁木齐：新疆教育出版社，2006年；新疆维吾尔自治区文物管理委员会、库车县文物保管所、北京大学考古系编：《中国石窟·库木吐喇石窟》，北京：文物出版社，1992年；中国壁画全集编辑委员会编：《中国美术分类全集·中国新疆壁画全集　库木吐拉》，沈阳：辽宁美术出版社、乌鲁木齐：新疆美术摄影出版社，1995年；中国壁画全集编辑委员会编：《中国美术分类全集·中国新疆壁画全集（森木塞姆·克孜尔尕哈）》，沈阳：辽宁美术出版社、乌鲁木齐：新疆美术摄影出版社，1995年；新疆龟兹石窟研究所编：《库木吐喇石窟内容总录》，北京：文物出版社，2008年）除了直接与净土图像相关的图像外，库木吐喇石窟和阿艾石窟中也存在一些表现各种净土中的教主及胁侍菩萨的单尊像。鉴于它们的具体含义在不同的图像语境中往往有所不同，故而在本文中，仅列出与西方净土信仰直接有关的阿弥陀佛和大势至菩萨作为正文说明的补充材料。

廊宇轩窗罗网皆七宝成，亦如西方极乐世界功德庄严。①

此佛誓愿不可思议，若有人身患重病，死衰相现，眷属于此人临命终时昼夜尽心供养礼拜药师佛，读诵药师如来本愿功德经四十九遍，燃四十九灯，造四十九天之五色彩幡，其人得以苏生续命。

药师佛亦为报身佛，与阿弥陀佛信仰一样，是他力信仰。如果众生信仰他，不仅可得往生东方药师净土，不再退转，最终成佛，而且能解决现实中的各种苦难，其兼具现世和来世的两重性质，自然对有情众生的吸引力很大，从而成为宋元时期汉传佛教地区的流行信仰。

记载药师信仰的佛经是《药师经》。此经在佛教史上有多种汉文译本。最早的译本是东晋僧人帛尸梨蜜多罗译，名叫《佛说灌顶拔除过罪生死得度经》。最流行的译本是唐代玄奘于永徽元年（650）所译的《药师琉璃光如来本愿功德经》。

依据各种药师经经本绘制的经变画和单尊造像在龟兹地区也有发现。

库木吐喇石窟第16窟主室右侧壁就绘制有药师经变。②

经变画残损严重，情节多不辨。但保存着汉文榜题。内容为“十二大愿”。尚存可见者：“第二愿者使我来世自身光明”“琉璃内外明彻净无瑕秽妙”“功德巍巍安住十方”“如日临世”“众生悉蒙开晓”“第三愿者……也”“……益”“无饥……想……”。③

根据学者研究，该榜题文字系摘自东晋帛尸梨蜜多罗所译《佛说灌顶经》，而所绘壁画为药师经变。④

单尊的造像则发现在阿艾石窟主室右侧壁上，共绘有两身，附有榜题（图3）。两身均为立姿，内着僧祇支，束帛带，外披双领下垂式袈裟。左手作吉祥印并持药钵，右手持锡杖。在第二身药师左侧还绘有七身小坐佛和一身供养人像。此外，券顶的榜题里还有

图3 阿艾石窟主室右侧壁药师佛

① 《大正藏》，第14册，第413页。

② 库车地区出土了两件与药师信仰有关的汉文文书，均由大谷探险队获得。两件《药师经》抄本残件序号分别为第41和第69号。第41号文书现存21行汉文，墨书竖写。除第一行上端有缺字外，其余各行均文字完整。经日本学者熊谷宣夫与诸译本对勘发现，此文书虽尾题为“药师经一卷”，现存文字却与东晋帛尸梨蜜多罗所译的《佛说灌顶拔除过罪生死得脱经》第12卷的有关章节最为接近，相当于《大正藏》No.1331，第21卷第536页上段第6行至中段6行。第69号文书现存15行汉文，墨书竖写。第一行首尾都有缺字，其余各行均是下端缺字。这15行文字，相当于《大正藏》No. 1332, 第21卷第535页下段第28行至第536页上段第11行。见龙谷大学佛教文化研究所编：《龙谷大学善本丛书一》，法藏馆，1980年，“研究册”第78—79、120—121页。

③ 马世长：《库木吐喇的汉风洞窟》，收入新疆维吾尔自治区文物管理委员会、库车县文物保管所、北京大学考古系编著：《中国石窟·库木吐喇石窟》，北京：文物出版社，1992年，第207页。

④ 马世长：《库木吐喇的汉风洞窟》，第208页。鉴于该榜题文字的来源为东晋龟兹人所译，可能这一经本早在这一地区流传，与其相关的药师信仰可能在龟兹地区就已存在。这为我们探索汉传佛教药师佛信仰在龟兹地区的传播情况提供了一个有益的视角，值得进一步发掘。

四条提及供养七佛。综合考虑，这些图像和榜题文字可能与药师七佛有关。[①]

（三）永远的释迦佛

释迦牟尼在菩提树下成佛后，度化众生，创立了佛教。传教40年后，他在娑罗树下入灭。佛陀是个历史上的真实人物，他引导信众走上追求的圣道。

释迦牟尼去世后，佛教继续发展。然而随着距离佛在世时间的愈益遥远，信徒们对佛陀的思念愈益强烈。在他们的心中，释迦牟尼不仅仅是个圣者和导师。这样，他的人格属性日益淡漠，而日益被神话。

《法华经》认为释迦牟尼佛久远就已成佛，佛寿无量：

> 尔时世尊知诸菩萨三请不止，而告之言："汝等谛听，如来秘密神通之力。一切世间天、人及阿修罗，……我实成佛已来无量无边百千万亿那由他劫。……自从是来，我常在此娑婆世界说法教化，亦于余处百千万亿那由他阿僧祇国导利众生。……如是，我成佛已来，甚大久远，寿命无量阿僧祇劫，常住不灭。"[②]

并且分身度化十方世界的众生，是万佛之根本（本），其他的分身仅仅是他的化现之身（迹）。佛告大乐说菩萨摩诃萨：

> ……我分身诸佛——在于十方世界说法者，今应当集。[③]

《法华经》久远释迦的佛身观，认为真正的释迦牟尼佛早在久远就已断恶现善，成就佛道，不生不灭。释迦佛的寿命是无量的，法身不灭，佛佛时间上是同一；佛的分身教化各方，佛佛在空间上是统一。[④]

释迦佛的色身，仅仅是释迦牟尼为度化众生中根机粗钝者而采取的方便之道，权宜之法，是将他们导向正道的手段。

库木吐喇石窟第16窟的法华经变就是对法华永远释迦佛观念的阐释。

法华经变绘于该窟主室正壁的上部，为绘塑结合。主室正壁上部龛中原塑有释迦牟尼像，像后影塑身光。佛像坐于两树下，佛头上方的券顶内，飞天吹箫奏乐。表现的正是世尊在灵鹫山为诸菩萨、阿罗汉等说法的情景。当此之时——

> 天雨曼陀罗华、摩诃曼陀罗华、曼殊沙华、摩诃曼殊沙华，而散佛上、及诸大众。[⑤]

佛龛外左右对称绘制文殊菩萨与普贤菩萨及胁侍人物。龛左侧绘骑狮文殊菩萨，项饰瓔珞，臂腕配钏，左足踏莲花，半结跏趺坐于狮子上。周围绘制三身胁侍菩萨。文殊菩萨及周围胁侍菩萨丰腴华美。文殊菩萨左下方绘制一身牵狮昆仑奴，昆仑奴及狮子均踏莲花（图4）。[⑥]龛右侧绘制骑象普贤菩萨，其周围也绘制三身胁侍菩萨，普贤菩萨左侧绘制一身牵象奴，象奴通身黝黑与象均踏莲

---

① 霍旭初：《阿艾石窟题记考识》，《西域研究》2004年第2期，第50—59页。

② 《大正藏》，第9册，第42页。

③ 同上，第32—33页。

④ 同上。

⑤ 同上，第2页。

⑥ 此资料由德国柏林亚洲艺术博物馆提供。

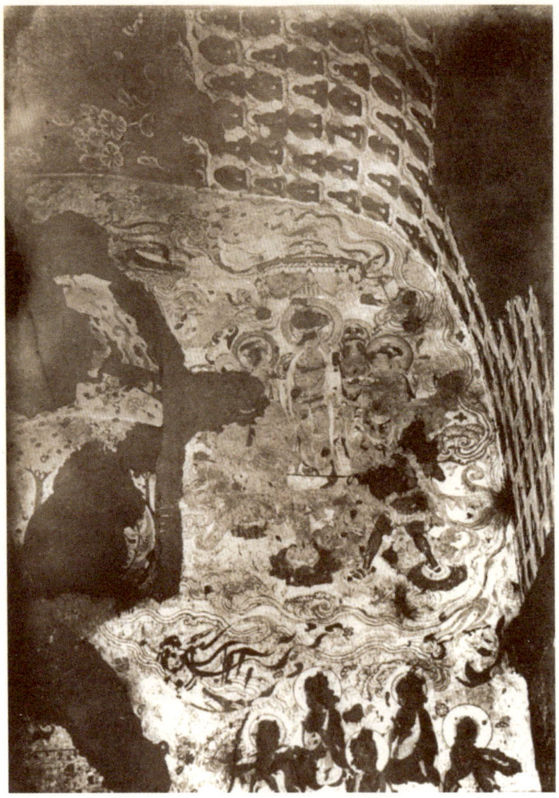
图 4 库木吐喇石窟第 16 窟主室正壁局部

花。[①] 文殊和普贤周围云气环绕，飞天供养。

文殊和普贤是法华会上的两个大菩萨，文殊菩萨代表智、慧、证，普贤菩萨代表理、定、行，两者居于世尊两侧，体现了本尊理智、定慧、行证的完备圆满，正是他们协助世尊完成了《法华经》的宣化，并且在将来卫护和供养受持和诵读《法华经》的众生。[②]

文殊和普贤两侧下方各绘五身坐佛像，四周祥云围绕，天花飞舞。主室正壁上方的券顶除中脊和叠涩外，均绘有坐于莲座上的小坐佛，表现了法华会上——

> 释迦牟尼所分之身，百千万亿那由他恒河沙等国土中诸佛，各各说法，来集于此；如是次第十方诸佛皆悉来集，坐于八方。[③]

第 16 窟主室正壁上绘制的法华经变主要依据《法华经·序品》绘制，但是画师也增加了一些其他品的内容。例如龛左侧骑着狮子的文殊菩萨和龛右侧乘象的普贤菩萨。文殊是法华会上重要的大菩萨之一，但是现存汉译《法华经》中，均没有提及他骑狮。赴法华会的菩萨中，没有普贤菩萨，普贤乘象的情节出现于《法华经·普贤菩萨劝发品》。此种将骑狮文殊和乘象普贤对称布置的法华经变的图像在初唐时期就已出现于敦煌的第 220 窟和第 331 窟中。

根据学者的研究，在汉传佛教造像系统中，只有释迦牟尼佛和卢舍那佛以文殊和普贤作为胁侍，但是他们出现的时间有所不同。一般来说，包括释迦牟尼、文殊和普贤的所谓释迦三尊像出现在中唐以前，而包括卢舍那佛、文殊和普贤的华严三圣则出现在中唐以后。[④] 库木吐喇第 16 窟具有浓郁的盛唐风格特点，结合龟兹地区历史背景，其绘制时间可能是武周政权重新确立对龟兹地区控制的 7 世纪左右。因而，尽管该窟正壁龛内的塑像已无存，我们大致可以断定正壁上部绘塑内容为法华经变。

（四）宇宙主卢舍那佛

卢舍那佛，梵文 Locanabuddha，即报身佛，是表示证得了绝对真理，获得佛果而显示佛智的佛身。“卢舍那”的意思就是智慧广大，光明普照。卢舍那这个名字其实就是法身“毗卢遮那”的简称，

---

① 此资料由德国柏林亚洲艺术博物馆提供。
② 《大正藏》，第 9 册，第 61—62 页。
③ 同上，第 33 页。
④ 镰田茂雄:《华严三圣像的形成》，收入杨曾文、方广锠编:《佛教与历史文化》，北京：宗教文化出版社，2001 年，第 362—369 页；殷光明:《从释迦三尊到华严三圣的图像转变看大乘菩萨思想的发展》,《敦煌研究》2010 年第 3 期，第 1—10 页；潘亮文:《敦煌唐代的文殊菩萨图像试析》,《敦煌研究》2013 年第 3 期，第 86—102 页。

释迦牟尼佛在立名时，把他的报身和法身立在同一个名中，表示法、报不二。佛有三身，法身即最本质、最圆满的智慧，是无相可言的。法身佛就是宇宙的人格化，一切佛的智慧和宇宙本身平等不二，所以一切佛的法身根本无分别，都是摩诃毗卢遮那佛（汉译为大日如来）。它是过去现在存在于不同空间的佛产生和存在的本原。永恒存在，是诸佛之母。[①]该法身相好庄严，清净常寂，普照十方。[②]

报身是佛的修行依因果感召而来的报应身，是修行圆满、大彻大悟的表现。阿弥陀佛、药师佛等都属于报身佛，卢舍那佛也是。释迦牟尼佛原本是莲华藏世界中，卢舍那佛座下的十地菩萨，也是卢舍那佛的化身、分身之一，他来到娑婆世界，依照法门修行而成就了卢舍那佛的报身。简而言之，毗卢遮那佛是法身佛，卢舍那佛是报身佛，释迦牟尼佛是应身佛。

图 5　阿艾石窟右侧壁卢舍那佛

阿艾石窟主室右侧壁绘有一幅卢舍那佛，使我们对盛唐时期汉传佛教卢舍那佛信仰在龟兹的传播情况有所了解。

此身卢舍那佛立姿，着通肩袈裟，左手作与愿印，右手作施无畏印，左肩绘一钟，右肩绘一鼓。左臂从肩至肘依次绘：一坐姿天人、阿修罗和白象。右臂从肩至肘依次绘：一天人上部和不明动物的身体后半部（仅见躯干、两条后腿及尾巴）。胸部绘一身菩萨及四身跪姿礼拜天人，菩萨似正在说法，这几身人物均位于天宫中。腹部上部绘大海，下部绘须弥山，须弥山上部两侧绘日、月，中部绘四条蛇，左右各两条。腹部下部绘奔马。股部绘画脱落，仅见两结跏趺坐人物的双腿。左膝处绘两身立姿供养胡人，一男一女。右膝绘两身披甲武士（均有头光）。膝盖以下部位脱落（图 5）。

阿艾石窟中的卢舍那佛身上绘有多个展现庄严法身以及法身特点的物象，包括绘于左右肩部的鼓和钟，绘于腹部下部的奔马。

钟鼓作用相似，为寺院行事报时所用，鼓在诵经时也用。它们还都具有警醒睡眠和冥昧的功能。《华严经》中记载，鼓钟能发出妙音，给修行者劝勉。[③]

奔马，则是对法身空寂，亦有亦非特点的譬喻：

> 诸法空寂无生灭，解达非有亦非无，譬如野马水月形，亦如幻梦镜中像，诸法无主悉空寂，因是得成慧灯光。[④]

---

① “去来今佛，一切悉等，为一法身。”《大正藏》，第 10 册，第 592 页。
② 《大正藏》，第 9 册，第 399、736 页。
③ 同上，第 423、436、652 页。
④ 同上，第 436 页。

卢舍那佛也是世界万物的起源，是卢舍那佛的愿力化现了无量的三界六道和万事万物：

> 重观普贤一一身分、一一肢节、一一毛孔中，悉见三千大千世界……如是等事，皆悉显现；十方一切世界，亦复如是。如此娑婆世界，卢舍那如来、应供、等正觉，所现自在力。①

可以看出，阿艾石窟的卢舍那佛身上从上至下依次绘出了天界、阿修罗、人道、畜生道，袈裟的下部已脱落，可能绘有饿鬼和地狱道。正是对有情娑婆世界的描绘。

娑婆世界也是卢舍那佛的度化对象：

> 一切见者两足尊，哀愍众生现神力，令此种种诸天乐，普发妙音咸得闻。于一毛端百千亿，那由他国微尘数，如是无量诸如来，于中安住说妙法。……于彼一切刹土中，悉有如来演妙音，随顺一切众生心，为转最上净法轮。刹中种种众生身，身中复有种种刹，人天诸趣各各异，佛悉知已为说法。②

卢舍那佛身体各部位绘制的六道多位于椭圆形中，正表现了卢舍那佛身放光明照耀、度化众生的情况。

（五）三世十方佛

十方诸佛观念是大乘佛教佛陀观的一个重要内容。这种观念早在部派佛教中的大众部中就已出现，佛教发展到大乘阶段后，这种观念成为所有大乘教派的基本观念。

大乘佛教认为，我们生活的世界，无量无边，不仅有我们生活的娑婆世界，还存在无量的其他世界。这些世界的分布地域从空间方位上可分为东、西、南、北、东南、西南、东北、西北、上、下十个方向。十方有无数世界及净土，称为十方世界、十方法界、十方净土、十方刹等。其中之诸佛及众生，则称为十方诸佛、十方众生。

十方佛的观念至迟在公元 2 世纪就已经在中亚地区出现，而且已与三世佛观念结合起来。这种情况可以在 2 世纪由月氏僧人支娄迦谶译出的《佛说般舟三昧经·问事品》中见到：

> 佛告飚陀和。有三昧名十方诸佛悉在前立。能行是法。汝之所问悉可得也。飚陀和白佛。愿为说之。今佛说者。多所过度安隐十方。为诸菩萨现大明相意善解便离欲，常念佛有威德……悉见知无数变，过去佛及当来，并现在人中尊，诸相好若干种。③

北朝时期及其以后，千佛一直是敦煌石窟中非常流行的题材，其表达的具体内涵也是多种多样。其中表达三世十方佛也是其内涵之一。④

龟兹石窟中具有相似特点的千佛图像被保存在库木吐喇第 11 窟、14 窟、16 窟、37 窟和阿艾石窟中。

---

① 《大正藏》，第 9 册，第 784 页。

② 《大正藏》，第 10 册，第 198 页。

③ 《大正藏》，第 13 册，第 897—899 页。

④ 贺世哲：《关于北朝石窟千佛图像诸问题》，《敦煌研究》1989 年第 3 期，第 1—10 页；陈慧宏：《敦煌莫高窟早期的千佛图》，第 48 页，台湾大学硕士论文，1994 年；赖鹏举：《丝路佛教的图像与禅法》，财团法人圆光佛学研究所，2002 年；梁晓鹏：《敦煌莫高窟千佛图像研究》，北京：民族出版社，2006 年；沙武田：《千佛及其造像艺术》，《法音》2011 年第 7 期，第 55—64 页。

图 6　阿艾石窟主室券顶千佛

其中具有明确题记的是阿艾石窟。（图 6）

阿艾石窟为方形窟。主室正壁绘一铺观无量寿经变图。左、右侧壁绘：药师佛、卢舍那佛、药师佛、文殊菩萨、观音菩萨、弥勒菩萨和地藏菩萨等。券顶原遍绘汉式小坐佛，现保存右侧券腹部分。券顶小坐佛间出现了造“七佛”和“十方佛”的汉文题记。说明其表达的是三世十方佛的观念。至于在本窟中绘出千佛的目的，《佛说观无量寿经》记载：

> 尔时世尊放眉间光，其光金色，遍照十方无量世界；还住佛顶，化为金台，如须弥山。十方诸佛净妙国土，皆于中现。……令韦提希见……尔时世尊告韦提希：……此三种业，乃是过去、未来、现在三世诸佛净业正因。①

可以看出，经中提到了十方佛在佛的法身中展现，凸显了释迦牟尼佛的神圣性和超越性；为了强调西方净土修行法的权威性，专门谈到过去现在未来千佛就是按照这种修行方法成佛的。

库木吐喇第 14 窟亦为方形窟，纵券顶，主室正中有一方形坛基。

主室正壁绘阿弥陀经变。前壁下部坍塌，现仅存上部少许绘画，应为经变画，但内容不可辨识。左右侧壁壁画多不存。券顶绘汉式千佛，表现的应当也是三世十方佛。

据《佛说阿弥陀经》记载：

> 今佛独当念，诸已过去佛，诸当来佛，若他方佛国，今现在佛，独展转相思念故，佛面色光明乃尔耳！②
>
> 其人寿命欲终时，阿弥陀佛即自与诸菩萨、阿罗汉，共翻飞行迎之，则往生阿弥陀佛国，便于七宝水池莲华中化生。即自然受身长大，则作阿惟越致菩萨。便即与诸菩萨，共翻辈飞行，供养八方、上下诸无央数佛。即逮智慧勇猛，乐听经道，其心欢乐。所居七宝舍宅，在虚空中，恣随其意。在所欲作为，去阿弥陀佛近。③

这里，十方三世千佛又成为供养的对象和佛的总称。

库木吐喇第 16 窟主室正壁塑绘结合表现法华经变。左侧壁原绘有观无量经变，右侧壁原绘药师经变。主室券顶绘汉式千佛，其样式也与前面二例完全相同。

据《法华经》记载：

① 《大正藏》，第 12 册，第 341 页。

② 同上，第 300 页。

③ 同上，第 309 页。

> 尔时佛放白毫一光，即见东方五百万亿那由他恒河沙等国土诸佛……是时诸佛各将一大菩萨以为侍者，至娑婆世界。……尔时诸佛各于此座结加趺坐，如是展转遍满三千大千世界，而于释迦牟尼佛一方所分之身，犹故未尽。时释迦牟尼佛，欲容受所分身诸佛故，八方各更变二百万亿那由他国，皆令清净。……如是次第十方诸佛，皆悉来集坐于八方。尔时一一方四百万亿那由他国土，诸佛如来遍满其中。[①]

尽管经文中仅仅说到了十方佛，没有提到过去现在未来三世佛，但是在其异译本《正法华经·药王如来品第十》中却提到了“去来今佛皆从是出。若族姓子族姓女，欲得供养十方诸佛，即当受持正法华经”[②]。说明三世十方佛也是法华信仰的重要组成部分，它们一起见证了《法华经》的真实不虚，不生不灭。

此外，尽管由于洞窟壁画保存不全，库木吐喇石窟第11窟和第37窟的整体内容无法得知，但是券顶的千佛基于其形式完全一致，其可能表现的也为三世十方佛。

三

汉地佛教佛陀观在龟兹地区的传播，对本土传统佛陀观念造成了一定的冲击。一个明显的表现就是反映汉地净土因素的图像在龟兹风洞窟中的出现。它反映了汉传佛教佛陀观对龟兹本土佛教的渗透。

库木吐喇石窟第58窟为一中心柱窟，现存主室和后室，后室由左右后三甬道组成。主室平面呈方形，纵券顶。主室正壁中下部开拱形的大龛，龛内正壁绘一棵圆冠形的树，树干上系有绿色的飘帛，下部似绘有方座，但已残损。树上残存树神形象，此外还绘有多种乐器，包括琵琶、鼓、腰鼓、锣、筚篥。乐器的空间饰以莲蕾（图7）。龛外左右两端绘五髻乾达婆和帝释天夫妇。上部的半圆面绘一幅场面巨大的伎乐图，背景为菱格山形，人物形体较大，两侧共绘八身伎乐，中部的菱格内绘禅修的婆罗门与动物。左右侧壁原绘说法图。前壁上方半圆端面绘补处菩萨兜率天说法，左侧壁面残存龙王形象。主室券顶中脊绘天相图，券腹绘菱格塔中坐佛。左右后甬道壁画全部脱落。

图7　库木吐喇第58窟主室正壁龛

从保存的壁画看本窟壁画无论是构图布局和艺术风格，依然为龟兹本地特点，如主室正壁开龛，侧壁绘说法图，前壁上方绘补处菩萨在兜率天说法，券顶中脊绘天相图，券腹塔中坐佛为菱格构图。但是在作为洞窟中最重要的主龛的背景中绘出净土图像，券顶绘千佛，则说明此窟主尊已非人格化的释迦。

① 《大正藏》，第9册，第32—33页。

② 同上，第100页。

本窟主室大部分题材均属龟兹传统题材，表现释迦的各种事迹。按照佛教的教义，这些事件的发生地均在我们有情众生生活的娑婆世界。

有情世界的净土一般认为有两个，一个是未来弥勒下生时的人间净土，一个是《法华经》中所说的灵山净土。根据整窟的图像内涵，笔者以为第58窟可能反映的是永远的释迦佛说法的灵山净土。[①]

依据《法华经》的记载，释迦牟尼成佛以来，

> 甚大久远，寿命无量阿僧祇劫，常住不灭。[②]
>
> 常在此娑婆世界说法教化，亦于余处百千万亿那由他阿僧祇国导利众生。[③]

释迦牟尼佛示现涅槃，而实非涅槃。

> 尔来无量劫，为度众生故，方便现涅槃，而实不灭度，常住此说法。[④]

久远劫来的释迦牟尼佛，其常住国土就在这娑婆世界，如来常在此说法，

> 常在灵鹫山，及余诸住处。[⑤]

释迦牟尼过去久远，行菩萨道时，发愿度脱娑婆世界六道众生，成佛后，以清净心成就其净土。净土成就后，为使众生成佛，释迦牟尼佛于此娑婆世界示现法华净土。

法华净土——

> 其地琉璃，坦然平正，阎浮檀金以界八道，宝树行列，诸台楼观皆悉宝成，其菩萨众咸处其中。[⑥]
>
> 园林诸堂阁，种种宝庄严，宝树多花果，众生所游乐。诸天击天鼓，常作众伎乐，雨曼陀罗花，散佛及大众。[⑦]

此法华净土，在世界劫难来临时，安稳快乐，不受影响：

> 众生见劫尽，大火所烧时，我此土安隐，天人常充满。[⑧]

依据《法华经》的记载，此法华净土，既无三界之秽恶，又不离三界而另存，就包含我们所在的南阎浮提，这是此净土的殊胜之处。然而众生由于心识的不同，也是释迦牟尼佛为度化众生的需要，众生所见和释迦示现的世界是不同的。六道众生所见为有漏的秽土世界，而证得智慧的菩萨所见和佛所示现的则为无量珍宝庄严的佛土。

---

① 参见方立天:《佛教哲学》，北京：宗教文化出版社，2013年，第169页；方立天:《方立天讲谈录》，北京：九州出版社，2014年，第167—170页；汪志强:《印度佛教净土思想研究》，成都：巴蜀书社，2010年，第5页。

② 《大正藏》，第9册，第42页。

③ 同上。

④ 同上，第43页。

⑤ 同上。

⑥ 同上，第45页。

⑦ 同上，第43页。

⑧ 同上。

这种差异体现了三界唯心，万法唯识，一切无非唯心所现的观念。灵山净土属唯识净土，唯识所变，故随其心净，则佛土净。众生只要敬信供养，即可得佛显现净土：

> 众见我灭度，广供养舍利，咸皆怀恋慕，而生渴仰心。众生既信伏，质直意柔软，一心欲见佛，不自惜身命。时我及众僧，俱出灵鹫山……余国有众生，恭敬信乐者，我复于彼中，为说无上法。①

该窟窟顶千佛当是对十方佛的表现，笔者前文中有所阐释。

同样描绘有净土场景的还有库木吐喇第 50 窟。该窟亦为一龟兹式中心柱窟，中心柱正壁开龛，主室中脊绘天象图，主室正壁龛侧壁及顶、龛外壁面、左右侧壁及券腹，左右后甬道大部壁面均绘方格因缘。根据学者研究，正壁龛内绘制的因缘故事表现的是过去佛的供养事迹②，其他壁面估计也是相同的内涵。此外，该窟左甬道外侧壁开龛，龛正壁、左右侧壁下部均绘一列菩萨，应当也是对过去佛的表现。这些内容基本上还属于龟兹本土佛陀观的内涵。

但是，有意思的是，主室正壁龛的正壁以及左甬道内侧壁龛的正壁上绘出树冠、方座，作为佛的背景（图 8）。这在龟兹本土佛教中不多见，而在同时期汉地佛教中常见。主室前壁门上方半圆端面正中绘一佛二菩萨，两身菩萨下方各绘两身莲花童子作供养（图 9）。这些图像在汉地净土图像中多见。尽管上述造像中的主尊尚无法确定，但本窟所反映的佛陀观念，远远不是小乘佛陀观所能涵盖，体现出浓厚的大乘佛陀观色彩，这与汉地佛教的传入是密不可分的。

图 8　库木吐喇第 50 窟主室正壁龛正壁（局部）

图 9　库木吐喇第 50 窟主室前壁（局部）

① 《大正藏》，第 9 册，第 43 页。

② 荻原裕敏：《试论库木吐喇第 50 窟主室正壁佛龛千佛图像的程序》，《西域研究》2015 年第 3 期，第 36—42 页。

The Spread and Influence of Central Plain Buddhism in Kucha in Tang Dynasty

—Focus on the Buddha Concept

Miao Lihui (Remin University of China/Xinjiang Kucha Academy)

Abstract: In Tang dynasty, a large of the soldiers and the mass of Han nation, as the same time, the Buddha ideas of Central Plain Buddhism, including the believes of Amitabha Buddha, Healing Tathagata BuddhaViroc, ana Buddha, unextinguishable Sakyamuni Buddha and all buddhas of the ten directions and three times, spread into Kucha. Affected by the background, the local mass accepted the ideas about Amitabha Buddha and unextinguishable Sakyamuni Buddha.

Keywords: Central Plain Buddhism; Buddha ideas; Kucha

中国伊斯兰经学派在明末清初的创立和发展 *

沈一鸣（北京大学）

摘　要： 目前学界普遍认为中国穆斯林的经堂教育和知识传承源于明末伊斯兰经师胡登洲（1522—1597）。但是本文通过对史料和文本的分析研究，可以发现胡登洲所创立的伊斯兰经学派在明末清初的发展过程中很可能受到了教内穆斯林的质疑和反对。在选经、读经、讲经、传经、译经、注经和写经过程中，伊斯兰经学派借鉴了中国哲学经注传统，采用书字阐释伊斯兰教义。在伊斯兰经学派争取教内对书字阐释伊斯兰教义合法性和权威性认同的同时，中文伊斯兰经书的读者群也得以扩大，并逐渐获得了儒家社会的了解和认可，从而令以胡登洲为代表的中国伊斯兰经学派在明末清初阐释伊斯兰教义的竞争中最终胜出并传承至今。

关键词： 伊斯兰经学派；胡登洲；书字；经堂教育

前言

伊斯兰教自唐代进入中国。随着蒙古人对亚洲的征服，大量来自中亚及更远地区的穆斯林移居到中国中原地区。在蒙古人统治的元朝覆灭之后，由汉人建立的明朝见证了穆斯林移民的本地化和中国穆斯林社群的发展。由胡登洲开创的中国伊斯兰经学派即产生于这一时期。“经学”一般指儒家经典的注释传统，可以追溯到西汉时期。在中国穆斯林的语境下，经学特指对伊斯兰经典的研习和注释。当代学者一般认为今日中国中原地区的伊斯兰教育，即经堂教育，起源于经学派胡登洲（1522—1597）。① 然而，对于这一观点有以下两方面值得商榷：

首先，“经堂教育”这一名词出现于 20 世纪初，强调了中国伊斯兰教教学的地点为清真寺。尽管清真寺在伊斯兰教创立之初就作为穆斯林祈祷的场所，以及资讯交流和教育的中心②，但是现存史料中并没有明末之前在中原的清真寺中进行伊斯兰教学活动的证据③。而胡登洲的传记说其“设馆于

*　本文由国家社会科学基金项目《明末清初回儒舍起灵（蕴善）汉译作品研究》支持，项目编号 16CZJ017，项目类别：青年项目。

①　丁世仁：《中国经堂教育溯源》，《回族研究》2012 年第 2 期，第 106 页；冯增烈：《胡登洲》，中国伊斯兰百科全书编辑委员会编：《中国伊斯兰百科全书》，成都：四川辞书出版社，2007 年第 2 版，第 226 页。

②　有关穆斯林世界的教育历史，参见 H. Khan, *History of Muslim Education*, Karachi, Acedemy of Educational Research, All Pakistan Educational Conference, 1967-1973。有关中亚地区的穆斯林教育史，参见 Maria Eva Subtelny and Anas B. Khalidov, “The Curriculum of Islamic Higher Learning in Timurid Iran in the Light of the Sunni Revival under Shāh-Rukh”, *Journal of the American Oriental Society*, 2, 1995, pp. 210-236。

③　参见丁世仁：《中国经堂教育溯源》。

家"[①]，说明那一时期中国伊斯兰教学场所有可能为家塾，而非清真寺。这一家塾的教学传统尚不知从何时开始，但是可以推测，自胡登洲始可能一直持续了至少三代。直至胡登洲的第四代弟子冯养吾（生卒年不详）时，才第一次被明确提及在"寺"，即清真寺中接受了伊斯兰教育。[②]

其次，在明末清初的穆斯林社群本地化的发展过程中，除了胡登洲所创始的"经学派"以外，应该同时存在其他穆斯林群体在从事伊斯兰经典诠释和穆斯林教育，而这些群体对于读经和教育的方式持有不同观点。金宜久在《中国伊斯兰探秘——刘智研究》一书的导言中也提到了中国伊斯兰教育的发展过程中"不乏争辩和挫折"，只是"它究竟受何挫折、其争辩的对象究系何人，限于资料还难以说明"。[③]

由此可见，目前学界将经堂教育直接归宗于经学派开创者胡登洲是不妥当的。伊斯兰经学派与经堂教育有着密切的关联，但是从教学活动地点、教学内容和方法上来看，并不完全等同于今天所说的经堂教育。虽然有学者认识到在穆斯林教育的发展过程中，伊斯兰经学派经过了激烈的竞争和质疑，但是对于这一竞争的过程，以及经学派学者如何应对等问题尚没有相关研究进行充分的讨论。通过对经学派学者赵灿所撰写的穆斯林传记集《经学系传谱》（1713）等史料以及相关中文伊斯兰著作的研究，本文将梳理中国伊斯兰经学派的出现和发展，并讨论在与其他穆斯林群体的竞争中，经学派如何逐渐获得权威性，并最终成为今日中国穆斯林教育的主流。

一　中国伊斯兰经学派的产生背景和定义

伊斯兰教进入中国后，唐、宋时期的中文材料很少提及穆斯林在中原地区的活动，似乎他们与当地人保持着种族和文化上的隔离。[④] 随着蒙古人征服亚洲，来自中亚及更远地区的大量穆斯林移居中国。在此期间，穆斯林在蒙古统治者的支持下参与到中国的内部政务中，其地位和角色都发生了重大变化。与此同时，一些穆斯林将科技知识带入中国，在天文、历法、数学和医药等方面对中国文化做出了巨大贡献。根据《元秘书监志》所述，至1273年，皇家天文台的图书馆共收集了195部阿拉伯文和波斯文文献，其中大部分为科学文献，只有一小部分涉及哲学和文学。[⑤] 自元代中期至明代早期，穆斯林知识分子开始更主动地参与到中国主流社会文化的发展中。他们中的一些人在人文和军事等领域取得了卓越的成就，并被儒家社会所认可，但这其中的大多数人的姓名仍旧取自母语波斯语或者阿拉伯语，说明他们与中国主流社会仍旧保持着一定的距离。[⑥]

元朝覆灭后，由汉人统治的明朝继承下大量的阿拉伯文和波斯文文献，由此开启了这些文献的汉译工作。洪武十五年（1382），皇帝命令钦天监——来自西域的穆斯林后裔翻译从元代皇家图书馆承袭

① 赵灿：《经学系传谱》，《清真大典》影印清抄本，页46上。

② 同上，页59上。

③ 金宜久：《中国伊斯兰教探秘——刘智研究》，北京：中国人民大学出版社，2010年，第11页。

④ Donald Leslie, "Living with the Chinese: The Muslim Expansion in China, T'ang to Ming", *Chinese Ideas About Nature and Society: Studies in Honour of Derk Bodde*, Hong Kong, Hong Kong University Press, 1987, p. 176; 刘迎胜：《回族语言800年发展史简要回顾——从波斯语到"回族汉语"》，《回族研究》2003年第4期，第144页。

⑤ 王士点、商企翁：《元秘书监志》，扬州：江苏广陵古籍刻印社，1988年，卷七，页13下—14下。马坚：《元秘书监志"回回书籍"释义》，《光明日报》1955年7月7日。

⑥ 参见陈垣：《元西域人华化考》，上海古籍出版社，2000年；田坂兴道：《中国における回教の传来とその弘通》，东洋文库，1964年，第2卷，第1149页。

的阿拉伯文和波斯文文献。[①] 正如《明译天文书》所载："（太祖）且命之曰：尔西域人，素习本音，兼通华语。"[②] 皇帝更进一步要求这些官员"其口以授儒，尔儒译其义，辑成文焉"[③]。也就是说，当时的汉译工作是由通晓原文的西域移民后代与儒家学者共同完成。由此可以推测，明初服务于天文台的西域穆斯林移民后裔能够阅读阿拉伯文和波斯文原文，并转化成中文，但是他们的书面写作能力似乎还没有被儒家社会所认可。因此，以《明译天文书》为代表的这一时期翻译作品的文字实际上夹杂了阿拉伯语和波斯语科技术语的中文音译以及中国传统语文表述方式，是穆斯林和儒家学者的合作成果。

自15世纪开始，一部分穆斯林移民后裔逐渐融入儒家社会，他们的穆斯林身份大多只能通过家谱来判断，这些人包括马文升（1426—1510）、海瑞（1514—1587）、李贽（1527—1602）等。就如毕敬士（Claude L. Pickens，1900—1985）所说："通常那些被认为做出了贡献的人们都不被认为是穆斯林。"[④] 在同一时期，来自穆斯林记录的文献表明，另有一些穆斯林后裔在保持他们的宗教信仰和传统的同时，对于学习中国儒家经典产生了浓厚的兴趣和急迫的需求。据《经学系传谱》所载，胡登洲年幼时跟随一名高姓老师在家馆中学习伊斯兰经书[⑤]，然而在学习期间感到"虽明义理，然只可符以汉音之鄙俗者"[⑥]。因此，胡登洲"每欲谋习儒学，贯通一家……可启后世之蒙，能泄先天之秘"[⑦]。可见，中国的穆斯林在16世纪已经能够掌握阿拉伯语、波斯语和汉语，但是他们对于汉语的表达能力仍不甚满意。他们意识到只有将儒学与伊斯兰教义融会贯通，方能阐明伊斯兰真理。基于这样的认识，胡登洲年过半百之时，仍师从一儒家学者研习儒家经典。[⑧]

以胡登洲为代表的这一类中国穆斯林知识分子群体的出现，标志着中国伊斯兰经学派的诞生。他们既不同于专长于科技知识的穆斯林早期移民，也不同于与他们同时代的流淌着穆斯林先人血液，但实际上已经被界定为儒家学者的群体。他们在保持伊斯兰信仰和传统的前提下，认识到儒家传统文化对于理解和阐述伊斯兰教义的重要性，希望通过"以儒诠经"将伊斯兰哲学思想介绍到中国主流社会。

二　经学派之原文经典

按照伊斯兰经学派的观点，"初吾教自唐迄明，虽有经籍传入兹土，而其理艺难传，旨义难悉，故世代无一二精通教理之掌牧，以致多人沦落迷途，漫漫长夜而甘醉梦之不觉也"[⑨]。也就是说，在胡登洲之前，虽然有伊斯兰经书传入中原地区，但是并没有人能够正确释读这些经书所传达的教义，以至于许多人误入歧途而不自知。经学派认为，只有自胡登洲开始，"宣天房之秘，漏泄其微，按东土

① 《明实录·明太祖实录》卷一四一，台北："中研院"历史语言研究所，1962—1966年，第3页。同见阔识牙儿：《明译天文书》，马明达、陈静辑注：《中国回回历法辑丛》，兰州：甘肃民族出版社，1996年，第1—2页。

② 阔识牙儿：《明译天文书》，第2页。

③ 同上，第1页。

④ Claude L. Pickens, *Annotated Bibliography of Literature on Islam in China*, Hankow, Society of Friends of the Moslems in China, 1950, p. 64.

⑤ 《经学系传谱》，《清真大典》影印清抄本，页43上："高太师馆中习读"。同见于振贵、雷晓静主编：《中国回族金石录》，宁夏人民出版社，2001年，第513页："长随同乡高师祖习受本教之学"。

⑥ 《经学系传谱》，《清真大典》影印清抄本，页43上。

⑦ 同上。

⑧ 同上，页44上至44下。

⑨ 同上，页1下。

之音配合其节，究于理之赅而不偏，辞之平而有味，且好学不厌，诲人不倦”[①]。胡登洲因此声名远播，上门求道的学生络绎不绝，经学派也因此创立并传承下去。

对于以“经”为中心的中国伊斯兰经学派而言，要研读和诠释经典，首先必须获得经书。由于自明代以来中央政府控制了边境的民间交流，明清时期中国穆斯林作为中原地区的少数族群，与其先辈相比较，和当时的境外穆斯林的交流更少，生存环境也变得相对闭塞。这一时期，除了来自中亚的穆斯林商人和苏非旅行者随身携带的抄本之外，一些之前散落在民间的抄本也成为中国穆斯林学者争相寻访的目标。

从《经学系传谱》中经学派穆斯林学者的传记内容看，寻访并收集伊斯兰原文经典的过程充满了各类轶事，是这些人物传记中必不可少的内容。这些轶事既体现了获得真经抄本的不易，也暗示了传主因为拥有这些经书而在诠释伊斯兰教义上具有权威性。例如，胡登洲在新丰（今陕西省境内）遇到了一名据说来自天房[②]的缠头叟。胡登洲见到这位老人带着一本名为“《母噶麻忒》，兹土未见之经也”[③]。但缠头叟拒绝把这部经书卖给胡登洲。几个月后，胡在北京街市上偶遇一位穆斯林老妪，发现她保存有这部经书的另一个抄本，胡登洲即刻买下了它。该经书后来成为了经学派的一部重要经文。

尽管经学派的穆斯林学者热衷于收集原文经书的抄本，但是并不是他们收集的每一部经书都被该学派所认可。只有经过“精研确核”[④]以确定“正典”[⑤]之后，被认可的经书方能被研读、注释和传承。

据《经学系传谱》所载，17 世纪和 18 世纪有近千名来自中亚及更远地区的穆斯林进入中国。[⑥]这其中，大多数人被经学派认为是“游食者”[⑦]和“碌碌张罗”[⑧]，只有一小部分在中国从事伊斯兰经文的传授工作。其中一些人被认为在传播和解释“正学”[⑨]，“厘正教款”[⑩]，被形容为“廉介不贪”[⑪]，受到了伊斯兰经学派的肯定。这些人包括极料理、逸蛮阿訇、厄蒲杜勒直利黎和噶信。[⑫]通过与这些外来穆斯林的交流，经学派的穆斯林学者们拓宽了视野，对伊斯兰经典的理解更加深入和透彻，促进了经学派的发展。例如，经学派的常志美（1610—1670）对《米而萨德·阿巴德》（*Mirṣād al-ʿIbād*）的经注

① 赵灿:《经学系传谱》,《清真大典》影印清抄本，页 2 下。

② “天房”，又有同音词“天方”，又称“克尔白”，一般指伊斯兰教圣城麦加。

③ 赵灿:《经学系传谱》,《清真大典》影印清抄本，页 43 下。

④ 同上，页 21 下。

⑤ 同上。

⑥ 同上，页 92 上。

⑦ 同上。

⑧ 同上，页 92 下。

⑨ 同上，页 92 上。

⑩ 同上。

⑪ 同上，页 92 下。

⑫ 同上，页 92 上—91 下。“极料理”“厄蒲杜勒直利黎”这样的名字应是原名的音译转写，其他人名有的说明了其所有者的家乡，例如“逸蛮阿訇”中的“逸蛮”应为“也门”一词的音译转写；而有的则说明了职位，例如“阿訇”说明了教内职位，“噶信”则可能是“法官”一词的波斯语音译转写。一些学者试图通过其他历史材料，例如碑文和地方志来确定这些穆斯林的身份，但是到目前为止还没有找到可信的证据。参见马景:《〈经学系传谱〉中“逸蛮阿訇”考辨》,《中国穆斯林》2001 年第 2 期。

主要依据了一部名为《富而斯》的经书，而这部经书正是来自于极料理。[①] 与此同时，在这些传播经文的外来穆斯林中，也有被经学派所批判的人物。例如明末有个叫作失利夫的穆斯林，来自“虎喇撒国”[②]，就被形容为一个爱卖弄的人，而他的经注也被经学派批判为“文风舛错，义理乖张”[③]。

对于经书内容，虽然《经学系传谱》列出了失利夫带入中原地区的27本非正统经书书名，但这些书名用潦草的阿拉伯字母拼写，且并没有像《经学系传谱》中列举的正统书籍那样提供中文音译转写，因此无法根据这些简单的标题而确定经书原本。关于这些经书的内容，仅有的线索即赵灿在《经学系传谱》中转述的失利夫经书中的一个故事，即圣人割下自己身上的肉去喂一只鹰。[④] 这则轶事被赵灿批判为“不通机宜，不知资盗之义耳。岂不知鹰乃伤鸟害众之禽乎。此乃释家经典中有此悖理之言也”[⑤]。经学派穆斯林认为，如此非正统的经文只会让读者困惑，即使他们完成了穆斯林的功课[⑥]，“岂但不能招福，而反由斯获罪矣”[⑦]。而对于整个中国穆斯林社会而言，教内的冲突与不和也当归因于这些经书的传播。[⑧] 因此，穆斯林学者在辨析经文时应当“细心稽究，以辨虚实”[⑨]，那些被认为是“不符教理”[⑩] 或者“绝无意味”[⑪] 的经书应该被舍弃。

与经书收集的热情相对比的是，穆斯林学者对于已经获得的经书抄本的态度颇为保守。一旦获得了被认为是正典的经书抄本，穆斯林就将其珍藏在私人图书馆中，无论去哪里旅行都随身携带，且不轻易展示于世人。甚至对于自己的学生，也只是口授经书，至多让学生们抄录需要的章节。到了经师临终时，这些抄本只会传给他的某一位继承人，通常是其儿子或学生。例如，前文所述的胡登洲所收集的《母噶麻忒》经书抄本，在18世纪早期已经被传至一个在长安的穆斯林家庭。据说抄本的主人非常珍爱这一抄本，他只允许人们看一眼外观，“予百金弗售也”[⑫]。

穆斯林学者对于原文经书抄本的态度直到19世纪晚期都没有改变。法国都隆（d’Ollone）教团在1906年到1909年间访问了北京和兰州的清真寺，以调研中国的伊斯兰抄本现状。他们的报告指出这些伊斯兰抄本被认为是私人财物，其拥有者不愿展示给外人，而只同意提供收藏目录。[⑬] 到了20世纪初，中国穆斯林学者马坚（1906—1978）在埃及留学时发表的有关中国穆斯林概况一文中，也如此描写当时他遇到的情况：“学生们不知道第一手资料，只是从他们的老师那里通过中文口授学习……阿拉伯语书在中国是抄本，而学生抄录下他们需要的章节。”[⑭]

综上所述，16世纪中原地区的穆斯林社会中流传着类型和内容各异的原文经书，并被不同的人

① 《经学系传谱》,《清真大典》影印清抄本，页90上。
② 波斯文音译转写，即今天伊朗东北部的霍拉桑省。
③ 《经学系传谱》,《清真大典》影印清抄本，页22上。
④ 同上，页77下。
⑤ 同上。
⑥ 即穆斯林五功“念、礼、斋、课、朝”。
⑦ 《经学系传谱》,《清真大典》影印清抄本，页22下。
⑧ 同上，页23上：“一教似分两途，总由此经而起。”
⑨ 同上，页23下。
⑩ 同上，页22下。
⑪ 同上，页23下。
⑫ 同上，页46下。
⑬ A. Vissiére, “Catalogues De Livres”, *Revue Du Monde Musulman*, VI, 1908, p. 697.
⑭ Ma Jian, “The Views of a Chinese Moslem” , translated by Philip Blackwood, *The Moslem World*, 26, 1936, pp. 73–74.

群所释读。因此，这种多元化的局面可能产生了中国穆斯林社群内部的争论和矛盾。对于伊斯兰经学派而言，对其收集的经书进行分辨的标准分为两部分，一是对推荐和阐释经书的穆斯林能力的评估，如尊极料理、贬失利夫；二是对经书内容的评估。一些经书，例如《米而萨德·阿巴德》《母噶麻忒》随着经学派的发展逐渐被这一学派的穆斯林学者所确定并传承，而另一些经书因其内容不宜，则被经学派批判并舍弃。

到了19世纪末20世纪初，经学派最核心的经书被认定为“十三本经”[①]，一个内容涵盖了阿拉伯语和波斯语语法、文学、哲学和宗教的经书清单。通过对20世纪初西方传教士在中原地区穆斯林学者那里抄录的多份私人藏书单的研究，可见每一个书单的书目虽不尽相同，但大部分书籍都可以对应于“十三本经”，由此也印证了经学派通过对经书的收集和辨析，最终确立了以“十三本经”为基础的正统经书书目。

三 经学派之中文伊斯兰经书

相比于对原文经书抄本的保守态度，经学派穆斯林似乎对中文伊斯兰经书，包括原创作品和原文经书汉译本的流传报以容忍，甚至是鼓励的态度。从现存的中文伊斯兰著作看，经学派的汉译早于中文原创作品，而汉译工作可以说传承于早期穆斯林移民的科技翻译，开始于胡登洲时期。在《经学系传谱》的序言中，赵灿说胡登洲“慕本教经书，欲译国语，以为斯土万世法”[②]。但现存的材料不能确定胡登洲是否完成了书面的汉译作品并传世。目前有确切证据的最早完成中文伊斯兰著作的人是马君实（约1600—1680）。[③] 他的中文经注《卫真要略》据说“江浙多受其益”[④]。此后，穆斯林学者越来越多地参与到翻译和创作中文伊斯兰经书的实践中。

基于自胡登洲开始的对“以儒诠经”的重视，经学派穆斯林一直在提高自身的儒学水平。17世纪到19世纪，经学派穆斯林学者已经能够运用成熟的中国传统哲学表述方式来阐释伊斯兰教义，由此创作并出版了大量的中文伊斯兰著作，从而形成了一个新的著作种类，叫作“汉克塔布”，即综合了中文词“汉”以及阿拉伯词“Kitāb”（书）的音译转写的新词汇。这一类别的代表作包括王岱舆（约1584—1670）创作的《正教真诠》《清真大学》《希真正答》，张中（约1583—1663）编译的《归真总义》，伍遵契（约1598—1698）翻译的《归真要道》，舍起灵（1638—1703）翻译的《昭元秘诀》，马注（1640—1711）创作的《清真指南》，刘智（约1655—1745）创作的《天方典礼》和《天方性理》，以及译作《真境昭微》等。

对于一部被确定为正典的原文经书，不同时期也会流传不同译者的版本。例如，由波斯苏非纳吉姆·丁·拉奇（Najm al-Dīn Rāzī，1177—1256）创作的《米尔萨德·阿巴德》在1668年前后被舍起灵翻译为《推原正达》，约1678年由伍遵契翻译为《归真要道》。在《天方性理》中，刘智将《米尔萨

① 参见庞士谦：《中国回教寺院教育之沿革及课本》，马松亭编：《禹贡：回教专号》，东方文化书局，1973年，第153—158页。

② 《经学系传谱》，《清真大典》影印清抄本，页2上。

③ 马君实被认为是王岱舆的老师。尽管确信马君实的《卫真要道》早于王岱舆的《正教真诠》的完成，但是基于《正教真诠》的传播和影响力，学界仍普遍把《正教真诠》看作最早的中文伊斯兰著作。参见马景：《马君实生平著述考》，《回族研究》2011年第2期。

④ 《经学系传谱》，《清真大典》影印清抄本，页81下。

德·阿巴德》的经名翻译为《道行推原经》，并引用了其中的片段，但不确定刘是否完成了全文翻译。

此外，一些著作和译作还一直再版，例如王岱舆的《正教真诠》一书在1949年之前至少有六个版本问世，最早的版本可以追溯到1657年，而参与的出版社也遍布中原广大区域，包括广州（1801年版）、成都（1873年版）、镇江（1904年版）等。[①] 刘智的《天方典礼》直至20世纪前半叶被印刷了近20次，印刷地点分布于成都、广州、北京等地。由此可见“汉克塔布”在穆斯林社会之流行。

然而，并不是所有用中文写作的伊斯兰经书都得到经学派的认可。即使是列于同一作者名下的作品，也会有所区别。例如，舍起灵的《觉世省迷录》[②] 一书据称是对一本名为《穆难必哈提》或《摸喃哷哈哈》的阿拉伯文或者波斯文经书的注释，是张问行对其师舍起灵课堂讲授该经文所做笔记的整理。虽然这部作品在印刷出版时列舍起灵为作者，但在《经学系传谱》的舍起灵传记中并没有被提及。同样，刘智的《天方性理》《天方典礼》以及《真境昭微》等译作和原创作品被认为是经学派的经典，但是《五更月》和《天方三字经》等作品则仅用于穆斯林启蒙教育。《觉世省迷录》和《五更月》等这类作品都有一个共同点，即用汉语口语或者歌谣形式完成。这说明，书写经书的汉语语言类型是判断中文伊斯兰经书的关键标准之一。

在《经学系传谱》中，赵灿认为伊斯兰经书用三种类型的文字书写，分别是“经语”“汉音”和“书字”。经语指原文经书所使用的语言，也就是阿拉伯语和波斯语。阅读经语不难，然而读懂经语里的每一个单词，理解经语所阐释的伊斯兰教义并不容易。极料理曾向他的学生马明龙（生卒年不详）指出，“尔所知亦乃白纸行中徒认墨字耳”[③]，“盖经学之字义变化万端，一字数呼”[④]，只有准确理解了每一个单词的含义之后，读者才能“深获入道之就里矣”[⑤]。

汉音是指在传授伊斯兰经书中所使用的汉语口语，上述舍起灵的《觉世省迷录》即可被认为用汉音完成。汉音保持了原语言的句法结构顺序和语法，中间夹杂了阿拉伯语或者波斯语的伊斯兰术语的音译转写，可以说是今日经堂语的前身。[⑥] 例如，在《觉世省迷录》中，我们可以看到这样的文字表述：“真主命道他们若不信我的经典，不遵我的命令，不远我的禁止，我要用洪水淹死他们。”[⑦] 在这一句话中，“不遵我的命令，不远我的禁止”一句，并不符合汉语的表达习惯，而“我要用洪水淹死他们”则是汉语口语的表达方式。因此，用汉音写作的伊斯兰经文针对的是有一定阿拉伯语或者波斯语基础，能够理解伊斯兰原文术语的读者。可见，汉音的读者群仍局限在掌握经语的穆斯林中。如前文所述，胡登洲在研习原文经书时，“虽明义理，然只可符以汉音之鄙俗者”[⑧]，说明其把汉音看作是不登

---

① 杨晓春:《关于1931年中华书局刊本〈正教真诠〉的版本渊源及相关问题》,《西北第二民族学院学报》(哲学社会科学版）2008年第3期，第39页。

② 《觉世省迷录》，又称《省迷录》，有两个现存的版本。一个是根据买虚吾保存的版本，由马骏（1882—1945）校勘，由马福祥（1876—1936）在1923年印刷的铅字版。另一个是由北京牛街清真书报社于1927年出版的版本。埃塞克·梅森（Issac Mason，1870—1939）曾经提到另一个在北京印刷，于1909年在天津出版的版本，但笔者尚未找到该版本。参见Isaac Mason, *Notes on Chinese Mohammedan Literature*, Beijing, Wendiange shuzhuang, 1938, p. 202。

③ 《经学系传谱》,《清真大典》影印清抄本，页68下。

④ 同上，页69上。

⑤ 同上。

⑥ 杨宗山、冯增烈:《经堂语》,《中国伊斯兰百科全书》，第265—266页。

⑦ 舍起灵:《觉世省迷录》，牛街清真书报社，1927年，第2页。

⑧ 《经学系传谱》,《清真大典》影印清抄本，页43上。

大雅之堂的文字，且对于用汉音诠释伊斯兰教义持否定态度。

在经学派看来，只有用书字完成的中文伊斯兰作品，才能够在特定情况下完全替代阿拉伯语或者波斯语原文经典，使读者可以“终则亦能悉通教范，精达先天之理”[①]。在伊斯兰经学的语境下，“书”特指“儒者之经史子集及杂家之书”[②]，对应于天方之“经”、释“藏”、道“藏”等其他哲学经典[③]。书字因此被认为是一种基于儒家传统哲学经典的表达方式。在这类经文中，译者一般通过借用中国传统哲学术语或者创造新术语来对应原文，很少采用伊斯兰哲学术语的音译。例如，对于波斯苏非学者贾米（Jāmī，1414—1492）两部作品《阿施阿特·拉玛阿特》（*Ashi'at al-Lama'āt*）和《勒瓦一合》（*Lavāyih*）中的同一个伊斯兰术语，舍起灵和刘智采用了相同的翻译策略。如下表所示：

《阿施阿特·拉玛阿特》[⑤] 和《勒瓦一合》[⑥]			《昭元秘诀》[⑦] 和《真境昭微》[⑧]	
波斯语 / 阿拉伯语	拉丁转写	含义[⑨]	汉译	含义
وحدت	vahdat	Oneness	一	one
وجود/هستی	vujūd/hastī	existence/being	有	existence
حق	Haqq	Real	真	real
هستی حق	hasti-yi Haqq	Real being	真有	real existence
ذات	dhāt	Essence	体	substance/body
ظاهر	zāhir	manifest	表	appear
			显	manifest
باطن	bātin	non-manifest	里	inside
			隐	conceal
مرتبه	martaba	level	品（第）	grade/level
عالم	'ālam	world	世（界）	world

此外，用书字完成的中文伊斯兰著作的句式也类似于中国传统哲学经注的表达方式。例如，在描述伊斯兰哲学的“真主独一”思想时，刘智在《真境昭微》中的翻译如下：

> 此非加谨用力，克去己私，不易得也。私愈克，则道愈明。臆愈除，则道愈健。谨则纷杂之虑避去，真有之光昭至矣。万物皆备于己，无外物之烦扰矣。不自觉，不觉其不自觉。无所为，独一真主矣。[⑨]

---

① 《经学系传谱》，《清真大典》影印清抄本，页 32 上。

② 刘智：《天方至圣实录年谱》，《清真大典》影印清同治八年（1869）锦城宝真堂重刊本，页 76 上。

③ 同上，76 页上。

④ 参见 Jāmī, *Ashi'at al-Lama'āt*, Edited by Hādī Rastgār Muqadam Gawharī, Qom: Mu'asisa-yi Būstān-i Kitāb-i Qum, 2004。

⑤ 参见 Jāmī, *Lavāyih*, Edited by Yann Richard, Tehran: Intishārāt-i Asātīr, 1994。

⑥ 参见舍起灵：《咧母嗯惕：昭元秘诀》，哈佛大学燕京图书馆藏光绪十六年（1890）抄本。

⑦ 参见刘智：《真境昭微》，牛街清真书报社，1925 年。

⑧ 为了客观地对比波斯文和阿拉伯文词汇以及相对应的汉译词汇含义的异同，此处采用英语作为第三方语言来对原文和译文词汇进行释义。

⑨ 刘智：《真境昭微》，牛街清真书报社，1925 年，第 10 页。

从上述例子可以看出，用书字完成的中文伊斯兰经文在行文上与中国传统哲学著作颇为相似。能够用书字完成中文伊斯兰作品，说明中国穆斯林作者或译者已经兼备伊斯兰原文经文的阅读能力以及用中国传统哲学语言进行表述的能力。与明初翻译《明译天文书》的先辈相比，书字的运用标志着明末清初的穆斯林学者在中文的运用能力上取得了长足进步。

对于经学派的语言策略，穆斯林内部很可能产生过激烈的辩论。虽然我们没有经学派以外的文字材料佐证，但经学派早期文献中几乎都出现了对中文阐释伊斯兰教义合法性的辩护。早在王岱舆的《希真正答》这一问答式语录中，就有人提问："若以哈他文字注释正教之经旨，岂不大悖乎？"① 这里的"哈他"一词为阿拉伯语单词的音译，意为差错、偏差。② 王岱舆"答云：此说有之，但今之为此说不明耳。所谓'哈他'者，乃其教导而非文字也。……须知文字比如土木，可以建礼拜寺，可以造供佛堂，正道异端互相取用，其功过不在材料，唯论人之所用何如耳"③。这是说，文字只是工具，是传达教义的载体，真正错误的是文字所要表达的含义。可见，最初的争论主要着眼于用中文阐释伊斯兰经文是否具有合法性。

刘智在编写《天方典礼》一书时，在其"例言"中说："是书语气与经堂语气既不相合，则不能不起物议。"④ 说明当时穆斯林社会的争论已经从能否用中文阐释，转变为如何用中文阐释。从刘智的这句话可以推测，似乎经堂语，即汉音已经被认可阐释伊斯兰教义，但是对于书字的使用，刘智很可能感觉到很大的反对声音，因此在著作开篇即向他的读者进行解释。

在同样用书字完成的《天方性理》中，刘智又一次在"例言"中解释了他对于运用书字阐释伊斯兰教义的原因："是书语义，悉本天方之经，间有经文难于汉译，不得不用别文以传之。文虽不合，义无不合也。"⑤ 这里所说的"天方之经"即阿拉伯文或波斯文原文经典，"文"是相对于"经堂语气"而言，应该就是指的《经学系传谱》中所说的"书字"。刘智在这里认为用汉音翻译原文经文有所困难，因而不得不采用"别文"，即儒家传统阐释习惯来另行表述。在刘智的解释中，使用书字表述似乎是一个折中的办法，虽然译文不能够完全对应于原文，但是在含义上是对等的。

经学派这一折中的态度也表现在对于原文经典和中文伊斯兰著作读者群的界定和划分上。如赵灿所述："或有知书学，而不能深入吾教之经学者，则授以所译之《归真必要》等经。"⑥ 这说明用书字完成的伊斯兰经书的读者并不要求掌握阿拉伯语或者波斯语。赵灿又说："凡通儒学者沾益最多，而求道之礼备焉。"⑦ 也就是说，只要具备中国传统哲学素养，特别是熟悉儒家哲学思想，通过研读用书字写作的中文伊斯兰作品也可以达到理解伊斯兰教义的目的。与此同时，对于原文经典和中文著作，刘智认为："然而无庸议也，是书非为不知文者作也。盖不知文者，经师遵经训之，无须是书。而须是

① 王岱舆：《正教真诠，希真正答，清真大学》，银川：宁夏人民出版社，1996 年，第 284 页。

② "哈他"也可以理解为波斯文 *Khatā* 一词的音译转写，意为"契丹"，特指中国，因此该处"哈他"似有双关含义。但结合下文引文中王岱舆对于"哈他"文字的讨论，王岱舆所指"哈他"更倾向于阿拉伯语中"错误"的含义，而非波斯语"契丹"之意。

③ 王岱舆：《正教真诠，希真正答，清真大学》，第 284—285 页。

④ 刘智：《天方典礼择要解·例言》，《清真大典》影印清康熙四十九年（1710）杨斐菉刻本，页 2 下—页 3 上。

⑤ 刘智：《天方性理·例言》，影印 1922 年刊本，黎明文化事业公司，页 1—2。

⑥《归真必要》是舍起灵译自波斯苏非哲学散文阿齐兹·丁·那萨菲（'Azīz al-Dīn Nasafī，约 13 世纪）的《玛格萨德·阿格萨》（*Maqsad-i Aqsa*）的中译本，已失散。参见《经学系传谱》，页 32 上。

⑦《经学系传谱》，《清真大典》影印清抄本，页 138 下。

书者，必通习三教，未知吾教之礼者也。读其文，会其义，自有裨益。知我罪我，听之斯世。”①

由此，经学派将读者群根据经书的语言和表述方式进行分类。能够读懂原文的穆斯林可以研习原文经书，而不能读懂原文经书，但是对中国传统哲学有所了解的读者则可以通过研读用书字撰写的伊斯兰经书来通达伊斯兰教义。面对其他穆斯林学者对书字阐释伊斯兰经文的质疑，经学派在为书字的权威性进行辩论的同时，也承认原文经典的权威性和神圣性。这很可能是经学派的一个策略，旨在一定程度上缓解与其反对者的矛盾。

中国穆斯林对于用中文诠释伊斯兰教义合法性的争论在伊斯兰经书翻译史上并非个案，类似的讨论也出现在8世纪用波斯语翻译《古兰经》的合法性讨论中。②承认书字在诠释伊斯兰教义上的功能和权威，为经学派提供了翻译和创作中文伊斯兰著作的理论基础。经学派学者一方面在理论上为书字的合法性进行辩驳，另一方面一直在进行实践。通过书字的运用，中文伊斯兰作品扩大了中国读者的范围，因此逐渐受到儒家主流社会关注。

在中国伊斯兰教外，由于《天方典礼》曾被列为《四库全书》备选书目，刘智在《四库全书总目提要》中获得了一个简短的词条介绍，成为在《提要》中唯一一位被提及的中文伊斯兰著作的穆斯林作者。这一词条如此评价刘智及其作品："回回教本僻谬，而智颇习儒书，乃杂援经义以文其说，其文亦颇雅赡。然根柢先非，巧为文饰无益也。"③在这段文字中，由于作者的历史局限性而对伊斯兰教存有偏见。虽然《天方典礼》的内容受到质疑，但是刘智用书字写作的能力获得了儒家学者的肯定，这也说明了书字在阐释伊斯兰教教义上的使用增加了穆斯林学者在儒家主流社会中获得的关注和认同。

经过经学派的努力，用书字写作的中文伊斯兰经书被确定在特定情况下能够用来阐释伊斯兰教义，具有与原文经书同样的功能。虽然没有直接的证据，但是可以推测，儒家社会对于中国穆斯林学者文字阐释能力的认可，也反过来提高了经学派在中国穆斯林社会中的地位和权威，使得经学派在阐释伊斯兰教义的竞争中得以最终取得决定性胜利。20世纪初，一个在中国西北创立的名为西道堂的苏非教团甚至直接采用中文伊斯兰作品作为他们的教义经典。④

结 语

来自中亚及更远地区的穆斯林移民自唐代进入中国后，经过几个朝代的更迭，自明末清初出现了一个在保持原有信仰的同时，专注于对伊斯兰经文的学习和研究，并用中文翻译和诠释伊斯兰教义的穆斯林知识分子群体，他们被称为经学派。这一学派由胡登洲开创，主要在中原地区发展。在收集、整理、辨伪、研读、注释和传播原文经书的同时，这一学派积极学习中国传统哲学经典，并将其融入到翻译和创作中文伊斯兰著作当中。经学派将这种用中国传统哲学术语和表达方式诠释伊斯兰教义的语言称为书字，通过赋予书字阐释伊斯兰教义的权威性，将伊斯兰经书的读者范围扩大至不懂阿拉伯语或者波斯语的中国伊斯兰教内外人士。在这一过程中，经学派遭遇了教内对于确定和辨析正统经文，能否使用中文以及如何用中文经注等各方面的辩论和挑战。

---

① 刘智：《天方典礼择要解·例言》，《清真大典》影印清康熙四十九年（1710）杨斐菉刻本，页2下—页3上。

② Travis E. Zadeh, *The Vernacular Qur'an: Translation and the Rise of Persian Exegesis*, Oxford: Oxford University Press, 2011.

③ 永瑢等编：《四库全书总目》，北京：中华书局，1965年，第1085页。

④ 马通：《西道堂》，《中国伊斯兰百科全书》，第605—606页。

用书字写成的中文伊斯兰作品扩大了伊斯兰经书的读者群，为中国传统哲学和伊斯兰哲学之间建立了桥梁，也为伊斯兰世界贡献了中文经注传统。伊斯兰经学派通过中文伊斯兰著作获得了儒家主流社会的关注和认可，反之又加强了该学派在中国伊斯兰社会中的权威性，并最终在明末清初的伊斯兰经书诠释和伊斯兰教育的竞争中胜出，成为今日中国经堂教育的主体。

The Development of the School of Islamic *Jingxue in* China Proper during the Late Ming and Early Qing Dynasties

Shen Yiming (Peking University)

Abstract: Modern scholars consider that Islamic education in China proper was initiated by Hu Dengzhou (1522-1597), a Chinese Muslim scholar in the Ming dynasty. In this paper, however, the study of historical materials and Chinese Islamic texts indicates that the group initiated by Hu Dengzhou, namely the school of Islamic *Jingxue*, in all probability had been questioned or opposed in Chinese Muslim community. In the process of selecting, reading, interpreting, disseminating, translating and writing the Islamic scriptures, the school of Islamic *Jingxue* imitated the exegetical tradition of Chinese philosophy and applied *shuzi*, a language derived from Chinese exegetical writings, to interpret Islamic doctrines. While the school of *Jingxue* argued in the Muslim community for the legitimacy of applying *shuzi* to interpret Islamic scriptures, the readership of Chinese Islamic texts written in *shuzi* had been extended and gradually received the recognition from the Confucian society. Consequently, the school of *Jingxue* won the competition of interpreting Islamic doctrines and lasted until today.

Keywords: the school of *Jingxue*; Hu Dengzhou; *shuzi*; *Jingtang jiaoyu*

明清时期广州口岸望远镜传用考述

黄佳欣（中山大学）

摘　要： 望远镜是世界科学发展史上的重要发明。自17世纪初发明之后，望远镜成为人类探索宇宙强有力的工具。在其发明后不久，来华传教的天主教耶稣会士将望远镜带入中国，并翻译相关书目，望远镜始为中国人所知，并开始在中国流传。本文主要从两个方面展开论述，第一部分，分析望远镜在中国的不同称谓以及不同名称背后的文化传统意涵以及使用范围。第二部分，重点讨论广州口岸在望远镜传播过程中的历史内容。广州是西洋望远镜捷足先登的地方，这里的社会上层人士有着先睹为快的机会。从康、乾到嘉、道年间，有幸在此鉴赏把玩过望远镜者，分属于官、商、儒、释、道各界，由于各人身份的不同，他们的望远镜观感也大异其趣。这一部分通过解读不同人士眼中的西洋望远镜，旨在探讨由奇器引发奇想，以深化对中西文化交流的复杂性和微妙性的认识。

关键词： 望远镜；广州；阮元（1764—1849）；潘有度（1755—1820）；成鹫（1637—1722）；屈大均（1630—1696）；李明彻（1751—1832）

前言：问题与方法

17世纪的欧洲被誉为天才的世纪，伽利略、开普勒、帕斯卡、笛卡儿等一长串闪烁古今的名字载入史册，在全面向科学进军的浪潮中，望远镜应运而生。望远镜本身的发明，是利用光学原理的偶然成果，但在伽利略的手中，望远镜经过改良，运用到天文领域的观测，有着跨时代的意义，不论技术史还是天文学史，望远镜的发明都是重要的一页。① 这几乎是所有科学史书籍都要加以阐述的历史性事件。②

望远镜使得人类对于宇宙天体的探索迈开了一大步。除了天文计算，人们还可以直接观察到天体表面的细节与星体运行。伽利略利用望远镜，发现了月亮凹凸不平的表面，发现太阳黑子，发现了木

① 关于伽利略，笔者参考鲍·格·库兹涅佐夫:《伽利略传》，陈太先、马世元译，北京：商务印书馆，2001年；达娃·贝索尔:《伽利略的女儿——科学、信仰和爱的历史回忆》，谢延光译，上海译文出版社，2002年；Jean-Pierre Maury:《伽利略——揭开月亮的面纱》，金志平译，上海书店出版社，2000年；亚历山大·柯瓦雷:《伽利略研究》，刘胜利译，北京大学出版社，2008年；伽利略:《星之信使》（Starry Messenger, 1610），徐光台译，台北：天下文化出版公司，2004年；Pasquale M. d' Elia, *Galileo in China: Relations through the Roman College between Galileo and the Jesuit scientist-missionaries (1610-1640),* Harvard University, 1960。

② 科技史方面，笔者参考贝尔纳:《历史上的科学》，伍况甫等译，北京：科学出版社，1959年；A.N. 怀特海:《科学与近代世界》，何钦译，北京：商务印书馆，1959年；戴维·林德伯格:《西方科学的起源》，王珺等译，北京：中国对外翻译出版公司，2001年；布罗诺斯基:《科学进化史》，李斯译，海口：海南出版社，2006年；詹姆斯·E. 麦克莱伦第三:《世界史上的科学技术》，上海科技教育出版社，2003年；亚·沃尔夫著:《十六、十七世纪科学、技术和哲学史》，周昌忠译，北京：商务印书馆，1997年；艾伦·麦克法兰、格里·马丁:《玻璃的故事》，管可秾译，北京：商务印书馆，2003年。

星的卫星，发现了金星也如月亮般的盈亏，发现了银河由无数的星体组成，这些都是人类眼力所不能及的发现。而此后三百多年间，望远镜不断发展，一直是天文学家们有力的观测工具，对人类认识宇宙起到至关重要的作用。而不同于繁杂的天文计算、抽象的推论，只要使用望远镜，普通民众也可以切身感受到宇宙的浩瀚与星体的奇妙。

17 世纪也是中西经济贸易交流开展的重要时期。英国、荷兰、法国、丹麦诸国先后成立东印度公司，开启了帆船时代东西方大规模的远洋贸易。与此同时，天主教耶稣会士也搭乘洋舶，来到遥远的东方传教，东西方两种异质文明开始了大规模的正面接触，西学东渐之潮泛起，西方奇器与思想也随商人与传教士一同进入中国。

在逐渐泛起的西潮中，望远镜也在其诞生后的十余年间，被天主教耶稣会士带到了中国。望远镜的传入，被李约瑟誉为是西方科学传入中国的一个高峰。[①] 这件在欧洲已经引起轰动的器物，在中国会有怎样的命运呢？回顾以往的研究，望远镜在中国的研究有两种取向，一种是从科技史角度，考察望远镜入华后中国人如何理解望远镜的光学原理并加以仿照，以及如何将望远镜运用于天文观测、历法计算等领域的情况；另一种研究则是从社会文化史角度，对中国人望远镜观感进行文化分析。

望远镜初入中国的时间，学界已有共识。方豪在《望远镜传入中国考》一文中，最先考出了望远镜传入中国的确切年代[②]，复由戴念祖进行详细论证[③]。从科技史角度研究望远镜的论著，材料多依据某些古籍，如《天问略》[④]《远镜说》[⑤]《交食历指》《镜镜詅痴》[⑥]《镜史》[⑦]。在科技史方面，本文不拟多所发挥，但希望通过这些常用的科技史材料，以及其他提及望远镜的明清史料，探讨望远镜在华的"曾用名"及命名缘由。而在西方学界，亦有一书专门探讨"望远镜时代"人类探索月球的里程[⑧]，月球观测由于望远镜不同时期发展，逐步深入的过程。

至于从社会文化史角度探讨望远镜的历史，蔡鸿生在《清代广州的荷兰商馆》一文"荷兰馆与中西文化交流"一节中，首次指出望远镜不仅是广州荷兰馆中的重要奇器，而且望远镜所带来"西学东渐"的渗透现象值得深入分析。[⑨] 接下来王川在其《阮元望月歌与西洋望远镜》一文中，沿着蔡先生

---

① 李约瑟:《中国科学技术史》第 4 卷"天学"，第 2 分册，北京：科学出版社，1975 年，第 643 页。

② 该文原收录于方豪:《中外文化交通史论丛》第 1 辑，独立出版社，1944 年，复收录于《民国丛书》第 4 编，第 40 册，上海书店，1992 年，第 37—47 页。本文参考民国丛书版本。

③ 戴念祖:《明清之际望远镜在中国的传播及制造》,《燕京学报》新第 9 期，2000 年，第 123—150 页。

④ 关于《天问略》的研究可见姚立澄:《关于〈天问略〉作者来华年代及其成书背景的若干讨论》,《自然科学史研究》第 24 卷第 2 期，2005 年，第 156—164 页。

⑤ 关于《远镜说》的讨论可见赵栓林:《关于〈远镜说〉和〈交食历指〉中的望远镜》,《内蒙古师范大学学报》(自然科学汉文版)第 33 卷第 3 期，2004 年，第 332—335 页。

⑥ 关于《镜镜詅痴》的讨论见宋子良:《郑复光和他的〈镜镜詅痴〉》,《中国科技史料》1987 年第 3 期，第 41—46 页；钱长炎:《关于〈镜镜詅痴〉中透镜成像问题的再探讨》,《自然科学史研究》第 21 卷第 2 期，2002 年，第 135—145 页。

⑦ 李迪:《关于徐光启制造望远镜问题》,《自然科学史研究》第 6 卷第 4 期，1987 年，第 372—376 页；王广超等:《明清之际望远镜的传入对中国天文学的影响》,《自然科学史研究》第 27 期第 3 卷，2008 年，第 309—324 页；孙承晟:《明清之际西方光学知识在中国的传播及其影响——孙云球〈镜史〉研究》,《自然科学史研究》第26卷第3期，2007年，第363—376页。

⑧ William P. Sheehan, Thomas A. Dobbins, *Epic Moon, A history of lunar exploration in the age of the telescope*, Richmond, Willmann-Bell, Inc, 2001.

⑨ 蔡鸿生:《清代广州的荷兰商馆》，收入蔡鸿生主编:《广州与海洋文明》，广州：中山大学出版社，1997 年，第 349—351 页。

的思路，深入分析阮元在使用望远镜观月质疑月亮神话的真实性、发出了“广寒玉兔尽空谈”感叹的原因，指出这与其西学造诣有关。[①] 蔡鸿生此后还撰写《清代广州行商的西洋观》一文，详细考察分析广州行商潘有度所创作的《西洋杂咏》，当中包括了潘有度有关望远镜的观感，蔡鸿生指出了商人潘氏与身为两广总督阮元的观月感在思想境界上的差别。[②] 另外，台湾学者邱仲麟搜寻了大量明清以降的材料，探讨各式西洋镜对士人生活的影响，作者认为望远镜等西洋镜的传入意味着新视觉时代的来临，它们丰富了文人的想象，为诗文增添了新的主题和内容，通过他们于西洋镜等器物所作诗文，可以探索文人背后的心灵。[③]

本文拟在前人研究的基础上，进一步分析广州官、商人士所留下的有关望远镜观感的文字，进而挖掘儒、释、道等不同身份人士，力图从社会背景、文化背景的不同，来分析他们对望远镜这种新事物的不同感受，力求从多角度了解望远镜所带来的“西学东渐”渗透现象。

综上所述，本文打算分两个部分对望远镜入华进行再讨论，第一部分是考察明清时期望远镜名称背后的文化成因，第二部分是对清代前期广州人士观镜感受的文化分析。全文以第二部分为重点，根据目前掌握的资料，按观镜者的社会属性，分为官、商、儒、释、道五类，考察其观感的多样性，希望能够对“西学东渐”时期“器”与“道”关系的认识有所推进。

一　望远镜的华化名称及文化成因

（一）“远镜”的由来

虽有文献提及利玛窦首先带望远镜来华，但方豪早已指出此说不足信。[④] 明代万历四十三年，即1615年，葡萄牙耶稣会士阳玛诺（Emmanuel Diaz，1574—1659）在《天问略》（图1）中第一次提及望远镜这一“巧器”：

> 凡右诸论，大约则据肉目所及，测而已矣。第肉目之力劣短，曷能穷尽天上微妙理之万一耶？近世西洋精于历法一名士，务测日月星辰奥理，而哀其目力尪羸，则造刱一巧器以助之，持此器观六十里远一尺大之物，明视之无异在目前也。持之观月，则千倍大于常。观金星，大似月，其光亦或消或长，无异于月轮也。观土星，则其形如上图，圆似鸡卵，两侧继有两小星，其或与本星联体否，不可明测也。观木星，其四围恒有四小星，周行甚疾，或此东而彼西，或此西而彼东，或俱东俱西，但其行动与二十八宿甚异，此星必居七政之内，别一星也。观列宿之天，则其中小星更多稠密，故其体光显相连，若白练然，即今所谓天河者，待此器至中国之日，而后详言其妙用也。[⑤]

在这段不长的材料中，阳玛诺虽然没有为望远镜这种“奇器”命名，但已将伽利略最新的观测成

① 王川：《阮元望月歌与西洋望远镜》，收入黄时鉴主编：《东西交流论谭》第2集，上海文艺出版社，2001年，第148—155页。

② 蔡鸿生：《清代广州行商的西洋观》，收入《中外交流史事考述》，郑州：大象出版社，2007年，第375—376页。

③ 邱仲麟：《晚明以来的西洋镜与视觉感官的开发》，收入《中国史新论》（生活与文化分册），台北：“中研院”历史语言研究所，2013年，第377—447页。

④ 同上，第38页。

⑤《天问略》在四库全书本中并无“近世西洋精于历法一名士”一段，丛书集成本据《艺海珠尘》本恢复。阳玛诺：《天问略》，《丛书集成初编》，上海：商务印书馆，1936年，第104—105页。

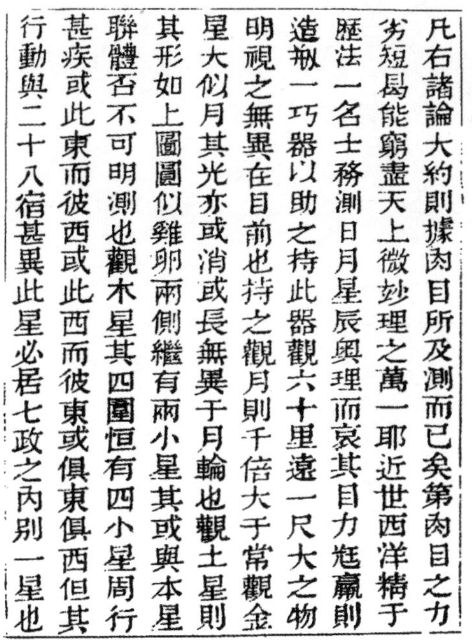
天問略

凡右諸論大約則據肉目所及測而已矣第肉目之力劣短曷能窮盡天上微妙理之萬一耶近世西洋精于歷法一名士務測日月星辰奥理而哀其目力尪羸則造剏一巧器以助之持此器觀六十里遠一尺大之物明視之無異在目前也持之觀月則千倍大于常觀金星大似月其光亦或消或長無異于月輪也觀土星則其形如上圖圖似雞卵兩側繼有兩小星其或與本星聯體否不可明測也觀木星其四圍恒有四小星周行甚疾或此東而彼西或此西而彼東或俱東俱西但其行動與二十八宿甚異此星必居七政之內別一星也

一〇四

图 1 《天问略》中论及望远镜的书页

果全部介绍到中国，意义非凡。

虽然《天问略》的书名已经非常华化，取自屈原名作《天问》，但仔细对比《天问》与《天问略》当中的内容，两者实则有很大的不同。《天问》在形式上有问而无答，而《天问略》的重点不在于问，而在于答，里面不仅有问有答，而且回答详尽系统，字里行间对答案成竹在胸。阳玛诺在此书中，几乎处处显示出他在天文领域的自信，希望以天文方面渊博的知识来打动中国人，从而为传教赢得主动权。其实，如果不是为了照顾华情，而是从内容归纳出发，那么取名《天问答略》可能更合适。

正是在这种问答的形式下，作为“巧器”的望远镜，在书中最后一段才呼之欲出。原来阳玛诺书中能全面回答天文问题，是依赖一种“巧器”的观测，但书中却未给予其华味的名字。这既是一种卖关子的写法，让中国的读者对于未知器物充满好奇。而“巧器”一名只是西洋舶来品的通称，这说明当时中国尚未有人接触到望远镜。

直到天启六年（1626），耶稣会士汤若望（Johann Adam Schall von Bell，1591—1666），真正首次携望远镜到中国，汤若望还翻译了《远镜说》，详细介绍了望远镜的构造与使用（图 2、3）。“远镜”是目前所知望远镜入华后的第一个名字。《远镜说》开篇就解释了“远镜”一词的来历：

> 夫远镜何昉乎，昉于大西洋天文士也。其用之利可胜言哉。盖凡人视近与大易，视远与小难，远镜则无远近，无大小者也。天象地形，不出其照。①

“远镜”一词在望远镜传入中国后，基本上就成为了特有的名词。出现于《格致草》《新法算书》《谈天》《畴人传》等诸多明清天文、历法著作中。汤若望还将“远镜”一词介绍到了军事领域，由汤若望授、焦勖撰的《火攻挈要》便论及“远镜”在不同军事战术中的使用方法：

> 惊远说略：凡敌兵远来，我欲令彼惊溃，则先以远镜看明敌营所在，次则测量地步远近如何，再以铳规算合所到度数。出其不意以飞龙大铳，炤准营头，连发数弹，如雷从天降，即虽强敌，亦未有不惊散而奔溃也。
>
> 守城说略：另筑眺台二层，高三丈，上设视远镜，以备瞭望。
>
> 水战说略：先以一人，坐于桅斗之上，用远镜窥望，俟敌船将近数里之內，用铳对准击放，不必数弹，敌船立成齑粉，敌兵尽为鱼虾。②

① 汤若望：《远镜说》，早稻田大学藏抄本，无页码。

② 焦勖：《火攻挈要（附火攻诸器图）》卷下，丛书集成初编本，上海：商务印书馆，1936 年，第 54—56 页。

又如明末筹划城邑防守的兵书《金汤借箸》，也有“望远镜”一条：

望远镜：望远镜出自大西洋国，用筒数节安玻璃两端，置架上，视远如近，视小为大，远望敌人营帐人马，器械辎重，毫发不爽。我可预备战守，安放铳砲，必不可少者。①

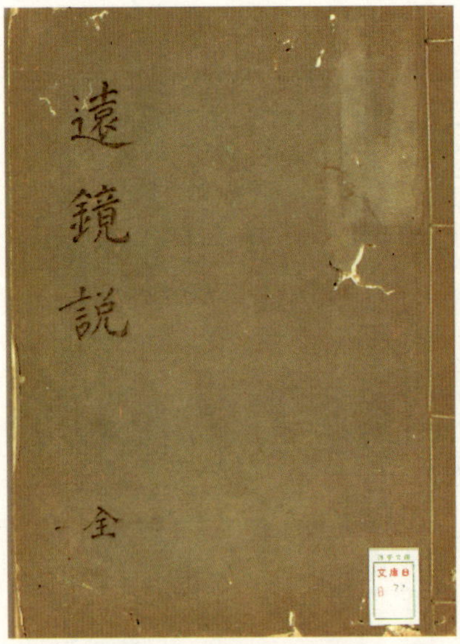

图 2 《远镜说》早稻田大学抄本封面

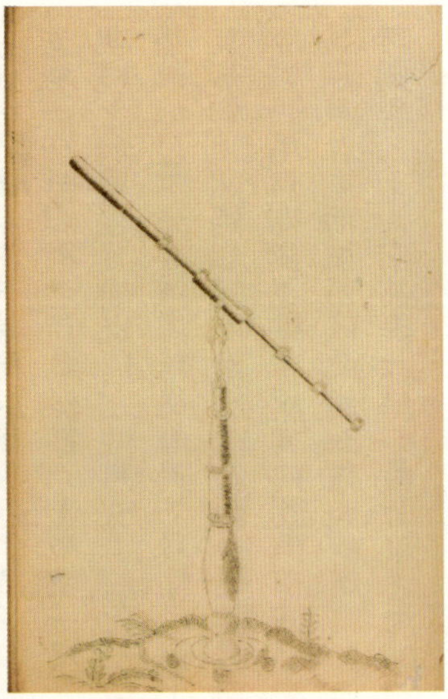

图 3 《远镜说》中的望远镜

屈大均的《广东新语》之中，提到葡萄牙殖民者利用远镜辅助大炮射击，击退来犯的荷兰殖民者：

澳夷乃仿为之，其制比红毛益精，安置南北两台，以守要害。发时，以尺量之，测远镜度之，无不奇中，红夷乃不敢犯，用于中土，则诚攻守重器也。②

可见，军事上对于“远镜”的使用，主要是取其观远之奇效。

（二）“窥管”词义的变迁

“窥”字，《说文》：小视也，从穴，规声。有从小孔望出之意。《庄子·秋水》：“是直用管窥天，用锥指地也，不亦小乎。”③《庄子》之后，“以管窥天”成为成语，用于比喻见闻狭窄，与“坐井观天”同义。如《文选·东方朔〈答客难〉》中：“语曰：‘以筦窥天，以蠡测海，以筳撞钟。’岂能通其条贯，考其文理，发其音声哉！”④以管窥天，既是自谦用语，又可作贬义之用。另外，窥管也是古代的天文仪器，宋代著名科学家沈括就曾利用窥管观察星象：

熙宁中，予受诏典领历官，杂考星历，以玑衡求极星，初夜在窥管中，少时复出，以此知窥管小，不能容极星游转，乃稍稍展窥管候之，凡历三月，极星方游于窥管之内，常见不隐，然后知天极不动处，远极星犹三度有余。每极星入窥管，别画为一图。图为一圆规，乃画极星于规中。具初夜、中夜、后夜所见各图之，凡为二百余图，极星方常循圆规之内，夜夜不差。予于熙宁历奏议中叙之甚详。⑤

---

① 周鉴：《金汤借箸》卷一一《营阵部》，《四库存目丛书·子部》第 34 册，北京出版社，1995 年，第 292 页。

② 屈大均：《广东新语》，北京：中华书局，1997 年，第 442 页。

③ 王先谦撰：《新编诸子集成·庄子集解·庄子集解内篇补正》卷四，《秋水》第一七，北京：中华书局，1987 年，第 147 页。

④ 萧统：《文选》卷四五《设论·答客难》，上海古籍出版社，1986 年，第 2003 页。

⑤ 沈括撰，胡道静校注：《新校正梦溪笔谈》卷七，北京：中华书局，1957 年，第 81 页。

《元史·天文志一》中提到：

> 于是太史郭守敬者，出其所创简仪、仰仪及诸仪表，皆臻于精妙，卓见绝识，盖有古人所未及者。其说以谓：昔人以管窥天，宿度余分约为太半少，未得其的。乃用二线推测，于余分织微皆有可考。而又当时四海景测之所凡二十有七，东极高丽，西极滇池，南踰朱崖，北尽铁勒，是亦古人之所未及为者也。①

此段材料中的“以管窥天”，便有着双重的含义。其一指测量工具观察观测星象，其二是指以管窥天的方法不够高明，略显狭隘，以至观测精度不准确，郭守敬最新发明的简仪、仰仪，有效解决了这些问题。但是令郭守敬万万没有想到的是，在数百年后，正是“管”成为中国天文学家们用以窥天的强大的工具。这是望远镜传入中国后的巨大改变,《明史·志第七·历一》载：

> 《天经》又言:“臣于闰八月二十五日夜及九月初一日夜，同礼臣陈六韐等，用窥管测，见积尸为数十小星团聚，木与积尸，共纳管中。盖窥管圆径寸许，两星相距三十分内者，方得同见。如觜宿三星相距三十七分，则不能同见。而文魁但据臆算，未经实测。据云初二日木星已在柳前，则前此岂能越鬼宿而飞渡乎？”②

这样的观测精度只有望远镜才能达到，是简仪时代的郭守敬无法想象的。《庄子》中“以管窥天”的贬义，在《元史》中获得延续，而望远镜在晚明传入后，却彻底发生改变，视野窄小变成了洞察清晰。此为外来器物传入中国后，改变中国原有词义的一例。

另外，李约瑟认为带窥管的转移钟是望远镜前身③，但即使以窥管加上测量方向的仪器，也没有望远镜中最重要的“核心技术”——光学原理以及光学玻璃材料的运用，对于天象的观察，并不能带来清晰度上质的改变。因此并不能认为“窥管”是望远镜的前身。

（三）“千里镜”名称在广州口岸的广泛传播

在望远镜入华后，“千里镜”之名在民间流传甚远，几乎成了望远镜最流行的名称。千里镜在广州口岸是常见的。如屈大均（1630—1696）的《澳门》组诗中，便在描绘船上的瞭望、导航设备时提到千里镜：

> 五月飘洋候，辞沙肉米沉。窥船千里镜，定路一盘针。
> 鬼哭三沙惨，鱼飞十里阴。夜来咸火满，朵朵上衣襟。④

屈大均描写的应该是一艘赴东南亚进行贸易的广舶。五月东南季风起，正是出海的好时节，“辞沙肉米沉”说明该船延循中国传统的出海前祭拜海神的习俗。清初中国船只使用望远镜，史籍少载，但望远镜于航海者，实用意义非常大，在海上航行中，船上人员应该比陆上的官员更早认识到望远镜的重要性，只是船员、水手作为历史上“失语的人群”，通常不受关注。当时他们

---

① 《元史》卷四八《天文志一》，北京：中华书局，1976年，第989—990页。

② 《明史》卷三一《历志一》，北京：中华书局，1974年，第536—537页。

③ 李约瑟:《中国科学技术史》第4卷“天学”，第2分册，北京：科学出版社，1975年，第696页。

④ 章文钦:《澳门诗词笺注》(明清卷)，珠海出版社，2002年，第80—81页。

是不是也称望远镜为千里镜呢？目前不得而知。屈大均此诗为我们留下了当时中国船员所带装备的宝贵记录。

屈大均所知千里镜不仅来自洋舶，也来自澳门的天主教堂，他参观大三巴教堂时，见识到了诸种舶来品：

> 西望洋寺，中一寺曰三巴，高十余丈若石楼，雕镂奢丽。……有风乐藏革柜中……有玻璃千人镜……有千里镜……有显微镜……有自鸣钟、海洋全图璇玑诸器。①

除了屈大均外，还有另外几位诗人在澳门看过望远镜，他们不约而同都用望远镜来看海。

武将出身的汪后来（1678—约1752），在《澳门即事同蔡景厚六首》中之一首，也提到他曾在澳门的南环借洋人的望远镜进行瞭望，其诗如下：

> 南环一派浪声喧，锁匙惟凭十字门。借得西洋千里镜，直看帆影到天根。②

顺德人氏张琳（1770—1825），字逸芳，曾作《澳门竹枝词》七首，也是在澳门携望远镜凭眺：

> 回环数里枕波间，路接南湾又北湾。凭眺时携千里镜，外洋远舶影如山。③

新会人钟启韶（1771—1823），字琴德，曾作《澳门杂诗十二首》：

> 十字门当槛，零丁港近墙。都归千里镜，直过九洲洋。
> 关闸沙为界，波罗蜜是乡。皇心正柔远，荒徼此来王。
> （十字门诸山夐立海面，接零丁洋，又有九洲洋。登白鸽巢园石顶亭。以大千里镜瞩之，当面了了，不知其远涉日余也。波罗蜜树高数寻。④）

其实，在澳门诗词中频见千里镜一词，已说明该物在澳门流行之广。修于道光年间的《粤海关志》，也可以提供佐证。千里镜多次出现于不同分类商品的税则之中，如“各色竹木器”中：木小千里镜，每二十个各税四钱；“烧料器”类中：千里镜大者每一个、小者每四个，……各税四钱；“骨角皮革器”类中：千里镜（小牛角）每十个各税四钱。⑤可见至迟到了道光年间，千里镜已经成为配备各种装饰且样式颇多的商品。显然，望远镜已经远远不止天文航海观测单一的功能，而成为一种时兴的新奇玩意，通过不一样的装饰还可以彰显用家的消费品位。

而卷九《右正税》中，以“千里镜”作为关税比价者为数众多，如大洋鸟枪、小洋鸟枪、金标、银规矩、剃头小规矩、风琴、时辰标、洋法蓝标、玻璃球（大）、银标钟、大铜标、番琴、千里影、镶金丝玛瑙规矩、铜自行珠箱、小番琴、镶花石金标、铜规矩、铜架大显微镜、番铜花、玛瑙镶金推

① 屈大均：《广东新语》，第36—37页。
② 章文钦：《澳门诗词笺注》（明清卷），第101页。
③ 同上，第260页。
④ 同上，第267—268页。
⑤ 梁廷枏：《粤海关志》卷九，收入沈云龙主编：《近代中国史料丛刊续编》第19辑，第182册，台北：云海出版社，第630—633页。

钟、金推钟、花石金标、镀金镶标玻璃圆手镜、挂推钟金亭、小金亭镶标、玻璃日规、蜜珀镜架、镶水晶石架标、针金铜柱棹表、挂金标金亭座、酒杯嵌时辰标、嵌表镶料石牙扇、珐琅牙签筒、镶标珐琅洋小刀、镶料石嵌标洋腰刀、镶宝石牙扇、镶宝石玻璃嵌表烛台、镶桃式嵌表双开鼻烟盒、洋珐琅带表小千里镜。[①] 真是多不胜数，当中多为金属制的工艺品。而在接下来一章对广州人士使用望远镜观感的分析中，望远镜便主要是以“千里镜”名字出现的。

“远镜”“窥管”“千里镜”这三个望远镜的曾用名，使用范围各异，军事上亲睐其“远”之效用，天文观测上取其“窥”之洞察，而民间则惊叹其“千里”之神奇。同一件舶来品，在中国由于不同的使用领域，因为使用者出发点与文化背景的不同，赋予了其不同的名字，望远镜折射出异样的光辉。

二　广州人士望远镜观感的文化分析

在上一部分中，分析了望远镜进入中国之后出现的不同名字，当中多有在澳门接触到望远镜的实例。作为中国与西方世界接触的桥头堡，广州口岸在一口通商时代独具优势。从流通渠道来说，基本是贡品与商品两类，贡品主要是由传教士带入，而商品主要是由行商从外商手中购入。如美国学者马士的著作《东印度公司对华贸易编年史》中，便举出1794年石琼官的资产清单中，“钟、表、千里镜等”一栏价值达222650两白银之多，数额巨大，竟然接近了石琼官未售的新旧茶叶（229428两），超过了未售的存栈货物（130075两），马士分析，这有可能是收藏家的嗜好，也有可能是作为礼物送给官员及其属员。[②] 货物之中当有一定比例为商品，这数量众多的奇器，足以引导广州的消费时尚。这是海关将千里镜作为舶来品税制比价的佐证，也成为广州地区人士接触望远镜的先决条件之一。本部分便主要以广州地区的不同人士使用望远镜后的观感为例，略作文化分析。

月亮是地球的卫星，也是离地球最近的星体，夜晚肉眼所见最明亮的天体。月亮还是世界各地共同的神话元素，中国的月亮神话有着悠久的历史。[③] “嫦娥奔月”的故事流传数千年之久。[④] 据新近的研究，早在战国初年，“嫦娥奔月”就已经流传。[⑤] 千百年来，人们撰写了多不胜数的诗文，来表达遥望月亮时的所思所想。[⑥] 到了17世纪后，由于望远镜的发明，人类终于可以近距离一睹月亮的真容。当伽利略改造了望远镜之后，第一时间也将望远镜对准了月亮，他绘制了世界上首张月球表面图，此图也被收录于《远镜说》当中。而当望远镜来到中国，来到广州，在诸多观感当中，最有吸引力的无疑就是观月。

---

① 梁廷枏：《粤海关志》卷九，如“大洋鸟枪，每枝比大望远镜一个，每个四钱”，第648—677页。

② 马士：《东印度公司对华贸易编年史》（第1、2卷），第50章“石琼官的破产”（1794年），区宗华译，广州：中山大学出版社，1991年，第576页。

③ 吴天明：《中国神话研究》第6章“月亮神话”，北京：中央编译出版社，2003年，第271—312页。

④ 关于嫦娥研究可参见袁珂：《嫦娥奔月神话初探》，《南充师范学院学报》（哲学社会科学版）1980年第4期，第1—9页。

⑤ 有学者对出土的王家台秦简《归妹》进行研究表明，“嫦娥奔月”神话出现时间可以推早到战国中早期。见戴琳、蔡云章：《秦简〈归妹〉卦辞与“嫦娥奔月”神话》，《史学月刊》2005年第9期，第16—21页。

⑥ 关于月景诗研究可参见韩烈文：《月景诗与民俗文化》，《四川师范大学学报》1989年第3期，第15—22页。

（一）官员的观镜感受

阮元（1764—1849），字伯元，号芸台，江苏仪征人，是清朝中期著名的封疆大吏。阮元早年曾学习钻研自然科学，在入官之后，致力于推动科学研究的工作，强调科学的重要性。他曾编纂《畴人传》，又赞助刻印广州道士李明彻（1751—1832）的科学著作《圜天图说》。嘉庆二十五年（1820），阮元时年57岁，任两广总督，表达观镜感受的诗作《望远镜中望月歌》正是在这一年写下的：

> 天球地球同一圜，风刚气紧成盘旋。阴冰阳水割向背，惟仗日轮相近天。
> 别有一球名曰月，影借日光作盈阙。广寒玉兔尽空谈，搔首问天此何物？
> 吾思此亦地球耳，暗者为山明者水。舟楫应行大海中，人民也在千山里。
> 昼夜当分十五日，我见月食彼日食。若从月里望地球，也成明月金波色。
> 邹衍善谈且勿空，吾有五尺窥天筒。能见月光深浅白，能见日光不射红。
> 见月不似寻常小，平除如波高处岛。许多泡影生魄边，大珠小珠光皎皎。
> 月中人性当清灵，也看恒星同五星。也有畴人好子弟，抽镜窥吾明月形。
> 相窥彼此不相见，同是团团光一片。彼中镜子若更精，吴刚竟可窥吾面。
> 吾与吴刚隔两洲，海波尽处谁能舟？羲和敲日照双月，分出大小玻璃球。
> 吾从四十万里外，多加明月三分秋。①

该诗作值得玩味的地方很多。其娓娓动听地叙述：拿起望远镜，先绕可视的天球，扫视了一圈，然后再将目标对准了月球，开始了详细的观察，若有所悟，遂阐发了各种联想。

“广寒玉兔尽空谈，搔首问天此何物”是本诗中惊人的亮点，也是阮元观月的第一感受。当他从镜中看到月亮时，肯定与其想象相距甚远，镜中当然看不到他所熟知的广寒宫与玉兔，流传千年的月亮神话在阮元的眼中破灭了。由此，他开始思索应如何重新理解月亮，他设想月球应该是与地球一样的星球，上面也有山有水，可能还住着“月球人”，他们应该生性清灵，甚至月球上也有天文学家、物理学家，而他们也会用望远镜遥望地球。到了倒数第三、四句却峰回路转写道：“彼中镜子若更精，吴刚竟可窥吾面。吾与吴刚隔两洲，海波尽处谁能舟？”这与前诗否定“广寒玉兔”产生了矛盾，广寒玉兔都不在了，吴刚怎么还会在月球呢？有关月亮的神话，似乎在阮元的心头挥之不去。

其实透过《望月歌》全诗，可看出阮元于当时主流的天文学知识，如天球、地球等等，已颇多知晓，但这些天文学知识并不是他用望远镜观察得来的。在观月的同时，他并没有忘记自己所非常关心的“畴人”，体现出他对于科学事业的热情。望远镜触发了阮元新的灵感，引出了新的想象，使得诗意独特而玄妙，在诗歌创作中可谓独树一帜。而在阮元心中，神话可以破灭，但仍可以继续借喻。科学与神话也可以并行不悖，一个代表传统，一个代表新知，阮元心中把握有度。

从《望远镜中望月歌》可以看出，望远镜带给阮元最大的启示应该是，既然已有工具能使月球视远而近，那么是不是有朝一日，也会有工具帮我们“奔月”呢？这是个非常大胆的飞天之梦，正是望

---

① 阮元：《研经室四集》卷一一，见邓经元点校本《研经室集》下册，北京：中华书局，1993年，第971—972页。

远镜引发了这个梦。

（二）商人的观镜感受

潘有度（1755—1820）[①] 又名潘致祥，字宪臣，又字容谷，出身广州番禺的行商世家，其父潘振承创同文行，是广州十三行的元老之一。潘有度是乾嘉时期的重要行商，他对西洋事物抱有很大的热情，曾著《西洋杂咏》20首[②]，内容涉及商业习惯、宗教信仰、生活风尚、婚丧礼俗、科学技术、外洋争战[③]，其中第12首便是描写其看千里镜的感受：

> 万顷琉璃玉宇宽，镜澄千里幻中看。朦胧夜半炊烟起，可是人家住广寒？

自注云：

> 千里镜，最大者阔一尺长一丈，傍有小镜看月，照见月光约大数丈，形如圆球，周身明彻，有鱼鳞光。内有黑影，似山河倒照，不能一目尽览，惟向月中东西南北分看，久视则热气射目。夜静，有人用大千里镜照见月中烟起，如炊烟。

还有第19首：

> 术传星学管中窥，风定银河月满地。忽吐光芒生两乳，圭形三尺最称奇。
> （夜用外洋观星镜，照见一星圭形，长三尺，头尾各穿一孔）

由这两首诗中，潘有度使用了两种不同的望远镜。大千里镜，《粤海关》税则中业已出现，应是较为常见的舶来商品，潘有度作为行商，当能准确划分大小望远镜及不同的税率，这与其他职业人士有所不同；外洋观星镜，应相当于现在的天文望远镜，放大倍数比普通望远镜更大，光学效果更出众。潘有度与阮元均用镜观月，但观感不同，在潘有度的眼中，通过望远镜，他看到的是月亮上的炊烟，商人本色尽显无遗，即使是在静夜中把玩西洋千里镜，脑中想到的依然是人间烟火，也即是生计的问题。

（三）僧人的观镜感受

成鹫和尚（1637—1722），广州番禺人，俗姓方，中年后在华林寺剃度出家，成鹫和尚曾自撰年谱《纪梦编年》，既是回忆录，又是反思录，表达其明遗民情结。[④] 成鹫一生著录颇丰，曾著《楞严直说》《金刚经直说》《老子直说》《注庄子内篇》《鹿湖草》《诗通》《不了吟》《自听编》《鼎湖山志》《渔樵问答》《咸陟堂集》。[⑤] 其中《咸陟堂集》是其诗文集，其中《小匡庐溪月草堂记》一文记录了成鹫和尚曾使用显微镜和望远镜：

> 客从番舶来，遗予奇货二：一为演微镜，其大如钱，外赘一物乃瓜子白也，中有细纹如蜘

---

① 关于潘有度的生平，可参考陈国栋：《潘有度（潘启官二世）：一位成功的洋行商人》，收入陈国栋：《东亚海域一千年：历史上的海洋中国与对外贸易》，济南：山东画报出版社，2006年，第309—348页。

② 潘仪增、潘飞声：《番禺潘氏诗略》，第2册《义松堂遗稿》，清光绪二十年（1894）刊本，第2—4页。

③ 蔡鸿生：《清代广州行商的西洋观——潘有度〈西洋杂咏〉评说》，《中外交流史事考述》，第373页。

④ 蔡鸿生：《清初岭南佛门事略》第5章“成鹫法师的遗民梦”，广州：广东高等教育出版社，1997年，第98—147页。

⑤ 杨权：《成鹫及其〈咸陟堂集〉》（《咸陟堂集》前言），清初岭南佛门史料丛刊，广州：广东旅游出版社，第2008年。

蛛丝绸缪不可辨识。持镜演之，白中丝缕忽现为山川人物、茂林修竹、豆觞匕箸、博弈赌胜之具，种种备有，饮酒者七人，侍坐五人。瓜子白仅豇豆比耳，纳于镜，影现尺幅，向之丝缕绸缪者，俨若云林笔意。已而去镜索像，山川人物复为丝缕。此大小之喻也。一为千里镜，其状如筒，筒函三镜，镜竟筒口，中杀二之一，侧筒置窗穴中，从内觑外，莽苍人物移而接于眉睫，若可舒手及也；倒置筒管，咫尺人物又可推而出之莽苍之外，攀跻如不及。此远近之喻也。由是恍然有得，宇宙之内，人物之颐，大小远近之数，尽属幻形，因幻形而成幻影，因幻影而成幻见，因幻见而成幻想，世间所有种种事物，悉从幻生，语言文字之所发挥，丹青图画之所名邈，皆幻也。明知其幻，日游戏于幻中，能超然于幻外，惟香山广文石子铁霖，与东樵之老樵相视莫逆，别去一载余，犹昨日也。……鼎湖去小匡庐甚远，去大匡庐远甚，因阅小匡庐之记，恍为大匡庐之游。俄而移近附远，俄而缩远就近，其千里镜中所有种种人物耶？幻耶？真耶？吾不得而知也。[①]

成鹫和尚的望远镜来自外国船只，除了带来望远镜，还有一架显微镜。此篇《小匡庐溪月草堂记》，应是其应庆云寺方丈契如元渠之邀到肇庆修纂《鼎湖山志》结束后所写的，成鹫和尚时年六十二。[②]

成鹫和尚在17世纪末期所使用的望远镜，应该是当时较为先进的反射式望远镜，是由牛顿所改造发明的。其特点就是“筒函三镜”，而且他所使用的望远镜不是从底端往前端观看，而是“侧筒置窗穴中，从内觑外”，这都是反射式望远镜基本的特点。[③]

“幻”是佛教常用的术语，是空法十喻之一，佛教认为一切事象皆无实体性，唯现出如幻之假相。而成鹫所引以“幻”开头的诸词，历代佛经常见，兹列如下：

幻形：根尘虽同于法体，相表特异于幻形。既云在凡之境。亦应随机之教。[④]

幻影：太师真隐居士赞曰：瞻彼连师色粹而温，礼义是皆诗书是敦。虽精止观实祖儒门，鹤飞寥廓蝉蜕尘氛，遂令听者去缚解纷，五住大刹籍籍有闻。晚居延庆其道弥尊。伊惟台教垂裕后昆。前有法智后有觉云。意此幻影与法常存。[⑤]

幻见：若复怜愍一切诸众生故。为之积集功德智慧。断除一切虚诳幻见。得坚固勇猛求一切善如说修行。[⑥]

幻想：识智非智，一切不著；若知于法，识如幻想。[⑦]

幻生：五受众亦如是，先业因缘，幻生今五众，受五欲，生贪瞋。[⑧]

---

① 收于《咸陟堂集》(三)，第35—36页。

②《纪梦编年》载：“次年戊寅，予年六十有二。……至夏，入鼎湖安居。时契如装公主席，委修山志。”转引《清初岭南佛门事略》，第136页。

③ 吴鑫基、温学诗：《现代天文学十五讲》，北京大学出版社，2005年，第24—25页。

④ 赞宁：《宋高僧传》卷一〇《唐洪州开元寺道一传》，北京：中华书局，1987年，第221页。

⑤ 志磐：《佛祖统纪》卷一六，《大正新修大藏经》第49册，第231页。

⑥ 昙无谶译：《大方等大集经》卷五〇，《大正新修大藏经》第13册，第326页。

⑦《不退转法轮经》(失译者)，《大正新修大藏经》第9册，第240页。

⑧ 鸠摩罗什译：《大智度论》，《大正新修大藏经》第25册，第376页。

幻中：又曰。世间无非幻。人处幻中不知万古纷纷。喜怒爱恶从何而起。以为本有则物不形。以为本无不可责之。[①]

幻外：师曰：心名大幻师，身为大幻城，名相为大幻衣食，河沙世界无有幻外事，凡夫不识幻，处处迷幻业。[②]

可见诸幻皆有出处，成鹫和尚参悟之深，由此可见。他不仅觉得望远镜所看到的景物是“幻”，就连文字、书画，都没有实体的意义。而能超脱到幻外的，只有两位莫逆之交。

从客观上来讲，以“幻”来理解望远镜中的成像是准确的。望远镜的成像在光学上属于“虚像”，只是由于远处物体的任何一点上的光线都相交在影像上，而并非实像。成鹫和尚应非懂得光学原理，只是使用望远镜时，同时参悟佛法，深化了自身的幻觉。

（四）文人的观镜感受

屈大均被誉为广东清初三大家之一，诗文、书画俱佳，虽然他也在中年以后遁入空门，但与成鹫和尚不同，毕竟在佛法上并没有多少造诣，倒是诗文充满了生活气息。他对新鲜的舶来品，也保持着浓厚的兴趣，在《广东新语·澳门》一节中，他便介绍了很多的舶来品，望远镜是其中一件。

同样是用望远镜观月，在澳门使用过望远镜的屈大均，不像成鹫在镜中看到了诸般虚幻的景象，他把看到的景象与现实中的事物紧密地联系在一起：

有千里镜，见三十里外塔尖，铃索宛然，字画横斜，一一不爽。月中如一盂水，有黑纸渣浮出，其淡者如画中微云一抹。其底碎光四射，如纸隔华灯，纸穿而灯透漏然。[③]

屈大均的观月感受，在科学气氛浓厚的望远镜史料中，显得特别：看到30里外的塔尖，用“字画清晰可辨”来比喻；月亮用“一盂水”来比喻，月亮阴影的部分用纸渣来比喻；把整体的观感比作一幅朦胧素色的水墨画。而月亮表面发光又朦胧的状态，则用“纸穿而灯透”来比喻。可见在描写光影上，屈大均相当出色。屈大均并没有探索夜空的好奇，他的观月感受，被渲染成文人画在太空的再现，与潘有度的“炊烟”说，是大异其趣的。

（五）道士的观镜感受

上述提到诸广州人士使用望远镜，实际均未真正触及望远镜的观测功能，望远镜在他们手中，只是触发联想与诗兴的新奇舶来品。实际上，当年在广州也有利用望远镜进行观测的天文学家，那就是纯阳观的创始道长李明彻。[④] 冼玉清教授这样评价李明彻：“古来方外之士，能诗文者甚多，而能推步之术者甚鲜。……以粤人而精推步又为方外之士者，当推番禺李明彻。”[⑤]

李明彻著有广东省第一部天文著作《圜天图说》，其中的《七政形象大小说》提到“窥管”：

---

① 觉岸编：《释氏稽古略》，《大正新修大藏经》第49册，第889页。

② 道原纂：《景德传灯录》，《大正新修大藏经》第51册，第442页。

③ 屈大均：《广东新语》，第37页。

④ 关于李明彻，参见冼玉清：《天文家李明彻与漱珠冈》，收入《冼玉清文集》，广州：中山大学出版社，1995年，第193—214页；甄鹏：《清朝道士李明彻及其科学成就研究》，山东大学博士论文。

⑤《冼玉清文集》，第193页。

七政形象各有大小不同，土星远于赤道，其星圈所占甚宽，本体一星长圆，彷佛卵形左右，继有两小星或时与本星联体，外又排定小星五点，绕土星之体面行，观其所动，与恒星各异，故知此星是居七政之内，又别一星也。……此管窥实测也，但人目所睹近者虽小亦大，远者虽大亦小，不可以井窥泥也。①

在《圜天图说续编》的《金水二星伏见说》一章中，李明彻详尽描写了他所知道的望远镜：

泰西有推步名家，做成管窥望远之镜，管窥之器，以一独木杵架乘之，约高五尺，下有三足着地，上有□月□以座管寅筒，能旋转左右，随景高低。此观星之活用也。其管窥镜以□为筒，长约数尺，其大小各四五筒叠套内小镜□□□之见大为小，外大筒窥向物视之，见小为大，□□甲之遥无云霞，所隔视见人须眉嬉笑如在目前方，乃万历年间始有。此器能测天之高低，观星宿多少，深浅之度数，皆由此器也。测观土星两旁有二小星，如附耳焉，外有小星，五点围绕旋行。木星旁亦有四小星，周行甚疾，太白星所行亦有时晦时光，有时若上下两弦，如月相似。然则水星之见，必须平望高舂桑榆之间，切地上浮游之气，亦可影小为大，如眼带镜看字，又可影远为近，如着钱于水盂中相此焉。水星自有本天又有附次轮运行之天，此即轨迹圈也。其次轮颇大，故能随日旋绕，或在日前或在日后，附次轮而行，行至轮上，则远于地，此为远地，次轮弦行至轮下，则近于地，此为近地，次轮弦因次轮旋行之天心，不能与地心相对，以不对地心之运行，所以有远地心之处，有近地心之处，故水星随次轮运行，有时近地，则可见之以平望切浮游之气，影之则见大，又其所循。次轮弦既与地切，而本天之动，又与地近，备此三端，所以得见，故推测甚难也，若恒星微渺难见者，如昴宿传云七星，唯据目力所见而定也，但用管窥实测细微者，有三十七星如鬼宿中白质传云积尸气，其中实有三十六星，又如牛宿，本体质亦甚小，尾宿东之鱼星，并传说星觜宿南星，皆在六等星之外，微渺难见，必须用管窥镜观之，分明显见，多星列次甚近，又如觜宿南一星，实测有二十一星，大小不等，可见恒星无数，三垣二十八舍，共三百六十未易悉列，然其有名者，中外星官通共一千八百一十二星之外，樊然淆乱，非上圣高真容成隶首，则不能穷究也。②

由上述两段引文可见，李明彻与其他人士的不同，成鹫和尚看出佛家的“幻”，但李明彻并没有看到道家的“玄”，他视望远镜为观测天象重要的工具。由于对天文的深入研究，月亮的神话不为他所关注，他看到了更深层次的问题：其他的行星也如月亮一样，时盈时亏。

仔细分析李明彻对于望远镜的描述，他称望远镜为管窥镜、窥管，由上文分析，这是流行于天象观测专业领域里的术语，或许与他曾去钦天监观摩学习有关，其时他肯定对望远镜有所耳闻。而他对望远镜的描述，比其他人要详细。“左右旋转、随景高低”，可见望远镜对于他真是一件有用的工具，大大帮助了李明彻的天文观测，他观测了金星、土星、木星、水星的运行状况，同时也观测了很多星宿中等级较小的恒星，这是以前用肉眼看不到的。

李明彻与阮元关系密切，曾经帮助阮元编修《广东通志》制图，他有可能从阮元处获得望远镜。

---

① 《圜天图说》卷上，四库未收肆辑26册，北京出版社，2000年，第260—261页。

② 同上，第359—360页。

另一方面，李明彻与外国商人传教士频繁接触的十三行商人亦有来往，冼玉清教授指出，纯阳观的捐款石碑中，有多家行商捐款的名录[①]，他亦有可能从行商处获得望远镜。

结语

明清时期西学东渐，广州口岸首当其冲。西洋“奇器”望远镜，也经常由此输入。粤海关的“税制”规定，望远镜每架征关税4两，并以此作为若干舶来品税率的折算依据。当年的广州督抚和海关监督，在其《宫中进单》中，也往往列望远镜为贡品。如雍正十一年（1733），两广总督鄂弥达贡“千里镜九架”，广东巡抚杨永斌贡“千里镜五枝”，粤海关监督毛克明贡“千里镜”五架，等等。[②]

广州既是西洋望远镜捷足先登的地方，广州的上层人士也就获得先睹为快的际遇。如前所述，从康、乾到嘉、道年间，有幸观镜者，分属于官、商、儒、释、道各界。这种独特的时地人的历史组合，表明“一口通商”时期的广州，确实是得“洋气”之先的。由于观镜者的社会文化背景不同，观感也因人而异。于是，西洋望远镜变成了文化万花筒。器同道异，人言言殊。奇器引发奇想，科技与心态不能截然分开，中西文化交流的复杂和微妙，于此可见一斑。

① 《天文家李明彻与漱珠冈》中《纯阳观与十三行》一节，第212—214页。

② 杨伯达：《中国古代艺术文物论丛》，紫禁城出版社，2002年，第326—328页。

The Spread and Use of Telescopes in Canton Port during Ming and Qing Dynasty

Huang Jiaxin (Sun Yat-sen University)

Abstract: Telescope was one of the most important invents in scientific history of the world. Since the 17th century, telescope has become a powerful tool for people to explore the universe. Short after its invention, the Catholic Jesuits have taken telescopes to China. They also translated some books about telescopes into Chinese. After that, telescopes began to be known and spread in China. The dissertation would be divided into two parts. When telescopes spreaded in China, there were some different names using Chinese in the same time. In the first part of the dissertation, I will analysis the traditional cultural meaning and usage range of the different names. In the second part of the dissertation, I will focus in Canton Port, which was the place that telescopes first landed. The higher range people in Canton can be easier to watch them. From Kangxi, Qianlong Dynasty to Jiaqing Daoguang Dynasty, people who were lucky to watch the monoculars, belong to officers, businessmen, Confucians, monks and Taoists. Because of the different personal background of the watchers, their feelings were also different. This part will focus on them. Special implements caused special thinking, we can't divide technology from mentality. That's an example to prove the complication and delication which between the Sino-western culture exchange.

Keywords: Telescopes; Canton (Guangzhou); Ruan Yuan (1764-1849); Pan Youdu (1755-1820); Cheng Jiu(1637-1722); Qu Dajun(1630-1696); Li Mingche(1751-1832)

在喀什开展巴基斯坦研究的必要性和可行性分析

姑丽娜尔·吾甫力（喀什大学）
王晓东（广东金融学院）

摘　要：喀什与巴基斯坦接壤，经济贸易往来历史悠久，喀什地区是"中巴经济走廊"起始点和核心区，同时也是国家安全形势最为敏感的地区，对"一带一路"倡议实施过程中的稳定安全具有决定性的影响。目前，具有重大意义的"中巴经济走廊"建设与新疆互动等方面的研究还滞后于国家"一带一路"倡议的需要。因此，在喀什开展"中巴经济走廊"研究、巴基斯坦研究的必要性和重要性可见一斑。

关键词：喀什；巴基斯坦；"中巴经济走廊"

一　问题的提出

作为古老丝绸之路上的重镇，历史上喀什在中亚、南亚的社会和谐、稳定、发展中发挥了重要的作用；作为中国大陆第一个信仰伊斯兰教的地区，喀什历史上很好地处理了宗教信仰与世俗国家的适应、融合，很好地处理了伊斯兰教与多元文化、多种宗教相融合，其成功经验可以为中国促进世界和平提供良好的话语权。也就是说，喀什地区的稳定、发展，能为中国的"一带一路"倡议实施提供"新疆地方经验"，这些经验需要有科研团队进行研究、梳理、总结。

2015年5月初，国家主席习近平正式访问巴基斯坦，中巴双方达成具有重大意义的多项协定，备受国内外关注的"中巴经济走廊"建设即是其中之一。两国智库召开的"中巴经济走廊战略研讨会"指出，"中巴经济走廊"的重要意义在于对国家推进"一带一路"建设的示范和引领作用。

"中巴经济走廊"北起新疆喀什，南至巴基斯坦境内的印度洋出海口瓜达尔港。2013年5月李克强总理访问巴基斯坦期间，两国同意启动经济走廊建设。两个月后，中巴两国成立"中巴经济走廊"远景规划联合合作委员会（简称"联委会"），以推动制定走廊远景规划。其重要意义在于：

第一，是"一带一路"倡议推进的"试点区"，更是"一带一路"构想实施的里程碑项目。在国家推进"一带一路"建设中，"中巴经济走廊"是最有可能实现早期收获的重点项目；

第二，是"一带一路"倡议成效的"示范区"。基于中巴之间睦邻友好关系典范，"中巴经济走廊"涉及港口建设、能源管道、交通基础建设、产业合作等重点领域，一定程度上具有较强的示范效应。"中巴经济走廊"看起来是双边的，实际上其功能和方式会辐射到相邻多边区域，会对"一带一路"更大区域产生重大影响；

第三，是"一带一路"倡议实践的"创新区"。作为"海上丝绸之路"的一个重要连接点，巴国南部瓜达尔港也是“中巴经济走廊”建设的一个起始点。“中巴经济走廊”正是打通“21世纪海上丝绸之路”与“丝路经济带”两个战略的连接区、交汇区、受益区，正在成为中巴深层经贸合作的新平台，“中巴经济走廊”项目具有崭新的开创性。

“中巴经济走廊”在国家战略规划和“一带一路”建设中受到越来越多的关注。但是，目前“中巴经济走廊”建设中新疆的战略价值和意义，中国新疆和巴基斯坦经贸交通及文化交流等关系，以及这个战略实施过程中对新疆尤其是南疆的多维度影响，似乎没有能够得到应有的关注，已有的研究成果滞后于国家“一带一路”建设的需要。特别是在对两国之间发展的自然环境与文化环境、推动项目落地的运作机制、必然出现的涉及新疆尤其是南疆的传统安全和非传统安全问题，目前在新疆尚无专门机构涉足研究。虽然国内已有几所高校和研究机构建立了巴基斯坦研究中心（如北京大学巴基斯坦研究中心、清华大学巴基斯坦文化传播研究中心、四川大学巴基斯坦研究中心、云南民族大学巴基斯坦研究中心），但是据我们调研分析，这些研究机构大多从事国家层面战略研究或教育交流方面的研究。

对于“中巴经济走廊”的专项研究，巴基斯坦已经开始推动。2017年2月，“中巴经济走廊”沿线城市卡拉奇的总领馆和位于卡拉奇的巴基斯坦信德大学建立了“中巴经济走廊”研究中心。尽管“中巴经济走廊”大部分在巴基斯坦境内，但喀什是“中巴经济走廊”的一个端点，“中巴经济走廊”建设的目的之一就是发展喀什。因此，在喀什开展全方位的巴基斯坦研究和“中巴经济走廊”研究，有助于发挥喀什的“当事人”的天然优势，有助于喀什地区参与“中巴经济走廊建设”，有助于“中巴经济走廊建设”政策、项目的快速推进，有助于助推落实国家关于喀什发展的战略布局，有助于喀什大学学术水平和学术地位提升，形成具有鲜明地方特色的学术研究领域。

二　在喀什开展巴基斯坦研究的必要性

（一）中国国家发展战略和自治区政府的重视。习近平主席最近访问巴基斯坦，与巴方启动的“中巴经济走廊”建设战略，其意义十分重大。特别是从喀什地区作为“中巴经济走廊”的廊桥和桥头堡，与这个战略实施关系极为重要。喀什地区是“中巴经济走廊”的核心区，同时是国家安全形势最为敏感的地区，对“一带一路”倡议实施过程中的稳定安全具有决定性的影响。根据新疆政府工作报告，2015年新疆将加快建设丝绸之路经济带核心区，对接“一带一路”和“中巴经济走廊”及面向中西南亚和欧洲的物流通道、信息通道建设，构建对内对外开放型经济新格局。因此，在喀什开展巴基斯坦研究，设立巴基斯坦研究中心，形成上述稳定的具有地缘优势的本地研究智库，为喀什地区、为新疆主动参与“中巴经济走廊”战略，自觉承担区域经济发展和社会稳定的任务提供预测研究、咨询建议的智力支持。

（二）当代国际文化交流合作发展的客观要求。最近由中国政府有关部门发布的《推动共建丝绸之路经济带和21世纪海上丝绸之路的愿景与行动》，进一步把促进文化相互理解、沟通和交流的重大意义推向了范围更广的国际平台。“一带一路”倡议特别强调在不同民族和不同文化类型间的“民心相通”，希望通过跨文化的“民心相通”奠定多边合作的民意基础，互联互通，互助合作，结成牢固的“命运共同体”。这对于新疆和喀什地区，尤其需要建立一个研究机构从事相关研究。

（三）“中巴经济走廊建设”的客观需要。喀什是中巴经济大通道的起点，是“中巴经济走廊”的桥头堡。"中巴经济走廊"的建设实施，新疆喀什有其独特的战略地位。如何作为？喀什的产业转移园如何与巴基斯坦的跨国产能合作产业园互动？喀什产业链与"中巴经济走廊"产业链如何协同？喀什的金融贸易区如何紧密支持"中巴经济走廊建设"？喀什的国际人才教育和培训如何支持"中巴经济走廊建设"？这些都是在喀什开展巴基斯坦研究的主要的出发点，将力争为国家"中巴经济走廊"建设提供来自喀什的第一手资料。

（四）区域经济文化交流融合的需要。喀什与巴基斯坦接壤，经济贸易往来历史悠久。红其拉甫口岸是国家批准对外开放的一类口岸，红其拉甫口岸历史上就是古丝绸之路前往印度、中亚、西亚直至欧洲的咽喉要道，是我国与巴基斯坦唯一的陆路进出境通道，是通往南亚次大陆乃至欧洲的重要门户，也是我国与西亚、南亚以及欧洲经济、文化交流的重要通道。

历史上喀什在中亚、南亚的社会和谐、稳定、发展中发挥了重要的作用，在中西亚及南亚社会中具有特殊的地位，经济文化的繁荣使其在历史上有"小布哈拉"之称。作为中国大陆第一个信仰伊斯兰教的地区，喀什历史上很好地处理了宗教信仰与世俗国家的适应、融合，很好地处理了多元文化、多种宗教与伊斯兰教的融合，同时培养了有较高科学文化知识、深厚文学功底和极深宗教造诣的思想家，成为当时中亚、西亚和南亚的思想文化中心，有"小麦加"之称，其成功经验可以为中国促进世界和平提供良好的范例。也就是说，喀什地区的稳定、发展，能为"一带一路"倡议提供"新疆地方经验"，有助于新疆和中南亚国家的区域经济文化融合交流，可以帮助喀什、巴基斯坦逐步摆脱经济落后状况，还可以帮助喀什、巴基斯坦更好地加强联合，互利合作，打击恐怖主义和暴力极端主义。喀什所积累的"新疆地方经验"需要有科研团队进行研究、梳理、总结，为中央政府、新疆自治区、喀什地区政府提供决策咨询依据。

（五）新疆各族人民和谐发展的需要。"中巴经济走廊"建设给新疆特别是喀什带来了前所未有的发展机遇。我们需要进一步研究，怎样使这个战略的实施与新疆本土社会实现长治久安和跨越式发展相结合；本土文化传统得到保护与现代文化得以健康培育和发展相结合；国家社会区域进步发展与有益于本土人民的福祉等结合起来，实现新疆和喀什地区与"一带一路"相关国家实现共赢乃至多赢等等。这样我们就必须深入了解巴基斯坦社会、经济、文化乃至于宗教，深入研究在"中巴经济走廊"建设过程中所发生的一切，分析"中巴经济走廊"建设所引发的区域、社会、经济、人文的嬗变，深入研究如何将此战略的实施建立在培育和发展人民对人民的交往和友谊上，使其有厚重的本土社会的和人民群众的支持基础。

三　建立研究机构的可行性

（一）喀什在丝绸之路经济带空间布局中区位优势浑然天成。喀什处于丝绸之路的南通道，自广州经长沙、重庆、成都、格尔木由若羌进入新疆，经和田、喀什，南下印度洋沿岸的瓜达尔港，是一条极具战略意义的通道。喀什地处欧亚大陆中心，是古丝绸之路南北两道交会的国际商业城市，也是国家新丝绸之路南通道上极具战略意义的重要节点城市。

（二）地区之间悠久的历史交往经验和文化交流基础。喀什自古以来与中亚、南亚有悠久的交往历史和传统，即使是在当代，这种传统仍在保留、发展，可以为中国"一带一路"通过中亚、南亚通向世界奠定较好的基础。交流和交往主要表现在以下几个方面：

第一，经济交往。喀什与中亚各国，特别与巴基斯坦和阿富汗的民间往来十分频繁。这些国家要从中国喀什进口大量肉制品、建材、服装、果蔬等产品。可见，喀什传承了与中亚、南亚的民间自觉自愿交往，能够达到凝聚人心、文化互通共荣的目的，这亦是“一带一路”倡议的目的之一。因此，关注喀什历史上与中亚、南亚国家的经济关系及其地位，关注喀什今天与中亚、南亚国家的特殊的民间交往模式，可以给国家提供很好的“一带一路”建设的经验。

第二，文化艺术交流。喀什作为维吾尔文化的中心，其悠久的历史中，许多民间叙事长诗、民间著名诗人都与中亚、南亚国家共享，且有许多共同的文学、民俗话题，彼此之间还有频繁的音乐绘画艺术的交流，具有丰富的对话交流的历史和经验，喀什是有地方民族特色的伊斯兰文化，为伊斯兰文化的中国化奠定了基础，为中国与中亚、南亚伊斯兰文化的交流提供较好的范式。

第三，民族交流通婚。目前喀什民间与巴基斯坦等国民众在经贸往来过程中催生的巴基斯坦等国居民在喀什通婚、定居，与维吾尔民众和谐相处，已经有较好的民间凝聚力基础。但是目前这样的民族交流形式并没有很好地得到足够的重视。

（三）喀什将成为“中巴经济走廊建设”培养人才的基地。刚刚批准成立的喀什大学，坐落在历史文化名城喀什，具有较好的科学研究传统，目前有五个自治区级重点研究机构，承担多项国家研究课题；有较好的专业研究队伍，特别是喀什大学建设过程中，对学科专业进行调整，更加面向社会所需，重点面向国家“一带一路”建设对喀什的跨学科人才需求。新开设的经济统计、财务管理、国际贸易、土木工程、清真产业、旅游文化产业等相关的专业，对集聚人才、满足南疆社会对人才的需求具有十分积极的作用。

（四）2014年喀什噶尔研究院的成立。喀什噶尔研究院是由喀什地委、行署支持成立的旨在为喀什丝绸之路经济带战略服务的地方智库，所聘请的专家包括中国社会科学院、北京大学、清华大学以及新疆地方高校科研院所的专家学者，为“中巴经济走廊”双边研究奠定了科技人才基础和科研成果基础。

四　在喀什开展巴基斯坦研究的初步构想

在喀什开展巴基斯坦研究，可以依托喀什大学、喀什噶尔研究院建立“巴基斯坦研究中心”。该研究中心拟不涉及国家层面的宏观战略研究，而是建议喀什大学、喀什噶尔研究院与疆内外高校及研究机构合作，把研究重点集中在新疆尤其是喀什在“中巴经济走廊”战略实施中应该做些什么，经济贸易实践中应该聚焦于哪些方面，如何运用喀什与巴基斯坦相通的民间文化、宗教来化解矛盾，支持“中巴经济走廊”建设中的各类项目的落实和运营，喀什金融如何与巴基斯坦等国的伊斯兰金融合作，“中巴经济走廊”建设将会给喀什当地人民的生活带来什么变化，当地人民如何适应这些变化。基于我们的本土经验，对“中巴经济走廊”战略实施过程中可能对喀什和新疆带来的复杂影响，向新疆和中央政府提出“预测性”研究成果和咨询建议，以减少和避免可能发生的“负面影响”（包括传统安全和非传统安全的影响）。

还有与此有关的其他问题，比如“中巴经济走廊”战略实施与新疆本土社会如何实现社会稳定和长治久安？新疆本土文化传统如何得到保护？现代文化怎样健康培育和发展？“中巴经济走廊”建设怎样和人民福祉结合起来？只有将这些问题结合新疆社会、经济和文化的实际状况开展研究，才能得到第一手的资料，才能提出更有地方视角的建议。成立该研究机构正是为国家“一带一路”倡议在新疆实施培养本土专家和科研人才，进而为喀什地区和新疆维吾尔自治区参与“中巴经济走廊”建设提供接地气的咨询和决策建议。

（一）理论依据：近期国家发展改革委员会、外交部、商务部联合发布了《推动共建丝绸之路经济带和21世纪海上丝绸之路的愿景与行动》，我国将进一步促进多民族文化相互理解、沟通和交流的重大意义推向了范围更广的国际平台。倡议推进务实合作，打造政治互信、经济融合、文化包容的利益共同体、命运共同体和责任共同体。“一带一路”特别强调了在不同民族和不同文化类型之间需要合力实现“民心相通”，希望通过跨文化的“民心相通”，互通互联，相互合作，多边共赢，奠定多边合作的民意基础，结成牢固的“命运共同体”。国家的战略思路为喀什大学建立“巴基斯坦研究中心”提供了理论依据。

（二）科研协作：在刚刚成立的喀什大学建立“巴基斯坦研究中心”，与喀什地区建立的喀什噶尔研究院相互整合、相得益彰。喀什大学是一所综合型大学，是国家、教育部和自治区党委根据喀什未来的发展形势需要特别批准由原来的喀什师范学院更名建设的一所综合性大学。国家在南疆喀什建设综合型大学，旨在推进“一带一路”建设，为南疆地区培养科技创新和社会发展人才。“巴基斯坦研究中心”设立在喀什大学，有可能发展成为喀什地区社会经济发展与对外开放的一个地方性智库，也可能成为新疆研究中巴双边关系的研究机构和创新平台，填补新疆乃至国家在中巴关系以及涉及的国家传统安全和非传统安全研究领域中的不足。

（三）团队建设：以“巴基斯坦研究中心”为平台的研究团队由三部分组成：喀什大学、喀什地区相关部门、喀什噶尔研究院本土专家和部分新疆专家组成核心团队。本土专家有地域、社会、民族、文化、心理、信息、经济、金融、物流等方面第一手资料的优势，但是在与国际学术界的接触对话以及研究方法等方面有明显不足；外聘北京大学巴基斯坦研究中心、四川大学巴基斯坦研究中心、中国社会科学院、复旦大学和中国国际关系研究院数位相关专家组成国内支持团队，聘请两三位（包括巴基斯坦的）国外学者组成顾问团队，以补充疆内本土专家和国内专家在研究中国际视野相对不足的缺陷，为培养新疆本土人才创造条件。

团队主要优势：首先，研究团队主要成员均在喀什大学，本土研究者具备一定的研究实力，特别是当地有较好的民间经贸交往资源和语言资源。因为商贸关系，喀什有一定数量的民间群体掌握乌尔都语，长期与巴基斯坦有民间商贸合作。喀什大学已经有了关于喀什历史、文化、经济、政治方面研究的成果和平台（自治区重点学科、自治区重点人文社科研究基地等），特别是目前引进和培养的一批青年学者的研究实力和研究视野都有较好的基础；其次，开放研究，积极与国内外展开合作。本中心将积极与北京大学、四川大学的巴基斯坦研究中心和中国社科院、复旦大学（包括巴基斯坦相关高校）等开展合作研究，得到研究优势互补；再次，本中心研究将发挥地域、文化优势，侧重点将不在理论、政策研究，而重在实际问题研究。如“一带一路”倡议背景下沿线国家社会民俗、文化现状、经济社会发展、对“一带一路”的需求、可能存在的现实风险和存在隐患，以及为政府及企业提供咨询服务。

研究目标：喀什的巴基斯坦研究，将以成立“喀什大学巴基斯坦研究中心”为平台，集中研究两大部分问题，一是研究在“中巴经济走廊建设”背景下与新疆有关的社会、经济、文化和非传统安全问题，该问题在可行性和必要性中已有专门阐述；二是从宗教、文化的内视角，探索国家打击恐怖势力的新思路，总结历史上新疆反对宗教极端势力的经验和存在的问题，维吾尔族伊斯兰文化与多元文化相融合的优秀经验和历史教训。挖掘历史文献资料，使维吾尔族等新疆少数民族在“一带一路”倡议与沿线伊斯兰国家互利共赢的建设中、在国家反恐工作中发挥桥梁纽带和正面的积极作用，并由此完成自身的文化转型。

结 语

“一带一路”是一个长期的工程，“中巴经济走廊”建设将造福于中国和沿线其他国家及地区的30亿人口，牵动着该地区社会、经济、文化更加广泛地交流。喀什在“中巴经济走廊”建设中处于中方的始点，其政治、经济、外交和对外开放交流的重要性自不待言，在喀什大学建立“巴基斯坦研究中心”，可以为自治区参与“中巴经济走廊”建设、促进新疆与巴基斯坦的友谊和合作、同时为可能出现的各种复杂因素和局面提供具有地方和国际视角结合的咨询建议，有利于国家确定的“中巴经济走廊”建设战略的实施，也有利于新疆和喀什地区参与这个战略的实施。

An Analysis on the Necessity and Feasibility of Carrying out Pakistan Studies in Kashgar

Gulinaer · Wupuli (Kashgar University)
Wang Xiaodong (Guandong University of Finance)

Abstract: Kashgar has a common border with Pakistan, and has a long history of economic and trade exchanges with Pakistan. Kashgar Prefecture has a decisive influence on the security and stability during the implementation of the Belt and Road Initiative, for its initial point and core area position of "Chinese and Pakistani economical corridor", as well as the most sensitive area of the national security. Now, the research about integrated relationship between "CPEC" and Sinkiang still lag to the need of the Belt and Road Initiative. So, it is very important and necessary to carry out the Chinese and Pakistani economical corridor research and Pakistan studies in Kashgar.

Keywords: Kashgar; Pakistan; Chinese and Pakistani Economical Corridor

《丝绸之路研究》用稿声明及引文规范

为便于学术交流和推进本刊编辑工作的规范化，在借鉴其他人文社科学术期刊的论文格式及引文注释规范的基础上，我们对原有论文格式及引文注释规范进行了补充和完善，并声明供稿注意事项，以制定《丝绸之路研究》用稿体例，供作者参考。

一、研究论文请附中英文论文摘要（200—300 字）及关键词（3—5 个）。中英文摘要应全面准确地概括论文的主要内容和观点，关键词应为具有检索价值、能够反映文章主题的名词性术语，基金项目文章需标注基金项目名称和项目编号。

二、投稿者应自觉遵守学术规范，认真核对引文、注释和文中使用的资料，确保引文、注释和相关资料准确无误。如使用转引资料，应注明转引出处。

三、来稿正文需用 5 号宋体字，行距应大于 1.25，一般文稿字数在 1.5 万字以内为宜。本刊将以简体中文版发表，文字如无特殊需要，不用繁体、异体及俗体字。

四、本刊一律使用新式标点符号，除破折号、省略号各占两格外，其他标点均占一格，中文书刊与论文题日均用书名号。

五、引文注释采用页下注（脚注）的形式，以①、②、③……为序号，其位置在标点符号前（引号除外）的右上角，每页重新编号。再次征引，用“同上，XX 页”“同注 X，XX 页”或“同注 X，XX 文，XX 页”格式，不用合并注号方式。

六、除常见的《旧唐书》《新唐书》《册府元龟》《资治通鉴》等外，引用古籍，应标明著者、版本、卷数、页码；引用专书及新印古籍，应标明著者、章卷数、出版者及出版年代、页码；引用期刊论文，应标明期刊名、年代卷次、页码。如：

1. 和宁:《回疆通志》，民国十四年（1925）沈瑞麟校印本，卷三叶一三背。

2. 刘肃撰:《大唐新语》，许德楠、李鼎霞点校，北京：中华书局，1984 年，第 138 页。

3.《金史》卷二《太祖本纪》，北京：中华书局，1975 年，第 30 页。

4. 吴玉贵:《突厥汗国与隋唐关系史研究》，北京：中国社会科学出版社，1998 年，第 429 页。

5. 谢弗:《唐代的外来文明》，吴玉贵译，西安：陕西师范大学出版社，2005 年，第 100 页。

6. 荣新江:《十世纪西域北道的粟特人》，李肖主编:《第三届吐鲁番学暨欧亚游牧民族的起源与迁徙国际学术研讨会论文集》，上海古籍出版社，2010 年，第 449 页。

7. 林梅村:《佉卢文书及汉佉二体钱所记于阗大王考》,《文物》1987 年第 2 期，第 35 页。

8. 文欣:《中古时期于阗国政治制度研究》，北京大学历史系硕士论文，2008 年 6 月，第 23 页。

引用西文论著，依西文惯例，书刊名用斜体，论文加引号。如：

1. Helen Wang, *Money on the Silk Road: The evidence from Eastern Central Asia to c. AD800*, London, The British Museum Press, 2004, p. 94.

2. E.G.Pulleyblank, “A Sogdian Colony in Inner Mongolia”, *T'oung Pao*, 41, 1952, pp. 317-356.

引用网上资料时，格式如下：

1.http://westernregion.goosuudata.com/index.php？m=cndex&a=category&catid=131&type=1

以上引用，再次出注时，可以省略版本、出版者、出版年代、期刊名、年代卷次等项。

七、凡向本刊投稿，如未特别注明，均视为专投本刊，严禁一稿多投。自投稿之日起三个月内未接获刊用通知者，可自行处理。

八、本刊编辑部对来稿有权删改，凡不同意删改者，请在投稿时予以说明。

九、我刊将加入“中国学术期刊全文数据库”（CNKI）及CNKI系列数据库，凡在我刊发表的论文，如作者不特别声明我们将视为作者同意编入以上数据库，我编辑部所付稿酬包含此项著作权使用费。